Strikes, wars, and revolutions in an international perspective

Strikes, wars, and revolutions in an international perspective

Strike waves in the late nineteenth and
early twentieth centuries

Edited by

LEOPOLD H. HAIMSON
CHARLES TILLY

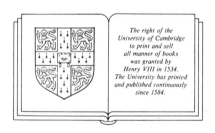

CAMBRIDGE UNIVERSITY PRESS

Cambridge
New York   New Rochelle
Melbourne   Sydney

and

EDITIONS DE LA MAISON
DES SCIENCES DE L'HOMME

Paris

Published by the Press Syndicate of the University of Cambridge
The Pitt Building, Trumpington Street, Cambridge CB2 1RP
32 East 57th Street, New York, NY 10022, USA
10 Stamford Road, Oakleigh, Melbourne 3166, Australia

331.892
S917

First published 1989

Printed in the United States of America

Library of Congress Cataloging-in-Publication Data
Strikes, war, and revolution: comparative studies and quantitative
analyses of strike waves in six major industrial countries in the
late ninteenth and early twentieth centuries/edited by Leopold
Haimson and Charles Tilly.
p.   cm.
1. Strikes and lockouts – Europe – History.   2. Strikes and
lockouts – United States – History. I. Haimson, Leopold H.
II. Tilly, Charles.
HD5364.A6S77 1988   87-30958
331.89′294 – dc19   CIP

British Library Cataloguing in Publication Data
Strikes, war and revolution: comparative
studies and quantitative analysis of
strike waves in six major industrial
countries in the late nineteenth and early
twentieth centuries.
1. Industrial relations. Strikes, 1870–1922
I. Haimson, Leopold   II. Tilly, Charles,
1929–
331.89′29034

SBN 2 7351 0291 2   France only
ISBN 0 521 35285 1

Contents

List of contributors   *page* ix
Preface   xi

Part I: Introductions   1
1. Theories and realities   3
    CHARLES TILLY
2. The historical setting in Russia and the West   18
    LEOPOLD H. HAIMSON

Part II: Models and realities   33
3. Introduction   35
    LEOPOLD H. HAIMSON, ERIC BRIAN
4. Changing forms of labor conflict: secular development
    or strike waves?   47
    FRIEDHELM BOLL
5. Strikes and power in Britain, 1870–1920   79
    JAMES E. CRONIN
6. Two strike waves in Imperial Russia, 1905–1907, 1912–1914 101
    LEOPOLD H. HAIMSON, RONALD PETRUSHA
7. Strikers in revolution: Russia, 1917   167
    DIANE KOENKER, WILLIAM G. ROSENBERG
8. Strikes in Imperial Russia, 1895–1913:
    a quantitative analysis   197
    V. I. BOVYKIN, L. I. BORODKIN, Y. I. KIRYANOV
9. Labor conflicts in Italy before the rise of fascism, 1881–1923:
    a quantitative analysis   217
    LORENZO BORDOGNA, GIAN PRIMO CELLA, GIANCARLO PROVASI

v

Contents

10. Strikes and politics in the United States, 1900–1919   247
P. K. EDWARDS

Part III: Workers in metal-processing enterprises in comparative perspective   259

11. From the mechanic to the metallo   261
MICHELLE PERROT

12. Strikes of machinists in the United States, 1870–1922   269
DAVID MONTGOMERY

13. The political economy of British engineering workers during
the First World War   289
KEITH BURGESS

14. The rationalization of class struggle: strikes and strike strategy
of the German Metalworkers' Union, 1891–1922   321
ELISABETH DOMANSKY

15. Scientific management and the changing nature of work in the
St. Petersburg metalworking industry, 1900–1914   356
HEATHER HOGAN

16. Structural processes of change and changing patterns of
labor unrest: the case of the metal-processing industry in
Imperial Russia, 1890–1914   380
LEOPOLD H. HAIMSON

17. Social characteristics, attitudes, and patterns of strike behavior of
metalworkers in Italy during the First World War   402
BRUNO BEZZA

Part IV: The effects of short-term variation   431

18. Introduction   433
CHARLES TILLY

19. Economic cycles and labor conflicts in Germany during the
first quarter of the twentieth century   449
FRIEDHELM BOLL

20. The crisis of state and society in Britain, 1917–1922   457
JAMES E. CRONIN

21. Strikes and the war   473
HUGUES LAGRANGE

22. Labor unrest in Imperial Russia on the eve of the
First World War: the roles of conjunctural phenomena, events,
and individual and collective actors   500
LEOPOLD H. HAIMSON

23. Strikes in Russia, 1917: the impact of revolution   512
DIANE KOENKER, WILLIAM G. ROSENBERG

Part V: Conclusion   523
24. Conclusion   525
LEOPOLD H. HAIMSON

Contributors

LEOPOLD H. HAIMSON
Columbia University
New York, New York

CHARLES TILLY
New School for Social Research
New York, New York

ERIC BRIAN
Maison des Sciences de
 l'Homme
Paris, France

FRIEDHELM BOLL
Friedrich-Ebert Stiftung
Bonn, West Germany

JAMES CRONIN
Boston College
Chestnut Hill, Massachusetts

RONALD PETRUSHA
Columbia University
New York, New York

DIANE KOENKER
University of Illinois at
 Urbana-Champaign
Urbana, Illinois

WILLIAM ROSENBERG
University of Michigan
Ann Arbor, Michigan

V. I. BOVYKIN
Institut istorii SSSR
Moscow, USSR

L. I. BORODKIN
Moskovskii Gosudarstvennyi
 Universitet
Moscow, USSR

Y. I. KIRYANOV
Institut istorii SSSR
Moscow, USSR

LORENZO BORDOGNA
Universita di Trento
Trento, Italy

GIAN PRIMO CELLA
Universita di Trieste
Trieste, Italy

GIANCARLO PROVASI
Universita di Brescia
Brescia, Italy

List of contributors

PAUL EDWARDS
Warwick University
Coventry, England

MICHELLE PERROT
Universite de Paris
Paris, France

KEITH BURGESS
Roehampton Institute
London, England

DAVID MONTGOMERY
Yale University
Yale Station, Connecticut

ELISABETH DOMANSKY
University of Chicago
Chicago, Illinois

HEATHER HOGAN
Oberlin College
Oberlin, Ohio

BRUNO BEZZA
Universita di Milano
Milan, Italy

HUGUES LAGRANGE
Centre National de Recherches
    Scientifiques (CNRS)
Paris, France

Preface

Most of the contributions to this volume have been drawn, in revised form, from papers originally presented at an international colloquium in comparative labor history held in Paris in June 1982, under the sponsorship of the Maison des Sciences de l'Homme, and from the discussions to which these contributions gave rise. The major object of the participants in this colloquium was to discuss, in a comparative perspective, the patterns of continuity and change in industrial labor conflicts in major industrialized countries before, during, and in the immediate aftermath of the First World War, and to explore the similarities and differences in these patterns of labor unrest and their underlying dynamics, with particular emphasis on the application for this purpose of quantitative methods. The participants included specialists in labor history and in the application of quantitative techniques to the analysis of industrial labor conflicts from seven countries: Austria, France, the Federal Republic of Germany, Great Britain, Italy, the United States, and the USSR. (Their involvement was supported, in most cases, by research institutions and learned societies of their countries of origin.)

At the conclusion of this colloquium, most of the participants expressed the desire to pursue jointly certain of the major substantive and analytic problems addressed in its proceedings, and in particular to explore further the possibilities of analyzing them in a comparative perspective through the application of quantitative methods. An international working group was created for this purpose, and assigned the task of designing and launching a cooperative project to further these objectives. To assist the implementation of this project, an international cooperative framework was established through the conclusion of accords involving the Maison des Sciences de l'Homme (Paris), the International Research and Exchanges Board (New York), the Academy of Sciences of the USSR, and the eventual cooperation of the Friedrich Ebert and Feltrinelli Foundations. The tasks pursued by this Project of date include:

xi

Preface

1. The creation of an international data bank to make available, in computer readable form, the statistical data on industrial labor conflicts recorded in the official and other major sources for the seven countries eventually encompassed in our Project design (Austro-Hungary, France, Great Britain, Italy, Germany, Imperial Russia, and the United States) from the inception of these sources (usually in the late nineteenth century) through the years of the First World War and of its immediate aftermath. For each of the countries concerned, data are to be provided on the overall intensity of industrial labor conflicts, as well as on their causes, durations, and outcomes, at the finest available level of aggregation (by branch of industry and/or geographical jurisdiction), along with major objective indices for the branches of industry and work forces for which these strike data were presented. The magnetic tapes on which these data are being recorded will be distributed at cost by the Maison des Sciences de l'Homme along with appropriate documentation for their use, to existing data banks as well as to interested individual scholars.

2. The organization, under the sponsorship of the Project, of other colloquia in the field of comparative labor history. In addition to our 1982 colloquium, the following meetings have been held to date, or are currently planned:

a. A colloquium convened in Cortona, Italy, in June 1986, under the sponsorship of the Feltrinelli Foundation, in cooperation with the Maison des Sciences de l'Homme, the International Research and Exchanges Board, the Friedrich Ebert Foundation, and the USSR Academy of Sciences. The proceedings of this colloquium were devoted to more detailed discussions of patterns and dynamics of labor unrest during the period of the First World War and its immediate aftermath. The papers presented included qualitative as well as quantitative analyses of patterns of industrial labor conflicts in major European countries during these years, of the pressures and dislocations induced by the war that contributed to these labor conflicts, and of the roles played by certain of the major actors drawn into these labor conflicts and in the efforts at their organization and eventual resolution: employers, trade unions and other labor organizations, and the agencies of the state. But the most distinctive feature of this colloquium was the emphasis laid on the presentation of case studies of particular cities, regions, and branches of industry, in each of these belligerent countries that were beset during these years by particularly intense labor unrest. These case studies were discussed in a comparative perspective in an effort to bring out the similarities and differences that distinguished the dynamics of industrial labor conflicts in these epicenters of labor unrest.

b. A colloquium held in the Federal Republic of Germany in the spring of 1989, under the sponsorship of the Friedrich Ebert Foundation, which was devoted to analyses, in greater depth and longer term historical perspective, of the revolutionary and protorevolutionary situations that surfaced in a number of European countries at the end of the First World War in the interaction between industrial workers and other major political and social actors.

c. An international conference to be convened in Leningrad in 1990 under the sponsorship of the Institute of History of the USSR of the Soviet Academy of Sciences, which will pursue these themes in Russia's historical experience, and in particular the analysis of the dynamics of labor unrest, in the context of the "krizis verkhov" and "krizis nizov" – the crises that unfolded in the upper and lower strata of the Russian body politic – from the turn of the century up to the October Revolution.

3. The joint publication program, which has been designed in connection with these activities of the Project, includes:

a. The publication, in revised form, of the proceedings of the international colloquia listed above. (Those of the Cortona colloquium of June 1986 are to appear in an English language volume, as part of the *Annali* of the Feltrinelli Foundation, in a joint publication with the Maison des Sciences de l'Homme.)

b. Critical analyses of the major statistical sources used in the creation of the Project's data bank on industrial labor conflicts, contributed by specialists in the labor history of the various countries concerned. A volume incorporating Russian language versions of these contributions has recently been published by the Institute of History of the USSR of the Soviet Academy of Sciences. An English language version, being prepared under the sponsorship of the Maison des Sciences de l'Homme, is to include statistical tables presenting the aggregate data recorded for the Project's data bank about the intensity and character of industrial labor conflicts, as well as the objective indices provided about the branches of industry and geographical areas for which they were recorded. Certain of the data presented, in particular for France and Imperial Russia, have not previously been available in any published form, and include aggregations newly constituted for the Project's data bank on the basis of strike-by-strike data. A morphological analysis of the aggregate data presented in the major sources for each of the countries concerned will seek through the application of descriptive quantitative techniques to regroup the original aggregations, in an effort to suggest certain criteria to be used in comparative analyses of the indices they provide on the intensity and character of industrial labor conflicts.

The contributions incorporated in this volume have thus been conceived as the first of a series of efforts to assist the further development of studies in the field of comparative labor history, and in particular to further the application of quantitative techniques to the analysis of industrial labor conflicts in a comparative perspective. We have listed these activities here partly to bring them to the attention of interested scholars, but also to express our gratitude to the specialists from various countries who are participating in this truly international cooperative effort, as well as to those individuals and groups whose support has made it possible.

In this connection, we owe a special debt of gratitude to Messrs. Clemens Heller and Maurice Aymard of the Maison des Sciences de l'Homme, whose intelligence, generosity, and tolerance saw us through our first stumbling steps. We also need to express our appreciation to I.D. Koval'chenko, V.I. Bovykin, and their associates at the Academy of Sciences of the USSR, to Wesley Fisher and his colleagues at the International Research and Exchanges Board, and to the staffs of the Friedrich Ebert and Feltrinelli Foundations, all of whom have contributed at various stages to the fulfillment of our Project's research objectives. Finally I wish to express my personal gratitude to Jan Sammer, Marianne Dumont, and Laura Elwyn for their respective contributions to the preparation of the manuscript of this volume.

LEOPOLD H. HAIMSON

I

Introductions

1

Theories and realities

CHARLES TILLY

Connections and comparisons

In what ways does the tide shape the beach, and the beach contain the tide? Clearly they depend on each other somehow, yet their interdependency is as subtle and hard to trace as is the connection between industrial and political conflict. Anyone who examines the history of World War I and its settlement in Europe, for example, notices the interplay among warmaking, wartime control of labor, mass strikes, and socialist bids for power. But in what sense, and how, did these varieties of conflict shape each other?

Formidable obstacles stand in the way of any straightforward answer to the question: the vagueness of such terms as "industrial and political conflict"; the variability of experience among countries, regions, and industries; the likelihood of further causes such as fluctuations in production and military expenditure; the probable complexity of any such causal web. Still, the relations badly need untangling. Our book follows some strands of the web within an important but relatively restricted frame: Europe and North America from 1890 to the early 1920s. It examines the interplay of politics and industrial conflict in Russia, Germany, France, Italy, Great Britain, and the United States.

Within that frame, we have a chance to make new, important comparisons. Fresh evidence concerning industrial conflict in Russia before the 1917 Revolution prompted the work that eventually produced this volume. Over the last decade, through research decribed in several papers appearing later in the book, it has become possible to document Russian strike activity by locality, industry, and period from 1890 to 1917 with far greater richness and accuracy than earlier researchers had managed. The availability of the new evidence raised the possibility of comparisons between Russian experience and that of other countries for which good documentation and interesting analyses already existed.

The broad comparison, in its turn, led to further questions: to what extent each country had a distinctive history of industrial conflict that grew from the character of its state and the nature of its working classes, whether skilled workers and capital-intensive industries generally played an exceptional role in the politicization of strike activity, how strike waves articulated with large-scale political conflicts, and so on. It led back to an old, unresolved question: how distinctive a path to revolution did Russia follow? To what extent did other countries follow similar paths, only to turn away from them? What accounts for the differences between the Russian path and the others? Such questions and comparisons inform all parts of our book.

If the book reports international comparisons, it also results from international cooperation. The authors currently work in France, the United States, Italy, the Soviet Union, the German Federal Republic, and the United Kingdom. They examine the same set of countries, but not in neat congruence between country of origin and object of study; in nine of the twenty-one papers, authors report on countries other than their own. Even when scrutinizing their home ground, the authors typically do so with deliberate *Entfremdung* – standing off and placing familiar experience in comparative perspective in order to see its essential characteristics more clearly.

Why 1890 to the early 1920s? No doubt World War I and the Russian revolutions of 1905 and 1917 give anyone who finds the interaction of industrial and political conflict interesting reason enough to examine the period with care. But many more wars and domestic conflicts engaged our six countries during those years. The list of major events by the year they began (Small and Singer 1982, 79–80, 225–7) includes:

Year	International wars	Revolutions and civil wars
1894	Franco–Madagascan	
1895	Italo–Ethiopian	
1898	Spanish–American	
1904	Russo–Japanese	
1905		Russia
1911	Italo–Turkish	
1914	World War I	
1917		Russia
1919	Russo–Polish	Russia
	Hungarian–Allies	Hungary

Our six countries also were involved indirectly in a number of other wars. The United States, for example, hovered over the Cuban insurrection of 1895 and the Philippine wars of 1896 and 1899. Russia attempted to mediate in the Balkan wars of 1912 and 1913. And all of our countries carried on military actions in their colonies.

4

International and civil wars, to qualify for the Small–Singer catalog, had to involve at least 1,000 deaths from battle. Many less lethal events occurred in both categories. In Italy, for instance, important conflicts of our period included the Sicilian Fasci (1893–4), the Massa–Carrara insurrection (1894), the Fatti di Maggio (1898), Red Week (1914), the Fatti di Agosto (1917), the factory occupations (1920), and the repeated struggles between Fascists and their enemies (1919 onward). In Germany, major confrontations included the worker–police battles of Berlin (1980), Polish resistance to Prussian schools (1901), anti-Prussian actions in Alsace (1913), not to mention the mutinies and socialist insurrections of 1918 and 1919. If we then interpolate the multiple waves of strikes over the same span of time, the problem begins to define itself: How did these various forms of conflict interlock? To what extent did they flow from common causes? To what degree, and how, did one struggle – international or domestic, industrial or political, lethal or not – lead to another? Did all states face an opportunity for revolution at the end of World War I? If so, why did the struggle work itself out so differently in Russia, the United Kingdom, Italy, Germany, France, and the United States?

In order to get at such questions, we clearly must learn a great deal about local and national histories. But we must also compare across national boundaries. The varied revolutionary movements in Western Europe from 1918 to 1920, for instance, become more intelligible in comparison, and in connection, with the Bolshevik Revolution in Russia. A comparison between Britain and Germany, on the other hand, establishes that the presence of a large number of workers in capital-concentrated industry alone did not suffice to produce a widespread revolutionary movement after World War I. Again anarchism, syndicalism, and their amalgams played larger parts in the working-class politics of Italy and France (not to mention Spain) than in Russia, Great Britain, or the United States; here a comparison suggests examining the influence of organized agricultural workers and small-town artisans on working-class political temper.

Our six countries deserve comparison. Broad similarities among their experiences in the nineteenth and twentieth centuries make comparisons at least thinkable. The United States, Great Britain, Germany, France, Italy, and Russia all went through considerable industrialization, urbanization, capital concentration, and population growth after 1860 – even though differences in the pace, timing, and character of those changes usually attract our attention first. Seen in the context of all the world's nations, these six countries also had relatively similar experiences with economic growth. As Figure 1 shows, all of them reached 1900 with GNP per capita above 200 U.S. dollars (1960), when "developed countries" as a whole stood at 475 dollars and Third World countries having market economies at 170 dollars (Bairoch 1981). As Figure 1 shows, GNP per capita rose in all six countries between 1860 and 1929, and was rising

5

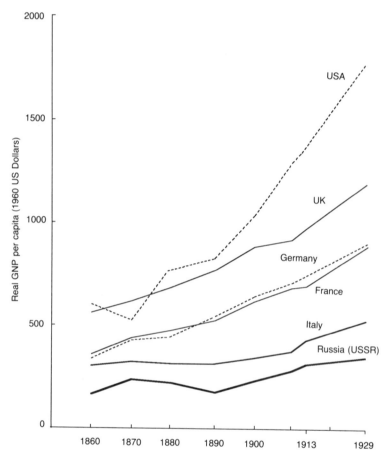

Figure 1. Real GNP per capita in six countries, 1860–1929 (Source: Bairoch 1976:286; Bairoch 1981:10)

more rapidly than usual over the period that concerns us most, 1890–1924. Russia and Italy started lowest and experienced the least growth in per capita production, while the United Kingdom and the United States led the way. Thus we have both similarities and differences to explain.

In the realm of industrial conflict, we likewise have significant differences among countries to place in the context of broad similarity. We can, for example, compute number of strikes and number of strikers per 100,000 workers in all industries for dates around 1900. (In the case of Russia, the numbers of strikes and of strikers involved in the two estimates are those reported by the factory inspectors only; the low estimate compares those

Country	Strikes/ 100,000	Strikers/ 100,000	Percentage of workers in manufacturing
Great Britain	4.0	1159	37.6
Germany	8.6	1883	28.5
France	3.7	900	25.4
Italy	3.8	831	23.7
U.S.A.	6.5	1993	21.8
Russia	0.5–7.2	207–1703	13.2

numbers to the entire labor force and the high estimate to the labor force in the firms covered by the factory inspectors. The true rates should lie between these two extremes.) Since strikes tended to concentrate in manufacturing, some of the differences are undoubtedly due to variations in the proportion of national labor forces in manufacturing. We cannot, however, simply exclude nonmanufacturing workers from consideration; in Italy and France, for instance, agricultural laborers struck fairly often. Thus the broad national differences immediately call forth finer comparisons.

Yet comparison poses its own difficulties: not only the obvious requirements of making the evidence and the categories comparable, but the more obscure choices of logic and scale of comparison. If the efforts of bureaucrats and scholars have put strike data into ostensibly similar forms, for example, the legal definitions separating strikes from other forms of conflict (such as demonstrations and "riots") themselves result from previous struggles among workers, employers, and government officials. They vary from one country and era to another. Other complications follow: Workers in different countries sometimes pursue similar ends by very different means (including strikes, demonstrations, and what authorities call riots), and in moments of deep political division, observers and participants assign different meaning to strikes than in moments of relative tranquility.

It is not certain, furthermore, that national states provide coherent frames for the comparative study of industrial conflict; if we want to get at the relationship between the structure of capital and the character of conflict, for example, a comparison between the coal and textile regions that span the borders of France and Belgium may well serve us better than a global comparison of France and Belgium. At a minimum, any analyst who insists on comparing national states must take into account profound national differences in industrial composition, regional distribution, labor force characteristics, and political control over industry. Often a comparison of industries and localities within and across national boundaries will yield more understanding than an equally extensive comparison of national aggregates. Both sorts of comparisons, will occupy us as this book proceeds.

7

Theoretical stakes

Theoretically, much is at stake in such comparisons. The study of industrial and political conflict from 1890 to 1922 can draw on four main literatures:

1. political and economic history at the level of the historical era;
2. economic analyses of strikes at the individual level;
3. treatments of political mobilization at the group level;
4. theories of revolution at the level of states.

Political and economic history of the period 1890–1922 generally organizes around a few major events and processes: the transformation of capitalism, the development of big industry, the rise of Fascism, World War I, the Russian revolutions. To the extent that it goes beyond narrative, it stresses the causes and consequences of these events and processes. The literature rumbles with controversy over such questions as the causes, consequences, and avoidability of World War I. By examining the diverse trajectories of industrial and political conflict in six countries during the three decades after 1890, we will necessarily join many of the controversies.

Economic analyses of strikes characteristically seek to identify the sufficient conditions for workers' decisions to strike, drawing on such factors as the organization of production, the structure of labor markets, the business cycle, and changes in the political climate. Although most theories, strictly speaking, concern individual strikes, empirical work rarely deals with one strike at a time. Research in this field often involves the statistical estimation of equations representing a hypothetical set of relations among those factors, using aggregate strike data as evidence. One of the controversies in the field – as we shall see – concerns the degree to which (or conditions in which) strikes connect with struggles for control of the state and therefore acquire a political edge.

Treatments of *political mobilization* commonly seek to explain why groups of people vary so widely in their readiness to organize and act together on their shared interests. Theories of political mobilization divide roughly into *cumulative* and *constructive*. On the cumulative side, the typical model sees individuals responding to the stresses and cleavages produced by rapid social change, developing personal grievances, and joining with other likeminded individuals (often under the leadership of charismatic figures) in some organization or collective action that expresses the common grievances; shared consciousness thus becomes the sine qua non of collective action.

On the constructive side, the quintessential scheme treats interests as resting on the everyday organization of production and coercion, portrays a carryover of existing social ties into collective action, and stresses strategic interaction among parties characterized by well-defined divisions of interest. Controversies concerning political mobilization therefore occur at several levels: the nature of

8

the phenomenon in general, the relevance of different social changes to particular kinds of mobilization, the explanation of group differences with respect to involvement in crucial conflicts and collective actions.

Theories of *revolution* customarily operate at the level of national states. The division between cumulative and constructive analyses that appears in studies of political mobilization reappears, unsurprisingly, in discussions of revolution. Theories of revolution differ, broadly speaking, according to whether they imagine a massive, aggrieved, simultaneous popular response to disruption or the transformation of existing interests and social cleavages into a struggle for national power. But they also differ with respect to scope. As Jack Goldstone puts it:

> In the first part of this century, one group of theorists, the natural-history school, defined revolution narrowly. They examined only the great revolutions and sought regularities in the way such revolutions occurred. In reply, later theorists argued that to develop and test generalizations about social behavior one must study large numbers of events. As the number of great revolutions was rather small, this general-theory school sought to include revolutions within the framework of more common events. Grouping great revolutions with peasant revolts, riots, unsuccessful revolutions, and sometimes civil wars, they sought to ground the common causes of all these events in a general theory of collective political violence.
>
> Recently a third generation of theorists, the structural-theory school, has sought to avoid either too narrow or too broad a definition. They have insisted that although the various forms of collective political violence are in some sense similar, they are still different kinds of events, and develop from quite different circumstances. Thus they have separated these events into distinct clusters – successful revolutions, unsuccessful revolutions, revolutionary coups, etc. – and asked: What kinds of states have a political structure that is vulnerable to revolution? What kinds of government and social organization are prone to revolutionary coups? What kinds of states are so structured that they are likely to be stable, or likely to experience only unsuccessful revolutions? In sum, this school is interested in the vulnerability of different kinds of states and social organization to different kinds of events (Goldstone 1982: 189).

Since the Russian Revolution of 1917 initiated much of this theorizing about revolution, and invariably figures in comparisons of great revolutions, the literature bears directly on our book's subject matter.

The study of industrial and political conflict from 1890 to 1922 promises to draw on and contribute to all four of these lines of thought: political and economic history, economic analyses of strikes, treatments of political mobilization, and theories of revolution. All four converge at a precise point when we ask about the role of industrial conflict in revolution. How much, and how, does the pattern of conflict among workers, employers, and government officials

9

reflect or constrain the character and likelihood of revolutionary struggles for power? the outcome of those struggles? Is it true (as Koenker and Rosenberg say later in this book) that revolution "inverts the relationship between strikes and the system of industrial relations," since revolutionary strikes themselves alter the terms and stakes of industrial conflict? These questions – long standard in Marxist analyses of revolution – turn out to be pivotal for our whole enterprise.

Other questions also matter: Who are the actors? What difference does their action make? In analyzing strikes, it is easy to slip into the supposition that all that has to be explained is the action of workers. A little reflection on the forms of industrial conflict, however, dispels that illusion. During our period, the industrial conflicts of our six countries most often took the forms of firm-by-firm strikes; communitywide turnouts of all the workers in a trade; employer-initiated lockouts; attacks on owners, employers, strikebreakers, or their property; demonstrations; public meetings; electoral campaigns; and similar events. A number of forms that had often appeared early in the nineteenth century – including shaming ceremonies and retaliatory destruction of machines – had by then become rare. But the old forms and the new all involved at least two parties in sustained interaction.

The politics of industrial conflict

In the long run, each of the more recent forms of conflict acquired a kind of legal standing through repetition, negotiation, and compromise. Workers, employers, officials, police, judges, and other parties to the conflicts fought out rules and understandings. The rules and understandings were often implicit but powerful; no country, for example, explicitly legalized demonstrations as such, but in all our countries, police, troops, officials, and demonstrators hammered out limits within which some groups could voice demands and grievances by assembling at their own initiative in public space – that is, demonstrate – without great danger of immediate repression.

Sometimes the rules and understandings were explicit; with many qualifications, all our countries except Russia established a legal right to strike at some time before 1900. In the United States, courts construed the eighteenth-century Bill of Rights as granting a limited right to strike. Great Britain first legalized some forms of the strike in 1824, Saxony in 1861, France in 1864, Prussia in 1869, Italy in 1889 (very restricted, with fuller rights in 1901). As guarantors, monitors, and repressors, governments remained parties to industrial conflict throughout our period.

In the short run, to be sure, both governmental intervention and the involvement of governments as the objects of strikes varied from one circumstance to another. From 1890 to 1922, workers rarely aimed their strikes directly at governments, or built into them demands concerning the structure of political power. The one-day strike on the First of May, which began to generalize in Western Europe and North America toward 1890, constituted the chief exception. At the municipal level, the theory and practice of the general strike were just coming into existence. Milan's general strike of 1904, which pitted workers from the full range of trades against employers and the municipality, was the first of its kind anywhere.

Most strikes pitted the employees of a single firm against their own bosses. Local governments stood by to contain the action, but did not intervene directly; the national state did no more than collect data about the strike. In French strikes from 1893 to 1914, local Justices of the Peace attempted to organize some form of conciliation in about 45% of all conflicts, but official representatives of the national state only entered the formal resolution of about 5% (Shorter and Tilly 1974: 40–41). During 1919–24, however, formal governmental intervention rose to 14% of all French strikes. Furthermore, in the great majority of strikes, worker demands concerned earnings, employment, and working conditions rather than anything one could reasonably call "political." The political implications of strikes lay rather in their legal context, their tendency to rise and fall as a function of the political strength of labor, and their potential as a weapon in regional and national struggles for power.

In the late nineteenth and early twentieth centuries, the prevalent forms of industrial conflict always involved at least two actors: a group of workers who pressed claims on their employers, and the employers themselves. But government officials, local and national, often became involved as mediators, allies, and repressors. Other groups of workers, shopkeepers, local dignitaries such as priests, and spectators likewise took part in industrial conflicts repeatedly, if not always willingly; when conflicts became acute, all members of a community sometimes had to choose sides and lend aid to their allies. In some of our countries, notably the United States, employers hired private police to maintain order, restrain workers, and protect property or personnel, sometimes breaking a strike. All these parties, then, played their parts in industrial conflict. And the responses of several of them – not only employers, but also police and governmental officials – to workers' actions regularly made a large difference to the struggle's outcome.

If so, it makes little sense to limit analyses of industrial conflict to the conditions of workers. The *relationship* of workers to other groups determines the frequency and character of collective conflict. Within routine labor relations, strikes are rare when the positions of management and labor are very unequal; they become much more frequent as the two parties approach equality. The same principle applies more generally: The frequency of industrial conflict fluctuates as power balances change – not only between workers and employers, but also with regard to officials, allies, and other parties to the conflict. Struggles

11

within the work force sometimes precipitate strikes, especially when several organizations compete for the allegiance of workers by attempting to demonstrate their militancy and effectiveness. This strategic character of industrial conflict helps account for the sharp fluctuations in its intensity from one year to the next, and requires that any sensible models and explanations of strikes focus not on the condition of workers alone but on the interaction between workers and others.

Our questions

Every author in this volume pursues an individual set of questions, questions that reflect the separate countries, periods, and theoretical orientations of a diverse set of studies. Nevertheless, some questions recur. Those questions knit our volume together. More than anything else, the following papers ask under what conditions industrial conflict – and more specifically strikes – acquired revolutionary potential. That vast problem leads to others: To what extent did the industrial conflict of other countries resemble Russia's, and what accounts for the differences? Did the industrial conflicts of apparently revolutionary moments in such countries as Italy and Germany resemble those of Russia? Outside of revolutionary moments, how often and when did industrial conflict converge with overt national struggles for power? What determined the variations in the impact of World War I in this regard?

In order to discipline the answers to these questions, we have divided our book into three main parts. The first, Models and Realities, takes general ideas concerning industrial and political conflict, and confronts them with evidence from single countries. After Leopold Haimson and Eric Brian's introduction, Friedhelm Boll treats German strike waves; James Cronin reports more generally on strikes and political power in Britain; Leopold Haimson and Ronald Petrusha deal with the strike waves of 1905–7 and 1912–14 in Russia; Diane Koenker and William Rosenberg close in on the Russian strikes of 1917; V. I. Bovykin, L. I. Borodkin, and Iu. I. Kiryianov report on time series of Russian strikes from 1895 to 1913; Lorenzo Bordogna, Gian Primo Cella, and Giancarlo Provasi present analyses of Italian strike activity; and P. K. Edwards takes up strikes and politics in the United States.

The next section, Metalworking Industries in Comparative Perspective, narrows the focus to a crucial set of industries. Michelle Perrot introduces that section, followed by David Montgomery on machinists' strikes in the United States from 1870 to 1922, Keith Burgess on British engineering workers during World War I, Elisabeth Domansky on the German metalworkers' union from 1891 to 1922, Heather Hogan on St. Petersburg from 1900 to 1914, Leopold Haimson on Russia as a whole from 1890 to 1914, and Bruno Bezza on Italian metalworkers during World War I.

The final section concerns Effects of Short-term Variation. There, after Charles Tilly provides an introduction, Diane Koenker and William Rosenberg look at the impact of revolution on the Russian strikes of 1917, Leopold Haimson examines conjunctural factors in the Russian strikes wave of 1912–14, Friedhelm Boll writes on strikes and economic fluctuations in Germany, and Hughes Lagrange takes up variation in French strike activity during World War I.

After these three major parts comes a concluding essay by Leopold Haimson. We will not have answered all of our questions by the time we arrive there but we will have a much clearer idea how the experiences of the United States, the United Kingdom, France, Germany, Italy, and Russia bear on the relationship between industrial and political conflict.

References

Adams, Graham, Jr. 1966. *The Age of Industrial Violence.* New York: Columbia University Press.

Amsden, John, and Stephen Brier. 1977. "Coal Miners on Strike: The Transformation of Strike Demands and the Formation of a National Union." *Journal of Interdisciplinary History* 7: 583–616.

Ashenfelter, Orly, and George E. Johnson. 1969. "Bargaining Theory, Trade Unions, and Industrial Strike Activity." *American Economic Review* 59: 34–49.

Bain, G. S, and F. Elsheikh. 1976. *Union Growth and the Business Cycle: An Econometric Analysis.* Oxford: Blackwell.

Bain, G. S., and Robert Price. 1980. *Profiles of Union Growth. A Comparative Statistical Portrait of Eight Countries.* Oxford: Blackwell.

Bairoch, Paul. 1976. "Europe's Gross National Product: 1800–1975." *Journal of European Economic History* 5: 273–340.

1981. "The Main Trends in National Economic Disparities since the Industrial Revolution." In Paul Bairoch & Maurice Levy-Leboyer, eds., *Disparities in Economic Development since the Industrial Revolution.* London: Macmillan.

Banks, J. A. 1970. *Marxist Sociology in Action.* London: Routledge & Kegan Paul.

Batstone, Eric, Ian Boraston, and Stephen Frenkel. 1978. *The Social Organization of Strikes.* Oxford: Blackwell.

Bean, R., and D. A. Peel. 1976. "Business Activity, Labor Organizations and Industrial Disputes in the U.K., 1892–1938," *Business History* 18: 205–11.

Boll, Friedhelm. 1981. *Massenbewegungen in Niedersachsen 1906–1920.* Bonn: Verlag Neue Gesellschaft.

Bonnell, Victoria. 1983. *Roots of Revolution: Workers' Politics and Organizations in St. Petersburg and Moscow, 1900–1914.* Berkeley: University of California Press.

Case, Millard. 1957. "The Relationship of Size of Firm and Strike Activity," *Monthly Labor Review* 80: 1334–444.

Cedarqvist, Jane. 1980. *Arbetare i strejk. Studier rorande arbetarnas politiska mobilisering under industrialismens genombrott. Stockholm 1850–1909.* Mongrafier utgivna av

13

Stockholms Kommun, 41. Stockholm: GOTAB.

Cella, G. P., ed. 1979. *Il movimento degli scioperi nel XX secolo.* Bologna: Il Mulino.

Christman, Lillian J., William R. Kelly, and Omer R. Galle. 1981. "Comparative Perspectives on Industrial Conflict." In Louis Kriesberg, ed., *Research in Social Movements, Conflict, and Change* 4: 67–93.

Churnside, R. J., and S. W. Creigh. 1981. "Strike Activity and Plant Size: A Note." *Journal of the Royal Statistical Society*, ser. A, vol. 144, pt 1: 104–11.

Clegg, H. A. 1976. *Trade Unionism under Collective Bargaining.* Oxford: Blackwell.

Cousineau, Jean-Michel, and Robert Lecroix. 1976. "Activité economique, inflation et activité de grève," *Relations industrielles* 31: 341–57.

Cronin, James E. 1979. *Industrial Conflict in Modern Britain.* London: Croom Helm.

Cronin, James E., and Jonathan Schneer, eds. 1982. *Social Conflict and the Political Order in Modern Britain.* London: Croom Helm.

Crouch, Colin, and Alessandro Pizzorno, eds. 1978. *The Resurgence of Class Conflict in Western Europe since 1968.* 2 vols. London: Macmillan.

Della Rocca, Giuseppe. 1976. "L'offensiva politica degli imprenditori nelle fabbriche." In Aris Accornero, ed., *Problemi del movimento sindecale in Italia, 1943–1973.* Milan: Feltrinelli.

Durand, Claude. 1981. *Chômage et violence. Longwy en lutte.* Paris: Galilee.

Durand, Claude, and Paul Dubois. 1975. *La grève. Enquête sociologique.* Paris: Armand Colin.

Durand, Michelle. 1977. *Les conflits du travail. Analyse structurelle.* Paris: Centre de Recherches en Sciences Sociales du Travail, Universite de Paris-Sud.

Edwards, Paul K. 1979. "The Social Determination of Strike Activity: An Explication and Critique." *Journal of Industrial Relations* 21: 198–216.

——— 1981. Strikes in the United States, 1881–1974. Oxford: Blackwell.

Eldridge, J. E. T. 1968. *Industrial Disputes: Essays in the Sociology of Industrial Relations.* London: Routledge & Kegan Paul.

Evans, E. W., and S. W. Creigh. 1977. *Industrial Conflict in Britain.* London: Frank Cass.

Forchheimer, K. 1948. "Some International Aspects of the Strike Movement." *Bulletin of the Oxford Institute of Statistics* 10: 9–24.

Franzosi, Roberto. 1981. "La conflittualita in Italia tra ciclo economico e contrattazione collecttive." *Rassegna Italiana de Sociologia* 22: 533–75.

Galambos, P., and E. W. Evans. 1966. "Work-Stoppages in the United Kingdom. 1951–1964: A Quantitative Study." *Bulletin of the Oxford University Institute of Economics and Statistics* 28: 33–55.

Goldstone, Jack A. 1982. "The Comparative and Historical Study of Revolutions," *Annual Review of Sociology* 8: 187–207.

Gouldner, Alvin. 1954. *Wildcat Strike: A Study in Worker–Management Relationships.* Yellow Springs, Ohio: Antioch College Press.

Gubbels, Robert. 1962. *La grève, phénomène de civilisation.* Brussels: Institut de Sociologie, Universite Libre.

Hanagan, Micheal P. 1980. *The Logic of Solidarity. Artisans and Industrial Workers in Three French Towns, 1871–1914.* Urbana: University of Illinois Press.

Hendricks, Wallace. 1975. "Labour Market Structure and Union Wage Levels." *Economic Inquiry* 13: 401–6.

Hibbs, Douglas A. 1978. "On the Political Economy of Long-Run Trends in Strike Activity." *British Journal of Political Science* 8: 153–75.

Ingham, Geoffrey K. 1974. *Strikes and Industrial Conflict. Britain and Scandinavia.* London: Macmillan.

Jenkins, J. Craig. 1983. "Resource Mobilization Theory and the Study of Social Movements." *Annual Review of Sociology* 9: 527–53.

Kaelble, Hartmut, and Heinrich Volkmann. 1973. "Konjouktur und Streik in Deutshland während des Uebergangs zum organisierten Kapitalismus." *Zeitschrift fur Wirtschafts- und Sozialwissenschaften* 92: 513–544.

Kassalow, Everett M. 1969. *Trade Unions and Industrial Relations: An Interational Comparison.* New York: Random House.

Kelly, John E., and Nigel Nicholson. 1980. "The Causation of Strikes: A Review of Theoretical Approaches and the Potential Contribution of Social Psychology." *Human Relations* 33: 853–83.

Knowles, K. G. J. C. 1974. *Strikes: A Study of Industrial Conflict with Special Reference to British Experience.* Oxford: Blackwell.

Kornhauser, Arthur, et al., eds. 1954. *Industrial Conflict.* New York: McGraw-Hill.

Korpi, Walter, and Michael Shalev. 1979. "Strikes, Industrial Relations and Class Conflict in Capitalist Societies." *British Journal of Sociology* 30: 164–87.

1980. "Strikes, Power and Politics in the Western Nations, 1900–1976." In Maurice Zeitlin, ed., *Political Power and Social Theory.* Greenwich, Conn.: JAI Press.

Kumar, Krishnan. 1983. "Class and Political Action in Nineteenth-Century England. Theoretical and Comparative Perspectives." *Archives Europeennes de Sociologie* 24: 3–43.

Lay, Adriana, Dora Marucco, and Maria Luisa Pesante. 1973. "Classe operaia e scioperi: ipotesi per il periodo 1880–1923." *Quadernia Storici* 8: 87–147.

Lequin, Yves. 1977. *Les ouvriers de la région lyonnaise (1848–1914). 2 vols.* Lyon: Presses Universitaires de Lyon.

McKibbin, Ross. 1984. "Why Was There No Marxism in Great Britain?" *English Historical Review* 99: 297–331.

Maitland, Ian. 1983. *The Causes of Industrial Disorder. A Comparison of a British and a German Factory.* London: Routledge & Kegan Paul.

Mayhew, K. 1979. "Economists and Strikes." *Oxford Bulletin of Economics and Statistics* 41: 1–20.

Merriman, John, ed. 1979. *Consciousness and Class Experience in Nineteenth-Century Europe.* New York: Holmes and Meier.

Mottez, Bernard. 1966. *Systemes de salaire et politiques patronales. Essai sur l'evolution des pratiques et des ideologies patronales.* Paris: Editions du Centre National de la Recherche Scientifique.

Parsley, C. S. 1980. "Labor Union Effects on Wage Gains: A Survey of Recent Literature." *Journal of Economic Literature* 18: 1–31.

Pencavel, John H. 1970. "An Investigation into Industrial Strike Activity in Britain." *Econometrica* 37: 239–56.

Perrot, Michelle. 1974. *Les ouvriers en greve. France 1870–1890.* 2 vols. Paris: Mouton.

Peterson, Florence. 1938. *Strikes in the United States, 1880–1936.* Washington, D. C.: U.S. Bureau of Labor Statistics.

15

Porta, Donatella della, and Gianfranco Pesquino, eds. 1983. *Terrorismo e violenza politica.* Bologna: Il Mulino.

Rimlinger, Gaston V. 1960. "The Legitimation of Protest: A Comparative Study in Labor History." *Comparative Studies in Society and History* 2: 329–43.

Romagnoli, Guido, and Maurizio Rossi. 1980. "La sindacalizzazione in Italia fra ciclo economico, conflitto e facilitazioni istitutionali." In Guido Romagnoli, ed., *La sindacalizzazione tra ideologia e pratica.* Rome: Edizioni Lavoro.

Ross, Arthur M., and George W. Hartman. 1960. *Changing Patterns of Industrial Conflict.* New York: Wiley.

Sabel, Charles F. 1982. *Work and Politics. The Division of Labor in Industry.* Cambridge: Cambridge University Press.

Sapsford, D. 1977. "A Time Series Analysis of U.K. Industrial Disputes." *Industrial Relations* 15: 242–9.

Shorey, John C. 1976. "An Inter-Industry Analysis of Strike Frequency." *Economica* 43: 349–65.

1977. "Time Series Analysis of Strike Frequency." *Industrial Relations* 15: 63–75.

Shorter, Edward, and Charles Tilly. 1974. *Strikes in France, 1830 to 1968.* Cambridge: Cambridge University Press.

Small, Melvin, and J. David Singer. 1982. *Resort to Arms. International and Civil Wars, 1816–1980.* Beverly Hills: Sage Publications.

Snyder, David. 1975. "Institutional Setting and Industrial Conflict. Comparative Analyses of France, Italy and the United States." *American Sociological Review* 40: 259–78.

1976. "Theoretical and Methodological Problems in the Analysis of Governmental Coercion and Collective Violence." *Journal of Political and Military Sociology* 4: 277–93.

Snyder, David, and William R. Kelly. 1976. "Industrial Violence in Italy, 1878–1903," *American Journal of Sociology* 82: 131–62.

Stearns, Peter N. 1968. "Against the Strike Threat: Employer Policy toward Labor Agitation in France, 1900–1914." *Journal of Modern History* 40: 474–500.

1975. *Lives of Labor. Work in a Maturing Industrial Society.* New York: Holmes & Meier.

Stern, Robert N. 1978. "Methodological Issues in Quantitative Strike Analysis." *Industrial Relations* 17: 32–42.

Taft, Philip, and Philip Ross. 1969. "American Labor Violence: Its Causes, Character and Outcome." In Hugh Davis Graham and Ted Robert Gurr, eds., *Violence in America: Historical and Comparative Perspective.* Washington, D. C.: U.S. Government Printing Office.

Tarrow, Sidney. 1983. *Struggling to Reform: Social Movements and Policy Change during Cycles of Protest.* Western Societies Program, Occasional Paper no. 15. Ithaca, N.Y.: Center for International Studies, Cornell University.

Tenfelde, Klaus, and Heinrich Volkmann, eds. 1981. *Streik. Zur Geshichte des Arbeitskampfes der Industrialisierung.* Munich: Beck.

Turner, H. A., Garfield Clack, and Geoffrey Roberts. 1967. *Labour Relations in the Motor Industry.* London: George Allen & Unwin.

Volkmann, Heinrich. 1977. "Modernisierung des Arbeitskampfs? Zum Formwandel von Streik und Aussperrung in Deutschland 1864–1975." In Hartmut Kaelble et al.,

16

Probleme der Modernisierung in Deutschland. Sozialhistorische Studien zum 19. und 20. Jahrhundert. Opladen: Westdeutscher Verlag.

Wardell, Mark L., Charles Vaught, and John N. Edwards. 1982. "Strikes: A Political Economy Approach." *Social Science Quarterly* 63: 409–27.

Wolman, Leo. 1976. *Ebb and Flow in Trade Unionism.* New York: Arno Press.

Zald, Mayer N., and John D. McCarthy, eds. 1979. *The Dynamics of Social Movements. Resource Mobilization, Social Control, and Tactics.* Cambridge, Mass.: Winthrop.

Zimmerman, Ekkart. 1983. *Political Violence, Crises and Revolutions.* Cambridge, Mass.: Schenkman.

2

The historical setting in Russia and the West

LEOPOLD H. HAIMSON

The role of strike actions as weapons in the struggle of industrial workers for power and autonomy in the workplace and also in the polity as a whole, and the interrelationships to be discerned between the various aspects of this labor struggle, have reemerged in recent years as a major theme in historical studies of labor unrest and of workers' movements. Yet, however obvious the relationship of strikes to politics appears – particularly when one focuses attention on major strike waves, which challenge most openly and directly the whole structure of power and authority governing workers' conditions of life and work – the processes underlying the outbreak, the unfolding, and the eventual outcomes of such major strike waves are by no means easy to establish, especially when one considers them in a comparative historical perspective.

To what extent and in what respects do major waves of labor unrest expose long-standing fissures in the societies in which they break out? To what degree do they in turn contribute to the widening, if not to the opening, of these fissures? What significance is to be assigned, in this connection, to the role of relatively long-term structural processes of change in the conditions of life and work of various strata of industrial workers, and their cumulative effects on these workers' mentalities, attitudes, and patterns of collective action? What role is to be attributed, on the other hand, to historically more circumscribed political and economic conjunctures, and to specific historical events? Last but not least, how can the interplay between these longer- and shorter-term processes be effectively examined in quantitative and qualitative analyses of continuities and changes in patterns of labor unrest, particularly when one considers them in a comparative perspective?

No period in European labor history poses these issues as acutely – or at least as dramatically – as the experience that European labor movements underwent in the early twentieth century, and especially during the period stretching from

18

the eve through the immediate aftermath of the First World War. In the accounts of most contemporary observers, and indeed of most historians who have scrutinized them retrospectively, the years immediately preceding the outbreak of the First World War stand out as a period in which effective institutional mechanisms emerged to defuse, if not to contain, industrial labor conflicts, and to serve as organizational instruments through which workers could make their weight effectively felt in the functioning of their industrial economies and bodies politic.

To be sure, even in the eyes of the most sanguine observers, there still appeared, as of 1914, some signal exceptions to this essentially optimistic vision of the involvement of industrial workers in the shaping of their respective polities. The Russian Empire provided the major case in point. In fact, as we shall try to show, Russia was only a partial exception to the patterns generally observable on the European labor scene, if not to the inferences that were drawn from them. But in the view of most contemporary observers, if prewar Russia was then experiencing a wave of labor unrest that was becoming increasingly explosive if not revolutionary in character (and was so reported in the contemporary European press), it was because Russia had not yet attained an institutional framework comparable to that of more advanced European countries – including the legal guarantees required for the maturation of a mass labor movement and labor party. As of the eve of the war, this view and the sense of Russia's backwardness that underlay it – relegating its contemporary labor experience to an exception that confirmed the rule – were widely shared by the various groupings of Russian Social Democracy, including the most radical of its factions. Need we recall that even in the eyes of Lenin and his followers, German Social Democracy and its leaders still represented, circa July 1914, the veritable exemplar of a mature labor party and labor movement?

In most European countries, the early years of the First World War appeared to confirm – indeed to accentuate dramatically – the centripetal tendencies at work in the relationship between the working classes of most European countries and their respective polities, even while they appeared to dispel the dreams of working-class solidarity that had also been nurtured, especially from the turn of the century onward, by the circles of the Socialist International. The outbreak of the war saw the socialist parties of most belligerent countries, or at least their majorities, rally to their respective governments, and in most cases actually join governments of national unity. Most of the trade union organizations through which workers had sought to exercise their influence on the functioning of the industrial economy also supported these countries' war efforts. As pressures inexorably mounted for full-scale industrial mobilization, the war years saw an unprecedented degree of intervention by the organs of the state, now bolstered by official representatives of working-class and employers' organizations, in the regulation of industrial relations, including the mediation

19

if not the arbitration of labor conflicts. Last but not least, most industrial workers in most belligerent countries actually rallied, at least at first, behind their official leaderships in support of their respective governments and indeed shared, however passively, the visions of national interest and national aims that they articulated and acted out.

The conclusion of the First World War was to shatter – equally dramatically – these representations of national unity, and the realities that underly them of the ties that has been forged between the industrial workers of Europe's various national societies and their respective polities. Indeed, in some of these polities, and particularly in those most sorely tried and bled by the war, the Russian Revolution of 1917 provided, even before the conclusion of military hostilities, an unexpectedly powerful catalyst for the outbreak of labor unrest. The end of the war was to see this unrest escalate – especially in the defeated, but even in some of the victorious countries – into waves of industrial strikes, which challenged more powerfully, more directly, and more openly than had been the case in European experience since at least the mid-nineteenth century, the very foundations of these countries' established political, social, and economic orders, and structures of authority.

One feature of this challenge appears especially ironic in the perspective we have sought to trace. The experience of the Russian Revolution emerged in the eyes of many of the workers who became involved in these waves of labor unrest as a meaningful example to follow in their challenge of their own *ordre etablit*. Indeed, the specific institutional forms that this experience publicized of the ways in which workers could organize for this challenge, if not of the goals that they should seek to pursue, suddenly appeared, however differently perceived by various strata of workers, as models to adopt in their own struggle for power and autonomy. This was the case of the role played by soviets of workers' deputies, workers' councils, and factory committees, as instruments for the achievement of workers' control of the body politic, of the national economy, and of their conditions of life and work in the enterprise. Thus, in four short years, in the eyes of millions of European workers, and of many of their leaders and supporters of other strata of society, Russia turned from a dramatic example of backwardness into a model of revolutionary struggle, if not of future political, social, and economic development.

It is easy for one to forget, over half a century later, the realities of this experience in European labor history, and especially the scope and intensity of the convulsions that it set off. The waves of labor unrest that it unleashed spread to the entire European continent, across the Channel, and indeed – in however mitigated a form – to other continents, and in many of the countries concerned, these waves did not subside until the early or mid-1920s. For students of labor history, these great strike waves pose in the most dramatic fashion the issue of how to study, in a comparative perspective, the patterns of labor unrest that they brought to the surface. They especially pose the problem of how to analyze effectively in such a perspective the factors that underlay the outbreak of these labor conflicts, the character and the intensity that they assumed, as well as their eventual outcomes – including the changes that these strike waves induced, or failed to induce, in the structures of the national polities that they so powerfully challenged.

The thorniness of the issues involved in such a comparative analysis and the need to consider in this connection the complex interplay between long-term and short-term processes of change, appear especially evident when one approaches these problems from the perspective of Russia's historical experience. As readers will have occasion to infer from some of the contributions to this volume, certain extraordinarily inviting similitudes suggest themselves between the strike waves that broke out in other European countries at the end and in the immediate aftermath of the First World War and those that unfolded in Russia, not only during the Revolution of 1917 but also in earlier years: from the summer of 1915 to February 1917, but also during the immediate prewar period – from the Lena goldfields massacre of April 1912 up to July 1914, if not in the course of the revolutionary period of 1905–7.

First and foremost, such similitudes suggest themselves about the patterns of labor unrest that surfaced in the course of these various strike waves: in the degree to which ostensibly economic as well as political strikes came to focus explicity on issues of power and authority, and especially in the acuteness of the sense displayed by many of the workers who participated in them of the inextricable connections between the grievances and aspirations generated by their roles in the production process and their relationships with the supervisors adminstering it on the shop floor, and their position in the polity as a whole. It was this instinctive sense – far more than the appeals of any outside agitators – that contributed to the mutual reinforcement and sometime fusion of the various economic, social, and political grievances and aspirations that surfaced among the workers who were drawn into these strike waves into a struggle against the whole structure of power and authority that governed their lives.

Major similitudes, worthy of further exploration, also suggest themselves about the social characteristics of those strata of industrial workers who became most militantly involved in the various dimensions of this struggle of power, and who indeed provided the catalysts for the unleashing of the various strike waves on the European continent at the end of the war, but also in prewar Russia. One was the degree of concentration of labor unrest, especially in the early phases of these strike waves, in large urban centers where industrial workers were represented in large numbers and in close proximity to other groups of urban society, including members of the professional classes. Almost as uniform was the degree of concentration of the most highly politicized, if not revolutionary, forms of this unrest, especially at the outset, in those capital cities

21

of the various countries concerned that were distinguished by such large concentrations of industrial workers. Complementing and usually reinforcing these patterns of urban concentration was the perhaps even more notable, and certainly more novel, concentration of the more militant forms of labor unrest – of those involving the most direct confrontations of power and authority in the workplace, as well as in the polity as a whole – among workers of mechanical and metal-processing enterprises.

More often than not, these two patterns of the distribution of labor unrest proved mutually reinforcing, given the disproportionate concentrations of metal-processing and mechanical enterprises in large urban centers. These patterns also appeared to contribute to the fusion of the various dimensions of the struggle for power that so strikingly emerged as the major theme of these strike waves: of their participants' struggle for power and autonomy in the work-place, in their local communities, and in the body politic as a whole.

It is not difficult to discern, especially in comparative perspective, what the wartime conjuncture contributed to the highly politicized, if not revolutionary, character that labor unrest assumed among these specific strata of workers of various belligerent countries. The grounds for the politicization of labor unrest among workers of metal enterprises were, after all, laid down by the unprecedented responsibilities that the state assumed in the course of the war in the mobilization and control of the national economy, including the mediation and arbitration of labor conflicts. Most prominent and most pervasive in this regard was the role that the organs of political authority played in the regulation of labor relations in metal processing and mechanical enterprises working for defense. By the same token, once the "union sacree" that has provided the justification of this intervention broke down, the workers employed in defense-related industries were irresistibly drawn to turn their pent-up grievances and aspirations not only against their employers, but also against the state, which had assumed this unprecedented accountability for their fate and which, once the war was over, withdrew it in many cases equally abruptly. Among no strata of workers was the impulse for such a direct challenge of political authority more irresistibly felt than in those European capitals – the seats of political authority – where workers of metal-processing and mechanical enterprises were concentrated in large numbers.

But even while a comparative perspective brings out so sharply the catalytic effects of the First World War on the dynamics of labor unrest, it also raises even more basic issues about the contribution of certain common patterns in European experience since the late nineteenth century to the character that these strike waves eventually assumed – however submerged or obscured the workings of these longer-term processes may have been in other European countries than Imperial Russia before the First World War. In this more long-term perspective, two mutually reinforcing processes that had been at work in the crystallization of European nation states, and in the involvement of European workers into their respective polities that these processes induced, invite further exploration.

One was the growing intervention on the part of the state, in most of the countries concerned, in the regulation of the industrial economy, including labor relations, and even more broadly, the extension of the assumption by the state of responsiblity for workers' conditions of life and work implicit in the social and welfare legislation issued during these years. The other common pattern European experience was of course the growing involvement of industrial workers in the political process – in part stimulated by, but also reinforcing, the sense of accountability for their welfare assigned to political authority. What was particularly distinctive of the evolution of European polities in the early twentieth century in this regard was not merely the extension of political suffrage to industrial workers, but also the emergence and involvement in the political process of major labor and/or socialist parties. These groups were now explicitly identified by industrial workers as their political representatives as a distinct social group if not as a "class" in the polity, and indeed as the vessels for the articulation of these workers' own grievances and claims, rather than as the patrons, however benevolent, of these claims.

Both of these dimensions of the evolution of European nation-states in the late nineteenth and early twentieth centuries – the extension of the responsibilities assumed by the state for the conditions of life and work of industrial workers, and the involvement of workers in the political process as a distinct group in the polity – were themselves reinforced by the processes of consolidation of the industrial economies that the countries concerned experienced to different degrees during these years at the national, and indeed the international, level. These processes of industrial consolidation, in the various forms that they assumed – the merger and consolidation of industrial firms (usually in the form of stock companies), the growing predominance in certain sectors of large enterprises benefiting from economics of scale, the emergence of trusts and cartels to control and divide markets, and the leading role often assumed in these processes by investment banks – contributed to major changes in the character and production of work processes, with effects on patterns of labor relations and ultimately on labor unrest, to which we shall presently return. Almost from the outset, these processes also made possible a greater degree of militance on the part of individual employers, and of unity on the part of employers' organizations, in their confrontation of workers' demands and of their efforts to organize collectively. (Employers could now afford to display such greater militance given their greater degree of control over their markets, and hence lesser vulnerability to strikes).

By the same token, these processes of industrial consolidation increased the pressures on workers not only to organize at the national level, but also to turn

23

to the state and to the political process to redress the balance in their confrontation of employers. Faced as it was by these tendencies toward the organization of both management and labor on a national scale, and by the tensions they induced on the political and economic scene, the state, however reluctantly in many cases, was increasingly pulled to intervene.

The experience of the First World War accentuated these, as well as other long-term tendencies at work in the consolidation of European nation-states and of their industrial economies. Indeed, as we already noted, the pressures of war induced the absorption of workers' and employers' organizations, now officially recognized by the state as partners at the national level, into the institutional mechanisms created to mobilize the industrial economy and regulate labor relations. But the unfolding of the war also eventually unveiled the potential of these various processes – and in particular of the growing involvement of the state into the life of industrial workers, and of workers in the functioning of the polity as a whole – for the accentuation rather than the resolution of political, social, and economic conflicts, and indeed for their eventual fusion.

Russia was no exception to the unfolding of these longer-term processes. It merely brought out their essentially ambiguous and potentially negative implications for the stability of the body politic earlier than was the case in most other European polities. Due to the acuteness of the crisis that it had endured, given its dependence on foreign investments, during the international recession at the turn of the century, Russia's heavy industry had in fact undergone a process of consolidation and reorganization more radical than that experienced by most other European countries during these years. This reorganization, spurred by Russian investment banks and foreign investors acting partly through them, had led to the creation of trusts, cartels, and eventually of employers' organizations that after the Revolution of 1905, increasingly sought to follow concerted policies in their efforts to resist labor demands. The most notable case in point was the St. Petersburg Society of Manufacturers and Mill Owners, and especially its Council of Mechanical Enterprises, which by the eve of the war was resorting on a systematic basis to blacklists and collective lockouts to crush labor unrest. This organization eventually induced the officials in charge of the state enterprises of St. Petersburg's metal industry to join it in these repressive measures.

In the perspective that we have sought to trace, it should be recalled as well that Russia's political experience after 1905 witnessed not only the establishment of new national representative institutions and the extension of political suffrage to industrial workers (as indeed to all other major groups of the Russian polity), but also the emergence of Social Democracy as the political spokesman of Russia's industrial workers. Indeed, the elections to the four state dumas, between 1906 and 1912, dramatically demonstrated the consolidation, at least among those workers who participated in the electoral process, of the conviction – only reinforced by the bitter divisions that opened between Bolsheviks and Mensheviks – that Russia's Social Democratic Labor Party was their own workers' party, whose unity should at all costs be preserved.

The character of the curial electoral system adopted after 1905 to define the new political nation substantially contributed to this sense of identification. The creation of a separate curia for industrial workers was designed not only to diminish their weight in the body politic but also to insulate them from the influence of "outside" radical agitators. Instead, it reinforced among those workers who participated in the political process a sense of class identity and class consciousness, even as their involvement in this process contributed to the translation and extension of their sense of class interest and class identity into a vision of the society as a whole.

Russia's post-1905 political experience also partially rejoined that of other European polities in the issuance by organs of political authority of legislation that eased the efforts of industrial workers to organize and act collectively in their struggle with employers. It also saw, however modestly, the issuance of welfare legislation, such as the enabling legislation for the establishment of workers' health self-insurance funds enacted in 1913, which just as in other European countries substantially extended the responsibility, and hence the accountablility, of the state for workers' conditions of life and work. We should also note that this 1913 legislation provided for the participation of workers' elective representatives in the administration of these health insurance funds. The pressures generated by the war would in turn lead, by the summer of 1915, to the establishment of elected labor groups to participate, along with representatives of employers and public organizations, in the work of the war industrial committees that were established to mobilize the industrial economy.

To be sure, all of these pieces of legislation and institutional innovations were riddled with reservations and/or contradictions that, far more than was the case in Western European countries, crippled their effectiveness, and thus aroused workers' discontent even while they facilitated their ability to articulate it. For example, the right of workers to "participate" in economic strikes was now legally sanctioned, but "incitement" to economic strikes continued to be prosecuted. Workers were allowed to organize into trade unions, or more precisely into societies of mutual aid, but the latter were forbidden to interfere in industrial labor conflicts, including economic strikes.

These contradictory pieces of legislation inevitably came to provide a focus and a stimulus for political struggle. By the same inexorable logic, the various organs of the "open" labor movement for which they provided however flimsy legal protections – the trade unions, the workers' cooperatives and clubs of enlightenment, the open labor press, workers' health insurance funds, and eventually the labor groups of the war industrial committees – increasingly assumed the role of instruments for the mobilization and organization of political unrest. And so did the strike weapon itself, notwithstanding the continued absence of any legal protection for participation in political strikes. (As we shall see, no earlier period in Russian labor experience – including the revolutionary years 1905–7 was marked by such a preponderance of political, as against economic, strikes.)

Just as inevitably, the objectives of this struggle, the strategy and tactics to be adopted in seeking to achieve them, and the use to be made in this connection of the organs of the open labor movement, increasingly became the focus of the conflicts between the "reformist" and "orthodox" revolutionary currents in the RSDRP. At issue in these conflicts was not the legitimacy of political struggle per se, or indeed the centrality of the role that the RSDRP should perform in mobilizing Russian workers to pursue this struggle. Notwithstanding the label of "Liquidators" that was applied to them by their Bolshevik opponents, not even the most reformist-minded elements of the coalition that the Mensheviks sought to forge in opposition to the Bolsheviks really disputed the legitimacy of the pursuit of political objectives by the organs of the open labor movement, or indeed the definition of these objectives by the RSDRP. Rather, what they argued with increasing vehemence and desperation by the eve of the war was that these political objectives, and the strategy, tactics, and forms of organization used to pursue them, should be designed to win from the Czarist regime specific and delimited political and legal concessions – most notably, the freedom for workers to organize and bargain collectively. These political and legal concessions would, in turn, permit the emergence on Russian soil of a "Europeanized" mass labor movement and labor party, based first and foremost on the model of German Social Democracy. For the Bolsheviks, on the other hand, the use to be made of the open organizations of labor had come by the eve of the war to be subordinated entirely to the realization of the goal – which increasingly appeared to them within reach – of achieving a wholesale overturn of the existing political and social order, which would bring the Russian proletariat and its "allies" among the masses of the peasantry to full and undivided control of the country's destiny.

Be that as it may, in the setting created by the new wave of industrial strikes that unfolded between the end of the Lena goldfields massacre and the outbreak of the war, the chief focus of the conflicts between Bolsheviks and Mensheviks became the proper use to be made of the strike weapon itself. The Bolsheviks' perception of all industrial labor conflicts, economic as well as political – and of the way in which they were to be exploited and pursued – came to be shaped entirely by their vision of an increasingly revolutionary wave of labor unrest leading to a general political strike, culminating in an armed uprising that would bring about the establishment of a "firm democratic" regime.

In the eyes of the Mensheviks, who did not share these expectations of an immediate revolutionary overturn – especially in the maximalist variant outlined by Lenin and his followers – the Bolshevik strategy and tactics increasingly appeared to be leading the workers' movement to disaster. The Bolsheviks' "indiscriminate use of the strike weapon" had contributed, so the Mensheviks felt, to the unleashing of a wave of labor unrest that was becoming increasingly diffuse, chaotic, "elemental" in character – indeed, more reminiscent in its primitive *buntarstvo* of the peasant uprisings of the seventeenth and eighteenth centuries than of a "conscious," modern, Europeanized workers' movement.

The Bolsheviks discerned in the explosive character that this labor unrest increasingly assumed, including the exceptionally high proportion of defeats that workers suffered in economic strikes, the very dynamics conducive to their objective of unleashing a general revolutionary strike leading to an armed uprising. The Mensheviks, on the other hand, viewed these dynamics as contributing inevitably to the exhaustion of the strikers, and to their eventual relapse into apathy, under the weight of the increasingly repressive measures of organs of political authority and employers.

In these conflicts between Bolsheviks and Mensheviks on the eve of the First World War, and especially in the differences of perception that underlay them, one could easily discern – notwithstanding the twists imposed on them by the peculiarities of Russia's historical experience – certain of the basic themes that had animated since the turn of the century the debates between the moderate and radical wings of most European socialist parties. But these conflicts also brought into sharp relief the ultimately ambiguous implications of the propositions that both the reformist and orthodox currents of European and Social Democracy had come to share by the turn of the century in their respective prescriptions for the relationship of workers' movements to the polity as a whole.

Since the 1880s and 1890s, most of the major spokesmen of European Social Democracy had been pressing the proposition that only be developing a vision of the polity as whole and translating this vision into an alternative conception of a legitimate political, social, and economic order, would industrial workers develop a genuine class consciousness, and eventually become the dominant actors in their respective polities and in the international community as a whole.

Perhaps the clearest demonstration of this consensus, and of the sharpness of the repudiation that it involved of any parochial, "particularistic" definition of working-class interests and working-class struggle, was the agreement among various spokemen of international social democracy by the turn of the century – including Kautsky and Lenin, but also Eduard Bernstein – that socialist consciousness had been brought to the working class from outside its own ranks by intellectuals from other classes.

By the turn of the century, the evolution of Russian social democracy provided perhaps the sharpest demonstration of the crystallization of this consensus as well as of its ultimate fragility. It was P. B. Akselrod, one of the spokesmen of the "orthodox" current in the RSDRP at the turn of the century (and a major ideologue of the Menshevik movement after 1905), who insisted most unequivocally that Russia's workers could come to perceive the differences of interests that separated them from other social groups and develop genuine class consciousness only by becoming conscious of the interests of the polity as a whole. It was also Akselrod who, at the turn of the century, drew most sharply from this proposition the conclusion that Russia's proletariat should assume the leadership of the all-nation struggle for political freedom, and indeed the role of *gegemon* in the "bourgeois" revolution that Russia was still historically destined to undergo.

Due to the character of the political settlement that followed the Revolution of 1905, the prewar experience of Russian Social Democracy would be the first to bring out the revolutionary implications of these prescriptions for the development of the working class: their potential for the radicalization of the industrial workers if the aspirations that they necessarily aroused were to be denied. Russia's experience also demonstrated before the outbreak of the war that among no strata of industrial workers would these broader aspirations be generated as powerfully, nd the denial of their realization exercise as explosive effects, as among workers 'ving in large urban centers in close proximity to more privileged elements of s, ety. In fact, Russia's prewar experience clearly suggested that these explosive , erns of labor unrest were displayed most dramatically be those strata of urba. vorkers who had undergone most fully the processes of urbanization that exposed them to the attraction, as well as the ultimate denial, of the models of "cultured" civilized existence enjoyed by more privileged groups of urban society. Among these urbanized strata of workers, none drew more sharply the political implications of the denial of these broader aspirations than those of the capital city of St. Petersburg. Indeed, the emergence of the workers of St. Petersburg as the fulcrum of the strike movement, and eventually as the catalyst of the Russian Revolution, provides perhaps the clearest motif in the evolution of labor unrest in Imperial Russia from the 1890s up to 1917.

Within St. Petersburg's working class, these changing patterns of labor unrest were displayed most sharply by workers employed in metal-processing and mechanical enterprises, who by 1914 constituted some 40% of the industrial workers of the capital. Throughout the 1890s, hardly any industrial labor conflicts had broken out in St. Petersburg metal-processing and mechanical plants. The situation began to change at the turn of the century, and by 1905 St. Peterburg's metalworkers had clearly emerged as the most politically militant strata of workers in the capital. Their degree of involvement in economic as opposed to political strikes, however, still remained well below that of workers in St. Petersburg's textile industury. It was only in the immediate prewar period that the work forces of mechanical and metal-processing enterprises, in the capital and in the country as a whole, emerged as the most militant participants in those ostensibly economic strikes that challenged more sharply and most directly the organs of authority that ruled over them on the factory floor. After the brief lull that followed the outbreak of the First World War, St. Petersburg metal enterprises reemerged, already by the fall of 1915, as the epicenters of labor unrest in Imperial Russia. During the February days of 1917, it was the workers employed in these enterprises, especially those in the Vyborg district, who provided the spark that ignited the explosion of the Russian Revolution.

Indeed, the regularity of the patterns in the emergence of metalworkers as the vanguard in the outbreak of the most explosive manifestations of labor unrest – in Russia, already before the outbreak of the First World War; in other European countries, most sharply toward the end of the war and in its immediate aftermath – brings us to still another common feature of European labor experience in the early twentieth century. This second dimension of shared experience was the series of changes in the character and organization of work processes that certain branches of industry – most notably those, like mechanical enterprises, that had hitherto engaged in semiartisanal forms of production – experienced under the impact of processes of industrial consolidation, and of the role assumed in them by investment banks. As we shall see in certain contributions to this volume, the workers of Russia's mechanical enterprises were also exposed to the various dimensions of this experience in the years after the Revolution of 1905. Especially in mechanical enterprises affiliated with foreign firms, managers and supervisors sought to achieve greater productivity and economy of costs through the introduction of greater division of labor and higher levels of mechanization in production processes, but also through the imposition of new forms of supervision and financial remuneration designed to achieve economies in the time spent in the completion of work tasks.

To be sure, in all belligerent countries (including Russia), the pressures of the war induced in all defense-related industries a sharp acceleration in the pace and scope of these changes in the character and organization of production processes – partly in an effort to achieve gains in productivity but also to facilitate the employment of higher proportions of unskilled and semiskilled workers, including larger numbers of women. But in many Western European countries, these changes in industrial organization – and in particular those attendant to the introduction of the "American system of wage rates," with its bonuses for economies of time – had proceeded apace in metal-processing and mechanical enterprises at least since the turn of the century. By the eve of the war, they were being applied for systematically in the home enterprises of German metal firms, for example, than in their *Russian filialy*. Given this fact, the apparent lag in the translation of the effects of these changes – and particularly of the erosion they induced in the autonomy that skilled and semiskilled workers had tradi-

29

tionally enjoyed – into forms of labor unrest among Western European workers comparable to the explosive character that this unrest already assumed among Russia's metalworkers by the eve of the war is one of the most difficult problems to be unraveled in any comparative analysis of European labor experience during these years.

This lag brings into sharp relief the general issue we raised at the beginning of this discussion of the respective roles of structural phenomena, conjunctures, and events in accounting for the timing, as well as the character and intensity, of the major strike waves that unfolded in various European countries under our scrutiny during this period.

In each of the industrialized countries that would eventually be drawn into the First World War, what did the two longer-term processes of structural change to which we have drawn attention – processes of urbanization and changes in the character and organization of production processes – respectively contribute to the crystallization of a sense of class identity as well as of nationhood among the workers who were exposed to them, and to the complex interplay between these two orders of representation in the shaping of these workers' mentality and attitudes?

What differences in the economic, social, and political environments in which these processes unfolded, and especially in the roles played by the individual and collective actors who became involved in the launching, organization, and resolution of labor conflicts, induced the industrial workers of these various European countries to follow up to the outbreak of the First World War such seemingly different paths in their labor struggles – in the grievances and aspirations that they articulated, and thus in the content that they infused into their sense of nationhood and class identity?

By the same token, what common features in the wartime experience to which these workers were exposed caused the seemingly so different currents of the European workers' movement to rejoin at the end of the war, or at least to unleash waves of labor unrest in which the various grievances and aspirations that animated the workers who participated in them were generalized into challenges of the whole structure of power and authority that had contained their lives?

And last but not least, what induced these various strata of European workers – at the peak of their respective challenges to existing authority – to be so powerfully attracted by the example of the Russian Revolution, and indeed to seek to adopt similar models to those that it provided for the assertion and exercise of their power in the workplace and in the polity as a whole?

The sudden and dramatic changes in their perception of Russian experience that Western European labor movements displayed after the outbreak of the Revolution of 1917 and the end of the First World War, the deeper changes that these new representations reflected in the sense of national and class

30

identity of Western European workers, and the reflection of these changes in these workers' patterns of collective action, raise perhaps more sharply than any other example, the issues of the continuities and changes to be discerned in the facets of European labor history in the early twentieth century on which the contributions to this volume will be focusing attention.

II

Models and realities

3

Introduction

LEOPOLD H. HAIMSON, ERIC BRIAN

A wide range of contributions reflecting a variety of concerns appear in this section: descriptive studies that examine the strike waves that broke out in various European countries on the eve, during, and in the immediate aftermath of the First World War, and compare them with earlier strike waves in these countries' labor histories; more theoretical treatments that scrutinize these strike waves in the perspective of the overall evolution of patterns of labor unrest in the countries under their scrutiny in the second half of the nineteenth and in the early twentieth centuries, and assess the adequacy of the models that have been applied to analyze their dynamics; and a number of quantitative studies that seek in a variety of ways to test the statistical validity of these and other approaches in accounting for the scope, intensity, and character that certain of these strike waves assumed, especially after the turn of the century. Yet, however implicitly in some cases, all of these contributions have had to confront, and challenge at least to some degree, the adequacy – at least in accounting for the phenomenon of strike waves – of two major theoretical models that have dominated the analysis of industrial labor conflits, especially in quantitative studies.

The first of these models, largely developed by economists and economic historians, has focused attention on the relationships between patterns of labor unrest and short-term as well as long-term cycles in economic and particularly industrial development. Scholars using this approach have sought to examine the statistical relationships between the number of strikes, participants, and work-days lost in industrial labor conflicts, as well as their attributed causes and eventual outcomes, and the movement of various economic indices: indices of the volume and value of industrial production, of the numbers of workers employed and unemployed in various branches of industry, and in industry as a whole, and of the movement of workers' nominal, as well as real wages.

35

The general impressions, or at least the common wisdom, usually drawn from these studies can be easily summarized. They are that strikes, and especially offensive economic strikes, tend to be concentrated during upturns in economic cycles. Especially at the beginning of these upturns, workers perceive themselves to be in a stronger bargaining position with employers, given their growing demand for labor, and seek to obtain from them higher wages, shorter hours of work, and improved working and/or living conditions – partly to make up for the losses these workers have suffered during periods of industrial recession, as well as to catch up with the increases in the cost of living also characteristic of the initial phases of these economic upturns. By the same token, defensive strikes are seen as tending to be clustered at the beginning of the downturns of economic cycles, in response to the worsening terms of employment that firms then seek to impose on their work forces. The bottoms of economic cycles are viewed as distinguished by the lowest indices of strike propensity as workers, sensing the great weakness of their position on the labor market, relapse into apathy.

Most of the contributions to this volume, including those that concede a degree of validity to this approach – in accounting, at least during certain periods of labor history, for general "trends" in the number of economic strikes (if not necessarily for their numbers of participants) and for the "offensive" or "defensive" character that strike actions assumed – question the adequacy of this model of the dynamics of labor conflicts for an understanding of the phenomenon of strike waves. Some of these contributions, particularly those involving quantitative analyses of labor unrest in the early twentieth century in a number of the countries under our scrutiny (Italy, Imperial Russia, and to a degree Imperial Germany), do not discern *any* significant statistical relationships between the strike waves that broke out in these countries during the years of the First World War and in its immediate aftermath and the movements of the various economic indices incorporated in their analyses. Other contributions, especially those surveying the phenomena of strike waves over longer time spans (e.g., the studies by James Cronin of strike waves in Britain and by Friedhelm Boll of strike waves in Germany in the late nineteenth and early twentieth centuries) concede the relevance of this model in accounting for the timing of many of these strike waves (seeing most of them as indeed breaking out, at least up to the eve of the First World War, at the beginning of upturns of economic cycles). But even these contributions question the adequacy of this approach in accounting for the massive number of workers who became involved in these major strike waves, and especially for the nature of the grievances and aspirations that they brought to the fore. One also draws the impression that in the eyes of most of the contributors, the model – whatever its degree of relevance for patterns of labor unrest in the second half of the nineteenth century – is found especially wanting in accounting for the degree of intensity and character

36

that industrial strikes assumed by the eve of the First World War, and especially during the war years and the immediate postwar period.

In their search for more adequate explanations for the dynamics of strike waves, most of our contributors were therefore induced to consider the significance of other factors – including political processes, conjunctures, and events (a subject to which we shall return) – and especially to take account of the roles played by the various individual and collective actors who were or became implicated in the outbreak, organization, and ultimate resolution of the massive labor conflicts that these strike waves involved. In these explorations, several of our contributors have been impelled to confront another model that has become prominent in recent analyses of the historical evolution of patterns of industrial labor conflicts: a model of the forms that these conflicts assumed, and the ways in which they were organized, and ultimately resolved.

According to this model, the evolution of the intensity and character of labor conflicts was dictated by patterns of industrial development, and especially by changes in the nature of production processes. These changes are seen as having occurred in spurts, which periodically induced developmental imbalances between the character and organization of work processes and that of production relations – including the power relationships between employers and labor forces, but also the capacity of the state and of the polity as a whole to institutionalize these relationships. In this perspective, the outbreaks of industrial strikes, and especially of strike waves, are seen as a reflection of the imbalances created by these spurts in industrial development. But they are also perceived as efforts, ultimately successful by and large, to redress the balance in these power relationships through the emergence of more effective forms of organization among the workers involved in these labor struggles, and through the stimulus that these struggles provided for the state to create more effective mechanisms to contain and defuse labor conflicts. Indeed, as Friedhelm Boll describes it in his contribution to this volume, this approach rested, at least originally, on a highly optimistic view of the long-term tendencies at work in processes of "modernization of labor conflicts," as reflected in the *forms* that these conflicts gradually assumed in the course of industrial development. According to this view, in the early phases of industrialization, labor conflicts generally conformed to a "protest" model – strikes, usually involving small numbers of workers engaging in essentially defensive and poorly organized actions, usually of short duration, and eventuating in a very high proportion of labor defeats. With the emergence of trade unions in the middle and late nineteenth century, industrial strikes are seen as having increasingly assumed the character of "confrontations" between labor and management – strike actions typically tending to involve larger numbers of participants and to display greater persistence (as reflected in the indices of numbers of days lost per striker). These strikes are also seen as having resulted in growing proportions of labor victories and compromises,

37

partly because of their more effective organization by trade unions – including these unions' control over the formulation of strike demands and the timing of strike actions. (Thus it is argued that strikes were now more typically launched during upturns in the business cycle, and especially at the inception of these upturns, when workers were in the strongest bargaining position with employers.) Finally, the most recent phase in this process of modernization of labor conflicts is viewed as distinguished by the growing predominance of a "demonstrative" model of labor conflict – strikes typically becoming smaller in number and shorter in duration, even while involving more massive numbers of participants – and playing chiefly the function of providing "signals" for the inception and/or resumption of collective bargaining, usually within the institutional framework created by the state. This last phase in the modernization of labor conflicts is viewed as marked by a dwindling number of labor defeats and a growing proportion of compromises in the outcomes of strike actions, and by a growing number of collective agreements reached through collective bargaining without the actual outbreak of strikes.

The reader will find in Boll's contribution a more detailed description and critique of this essentially teleological view, as well as of the qualifications and modifications that its authors have been impelled to introduce in the course of subsequent research. But let us summarize the ways in which other contributors to this volume have found the models that it distinguishes in the evolution of the forms of labor conflicts wanting in accounting for the phenomena of strike waves, and particularly for those that unfolded during the years of European labor history that especially concern us. The thrust of their criticism may be summarized as follows:

It is that *all* strike waves, and indeed *all strikes*, necessarily involve, to a greater or lesser degree, dimensions of protest, confrontation, and demonstration (the latter, at least in the sense of explicit or implicit appeals to other political and social actors for intervention and support). It is, by the same token, that all strike waves are in fact responses to significant developmental "imbalances" in the relations between workers and employers. And last but not least, it is that the imbalances in these power relationships became more, rather than less, pronounced by the eve of the First World War.

Indeed, in the view of many of our contributors, by the eve of the war, all of the major, established, organized collective actors implicated in labor conflicts – employers, agencies of the state, and in many instances also the official leaderships of trade unions and of existing political parties – displayed a growing unwillingness, or inability, to recognize the legitimacy, if not to apprehend the very nature, of the grievances and aspirations of the workers who were drawn into these labor conflicts. By the same token, the leadership of established working-class organizations proved increasingly incapable of organizing effectively these workers' patterns of collective action.

38

Specifically, it was the incapacity of all of these major collective actors to recognize, or at least to respond to, workers' grievances and aspirations that accounted for the character that most of these strike waves assumed – of initiatives from below, involving large numbers of hitherto unorganized workers, and of already organized workers revolting against their official leaderships. The power imbalances between workers and employers to which they contributed also help account for the "unorthodox" forms of collective action that distinguished these strike waves, especially by the eve of the war. As other more institutionalized and accepted forms of conducting labor conflicts proved ineffective – especially given the unwillingness of the established leaderships of workers' organizations to lead them – workers increasingly resorted to "wildcat" strikes (in breach of contract and/or without the approval of trade unions), "Sicilian" strikes (slowdowns of production processes initiated without the actual calling of strikes), "sitdowns" (workers remaining at the bench, but refusing to work), and eventually more open and explicit forms of "occupation" and "seizure of control" of enterprises.

This process of "deinstitutionalization," or more precisely of the emergence of new forms of organization of labor conflicts, was to a degree characteristic of all the major strike waves scrutinized in this volume – even if in the labor experience of certain of the countries concerned (e.g., Great Britain), they frequently resulted in redressing the balance in the power relationships between workers and employers through the reorganization of trade unions, the extension of trade-union membership to hitherto unorganized workers, and/or the emergence of new institutional mechanisms for the structuring and resolution of labor conflicts. But by the eve of the war, these power imbalances in the organization of labor conflicts were becoming increasingly difficult to redress, given the unwillingness of employers, state officials, and indeed established trade leaders, to recognize the legitimacy of the grievances inspired (especially among metal-workers) by the rationalization of production processes, as well as due to the growing ability of employers to counter successfully the forms of collective action to which unions resorted in their organization of labor conflicts.

The unwillingness of the dominant actors in the polity to recognize their legitimacy may also help explain the often submerged character of the basic grievances that underlay many of these strikes, and their tendency to be transmuted into the more commonly recognized, if not "legitimized," forms of demands for higher wages and for shorter hours. The failure to recognize the nature of these grievances also helps account for the political dimensions that many of these labor conflicts eventually assumed, once an appropriate political climate for this process emerged.

We shall return to this issue of the politicization of these labor conflicts – and to the general problem that they pose of the relationship of strikes to politics – but let us consider first certain more difficult if not intractable problems in-

39

volved in the scrutiny, particularly through quantitative studies, of the distinctive characteristics and dynamics of strike waves, and especially of those that broke out after the turn of the century. The problems lie in part in the nature of the statistical sources at our disposal for this purpose, and in the *implicit* representations of the character and dynamics of industrial strikes on which these sources rest.

In the best of cases, statistical data on labor unrest are provided by three major sources: those assembled by governmental agencies, by employers' organizations, and by trade unions. In most of the countries concerned, the collection of information about industrial strikes in official sources was initiated by the agencies of the state charged with the maintenance of public order (e.g., usually under the jurisdiction of their ministries of internal affairs), for which strikes represented actual or potential infringements of public order and security, if not outright violations of existing statutes or legal precedents. But such data really began to be assembled on a systematic basis when, and only when – even in those countries where strikes were not explicitly legalized – labor conflicts came to be viewed as regular, if not normal, phenomena of economic life. Specialized agencies were therefore created to regulate labor relations, if not actually to mediate labor conflicts, and in the process began to collect information about their character and sources. The emergence of the representation of strikes as essentially economic phenomena was most readily apparent in those countries such as Imperial Russia in which the new agencies for the regulation, and hence the collection of information about industrial labor conflicts, were placed originally under the jurisdiction of the Ministry of Finance (and in Russia, eventually under the Ministry of Trade and Industry), but to a greater or lesser degree it also surfaced in countries where special labor departments, and eventually labor ministries, were established for this purpose.

Given this increasingly economic but also institutionalized approach to labor conflicts, the official agencies charged with the collection of statistical information about industrial strikes also came to represent them as conflicts essentially focused on the terms of employment, and began to record – on a systematic basis, in many cases – information about wages, hours of work, and working conditions in enterprises struck, before and after the resolution of these labor conflicts. Given this perspective, political strikes were usually not included in the statistics of labor conflicts assembled by these agencies. Even if they were, they were usually assigned to a residual category of strikes without identified causes.

In fact, in certain of these official statistics, the very methods used to classify industrial labor conflicts came to draw an increasingly close relationship between the attributed *causes* and *outcomes* of strikes. In those of the Factory Inspectorate in Imperial Russia, for example, one of the criteria applied to define "the chief cause" of economic strikes whose participants had advanced a series of grievances and demands became (for those conflicts that did not eventuate in out-right labor defeats) that grievance or demand whose settlement had been followed by the strikers' return to work. By the same token, the outcomes of labor conflicts in which such settlements were reached were classified as labor victories or compromises, depending upon whether the workers' demands with respect to this one issue – and one issue alone – had been satisfied in whole or only in part. By the same circular logic, political strikes, along with "solidarity" – that is, sympathy – strikes, and strikes for which no causes could really be assigned, were classified up to 1905 in a residual category (other strikes), for which no identifiable outcomes – no labor victories, compromises, or labor defeats – and therefore no identifiable causes, could be established.

In Russia, although not in most other countries, political strikes emerged as an identified phenomenon in the statistics of the Factory Inspectorate in 1905 (originally both in the form of strikes with attributed "mixed" political and economic motifs, and as a separate category to which purely "political-demonstrative" strikes, with no attributed economic causes, were assigned). Indeed, it was inevitable that this should be so, given the massiveness that political protest assumed in labor unrest among Russia's workers during this revolutionary year. By 1907, the number of labor conflicts classified in the reports of the Factory Inspectorate as strikes with mixed political and economic motifs dwindled to insignificance – almost all strikes with attributed political causes were now assigned to the category of purely political-demonstrative strikes. This evolution reflected a complex interplay between the changing representations of labor conflicts entertained by the official agencies charged with their control and regulation, the changing nature of the constraints that these agencies imposed upon them (including the ostensible legalization in 1906 of "economic," but not of "political" strikes), and the changes in the representations that workers themselves came to hold of the strike weapon and of the different uses to which it could be put, partly as a result of these legal changes.

The dynamics involved in the evolution of the treatment of political strikes in Russia's official labor statistics are discussed more fully in our contribution to this part of the volume. But let us take note of the analytic problem that they pose – that of the interplay between the actual character of labor conflicts and the representations entertained of them by the various actors involved in these conflicts, and of the reflection of this interplay in the categories to which strike actions were assigned (if indeed they were taken into account) in the records kept of these labor conflicts. This analytic problem arises just as sharply with respect to a second major statistical source on industrial strikes that became available in many of the countries under our scrutiny after turn of the century: the reports of employers' organizations. In the Russian case, to be sure, political strikes surfaced as a prominent phenomenon in the statistics of labor unrest that the Societies of Manufacturers and Mill Owners of St. Petersburg and of the Moscow Industrial Region began to compile by the eve of the First World War. (Indeed, these employers' organizations were all too readily inclined, especially at first, to attribute to political causes, and thus to absolve themselves of any responsibility for, the industrial conflicts that broke out with such massiveness among their work forces in the course of the post-Lena strike wave). But in the data compiled by the St. Petersburg Society, the basic issue of the representation – and hence of the very recognition – of the character and sources of labor conflicts surfaced during these years with respect to strikes over "order in the enterprise."

These conflicts, which perhaps more sharply than any others challenged the power and authority of management, had become by 1913 (when these statistics of the St. Petersburg Society began to be compiled) a major motif of labor unrest in metal-processing firms affiliated with it – involving, often implicitly, protest actions against the efforts of these firms to rationalize processes and relations of production. Yet these and other strikes over "order" were assigned in the contemporary statistics of the St. Petersburg Society to a residual category entitled "demonstrative strikes." They very label suggested the problem posed for these St. Petersburg employers and their administrative staffs of "representing" the character of labor conflicts that – in contrast to strikes over wages, hours, or by this time even political strikes – appeared to them to be breaking out for no clearly recognizable or at least reasonable cause, involving as they did prerogatives that these employers considered peculiarly their own.

This basic problem of representation, and indeed of recognition, arose even more sharply in both official and employers' statistics, especially during this period in the labor experience of Russia and other countries, with respect to forms of labor conflicts that broke out of the conventional mold, partly as a result of the growing ineffectiveness of more traditional forms of strike actions. Sicilian strikes, work stoppages during which workers remained in the shop or indeed at the bench, and the like did not fit the representations that officials and employers entertained of the very nature of labor conflicts, and tended, therefore, to be undercounted, if not entirely discounted, in their statistical records of industrial strikes.

The same general observations apply with respect to the third major statistical source that in many of the countries under our scrutiny, became available by the turn of the century on the number and character of labor conflicts: the reports compiled by trade union organizations. Indeed, the discounting of labor actions that assumed unorthodox forms was especially characteristic of trade-union statistics: they almost invariably tended to ignore wildcat strikes, which broke out without the official sanction of these unions' official leaderships. This is obviously a serious limitation, in view of the prominence that wildcat strikes in fact assumed in labor conflicts even before the First World War (in the

42

German metal-processing industry, for example), and especially during the war years and the immediate postwar period.

But even more broadly, given the features that the contributors to this volume have discerned in the strike waves they have scrutinized – that of initiatives from below bringing to the surface, through new forms of collective action, the hitherto unrecognized grievances of large masses of unorganized workers, and of organized workers rebelling against their official leaderships – it should be readily apparent how the limitations we have observed in these various statistical sources, and the representations of the very nature of the labor conflicts that they reflect, have contributed to obscuring the scope, character, and dynamics that these strike waves actually assumed. It should be obvious, by the same token, how the very character of these statistical sources also tended to reinforce the two major stereotypes of the nature of labor conflicts that we summarized at the beginning of this discussion: the representation of the intensity and character assumed by industrial strikes as essentially economic phenomena, and indeed as functions of economic cycles, as well as the models we have described of the gradual rationalization and institutionalization of the forms of labor conflicts.

Also contributing to the predominance of these models and to obscuring the phenomenon of strike waves is the nature of the techniques that usually have been applied to the analysis of these statistical sources in quantitative studies of the dynamics of industrial labor conflicts. The prevalent use of time series in this connection has tended to reinforce the impression of regularities in the dynamics of patterns of labor unrest (which each of these models, in its own fashion, emphasizes), and by the same token has contributed to the difficulties of analyzing, if not to the discounting of, the phenomenon of strike waves. Two major characteristics of this approach particularly account for these tendencies.

The first is that the use of time series – whether through the study of *natural* time series, or of series discounting for *trends* in the evolution of patterns of labor unrest – necessarily discounts in large measure the phenomenon of strikes waves as "aberrations" in the overall evolution of patterns of labor unrest, or more precisely treats them as "residues" in the fluctuations observed in indices of labor unrest and the relationships that they bear to the indices for other factors under consideration. The second is that the statistical relationships considered – those obtaining during the periods under scrutiny *between* the *fluctuations* of the indices for the various factors considered, rather than between the *factors themselves* – makes it exceedingly difficult to analyze the aberrations recorded for periods of strike waves from the patterns generally discerned in the relationships between these fluctuations.

As some of the contributions in this volume suggest, sectorial analyses, in which the actual relationship between the factors considered (rather than between their fluctuations) are considered during period strike waves and then compared with those observable during time periods immediately preceding and following these waves, appear more appropriate to determine the statistical significance of these factors in accounting for the scope and character that these strike waves assumed. Admittedly, a sectorial approach – whether it takes the form of correlational, regression, or factorial analysis – raises its own problems of interpretation, given its tendency to treat as *regularities* in the patterns observed individual aberrations that may appear in the relationships among the variables considered during periods of strike waves. But the effects of these aberrations can at least be examined in a more systematic fashion, especially through the descriptive methods of factorial analysis. An example from the quantitative analyses presented in this volume of the dynamics of labor unrest in prewar Imperial Russia may serve to clarify and illustrate the point.

In the time series examined by V. I. Bovykin et al. of the relationships between patterns of labor unrest and the movement of indices of the value of industrial production during the period 1895–1913, the metal-processing industry (Group VIII) emerges as a major exception to the general conclusion suggested by the analysis of the absence of any positive statistical relationship between the evolution of patterns of labor unrest and that of the value of industrial production during these years (see Tables 4 and 5). In the sectorial analysis conducted by Haimson and Petrusha on the other hand, the strike behavior of workers in the metal-processing industry emerges as an extreme *illustrative* case of patterns of labor unrest during the post-Lena strike wave and of the statistical relationships accounting for these patterns brought out among the variables considered in the analysis. Such a conclusion could legitimately be drawn only on the basis of a systematic comparison (through the use of factorial analysis) of the patterns and relationships suggested when the metal-processing industry was, and was not, included within the framework of the analysis.

What the picture we have sought to draw suggests is that not only the theoretical models to which we have drawn attention, but also the statistical techniques that have predominantly been used in quantitative studies of labor conflicts, and indeed the statistical sources on which these studies have had to draw, have rested, however implicitly, on certain commonly shared representations of the nature of labor conflicts. These common representations have tended to reinforce one another and in the process to minimize, if not to ignore, the character and underlying dynamics of the phenomenon of strike waves.

But let us return to the more basic conceptual and analytic issues posed at the outset of this discussion concerning the strikes waves that unfolded, in Russia already by the eve of the First World War and in other European countries during the war years and their immediate aftermath. As we noted in the general introduction, what distinguished these specific strike waves from the earlier labor experience of many of the countries concerned was not merely the degree to which the labor conflicts that surfaced in them – including economic strikes – came to focus explicitly over issues of power and authority. It was also the acuteness of the sense that the workers drawn into these strike actions came to display of the inextricable links between the grievances and aspirations generated by their position in the workplace and their position in the polity as a whole. These features have induced the contributors to this volume to recognize in the waves of labor unrest that unfolded during these years a more highly politicized character than in earlier strikes waves, as well as to discern in them more generalized and more explicit challenges of the entire structures of existing authority in these various polities. But in the light of the analytic issues that we have sought to draw, we should now pose certain more specific questions concerning the more highly politicized character that these strike waves assumed.

All strike waves, and indeed the outbreak of all strikes, involve an elaborate process of translation of a sense of deprivation into specific grievances and aspirations, and of these grievances and claims into concerted patterns of collective actions. Given this fact, what conditions and circumstances accounted, in certain of the strike waves under scrutiny but not in others, for the translation of these grievances and aspirations into the specific forms of concerted action involved in *political* strikes, by comparison with other categories of strikes, and also with other forms of collective action – from riots, demonstrations and other forms of participation in the political process, to actual insurrections against the existing order? By the same token, if all strikes involve a struggle for power, what features in the power relationships among the various individual and collective actors implicated in these strike waves – in their perceptions of the issues involved ("power over what?"), and of the sources of power to be mobilized, appealed to and/or neutralized in these labor struggles – impelled their participants to resort so extensively to the weapon of political strikes?

The case studies presented in this volume, in particular those of labor unrest in prewar Russia and in 1917, induce us in turn to pose two further questions about the dynamics that distinguished these particular strike waves in European labor experience. What conditions and circumstances in certain of the countries under our scrutiny contributed to the escalation of political strikes into other forms of collective action, including revolutionary insurrections that culminated in the overthrow of their existing structures of political authority, if not of their entire political, social, and economic order? And by the same token, as the case study of Russia's 1917 labor experience presented in this volume suggests, what conditions and circumstance contributed, even under these revolutionary conditions, to the decline if not disappearance of political strikes as a meaningful form of collective action – particularly for the more militant and radicalized strata of workers who in earlier years had in fact accounted for the large bulk of political strikes?

These questions bring into focus the broader issues concerning the relationships of strikes to politics that various contributions to this volume address in their analyses of the strike waves that broke out at the end and in the immediate

45

aftermath of the First World War, and of the patterns that distinguished them from earlier strike waves in the countries under their purview. These questions appear so fundamental for an understanding of the dynamics of these specific strike waves, and of the relationships that they bore to the historical settings of war and revolution in which they unfolded, that we shall return to them in the concluding section of this volume, after considering the suggestions that our various contributors have made concerning the issues that they pose.

4

Changing forms of labor conflict: secular development or strike waves?

FRIEDHELM BOLL

Two major approaches resting on different theoretical models are currently influencing quantitative research on industrial strikes in Germany. The first of these focuses on long-term tendencies at work in the evolution of industrial labor conflicts, as reflected in longer-term changes in form that strikes allegedly underwent in the course of industrial development. The other stresses the discontinuities in patterns of labor unrest reflected in the phenomenon of strike waves.[1] These two approaches were originally used separately, but most recently have been combined in quantitative studies. The following observations are intended to contribute to reflection on the development of these two approaches, and particularly on the further possibilities for their joint application in quantitative studies of industrial strikes.

1. H. Volkmann, "Modernisierung des Arbeitskampfes? Zum Formwandel von Streik und Aussperrung in Deutschland 1864–1975," in H. Kaelble et al., *Probleme der Modernisierung in Deutschland* (Opladen, 1978), pp. 110–70; "Organisation und Konflikt. Gewerkschaften, Arbeitgeberverbaende und die Entwicklung des Arbeitskonflikts in spaeten Kaiserreich," in W. Conze and U. Engelhardt, *Arbeiter im Industrialisierungsprozess. Herkunft, Lage under Verhalten.* (Stuttgart, 1979), pp. 422–38; and the somewhat earlier essay by H. Kaelble and H. Volkmann, "Konjunktur und Streik waehrend des Uebergangs zum organisierten Kapitalismus in Deutschland," in *Zeitschrift fue Wirtschafts- und Sozialwissenschaften* 92 (1972): 513–44.

For the model of strike waves, see J. E. Cronin, *Industrial Conflict in Modern Britain* (London and Totowa, 1979), and "Theories of Strikes: Why Can't They Explain the British Experience?" *Journal of Social History* (1978/79): pp. 194–220; E. Shorter and C. Tilly, *Strikes in France, 1830–1968* (Cambridge, 1974); F. Boll, "International Strike Waves: A Critical Assessment," in W. J. Mommsen and H. G. Husung, eds., *The Development of Trade Unionism in Great Britain and Germany, 1880–1914* (London, 1985), pp. 78–99; H. Volkmann, "Die Streikwellen von 1910–13 und 1919–20. Kontinuitaet und Diskontinuitaet der Arbeitskampfentwicklung," in J. Bergmann et al., *Arbeit-Mobilitaet-Partizipation-Protest* (Opladen, 1986). In this essay Volkmann changed some of his earlier opinions about the modernization of strike patterns. Now he links the two interpretations, which he calls the models of continuity and of discontinuity. See the introduction of H. Kaelble, H. Volkmann et al., *Probleme der Modernisierung in Deutschland* (Opladen, 1978).

I

For the benefit of the non-German reader, I shall first summarize the major propositions about the changes in form that strikes purportedly underwent in the course of industrial development, and the general thesis concerning the rationalization of strike behavior on which these propositions rest.

According to this thesis, articulated in German research by H. Volkmann in the course of his work on modernization processes, the changes in production techniques and organization that took place in the course of the industrial revolution created an entirely new framework for labor relations. The fact that processes of industrial development unfolded in cycles contributed – given their effects on the recruitment of work forces – to gaps between changes in the character and forms of production on the one hand, and changes in industrial relations, conflict-solving methods, and political participation on the other. Volkmann calls these gaps "development disparties."[2] His view is that sharp social conflicts were at once a direct result of these disparities and one of the main forces helping to close the gap between them, that is, the revolutionary modernization of the mode of production was followed by a modernization of industrial relations, and of the social and political system as a whole. On this subject Volkmann writes, "Social conflict is a result of modernization in that it is a reaction to development disparities. Insofar as it aims to forcibly overcome these disparities it is also the driving power of modernization."[3] Volkmann calls this second form of modernization the innovation process of society, "which – as a reaction to social challenge through changed modes of production and organization of the economy – not only imposes the appropriate forms of economic and social order but also conceives and applies the instruments for their realization."

In this perspective strikes become the central indices of the state of industrial relations. Intensive and frequent labor conflicts, which were characteristic of the years between the end of the nineteenth century and the economic world crisis at the beginning of the 1930s, were indicative of a disparity between rapid industrial development and a backward social system. The relatively small number of strikes in West Germany signalled, by the same token, a particularly well adjusted social, economic, and political system: The gap caused by development was again being closed and the "basic supportive structures" of society were once again properly aligned.

Modernization theory was not again touched upon in Volkmann's later essays. The assumption that the outbreak of labor conflict during phases of rapid industrial development was followed by their largely dying away during the phase

2. Kaelble et al., *Probleme der Modernisierung*, p. 7.
3. Ibid.

48

of restored "alignment" of the basic social structures of society may have been too abstract a construction.[4] The increased number of strikes in the early 1960s, and especially starting in the mid-1970s, has refuted the expectation drawn from modernization theory that strikes would "wither away."[5] Nonetheless, the major focus of this approach has remained at the center of labor conflict research: the "rationalization" of labor conflict through the organization of the parties and procedures. In a recent essay Volkmann outlined this concept once again:[6]

> The instruments developed by workers in order to improve their working and living conditions are becoming more and more rational, i.e. are being used with increasing attention to the probable cost-effect ratio and thus influence the behavior of an employer as the direct adversary in a conflict, and are also reflected in the general understanding of conflict in the society. Labor conflicts are concentrated in periods of upturns in the economic cycle, when the bargaining position of workers is stronger. The number of participants in strikes increases. The conflicts are shorter, i.e. more effective. Their frequency declines. Strike-free methods of wage bargaining are developed and applied. Negotiations and collective agreements become the norm, strikes and lockouts, the exceptions. Law, common law and collective contracts replace the more or less spontaneous clash of forces during a conflict. The precondition for this development is the institutionalization of the conflicting interests between the unions and organizations of employers. They intervene increasingly in the conduct of labor conflicts and subject them to their tactical and strategic considerations. Each side thus not only represents the expectations of its own members but must also take into account the reactions of the other, which are deteremined by self-interest. The other side is not only an adversary, but also a negotiating and contracting partner. Put in a nutshell, this concept suggests a continuous process aiming at an efficient balancing of interests. In this process, the generally insoluble conflicts about the conditions of utilizing labor are subjected to generally accepted procedures and are integrated into the constitution of society. Although this concept has been illustrated with the findings of international strike comparisons, the German situation is regarded as the preferred example, and reference is made to the mainly reformist policy of the social democratic trade unions.

4. For several criticisms of the modernization theory, see W. Conze's review of H. Kaelble, H. Volkmann et al., *Probleme*, in *Archiv für Sozialgeschichte* 21 (hereafter *AfS*) (1981), pp. 734ff.
5. A. M. Ross and P. T. Hartmann, *Changing Patterns of Industrial Conflict* (New York and London, 1960). For the history of social conflict before 1848: H. Volkmann and J. Bergmann, eds., *Sozialer Protest. Studien zur traditionellen Resistenz und kollektiven Gewalt in Deutschland vom Vormaerz bis zur Reichsgruendung* (Opladen, 1984); cf. esp. A. Griessinger, *Das symbolische Kapital der Ehre. Streikbewegungen und kollektives Bewusstsein deutscher Handwerksgesellen in 18. Jahrhundert*, (Frankfurt/M u.a., 1981); H. G. Husung, "Kollektiver Gewaltprotest in norddeutschen Vormaerz," in W. J. Mommsen and G. Hirschfeld, *Sozialprotest, Gewalt, Terror. Gewaltanwendung durch politische und gesellschaftliche Randgruppen in 19. und 20. Jagrhundert* (Stuttgart, 1982), pp. 47–63.
6. Volkmann, "Die Streikwellen."

Volkmann's methodological approach concentrates on three areas: the changing forms of conflict, the changing procedures of conflict and the effectiveness of balancing opposing interests.

The *changing form* of conflict means the changes in duration, number of participants, intensity, frequency, and the success/failure rate. Changes derive from the effects of increased organization by the conflict parties. The *changing procedures* of conflict refer to the transition from militancy to collective bargaining without strikes: ". . . to the same degree to which the progress of organization leads to a rationalization and formalization of conflict, forces become effective which prevent fighting. The process assumes a new quality. Strikes and lockouts are increasingly replaced by collective bargaining."[7] The strike is reduced in importance and its main use becomes that of a demonstration, a threat. The total cycle of these changes of function typically unfolds as protest – trial of strength – demonstration.[8] Volkmann hints that this cycle unfolded in successive phases of historical development: a protest phase up to 1891, followed by a trial of strength phase until the 1920s, and a demonstration phase in the post – World War II period.

Today's system of labor relations is seen as the product of an evolution from class conflicts to social partnership. By comparison with the extremely severe labor conflicts during the last years of the Kaiserreich and during the Weimar Republic, it is viewed as an effective balancing of interests, which is an integral part of the society's social constitution. Some figures are advanced to emphasize this point: the average number of workers participating in strikes or affected by lockouts (as a ratio of 1,000 employees per year) increased to 14 during the Kaiserreich and to 35.6 during the Weimar Republic; during the lifetime of the Federal Republic of West Germany it has declined to 6.5. This decline is shown even more clearly when the very much shorter duration of strikes and lockouts is taken into account. The number of working days lost, which decreased about four to five hours per employee per year during the Kaiserreich and the Weimar Republic, is now about seventeen minutes. During the same period the average number of companies involved in each labor conflict increased from 4.6 per strike to 16.3.[9]

The approach just outlined thus emphasizes "rationalization through organization" and has found favor with historians concentrating on the organizational development of the labor movement.[10] It has been criticized by those who

7. Volkmann, "Modernisierung," p. 167.
8. Ibid.
9. Ibid., p. 127.
10. For example, K. Tenfelde and G. A. Ritter, *Bibliographie zur Geschichte der deutschen Arbeiterschaft und Arbeiterbewegung, 1863–1914*, pp. 92–5; K. Schoenhoven, "Arbeitskonflikte in Konjunktur und Rezession. Gewerkschaftliche Streikpolitik und Streikverhalten der Arbeiterschaft vor 1914," in K. Tenfelde and H. Volkmann, *Streik. Zur Geschichte des Arbeitskampfes in Deutschland waehrend der Industrialisierung* (Munich, 1981), pp. 177–93.

emphasize "spontaneity" and grass-roots movements, the so-called history from below, to be the central points of interest in labor history.[11] The "strike waves" approach attempts to do justice to these research interests while using the methodological tools of the organizational approach, that is those of quantifying historians. Thus, on the basis of this approach, it should be possible to verify the claims of rationalization theory to "describe essential structural changes" and "provide an appropriate periodization".[12]

The criticism leveled against the modernization approach is worth summarizing, as it has led Volkmann to modify his approach and make its claims more precise. The major objections to it were directed against its teleological view tailored to fit the development of West Germany: Labor conflicts of previous eras were seen only as "pre-history," denying them significance in their own right.[13] By the same token, there was an at least implicit notion that progress in the organization and rationalization of labor conflicts was characteristic of the Kaiserreich and the Weimar Republic. On this point G. D. Feldman has criticized the modernization view and its variants, such as "organized capitalism," for their "exaggerated functionalization of historic development and homogenization of the national experience." To substantiate his argument Feldman shows how the politicization of strikes and the role of the state assumed special importance in labor conflicts during the Weimar Period.[14] Despite enormous progress in the organization of the conflict parties and conflict procedures, this period was marked by the highest strike frequency in German labor history.[15] In terms of modernization theory, however, the improved organization of labor conflicts after 1918 should have brought a significant reduction in strikes. In fact, notwithstanding social, political, organizational, and technological progress during the 1920s, the expected "conflict-preventing forces" only came to bear after the experience of fascism. Ilse Costas has pointed out in this context that the modernization approach simply ignored structural breaks in labor history. Thus, "it makes little sense to interpret the development of strike variables in the Federal Republic of Germany as a 'streamlined' continuation of the tendencies of the Weimar Republic and, in the process, simply to sweep fascism under the carpet. The strike behavior of the 1920s has rather to be interpreted as the historical chapter preceding fascism, in the sense of an offensive

11. See footnote 15.
12. H. A. Winkler, characterizing the notion of the "organized capitalism" in Winkler, ed., *Organisierter Kapitalismus* (Goettingen, 1974), Introduction. Cf. also. Volkmann, "Modernisierung," p. 165.
13. Costas, "Arbeitskaempfe in der Berliner Elektroindustrie 1905 und 1906," in Tenfelde und Volkmann, *Streik*, pp. 91–108, 109; L. Machtan, *Streiks im fruehen deutschen Kaiserreich* (Frankfurt and New York, 1983), pp. 124ff.
14. G. D. Feldman, "Streiks in Deutschland 1914–1933: Probleme und Forschungsaufgaben," in Tenfelde and Volkmann, *Streik*, p. 276.
15. The data are available in ibid., Appendix.

51

by capitalism, withdrawing step-by-step the concessions made during the November Revolution."[16]

A second major objection to modernization theory was directed at its exaggeration of the increase in the numbers of labor conflicts settled without strikes during the Kaiserreich, and at the claim that there was a decrease in strike activity from 1906–7 onward due to the success of integrationist forces.[17] A more general objection was directed against the attempts to provide a typology and periodization of labor conflicts. Kaelble and Volkmann took as a starting point Hobsbawm's observation that whereas during the early phases of industrialization strikes took place mainly during economic crises, in the course of further economic development they broke out increasingly during periods of industrial expansion. For the early industrialization period Kaelble and Volkmann suggested the application of a *protest model*, according to which spontaneous reactions to deteriorating conditions of life led to strikes that were, on the whole, not very successful, usually short-lived, and often violent. Only with the organizational and financial support, as well as publicity capabilities provided by unions, did the timing of strikes improve. Better adjusted to the economic cycle, this pattern was termed the *adjustment model*, and is claimed to have gained predominance beginning in the 1890s.[18]

A study of the strike behavior of individual groups of unions before 1914 has brought out that the patterns suggested by the rationalization thesis could be confirmed only in those few instances in which employers were organizationally weak.[19] In a more recent essay Volkmann has sought to account better for developments before and after the First World War by combining the concept of the *changing form* of conflict with that of *strike waves*.[20] We shall now follow the same methodological path.

For this purpose we have to summarize the *strike waves* approach. It also rests on quantifiable phenomena: the extremely strong wave characteristics of the intensity of strikes and lockouts when indices are compared over several years. In their quantitative study of strikes in France, Shorter and Tilly found that strike waves occurred in rather regular intervals, beginning in 1890.[21] They also found that besides the economic cycle, political events such as elections, representation of workers in government, May Day actions, and foreign affairs

16. Costas, "Arbeitskaempfe," p. 104.
17. D. Groh, "Intensification of Work and Industrial Conflict in Germany, 1886–1914," in *Politics and Society* 8 (1978): 349–97. K. Saul, *Staat, Industrie, Arbeiterbewegung im Kaiserreich. Zur Innen- und Sozialpolitik des Wilhelminischen Deutschland 1905–1914*, (Duesseldorf, 1974) and "Zwischen Repression und Integration. Staat, Gewerkschaften unde Arbeitskampf im kaiserlichen Deutschland 1884–1914," in Tenfelde and Volkmann, *Streik*, pp. 209–36.
18. Kaelble and Volkmann, "Konjunktur und Strei"; Griessinger, *Kapital*, pp. 287ff.; F. Boll, "Economic Cycles and Strikes," in this volume.
19. Volkmann, "Organisation und Konflikt."
20. Volkmann, "Die Streikwellen."
21. Shorter and Tilly, *Strikes in France*, p. 106.

(e.g., wars) were significantly associated with the intensity of strikes. Another line pursued showed that characteristic of strike waves was an initial phase of strikes with above average success rates, followed by their spread into branches and regions with little previous experience of labor conflict, and finally the use of militant tactics (sit-ins, undeclared strikes, slowdowns, etc.). Particular importance was assigned, especially in the case of Britain, to the combined effects of spontaneous elements in strikes and of the eventual strengthening of the ideological and organizational contributions of unions.[22] It is not justified, therefore, to consider the strike waves approach onesidedly as a protest model.[23] Its objective rather is to provide quantitative evidence of the periodic emergence of more spontaneous forms of strikes and labor organization, as well as of ideologically new approaches. The objective is to combine systematically the description of individual cases characteristic of the "history from below" with the methods of quantitative research.[24] In contrast to the views expressed in some German research, spontaneity and organization need not be seen as contradictory. So-called spontaneous movements and forms of expression are often not entirely unplanned, unstructured, and unorganized, but rather new and different forms of action and organization. Seen in this light, the connection between strike waves and the launching of new forms of labor conflict and strike organization (such as the New Unionism and the shop stewards movement) can be better understood.

Because such changes are only partly quantifiable, evidence that there are strike waves and cyclical change in the form of strikes only serves as a pointer for further studies.[25] This suggestive function of quantitative analysis also applies to the downswings of strike waves. These are generally characterized by 1) an increased number of employer counteroffensives and, thus, defensive strikes of considerable duration culminating in higher proportion of labor defeats; 2) a decline of strike activity in weakly organized branches and regions; and 3) a decreased degree of mobilization during strikes. In contrast to the rationalization approach, the strike waves model emphasizes the continuity and inevitability of conflict.

On the basis of quantitative methods a combination of both approaches poses no problem, but the same does not hold for their interpretative models. The relatively narrow emphasis on modernization and sociological conflict characteristic of the rationalization approach rests on a collective bargaining model. By

22. Cronin, *Industrial Conflict*, pp. 74ff.
23. Like Volkmann, "Die Streikwellen."
24. Cronin, "Theories of Strikes." Cf. F. Boll, "Spontaneitaet und Organisation in der Arbeiterbewegung. Methodische Ueberlegungen zu ihrer Behandlung in der Geschichtsschreibung," in *Internationale Tagung der Historiker der Arbeiterbewegung*, 1983, ITH Tagungsberichte 20, (Wien, 1985), pp. 413–31.
25. See Cronin's recourse to Hobsbawm's "Economic Fluctuations and Some Social Movements since 1800," in *Labouring Men* (London, 1964).

53

contrast, the strike waves approach is much more open to interpretation. Shorter and Tilly largely restricted themselves to advancing their research results, which nonetheless enabled them to refute economically oriented approaches.[26] Cronin, by contrast, seizes on Marxist intimations that changes in the relative power of the parties, together with changes in the economic cycle, periodically led to new struggle phases for the workers and their employers. In addition to the economic cycle, he argues that the union structure and ideology had particular effects on the changing strength of the conflicting parties and, in connection with this, on changes in production technique and organization.[27] Changes in the level of qualification, structure, and the consequent ideological orientation of the labor force, together with changes in the economic cycle, periodically led to new struggles on the part of workers and their organizations.[28]

It is not surprising that such an interpretation has been developed for British labor history, in which a series of conflicts resulted from a slow process of technological change resisted by a union force strongly adhering to work rules. Further research efforts are required to find out to what degree this specific combination of factors bears on the German situation, because the outbreak of strike waves also characterized the history of German labor conflicts.[29]

II

I shall seek to shed more light on these problems by a comparison of statistical methods and results.

Volkmann used for his linear continuity analysis statistics and diagrams based on five-year averages, which brought out the long-term course of developments very clearly. The most common movement, as seen in Figure 1, had a shape roughly like an arch,[30] describing a secular increase in the number of strikes

---

26. E. Weede provides a good survey on the state of international comparative research into the macrosociological aspects of strikes in his "Der Streik in den westlichen Industriegesellschaften. Eine kritische Ueberschrift der international vergleichenden und quantitativen Streikforschung," *Zeitschrift fuer die gesamte Staatswissenschaft* 135 (1979): 1–16.

27. Cronin, "Theories of Strikes."

28. See R. Price, *Masters, Unions, and Men. Work Control in Building and the Rise of Labour, 1830–1914* (Cambridge, 1980); D. Groh, "Intensification."

29. For the miners, see K. Tenfelde, *Sozialgeschicte der Bergarbeitschaft an der Ruhr im 19. Jahrhundert,* (Bonn, 1981); idem, "Gewalt und Konfliktregelung in den Arbeitskaempfen der Ruhrbergleute bis 1918," in F. Engel-Janosi et al., (Hg.), *Gewalt und Gewaltlösigkeit* (Wien, 1977), S. 185–236; Tenfelde and D. Milles, "...Aber es kam kein Mensch nach den Gruben um anzufahren," *Arbeitskaempfe der Ruhrbergarbeiter 1867–1878* (Frankfurt and New York, 1983); Machtan, *Streiks,* Cf. also: H. Steffens, "Arbeitstag, Arbeitszumutungen und Widerstand. Bergmaennische Erfahrungen an der Saar in der zweiten Haelfte des 19. Jahrhunderts," in *AfS* 21 (1981): 1–54. For the metalworkers, see I. Costas, "Berliner Elekroindustrie", and R. Vetterli, "Konflikt und Konfliktregelung in einem schweizerischen Grossbetrieb 1890–1914, both in Tenfelde and Volkmann, *Streik,* pp. 91–108, 162–76, and H. Homburg, "Anfaenge des Taylorsystems in Deutschland vor dem Ersten Weltkrieg. Eine Problemskizze under besonderer Beruecksichtigung der Arbeitskaempfe bei Bosch 1913," in *Geschichte und Gesellschaft* 4 Jg., (1978): 170–94.

30. Volkmann, "Modernisierung," p. 126.

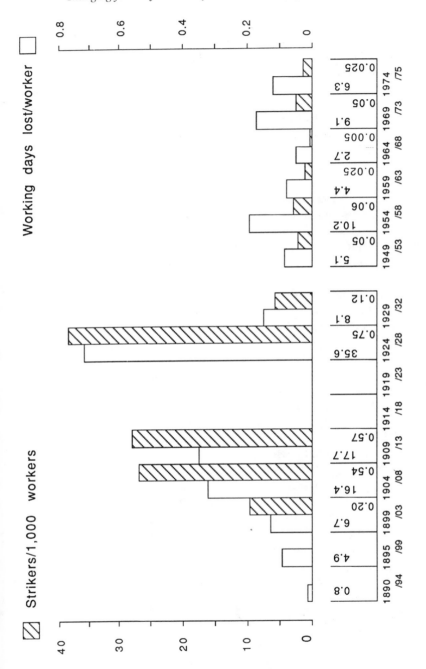

Figure 1. Volkmann's continuity model of decreasing strike frequency (in five-year steps)

roughly like an arch,[30] describing a secular increase in the number of strikes from the end of the nineteenth century to the middle phase of the Weimar Republic, and followed by a continuous decline beginning in the 1930s. Short-term aberrations were systematically leveled out and thereby ignored. In contrast, the analysis of strike waves rests on the consideration that data sectioned on a yearly basis bring out a much more erratic curve, which cannot be leveled statistically, as shown by Figure 2. A comparison of the variations in such economic indices as production figures and prices and wages with variations in strike intensity shows that strikers vary much more decisively. The most important indices of strike intensity, such as the number of strikes, strikers, and work days lost can increase or decrease many times from year to year.

The two figures clearly illustrate this contrast. Besides high fluctuation in the number of strikes and in working days lost, Figure 1 shows a clear increase in the numbers of strikers around 1889–90, 1905, 1910–12, and particularly 1919–23. These periods are followed from 1924 onward by continuously high strike activity that, with the exception of 1926, is well above the prewar average.[31]

A central definitional problem needs to be addressed: What is a normal increase in the number of strikes corresponding to the economic cycle and what is an exceptionally rapid fluctuation?[32] In those countries researched more thoroughly, some strike waves can be easily identified showing characteristics exceeding "normal" increases in strike activity: in Britain, the fighting years of the New Unionism in 1889–90 and of the rank and file movement between 1910 and 1913; in France, the years 1890–3, 1906, 1936, and 1968; in Germany, the important miners' strikes of 1889, 1905, and 1912; and in all three of these countries, the postwar strike waves of 1919–21.[33] The years 1919–21 are especially noteworthy in that they were recognized as particularly intensive strike years well before the conduct of quantitative analyses, having marked significant high points in both political and trade union activity.

The patterns of national strike waves, which have been closely examined elsewhere, highlight hitherto little noticed historical peculiarities of German labor conflicts.[34] Because of the pioneering work of Shorter and Tilly, France was initially regarded as the classic example of strike waves.[35] A comparison with Britain and Germany, however, shows that until the 1920s the wavelike

31. Figure 1, see K. Oldenberg, "Arbeitseinstellunge," in *Handwoerterbuch der Staatswissenschaften* (Jena, 1909), p. 950, and Tenfelde and Volkmann, *Streik*, Appendix, graphic 2. See Volkmann, "Modernisierung," p. 127, graphic 4.

32. See F. Boll, "International Strike Waves: A Critical Assessment," in W. J. Mommsen and H. G. Husung, eds., *The Development of Trade Unionism in Great Britain and Germany, 1880–1914* (London, 1985), p. 80, with some definitions.

33. Cf. ibid.

34. Ibid.

35. Cf. esp. C. Tilly and E. Shorter, "Les vagues de grèves en France," *Annales ESC*, vol. 28 (1973), pp. 857–87.

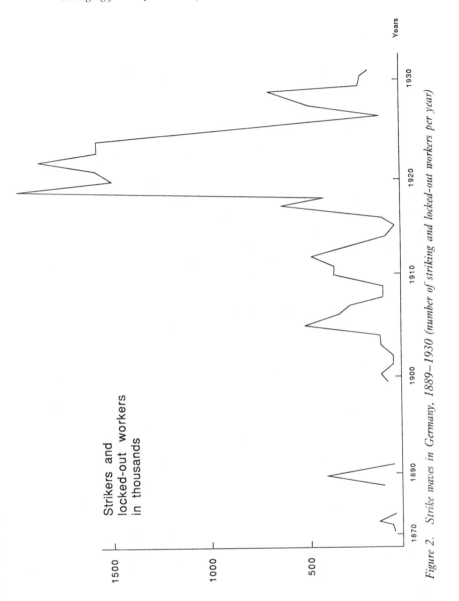

Figure 2. Strike waves in Germany, 1889–1930 (number of striking and locked-out workers per year)

This timing of the inception of statistical tabulations contributed to the false impression that the process of changes in the form of strikes during the Kaiserreich was rapid and irreversible. Actually, the forms of strikes changed in Imperial Germany in a cyclical pattern. Low strike frequency and participation, high number of individual strikes, and long duration of strikes were features of the economic downturn, and were particularly evident during the recession at the beginning of the 1890s. The sudden change in 1896, which appears to support the rationalization thesis, in fact corresponded to a change in the economic cycle from relatively low to high growth rates, which strongly favored an upswing of strike activity. Putting together more recent case studies with our general knowledge of strike waves, a new picture emerges with respect to the other indices discussed by the change of form school. Even taking into account the gaps in the data, we can safely assume that by 1914 the indices for the duration, success rates, and the average number of participants in strike actions, and their dependence on the economic cycle, changed little if at all in the direction suggested by the modernization approach.

As for the *duration* of labor conflicts, Volkmann came to the wrong conclusions because he overestimated the proportion of one-day strikes. He maintained that until 1880 strikes were very short (an average five days) and that a sudden increase in their duration to more than forty days occurred during the years 1890–4. Afterwards, a "secular" trend allegedly appeared toward the shortening duration of strikes, which was only interrupted briefly during the mid-1920s.[48] According to the strike statistics used by Volkmann, one-day strikes made up 48% to 93% of the total number during the years 1869 to 1890. The more recent data of Machtan and Milles, presented in Table 1, suggest and show for the randomly selected years 1873 and 1877 proportions of between 2.4% and 23%, and 18% and 42%, respectively.[49] (The lower figure in each case is for the number of known one-day strikes; the higher one includes the number of strikes with an unknown duration, i.e., when a one-day strike cannot be excluded as a possibility). Machtan's data for the years 1871–5 show an average strike duration of 21.3 days, increasing from 15.5 days in 1871 to 33.3 days by 1875, when the duration of strikes reached the average for the years 1899–1914. The fluctuations observed are characteristic of the development of strike waves: initially shorter, more successful strikes with greater participation, followed by periods marked by the declining success and increased duration of strikes.

The strike statistics of the Free Trade Unions used by Volkmann also do not support his claim of a clear-cut tendency toward the shortening of the strikes. The average duration of strikes and lockouts decreased from 31.2 labor days

48. Volkmann, "Modernisierung," p. 118, with references to Shorter and Tilly, *Strikes in France*, pp. 306ff.
49. Machtan, *Dokumentation*.

60

Table 1. *Duration and defeat in strike waves*

Year	Duration (in days)	Defeat (in %)
1872	17.3	25.8
1875	33.3	54.5
1889	—	36.4
1893	—	62.7[a]
1899	32.3	40.7
1901	40.0	53.8
1906	33.1	36.0
1909	34.6	47.3
1910	—	26.9
1912	22.3	—

[a] Data for Russia only.
Sources: See footnote 50.

lost during the period 1895–9 to 26.0 in 1904–8, climbing back to 30.6 days in 1909–13. Only for the years 1890–3, virtually all years of economic depression, was the figure significantly higher (40.9 days).

The range of fluctuation recorded in Table 1 confirms that one cannot speak of a significant shortening of strikes before 1914. An unmistakable deviation is noticeable only during the Weimar Republic when the comparable figure for working days lost through strikes and lockouts per affected worker fluctuated between 12.8 (1919–23) and 21.1 (1924–8). For the period of the Federal Republic of Germany, however, the picture looks entirely different, with the figures fluctuating generally between 5.6 and 3.9 days lost per affected worker (1964–8 is exceptional, with 1.1 days).[51]

The impression of relative stability suggested by the overall pre-1914 average, allowing for fluctuations corresponding to the economic cycle, is also confirmed for other "form categories." But in the 1880s strikes in Hamburg and Berlin – other data are not available for this period – achieved a very high level of average duration (see Table 3).

As for *average participation* in strikes and lockouts, Volkmann, too, noticed a continuous rather than incremental development. According to him this number remained around 100 for the years 1890–1913 and rose to between 400 and 500 participants for the period 1914–32.[52] Table 2[53] gives these figures,

50. Table 1 according to Machtan, *Dokumentation*, and to Oldenberg, "Arbeitsein-stellungen," p. 950, for the years 1889–94. For the rest of the period, *Statistik des Deutsches Reichs*, vol. 272 (Berlin, 1914), p. 27.
51. Volkmann, "Modernisierung," graphics I and II.
52. Ibid., p. 124.
53. Ibid., p. 146.

Table 2. *The ups and downs of strike waves in Germany*

Year	Strikes	Strikers	Strikers/Strike
1871	157	64,300	409
1872	362	108,800	300
1875	88	5,362	123
1879	15		
1881	15		
1886	77		
1889-90	1,131	394,440	349
1893[a]	150	10,000	67
1900	1,468	131,888	90
1901	1,091	60,776	57
1905	2,657	526,810	198
1906	3,626	349,327	96
1908	1,524	112,110	74
1910	3,228	369,807	115
1912	2,834	481,094	170
1915	141		

Note: See Table 1.
[a] Estimated data.

but for the strike waves of 1871–3 and 1889–90. During the intervening years of depression participation naturally decresased very sharply.

This fact, as well as fluctuations according to the economic cycle, also emerges in the illustrative cases of labor unrest in Berlin and Hamburg, which shed some light on the otherwise still little known strike wave of 1889–90. (See Table 3.)

In Table 3 the increases in the numbers of strikes and striking workers beginning in 1888 bring out that the strike wave of 1889–90 was not an isolated phenomenon. Rather, there was a preparatory phase of several years during which strike activity appears to have been far greater than in the first half of the 1890s. Calculating the figures for participation per strike only makes sense of the period from 1888 onward when relatively precise data become available. For the years 1888–90 these figures are above rather than below the mean for prewar strikes. The division into strikes per individual company and groups of companies during this strike wave is also of importance for our argument. Table 4 shows the distribution of group strikes from 1886 to 1896 and is based upon police statistics, which should be precise, particularly for group strikes with significant participation. The distribution of group strikes confirms the suggested pattern of the preparatory and main phases of the strike wave, followed by the abrupt replacement of group strikes by individual strike actions during the 1891 recession.

Table 3. *Strikes in Hamburg and Berlin, 1886–96*

	Hamburg			Berlin		
	Strikes	Strikers	Strikers/Strike	Strikes	Strikers	Strikers/Strike
1886	17	4,000	253	11	1,722	157
1887	12	5,000	416	9	1,318	146
1888	23	7,069	307	6	17,364	2,894
1889	17	7,000	412	20	34,287	1,715
1890	58	26,031	449	52	10,758	207
1891	17	1,446	85	46	2,901	63
1892	3	491	164	35	986	28
1893	7	800	114	47	1,609	34
1894	9	275	31	50	1,848	37
1895	11	461	42	73	1,796	25

Source: Calculated from *Stattsarchiv Hamburg,* pp. 1621, 2350, 2830, 3568, 4160, 4795, 1907, and *Staatsarchiv Potsdam,* Rep. 30 Bln C. Tit 94 Nr. 8552.

Table 4. *Strikes of individual companies and groups of companies in Hamburg and Berlin 1886–96*

	Hamburg		Berlin	
	Individual	Groups	Individual	Groups
1886			5	3
1887			4	5
1888	1	15	2	4
1889	0	10	17	13
1890	11	28	35	14
1891	13	3	67	1
1892	2	2	73	5
1893	3	2	51	6
1894	8	1	80	10
1895	10	1	ca. 700	ca. 16

Source: The data for group strikes is based on police statistics.

The *frequency* of strikes increased continuously until 1914. However, when one measures the number of participants relative to the number of workers employed, the picture changes to one of relative stability, again allowing for some fluctuations according to the economic cycle. Looking at Table 5, which takes into account only those years with high participation – that is, those of

63

Models and realities

Table 5. *Frequency of Strikes*

	Strikes/100,000 workers	Participants/1,000 workers
1871	34	10.2
1889	71	24.6
1905	149	29.6
1912	159	27.0

Source: Number of workers from G. Hohorst, J. Kocka, G. A. Ritter, eds, *Sozialgeschichtliches Arbeitsbuch II*, 2nd ed. (Munich, 1978), p. 67.

strike waves – the number of strikers and locked-out workers per 1,000 workers hardly increased after 1889. In fact, measured in terms of the most important form categories, the strike wave of 1889 had already reached the levels of the prewar period. The total number of striking workers was only exceeded twice thereafter (in 1905 and 1912), and average participation per strike (349) was far higher than subsequent years. The rates of success and partial success also reached their highest levels for the whole Kaiserreich period (see Table 1).

Even the timing of strikes according to the economic cycle was perfect, a view that is supported by the average decrease in strike activity caused by the recession that started in 1891. As has already been discussed, the well-planned use of the strike weapon according to the movements of the economic cycle was not the result of the influence of centralized unions. Working-class consciousness of the economic cycle developed in large measure through direct experience, independently of organization: direct observations of the increased demand for labor during upswings, as well as the reading of company reports.[54] The strike wave at the beginning of the 1870s already reflected the learning of these lessons in timing relative to the economic cycle, adopted for the launching of strikes, their preparation over the course of a year or more, and supportive measures, such as the building up of a strike fund, public relations activities, and appeals to government institution. These features, on the basis of Volkmann's periodization, should have appeared only after 1900.

Thus, when one takes the 1871–3 and 1889–91 strike waves into account, the history of labor conflict during the Kaiserreich presents itself in an entirely different light. The picture of a rapid and "continuous" increase from the 1890s disappears, and is replaced by one of a wave movement that did not end in 1889–90, but continued with increasing frequency until 1923.

The scheme of periodization that is central to the rationalization approach must now be reconsidered. It distinguishes between a phase of less well-timed strikes making for extremely long struggles with low mobilization and little

54. See F. Boll, "Economic Cycles and Strikes," in this volume, with references to Perrot, Andreani, Cronin, Machtan, and Engelhardt.

union planning, and a phase following of continuous "rationalization through increasing organization."

Without doubt, the frequency of individual strikes increased both absolutely and in accordance with the degree of union organization. The share of striking workers belonging to unions strongly increased before 1914, and the strengthening of the influence of unions on strike activities was reflected in an increase in group strikes, their relatively high rates of success, and the number of conflicts resolved through negotiations. Looking over *all* the form categories for which statistical data are available, however, we observe a preponderance of stagnating tendencies and of those contradicting the rationalization thesis. Average duration, the degrees of participation and mobilization within companies (measured by the numbers of striking and locked-out workers relative to the total labor force) stagnated, as did success rates calculated for each form of strike (individual or group strike, unfinished or finished strike). Given the fact that the numbers of successful lockouts remained high up to the war and that this militant tactic was used more and more frequently by employers, the success rates of labor struggles generally have to be viewed as declining.[55] The number of companies per strike also declined slightly before 1914.

III

This meager overall validity of the modernization approach is confirmed by an international comparison: labor conflicts in prewar Germany, despite a highly developed capitalism, were far less modern (in the meaning of the rationalization approach) than those in France or Britain. In terms of direct participation, they only reached a third to a half of the levels of British or French strikes. In terms of duration, they were 50% to 100% longer, and they were affected to much higher degree by lockouts. Yet, even though the rate of success of strikes in Germany did not match that of British or French strikes,[56] unionized labor was clearly stronger in the German Kaiserreich than in the other two countries.

Indeed, if we look at the changes in the form categories of strikes, a clear contrast emerges (with a few exceptions in individual industrial branches) between the growth of union organization and involvement in strikes, and changes in the forms of conflicts. The central thesis of a parallel evolution of union organization and of the forms of labor conflicts therefore appears incorrect. Such a conclusion may also be drawn concerning labor unrest during the First World War and the revolution, when a development in the opposite direction occurred: while union influence on strikes was rapidly declining, an equally

55. Volkmann, "Modernisierung," p. 146.
56. Boll, "International Strike Waves," p. 89.

rapid change in the form of conflicts was taking place (in the sense of the rationalization approach).[57] These events confirm the observations made about the timing of the strike waves during the nineteenth century. The working class was quite capable of exploiting politically and economically "favorable" turns of the economic cycle without centralized and highly organized unions, and partly even in opposition to them. It is worth recalling Geary's warning that the development of the strike as a weapon cannot be regarded as a simple chronological parallel to the creation of formal organizations.[58]

More detailed information on the relationship between changes in the organization and forms of labor conflicts can only be provided by specific studies of individual branches of industry, because some of the apparent contradictions are presumably a result of the high level of data aggregation. Before discussing local cases, it should be noted that the not very successful, and from 1906 clearly worsening, position of workers in labor conflicts has also been comprehensively discussed by the exponents of rationalization theory. Volkmann states in this context:

> The continuing efforts of the workers...meet increasing resistance by the employers. Organisation and concentration strengthen capital at the expense of labor, one could say, going by the criterion of strike success during the years 1899–1913, and as a critique of the concept of "organized capitalism": the modernization of labor conflict puts one side at a disadvantage.[59]

Yet, according to Volkmann, the rationalization of labor conflicts progressed even under the conditions of the Kaiserreich, when one considers a form of conflict not yet discussed in detail here: labor conflicts resolved locally without strikes. (These were officially registered in union statistics only from 1905 onwards.) Strike-free movements were by far more successful than strikes, affected more workers per movement, were less costly, and were therefore considered more "rational." Because their numbers rapidly increased from 1906 onward, they are said to have contributed to a kind of negative process of selection of strike movements. Given the labor successes achieved without strikes, analysts consider that only particularly hard-to-win conflicts culminated in strike actions. This is seen as an explanation for the stagnating success rates of strikes.[60]

Thus, the so-called strike-free movements demand closer scrutiny both because of their centrality to the rationalization argument and in order to be able to judge industrial relations in the Kaiserreich.[61] In the same way as

57. Volkmann, "Die Streikwellen."
58. D. Geary, *European Labor Protest, 1848–1939* (London, 1981), p. 37.
59. Volkmann, "Modernisierung," p. 146.
60. Ibid., p. 148.
61. See the criticism of G. A. Ritter, *Sozialdemokratie und Sozialgeschichte 1909–1914*, in AfS XVII (1977): 462 on D. Groh, *Negative Integration und revolutionaerer Attentismus. Die deutsche Sozialdemokratie am Vorabend des Ersten Weltkrieges*, (Frankfurt, 1973).

strikes, these movements have been integrated into a periodization scheme: the "older" form of conflict – strikes – was gradually replaced by the more "novel" form of collective agreement.[62] But it is worth noting that collective agreements on wages and working conditions were concluded between artisans and masters even in the preindustrial age.[63]

Our knowledge of these earlier collective agreements has many gaps. Even in the early days of the industrial age they were not recorded in writing. The unions that emerged during the strike waves between 1870 and 1889 were preoccupied with organizing strike support from beyond their regions; there was no time for reporting successful strikeless settlements. Besides, case studies of labor conflicts conducted by researchers after the event tended to focus on the spectacular, and to ignore collective agreements. Yet despite the unsatisfactory level of our knowledge, there should be no doubt that in the craft trades, which were the pillars of the early union movement, collective agreements on wages and working conditions, not strikes, were the main objective of workers' associations. Often this was a continuation of the guild tradition, when the "local wage" or "local tariff" was determined by a collective agreement if it had not already been fixed by the authorities. In the textile industry the so-called wage lists were usually negotiated collectively.[64] From a historical point of view, collective agreements and labor conflict were thus closely connected, and a chronological division between old (strike) and new forms of conflict (strike-free settlements) is artificial.

Indicative of the relationship between collective agreements and strikes is the case of the Hamburg building workers. Their union was founded in the 1860s with the objective of negotiating new tariffs with masters, and during a number of years this objective was achieved without a general downing of tools. The predominant form of conflict, however, is difficult to ascertain because there was no clear dividing line between wage movements with and without strikes. For example, it was said of the Hamburg carpenters: "After newcomers were kept away for awhile the demand was accepted; shorter working hours were introduced on 3rd June 1872."[65] Another pressuring device between collective agreements and strikes used by militant worker was "blocking" individual building sites or companies; pressure could also be applied through partial strikes before turning to the more powerful general downing of tools. We read about the Berlin carpenters of 1869–70: "Some partial strikes were sufficient to cause the masters to withdraw the already (individually) drawn contracts and

---

62. Volkmann, "Modernisierung," p. 148.
63. Griessinger, *Kapital.*
64. D. Dowe, "Legale Interessenvertretung und Streik. Der Arbeitskampf in den Tuchfabriken des Kreises Lennep (Bergisches Land) 1850," in Tenfelde and Volkmann, *Streik,* pp. 31–51, 39.
65. Brinkmann, *Zimmerer,* p. 50.

to respect the (collective) agreements of the previous year."[66] The parallels with the modern interplay between warning strikes, partial strikes, and collective bargaining without strikes is obvious.

These examples indicate that right from the beginning, particularly among craft-oriented workers, strikes were unmistakably aimed at an improvement of their collective bargaining position. That in this respect there appears to have been no change in the function of strikes in these branches of industry is also shown by the few figures available on the ratio between wage movements with and without strikes. In the case of the Hamburg carpenters and bricklayers, there is no doubt that the number of strike-free agreements with masters exceeded that of general strikes, after their unions were reorganized in the mid-1880s.[67] Individual site blockades or partial strikes served largely as a negotiating weapon to emphasize the strength of the union's position. For bricklayers, the first statistics on wage movements without strikes – in 1895 and 1896 – show that even at this time their number exceeded that of strikes; the ratio was 20:10 in 1895 and 40:38 in 1896.[68]

This connection between strike and collective agreement, however, can already be shown as early as the strike wave of 1869–73. Union reports at the time of the founding of the Kaiserreich provide a number of vivid descriptions of strikes and a list of towns where collective agreements on wages, hours, and working conditions were reached.[69] But these successes could not be sustained and had to be recovered in the next strike wave. The recession was too deep and lasting and the union organization still too weak, or the employers' counterpressure too strong, to safeguard these gains through difficult times.

However, with the sudden emergence of trade unions as mass organizations and the sustained economic upswing that started in 1895, it became possible for workers to safeguard their gains even in times of crisis. This can certainly be regarded as progress through organization, and may have even provided at times an alternative to strikes, but such means of organized pressure remained restricted to a few industrial branches during the Kaiserreich (parts of the engineering, printing, and building industries and the timber trade). Furthermore, victories won through a high degree of organization could be lost, because of technological changes or restructuring in the organization of work, or both (e.g., Siemens in 1905–6, Bosch in 1913).[70] British trade unionism also underwent

66. Ibid., p. 50.
67. Staatsarchiv Hamburg, Politische Polizei, V. 104 – 1/2, V. 104a Bd. 1 u. 2, S. 495 (Fachverein der Maurer).
68. *Protokoll des vierten ordentlichen Verhandstages* des Zentralverbandes der Maurer Deutschlands und verwandter Berufsgenossen (Sitz Hambury) 1897 (Hamburg, 1897), p. 13.
69. Brinkmann, *Zimmerer*, p. 135; Protokoll der zehnten Generalversammlung des Verbandes deutscher Zimmerleute 1891/92 (Hamburg, 1893), p. 8.
70. Costas, "Berliner Elektroindustrie"; Domansky's article in this volume; Homburg, "Taylorsystems."

time and time again the experience of having conflicts solved through bipartite agreements reignited quickly by technological changes.[71]

In summary, parallel wage movements with and without strikes were normal phenomena under a fully developed union system. This dual-front approach was already evident during the initial phases of union organization, and by the 1890s had been achieved in the construction industry. Exponents of the rationalization thesis recognize such progress only when there is a mutual recognition by unions and employers. Yet statistics on strike-free movements included actions and agreements by the work forces of companies in which unions were *not* directly involved or accepted as a controlling body. Finally, it must be remembered that strike-free agreements were often accepted by employers to delay strikes, stall unions, and weaken the determination of the labor force.[72]

The rationalization argument would gain strength if it could be established that there was a clear reduction of strikes in favor of peaceful agreements over time. The turning point in the increase in the number of strikes around 1906–7, which Kaelble and Volkmann mention, cannot be regarded as such evidence.[73] Rather, this period marked a change from smaller to larger strikes; only the number of strikes declined, not the number of workers involved in these conflicts. The growing intensity of these conflicts, the increase in the numbers of lockouts, which were mainly successful for the employers, and the high rate of strike failures confirm the view that the influence of trade unions was declining before 1914. When the years of the Weimar Republic are included in our purview, the thesis of a change of trend from confrontation toward partnership is further undermined. Despite the rapid increase in the number of strike-free movements, strikes and lockouts also increased drastically from 1918 onward and remained until 1928 at a level far exceeding that of the Kaiserreich. The clear decline in the frequency of strikes and the changeover to social partnership is most certainly a pattern that developed in the Federal Republic of Germany. It can presumably be explained, not so much by the logic of labor

71. Cronin, "Strikes and the Struggle for Union Organization"; J. Zeitlin, "Industrial Struture, Employer Strategy, and the Diffusion of Job Control in Britain, 1880–1920," in Mommsen and Husung, eds., *The Development*, pp. 325–37. For the printing workers: G. Beier, *Schwarrze Kunst und Klassenkampf. Geschichte der Industriegewerkschaft Druck und Papier und ihrer Vorlaufer seif dem Beginn der modernen Arbeiterbewegung*, vol. 1 (Frankfurt, 1966); and Oldenberg, "Arbeitsstelungen," 931, 933, 937, 940; Engelhardt, *Zur Entwicklung der Streikbewegungen*, pp. 559, 561ff, and "Von der 'Unruhe' zum 'Strike'. Hauptzielsetzungen und erscheinungsformen des sozialen Protests beim Uebergang zur organisierten Gewerkschaftsbewegung 1848/49–1869/70," in H. Volkmann and J. Bergmann, eds., *Sozialer Protest. Studien zur traditionellen Resistenz und kollektiven Gewalt in Deutschland vom Vormaerz bis zur Reichsgruendung* (Opladen, 1983), pp. 228–52.

72. See Domansky's essay in this volume.

73. Costas, *Auswirkungen der Konzentration des Kapitals auf die Arbeiterklasse in Deutschland (1880–1911)* (Frankfurt and New York, 1981), p. 87.

conflict as by factors such as the previous experience of Fascism and military defeat, as well as by the steady economic upsurge after 1945.[74]

When the phenomenon of strike waves is included in an analysis of the changes in the form of labor conflicts, Volkmann's trend analysis appears in a more differentiated light. Specific breakthrough phases emerge and the subsequent volatility of labor–management relations is highlighted, making obvious how fragile those new arrangements were. A brief outline of the strike waves in Germany after 1848 brings out these aspects.

The revolutionary years 1848–9 mark a turning point in the history of social conflict from tumultuous popular unrest to goal-oriented labor conflict. Previously, the predominating forms of conflict aside from strikes were the destruction of machinery and factories (Luddites), attacks on public workhouses, clothing shops, and furniture stores. The legalization of labor organizations resulted in a preference for strikes as one of the chief forms of conflict, supplementing already existing forms of collective action: workers' education, cooperatives, and organization itself.[75]

The years of reaction after 1848 brought the destruction of nearly all workers' organizations but not the existing networks of labor communication and front organizations. These facilitated the resurgence of the labor movement in the 1860s at a higher level. Once again, the legalization of workers' organizations led to a significant decline of "violent collective actions" in favor of strikes. Strikes were still viewed not as the only weapon, but as the ultimate one, in labor conflicts. And once again, education (especially through the workers' press) and free organization emerged. The years around 1870 are generally regarded as the period during which German trade unions established themselves. This process was accompanied by a wave of strikes and collective agreements, which displayed two outstanding features by comparison with developments in other countries: the consolidation of the trade union movement through centralized organization and political agreements on the basis of adherence to socialist views, and a strong organizational reaction on the part of the employers. Both features significantly affected later developments.

For the first time, a high rate of success during the initial stages of waves of labor unrest, short duration of strikes, and good timing with regard to the economic cycle – all typical features of strike waves – became common. Although there was hardly any supraregional organization of strikes and the number of unorganized strikers far surpassed that of striking union members, there was on the whole a high level of strike organization and a comparatively low level of violence. Artisan hostels, the remnants of the guild times, and the workers press played an important part in the coordination of labor struggles.[76]

74. Feldmann, "Streiks," p. 275; Volkmann, "Modernisierung," p. 169.
75. Engelhardt, "Unruhe."
76. Ibid.

Changing forms of labor conflict: secular development or strike waves?

In German labor experience, there was a particularly strong tendency to organize trade unions not only on a local or regional basis (as in England), but right from the beginning also as national institutions, thereby effectively suppressing local and regional rivalries. One of the main reasons for this was the presumably common origins and interdependence of the social and the national movements in the Revolution of 1848.[77] Against this background, the merger of the socialist branches of the labor movement at the Gotha Party Congress in 1875 may be seen as a result of the preceding strike wave in which party political divisions had played an extremely debilitatng role.

The depression and political repression during the years of the Anti-Socialist Law (1878–90) once more induced a break of organizational continuity. Even so, the next wave of strikes and union organization in the mid-1880s was of such momentum that it allowed a decisive breakthrough for German trade unions as mass organizations.[78] Union membership recorded an increase from 95,000 in 1887 to 294,000 by 1890. The number of strikes rose from about 50 to 1,131 during this period, and these strikes enjoyed a well above average rate of success and participation. On top of this, came two clear Socialist election victories in 1887 and March 1890. This upsurge culminated in unprecedented labor euphoria that exploded publicly during the May Day celebrations that took place for the first time in 1890, even before the Socialists had emerged from illegality (in the autumn of 1890).[79] The degree of spontaneity at the local level far exceeded the expectations of the leadership and could not be controlled.

This period of intense union struggle also strengthened the tendencies towards centralization on both sides of the labor scene. The Free Trade Unions founded a central body called the *Generalkommission*, which played a significant role in labor progaganda and in coordinating the efforts of union organizations. The smaller unions formed trade and even industrial organizations.[80] On the other side, employers also intensified their efforts at organization. During the May Day celebrations of 1890 there were regional lockouts affecting several industrial branches, particularly in the labor strongholds of Hamburg and Berlin. Other means for resisting the unions were also devised, such as lockout funds, blacklists, and employer-run hiring agencies.[81] After the 1889–90 strike wave, Germany emerged as the most centralized industrial nation as far as

77. Engelhardt, "Unruhe," has one interesting example. See also Engelhardt, "Nur vereint sind wir stark," *Die anfaenge der deutschen Gewerkschaftsbewegung 1862/63 bis 1869/70* (Stuttgart, 1977), 2 vol.; and W. Albrecht, *Fachverein – Berufsgruppengewerkschaft – Zentralverband. Organisationsprobleme der deutschen Gewerkschaften 1870–1890* (Bonn, 1982).
78. Ritter and Tenfelde, "Durchbruch."
79. Trade union membership: ibid., Appendix. Strike data: Oldenberg, "Arbeitseinstellungen."
80. Albrecht, *Fachverein*, pp. 475ff. K. Schoenhoven, *Expansion*.
81. W. D. Hund, "Der 1. Mai 1890," and Saul, "Verteidigung der buergerlichen Ordnung."

worker and employer organization and means of conflict were concerned. The centralization of labor conflicts was highly valued, as shown by the fact that the so-called localist unions, with particularly deep roots in Berlin, the center of the German labor movement, had no chance of successfully competing with labor organizations more widely organized in the Kaiserreich. It was not until the unsuccessful strike wave of 1910–12, and in particular the union crisis caused by the First World War, that a resugence of localist traditions occurred.[82]

British and American scholars have generally explained the outbreak of strike waves by focusing attention on the organizational structure and relative strength of the two sides in labor conflicts. Besides the role played in this regard by economic cycles and political developments, another instrumental factor was technological change and the resulting restructurings of the labor force.[83] Such changes assumed increasing importance in labor conflicts after the turn of the century.

Technological change induces structural changes in the labor force through the devaluation of traditional skills and a corresponding increase in the numbers of unskilled and semiskilled workers. In a long-term perspective, it is a process that unfolds in successive phases of growth and stagnation, with grave repercussions for the ability of the labor force to organize. In Germany new branches of industry emerged within a short time, and old industries with firmly established industrial relations (such as, the printing industry) were restructured. These developments required new and creative answers on the part of the labor movement. Yet, despite long-term preparatory work, union demands were often not clearly formulated until after the outbreak of strike waves.[84] Structural changes also shaped the history of German trade unions and industrial strikes in a decisive way. Before 1914 German unions rarely managed to get a foothold in the newly emerging large companies, employing small numbers of skilled workers, that emerged in the electrotechnical, chemical, and rubber industries.

In Britain the failure to organize certain groups of unskilled and semiskilled workers was justified mainly on ideological grounds and on the basis of existing union structures. These workers were in fact regarded as incapable of organization because they could not afford the unions' extremely high membership fees, these being inflated by numerous insurance provisions.[85] In Germany the weakness of union organization in large companies, especially in the steel and textile industries, was a result of the strongly antiunion-oriented organization

---

82. For the German localism, W. Albrecht, *Fachverein – Berfusgewerkschaft – Zentralverband*, 397ff.; and D. H. Mueller, "Syndicalism and Localism in the German Trade Union Movement," in Mommsen and Husung, eds., *The Development*, pp. 239–49.
83. Cronin, "Theories of Strikes."
84. Ibid.
85. Hyman, "Mass Organization."

of employers.[86] In Britain this obstacle had been overcome by 1914; in the Kaiserreich it remained until 1914, clearly reflected in the course that strike waves assumed after the turn of the century.

The Great Depression of the mid-1890s was followed by an increasingly rapid sequence of economic upturns. Organizational successes were being consolidated, as were collective agreements, and with each upturn these agreements were improved. Continuing inflation further insured that the next "wage round" would take place after only one or two years, so that the economic recovery from 1896 onward (which was only briefly interrupted by short periods of recession), automatically gave rise to a steadily increasing number of wage movements, with and without strikes. However, with the strike wave of 1910–12, the Social-Democratic labor movement apparently reached a threshold beyond which it could not pass without challenging the semiabsolutist political conditions of the Kaiserreich. This impasse is reflected statistically in the stagnation or declines of rates of average strike participation and strike success rates during lean years, as well as in an increase in the number of lockouts.

Apart from an increase in the number of strike-free movements and agreements, the comparatively successful strike wave of 1905–6 had also brought a number of limited breakthroughs in large-scale industries, particularly in metal and engineering.[87] Employers reacted with the intensified use of lockouts and the support of "yellow unions" (*Werkvereine*), which adhered to a no-strike policy and acted as strike-breakers in case of labor conflicts. These were the employers' two preferred weapons during the strike wave of 1910–12: In 1910, for the first time, the number of locked-out workers exceeded that of strikers. The number of working days lost through lockouts was about three times that of days lost through strikes at the beginning of this period of economic recovery.[88] Even more significant was the fact that the rate of new members joining the unions declined to 38% in 1909–12. Increase in union membership has been a typical feature of strike waves, and in 1887–90 and 1903–6 had reached about 90%. By the eve of the war, however, membership stagnated even in those unions that were the core of the union movement – that is, construction, timber, and metalworkers organizations.[89] German unions now displayed limitations that seemed almost insurmountable: In branches such as engineering (1912) and shipbuilding (1913), the results were meager; in mining

86. E. Domansky-Davidsohn, "Der Grossvertrieb also Organizationsproblem des Deutschen Metallarbeitsverbandes vor dem Ersten Weltkrieg," in H. Mommsen, ed., *Arbeiterbewegung und sozialer Wandel* (Wuppertal, 1980), pp. 95–116.
87. I. Costas, *Auswirkungen der Konzentration*, pp. 77ff, 132ff.
88. See footnote 32.
89. *Statistische Beilage des Correspondenzblattes der Freien Gewerkschaften Deutschlands 1914*; Schoenhoven, *Expansion*, pp. 141ff.

(1912) defeat had to be accepted.[90] Once more, unions were unable to penetrate branches of large-scale industry that had now become strongholds of the yellow unions.

These developments certainly reflected the structural changes experienced by the industrial labor force during the prewar decade, notably a rapid increase in the numbers of unskilled and semiskilled workers employed at the expense of skilled labor. The employers' antiunion strategy was especially successful among older workers and new workers, many of whom had recently immigrated from agricultural areas to industrial centers. Thus, the destabilizing effects of technological change, which previously had affected unions most seriously during periods of economic recession, were not recouped during the boom years 1910–12.[91]

Only with the political developments that took place during the war, including the passage of the Auxiliary Service Law (*Hilfsdienstgesetz*) and the accompanying official recognition of trade unions by employers and the state, was it possible for the unions to overcome their organizational limitations. Employers were eventually forced by the political pressure of the labor movement to drop the yellow *Werkvereine*, to open large companies to unionization, and to accept the eight-hour workday. The mass of workers rushing to join the unions – leading to a tripling of the membership by 1920 as compared to 1912 – naturally contributed an enormous destabilizing element for traditional union work structures. The war and the revolution resulted in the politicization especially of part of the older generation of workers with trade union experience. Along with the influx of new groups of workers, this phenomenon by 1919–20 produced a sharp increase in strike frequency and in the number of participants and companies involved in strike activities. According to Volkmann's data, the indices of the intensity of labor conflict increased as follows from the strike wave of 1910–13 to the strike wave of 1919–20: participation, 1:17; affected companies, 1:9; number of strikes, 1:25, working days lost, 1:4.

From Volkmann's point of view, enormous step toward the greater effectiveness of strikes was achieved in Germany after the end of the war; and the backwardness of conflict resolution in comparison with Britain disappeared during this period.[92] But these radical changes under the Weimar Republic

90. K. Saul, *Staat, Industries, Arbeiterbewegung im Kaiserreich. Sur innen- und Sozialpolitik des Wilhelminischen Deutschland 1903–1914* (Duesseldorf, 1974), pp. 269ff.; V. Ullrich, *Die Hamburger Arbeiterbewegung vom Vorabend des Ersten Weltkrieges bis zur Revolution 1918/19*, 2 Bde. (Hamburg, 1976), pp. 124ff.; M. Cattaruzza, " 'Organisierter Konflikt' und 'Direkte Aktion.' Zwei Formen des Arbeitskampfes am Beispiel der Werftarbeiterstreiks in Hamburg und Triest," in AfS XX (1980): pp. 325–55.

91. K. Mattheier, *Die Gelben. Nationale Arbeiter zwischen Wirtschaftsfrieden und Streik* (Duesseldorf, 1973).

92. Volkmann, "Die Streikwellen."

were certainly not the result of more effective union organization. In fact, the influence of trade unions on labor conflicts during these years drastically declined.[93]

Under the Weimar Republic the level of labor conflicts never descended to the levels of the prewar period. Fundamental changes were achieved in the way conflicts were conducted with the recognition of the right to negotiate collective agreements autonomously, and in the institutional framework with the establishment of the eight-hour workday and unemployment benefits. Are these changes in the dynamics of labor conflict also to be considered evidence of rationalization in the sense of a more cautious and goal-oriented, but gradually declining, use of militant tactics? Volkmann thinks so, despite the fact that strikes continued to be very frequent until 1928, and the number of working days lost through strikes and lockouts was far higher than the prewar average.[94] In light of the data available, it seems more reasonable to infer that the effective use of strikes achieved through organization and mobilization did not automatically lead to the decreasing frequency of strikes.

It also seems justified to argue that the frequency and intensity of conflicts during this period were caused by the employers' efforts to regain ground that the labor movement had won during the early years of the Weimar Republic. The legal safeguards of bipartite conflict resolution and other achievements of the labor movement, such as the eight-hour workday, became the starting point for renewed political fighting, and decisively contributed to the breakdown of the young republic. The advanced organization of both management and labor and of conflict resolution did not induce a "rationalization," but a reintensification of labor conflicts. Chartes Maier even speaks of an "over-organisation" of German capitalism during those years compared to the Italian situation. The importance of the employers' counterattack may be gauged by the fact that after the end of the revolution and the inflationary period, labor conflict was characterized by a decreased strike rate (1926), while the so-called stabilization phase of the Weimar Republic, the years 1927 to 1929, were marked by a particularly high number of lockouts. For each of these latter years the numbers of working days lost through lockouts was consistently higher than those lost through strikes.[95] The employers' counterattack persisted during the worldwide economic crisis (after the breakup of the government coalition in 1929), now resorting more to political means.[96]

Let us return to the applications of the modernization approach to labor conflicts during the Kaiserreich, in particular, in branch-by-branch analysis.

93. Boll, "*International Strike Waves,*" p. 89.
94. Volkmann, "Modernisierung," graphics 4, 5, pp. 127, 130.
95. Tenfelde and Volkmann, *Streik* Appendix, p. 309.
96. Costas, "Arbeitskaempfe," p. 104.

75

Such closer scrutiny appears all the more appropriate because hardly anywhere else in the industrialized world was labor conflict so strongly differentiated according to industrial branches.[97]

Volkmann attempted to test the rationalization thesis through a comparison of industrial branches. In this comparative analysis he examined how the degree of industrial concentration and organizational strength of labor and companies were related to conflict behavior.[98] His main argument that increasing organization leads not only to an effective use, but also to a clear reduction, of strikes could only be confirmed in the case of the printing industry. In 1912 the largest proportions of workers involved in collective agreements were in contruction (39.6%), printing (38.6%), and timber industries (25.1%).[99] Despite this relatively high proportion of collective agreements, the building and timber industries had high strike rates. In these two branches there was "a parallel existence of regulated and unregulated conflicts" of strikes and strike-free movements.[100]

The negative results of Volkmann's study actually confirm the findings of Costas and Groh. They found the cause for reduced union power and low strike rates in the employers' organizational superiority resulting from the high degree of concentration and large scale of industrial enterprises. This also explains the below average strike rates in the German heavy, electrotechnical, engineering, chemical, and textile industries.[101]

Volkmann provided additional important insights into the relationship between organization and conflict. He had to reject as too general a direct parallel between increasing organization and increasing "rationalization" of conflict behavior.[102] The branch comparison showed that increasing organization could result in intensified conflicts (e.g., in the construction industry), but that if organization developed one-sidedly among the employers, as in the textile industry, expressions of conflict could largely be suppressed. Thus, the organization of the opposing sides of industry showed itself to be a necessary but not sufficient explanation for bipartite conflict resolution. As an additional factor, Volkmann emphasized the changing relative organizational strength of the two sides. Citing once more the example of the construction industry, he found that the considerable union successes during the strike wave of 1905–6 and the high number of subsequently concluded collective agreements did not have a calming effect on the industry, but resulted in an intensification of conflict, mostly initiated by employers. Further variables mentioned as strongly in-

97. P. N. Stearns, *Lives of Labour* (London, 1975), p. 316.
98. Volkmann, "Organisation und Konflikt."
99. Ibid., p. 437.
100. Ibid., p. 434.
101. Stearns, *Lives of Labour*, p. 316; Volkmann, "Organisation und Konflikt" pp. 427ff.
102. Volkmann, "Organisation und Konflikt," p. 436.

fluencing conflict development were "the economic situation" and the "general political climate," factors that could mutually influence each other and lead to an alternation between "phases of fast development, stagnation and set-backs."[103] With these conclusions Volkmann implicitly confirmed the main findings of the strike waves approach. Hopefully, a revision of the rationalization thesis, no longer confined to organizational developments, will be forthcoming.

IV

According to the rationalization approach, strikes in Germany from the end of the nineteenth century onward became increasingly comprehensive, shorter, involved more companies, and tended to mobilize their entire work forces. On the other hand, the statistical data, arranged here on a sectoral basis, have shown changes in German labor conflict less as a continuous rationalization process than as a recurring wave movement. Changes took place in stages, with setbacks, followed by impressive further developments, of which the strike waves around 1869–73, 1889–90, and 1919–23 provide some of the most significant.

Thus, the rationalization thesis's one-sided emphasis on organizational development as the basis of changes in conflict behavior cannot be confirmed. The evidence of strike waves and that of stages of change demonstrate that besides economic factors, there were strong poltical influences. The learning processes induced by the political and military breakdowns were especially marked.

From a methodological point of view, the analysis of form change, as developed by Shorter and Tilly, emerges as the most fruitful approach, particularly as it can be detached from the rationalization approach and successfully combined with the strike wave method.[104] An appropriate methodological approach would, therefore, lay greater emphasis on the analysis of changes in forms of struggle and organization, the economic cycle, organizational strength, the structures and ideologies of the two opposing sides in industrial labor conflicts, and the political conditions and learning processes related to them. The strike wave approach is a useful tool in this context because it permits one to take into account factors that were distinctive of specific periods. But the strike wave method is inadequate in and of itself. Without the support of an approach showing long-term trends of change, it would one-sidedly emphasize specific conditions and spontaneous influences.

Since a combination of the form change and strike wave approaches appears the most fruitful methodological procedure, I suggest that the term "rational-

---

103. Ibid., p. 436.
104. For first steps in this direction, see Shorter and Tilly, *Strikes in France*, pp. 306ff. They discuss only three items of the form change: size of strike, duration, strikes per 100,000 workers.

ization of labor conflict" be entirely dropped. It reflects a point of view that overemphasizes the role of centralized, disciplined labor conflict led by union bureaucracies, and implies that all spontaneous forms of fighting and rank-and-file initiatives are irrational.[105] On the contrary, the rationale, purpose, and methods used in labor conflict cannot be measured with an arbitrarily defined yardstick. Each case has to be judged on its own merits.[106]

105. Ritter and Tenfelde, "Durchbruch," p. 91. This is an important criticism of the so-called rationalization of strike behavior: L. Machtan, *Streiks*, pp. 124ff.

106. Machtan, *Streiks*, pp. 124ff.; cf. also Milles, "...Aber es kam kain Mensch nach den Gruben, um anzufehren," pp. 83ff.

5

Strikes and power in Britain, 1870–1920

JAMES E. CRONIN

I

Not long ago, sociologists and labor economists used to talk confidently about the "natural history of the strike."[1] By that they meant its rather smooth progress along a line that supposedly rose rapidly in the early stages of industrial growth, gradually flattened out with the establishment of stable collective bargaining, and slowly fell as the strike proceeded to "wither away" in the prosperity of "advanced industrial society."

Such notions have much less currency today. Striking has not died out; industrial conflict continues at high levels and periodically erupts into massive confrontations. Newer scholarship, informed by different concerns and predilections, has little sympathy with the earlier work, and has moved in quite different directions. The historical analysis of strikes has been thoroughly transformed, and bears little resemblance to the older studies. The emphasis now is upon complexity and variation, and teleological concepts about long-term trends have been replaced by a much finer sense of the contingent nature of strikes and labor movements within regions or industries. The strike is coming to be understood in terms of specific social contexts and as a manifestation of relations between workers, employers and, in many instances, the

---

1. This essay seeks to extend and to document in some detail the argument first proffered in *Industrial Conflict in Modern Britain* (London, 1979), by focusing upon late nineteenth and early twentieth century developments in British strikes and by linking up the official statistical data, which begin in 1888, with the much less complete information available on the period just before that. The first fruits of this effort appeared as "Strikes, 1870–1914," in C. J. Wrigley, ed., *A History of British Industrial Relations, 1875–1914* (Brighton, 1982), pp. 74–98. The analysis was elaborated and put into a more comparative context for presentation to the 1981 Tutzing conference on the development of unions in Europe, and then refined and refocused upon Britain for the meeting at the Maison des Sciences de l'Homme in Paris in June, 1982, on comparative strike movements. This presumably definitive version is based largely upon the latter paper, though it reflects the comments and criticisms made at both meetings and by other colleagues.

79

state rather than as some unproblematic reflection of working-class interests and grievances.

No doubt the sum of this new work is a major advance in the understanding of strikes and of labor history more broadly. But it does seem that something has been lost in the excessively local orientation of research, and in the decomposition and disaggregation of overall strike indices. What is lost in particular is the way in which strikes feed upon each other and turn from single conflicts into strike movements with a momentum of their own. This omission is particularly obvious in the British experience, where the case study of the individual strike or the particular factory has left largely unexplored the forces that have produced strike waves, those occasional outbursts of militancy that so mark the history of industrial relations.[2]

So, although not wishing to argue for a return to "the natural history of the strike," I would like to urge the value of an analysis of the trends in strikes across British society.[3] There are, of course, problems with such aggregate level analysis, of which we are all aware. Aggregate data can tell us little about the dynamics of strike movements or the mode of transmission from one industry to another, but they can at the least inform us about when strike movements occurred, their dimensions and locations, and their interrelation with other key variables. That alone would seem a useful service. In this particular essay, however, the aim is to go a bit further and to attempt to cast some light upon four specific issues.

First, by combining the rather fragmentary evidence on strikes for the years 1870–90 with the much fuller information available in official statistics for the period following, it should be possible to refine existing notions about the transition from older to newer patterns of collective action.[4] More precisely, it will be argued that the changes that occurred in styles of mobilization were extremely uneven, that they do not fit into any neat dichotomy of traditional versus modern, and that the strike itself does not seem to have played a major role in working people's "repertoire of contention" until after 1867.

The second point that will be stressed is the importance of strike waves to the British record of industrial conflict and the linkages that seem to have existed between these periodic explosions of militancy and short- and long-term economic trends. The third argument qualifies this second point, for it

2. The importance of strike waves in labor history has been argued by Eric Hobsbawm, "Economic Fluctuations and some Social Movements since 1800," in *Labouring-Men* (Garden City, N. J., 1967); and by Friedhelm Boll, "International Strike Waves: A Critical Assessment," in W. J. Mommsen and H. G. Husung, eds., *The Development of Trade Unionism in Great Britain and Germany, 1880–1914* (London, 1985), pp. 78–99.

3. For a useful review under that very rubric, see E. W. Evans and S. W. Creigh, "The Natural History of the Strike in Britain," *Labour History* 39 (November, 1980): 47–61.

4. On the quality of the U. K. statistics and the methods involved in gathering and using them, see K. G. J. C. Knowles, *Strikes* (New York, 1952); and S. W. Creigh, "The Origins of British Strike Statistics," *Business History* 24, no. 1 (1982): 95–106.

will be suggested that beneath the considerable variation over time in the incidence and scale of strikes, there was a fundamental continuity to strike movements before 1914. What united these several outbursts of conflict was a broad effort to enroll ever larger sections of the work force into stable unions. This de facto objective seems, in retrospect, to have overshadowed issues of wages, hours, working conditions, and job control, however important these may have been at the moment or in specific situations.

Finally, the paper will conclude with a quick look beyond 1914 to the war and the postwar unrest. Based upon this, it will be argued that a major discontinuity entered the history of strikes and labor relations with the period of war. Somehow the war brought about a distinct widening of the aims of labor beyond the establishment of organization, and imparted a more aggressive and insurgent quality to working people's industrial and political activities. It was this new dimension to unrest, this new thrust for power that lay behind it, that made the postwar confrontation so deep and protracted. Though the details of this critical moment in the history of British industrial conflict are beyond the scope of this paper, the events of 1917–20 nonetheless constitute the terminus for the evolution sketched out here and, in this way, form an integral part of the empirical groundings for the analysis.[5]

II

"Striking has become a disease, and a very grave disease, in the body social," intoned George Phillips Bevan at the beginning of his learned lecture on strikes to the Royal Statistical Society on 20 January 1880. Worse still, the disease "as yet shows no sign of having run its course," and the concerned statistician could not bring himself "to believe in any speedy cure," whether "by legislative measures or any one course of action." Bevan's subject was the record of industrial disputes during the 1870s, which he compiled in a most thorough and useful fashion, and his judgment on this particular era in industrial relations was endorsed by the labor leader George Howell, who also had recourse to the metaphor from pathology. "This was a period of strike epidemics, not to occur again, let us hope," wrote Howell on the very eve of the next such epidemic in 1889.[6]

The figures produced by Bevan, and reproduced as part of Table 1, are indeed impressive: impressive enough to suggest that the early 1870s probably were the years when strikes became the dominant form of workers' collective

5. For some of the detail, see my "Coping with Labour, 1918–1926," in J. Cronin and J. Schneer, eds., *Social Conflict and the Political Order in Modern Britain* (New Brunswick, 1982); and also Keith Burgess, in this volume.
6. G. P. Bevan, "The Strikes of the Past Ten Years," *Journal of the Royal Statistical Society* 43 (March, 1880): 35–54; George Howell, "Great Strikes: Their Origin, Costs, and Results," *Cooperative Wholesale Societies Annual 1889*, p. 310.

81

Table 1. *Strikes, strikers and trade union membership in Britain, 1870–1920*

Year	Strikes			Strikers	Trade union membership	
	A (Bevan)[a]	B (Webb)[b]	C (Official)[c]	C (Official)[c]	TUC-affiliated unions	Official returns
1870	30				250,000[d]	
1871	98				289,000	
1872	343				256,000	
1873	365				750,000	
1874	286				1,192,000	
1875	245				818/540,000[e]	
1876	229	17			558,000	
1877	180	23			691,000	
1878	268	38			624,000	
1879	308	72			542,000	
1880		46			494,000	
1881		20			464,000	
1882		14			509,000	
1883		26			520,000	
1884		31			598,000	
1885		20			581,000	
1886		24			636,000	
1887		27			674,000	
1888		37	517	119,000	817,000	
1889		111	1211	337,000	885,000	
1890			1040	393,000	1,470,000	
1891			906	267,000	1,303,000	
1892			700	357,000	1,220,000	1,576,000
1893			782	599,000	900,000	1,559,000
1894			929	257,000	1,100,000	1,530,000
1895			745	207,000	1,000,000	1,504,000
1896			926	148,000	1,076,000	1,608,000
1897			864	167,000	1,093,000	1,731,000
1898			711	201,000	1,184,000	1,752,000
1899			719	138,000	1,200,000	1,911,000
1900			648	135,000	1,250,000	2,022,000
1901			642	111,000		2,025,000
1902			442	117,000		2,013,000
1903			387	94,000		1,994,000
1904			354	56,000		1,967,000
1905			358	68,000		1,997,000
1906			486	158,000		2,210,000
1907			601	101,000		2,513,000
1908			399	224,000		2,485,000
1909			436	170,000		2,477,000
1910			531	385,000,000		2,565,000

Table 1. (*cont.*)

Year	Strikes			Strikers	Trade union membership	
	A (Bevan)[a]	B (Webb)[b]	C (Official)[c]	C (Official)[c]	TUC-affiliated unions	Official returns
1911			903	831,000		3,134,000
1912			857	1,233,000		3,416,000
1913			1497	516,000		4,135,000
1914			972	326,000		4,145,000
1915			672	401,000		4,354,000
1916			532	235,000		4,644,000
1917			730	575,000		5,494,000
1918			1116	923,000		6,533,000
1919			1352	2,401,000		7,926,000
1920			1607	1,779,000		8,348,000

[a] Derived from various newspapers and reports by G. P. Bevan, "The Strikes of the Past Ten Years," *Journal of the Royal Statistical Society* (March 1880): p. 37.
[b] Collected from strikes mentioned in *The Times* by S. and B. Webb, The History of Trade Unionism (New York, 1920), p. 347n.
[c] Based on the *Reports on Strikes and Lockouts*, published by the Board of Trade, 1888–1914.
[d] Actually 1869.
[e] Two Congresses held that year.

activity. Thus, though the labor market was buoyant in 1870 – unemployment was only 3.9%, compared with 7.9% in 1868 and 6.7% in 1869 – only 30 strikes were recorded. The figure tripled in 1871, to 98, and more than that again in 1872, when 343 disputes were noted.[7] The levels remained high in the 1870s, as what Thomas Wright called "the alternation between 'flushes' and 'crashes'" shifted the balance of tactical advantage back and forth, and so prompted first workers and then employers to press their advantage to the fullest.[8] Indeed, the strike wave of the early 1870s was probably the first of those major explosions of militancy and union organization that have charac-terized much of the subsequent history of British industrial relations. Like the later waves of 1889–90, 1911–13, and 1919–20, it represented not merely an escalation of overt conflict between workers and employers, but also a shift toward the more inclusive organization of less skilled workers, together with an

7. The numbers in this table are to be taken as broadly indicative of the movement of strikes, but can in no way be regarded as definitive. This is especially the case for the years before 1888, and even for the period 1888–92. On this issue see the references in footnote 4 and also J. Cronin, *Industrial Conflict*, pp. 197–200.
8. Thomas Wright, "On the Condition of the Working Classes," *Eraser's Magazine* 4 (October, 1871): 427.

upsurge of local shopfloor activism, a rejection of the cautious advice of established officials, and a renewed emphasis upon the efficacy of strike activity.[9] Like later insurgencies, too, it was followed by a substantial counterattack by employers that succeeded in beating back workers' organization from its furthest and weakest extensions, but did not manage to turn the clock back to the state of organization or the lower level of strikes that had existed prior to the strike wave. The modes used to reestablish order within "the industrial relations system" also exhibited marked similarity during these successive counteroffensives: an odd mix of employer attempts to inflict symbolic defeats upon key groups of workers, together with efforts on the part of union leaders, state officials, and enlightened employers to elaborate restrictive conciliation schemes and procedures for resolving disputes.[10]

Despite certain earlier prefigurations, it seems reasonable to regard this pattern as basically novel and unique to the era beginning in 1870 and ending in 1914. Underlying this new pattern of strikes was the advance of worker organization from a very modest position in 1870 – about a quarter million trade unionists were organized and affiliated to the Trades Union Congress in that year – to the level reached at the end of World War I, when the bulk of the manual workers, skilled and unskilled, were organized in trade unions whose strength exceeded eight million. This massive achievement, which has yet to be properly appreciated, was accomplished by aggressive worker activity at the point of production.[11]

In this sense, the strike truly came into its own as workers' preferred form of action in the 1870s. To be sure, evidence of occasional strikes can be found much earlier than this, but these seem to have played a far less important role in

9. One implication of this recurring pattern is that the tension between entrenched union leaders and rank-and-file activists is a long-term, indeed structural, aspect of labor history, not peculiar to any particular moment but to those various periods when workers on the shop floor perceived a possibility of advance beyond what their leaders had come to expect. Ideological factors, generational differences, degrees of bureaucratization, and government policy all help to condition and mediate this tension, but its roots would seem to go much deeper. The evidence for this view is scattered widely throughout the record of British labor history, but one might begin the study of the unofficial character of virtually all insurgencies with George Howell. He claimed in 1890 that, "It is perhaps a bold thing to say, but the statement can be made with considerable confidence, that in ninety percent of the strikes which take place, the men directly concerned are the instigators and promoters, and that the union is the brake on the wheel which prevents too great precipitation, and liability to consequent failure." See Howell, *The Conflicts of Capital and Labour*, 2d ed. (London, 1890), p. 211 for the specific instance; and for a more general argument to this effect, Charles Sabel, "The Internal Politics of Trade Unions," in S. Berger, ed., *Organizing Interests in Western Europe* (Cambridge, 1981), pp. 209–44.

10. See J. H. Porter, "Wage Bargaining under Conciliation Agreements, 1870–1914," *Economic History Review* 23 (1970): 460–75; and R. Davidson, "Social Conflict and Social Administration: The Conciliation Act in British Industrial Relations," in T. C. Smout, ed., *The Search for Wealth and Stability* (London, 1979).

11. For the most recent overview, see E. H. Hunt, *British Labour History, 1815–1914* (London, 1981).

the broad array of popular protest and collective action.[12] Thus, while Charles Tilly makes a strong case for locating the birth of the modern "social movement" – with its tactics of mass mobilization, its national orientation, and its aggressive demands – around the political agitation of 1828–32, he nevertheless finds little indication that strikes were considered a major tool for processing grievances.[13] Strikes, and the effort to build unions, obviously became more important during the 1830s, and the 1842 Chartist strike centered in Lancashire clearly represented a dawning realization of the potential of working-class power at the workplace. And yet, these initiatives remained essentially inchoate: the organizations formed in the 1830s were beaten back, and the strike of 1842 would fail to bring tangible results. Chartism was and would remain essentially a political movement that, while drawing support from both old and new sections of the working people and adopting extremely novel strategies of mobilization, nonetheless spoke a language of popular radicalism inherited from the past. That language gave the Chartists a highly effective purchase on the political events of the 1830s in particular, but equipped them poorly for the new politics of the 1840s and even less well for the long-term tasks of building up working-class industrial and political capacity in the relatively stable environment of late nineteenth- and early twentieth-century Britain.[14]

Even the advances in tactics proved ephemeral, for there was little sign of a genuinely national social movement in Britain from 1848 to the mid-1860s. This seems in part to have been due to the temporary withdrawal of the state from overt involvement in the details of local government or social life. The efforts to reform municipal government and poor law administration that marked the 1830s abated, and the repeal of the Corn Laws removed yet a further spur to political activity. Working people, it appears, turned toward the building up of stable unions and, even more, of institutions of self-protection – friendly societies, cooperatives, and so on. They also managed to carve out for themselves a much larger sphere of local political activity, linked at times to the existing parties but often with a certain autonomy and independence.[15]

12. C. R. Dobson, *Masters and Journeymen, A Prehistory of Industrial Relations, 1717–1800* (London, 1980), esp. the appendix listing strikes; and John Rule, *The Experience of Labour in Eighteenth-Century England* (London, 1981), pp. 147–93.

13. Charles Tilly, "Britain Creates the Social Movement," in Cronin and Schneer, pp. 21–51.

14. A. G. Rose, "The Plug Plot Riots of 1842 in Lancashire and Cheshire," *Transactions of the Lancashire and Cheshire Antiquarian Society* 67 (1957): 75–112; James Epstein and Dorothy Thompson, eds., *The Chartist Experience* (London, 1983); I. Prothero, "William Benbow and the Concept of the 'General Strike'," *Past and Present*, no. 63 (1974): 132–71; Brian Brown, "Lancashire Chartism and the Mass Strike of 1842: the political economy of working-class contention," Center for Research on Social Organization – University of Michigan, Working Paper #203, 1979; and Craig Calhoun, *The Question of Class Struggle* (Oxford, 1982).

15. Harold Perkin, *The Origins of Modern English Society* (London, 1969), pp. 380–407; T. Tholfsen, *Working-Class Radicalism in Mid-Victorian England* (London, 1976); Derek Fraser,

85

It was upon these institutional gains that the agitation for political reform commenced again after 1865, culminating in the Second Reform Bill of 1867. Indeed, the years 1867–70 – into which were compressed the second installation of suffrage reform, the formation of the modern Liberal party with significant working-class support, and a major controversy over the status of unions and strikes – seem to have constituted a distinct rupture in patterns of collective action. Though the movement for reform involved many workers and their trade societies, it was conducted with the political tactics developed much earlier by the advocates of Catholic Emancipation in the 1820s and reformers of the 1830s, refined by the Anti-Corn Law League and the Chartists. Like the social movements of 1828–32, the reform agitation of 1865–7 did not much rely upon strikes as vehicles for mobilization, nor were industrial tactics seen as having much capacity either for influencing the authorities. The movement surrounding the Second Reform Act was accompanied, however, by the last substantial outbreak of food riots in the south – in Deptford and Greenwich, as well as in more rural areas such as Oxford and Devon. As a form of collective action, the food riot was certainly not predominant, but it was nonetheless at least viable in the mid-Victorian era. In an incident that reads like something from the eighteenth century, 500 women in Durham were moved as late as 1872 "to parade through the streets with banners, fire-irons, shovels and trays, 'with which they continued to beat, making wild and unearthly music,'" protesting the cost of meat, milk, and potatoes. The ostensible leader of the women threatened to burn in effigy any other woman who bought food at what were thought to be excessive prices. Community organization was strong enough, its "moral economy" meaningful enough, to make the threat effective, and the movement spread to other colliery villages in the county.[16]

Despite their occasional recurrence, most notably during the First World War, food riots did tend to disappear. Whether this reflected a maturation of protest is difficult to determine. One key factor seems to have been the decline in agricultural prices in the Great Depression, which reduced food costs by about 40% from 1877 to 1896. Even when overall prices began to rise again after 1905, the cost of food remained relatively stable and thus came to constitute a smaller proportion of workers' expenditure than it had before. The effect, it appears, was to shift attention from consumption to wages and

Urban Politics in Victorian England (Leicester, 1976); Patrick Joyce, *Work, Society and Politics* (Brighton, 1980) provide useful information on the organizational underpinnings of urban politics. On unions and strikes see National Association for the Promotion of Social Science, *Trades Societies and Strikes* (London, 1860); H. I. Dutton and J. E. King, *Ten Per Cent and no Surrender* (Cambridge, 1981); Richard Price, *Masters, Unions and Men* (Cambridge, 1980); and M. Holbrook-Jones, *Supremacy and Subordination of Labour* (London, 1982).

16. Donald C. Richter, "Public Order and Popular Disturbances in Great Britain, 1865–1914," (Ph.D. diss., University of Maryland, 1965), pp. 30–1; Robert Storch, "Popular Festivity, Social Protest and Public Order: The Devon Food Riots of 1867" (Pacific Coast Conference on British Studies Meeting, Los Angeles, April 1979).

conditions of employment, and to relocate protest from the marketplace to the workplace.

Though food riots became fewer, other types of riot continued to occur after 1870, and quite a substantial number took place in urban industrial centers. Still, the pattern was for the number of such outbreaks to decline, and for riots and strikes to become distinct, and ultimately antithetical, modes of action. (The exception, of course, was the continuation through 1914 of riots against the use of police and troops to protect blacklegs during strikes.) Thus, of 452 riots counted up between 1865 and 1914, 292 occurred in the quarter century ending in 1890, and only 160 in the next twenty-five years – a decrease of over 40%. More specifically, of the seventy-four situations in which riots were associated with strikes, fifty-six took place before 1895, but only eighteen from then until 1914. The gradual replacement of riots by strikes was noted explicitly by Thomas Brassey in the late 1860s, and the change was most welcome: "The conduct of the trade unionists, while out on strike, will probably be as much superior to that of the rioters in the manufacturing districts in the early part of the present century as the discipline of the standing army is to that of the guerilla band." No doubt when George Potter claimed in 1871 that, "instead of violence accompanying strikes as once it too often did, outrage of any kind is now the exception, and is so rare as to be scarcely that," he had an interest that was more than historical, but his claim was only somewhat premature.[17]

All this suggests that by 1870 British workers had become quite proficient in the waging of strikes in spite of sustained opposition from the articulate public, and persistent difficulties with the courts. The legal status of strikes and picketing remained precarious at least until 1906 – and despite the reform of 1875 – but by the 1870s unions were quite fluent with the law and adept at tailoring their actions to suit its restrictions. And if the "public" were still predominantly hostile to strikes, there were some notable cases where they did support strikes, as in the engineers' strike of 1871 and the dockers' in 1889 and, perhaps more importantly, they came to accept the inevitability of strikes. The shift in the discourse about strikes is evident in many forums, but nowhere more obviously than among social scientists. The famous investigation of the National Association for the Promotion of Social Science (NAPSS) in 1859 smacks of a sense of wonder, discovery, and novelty, while Bevan's paper to the Royal Statistical Society is greeted with a chorus of arguments that have obviously been rehearsed many times over. Even political economists were forced gradually to amend their arguments in the face of workers' sustained preference for behavior that was economically "irrational." With justice,

17. Richter, "Public Order and Popular Disturbances," pp. 85 and 260; Thomas Brassey, quoted in George Potter, "Strikes and Lockouts from the Workman's Point of View," *Contemporary Review* 15 (1870): 34–5; G. Potter, "Trades Unions, Strikes, and Lockouts: A Rejoinder," *Contemporary Review* 17 (1871): 535.

George Howell could assert in 1879 that "the right to strike is not...seriously disputed."[18]

III

Having thus "learned the rules of the game," British workers after 1870 took rapidly to organizing and to its necessary concomitant, strikes. Thomas Wright, The Journeyman Engineer, perceived this essential thrust to working-class activity as early as 1871:

> Average English workmen are not so political as continental, and especially French, workmen are.... They have not the type of mind for which theoretical or philosophical politics have fascination.... Their political thoughts and aspirations, though they scarcely recognize them as being strictly political, turn exclusively upon improving the position of labour in relation to capital. And this they seek to accomplish by direct action – as, for instance, by strikes and the strengthening of trades unions – and not by the establishment of entirely new social systems.[19]

The history of both unionism and strikes from 1870 through the war is concerned, therefore, with the spread of each downward and outward (and occasionally upward) to progressively larger sections of the working class. This extension is revealed clearly in the statistics of strikes, of strikers, and of trade union members from 1870 through 1914. These data suggest the main outlines of the second set of questions to be addressed in this paper. First, organization among workers increased dramatically and consistently throughout the entire period. Strike activity also grew, in the sense that strike propensity was higher across British industry at each successive peak in the curves of strikes and strikers. But the most distinctive aspect of industrial conflict was its tendency to occur in sharp explosions about every other decade. The problem, then, is to explain both the overall and spectacular advance of organization and the way

18. See W. Hamish Fraser, *Trade Unions and Society* (London, 1974), pp. 167–97, for a brief survey of the law regarding strikes; also John Orth, "Striking Workmen before the Courts, 1859–71," (University of North Carolina, School of Law, 1980). NAPSS, *Trades' Societies and Strikes* (London, 1860); the comments on Bevan follow his paper in the *Journal of the Royal Statistical Society* (March, 1880): 55–64. On the public support for the Newcastle engineers, see John Burnett, *Nine Hours' Movement. A History of the Engineers Strike in Newcastle and Gateshead*, (Newcastle, 1872); and, more recently, E. Allen et al., *The North-East Engineers' Strikes of 1871: The Nine Hours' League*, (Newcastle, 1971). On political economy, see also S. Pollard, "Trade Unions and the Labour Market, 1870–1914," *Yorkshire Bulletin of Social and Economic Research* 17 (1965): 98–112, which makes a rather pessimistic argument on the ability of unions to increase labor's share of national income. See also G. Howell, "Strikes: Their Costs and Results," *Fraser's Magazine* 20 (1879): 767.

19. Thomas Wright, "The English Working Classes and the Paris Commune," *Fraser's Magazine* 4 (1871): 62.

88

the three great strike waves of 1871–3, 1889–90, and 1911–13 fit into the process. Unfortunately, there has been surprisingly little attention paid by labor historians to either aspect of this problem.

This is not the place to review the reasons for labor historians' neglect of the problem, though that is an interesting topic in its own right. The intention is rather to begin to address the substantive issue. First, though, it is necessary to attend briefly to the formulation of the question. The norm for analysis in labor history has been to focus upon the accumulation of grievances, as if the relationship between the extent and character of oppression and the resistance to it was uniformly close and direct. By now, though, the sum of research on collective action showing the importance of strength and resources for mobilization ought to allow us to modify that approach considerably, so that the key question becomes not Why did workers fight? but rather, What allowed for or facilitated their translation of grievance into protest? It is important, secondly, to recognize that, because the transformation in organization and strikes occurred throughout industry, the critical factors should themselves be effective at a broad societal level. What one is seeking, therefore, are changes that cut across industries and that combine to enhance the collective capacity of working men and women to organize and resist. Let us review briefly the nature of this increase in organization in order to discern these social origins.

Before 1870, the social reach of unionism and of strikes was very narrow. Not without reason were unions in this period criticized for being the preserve of the skilled and best-paid of workers. "It is notorious," one hostile observer wrote, "that strikes and combinations have been most common among those portions of the working population whose wages are highest."[20] By 1914 this was no longer true in any sense; organization and strike-proneness had become common throughout the working class. The change is recorded in both the geography and the industrial distribution of strikes. (See Table 2.) In the 1870s, medium-sized towns exhibited the highest strike rates: Barnsley came just after London in the list of strike locations; Manchester saw fewer than Dundee or Merthyr; Sunderland outpaced Birmingham, Bradford, Bristol, and Belfast. A roughly similar pattern can be observed during the explosion of the "new unionism," despite the symbolic and psychological importance of the London dock strike. This reflected, it seems, the coming to union organization of operatives in basic industry located in these urban centers of modest size. The pattern shifted slightly after 1900, as many transport and service workers in the large provincial cities and in London finally succeeded in building stable unions, and so were able to launch effective strikes. These geographical patterns were manifestations of the continued extension of organization, from

---

20. Quoted in G. Potter, "Trades Unions, Strikes, and Lockouts," p. 529.

Table 2. *Major participants in strikes, 1871–1873*

Industry or occupation	Number of strikes
Agricultural laborers	3
Bakers	17
Boilermakers	8
Bricklayers	14
Building operators	20
Carpenters and joiners	65
Colliers	87
Cotton hands	19
Dock laborers	15
Engineers and fitters	37
Flax, linen, and jute hands	24
Ironworkers	44
Masons	31
Nail and chain makers	14
Navvies	5
Painters	8
Plasterers	9
Plumbers	81
Printers and compositors	10
Quarrymen	16
Railway and telegraph employees	13
Shipbuilders	28
Shoe and boot makers	48
Slaters	11
Tailors	24
All others	232
Total	806

Sources: G. P. Bevan, "The Strikes of the Past Ten Years," *Journal of the Royal Statistical Society* (1880): pp. 39–41.

the craftsmen in the largest cities to the operatives in the factory towns and the miners in their mining villages, then back to the relatively less skilled workers in the service industries of the big cities.

The industrial distribution of strikes reflected the same process: surprisingly broad in 1871–3, it broadened still further in the years approaching 1914. The militancy of 1871–3 touched at its peak agricultural workers, dockers, and other difficult-to-organize groups. Even among the engineers, the unorganized played a major role, as in Newcastle in 1871, when no more than 10% of the strikers were ASE members. From then until 1914, strike propensity was surprisingly evenly spread out in "the staple industries," as Bevan noted for the 1870s. Though some groups, like the miners, were more prone to strike (for reasons that have been discussed many times over), the really marked divergence between industries visible since the 1920s was much less clear before 1914. And the changes that do occur before 1914 – the slight decline in strikes among builders, the increase among transport workers – confirm the tendency for the differences between industries and between skilled and unskilled to lessen somewhat as organization advanced.[21]

So while strikes broke out and organization deepened among the skilled, the truly novel phenomenon was the enrollment of those without craft skills into the labor movement, and it was this that accounted for the massive growth in unions and in strike activity throughout the prewar era. Three sets of factors seem most compelling as explanations of this change. First, there was crude demography: The ranks of the semiskilled and unskilled increased substantially after 1870. This was intimately linked with a second factor: The nature of industrial development meant an increased demand for semiskilled, as opposed to skilled, labor, and this demand was filled largely, though not exclusively, by an upgrading in the status of unskilled or casual labor. Third, there is evidence that the social ecology of mid-Victorian cities, with their diverse and heterogeneous neighborhoods, slowly gave way to a more socially segregated pattern of residence during the massive urban growth of 1870–1914. The effect was to create a physical space for the development of a strong and distinctive working-class culture sustained by, and itself helping to sustain, a broad array of social and political institutions that together added substantially to the resources that workers could mobilize on their own behalf.[22]

To document the extent and impact of these changes throughout the different industries and communities in which British workers labored and lived would require a great deal more space than is available here. It is nevertheless possible to state that each of these trends is documented extensively in the literature on labor and social-structural change, and that when taken together and interpreted in terms of the balance of resources available to working people, they added up to a major change. At the point of production and in their communities, it seems, British workers found new sources of strength between 1870 and 1914. This was particularly important for those who did not possess a certified and marketable skill with which to bargain. In order for this set of changes in the underlying capacity of groups of workers to organize to eventuate in a wave of strikes and unionization, however, two additional condi-

---

21. Bevan, "The Strikes of the Past Ten Years," pp. 39–42, 45; Lynn H. Lees, "Strikes and the Urban Hierarchy in English Industrial Towns, 1842–1901," in Cronin and Schneer, pp. 52–72; and Cronin, *Industrial Conflict*, pp. 159–61, and, on mining in particular, pp. 179–83.

22. Richard Price, "The New Unionism and the Labour Process," pp. 133–49, and Richard Hyman, "Mass Organization and Militancy in Britain: Contrasts and Continuities," in Mommsen and Husung, *The Development of Trade Unionism*, pp. 239–99; and Eric Hobsbawm, *Workers: Worlds of Labor* (New York, 1984), pp. 176–213.

tions were necessary. The first was the long-term weakness of the employers and the positive predisposition of the state toward working-class organization. It is true that employers sought to match the workers' gains in strength by forming their own groups, but the fragmented structure of industry militated against successful employer combination. In most sectors of the economy, firms were small, specialized, and highly competitive. So while it was possible to put together a united front of employers for a brief confrontation with the unions, as happened in engineering in 1897–8, employers were unable to take advantage of their short-term victories to assert firm control at the workplace over the long run.

This weakness was compounded by the posture of the state. No doubt there were instances when the state intervened on the side of the employers and, as the Taff Vale decision amply demonstrated, the courts were capable of being used against unions as well during the 1890s and early 1900s. But most of the time the government preferred to mediate and conciliate, rather than to repress, and after 1906 its influence ordinarily favored the formation of stable organizations of workers and employers. With the coming of war in 1914, this tendency would be still further accentuated, and the state would end up virtually sponsoring greater organization on both sides of industry. The employers' rather feeble efforts to resist unionization therefore lacked the extra crucial dimension of state leverage, and overall the balance of advantage swung to the workers.[23]

The second factor was a favorable economic conjuncture. For if secular trends in the evolution of economy and society lay behind the great changes in industrial relations, it is nonetheless the case that the pace of development varied considerably from year to year. Both the growth of organization and the outbursts of strikes were concentrated in three "great leaps," in 1871–3, 1889–90, and 1911–13. What caused this distinctive clustering of forward movements? The vagaries of the trade cycle are no doubt part of the answer: Each of the strike waves occurred when the labor market was most favorable for workers. The wild boom of 1871–3 saw unemployment in the organized trades well below 2%; in the same industries only 2.1% were out of work in 1889–90, compared with 10.2% just two years before; in 1911–13, unemployment averaged just under 3%, whereas double that were out of a job in 1908–9. Clearly, a favorable labor market was something of a precondition for launching a wave of militancy.[24]

23. On these two issues, see W. R. Garside and H. F. Gospel, "Employers and Managers: Their Organizational Structure and Changing Industrial Strategies," and C. J. Wrigley, "The Government and Industrial Relations," in Wrigley, pp. 99–115, 135–58.

24. These statistics were taken originally from the Department of Employment and Productivity, *British Labour Statistics: Historical Abstract, 1868–1968* (London, 1971). They also appear in Cronin, *Industrial Conflict*, pp. 206–38.

A slightly broader view of economic conjuncture suggests a further feature common to these moments of insurgency. If one considers not simply the classic trade cycle of seven to ten years, but also the long waves of roughly half a century through which capitalist development seems to progress, it becomes clear that strikes and organization have tended to come during short-term upswings near the end of each phase of the long wave. The first great British strike wave in 1871–3 came during the speculative climax of the mid-Victorian boom; the "new unionism" broke through during the flurry of trade just before the last trough of the Great Depression; and the "labour unrest" swept Britain near the end of the long Edwardian prosperity. This quite marked pattern suggests a very intimate relation between the "Langen Wellen der Konjunktur," as Kondratiev called them, and labor militancy. It seems, in addition, that long waves were connected in important ways with the structural evolution of economy and society that brought about the enhanced capacity for workers' collective action after 1870.[25]

IV

Perhaps the best way to show these links and mediations and how they fit into the broader movement for organization is to describe briefly the most salient features of each of these major outbreaks of strikes and organization. Unfortunately, one must begin with what is surely the least well-documented of such episodes, the militancy of 1871–3. According to George Bevan's count, the number of separate strikes increased from a mere 30 in 1870 to about 150 for 1872 and 1873, an increase of well over ten times. Of these, however, very few find their way into George Howell's list of "Great Strikes" or a similar list compiled by the Board of Trade in 1889, so our knowledge of most remains scanty indeed. The best-known is the engineers' nine-hours strike on the Northeast in 1871, which seems to have been a stimulant to other workers. Several features stand out in the varied accounts of that struggle: the quality of the men's leadership, particularly John Burnett; the fact that most of the strikers were not members of the union; the recalcitrance of the owners and the public support generated by the workers. The demand for a shorter working day was extremely popular, and was widely emulated by workers in other industries. The initiative of the unorganized was also characteristic of the movement elsewhere, and these two characteristics often came together, as when "a massive strike wave" swept Sheffield in 1872, bringing over 1,200 smelters into the union around the demand for a shorter week. The strikes in general reflected a broad attempt to organize unions, so much so that membership in

25. J. Cronin, "Stages, Cycles, and Insurgencies: The Economics of Unrest," in T. Hopkins and I. Wallerstein, eds., *Processes of the World System* (London, 1980).

TUC affiliated societies grew from about a quarter of a million in 1870 to almost 1.2 million in 1874. The growth was particularly concentrated in heavy industry, like engineering and metalworking: the ironworkers grew from a mere 476 members in January 1869 to over 35,000 in 1874.[26]

Unions and strikes, though still strongest in the older, skilled trades, were clearly spreading into basic industry. (See Table 2.) Unskilled "boys" in shipbuilding, gas stokers, building laborers, dockers, even agricultural laborers, formed unions and/or struck in the early 1870s in what was by then the furthest extension of organization ever achieved. In 1874, for example, the National Union of Agricultural Workers claimed 100,000 members in approximately 1,000 branches. Among the miners, it was the South Wales coal field – newer than other fields, rapidly expanding, and previously less well-organized – that was the center of mining militancy. Generally, the strikes of 1871–3, whether in manufacturing or the older trades, were short, small, and successful, pushing organization to what were then its furthest possible limits.[27]

Inevitably, the depression of the late 1870s destroyed much of what was gained by 1874. Union membership was halved, but still remained almost twice as high as it had been in 1870. The footholds of unionism in agriculture, on the docks, and among other unskilled workers were lost, but advances made within industry were more stable. Overall, therefore, this foray into organizing beyond the skilled trades produced mixed results. One obvious weakness, it seems, was ideological and strategic. Specifically, the extension of organization downward and outward within the working class was not accompanied by a new set of political ideas, by any novel strategic thinking, or by anything that could serve as a new philosophy to guide the labor movement. Yet clearly the outlook and style inherited from the established unions were not well suited to the needs of the mass of workers.

The inability to maintain the gains of 1871–3 showed the inadequacy of the old unions and the old ideas for the new era of mass organization. In this sense, the subsequent Great Depression was a great teacher of labor. The defeats of 1878 in particular prompted changes in the cotton unions; the continuous fall in product prices gradually disabused the miners and others of the fondness for

---

26. See Table 1 above for details, as well as Bevan, "The Strikes of the Past Ten Years"; Howell, "Great Strikes," and the Board of Trade's *Report on Strikes and Lockouts in 1888, British Parliamentary Papers* (1889). On the iron and steel workers, see N. P. Howard, "Cooling the Heat: A History of the Rise of Trade Unionism in the South Yorkshire Iron and Steel Industry, from the Origins to the First World War," in S. Pollard and C. Holmes, eds., *Essays in the Economic and Social History of South Yorkshire* (Sheffield, 1976), pp. 59–73.

27. On shipbuilding, see J. F. Clarke, "Workers in the Tyneside Shipyards in the Nineteenth Century," in N. McCord, ed., *Essays in Tyneside Labour History*, pp. 109–31; on agricultural workers, see Howell, "Great Strikes," pp. 301–3; and R. Groves, *Sharpen the Sickle! The History of the Farm Workers Union* (London, 1949), pp. 39–92.

sliding scales; the railwaymen slowly discovered the need for an "all grades" strategy, even the engineers toyed repeatedly (if unsuccessfully) with plans for opening membership more broadly; and, most obviously, a new generation of activists came to the conclusion that a broad, inclusive strategy was the key to organizing the less skilled. These ideas and this strategic perspective crystallized in the new unionist explosion of 1889, but the antecedents go back to the 1870s. It is no doubt true, as Howell wrote in 1902, that very quickly the novelty of the "new unionism" wore off, that the "new unions" took on characteristics of the old and vice versa, but the net effect of the movement was nevertheless a major shift in the nature of the labor movement.[28]

Once again, in 1889–90, union membership jumped – from 817,000 in 1888 to 1,470,000 in 1890 – and the number of strikes increased a comparable amount from 517 in 1888 to 1,211 in 1889 and just over 1,000 in 1890; the workers involved grew by still more, from 119,000 in 1888 to just under 400,000 in 1890. As in 1871–3, strikes were relatively short and extremely successful. In 1889–90, 312,000 workers achieved clear-cut victories in strikes, a further 254,000 some sort of compromise, while only 143,000 experienced defeat. This is quite a remarkable record, for it is a commonplace in industrial relations that neither side is ordinarily anxious to claim or concede victory or defeat. The industrial spread of strikes was even broader than in 1871–3, with much increased participation by transport workers and by workers in metal, engineering, and shipbuilding, and somewhat reduced activity among the mostly skilled building trades. The shift toward heavy industry and toward the less skilled was thus further accentuated. Most significantly, the 1890s witnessed the first large-scale organization of women workers, mostly in textiles, but also in teaching and other white-collar occupations.[29]

Predictably enough, the wave of 1889–90 was followed by an employers' counterattack that began during the depression of 1892–3 and continued through the decade. The reaction was notable in several respects. First, it led to some of the most bitter, and occasionally violent, confrontations in the history of labor, among dockers, miners, engineers, quarrymen, boot- and shoemakers, and others. Second, the employers took the initiative in evolving new forms of organization with which to prosecute their aims. The Shipping Federation and the Engineering Employers gave the lead in organized strikebreaking, while

---

28. G. Howell, *Labour Legislation, Labour Movements, and Labour Leaders* (London, 1902). More generally, see Hunt, *British Labour History*, pp. 304–15, where the contrast between the "new unionism" and the old is reviewed. Hunt generally opts for the "revisionist" perspective that minimizes the difference between the two, but the evidence he marshals nevertheless makes clear that the labor movement was very different after 1889 than before.
29. See S. Lewenhak, *Women and Trades Unions* (London, 1977); and Hunt, *British Labour History*, pp. 299–300.

individual companies pursued the legal attack on unions that culminated in Taff Vale. The advance in workers' organization thus prompted counterorganization among employers that began to tip the balance of forces back in their direction. Third, despite the strength of the attack upon labor, union membership remained relatively stable through the 1890s and even began to creep up again after 1896. This was no doubt due to the much-improved labor market in the late 1890s, but whatever the cause, it meant that unions kept more of the gains resulting from the new unionism than they had from the 1871–3 strike wave. The mass organization of industry was gradually taking hold.[30]

The further development of unions and strikes was greatly hindered after 1900 by the combined effects of legal restrictions, which lasted until 1906, strong employer organizations, and a very uncertain economic climate. The underlying structural weakness of the British economy meant that the upswing beginning in 1896 was much weaker than in other countries, and unemployment from 1901–10 was on average double that of 1896–1900. Specifically, the numbers unemployed were below 3% during 1896–1900, but consistently above that every year after until the war. Faced with such disadvantages, union strength stagnated, and even declined slightly, from 1900 until 1905. The legislation of 1906, and a reasonably strong demand for labor, allowed a jump in that year, but membership declined again during 1907–9. By 1910, membership had just managed to creep over the 2.5 million mark, from which point a rapid rise ensued. Over 1.5 million new members were added during the next three years, as organization was consolidated and extended among transport workers – dockers and railwaymen primarily – and in basic industry.

The labor unrest of 1911–13 was thus, in the first instance, a great qualitative breakthrough in the extent of organization; and it was achieved in the teeth of sustained employer opposition. Inevitably, such a movement had to be initiated by the rank and file, and often even took the form of a rebellion against the union leaders. Not without reason did Sydney Buxton, President of the Board of Trade, complain in 1911 about "the serious diminution in the control which the leaders of the men used to exercise over their rank-and-file. . . ." It was also left to the rank and file, and to various militants, to articulate a new philosophy of mass unionism and direct action. Whether a great many workers grasped the key tenets of syndicalism or not, the syndicalist approach resonated well with the mood of the men and helped to express its essential thrust. The rebellion within the labor movement against the leaders can in a sense be viewed as the critical, preliminary skirmish in the struggle for

30. See E. Wigham, *The Power to Manage* (London, 1973), pp. 29–62, on the Engineering Employers' Federation; and J. Saville, "Trade Unions and Free Labour: The Background of the Taff Vale Decision," in A. Briggs and J. Saville, eds., *Essays in Labour History* (London, 1967), pp. 317–50, more generally.

another, qualitative advance of organization.[31]

The nature of strikes during 1911–13 reinforces this analysis. The spread of unions and of the capacity to strike is revealed in the mass character of disputes and in their industrial incidence. The size of the average strike increased from 350 during 1889–92 to 780 workers during 1910–13. As in 1889–90, these strikes were immensely successful, 1,135,000 strikers (44%) winning outright victories against employers, 1,080,000 (42%) being involved in compromises, and only 363,000 (14%) experiencing clear-cut defeats. The pattern of participation reveals a further shift away from skilled craftsmen toward the newer, more "proletarian" workers in industry and transport, with miners, dockers, railwaymen, and textile workers especially prominent.[32]

The transformation wrought by these waves of organizing and strikes by 1914 is perhaps best revealed by the changed role and attitude of the government. The government had become interested in fostering industrial peace in the late 1880s, appointing the Royal Commission on Labour of 1889–92, setting up a Labour Department of the Board of Trade just after this, intervening in the 1893 coal dispute, and actively fostering conciliation from 1896 onward. Faced with employer resistance and not pressed on by any crisis in industrial relations, such efforts languished from about 1897 to 1910. The wave of strikes that broke out in 1911, however, brought government back into the field for good. Troops were sent to Wales in 1910, to Liverpool and other ports in 1911; Lloyd George became involved directly in 1911–12 with the railwaymen and the miners; and throughout the turbulence the government's chief conciliator, George Askwith, was kept continually busy. The net effect of government intervention was problematic: On the one hand, its protection of blacklegs angered workers and assisted employers, while on the other hand, Lloyd Georges's efforts to mediate were resented almost as much by the employers. By 1913, in fact, the government was understandably disillusioned with the results of its efforts. The outcome of the contest on the docks and the railways remained in doubt, the possibility of major disputes in 1914–15 looming just over the horizon. It is especially unclear just what role government would have played in such a confrontation, but it seems unlikely it would have been able to withdraw. By 1914, workers were organized in some fashion in all the major industries, and their combined action could have dramatic con-

31. Buxton, quoted in C. J. Wrigley, *The Government and Industrial Relations in Britain* (Loughborough, 1979), p. 5. On rank-and-file movements and syndicalism, see B. Holton, *British Syndicalism, 1900–1914* (London, 1976); and Price, *Masters, Unions and Men*, pp. 238–67. For the view that the unrest was a matter of the trade cycle and little else, see H. Pelling, "The Labour Unrest, 1911–1914," in *Popular Politics and Society in Late Victorian Britain* (London, 1968). See also E. H. Phelps Brown, *The Growth of British Industrial Relations, 1906–1914* (London, 1959).
32. The general pattern of strikes is most clearly indicated in G. R. Askwith, *Industrial Problems and Disputes* (London, 1920).

sequences. Government could no longer remain aloof from the day-to-day conduct of industrial relations, and it no longer did.

V

With the coming of the Great War, the government's role would become even more significant, perhaps even decisive. Before describing the effects of the war upon the industrial relations, however, it might be useful briefly to recapitulate the relationship between strikes and organization prior to 1914. Judged by their timing, location, and strategic orientation, the successive strike waves of 1871–3, 1889–90, and 1911–13 are best understood as component parts of a long struggle to organize British industry. In each case, of course, the strike movement achieved a certain degree of inertia and momentum, but this was limited in scope and, it seems, subordinate to the overriding aim among workers to establish some collective power and organization at the workplace.

A clear indication of this is the statistical relation between the magnitude of strike waves and the scope of union organization efforts. The peak of strikes in each of the three explosions of militancy was slightly higher than the previous one, but only slightly. The peaks of strikers were higher, but were not sustained. The peaks of unionization, however, were much higher and they persisted. This suggests a relation that was not reciprocal: Strike movements built unions, but unions did not overall do a great deal to increase strike propensity.[33] Many possible reasons can be adduced for this asymmetrical relationship, but whatever the explanation, the reality was that the gradually increasing capacity of working people to organize, which was reflected in increasing unionization, was not reflected in as broad a resistance at the workplace as might have been possible.

The major effect of the war on industrial relations seems to have been to change this and to stimulate a much more aggressive consciousness and pattern of activity among the bulk of the working class. In this sense, the war brought about a major discontinuity in the long-term pattern of strikes. Most important, the new militancy was broader than ever before, and it was sustained for an extended period of time – until, in fact, the defeat of the General Strike in 1926. Even when the bottom fell out of the postwar boom in late 1920, workers continued to strike; and it took several more years to restore "order" in the

---

33. Thus, if one calculates the ratio of the number of trade unionists (in thousands) to the peak number of strikes during strike waves, one gets the following pattern of dramatic decline: 1871–3 = 1.01; 1889–90 = .77; 1911–13 = .36. No doubt part of the drop reflects underlying shifts in the organization of industry, and a further part the spread of organization from craft to semiskilled and unskilled occupations and the attendant sectorial differences entailed in that, but a portion of the change must certainly be attributed to a genuine relationship between organization and strikes.

industrial relations system. This process has been described in some detail elsewhere; for present purposes two simple pieces of evidence can be noted.

Prior to the Great War, the most massive outburst of strikes occurred in 1912, when over 1.2 million workers participated. But of that large number, a full three-quarters were miners. By 1919, the year of the greatest postwar participation, only a bit over a third of the 2.4 million strikers were miners. Truly massive numbers of other workers therefore took part in the labor upheavals after the war. And they did so without the stimulus of early victories that had helped to spread the earlier strike waves. From 1918 through 1922, the great majority of the strikers were engaged in struggles with mixed outcomes; even in 1919, approximately 60% could win only some sort of compromise, and in none of these years did those who won strikes outright outnumber those who lost outright. Nevertheless, the very ability to win compromises in the depressed years of 1920, 1921, and 1922 represented an impressive resilience, as did, of course, the revival of militance in 1925 and 1926.

In this context, the defeat of the General Strike in 1926 takes on quite serious proportions. There has been a tendency among labor historians and industrial relations specialists to see the General Strike merely as an anticlimax, as a relatively meaningless gesture of solidarity without lasting impact upon the position of labor in British society. It is possible to argue instead, both from the statistical evidence on strikes and from a reading of the broader context, that it was an absolutely critical moment in the construction of the postwar social order. Even if the British government was wrong in construing the contest as a battle over the constitution, it certainly was a battle over whose interests were to dominate in the industrial and social policy of the next two decades. That there had to be such a test in order to reestablish stability, that it was so long in coming, and that its outcome was so unpredictable, all testify to the novel dimensions of the labor insurgency of the era after the war.[34]

It would be much beyond the scope of this paper to attempt a comprehensive explanation of the origins of this new militancy.[35] The aim here has been primarily to point it out. I would like to conclude, however, by discussing two possible answers to the problem of origins. One possibility is that there is, or was, a certain threshold of working-class organizational strength, before which struggle is largely defensive and incapable of shifting the overall balance of social power, but beyond which the power of the workers becomes a much more

34. See, for example, G. A. Phillips, *The General Strike* (London, 1926). A view much closer to that expressed here is contained in Henry Phelps Brown, *The Origins of Trade Union Power* (Oxford, 1983), pp. 68–88.
35. The beginnings of such an interpretation are presented in my "Labour Insurgency and Class Formation: Comparative Perspectives on the Crisis of 1917–20 in Europe," in J. Cronin and C. Sirianni, eds., *Work, Community, and Power: The Experience of Labor in Europe and America, 1900–1925* (Philadelphia, 1983). For a different perspective, see Hugh Clegg, *A History of British Trade Unions since 1889*, vol. 2 (Oxford, 1985), pp. 239–311.

distinct threat to the prevailing social order, and that such a threshold was crossed in Britain during the war. The second possibility is that the war itself was the key factor in transforming strikes, both because of the edge it put upon workers' grievances and because of its politicizing effects. And perhaps the most satisfying explanation will be found by combining these two notions, and recognizing that the period of the war simultaneously strengthened workers enormously, angered them bitterly, and forced them to interpret their problems politically.

6

Two strike waves in Imperial Russia, 1905–1907, 1912–1914

LEOPOLD H. HAIMSON, RONALD PETRUSHA

Introduction

The quantitative analyses of labor unrest that we shall seek to summarize were originally conceived for the purposes of a broader study of the evolution of Russian society and politics on the eve of the First World War. In the perspective of this larger study, our original aim was to distinguish as precisely as possible the characteristics of the wave of labor unrest that broke out in April 1912, in immediate response to the Lena gold-field massacre, and to situate the character and scope that this labor unrest assumed up to the outbreak of the war in the context of the political and social crisis that built up during these years in the confrontation between the State power (and the landed nobility on which its political support increasingly rested) and the upper and lower social strata of urban, commercial, and industrial Russia. From its very inception, however, our analysis also involved an effort to compare the build-up of this prewar crisis with the processes that had culminated in the Revolution of 1905. Indeed, we were struck from the very outset by two major features that appeared to distinguish the character and dynamics of the political and social conflicts that the Russian body politic experienced during these prewar years from those that had surfaced in 1905–7.

The first was the degree to which, in such contrast to the social and geographical scope that Russia's first revolution had assumed among the rural as well as urban populations of the Empire, the prewar political and social crisis remained contained within urban Russia and, as far as any massive expressions of public protest were concerned, in a few of its major urban centers, including first and foremost the capital itself.

But a second, equally distinctive feature of this prewar crisis was the degree of acuteness of the political and social divisions that it unveiled almost from the very outset even *within* urban Russia; chiefly, but not exclusively, between the

101

upper, privileged elements of its "census" privileged society (including by this time most of its professional intelligentsia) and its increasingly explosive and rebellious masses of industrial workers. These conflicts – which mounted steadily, especially in Russia's urban centers, precisely as the prewar crisis matured – and even more notably the sharpness of their articulation in the consciousness and behavior of the political actors who sought to represent the constituent groups of Russia's urban society, provided an equally dramatic contrast to the majestic and seemingly harmonious build-up of the "all-nation" struggle against absolutism, at least up to the summer and fall of 1905.[1]

In this perspective, our studies of the post-Lena strike wave were intended to examine to what degree the patterns and dynamics that distinguished labor unrest during the prewar period reflected, but also contributed to, this twofold process of polarization in the Russian body politic – between urban and rural Russia, but also within urban Russia itself – and to compare them in these respects to the 1905–7 strike wave. As far as our quantitative analyses were concerned, this comparative dimension was intended to bring out the differences in the scope, intensity, and character that labor unrest assumed among various strata of industrial workers during these two periods, but also to consider the relationships that these differences bore to these workers' social characteristics and conditions of life and work, as well as to the features of the political and social environments in which their strike actions unfolded.

Most, though by no means all, of the objective indices used in our comparative analysis to distinguish these various strata of workers have been for over a century the objects of considerable attention and debate in the various treatments that have appeared about the industrial working class and labor unrest in Imperial Russia. But it is also the case that ever since the controversy that originally unfolded in the 1880s and early 1890s between the Marxist and Populist camps of the Russian intelligentsia, this debate has largely continued to be contained in two almost entirely contradictory interpretations.

The first has consistently found in the periodic explosiveness that labor unrest assumed in late nineteenth- and early twentieth-century Russia the manifestations of social tensions peculiarly characteristic of the early phases of industrialization, and stemming at least in part from the influx into industry of strata of workers drawn from – indeed still largely bound to – the countryside if

---

1. It was the acuteness of this twofold process of polarization – between urban and rural Russia, but also within urban Russia itself – that made for the tortuously halting and tormented character that the second Russian prevolution assumed, at least right up to the outbreak of the war, and which also accounted ultimately for the gravity of the convulsions that beset the Russian body politic in 1917 and during the Civil War aftermath. Leopold H. Haimson (ed.), *The Politics of Rural Russia (1905–1914)* (Indiana University Press, 1979), p. 296. See also Haimson, "Problems of Social Stability during the Last Decade of Imperial Russia," *Slavic Review*, Fall 1964 and Winter 1965, and "The Problem of Social Identities in Early Twentieth Century Russia," *Slavic Review*, Spring 1988 and Fall 1988.

not to agriculture, and as yet unadapted to their new conditions of urban life and industrial work. The other interpretation, pressed to this day with particular vigor by Soviet historians, has discerned in the exceptional intensity that this unrest assumed among certain strata of Russian workers, and especially in the catalytic role that these workers played in the inception and unfolding of both the 1905 and 1917 revolutions, the reflection of the early emergence on Russian soil (largely due to certain highly advanced features that Russia's industrial development already displayed by the 1890s) of a substantial stratum of "mature" and "conscious" proletarians, sharply differentiated both socially and psychologically from the still "inchoate" and "unconscious" masses of the peasantry.

To be sure, since their emergence nearly a century ago, both of these conflicting interpretations have undergone a variety of changing political and theoretical emphases. But notwithstanding the theoretical elaborations and reformulations that they have undergone since their original articulation, each of them has continued to focus attention on the role of the same objective factors in seeking to account for the intensity and character of labor unrest among Russian workers up to the advent of Soviet power. The interpretation originally advanced by the Russian Marxists has consistently emphasized the positive significance for labor unrest of higher concentrations of industrial workers in urban areas as well as in large enterprises, which (because of their generally greater investments in mechanization and the pressures thereby generated for year-round operation) are assumed to have contributed to severing their workers' ties to the countryside and the land. The articulation of this viewpoint in Soviet historiography has also laid stress, in accounting for the intensity of industrial labor conflicts, on the proportions of hereditary proletarians (i.e., of workers, one or both of whose parents were already employed in industry) represented among various strata of workers. Finally, with equal consistency and sweep, it has posited a dampening effect on labor unrest to the workers who continued to maintain ties to the countryside and to the land, and/or to engage in agricultural work on a part-time basis.

Just as consistently, proponents of the views originally espoused by the Russian Populists have laid sweeping emphasis, for all periods of Russian labor history, on the *positive* contribution to the intensity of labor unrest of the strength of these very ties to the countryside and to the land among Russian workers, and to the high proportions of rural immigrants represented among industrial workers employed in urban areas. However, in the applications by Western scholars of theories of modernization to Russian labor history, the precise significance assigned to the role of immigrants from the countryside in accounting for the intensity of labor unrest among Russia's industrial workers has ranged substantially. Some interpretations have stressed the sense of uprootedness, if not anomie, experienced by peasant recruits under the impact

103

of their new industrial and/or urban experience (a phenomenon sometimes considered to be typical of the early stages of modernization in all "traditional" societies). Others have emphasized the quite different proposition that during these early stages of industrialization, labor unrest in Russia, as in other countries, was disproportionately concentrated among groups of workers who were able to maintain a high degree of cohesion, and hence capacity for self-organization, precisely because of the persistent hold of their peasant pasts. Indeed, such cohesion and capacity to act, or more precisely to react, collectively has been attributed in certain of these applications of modernization theory not only to the homogeneity that distinguished the communities and conditions of life and work of industrial workers in rural settings and in "company towns" of relatively unmixed population, but also to the ability of peasant recruits into industry to transplant, even into the more highly mixed and unstable social settings of large urban centers, patterns of association and solidarity originally rooted in the countryside.

It is equally notable that even as the importance of these specific objective factors has been so consistently, if so differently, emphasized (even while left almost entirely untested) by exponents of these two viewpoints concerning the character and sources of labor unrest in Imperial Russia, the potential significance of certain other objective factors has been almost as consistently ignored or remained the object of almost entirely unscrutinized stereotypes. The last observation applies to the significance of such factors as the proportions of males and females represented among various strata of Russia's industrial workers, female workers being widely (and our analyses have suggested, incorrectly) assumed to have been less strike-prone than males throughout Russian labor history. It also applies to the effects on the relative intensity of labor unrest of differences in wage levels. The very notion that higher levels of pay could have been positively associated with the intensity of labor unrest obviously came into conflict with the basic assumptions underlying Populist and neo-Populist interpretations (as well as certain of the formulations of Western modernization theory). But it also ran sharply counter to the Marxist stereotype of a "labor aristocracy" inevitably drawn by higher economic rewards to "petty bourgeois" attitudes and social behavior.[2]

---

2. Only one of the conceptual categories highlighted in this historiographical debate warrants further comment at this point, if only because the paucity of available data has made it impossible to subject it to serious statistical analysis. This category is that of "hereditary proletarians," to which such great, and in our view, disproportionate significance has been assigned in the works of certain Soviet labor historians.* Even in the absence of the statistical data required for a serious quantitative analysis, it appears to us quite evident that this factor has little, if any, significance in accounting for the intensity of strike actions, at least during the years stretching from the mid-1890s to the outbreak of the First World War. One rather obvious reason for this is that the highest proportions of "hereditary proletarians" were to be found among workers employed in the oldest and most traditional industries and industrial regions of the Empire: most notably those of the

In the perspective of this still ongoing historiographical debate, one of the purposes of our study has been to subject the role of the objective factors highlighted in it, as well as of those it had largely ignored or obscured, to a careful quantitative analysis. But given the nature of our research objectives, we have also focused attention on the *changes* as well as the continuities discernible in the statistical relationships between these various objective factors and the character and intensity of labor unrest that our analysis has unveiled, even within the relatively narrow chronological span covered by our comparative studies of the 1905–7 and 1912–14 strike waves.

Major findings of quantitative analyses

We shall largely confine ourselves, for the purpose of this discussion, to the results obtained in our analyses of the quantitative data on the 1905–7 and 1912–14 strike waves recorded in a single source: the strike statistics provided in the reports of the Factory Inspectorate for the work forces employed in the branches of industry and geographical areas under its jurisdiction, which, on the eve of the First World War, represented some two-thirds of the total number of industrial workers of the Empire.[3] Despite the

---

iron industry of the Urals (whose origin lay in the Petrine period), but also those employed in the textile enterprises of the Central Industrial Region of European Russia (many of which dated back to the immediate post-Emancipation if not the pre-Emancipation period). At least from the late nineteenth century onward, the workers employed in these older and more traditional centers of Russian industry displayed, by and large, far lower strike rates than those employed in the more recently established metal and textile enterprise concentrated in urban centers. Indeed, in the light of the other criteria emphasized in Soviet interpretations of the sources of labor unrest, it is hardly surprising that this should have been the case. For these traditional branches of industry also included, even among the hereditary workers they employed, the highest proportions of workers still possessing land and/or cultivating it on a part-time basis – two of the indices so strongly identified in Soviet interpretations as retarding factors in the development of a modern working-class consciousness. *See particularly L. M. Ivanov, "Preemstvennost' fabrichno-zavodskogo truda i formivoranie proletariata v Rossii," *ANSSR*, Institut istorii, *Rabochii klass i rabochee dvizhenie v Rossii (1861–1917)* (Moscow, 1966).

3. Specifically outside the jurisdiction of the Factory Inspectorate were workers employed in such branches of the economy as mining and transport; and in manufacturing industries per se, workers employed in state enterprises (which constituted a significant proportion of metal-processing and mechanical plants, especially those engaged in the production of various types of arms and munitions as well as railroad equipment). Also excluded were very small private industrial enterprises (especially those not using any form of steam or electrical power), and finally, even those larger private enterprises located in geographical areas outside the jurisdiction of the Factory Inspectorate (largely in Russian Asia). Notwithstanding these and other limitations, the statistics of the Factory Inspectorate provide by far the most comprehensive and systematic compilations of data available about the intensity and character of industrial strikes during the years under our purview, as well as on the social characteristics and life and work situations of the work forces involved in these strike actions. However, whenever necessary, we shall also present the findings of analyses we have conducted of other data sets in our forthcoming volume on the three major strike waves in Imperial Russia (1905–7, 1912–14, and 1915–17), also to be published by Cambridge University Press.

limitations in their scope, these statistics afford the distinct advantage of encompassing a fairly stable and consistently defined universe of Russian industry and of the workers it employed from the mid-1890s up to 1917. These data were collected by the same institution, by and large under the supervision of the same executive personnel, and the definitions and criteria used in presenting and categorizing these data – about the number of strikes, strikers, and days lost in industrial labor conflicts, as well as their attributed causes and eventual outcomes – also remained relatively consistent over the entire period, making for a considerable degree of comparability in the various indices of labor unrest that they provide from year to year. Even more important for analytic purposes, the Factory Inspectorate also furnished, in a variety of publications, a wealth of statistical information about the industrial enterprises under its jurisdiction and the work forces they employed, including various objective indices concerning these workers' social characteristics and conditions of life and work. Since these additional data were broken down into the same geographical and industrial categories and subcategories as those that the inspectorate provided on labor unrest, they can easily be used to study the statistical relationships between the objective characteristics of the various strata of workers under Factory Inspection and the patterns of strike actions that these workers displayed.[4]

Even the aggregate data about the number of strikes and strikers recorded among workers under Factory Inspection between 1895 and 1914 (see Appendix 1) amply suggest the vertiginous upturns and downturns that distinguished the dynamics of both the 1905–7 and 1912–14 strike waves, as well as the catalytic role played by specific events – the massacre of the workers' demonstration led by Father Gapon on January 9, 1905, and of the strikers on the Lena gold fields in April 1912 – in focusing the grievances and unleashing the collective actions of the masses of workers who were drawn into these two strike waves.

4. The published reports on which we have drawn for the strike statistics compiled by the Factory Inspectorate during these years, all of them published under the editorship of V. E. Varzar by the Department of Industry of the Ministry of Trade and Industry (*Ministerstvo torgovli i promyshlennosti, Otdel promyshlennosti*), include: *Statisticheskiia svedeniia o stachkakh rabochikh na fabrikakh i zavodakh za desatiletie 1895–1904 goda* (St. Petersburg, 1905); *Statistika stachekh rabochikh na fabrikakh i zavodakh za 1905 god* (St. Petersburg, 1908); *Statistika stachek rabochikh na fabrikakh i zavodakh za trekhletie 1906–1908 goda* (1910); and the collections of these statistics published on an annual basis for the years 1909–14, *Svody atchetov fabrichnykh inspektorov* St. Petersburg, 1910–15). The statistical publications of the Ministry of Trade and Industry from which we have drawn the various objective indices used in our analysis of these strike data include (in addition to the *Svody otchetov fabrichnykh inspektorov*): *Statistika neschastnykh sluchaev s rabochimi na promyshlennykh predpriiatiiakh, podchinennykh nadzoru fabrichnoi inspektsii za 1905 god* (St. Petersburg, 1908); *Spisok fabriki zavodov Rossiiskoi Imperii* (St. Petersburg, 1912); *Stastisticheskii vremennik Rossiiskoi Imperii za 1910 god* (St. Petersburg, 1911); and *Goroda v Rosii v 1910 godu* (St. Petersburg, 1911).

106

Table 1. *Number of strikes, strikers, and days lost in strikes not classified as political-demonstrative and in all strike categories (1905–7, 1912–14)*

Year	Not political-demonstrative		
	Strikes	Strikers	Days Lost
1905	7,951	1,780,597	9,608,079
1906	3,164	593,552	4,385,760
1907	1,015	218,501	1,637,218
1912	732	175,678	1,865,564
1913	1,379	390,639	2,965,841
1914	1,239	351,803	2,924,132
	All categories		
1905	13,975	2,863,173	23,609,387
1906	6,114	1,108,406	5,500,652
1907	3,573	740,074	2,431,527
1912	2,032	725,491	2,378,057
1913	2,404	887,096	3,482,610
1914	3,534	1,337,458	4,691,088

As our tables indicate, throughout the decade preceding the outbreak of Russia's First Revolution, the numbers and proportions of strikers reported among workers under Factory Inspection had consistently remained exceedingly modest, and by the same token the number of strikers recorded in the course of 1905, and the percentage they constituted of the number of workers in the labor force (168%, when we do not discount for strikes in which workers struck more than once, as compared to 5.1% in 1904) dramatically reflects the veritable explosion of labor unrest that followed the massacre of the workers led by Father Gapon on Bloody Sunday. It may be argued that, by comparison at least, the strike wave that swelled in the wake of the Lena gold-field massacre surged from a higher base line, the aggregate data of the Factory Inspectorate already recording a substantial increase in the intensity of labor unrest in 1911 (largely reflecting, as we shall see, changes in the economic conjuncture). But exclusive reliance on aggregate data underestimates the dramatic changes that these two strike waves brought not only in the volume but also in the character of labor unrest. Almost no political strikes were reported in 1911 (or for that matter during the months of 1912 immediately preceding Lena), and the number of political strikes during the decade preceding 1905 had remained so modest that the phenomenon itself had not even been classified as an independent category in the statistics of the Factory Inspectorate.

But a more accurate sense of the differences and the similarities between these two strike waves may be drawn from Table 1, as well as Figures 1–3,

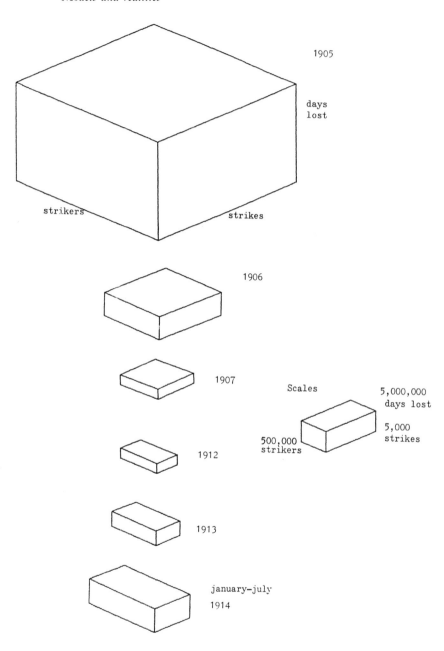

Figure 1. All cases of strikes

108

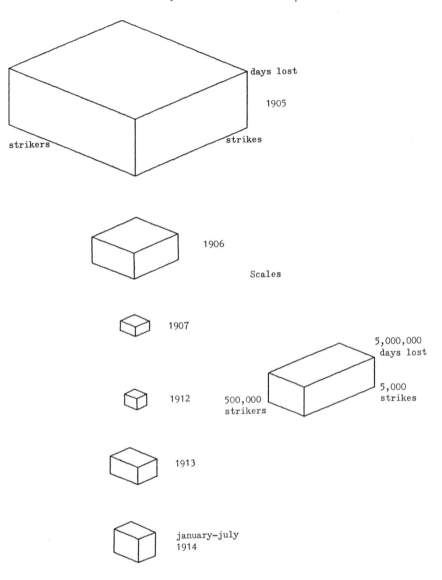

Figure 2. Economic strikes

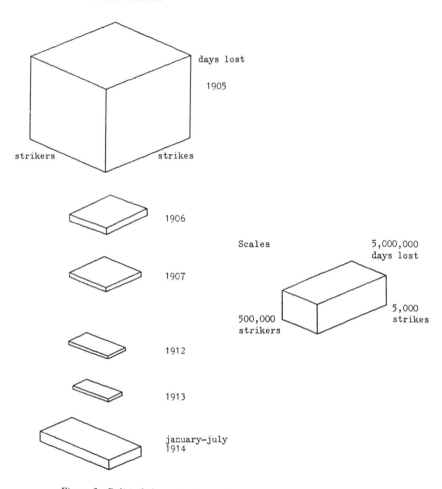

Figure 3. Political-demonstrative strikes

which present the "shape" of labor unrest – the number of days lost, strikes, and strikers recorded among all workers under Factory Inspection in economic and noneconomic strikes – in 1905–7 and 1912–14. Two major differences are strikingly brought out by these statistics.

The first is the much greater number of strikes, strikers, and days lost recorded in 1905–7, by comparison with all the years of the post-Lena strike wave in "economic" strikes, and more generally in all categories of strike actions *not* classified as "political-demonstrative" (i.e., as purely political in character). A second, even more glaring difference is the much smaller number of strikes and days lost in all strike actions, political as well as economic, in

110

Table 2. *Proportions of strikes to number of enterprises under Factory Inspection*

Year	Including repeated strikes	Discounting repeated strikes
1905	95.7%	34.4%
1906	42.1%	21.2%
1907	23.8%	16.9%
1912	11.7%	8.3%
1913	13.4%	11.0%
1914	25.2%	11.6%

enterprises under Factory Inspection throughout the post-Lena strike wave, by comparison with that of 1905–7.

But the different in scope between these two strike waves are even more sharply brought out when we discount in the aggregate data reported for them by the Factory Inspectorate for the phenomenon of *repeated* strikes (i.e., for the number of additional strikes recorded in enterprises that struck more than once in the course of these two strike waves), and calculate the proportions that the enterprises actually struck each year represented of all enterprises under Factory Inspection (Table 2).

As these figures indicate, labor unrest remained disproportionately concentrated throughout the post-Lena period in a small, indeed very small, proportion of the enterprises under Factory Inspection: in only 11.6% of them even in 1914, as against 34% in 1905. One of the major purposes of our quantitative analysis was to show to what degree the various objective indices available to us concerning the enterprises and work forces employed in the branches of industry for which these strike data were recorded, accounted statistically for these major differences in the scope that labor unrest assumed during these two strike waves.

The most detailed breakdowns of labor unrest that we could use for this purpose were also the most general in character, confined as they were to data about the total number of strikes, strikers, and days lost, without distinction between different types of strike actions. For both the 1905–7 and 1912–14 strike waves, such breakdowns were available for *each* of the major branches of industry represented in *each* of the provinces and other major geographical jurisdictions under Factory Inspection. The data sets thus available to us for the analysis of the *overall* intensity of labor unrest included 440 comparable cases for 1912, 456 for 1913, and 385 for 1914 (when, because of the partial occupation of the Kingdom of Poland following the outbreak of the war, the Polish provinces were excluded from the statistics published for that year by the Factory Inspectorate). The number of comparable cases for our analysis of the 1905–7 strike wave was 227.

111

For each of these cases (i.e., for each of the industrial groups represented in each of the provinces and other major geographical entities under Factory Inspection during these years), we were also able to assemble, from the various publications of the Inspectorate, data about the following objective characteristics of the work forces they employed: (1) their sexual and age distribution, including the number of male and female children (under 14 years of age), teenagers (15–17), and adult workers represented in them; (2) average annual levels of pay; (3) the distribution of work forces in enterprises of different categories of size (including most importantly, as we shall see, enterprises employing 500–1,000 and over 1,000 workers); and (4) the degrees of concentration of these work forces in urban as against rural areas, including more specific indices for concentration in urban centers of over 200,000 population, cities of 100,000–200,000, and towns of under 100,000. In most of our analyses, we also used as an additional and separate index the degree of concentration of the labor force in the capital city of St. Petersburg.

Let us consider the statistical relationships that appeared between these various objective characteristics and the index we used to measure the overall intensity of labor unrest during these two strike waves: the *proportions* of participants in *all* categories of strikes represented among the work forces considered in each of the cases under our purview.[5]

Bearing in mind the danger of reifying the findings obtained through regression models, it is important to note that in the first stages of our quantitative analyses, strong positive bivariate correlations appeared for all the years under our scrutiny between the overall intensity of labor unrest and higher proportions of adult workers; and more surprisingly, even stronger positive correlations for higher proportions of females in the labor force. Powerful positive correlations also appeared for the various indices we used to measure what we have termed industrial concentration: the absolute number of

---

5. Our inferences from the relationships observed between these various objective indices and the intensity of labor unrest during these years have been, from a strictly statistical standpoint, *indirect*, since these objective indices were drawn from the data provided about *all* the enterprises and work forces represented in the branches of industry scrutinized in each of these cases, rather than about those of them that were actually recorded as having struck. However, this qualification appears to us to carry considerably less weight for analyses of collective behavior – including the forms of collective action involved in strike actions, and especially in strike waves, than for analyses of individual behavior. Indeed, our various studies of the workers' movement during these years have consistently brought out the fact that patterns of strike actions bore a far closer relationship to the characteristics of the social environments in which these collective actions unfolded, and to the social composition and life and work situation of the collectivities of workers involved in them, than did the actions of any individual workers. (Consider, in this connection, the differences between these patterns of strike intensity and the voting behavior, almost invariably in support of candidates of the R.S.D.R.P., displayed by those *individual* workers who participated in the electoral process, even in provinces hardly beset by any labor unrest.)

workers employed in a particular branch of industry, and in all branches of industry, in each of the provinces under the Factory Inspectorate, as well as the proportions that these work forces represented of the total independent population of working age (including nonindustrial and industrial occupations). But most of these relationships consistently fell below the level of statistical significance after multiple regression – that is, after discounting for the even more strongly positive statistical relationships borne to the intensity of labor unrest by the other objective factors considered in our analysis. Indeed, after conducting these multiple regressions among the objective factors under our scrutiny (thereby discounting for the mutually reinforcing statistical effects that the congruence among these factors produced in the correlations between each of them and the intensity of labor unrest), we were largely able to focus attention on the relationships borne by only three major factors to the variations in the intensity of strikes during all the years of the post-Lena period, and in our comparison of these findings with those obtained in our analysis of the 1905–7 strike wave. (We did not drop from consideration in our final regression tables the relative proportion of males and females in the labor force, because of the statistically significant *positive* relationships that continued to appear, even after regression, between higher proportions of females in the work force and the overall intensity of labor unrest in our findings for 1905 and especially 1906, although not for any of the other years under our scrutiny.) The three objective factors that proved of such consistent statistical significance in our regression analyses of the overall intensity of strikes during all the years of the post-Lena period were:

1. the degree of concentration of work forces in urban areas;
2. average wage levels, particularly when weighted for the levels of pay earned by adult male workers (thereby discounting for the substantially lower wages earned by female and underage workers, even when engaged in the same tasks as adult males); and
3. the degree of concentration of the work force in enterprises employing 500–1,000 and especially over 1,000 workers.

Let us consider the statistical relationships that emerged for these three objective factors in our regression equations and the similarities and differences that they suggested about the character and dynamics of the 1905–7 and 1912–14 strike waves.

Urban concentration

The degree of concentration of the work force in urban areas is one of the few constants in the distribution of labor unrest among various strata of workers consistently noted in the analyses of the Factory Inspectorate for all the years covered by its published reports (1895–1914).[6] Our own findings confirm the overwhelming importance of this objective factor, even after discounting for the effects of other factors, but they also bring out one major difference in the relationships between patterns of urban concentration and the distribution of labor unrest in the course of the 1905–7 and 1912–14 strike waves. The difference lies in the extraordinary and disproportionate degree to which throughout the prewar period labor unrest remained concentrated in provinces with urban centers of over 200,000 population, and among these provinces, in the capital province of St. Petersburg. Indeed, the statistical relationships that appeared for these two specific indices of urban concentration proved so strong throughout the post-Lena strike wave, and those for the degrees of concentration of the work force in cities and towns of less than 200,000 comparatively so much weaker, that we were consistently able to drop from consideration in our final regression equations the degrees of concentration of the labor force in smaller cities and towns without appreciably diminishing the power and significance of the statistical relationships that the factor of urban concentration bore overall to variations in the intensity of labor unrest during these years. Our analyses of the effects of patterns of urban concentration on the intensity of labor unrest during the 1905–7 strike wave yielded, in this respect, strikingly different results: the degrees of concentration of the labor force in cities of 100,000 to 200,000 and even in towns of less than 100,000, proved very important in accounting for variations in the intensity of strikes, especially in 1905 and 1906.

These differences notwithstanding, the statistical relationship of urban concentration to the overall intensity of labor unrest was by far the most important of those that surfaced in our regression analyses of the post-Lena strike wave for the various factors under our scrutiny. Even in those regression tables in which concentration in the capital was not considered as a separate variable, the degree of concentration of the labor force in urban centers of over 200,000 in population accounted for approximately 16% of the variations in labor unrest recorded in 1912, 10% in 1913, and 13.5% in 1914. However, because of the exceptional intensity of labor unrest in the capital, the factor of urban concentration assumed even greater importance in our findings for the post-Lena strike wave when we treated the proportions of the work forces of the major industrial groups under Factory Inspection employed in St. Petersburg as a separate variable. In this case, our indices for concentration in the capital and in urban

6. These reports calculate that during the period 1895–1904, 75% of all strike actions were concentrated in urban areas of the Empire (which in 1900 accounted for only 42% of the total number of enterprises under Factory Inspection). The calculations for 1905–7 are even higher: 85% of the total number of strikes in 1905, 87% in 1906, and over 91% in 1907. Unfortunately, the Factory Inspectorate's reports for later years do not include information on the proportions of *strikes* recorded in urban areas.

centers of over 200,000 population *jointly* accounted for no less than 24.2% of the variations in the overall intensity of labor unrest in 1912 (part $r = 0.492$); for 13.8% in 1913 (part $r = 0.372$); and for 29% in 1914 (part $r = 0.538$).

Actually, the degree of concentration of labor unrest within urban Russia was even greater throughout the post-Lena period than these findings suggest. For exceptionally high strike rates were in fact recorded in only a *few* "select" provinces with urban centers of over 200,000 in population: aside from St. Petersburg *guberniia*, these included Lifliand and, to a lesser degree, Moscow, Kharkov, and Kherson *gubernii*. As we shall see, all of these provinces were distinguished by disproportionate concentrations in their urban centers of militant strata of industrial workers whose social characteristics were more fully brought out by the two other major objective factors that proved significant in our analyses of the variations in the overall intensity of labor unrest during the prewar period.

Average levels of pay

The second objective factor of statistical significance consistently brought out by our regression analyses was that of wage levels: The higher the average levels of pay, the greater the intensity of strike actions. This observed relationship between average levels of pay and the intensity of strikes was not confined to our findings for the post-Lena period. Indeed, the statistical relationships between this factor and the overall intensity of strikes proved consistently *stronger* in our findings about the 1905–7 strike wave, a difference explicable in part by two major considerations. The first is that in the final regressions of our comparative analysis of these two strike waves, no account was taken of the concentrations of workers in cities and towns of less than 200,000 in population, who were intensively involved in labor unrest in both 1905 and 1906 but not in the prewar period, and who, just as workers in large urban centers, typically earned higher levels of pay than those employed in rural areas. Secondly, it is also the case that workers in the Kingdom of Poland, who in both 1905 and 1906, but not during the post-Lena period, were generally even more intensely involved in labor unrest than the workers of Russia's interior (including those concentrated in most of its urban centers), also earned higher average levels of pay than did workers employed in the same occupations in most other provinces of the Empire. When we discount for both these phenomena, the importance of levels of pay in accounting for the intensity of strikes in both 1906 and 1907 becomes quite comparable with the power and significance that appear for this factor in our analyses of the post-Lena period. In 1905, however, even after excluding the Polish provinces from our purview and regressing for the disproportionate concentration of more highly paid industrial workers in cities and towns of less than 200,000 in population, levels

115

of pay continue to account statistically for over 16% of the variations in the overall intensity of labor unrest. The extraordinary strength of this relationship clearly indicates that even within urban Russia, it was workers earning higher levels of pay who were disporportionately drawn into labor unrest during 1905, most notably, as we shall see, into the wave of political strikes that culminated in the October general strike.

Average levels of pay also proved significant in the findings of our analyses of the overall intensity of the labor unrest throughout the post-Lena strike wave, but the strength of this factor, while markedly increasing as this strike wave unfolded, remained even by the eve of the war relatively modest by comparison with that of urban concentration. Levels of pay accounted in our final regressions for only 1.8% of the variations in strike intensity recorded in 1912, for only 3.9% in 1913, and 5.2% in 1914 (in all three cases, excluding workers employed in the Kingdom of Poland).

Size of enterprise

The last and most distinctive objective factor that proved statistically significant in our analyses of the overall intensity of strikes after Lena was the proportion of the work force employed in enterprises of 500–1,000, and especially of over 1,000 workers. In 1912, these two indices for concentration in large enterprises jointly accounted for some 5.6% of the variations in strike intensity, but in contrast to the growing importance of average levels of pay, the significance of this factor somewhat declines as the war approaches: to 5.2% in 1913, and to only 3.4% in 1914 (again, discounting for workers employed in the Kingdom of Poland).

The significance of the degree of concentration of the work force in large enterprises in accounting for the overall intensity of labor unrest appears, at least in the perspective of our comparative analysis of these two strike waves, as a novel phenomenon of the post-Lena period. No significant relationships surfaced between this factor and the overall intensity of strikes in our regression equations for any of the years of the 1905–7 strike wave. Given the contrary assumptions that have been articulated on the subject, this is a major finding, to the significance of which we shall need to return.

A related finding, which stands in equally sharp contrast to those obtained in our regression analyses of patterns of labor unrest in 1905–7, is that we observe throughout the post-Lena strike wave, significant two-way and three-way interactions among the three major objective factors highlighted in our analysis of the overall intensity of strikes: the degrees of concentration of the labor force in the capital and other urban centers of over 200,000 in population, its degrees of concentration in large enterprises, and average levels of pay. Thus, the proportion of the variations in strike rates accounted for by these three factors

116

Table 3. *Regressions of proportions of striking workers for indices of urban concentration, average level of pay, and concentration in large enterprises (1912–14, Poland excluded)*

	Regressions without interactions	Regressions with two-way interactions	Regressions with three-way interactions
1912			
No. of Cases	362	362	362
R^2	0.426	0.573	0.586
F	43.84	33.32	30.57
Degrees of freedom	6/355	14/347	18/345
1913			
No. of Cases	381	381	381
R^2	0.314	0.478	0.546
F	28.50	23.93	24.16
Degrees of freedom	6/374	14/366	18/362
1914			
No. of Cases	385	385	385
R^2	0.497	0.622	0.664
F	62.29	43.64	40.13
Degrees of freedom	6/378	14/370	18/366

Note: For regression equations, see Appendix 3.

in our regression tables for all the years of the post-Lena strike wave increased considerably when we considered the relationships that they bore to the intensity of labor unrest *in interaction* – that is, when we focused attention on the strike rates recorded during these years in those branches of industry whose work forces earned higher average levels of pay and were also more highly concentrated than the average in large enterprises and/or in large urban centers – than when we simply added up the *individual* contributions of each of these variables to the relative intensity of strikes. The order of magnitude of the differences is suggested by the Table 3, which summarizes the results of our regression analyses for the post-Lena period with and without two-way and three-way interactions among these three variables.

To illustrate the results recorded in Table 3 for readers unfamiliar with statistics: urban concentration, average pay levels, and concentration in large enterprises jointly accounted for, when simply added together, only some 50% – but after measuring the effects of three-way interaction between them, for over 66% – of the variations recorded in the overall intensity of labor unrest in 1914. In contrast, for all the years of Russia's First Revolution, we did not observe any statistically significant three-way interactions among these three factors, and the occasional two-way interactions of statistical significance remained consistently quite modest. (For regression equations, see Appendix 4.)

The powerful two-way and three-way interactions that surfaced in our analysis of the post-Lena strike wave clearly show the extraordinary degree to which, in contrast to the 1905–7 strike wave, labor unrest remained disproportionately concentrated throughout the prewar period among certain specific strata of workers. They show, in fact, that despite the undeniable spread of labor unrest between April 1912 and July 1914 among workers employed in different branches of industry and geographical areas of the empire, the intensity of this unrest *continued to mount even more rapidly* right up to the outbreak of war among the more militant strata of industrial workers distinguished jointly by our objective indices of concentration in the capital and in other large urban centers, concentration in large enterprises, and higher average levels of pay. The interest that these findings present lies in part in the fact that they provide a more general statistical framework for a systematic analysis and interpretation of certain examples of the extraordinary concentration of labor unrest during the post-Lena period already noted at the time by many observers of the Russian labor scene.

The first and best known of these was the extraordinary degree of concentration of labor unrest in the capital. In both 1912 and 1913, the workers of St. Petersburg *guberniia* (who then accounted for only 9% of the total number of workers under the Factory Inspectorate) were responsible for some 40% of the number of strikers recorded in the Factory Inspectorate's reports. Between January and July 1914, when war broke out, this proportion mounted to a staggering 54.3% (in this instance, including even the statistics recorded for the Kingdom of Poland). Notwithstanding the crucial role that St. Petersburg workers played in Russia's First Revolution, we do not observe, through most of this period, any comparable degree of concentration of labor unrest in St. Petersburg *guberniia*. Even in 1905, its workers (who then accounted for 9.3% of all industrial workers under the Factory Inspectorate) were responsible for only 22% of the number of strikers recorded in the Empire as a whole. For 1906, their share rose to 16.3%. Only in 1907, was the degree of concentration of labor unrest among the workers of the capital comparable to that of the prewar period, the workers of St. Petersburg *guberniia* accounting that year for 37.8% of the total number of strikers recorded by the Inspectorate.

But a more distinctive and extraordinary example of the concentration of labor unrest during the post-Lena period, presenting an even more dramatic contrast to the patterns observable during Russia's First Revolution, is provided by the workers employed in mechanical and metal-processing enterprises. In 1912, metalworkers (who then represented less than 16% of all workers under Factory Inspection) accounted for 51% of the total number of strikers recorded in all industries; in 1913, for 53%; in 1914, for 56%. By comparison, in 1905, workers of the metal industry (who then constituted 17.6% of the total number of workers under Factory Inspection) accounted for only 28.2% of the total number of recorded strikers; and in 1906 and in 1907, for only 26%.

Finally, let us focus attention on the eye of the storm of the labor unrest of the prewar period, the workers of the mechanical and metal-processing enterprises of St. Petersburg *guberniia*. In 1912, these workers (who then accounted for but a miniscule 2.5% of the total labor force under Factory Inspection) were responsible for about 20% of the total number of recorded strikers; in 1913, for 25.5%. And, in 1914, (when, with the Kingdom of Poland excluded from the annual published report of the Inspectorate, the metal-workers of St. Petersburg accounted for 4.1% of the recorded labor force), their contribution to the total number of strikers among workers under Factory Inspection rose to a staggering 32.6%. Notwithstanding the catalytic role played by St. Petersburg metalworkers in the inception of Russia's First Revolution, at no point during the 1905–7 strike wave did they account for a nearly comparable proportion of the number of strikers recorded among workers under Factory Inspection. In 1905, the metal workers of St. Petersburg *guberniia* (who then represented 2.8% of all workers under the Inspectorate) accounted for but 9.8%; in 1906, for but 5.6%; and, even in 1907 (when workers employed in *all branches of industry* of St. Petersburg *guberniia* figured most prominently in the strike movement), they accounted for but 12.6% of the total number of strikers recorded by the Inspectorate.

As we suggested earlier, the interest presented by these three well known examples lies partly in the fact that they provide striking, if extreme, illustrations of the statistical relationships between the intensity of labor unrest and the three major objective factors highlighted in our regression analyses of the post-Lena strike wave. For the workers involved in each of these three cases of extra-ordinary labor militance – those of St. Petersburg *guberniia*, of the metal-processing industry of the Empire as a whole, and most glaringly, of the metalworkers of St. Petersburg *guberniia* – were distinguished by the fact that, to differing degrees, they earned far higher average levels of pay, were concentrated in far greater proportions both in urban centers over 200,000 in population and in large enterprises employing over 500 workers than was characteristic of workers employed in other branches of Russian industry.[7]

An even more general observation is now in order. We noted earlier that the

7. To mention only the relevant indices for the epicenter of this phenomenon, the metalworkers of St. Petersburg *guberniia*: (1) 98% of them were employed in the capital, even while only 25.7% of all workers under the jurisdiction of the Factory Inspectorate were concentrated in urban centers of over 200,000 in population; (2) their average wage was 519 rubles, as against an average of 255 rubles a year for all workers under Factory Inspection; (3) 73% of the metalworkers of St. Petersburg *guberniia* were concentrated in enterprises employing over 500 workers, versus an average of 53.3% of all workers under the jurisdiction of the Inspectorate.

statistical relationship between the intensity of strike actions and the degree of concentration of workers in cities of over 200,000 in population in fact largely reflected the exceptional strike rates recorded during the 1912–14 strike wave only in certain "select" urban centers – St. Petersburg, Riga, and a few others – all of which were distinguished by the presence in their working-class workers whose social characteristics could more precisely be established by the populations of large numbers and proportions of especially militant strata of other objective factors highlighted in our analysis. And it is indeed the case that all of these select urban centers were marked by the presence in their working-class population of disproportionate numbers of metalworkers – and more generally, of work forces more disproportionately concentrated in large enterprises and earning substantially higher levels of pay than was the average among all workers under Factory Inspection. To account more fully for the exceptional strike rates recorded in these select urban centers during these years, we need to add two orders of explanation.

These exceptionally high levels of labor unrest obviously stemmed in part from the mutual encouragement that the more militant strata of workers distinguished by these two additional objective indices were able to draw from their concentration in large numbers and in close proximity to each other in these select urban centers, whether this mutual encouragement was expressed in the form of collective strikes, or merely of mutual financial and/or moral support in the conduct of their individual strike actions. But another factor clearly involved was the evident ability of the larger concentrations of more militant workers represented in these select urban centers to draw *other strata of workers in their proximity* into their wave of labor unrest.

This point is dramatically illustrated by the exceptionally high strike rates recorded during these years in urban centers such as St. Petersburg and Riga (where large numbers of metalworkers were congregated) not only by workers of the metal industry, but also by those employed *in almost all other branches of industry*. But a more general sense of the effects of such higher concentrations of metalworkers (and, we suspect, of workers in other branches of industry distinguished by the combination of higher wage levels and degrees of concentration in large enterprises) on the intensity of labor unrest among other workers congregated with them in large urban centers can be obtained by examining and comparing the power of two sets of statistical relationships. The first is the set of relationships between variations in strike rates among workers outside the metal industry and the proportions of such workers, as well as that of metalworkers, concentrated in large urban centers, when these two statistical relationships are considered in isolation, and their individual effects *simply added up*. The second is the strength of these two relationships *after interaction* (i.e., after considering the *combined statistical effects* of higher degrees of concentration of metalworkers and nonmetalworkers in large urban centers on

120

Table 4. *Regressions of percentages of striking workers recorded in all branches other than the metal industry for the proportion of non-metalworkers and metalworkers concentrated in large urban centers (i.e., more than 200,000 inh.)*

	Regressions without interactions	Regressions with two-way interactions
1912		
No. of Cases	523	523
R^2	0.215	0.281
F	71.09	67.73
Degrees of freedom	2/520	3/519
1913		
No. of Cases	541	541
R^2	0.174	0.238
F	56.68	55.78
Degrees of freedom	2/538	3/537
1914		
No. of Cases	447	447
R^2	0.229	0.378
F	65.90	89.90
Degrees of freedom	2/444	3/443

the strike rates recorded by workers employed in various industrial groups outside of the metal industry).

Recorded in Table 4 are the power and statistical significance of these two relationships, before and after interaction, for each of the years of the post-Lena period.

These interactions are so strong as to require only one further observation to be developed later.[8] It is that the extraordinary increase that we observe in the power of the interaction that we observe for 1914 coincides with the sharp increase in the number and, especially, the proportions of *political*, as against economic, strikes recorded in these select urban centers that year among workers employed in other branches of industry than metal processing. This fact suggests that the catalytic influence exercised by large concentrations of

8. As the figures recorded in Table 4 indicate, the proportions of metalworkers and nonmetal-workers employed in large urban centers accounted in 1914 for 23% of the variations in strike rates recorded among all nonmetalworkers under Factory Inspection, when we simply consider the additive effects of these two variables. But after interaction (i.e., in combination), these two variables together accounted for some 38% of the variations in strike intensity among workers outside the metal industry. The interactions observed in the comparable regression analyses that we have conducted of the strike rates among workers outside the metal industry during the 1905–7 strike wave consistently remained very modest, most of them below the level of statistical significance.

metalworkers on labor unrest among workers of other branches of industry congregated with them in these urban centers obtained first and foremost, as the post-Lena strike wave progressed, for the intensity of *political* strikes.[9]

Strikes by causes

The differences in the character and dynamics of the 1905–7 and 1913–14 strike waves are brought into much higher relief when we focus attention on the data concerning the intensity of the *different* categories of strike actions distinguished in the reports of the Factory Inspectorate. In these reports, labor conflicts involving the articulation of a *variety* of grievances and demands were classified according to the "chief causes" singled out for their outbreak by local Factory Inspectors. It was on the basis of these attributed chief causes that economic strikes were classified as follows: strikes over wages (usually broken down into subcategories of strikes for higher pay, strikes against reductions in pay, and over the methods of calculating and administering wage payments); strikes over hours (including separate subcategories for strikes over demands for and against reductions in the length of the work day, as well as over its organization and regulation); and finally, strikes over "order in the enterprise and other conditions of life and work" (including separate subcategories for strikes over the imposition of fines, working and living conditions, and conflicts with supervisory personnel). The category of "noneconomic" strikes came to include, after the outbreak of the 1905 Revolution, subcategories for strikes identified as purely "political-demonstrative" in character; and, from 1913 onward, for strikes over grievances and demands connected with the establishment of health insurance funds.[10]

9. Dramatic evidence of this trend is provided by another data set, drawn from the statistics provided in the reports of the St. Petersburg Society of Manufacturers and Mill Owners, about the numbers of strikes and strikers recorded in specific categories of strike actions in the various branches of industry represented among its member firms in 1913 and 1914. These data bring out a major shift in the character of strike actions between 1913 and the outbreak of the war in *all branches of industry* represented among the firms of St. Petersburg Society, but most notably in branches of industry other than metal processing and textiles. During 1913, workers employed in these other branches of St. Petersburg industry (including food processing, chemicals, and all forms of leather processing) were recorded as engaging in very high proportions of economic strikes, including strikes over wages. By 1914, however, workers in these other branches of St. Petersburg industry ceased *almost entirely* to engage in strikes over wage issues, while the relative proportions (although not the absolute numbers) of political strikes recorded for them actually exceeded those recorded among the politically more militant work forces of St. Petersburg's mechanical and typographical industries.

10. We fully recognize the formidable statistical and substantive problems involved in assessing the significance of the statistical relationships between the indices provided by these highly aggregated data on the objective characteristics of the work forces employed in the often quite different branches of industry that were agglomerated in these major industrial groups and our equally highly aggregated data on the patterns of labor unrest that these work forces displayed. In our effort to take these problems into account, we observed a number of major cautions. One was

Let us first review the indices we have drawn from the aggregate data for the number of strikers and days lost recorded in these various categories and subcategories of strikes during the 1905–7 and 1912–14 strike waves among *all* workers under Factory Inspection (see tables in Appendix 4). Even these aggregate data bring out some striking and distinctive features of the post-Lena strike wave: most notably, the extraordinary proportions of strikes and strikers recorded, especially in 1912 and 1914, in the subcategory of political-demonstrative strikes, that is, of strikes that did not involve the articulation of economic grievances *in any form*. The proportions of the total numbers of strikers recorded in such purely political strikes were 75.8% in 1912, 56% in 1913, and 73.4% in 1914. The percentage figures for 1912 and 1914 greatly exceed those recorded in 1905 (37.8%) and 1906 (46.2%), and are comparable only to those for 1907 (70.5%).

To be sure, the figures we have cited for 1905 and 1906 are somewhat deceptive, since they do not take account of strikes classified by Factory

to apply conservative standards in defining the threshold of statistical significance for the correlations obtained in our analyses of this data set (treating only correlations with a p of 0.05 or less – i.e., with a 5% or less chance of statistical error – as "statistically significant," while regarding those with a p of 0.05–0.09, as merely "suggestive"). We also focused attention not so much on the absolute power and statistical significance that any of these correlations assumed for any one year as on the patterns of continuity and change that they brought out, in the course of, and especially between, the two periods encompassed by these two strike waves. Last but not least, we sought to check the reliability of the inferences we drew from these correlations by resorting to other techniques of statistical analysis (such as analysis of principal components), as well as by scrutinizing, whenever possible, other less highly aggregated, if more fragmentary, data sets.

An additional order of problems stems from the classification by "chief causes" of strike actions, and especially of economic strikes, which in fact broke out – or came to include – the issuance of a variety of grievances and demands. But however formidable at first sight, the difficulties stemming from this system of classification were among the least obdurate of those that we confronted in our analyses. In the first place, the criteria used by Factory Inspectors to define chief causes appeared to us, by and large, quite sensible in both theory and actual practice. Even more importantly, to the degree that this system of classification necessarily involved distortions, these distortions appeared, on closer scrutiny of the data, to contribute to the attenuation rather than to the exaggeration of the distinctive patterns of labor unrest that our analysis brought out.

The difficulties posed by the highly aggregated character of breakdowns by major industrial groups proved far more formidable. In the first place, the small number of comparable cases that these data provided not only made for far less statistical reliability of the results than of those obtained in our analyses of the overall intensity of strikes, but they also made it impossible to study the effects of covariations and interactions among the various objective indices under our scrutiny. These analytic problems were, in turn, magnified by the fact that the major industrial groups under Factory Inspection constituted, as we already noted, agglomerations of branches of industry employing work forces whose objective characteristics were often quite different. In our analyses of the overall intensity of strikes, the distortions caused by these forms of aggregation were partially compensated by the uneven geographical distribution of the branches of industry agglomerated in these major industrial groups among the various provinces under Factory Inspection. The absence of such geographical breakdowns of our aggregations by major industrial groups for the causes of strikes greatly magnified the distortions of the various indices we had to use to analyze the variations in the intensity of different categories of strikes among the work forces agglomerated in these industrial groups.

Inspectors during these years as involving "mixed" economic and political motifs. There are two major reasons why these subcategories of mixed economic and political strikes figured so prominently in the strike statistics for 1905, and to a lesser degree in 1906, only to dwindle into insignificance by 1907. The first is that the legislation that legalized economic strikes (even while continuing to outlaw political strikes) came into effect only in the course of 1906. (It was issued in December 1905.) It was not until this legislation was actually applied, and its existence *perceived* by participants in labor unrest, that these workers really came to distinguish between political and economic strikes. But the absence of a legal distinction between political and economic strikes at the onset of Russia's First Revolution only reinforced the basic attitudes of most participants in labor unrest, at least until the onset in 1907 of economic recession and political repression. For until then, a major feature of labor unrest among most workers, including the politically most militant, most conscious, most radicalized ones, was a genuine striving to obtain a vast array of tangible economic gains (whether in the form of wage increases or of improvements in working and living conditions), and an equally firm expectation that these gains could in fact be obtained – wrested from employers in the here and now – even while these workers continued to press the political dimensions of their labor struggle. These patterns of labor unrest became even more prominent in 1906 than in 1905, and the expectations of tangible economic gains that underlay them were in fact confirmed and reinforced, until 1907, by the actual outcomes of strike actions.

Consider, in this connection, the indices provided by the aggregate data on the numbers of strikes and strikers recorded in economic strikes whose outcomes were classified in the reports of the Factory Inspectorate as "in favor of the workers," "compromises," and "in favor of the employers," during the years of the 1905–7 strike wave (Table 5). The contrasts that these figures present to the indices provided by the aggregate data of the Inspectorate on the proportions of labor victories, compromises, and labor defeats recorded in economic strikes during the post-Lena strike wave are indeed dramatic (Table 6).

The extraordinarily small and dwindling proportions of labor victories brought out by our indices for the post-Lena period and the equally extraordinary and rising proportions of labor defeats that they record, especially by 1914, find no real counterparts in our indices for the 1905–1907 strike wave, with the partial exception of the figures for 1907, a year during which St. Petersburg workers were already waging desperate rearguard actions, while those in the rest of the country were largely subsiding into apathy. But even more notably, when considered in combination with the different and changing proportions of participants in political strikes that we already observed in our comparison of the 1905–1907 and 1912–1914 strike waves (for which again,

124

Table 5. *Outcomes of economic strikes (1905–7)*

		1905	1906	1907
In favor	strikes	34.3%	40.7%	22.3%
of workers	strikers	23.7%	35.5%	16.3%
Compromises	strikes	43.7%	34.1%	32.3%
	strikers	46.9%	30.8%	26.2%
In favor	strikes	22.0%	25.2%	45.4%
of employers	strikers	29.4%	33.7%	57.5%

Table 6. *Outcomes of economic strikes (1912–14)*

		1912	1913	1914
In favor	strikes	13.7%	9.2%	9.1%
of workers	strikers	9.0%	8.9%	5.9%
Compromises	strikes	38.9%	51.5%	21.3%
	strikers	32.1%	35.2%	25.1%
In favor	strikes	47.9%	39.3%	69.6%
of employers	strikers	58.5%	55.9%	69.0%

1907 provides the only indices comparable to those of the post-Lena period), these differences in the percentages of labor victories, compromises, and labor defeats recorded in economic strikes consistently bring out an interplay between the causes and the outcomes of strike actions which we shall need to scrutinize more closely in our analyses of the dynamics of these two strike waves.

We obtain a sharper sense of the difference in these dynamics of labor unrest, and of the patterns specifically at work among politically more militant strata of workers, when we focus attention on the relationships observable during these two strike waves between the intensity of different categories of strikes in the various branches of industry under Factory Inspection and the various objective indices that were available to us to distinguish the patterns of urban – rural distribution, the social characteristics, and the conditions of life and work of the labor forces that were employed in them.

The published reports of the Inspectorate provide only highly aggregated breakdowns of strikes by causes: aggregations of the number of strikes, strikers, and days lost in different categories of strikes recorded for each of the major industrial groups in which the various branches of industry under Factory Inspection were classified (without the further geographical breakdowns by province provided in the Inspectorate's statistics on the overall intensity of labor

125

unrest). By the same token, the indices used in our analysis of the objective factors statistically associated with the variations in the intensity of these different types of labor unrest had to rest on equally aggregated data for each of these major industrial groups. (These indices included those already considered in our analyses of the overall intensity of strikes, but also additional indices for certain objective factors – such as the proportions of literate workers and the strength of workers' ties to the land and to the countryside among the work forces employed in these major industrial groups – the data for which were also available only in such highly aggregated form.)

Before seeking to summarize the patterns of continuity and change suggested by certain of the correlations obtained in our analyses of these highly aggregated breakdowns of strikes by causes by major industrial groups, let us consider the results of our analysis of a less highly aggregated, if more fragmentary, data set, which we were able to assemble from archival sources, on the intensity of different categories of strikes between January 1914 and the outbreak of the war.

The data on labor unrest incorporated into this additional data set were drawn from the breakdowns, provided in monthly confidential reports submitted by the Ministry of Trade and Industry to the Council of Ministers, of the number of strikes and strikers recorded during these last six months of the prewar period in the sixty-seven provinces under the jurisdiction of the Factory Inspectorate.[11] These breakdowns by province were classified in these reports according to the major categories used by the Factory Inspectorate to define the chief causes of labor unrest: political strikes, strikes over wages, hours, and order in the enterprise (without further breakdowns by subcategories). Also included, without more precise breakdowns, were statistics for each of these sixty-seven provinces on the number of days lost in political and economic strikes, as well as on the number of strikes and strikers recorded in economic strikes whose outcomes were classified by the Inspectorate as "in favor of workers," "compromises," and "in favor of employers."

From an analytic standpoint, these provincial breakdowns (although themselves not broken down by major industrial groups) presented the following major advantages over the aggregations by industrial groups (without further breakdowns by province) that were more generally available for our analyses of the intensity of strikes by causes and subcauses during the 1905–7 and 1912–14 strike waves:

1. These aggregations by province enabled us to draw a far less distorted sense of the statistical relationships observable between variations in the

---

11. These monthly reports, which were initiated in September 1913 and continued to be submitted through January 1917, are now deposited in *fond* 23 (Ministry of Trade and Industry) and *fond* 1276 (Council of Minister) in TSGIA (Central State Historical Archives) in Leningrad.

intensity of different categories of strikes and patterns of distribution of the labor force in urban and rural areas, the objective factor that had consistently proven so significant in our findings concerning the variations in the overall intensity of labor unrest during the 1912–14 and 1905–7 strike waves.

2. Even more important, the larger number of comparable cases provided by this additional data set (consisting of breakdowns for sixty-seven provinces, as against the maximum of twelve comparable cases provided by our aggregate data from major industrial groups) enabled us to apply in our analysis of these data, statistical techniques comparable to those already used in the analysis of our more detailed data sets on the overall intensity of strikes – that is, to conduct multiple regressions among the objective factors under our scrutiny, and to study the effects of interactions among those of these factors still found, after regression, to retain statistical significance. Indeed, great similarities emerged between the results obtained when we applied these comparable statistical techniques to analyze the aggregate data that this provincial data set provided on variations in the overall intensity of labor unrest between January and July 1914 and the findings of our earlier analysis of the more detailed breakdowns of these data (provided in the Factory Inspectorate's published annual report for 1914).

In the first place, the same three major objective factors emerged after regression, as strongly associated with variations in the overall intensity of strikes: the degree of concentration of the labor force in urban centers of over 200,000 in population, in enterprises employing 500–1,000 and especially over 1,000 workers, and higher average levels of pay. Secondly, the analysis of these provincial breakdowns also brought out significant interactions among these major objective factors after regression. Last but not least, the power of these three objective factors in accounting after interaction for the variations in the overall intensity of labor unrest between January and July 1914 in the sixty-seven provinces considered in this data set ($R^2 = 0.69$) proved quite similar to our findings for the 385 cases compared in the more detailed data set that had also been available to us to study these variations in 1914 ($R^2 = 0.66$).

The reassurance we drew from the compatibility of these results was all the more important because our analyses of the breakdowns that our 1914 provincial data set provided of strikes by causes *unveiled enormous differences* in the degrees to which the three major objective factors highlighted in our analysis of the overall intensity of strikes – that is, average levels of pay, and degrees of concentration of the work force in large urban centers and in large enterprises – were found to account statistically for the intensity of the *specific* categories of strikes distinguished by this second data set. Recorded in Table 7 are the proportions of the variations in the intensity of political strikes, strikes over wages, hours, and order in the enterprise that were found to be accounted for by these three major objective factors, before and after taking account of the

Table 7. *Regressions of percentages of workers engaged in different categories of strikes for indices of urban concentration, average pay, and concentration of workers in large enterprises (all provinces, including St. Petersburg, January–July 1914)*

	Without interactions	With two-way interactions
Political strikes		
Number of Cases	67	67
R^2	0.492	0.794
F	14.982	24.351
Degrees of freedom	4/62	9/57
Strikes over hours		
Number of cases	67	67
R^2	0.334	0.536
F	10.526	11.568
Degrees of freedom	3/63	6/60
Strikes over order		
Number of cases	67	67
R^2	0.264	0.367
F	7.521	5.800
Degrees of freedom	3/63	6/60
Strikes over wages		
Number of cases	67	67
R^2	0.116	0.127
F	2.748	1.458
Degrees of freedom	3/63	6/60

Note: For regression equations, see Appendix 6.

interactions between them, in our analysis of these provincial breakdowns for the period between January and July 1914.

But let us compare these findings with those obtained when St. Petersburg *guberniia* was excluded from the analysis, given the extraordinary degree of concentration of *certain* of these categories of strikes in the capital during these last months of the post-Lena strike wave (Table 8).[12]

The results recorded in both of these tables bring out enormous differences in the degrees to which the three major objective factors highlighted in our regression analyses were found to account for the intensity of political strikes, strikes over hours, and strikes over order, as against strikes over pay. But the

12. Our provincial breakdowns indicate that during the period between January and July 1914, the workers of St. Petersburg *guberniia*, who accounted at the time for only some 10% of the total number of workers under the jurisdiction of the Inspectorate, were responsible for some 60% of the total number of participants in political strikes, 25.1% in strikes over hours, 34% in strikes over order in the enterprise, and only 10% in strikes over wages recorded among *all* workers under Factory Inspection.

Table 8. *Regression percentages of workers engaged in different categories of strikes for indices of urban concentration, average pay, and concentration of workers in large enterprises (St. Petersburg excluded, January–July 1914)*

	Without interactions	With two-way interactions
Political strikes		
Number of Cases	66	66
R^2	0.398	0.590
F	10.073	8.948
Degrees of freedom	4/61	9/56
Strikes over hours		
Number of cases	66	66
R^2	0.226	0.431
F	6.026	7.441
Degrees of freedom	3/62	6/59
Strikes over order		
Number of cases	66	66
R^2	0.239	0.417
F	6.486	7.038
Degrees of freedom	3/62	6/59
Strikes over wages		
Number of cases	66	66
R^2	0.115	0.128
F	2.693	1.478
Degrees of freedom	3/62	6/59

Note: For regression equations, see Appendix 7.

tables also suggest certain notable differences in the results obtained, especially after interaction, when St. Petersburg *guberniia* was included in, and excluded from, our purview: the percentage of explained variations in the intensity of political strikes and strikes over hours declined significantly when St. Petersburg *guberniia* was excluded from the analysis, but increased markedly for strikes over order.

An examination of the regression equations obtained in the two analyses (see tables in Appendixes 6 and 7) suggests the following observations about the statistical relationships accounting for these substantial differences in their final results.

1. The major reason for the substantially higher r^2 obtained when St. Petersburg *guberniia* was included in the analysis is the greater power and statistical significance of the regression equation that emerges in that case for the factor of concentration in large urban centers, as well as of the interaction between this factor and that of higher average levels of pay. The greater power of these two relationships when St. Petersburg *guberniia* is included in the

analysis obviously suggests that not only were St. Petersburg workers more intensely involved in political strikes during the last prewar months than were workers employed in other cities of over 200,000 of population, but also that political strikes in St. Petersburg's *guberniia* were more disproportionately concentrated among work forces earning higher average levels of pay than was the case in other provinces with large urban centers.

2. Among workers outside St. Petersburg *guberniia*, the degree of concentration of the work force in very large enterprises and the interaction between this factor and higher average levels of pay (these two relationships in combination suggesting the distinctive characteristics of specific branches of industry) proved of far greater power and significance in accounting for the degree of intensity of strikes over hours than for that of political strikes.

3. Finally, the character of the regression equations that appeared for the intensity of strike over order when St. Petersburg *guberniia* was included in, and excluded from, the analysis suggests certain important differences as well as similarities in the motifs that underlay the intensity of strikes over order among workers of the capital and those employed in other large urban centers. The major similarity suggested by the regression equations obtained in both cases is that a major motif in strikes over order was the acuteness of the conflicts with supervisory personnel characteristic of labor relations in all provinces distinguished by higher degrees of concentration of their industrial labor force in very large enterprises, and especially of concentration in these very large enterprises of work forces earning higher average levels of pay (these two factors, especially in interaction, again suggesting the distinctive characteristics of specific branches of industry). But another motif underlying the intensity of strikes over order in 1914 is suggested by the interaction between the degree of concentration of the labor force in large urban centers and higher average levels of pay, and especially by the much greater power that this interaction assumes when St. Petersburg *guberniia* is excluded from the analysis. It is that among more highly paid work forces located in large urban centers outside of St. Petersburg *guberniia, including those employed in smaller enterprises,* strikes over order provided substitutes for political strikes in these workers' revolt against superordinate authority to a much greater degree than for workers of the capital. (We surmise that this difference stemmed, at least in part, from the much more systematic and effective repressions to which political strikes were subjected by local provincial authorities than they were in St. Petersburg, where these acts of repression were so much more effectively exposed to the light of publicity by opposition deputies in the State Duma as well as by the opposition press.)

The major findings suggested by our regressions equations concerning the patterns of labor unrest displayed on the eve of the war by the strata of workers

Table 9. *Correlations between variations in intensity of strikes*
(January – July 1914)

	Political strikes[a]	Strikes over hours	Strikes over order	Strikes over wages
(independent variable)				
St. Petersburg guberniia *included*	1.00	0.75	0.58	0.07
St. Petersburg guberniia *excluded*	1.00	0.73	0.74	0.06

[a] Independent variable.

distinguished by our various objective indices, and their underlying dynamics, were by and large also brought out by the correlation analyses that we conducted of the various data sets at our disposal about the intensity of different categories of strikes. First and foremost, these analyses brought into high relief the degree of polarization that distinguished by the eve of the war the patterns of labor unrest characteristic of politically *more* militant and *less* militant strata of workers, and the degrees of similitude observable in this regard between variations in the intensity of political strikes and that of strikes over hours and over order in the enterprise, but not of strikes over pay. Such intercorrelations emerged even in the analysis of our aggregate data on strikes by causes by major industrial groups, but they appeared even more sharply in the analysis of our provincial aggregates for 1914, which enabled us to assess much more clearly the effects of patterns of urban–rural distribution of the labor force on the character and the intensity of strikes.

Recorded in Table 9 are the correlations between variations in the intensity of strikes over hours, over order, and over pay, and the intensity of political strikes recorded among the provincial work forces under Factory Inspection between January and July 1914, with the St. Petersburg *guberniia* included in, and excluded from, the analysis.

In and of themselves, these correlations strikingly confirm two of the major findings already suggested by our regression analysis of this data set. On the one hand, they bring out with extraordinary sharpness the differences in the degrees of intensity with which politically more militant and more inert strata of workers throughout the empire engaged during this period in strikes over hours and over order, as against strikes over pay. On the other hand, the substantially higher correlations between the intensity of strikes over order and that of political strikes that appeared when St. Petersburg *guberniia* was excluded from the analysis also bring out the greater similitudes in the motifs that underlay the outbreak of strikes over order and of political strikes among workers outside St. Petersburg *guberniia* during these last prewar months than among those concentrated in the capital.

131

Our correlational analyses of the aggregations by industrial groups more generally available to us to study the distribution of strikes by causes among various strata of workers during these two strike waves also brought out, although less sharply, the statistical significance of the objective factors that we found so strongly associated in our regression models with the overall intensity of strikes throughout the post-Lena strike wave, and in our provincial data set for 1914 with the intensity of political strikes, strikes over hours, and over order, but not of strikes over pay.

This was particularly the case with respect to our indices for the proportions of participants and also for the number of days lost per worker in *political strikes*, which we found strongly correlated – for all the years of the post-Lena strike wave – with our indices for higher levels of pay, as well as for the degree of concentration of work forces in the capital, and in urban areas generally.

Strong positive bivariate correlations also appeared for all the years of the post-Lena period between higher levels of pay and the proportions of participants and days lost per worker in *strikes over hours*. But it was only for 1914 – precisely the year when our aggregate data for all workers under Factory Inspection showed a dramatic leap in the intensity of strikes over hours – that a series of statistically significant and suggestive relationships also surfaced in our correlations between the number of participants and days lost per worker in strikes over hours and several of the other indices we found strongly correlated with the intensity of political strikes: most notably, the degrees of concentration of the labor force in urban areas, and to a lesser degree, in the capital itself.

Even more notably, it was only for 1913 and 1914 that strong positive statistical relationships surfaced in the correlations between our indices for the intensity of strikes over order – and particularly for the number of days lost per worker in conflicts with advisory personnel – and certain of the objective factors that we also found so consistently associated throughout the post-Lena strike wave with the intensity of political strikes: higher levels of pay, and the degrees of concentration of the labor force in the capital, and in urban areas generally.

Indeed, the patterns brought out by these various correlations unmistakably suggest that notwithstanding the overwhelming preponderance of political strikes so characteristic of the post-Lena strike wave, and the disproportionate involvement in them of the strata of workers profiled by our various objective indices, what distinguished the evolution of labor unrest among these politically more militant workers during the prewar period was not so much the transmutation of their other grievances and aspirations into purely political strikes (a pattern in fact more generally characteristic of politically less militant strata of workers), but rather the mutual reinforcement of the predominant motifs in their economic and political strikes into a more and more generalized and

132

explosive struggle against *all* the forms of authority that were imposed on them, inside as well as outside the work place.

The analysis of our breakdowns by major industrial groups also brought out major differences, as well as a few similarities, between patterns of labor unrest during the post-Lena period – especially among more militant strata of workers – and those that characterized the dynamics of the 1905–7 strike wave. The major similarity was that for all the years of Russia's First Revolution, strong positive statistical relationships also appeared in our correlations between the proportions of participants and days lost per worker in political strikes and our indices for higher wage levels and for the degrees of concentration of the labor force in urban areas. Even in this respect, however, one important difference (already suggested in our regression equations for the overall intensity of labor unrest) was that in both 1905 and 1906, although not in 1907, political strikes appeared far more broadly distributed throughout urban Russia – including its smaller cities and towns – than at any time during the post-Lena period. (It is notable, in this connection, that for both 1905 and 1906 our correlations between the proportions of the participants and days lost per worker in political strikes and the degree of concentration of the labor force *in urban areas generally* proved *substantially stronger* than those for concentration in St. Petersburg, while the opposite pattern consistently surfaced in our findings for the post-Lena strike wave.)

But the most important and dramatic contrast brought out by our comparative analysis of the breakdowns by major industrial groups for these two strike waves was that *at no point* did our correlations for the 1905–7 period unveil differences even barely comparable to those that we observed by the eve of the First World War in the degrees of intensity with which the strata of workers distinguished by our various objective indices for their disproportionate involvement in political strikes *engaged in any category of economic strikes* by comparison with politically more inert strata of workers.

Let us consider more fully the significance of the factors of urban concentration, wage levels, and size of enterprise in accounting statistically, *especially in interaction*, for this unprecedented polarization of the character and intensity of labor unrest among the strata of workers distinguished by these three indices on the eve of the First World War. The interactions observed between these factors in the analysis of our provincial data set for 1914 appear, in this connection, all the worthier of further exploration when we consider that these interactions surfaced consistently in our analysis of the overall intensity of strikes throughout the prewar period, but not for any of the years of the 1905–7 strike wave.

As we shall have occasion to observe more fully in our discussion of the metal industry, one of the sources of these powerful interactions is that these three factors jointly bring out certain of the major social characteristics and conditions of life and work that distinguished the strata of workers who throughout the post-Lena period stood at the vanguard of the strike movement, and by the eve of the war became disproportionately involved in political strikes, strikes over hours, and over order, but not in strikes over pay. But the power of these interactions, we believe, also stems from the fact that these three major objective factors also bring out far more sharply and precisely *in combination* than they do separately, certain other social characteristics of the work forces distinguished by them. Let us pass in review a number of these submerged characteristics, which for lack of adequate statistical data could not be considered in our regression models.

Proportions of urban-born and urban-bred workers

One of the most obvious of these submerged factors is the proportion of urban-born and urban-bred workers represented in the labor force – an objective factor that is more clearly suggested by our indices for urban concentration and higher levels of pay in combination than by either of them separately, given the disproportionate numbers of urban-born and urban-bred workers represented in industrial occupations that required higher levels of skill, and therefore paid higher average wages. The empirical evidence at our disposal also suggests that it was the enterprises of branches of industry, such as machine construction and printing, employing disproportionate numbers of urban-born and urban-bred workers – especially in urban centers such as St. Petersburg and Moscow, where such enterprises were concentrated in large numbers – that were most strongly affected by labor unrest, and especially by political strikes, throughout the post-Lena period.

In St. Petersburg's metal industry, the prominent role played by urban-born and urban-bred workers in these most explosive forms of labor unrest had in fact been recognized since the turn of the century. To be sure, as late as 1905 such workers were relatively few in number, even in St. Petersburg's metal industry. The demographic evidence at our disposal, however, suggests that by the end of the decade their numbers and proportions had substantially increased, especially in branches of industry such as machine construction that experienced a stabilization, if not an actual contraction, of their labor force under the impact of the economic recession between 1905 and the end of the decade.[13] There is also little question that, especially by the eve of the war, such

13. For a more detailed analysis of these demographic changes in the capital and of their eventual impact on patterns of labor unrest among St. Petersburg workers in the course of the post-Lena strike wave, see Leopold Haimson, "Changements démographiques et grèves ouvrières,

urban-born and urban-bred workers constituted a substantially higher proportion of St. Petersburg's industrial labor force than they did of Moscow's. Indeed, this may have been one, if only one, of the objective factors underlying the disproportionately higher strike rates that St. Petersburg workers recorded during the post-Lena period than those of Russia's second capital, in contrast to the far more nearly comparable strike rates that the work forces of these two cities had displayed during the revolutionary year of 1905.

We should also note, however, that even the smaller proportion of workers born in the city of Moscow, which according to the 1912 Moscow municipal census figures accounted for only 10% of the city's industrial labor force, was very unevenly distributed among various trades and industrial occupations: the indices provided by this census range from 23.9% for workers in typographical enterprises, and 14.4% for metalworkers, to 4.5% for workers of the textile industry as a whole, and an even more miniscule 3.8% for workers employed in the weaving trades.[14] As we suggested earlier, such patterns of distribution were unquestionably a general phenomenon in urban Russia – a function of the different levels of literacy and skills required for the performance of various occupations. But the precise breakdowns that the Moscow 1912 municipal census affords us of the proportions of workers employed in various branches of industry who were born in Moscow (the only such municipal census data available) enable us to draw some sense of the relative significance of this factor, as against that of urban concentration per se, in accounting for the intensity of labor unrest, by engaging in a simple, if imprecise, statistical exercise.

The exercise involves a comparison of the power of two sets of statistical relationships. The first is the bivariate correlations for each of the years of the post-Lena strike wave between the strike rates recorded *throughout Moscow guberniia* by the work forces employed in the eight major industrial groups distinguished by the 1912 Moscow municipal census, and the proportions of these work forces recorded by this census as *being employed in the city of Moscow*. The strength of these relationships is then to be compared with the correlations obtaining for the same years between the intensity of labor unrest displayed by the workers of these eight major industrial groups of Moscow *guberniia* and the

le cas de Saint-Peterbourg a la veille de la Première Guerre Mondiale," *Annales* (Economies, Sociétes, Civilizations), no. 4 (juillet – aout, 1985): 781–803. The data of the municipal censuses of 1900 and 1912 compared in this article were compiled by the statistical division of the city (*gorodskaia*) *uprava*. These data eventually appeared in aggregate form in the following publications: *S-Peterburg po perepisi 15 dekiabria 1900 goda*, pod redaktsii N. A. Feduleva, S. Peterburg, 1903; and *Petrograd po perepisi 15 dekabria 1910 g.*, pod redaktsii V. V. Stepanova, Ch. 1 and 2, n.d.

14. The major data of the 1912 Moscow municipal census were published by the Statistical Division of the Moscow City Administration (*Statisticheskii otdel Moskovskoi gorodskoi upravy*) in *Glavneishie predvaritelnye dannye perepisi goroda Moskvy v Marte 1912 goda* (Moscow, 1913). The breakdown of Moscow-born workers and immigrants employed in various occupations appeared in *Statisticheskii ezhegodnik g. Moskvy i Moskovskoi gubernii, vypusk 2; "Statisticheskie dannye po g. Moskve za 1914–1925 gg."* (Moscow, 1927), pp. 68–71.

Table 10. *Bivariate correlations for indices of overall intensity of strike actions in eight major industrial groups of Moscow* guberniia *(1912–1914)*

	1912	1913	1914
Dependent variable			
Percentages of strikers (in Moscow *guberniia*)			
Independent variable			
Percentage of workers employed in Moscow	$r = .089$	.232	.135
(including immigrants and workers born	$p = .417$	.290	.374
in Moscow)			
Percentage of workers born in Moscow	$r = .582$	.671	.548
	$p = .065$	.034	.080

proportions of the workers employed in Moscow identified by the 1912 census as *having been born in Moscow*. Obviously, the exercise is imprecise since the indices used in both sets of correlations to measure the intensity of labor unrest are those we have had to draw from the strike statistics provided for the work forces of these industrial groups employed throughout Moscow *guberniia* rather than in the city of Moscow alone. But the objection loses much of its weight when we consider that the bulk of labor unrest, and especially of the political strikes recorded in Moscow *guberniia* throughout the post-Lena period, was in fact largely concentrated in the city of Moscow.

Recorded in Table 10 are the power and statistical significance of the correlations between the strike rates recorded by workers of these eight major industrial groups throughout Moscow *guberniia*, during each of the years of the post-Lena strike wave, and the two sets of objective indices that the 1912 municipal census affords us concerning those of them who were employed in the city of Moscow.

As Table 10 indicates, the correlations between the strike rates displayed by the provincial work forces employed in these eight major industrial groups and our indices for the proportions of them who were employed in the city of Moscow (immigrants and Moscow-born workers alike) prove to be during this period three to five times weaker than the correlations for the proportions of these workers recorded by the 1912 census as having been born in Moscow. However impressionistic, these findings surely go part way toward confirming the impression we have drawn from other data that it was in fact the work forces in branches of industry (such as metal-processing, mechanical, and typo-graphical enterprises) employing higher proportions of workers born in Moscow that also accounted, throughout the years of the post-Lena strike wave, for a disproportionate number of the participants in labor unrest (and especially in political strikes) in the city of Moscow, just as in Moscow *guberniia* as a whole.

Proportions of literate workers and levels of literacy

The proportions of literate workers represented in the work force, and especially the levels of literacy that workers recorded as literate actually displayed, constitute another set of submerged indices to which the factors of urban concentration and higher levels of pay point more sharply in interaction than they do separately – given the fact that higher proportions of literate, and especially more highly literate, workers were employed in industrial occupations (such as printing and machine construction) that required higher levels of skill and literacy, and therefore paid higher average wages. No adequate quantitative data were available to us to measure levels of literacy. But we were able to use certain indices to draw some sense of the statistical relationships between the percentages of literate workers represented in the major industrial work forces under our scrutiny and the strike rates that these work forces displayed in various categories of strikes.

The data available for this purpose were less than satisfactory, drawn as they were from the statistics provided by the 1918 industrial census about the percentages of literate persons represented among those of the workers of eight major industrial groups covered by this census *who had already been employed in these branches of industry before the revolution.* The indices that can be drawn from these data for our analyses of the 1905–7 and 1912–14 strike waves are obviously highly impressionistic, given the considerable number of workers employed in these eight branches of industry before the revolution who had left them by 1918 to engage in other occupations (partly as a result of the dislocation that certain of these industries suffered in the course of the revolution and especially in the early months of 1918). For this very reason we did not include these indices (the only ones available for such estimates of literacy) in our regression analyses. With these cautions in mind, let us consider what impressions may be drawn from a comparison of the correlations between these indices and the character of labor unrest during the 1905–7 and 1912–14 strike waves.[15]

15. As we noted earlier, we have generally attempted to cope with the difficulties involved in assessing the actual significance of the relationships suggested by the bivariate correlation we observed between our indices for the intensity of labor unrest in major industrial groups and the objective indices that were also available to us concerning the work forces employed in them, by seeking to observe two major safeguards – both of which had to be even more scrupulously observed in this instance, given the even smaller number of cases for which our indices of literacy were available (only nine out of the twelve major industrial groups under Factory Inspection), and the even less satisfactory character of the data themselves. The first of these

137

Table 11. *Bivariate correlations for number of strikers and days lost in nine industrial groups (1905–7, 1912–4)*

		1912	1913	1914	1905	1906	1907
Independent variable Percentages of literate workers							
Dependent variables Percentage of							
participants in political	$r =$ .671		.657	.777	.464	.063	.448
strikes	$p =$ .024		.027	.007	.088	.431	.097
Days lost per worker in	$r =$ .427		.578	.728	−.026	−.020	.329
political strikes	$p =$ .127		.051	.013	.472	.478	.177
Percentages of							
participants in strikes	$r =$ .523		.282	.506	.169	.116	.225
over hours	$p =$ .074		.231	.082	.320	.375	.266
Days lost per worker in	$r =$ .519		.552	.430	−.026	−.021	.324
strikes over hours	$p =$ .076		.062	.124	.472	.477	.180

Recorded in Table 11 are the power and statistical significance of those of the correlations for our indices of the proportions of literate workers represented in nine major industrial groups under Factory Inspection that emerged as statistically significant, as well as merely "suggestive," in accounting for the percentages of strikers and days lost per worker in political strikes and strikes over hours in the course of the post-Lena period, and the correlations we obtained for these same categories of strikes during the 1905–7 strike wave.

As these figures indicate, strong positive correlations appear for all the years of the post-Lena period between our indices for the proportions of literate workers represented in the labor force and the percentages of participants in political strikes. For 1913 and 1914, but not for 1912, such strong statistical relationships also surface for the *number of days lost per worker* in political strikes. These correlations are among the strongest of the relationships we observe for 1913 and 1914 between the various objective factors under our purview and the numbers of strikers and days lost per worker in political strikes. Some suggestive correlations, falling short of our threshold of statistical significance, also appear during this period for the number of participants and days lost per worker in strikes over hours.

In contrast to these findings, *no powerful correlations of any kind* appear between our indices of literacy and the intensity of *any* category of strikes during the 1905–7 strike wave. The correlations for these years between the

safeguards was to apply highly conservative standards in assessing the statistical significance of these correlations. The second was to focus attention not so much on the absolute power of the correlations that we obtained for any single year, as on the major differences that emerged in these relationships for the entire periods encompassed by these two strike waves.

proportions of literate workers represented in the labor force and the intensity of political strikes consistently fall short of statistical significance, and no relationships of even a suggestive character emerge for the intensity of any category of economic strikes, including strikes over hours.

Ties to the countryside and to the land

The strength of the ties to the countryside and to agriculture characteristic of the work forces employed in various branches of industry constitutes another submerged factor, itself closely related to levels of literacy, which is more sharply suggested by our indices of urban concentration, average levels of pay, and size of enterprise in interaction than by any of these factors separately. As we noted earlier, the size of enterprises bears a statistical relationship to this factor because of the greater degrees of mechanization generally characteristic of larger enterprises, and the greater capital investments needed to achieve them. These factors generated pressures for larger enterprises to operate all year round (rather than to shut down or slow down operations during the summer), thereby discouraging the peasant immigrants employed in them from returning to their native villages during the peak months of the agricultural season to engage in field work.

To explore the significance that these ties to the land bore to the relative intensity of labor unrest – an issue that for almost a century has been the object of such sustained historiographical controversy – the data of the 1918 professional census provide us with two sets of indices concerning the workers of ten major industrial groups who were already employed in these branches of industry before the revolution: the proportions of these workers who possessed – or whose families possessed – land before 1917, and/or who themselves engaged in agricultural work on a part-time basis.

Recorded in Table 12 are the power and statistical significance of the correlations between these two indices and the percentages off strikers and the number of days lost per worker in political strikes during the 1905–7 and 1912–14 strike waves in the ten major industrial groups for which these indices were available.

For all the years of the post-Lena strike wave, *negative* correlations surface between these two indices of ties to the land and the indices of strike intensity recorded for precisely the same two categories of strikes for which *positive* statistical relationships emerged in our correlations for higher proportions of literate workers: highly significant, but this time *negative*, statistical relationships between the strength of ties to the land and the intensity of political strikes, and suggestive negative relationships for the intensity of strikes over hours. In contrast, for all the years of the 1905–7 strike wave, no correlations even approaching statistical signficance appeared between these two indices of the

Table 12. *Correlations between two indices for strength of ties to the land and intensity of political strikes (1905–7 and 1912–14)*

	1912	1913	1914	1905	1906	1907

Dependent variable
Percentage of participants in political strikes in ten major industrial groups

Independent variables Percentage of workers						
possessing land	$r = -.613$	$-.565$	$-.685$	$-.353$	$-.132$	$-.321$
($N = 10$)	$p = .029$	$.044$	$.014$	$.143$	$.349$	$.168$
Percentage of workers						
engaged part-time in	$r = -.633$	$-.608$	$-.709$	$-.430$	$-.229$	$-.362$
agriculture	$p = .025$	$.031$	$.011$	$.094$	$.249$	$.137$

Dependent variable
Number of days lost per worker in political strikes in ten major industrial groups

Independent variables Percentage of workers						
possessing land	$r = -.337$	$-.553$	$-.694$	$-.081$	$-.089$	$-.319$
	$p = .171$	$.056$	$.013$	$.406$	$.397$	$.170$
Percentage of workers	$r = -.358$	$-.589$	$-.689$	$-.213$	$.217$	$-.403$
engaged part-time in	$p = .154$	$.036$	$.036$	$.265$	$.260$	$.109$
agriculture						

strength of ties to the land and the intensity of *any* category of labor unrest, *including political strikes.*

To be sure, the statistical relationships that we have unveiled for most of the post-Lena strike wave between the three submerged objective factors that we have reviewed up to this point and the intensity of political strikes, are in part redundant, given the high degree of correlation unquestionably present among these factors – that is, between the proportions of urban-born workers repre-sented in the work forces of various branches of industry, their proportions of literate workers, and the proportions of them who possessed land and/or engaged in agriculture on a part-time basis. But it may legitimately be argued by the same token that, for analytical purposes, these three sets of objective indices may be grouped under one common label: that of the degrees of "urbanization" (as against urban concentration per se) characteristic of the work forces em-ployed in various branches of industry. For it was clearly those workers in urban Russia who were urban-born, literate (and especially more highly literate), and had loosened, if not broken, their ties to the countryside and to the land who – by virtue of this combination of factors – were likely to have absorbed most fully the mores of urban life, and indeed to aspire most deeply to the levels of material well-being and *kulturnost* attained by more highly privileged groups of urban "census" society. By the same token, the differences brought out in our comparative analyses of the 1912–14 and 1905–7 strike waves for the significance of these various objective indices unmistakably suggest that by the eve of the war, far more clearly than had been the case during the years of Russia's First Revolution, the grievances and aspirations generated by processes of urbanization had come to provide a more powerful motive force for labor unrest, and especially for political strikes, than the factor of urban concentration of the labor force per se.

Levels of mechanization

Yet another set of "submerged" factors is suggested by the powerful interactions that surfaced in our regression analyses of the post-Lena strike wave; this one more closely associated with the distinctive and changing characteristics and forms of organization of production processes and their effects on labor relations than with the processes of urbanization that we have scrutinized up to this point. One of these additional submerged factors is the degree of mechanization characteristic of individual enterprises and branches of industry, a factor suggested more sharply by our indices for size of enterprise and urban concentration in combination than by either of these two factors in isolation.

Indeed, the degree of mechanization characteristic of individual enterprises (and of whole branches of industry) is one of the factors most consistently emphasized in the analyses of strike rates furnished by the Factory Inspectorate for all the years covered by its published reports. The fragmentary statistical data at our disposal suggest that by the eve of the war this factor had become even more closely associated with the intensity of labor unrest than had been the case during the years of the 1905–7 strike wave, indeed far more sharply so than the sheer size of enterprises.

For example, the strike statistics of the St. Petersburg Society of Manufacturers and Mill Owners consistently bring out that in all the branches of industry in which the enterprises of its member firms were classified (including, and indeed especially in, those enterprises employing work forces of predominantly lower skills and earning lower average wages), labor unrest was disproportionately concentrated throughout the post-Lena period in more highly mechanized factories and plants: among the enterprises of its Chemical Group, for example, in its highly mechanized rubber-processing factories; in its Food Processing Group in the large mechanized factories manufacturing cigarettes; in the Animal Products Group in the more highly mechanized enterprises producing certain types of shoewear. It was in such larger, but also more highly mechanized, enterprises that strike actions remained, right up to the First World War, disproportionately concentrated among member firms of the St. Petersburg Society (and particularly so, we repeat, in those branches of industry that employed predominantly work forces of lesser skills, earning lower pay, and including generally higher proportions of female workers).

Changes in the character, organization, and forms of supervision and compensation of work processes

In the published reports of the Factory Inspectorate one also occasionally encounters the observation that another objective factor underlying higher rates of labor unrest was the as yet unstable and uncrystallized character of labor relations characteristic of new enterprises, and especially of newly established branches of industry. (The example most frequently cited was the chemical industry, and in particular the rubber-processing enterprises classified in this industrial group.)

We do not dispute the validity of this observation, but would complement it with a corollary one to be developed later: It is that especially during the years of the post-Lena strike wave, the contribution of unstable patterns of labor relations to the intensity of labor unrest was not confined to newly established enterprises and branches of industry. It was even more marked in those already established branches of industry employing significant numbers of skilled and semiskilled workers – such as metal processing and especially machine construction – that experienced during these years the most profound *changes* in the character, and especially in the forms of organization, supervision, and compensation of their production processes.

Summary

Let us now summarize the patterns of continuity and change that have been brought out by the findings of our quantitative analyses of the 1905–7 and 1912–14 strike waves.

The greatest elements of continuity in our results were those that appeared with respect to the intensity of political strikes, which we found so strongly positively associated throughout these two waves of labor unrest with the degree of concentration of the work force in urban areas, as well as with higher average levels of pay. Even in this respect, however, important differences surfaced in the results of our comparative analysis. For not only did our findings for the post-Lena period consistently bring out a far greater degree of concentration of political-demonstrative strikes, even within urban Russia, among workers of the capital and other large urban centers, but they also unveiled far more sharply than did our correlations for any of the years of the 1905–7 strike wave, strong statistical relationships between the intensity of political strikes and our indices for higher proportions in the labor force of literate workers and lower proportions of workers possessing land, and/or cultivating land on a part-time basis. We did not hesitate to assign to these two sets of indices, and to the relationships that they bore to patterns of labor unrest, the designation of processes of urbanization, even though, strictly speaking, the data on which these indices were based did not distinguish patterns of urban–rural distribution. We were emboldened to do so for two major reasons.

The first and most obvious one was that the strata of workers distinguished by higher proportions of literate workers and weaker ties to the land were in fact disproportionately concentrated in urban, as against rural, areas. But a second and even more compelling reason was the conviction we drew, partly from certain of the quantitative findings we have summarized (most notably, the powerful interactions that appeared in our regression analyses of the post-Lena period), as well as from more fragmentary statistical evidence at our disposal, that the actual effects on labor unrest of these higher levels of literacy and of the loosening and/or severing of workers' ties to the countryside and to the land made themselves felt most deeply in the course of the post-Lena strike wave in urban Russia, and within urban Russia in St. Petersburg and certain other large urban centers.

In the capital and in a number of other major cities, the effects of these processes of urbanization surfaced most sharply in the intensity and character that labor unrest assumed among younger urban-born and urban-bred workers, who provided so disporportionate a number of the most militant elements of the labor movement during these years. But also, and perhaps even more important, they were reflected in the ability of these young urban-born and urban-bred workers to draw into their wake a growing number of young immigrants – including significant numbers of young female and male workers recruited from the peasant estate – who came to these cities in search of work, and were recruited in significant numbers into industry during the years of renewed industrial expansion after the end of the decade. Two additional observations may help account for the chemistry of this exceptionally rapid absorption of young immigrants into the wave of labor unrest, especially in St. Petersburg, during the prewar period.

First, the most dramatic increases in the numbers and proportions of literate workers recorded in the demographic studies we have conducted of the evolution of St. Petersburg's population between 1900 and the end of the decade surface precisely in our indices for the youngest age groups of immigrants to the capital recruited from the peasant estate, and especially for young female immigrants, who were drawn in increasing numbers and proportions during these years into such branches of St Petersburg's industry as textiles and food processing.[16] The other observation, already advanced in

16. See Haimson, "Changements démographiques."

our earlier studies of the problem of social stability in urban Russia, is that it was precisely during the prewar period that many in this new wave of peasant immigrants, especially in the youngest age groups, underwent in a particularly dramatic and concentrated form under the impact of the Stolypin land reforms the *psychological* effects of the *legal* severance of their ties to the countryside and to the land.[17] When viewed in combination with the emergence by the eve of the war of a "critical mass" of young urban-born and urban-bred workers – more highly urbanized than had ever before been the case – the higher levels of literacy and weaker ties to the countryside and to the land that became characteristic of the young immigrants who poured into St. Petersburg industry during this period help explain the rapidity of their absorption into the wave of labor unrest, as well as the character that the most explosive forms of this unrest increasingly assumed, as the war approached, of a veritable "revolt of the young" among urban-bred and immigrant workers alike.[18]

In these respects, at least, our findings for the post-Lena period come far closer than those obtained from our analyses of the 1905–7 strike wave to supporting the distinction between the political cultures of urban and rural Russia that the Russian Marxists drew in their polemics with the Populists in the 1890s about the future of Russia's industrial working class.

But even more sharply than the indices we found correlated with the intensity of political strikes, what distinguished the findings of our analyses of the post-Lena strike wave from those we obtained for the 1905–7 period was the differences that they brought out in the patterns of labor unrest displayed on the eve of the war by politically more militant and less militant strata of workers in strikes classified as economic. We shall not seek to trace once again the various features of this polarization of labor unrest and its underlying dynamics. But it is worth reemphasizing that what we observed by the eve of the war among the strata of workers most sharply distinguished in interaction by our indices for urban concentration, average wage levels, and size of enterprise, as well as by the submerged factors jointly suggested by these three sets of indices, was the *mutual reinforcement* of the different impulses for their revolt against the existing order into a now far more generalized and more highly explosive struggle against *all organs* and *all forms* of the exercise of superordinate authority – inside and outside the workplace.

17. See Leopold H. Haimson, "The Problem of Social Stability in Urban Russia," part 1, *Slavic Review* 23, no. 4 (December 1964).

18. See Haimson, "Changements démographiques."

Appendix 1

Table 1.1. *Strike data for all enterprises in the Empire under Factory Inspection*
(1895–1914)

Year	No. of strikes	No. of strikers	% of strikers in economic strikes		% of strikers in political strikes
1895	68	31,195	—		—
1896	118	29,527	—	U	—
1897	145	59,870	—	n	—
1898	215	43,150	—	k	—
1899	189	57,498	—	n	—
1900	125	29,389	—	o	—
1901	164	32,218	—	w	—
1902	123	36,671	—	n	—
1903	550	86,832	—		—
1904	68	24,904	—		—
1905	13,995	2,863,173	36.7		63.3
1906	6,114	1,108,406	41.3		58.7
1907	3,573	740,074	27.0		73.0
1908	892	176,101	47.2		52.8
1909	340	64,166	87.0		13.0
1910	222	46,623	91.9		8.1
1911	466	105,110	92.0		8.0
1912	2,032	725,491	24.2		75.8
1913	2,404	887,096	43.4		56.6
1914	3,534	1,337,458	26.3		73.7

Appendix 2: Regression analyses of overall intensity of strikes in all industrial groups represented in all provinces under Factory Inspection, 1911–1913.

Table 2.1. *Regression of workers striking in 1911, dependent variable, all cases*

Independent variable	B	Beta		F
Pay of one adult male, 1911	.00660	.058		1.37
% of workers in ent., 500+	.08950	.141 ⎫		9.18
% of workers in ent., 1,000+	.01084	.022 ⎭ $r = .143$		.20
% of workers in urban centers	.03694	.074 ⎫		2.28
% of workers in the capital	−.02743	−.028 ⎭ $r = .081$		.35
% females	.11669	.202		16.72

N of cases = 441; R^2 = .08915; F = 7.080; DF = 6/434; a = −2.735

Table 2.2. *Regression of workers striking in 1912, dependent variable, all cases*

Independent variable	B	Beta		F
Pay of one adult male, 1912	.047	.137		11.06
% of workers in ent., 500+	.194	.104 ⎫		7.72
% of workers in ent., 1,000+	.302	.214 ⎭ .238		29.11
% of workers in urban centers	.380	.268 ⎫		43.28
% of workers in the capital	1.202	−.430 ⎭ .492		121.42
% females	−.160	.097		5.91

N of cases = 440; R^2 = .39700; F = 47.513; DF = 6/433; a = −7.899

Table 2.4. *Regression of workers striking in 1913, dependent variable, all cases*

Independent variable	B	Beta		F
Pay of one adult male, 1913	.066	.194		20.83
% of workers in ent., 500+	.246	.126 ⎫		10.23
% of workers in ent., 1,000+	.273	.190 ⎭ .229		20.57
% of workers in urban centers	.324	.217 ⎫		27.12
% of workers in the capital	.920	.316 ⎭ .372		60.39
% females	−.038	−.023		.30

N of cases = 456; R^2 = .31825; F = 34.933; DF = 6/449; a = −15.96688

Table 2.3. *Regression of workers striking in 1912, dependent variable, all cases*

Independent variable	Two-way interaction			Three-way interaction		
	B	Beta	F	B	Beta	F
Pay of one adult male, 1912	-.002	-.005	101	.006	.017	.14
% of workers in ent., 500+	-.246	-.133	1.99	-.212	-.114	1.51
% of workers in ent., 1,000+	-.277	-.198	2.42	-.051	-.036	.08
% of workers in urban centers	-.424	-.299	4.35	-.037	-.026	.03
% of workers in the capital	-2.859	-1.023	14.32	9.302	3.327	5.12
% females	-.162	-.098	7.39	-.133	-.081	5.18
INT: pay & size 500+	.001296	.107	4.06	.001149	.183	3.27
INT: pay & size 1,000+	.001620	.382	7.68	.000866	.204	2.16
INT: pay – capital	.007915	1.227	23.00	-.020710	-3.210	4.59
INT: size 500+, capital	.051947	.371	16.84	-.780241	-5.570	8.94
INT: size 1,000+, capital	-.007320	0.123	2.59	.124858	2.105	2.88
INT: pay – urb. cen.	.001451	.406	7.56	.000401	.112	.45
INT: size 500+, urb. cen.	.010897	.163	12.72	.003430	.051	.05
INT: size 1,000+, urb. cen.	.009210	.203	20.92	-.047912	-1.058	14.38
INT: pay, size 500+, capital				.001910	5.830	10.26
INT: pay, size 1,000+, capital				-.000276	-2.069	2.93
INT: pay, size 500+, urb. cen.				.000021	.127	.31
INT: pay, size 1,000+, urb. cen.				.000149	1.292	21.02

Two-way interaction: N of cases = 440; R^2 = .52783; F = 33.936; DF = 14/425; a = 7.680
Three-way interaction: N of cases = 440; R^2 = .56228; F = 30.045; DF = 18/421; a = 4.914

Table 2.5. *Regression of workers striking in 1913, dependent variable, all cases*

Independent variable	Two-way interaction			Three-way interaction		
	B	Beta	F	B	Beta	F
Pay of one adult male, 1913	-.003	.008	.03	.014	.040	.77
% of workers in ent., 500+	-.229	-.117	1.12	-.188	-.096	.79
% of workers in ent., 1,000+	-.455	-.317	6.67	-.209	-.146	1.47
% of workers in urban centers	-.641	-.430	10.96	-.196	-.131	.83
% of workers in the capital	-4.351	-1.494	24.28	-10.099	-3.467	3.26
% females	.002	.001	.00	.426	.026	.50
INT: pay & size 500+	.001444	.219	3.28	.001273	.193	2.67
INT: pay & size 1,000+	.002122	.500	14.05	.001256	.296	5.08
INT: pay – capital	.011650	1.776	36.30	.024828	3.784	3.72
INT: size 500+, capital	.007199	.047	.29	.836110	5.495	11.32
INT: size 1,000+, capital	-.000703	-.012	.03	-.242969	-4.104	17.95
INT: pay – urban centers	.002015	.528	13.91	.000670	.175	1.19
INT: size 500+, urb. cen.	.009027	.127	6.08	-.001912	-.027	.02
INT: size 1,000+, urb. cen.	.006516	.140	8.79	-.045036	-.970	18.80
INT: pay, size 500+, capital				-.001884	-5.454	11.01
INT: pay, size 1,000+, capital				.000538	4.146	17.49
INT: pay, size 500+, urb. cen.				-.000031	.189	.78
INT: pay, size 1,000+, urb. cen.				.000134	1.174	26.30

Two-way interaction: N of cases = 456; R^2 = .47048; F = 27.988; DF = 14/441
Three-way interaction: N of cases = 456; R^2 = .52912; F = 27.281; DF = 18/437; a = -.394

Appendix 3: Regression analyses of overall intensity of strikes in all industrial groups represented in all provinces under Factory Inspection except those in the Kingdom of Poland, 1911–1914

Table 3.1. *Regression of workers striking in 1911, using percentage of workers in capital (Poland excluded)*

Independent variables	B	Beta	F
Pay of one adult male	.0037	.031	.301
% of workers in ent., 500–1,000	.0630	.099	3.625
% of workers in ent., 1,000+	.0257	.053	.904
% of workers in urban centers	.0073	.015	.074
% of workers in the capital	−.0272	−.031	.328
% female	.1222	.211	14.299

N of cases = 365; R^2 = .07193; F = 4.62437; DF = 6/358; a = −1.742961

Table 3.3. *Regression of workers striking in 1912, using percentage of workers in capital (Poland excluded)*

Independent variables	B	Beta	F
Pay of one adult male	.0494	.135	9.184
% of workers in ent., 500–1,000	.1605	.083	4.178
% of workers in ent., 1,000+	.3521	.247	32.272
% of workers in urban centers	.3777	.357	35.221
% of workers in the capital	1.1989	.454	113.196
% female	−.2244	−.130	8.950

N of cases = 362; R^2 = .42560; F = 43.83904; DF = 6/355; a = −7.523250

149

Table 3.2. *Regression of workers striking in 1911, using percentage of workers in capital (Poland excluded)*

Independent variable	Two-way interaction			Three-way interaction		
	B	Beta	F	B	Beta	F
Pay of one adult male	.000578	.005	.005	.000817	.007	.009
% of workers in ent., 500–1,000	.048595	.076	.383	.067683	.106	.688
% of workers in ent., 1,000+	-.041827	-.086	.212	-.046012	-.094	.217
% of workers in urban centers	.001413	.003	.000	.067534	.136	.351
% of workers in the capital	-.147574	-.167	.220	.389025	.439	.166
% female	.126971	.219	14.935	.128917	.222	14.688
INT: pay & size 500–1,000	.000073	.030	.056	.000007	.003	.000
INT: pay & size 1,000+	.000228	.147	.559	.000265	.170	.591
INT: pay & capital	.000359	.171	.250	-.001057	-.502	.179
INT: pay & urban center	.000009	.007	.001	-.000142	-.105	.185
INT: size 500–1,000 & capital	-.002017	-.056	.240	-.028375	-.784	.217
INT: size 1,000+ & capital	.000111	.006	.004	.000953	.048	.002
INT: size 500–1,000 & urb. cen.				-.23412	-.818	3.638
INT: size 1,000+ & urb. cen.				.001053	.067	.024
INT: pay, size 1,000+ & capital				-.000002	-.045	.001
INT: pay, size 500–1,000 & capital				.000070	.780	.189
INT: pay, size 500–1,000 & urb. cen.				.000063	.824	3.623
INT: pay, size 1,000+ & urb. cen.				-.000005	-.114	.006

Two-way interaction: N of cases = 365; R^2 = .07590; F = 2.40928; DF = 12/352; a = -1.032548
Three-way interaction: N of cases = 365; R^2 = .08773; F = 1.84848; DF = 18/346; a = -1.211950

Table 3.4. *Regression of workers striking in 1912, using percentage of workers in capital (Poland excluded)*

Independent variable	Two-way interaction			Three-way interaction		
	B	Beta	F	B	Beta	F
Pay of one adult male	-.005747	-.016	.098	.006492	.018	.140
% of workers in ent., 500–1,000	-.198348	-.102	.980	-.135779	-.070	.502
% of workers in ent., 1,000+	-.347282	-.243	3.340	-.042022	-.029	.052
% of workers in urb. centers	-.547829	-.373	6.286	.019942	.014	.008
% of workers in the capital	-2.772071	-1.049	13.618	9.371253	3.546	5.638
% female	-.204521	-.119	9.430	-.162660	-.094	6.617
INT: pay & size 500–1,000	.001089	.161	2.127	.000808	.120	1.275
INT: pay & size 1,000+	.001995	.450	9.515	.000940	.212	2.227
INT: pay & capital	.007725	1.267	22.175	-.020875	-3.424	5.065
INT: pay & urban center	.001833	.475	9.655	.000228	.059	.135
INT: size 500–1,000 & capital	.052880	.400	17.631	-.785790	-5.937	9.842
INT: size 1,000+ & capital	-.008217	-.147	3.230	.126795	2.263	3.217
INT: size 500–1,000 & urb. cen.	.009942	.123	7.461	-.010294	-.127	.299
INT: size 1,000+ & urb. cen.	.010470	.223	23.472	-.064545	-1.437	25.058
INT: pay, size 1,000+ & capital				-.000281	-2.231	3.291
INT: pay, size 500–1,000 & capital				.001925	6.220	11.306
INT: pay, size 500–1,000 & urb. cen.				.000059	.268	1.301
INT: pay, size 1,000+ & urb. cen.				.000199	1.716	34.564

Two-way interaction: N of cases = 362; R^2 = .57345; F = 33.32122; DF = 14/347; a = 9.202872
Three-way interaction: N of cases = 362; R^2 = .58638; F = 30.56817; DF = 18/345; a = 9.244630

Table 3.5. *Regression of workers striking in 1913, using percentage of workers in capital (Poland excluded)*

Independent variables	B	Beta	F
Pay of one adult male	.0736	.199	17.543
% of workers in ent., 500–1,000	.1982	.099	5.275
% of workers in ent., 1,000+	.3091	.211	20.437
% of workers in urban centers	.2760	.177	15.143
% of workers in the capital	.8877	.319	49.665
% female	−.0520	−.030	.408

N of cases = 381; R^2 = .31374; F = 28.49713; DF = 6/374; a = −15.75633

Table 3.7. *Regression of workers striking in 1914, using percentage of workers in capital (Poland excluded)*

Independent variables	B	Beta	F
Pay of one adult male	.1192	.228	31.686
% of workers in ent., 500–1,000	.3159	.094	6.262
% of workers in ent., 1,000+	.3813	.159	16.900
% of workers in urban centers	.4886	.189	23.713
% of workers in the capital	2.3784	.516	174.181
% female	−.2881	−.100	6.037

N of cases = 385; R^2 = .49717; F = 62.28999; DF = 6/378; a = −23.13404

Table 3.6. *Regression of workers striking in 1913, using percentage of workers in capital (Poland excluded)*

Independent variable	Two-way interaction			Three-way interaction		
	B	Beta	F	B	Beta	F
Pay of one adult male	.001967	.005	.011	.016116	.044	.787
% of workers in ent., 500–1,000	-.161637	-.081	.422	-.041802	-.021	.031
% of workers in ent., 1,000+	-.611081	-.417	10.078	-.343368	-.234	3.382
% of workers in urban centers	-.670816	-.430	9.550	-.087847	.056	.143
% of workers in the capital	-4.290192	-1.546	21.892	-9.882891	-3.561	2.969
% female	.008199	.005	.013	.036369	.021	.272
INT: pay & size 500–1,000	.001108	.154	1.347	.000640	.089	.490
INT: pay & size 1,000+	.002828	.638	19.357	.001865	.421	8.845
INT: pay & capital	.011500	1.840	32.852	.024294	3.887	3.381
INT: pay & urban center	.002055	.492	10.584	.000225	.054	.107
INT: size 500–1,000 & capital	.008132	.056	.346	.825778	5.699	10.486
INT: size 1,000+ & capital	-.002553	-.045	.320	-.242919	-4.310	17.038
INT: size 500–1,000 & urb. cen.	.005426	.117	4.637	-.041181	-.887	14.010
INT: pay, size 1,000+ & capital				.000535	4.328	16.407
INT: pay, size 500–1,000 & capital				-.001857	-5.645	10.153
INT: pay, size 500–1,000 & urb. cen.				.000118	.506	4.548
INT: pay, size 1,000+ & urb. cen.				.000123	1.077	19.149

Two-way interaction: *N* of cases = 381; R^2 = .47794; *F* = 23.93358; *DF* = 14/366; *a* = 4.106357
Three-way interaction: *N* of cases = 381; R^2 = .54569; *F* = 24.15674; *DF* = 18/362; *a* = -.1217619

Table 3.8. *Regression of workers striking in 1914, using percentage of workers in capital (Poland excluded)*

Independent variables	Two-way interaction			Three-way interaction		
	B	Beta	F	B	Beta	F
Pay of one adult male	.063197	.121	8.076	.079993	.153	14.094
% of workers in ent., 500–1,000	.333449	.099	1.559	.385430	.115	2.271
% of workers in ent., 1,000+	-1.216154	-.508	21.758	-.782814	-.327	9.270
% of workers in urban centers	-1.103051	-.426	9.813	.029508	-.011	.006
% of workers in the capital	-10.67950	-2.317	18.187	-15.33805	-3.327	1.402
% female	-.118876	-.041	1.272	-.082163	-.029	.668
INT: pay & size 500–1,000	-.000560	-.005	.422	-.000774	-.076	.919
INT: pay & size 1,000+	.004664	.694	34.135	.003238	.482	16.764
INT: pay & capital	.022881	2.529	28.833	.032730	3.618	1.643
INT: pay & urban centers	.003010	.475	11.888	.000129	.020	.016
INT: size 500–1,000 & capital	.099296	.376	13.311	.625339	2.368	2.378
INT: size 1,000+ & capital	-.009130	-.105	2.262	-.077594	-.986	28.424
INT: size 500–1,000 & urb. cen.	.022489	.150	13.513	.0415585	.278	1.342
INT: size 1,000 & urb. cen.	.008246	.105	5.607	-.077594	-.986	28.424
INT: pay, size 1,000+ & capital				.000202	1.195	.677
INT: pay, size 500–1,000 & capital				.001078	-1.985	1.720
INT: pay, size 500–1,000 & urb. cen.				-.000041	-.107	.195
INT: pay, size 1,000+ & urb. cen.				.000215	1.151	36.891

Two-way interaction: *N* of cases = 385; R^2 = .62283; *F* = 43.64171; *DF* = 14/370; *a* = -7.101466
Three-way interaction: *N* of cases = 385; R^2 = .66371; *F* = 40.13066; *DF* = 18/366; *a* = -12.72413

Appendix 4: Regression analyses of overall intensity of strikes in all industrial groups represented in all provinces under Factory Inspection, 1905–1907

Table 4.1. *Regression of percentage of workers striking in 1905*

Independent variable	Without interaction			With two-way interaction			
	B	Beta	F	B	Beta	F	r
Pay of one adult male	.814	.426	43.022	.794	.416	41.560	.502
% of workers in ent., 500–1,000	.117	.013	.048	−.428	−.047	.573	−.047
% of workers in ent., 1,000+	−.114	−.017	.075	−.035	−.054	.623	.117
% female	1.944	.194	9.763	1.802	.180	8.320	.235
% of workers in urban centers	.633	.089	1.965	−.589	−.082	.769	.261
% of workers in the capital	1.627	.142	5.689	−.266	−.023	.023	.253
INT: capital & size 1,000+				.0248	.092	1.005	.234
INT: capital & size 500–1,000				.0524	.116	.900	.248
INT: urb. cen. & size 1,000+				.0172	.088	1.390	.213
INT: urb. cen. & size 500–1,000				.0613	.192	6.438	.274

Without interaction: N of cases = 227; multiple R = .56235; R^2 = .31624; F = 16.95841; DF = 6/220; a = −135.9450
With two-way interaction: N of cases = 227; multiple R = .58415; R^2 = .34123; F = 11.18856; DF = 10/216; a = 111.7876; F (INT) = 2.05

Table 4.2. *Regression of percentage of workers striking in 1906*

Independent variable	Without interaction			With two-way interaction			
	B	Beta	F	B	Beta	F	r
Pay of one adult male	.362	.447	54.496	.308	.380	34.326	.533
% of workers in ent., 500–1,000	.030	.008	.020	−.013	−.003	.004	−.053
% of workers in ent., 1,000+	−.170	−.061	1.069	−.175	−.063	1.153	.112
% female	1.303	.307	28.038	1.275	.301	26.954	.334
% of workers in urban centers	.510	.169	8.144	−1.358	−.449	3.683	.375
% of workers in the capital	.228	.047	.720	−.344	−.071	.040	.160
INT: pay and capital				.0016	.139	.151	.163
INT: pay and urban centers				.0053	.663	7.435	.431

Without interaction: N of cases $= 227$; multiple $R = .63610$; $R^2 = .40462$; $F = 24.91869$; $DF = 6/220$; $a = -81.67934$
With two-way interaction: N of cases $= 227$; multiple $R = .65151$; $R^2 = .42446$; $F = 20.09683$; $DF = 8/218$; $a = -65.57334$; $F(\text{INT}) = 3.76$

Table 4.3. *Regression of percentage of workers striking in 1907*

Independent variable	Without interaction			With two-way interaction			
	B	Beta	F	B	Beta	F	r
Pay of one adult male	.144	.262	19.135	.140	.254	18.556	.419
% of workers in ent., 500–1,000	.078	.029	.299	−.026	−.010	.031	.005
% of workers in ent., 1,000+	−.036	−.019	.105	−.064	−.034	.297	.063
% female	.148	.051	.806	.112	.039	.463	.112
% of workers in urban centers	.183	.089	2.322	.089	.043	.255	.139
% of workers in the capital	1.684	.511	86.309	.572	.174	1.557	.570
INT: size 500 & urb. cen.				.0099	.107	2.410	.157
INT: size 1,000+ & urb. cen.				−.0020	−.035	.259	.053
INT: size 500 & capital				.0242	.186	2.755	.529
INT: size 1,000+ & capital				.0179	.230	7.560	.525

Without interaction: N of cases = 227; multiple R = .64654; R^2 = .41801; F = 26.33565; DF = 6/220; a = −19.19771
With two-way interaction: N of cases = 227; multiple R = .66943; R^2 = .44814; F = 17.54004; DF = 10/216; a = −14.63583; F (INT) = 2.95

157

Appendix 5: Regression analyses of overall intensity of strikes in all industrial groups represented in all provinces under Factory Inspection except those in the Kingdom of Poland, 1905–1907

Table 5.1. *Regression of percentage of workers striking in 1905 (Poland excluded)*

Independent variables	Without interaction			With interaction			
	B	Beta	F	B	Beta	F	r
Pay of one adult male, 1905	.90080	.44386	39.169	.88269	.43494	38.331	.518
% of workers in ent., 500–1,000	-.27322	-.02942	.219	-.81502	-.08775	1.788	-.029
% of workers in ent., 1,000+	-.66934	-.10191	2.117	-.79090	-.12042	2.637	.084
% female	2.63285	.25695	13.713	2.47639	.24168	12.040	.220
% of workers in urb. cent.	1.07791	.14872	4.901	.06098	.00841	.007	.312
% of workers in the capital	1.61204	.15342	5.456	-.29782	-.02834	.031	.296
INT: size 1,000+ & capital				.02759	.11149	1.315	.270
INT: size 500–1,000 & urb. cen.				.066061	.20894	6.814	.321
INT: size 500–1,000 & capital				.04835	.11690	.810	.287
INT: size 1,000+ & urb. cen.				.00306	.01624	.040	.213

Without interaction: N of cases = 186; multiple R = .58486; R^2 = .34206; F = 23.52492; DF = 6/179; a = −166.3143
With interaction: N of cases = 186; multiple R = .63204; R^2 = .39948; F = 11.64122; DF = 10.175; a = −144.8258

Table 5.2. *Regression of percentage of workers striking in 1906 (Poland excluded)*

Independent variables	Without interaction			With interaction			
	B	Beta	F	B	Beta	F	r
Pay of one adult male, 1906	.15255	.26201	14.679	.11675	.20051	7.889	.451
% of workers in ent., 500–1,000	.19592	.07352	1.474	.15714	.05897	.966	.056
% of workers in ent., 1,000+	−.06017	−.03193	.224	−.10541	−.05594	.689	.083
% female	.56982	.19384	8.393	.61487	.20916	9.804	.239
% of workers in urban centers	.75470	.36295	31.394	−.79625	−.38293	1.703	.434
% of workers in the capital	.82196	.27266	18.537	.18526	.06146	.025	.335
INT: pay & capital				.00169	.23459	.358	.336
INT: pay & urb. cen.				.00456	.78166	6.783	.467

Without interaction: N of cases = 186; multiple R = .64409; R^2 = .41485; F = 21.15045; DF = 6/179; a = −30.77727
With interaction: N of cases = 186; multiple R = .66109; R_3^2 = .43705; F = 17.17659; DF = 6/179; a = −20.83295

Table 5.3. *Regression of percentage of workers striking in 1907 (Poland excluded)*

Independent variables	Without interaction			With interaction			
	B	Beta	F	B	Beta	F	r
Pay of one adult male, 1907	.15559	.25493	14.591	.15196	.24898	14.491	.442
% of workers in ent., 500–1,000	.05088	.01821	.095	−.07949	−.02846	.277	.017
% of workers in ent., 1,000+	−.06708	−.03396	.266	−.12057	−.06104	.782	.044
% female	.05917	.01920	.086	.021949	.00420	.004	.058
% of workers in urban centers	.16622	.07626	1.455	.00763	.00350	.001	.103
% of workers in the capital	1.68295	.53258	74.261	.48726	.15420	1.050	.605
INT: size 500–1000, & urb. cen.				.01224	.12874	2.984	.141
INT: size 1,000+ & capital				.01887	.25360	7.849	.556
INT: size 1,000+ & urb. cen.				−.00076	−.01333	.031	.046
INT: size 500–1,000 & capital				.02667	.21443	3.143	.560

Without interaction: N of cases = 186; multiple R = .66538; R^2 = .44273; F = 23.70102; DF = 6/179; a = −19.13455
With interaction: N of cases = 186; multiple R = .69242; R^2 = .47945; F = 16.11801; DF = 10/175; a = −13.35053

Appendix 6: Regression analyses of strikes by causes in all provinces, January–July 1914

Table 6.1. *Regression analysis with percentage of workers engaged in political strikes, all provinces, January–July 1914*

Independent variable	Without interaction			With two-way interaction			With three-way interaction		
	B	Beta	F	B	Beta	F	B	Beta	F
% of workers in urban centers	1.1689	.5985	34.307	−6.5193	−3.3380	45.353	−0.2261	−0.1158	.006
% of workers in ent. 1,000 +	.2601	.1327	2.088	−0.4119	−0.2101	.917	−0.3285	−0.1676	.621
Average pay	.0516	.1199	1.380	−0.9235	−0.0546	.342	−0.0118	−0.0275	.092
INT: urban & pay				.0192	4.0394	51.127	.0012043	.2530	.021
INT: 1,000+ & pay				.0020	.3444	1.855	.001759	.2931	1.429
INT: 1,000+ & urban				−0.0030	−0.0572	.141	−0.161091	−2.9907	5.465
INT: 1,000+, urban & pay							.00044961	3.5755	5.328

Without interaction: No. of cases = 67; R^2 = .4902; F = 20.1999; DF = 3/63; a = −16.5321
With two-way interaction: No. of cases = 67; R^2 = .7917; F = 38.0151; DF = 6/60; a = 6.7957
With three-way interaction: No. of cases = 67; R^2 = .8089; F = 35.6959; DF = 7/59; a = 4.0176

Table 6.2. *Regression analysis with percentage of workers engaged in strikes over hours, all provinces, January–July 1914*

Independent variable	Without interactions			With two-way interactions		
	B	Beta	F	B	Beta	F
% in urban centers	.0209	.4309	13.605	−0.0027	−0.0572	.111
% in ent. 1,000+	.0116	.2379	5.134	−0.0411	−0.8423	6.823
Average pay	.0010	.0957	.673	−0.0026	−0.2453	3.150
INT: 1,000+ & urban				.0006502	.4847	6.806
INT: size 1,000 & pay				.0001764	1.180	10.045

Without interactions: No. of cases = 67; R^2 = .3336; F = 10.516; DF = 3/63; a = −0.3239
With two-way interactions: No. of cases = 67; R^2 = .5361; F = 14.103; DF = 5/61; a = .7368

Table 6.3. *Regression analysis with percentage of workers engaged in strikes over order, all provinces, January–July 1914*

Independent variable	Without interactions			With two-way interactions		
	B	Beta	F	B	Beta	F
% in urban centers	.0463	.2304	3.520	−0.3830	−1.9021	6.147
% in ent. 1,000+	.0611	.3025	7.511	.0550	.2722	6.676
Average pay	.0083	.1873	2.329	.0062	.1412	1.441
Urban & pay				.0010	2.1791	7.909

Without interactions: No. of cases = 67; R^2 = .2637; F = 7.521; DF = 3/63; a = −2.2795
With two-way interaction: No. of cases = 67; R^2 = .3470; F = 8.2369; DF = 4/62; a = −1.5469

Table 6.4. *Regression analysis with percentage of workers engaged in wage disputes, all provinces, January–July 1914*

	Without interaction		
Indepedent variable	*B*	Beta	*F*
% in urban centers	−.162938	−.1864	1.918
% in ent. 1,000+	.109848	.1252	1.071
Average pay	.066236	.3440	6.542
INT: urban & pay	—	—	—
INT: 1,000+ & pay	—	—	—
INT: 1,000+ & urban	—	—	—
INT: 1,000+ & urban & pay	—	—	—

Without interaction: No. of cases = 67; R^2 = .1157; F = 2.7481; DF = 3/63; a = −11.8577
No significant interactions.

Appendix 7: Regression analyses of strikes by causes in all provinces except St. Petersburg *Guberniia*, January–July 1914

Table 7.1. *Regression analysis with percentage of workers engaged in political strikes, January–July 1914 (St. Petersburg excluded)*

	Without interactions			With interactions		
Independent variables	*B*	Beta	*F*	*B*	Beta	*F*
% of workers urban centers	0.640	0.489	19.94	−3.880	−2.964	17.10
% of workers in enterprises, 500–1,000	0.025	0.009	0.01	−0.082	−0.030	0.12
% of workers in enterprises, 1,000+	0.199	0.169	2.80	0.159	0.135	2.44
Average pay of an adult male	0.0458	0.174	2.44	0.024	0.090	0.86
INT: urban & pay	—	—	—	0.1178	3.517	23.61

Without interactions: No. of cases = 66; R^2 = 0.398; F = 10.07; DF = 4/61; a = −12.671
With interactions: No. of cases = 66; R^2 = 0.568; F = 15.77; DF = 5/60; a = −4.426; F (int) = 23.61; sig (F (int)) = 0.0001

Table 7.2. *Regression analysis with percentage of workers engaged in strikes over hours, January–July 1914 (St. Petersburg excluded)*

Independent variables	Without interactions			With interactions		
	B	Beta	F	B	Beta	F
% of workers in urban centers	0.015	0.314	6.42	-0.002	-0.044	0.06
% of workers in enterprises, 500–1,000	0.004	0.038	0.11	0.00053	0.005	0.003
% of workers in enterprises, 1,000+	0.011	0.248	4.68	-0.040	-0.921	6.45
Average pay of an adult male	0.0010	0.105	0.70	-0.0026	-0.262	2.90
INT: pay & size 1,000+	—	—	—	0.0001748	1.270	9.66
INT: urban & size 1,000+	—	—	—	0.000553	0.377	4.12

Without interactions: No. of cases = 66; R^2 = 0.227; F = 4.48; DF = 4/61; a = -0.346
With interactions: No. of cases = 66; R^2 = 0.424; F = 7.24; DF = 6/59; a = 0.716

Table 7.3. *Regression analysis with percentage of workers engaged in strikes over order, January–July 1914 (St. Petersburg excluded)*

Independent variables	Without interactions			With interactions		
	B	Beta	F	B	Beta	F
% of workers in urban centers	0.048	0.213	3.01	-0.705	-3.162	14.05
% of workers in enterprises, 500–1,000	-0.007	-0.017	0.02	-0.025	-0.056	0.30
% of workers in enterprises, 1,000+	0.062	0.307	7.30	0.055	0.274	7.21
Average pay of an adult male	0.008	0.182	2.11	0.0045	0.100	0.77
INT: urban & pay	—	—	—	0.00196	3.437	16.29

Without interactions: No. of cases = 66; R^2 = 0.239; F = 4.79; DF = 4/61; a = -2.154
With interactions: No. of cases = 66; R^2 = 0.402; F = 4.79; DF = 5/60; a -0.780; F (int) = 16.29; sig (F (int)) = 0.0002

Table 7.4. *Regression analysis with percentage of workers engaged in strikes over wages, January–July 1914 (St. Petersburg excluded)*

| | Without interaction | | |
Independent variable	B	Beta	F
% in urban centers	−.177568	−.1805	1.885
% in enterprises 1,000+	.10⁹180	.1224	1.021
Average pay	.066062	.3336	6.409
INT: urban & pay	—	—	—
INT: 1,000+ & pay	––	—	—
INT: 1,000+ & urban	—	—	—

Without interaction: No. of cases = 66; R^2 = .1153; F = 2.6933; DF = 3/62; a = −11.7384
No significant two-way interactions.

7

Strikers in Revolution: Russia, 1917

DIANE KOENKER, WILLIAM G. ROSENBERG

Conceptualization

A comprehensive analysis of the strike movement in Russia during 1917 must have two distinct but related objectives. It must attempt to understand the strike process as a specific aspect of the broader patterns of Russian labor activism, relating such elements as the scope, intensity, duration, and outcome of strikes to the general social history of Russian workers; and it must also be an investigation of the ways in which elements common to the strike process generally, in Russia and elsewhere, both affected and were affected by the particular elements of the Russian revolutionary conjuncture. As such, a study of strikes in 1917 contrasts both to "longitudinal" studies, which analyze strikes over substantial periods of time, and to episodic studies, which look in detail at, say, the American Pullman strike of 1894 or the British general strike of 1926. An investigation such as ours is, in effect, a cross-sectional analysis of what amounts to a single strike wave, but one that has as its primary focus not so much the strike wave itself, as the interrelationships between this particular form of labor protest and the historical context in which it occurs.

For the comparative purposes of this volume, however, we minimize our attention in this paper to Russia's historical context, although that is the primary focus of our larger work. Our goal is to describe the role in Russia during 1917 of several factors that other studies in this volume have found to be important, and to make available the general results of our statistical analysis. We highlight, of course, those that seem of particular significance to Russia, and present as well some comparative data on strikes in Moscow and Petrograd as a way of displaying the differential patterns of two major urban centers caught up in the same general processes of revolutionary change. But for the most part, we will save for Part IV of this volume some brief observations about the

167

Russian historical context more broadly, and the likely reciprocal relationship between strikes and the Russian revolutionary conjuncture.

One obvious feature of Russia's historical context must, however, be emphasized at the outset. Virtually by definition, the Revolution of 1917 – and all similar revolutionary settings – involve great political uncertainty and unpredictability, as well as rapidly changing socioeconomic conditions. For workers in particular, the "ground rules" of strikes, which had remained more or less stable before the revolution, began in 1917 to dissolve. What is both exciting and analytically troublesome in investigating strikes in these circumstances is that the range of workers' assumptions about these rules rapidly expanded as events unfolded, changing the very nature of some strikes even as they were occurring. Labor activism and the strike movement in particular contributed simultaneously to defining new assumptions, both about strikes themselves and the possibilities of economic, political, and even social change. In other words, the strike process itself helped shape a new range of beliefs, attitudes, and values in 1917, affecting the limits of political and economic possibility, just as more broadly, the dynamics of proletarian activism as a whole structured the contest for power and ultimately gave historical definition to the nature of proletarian dictatorship as realized and implemented by Lenin and the Bolsheviks. Thus the quantitative data and objective relationships we will describe must ultimately be integrated not only with aspects of a rapidly changing political, social, and economic milieu, but also, even if here only by implication, with complex and analytically quite slippery subjective material, including most particularly the values and perspectives of those who exercised power, those who organized workers and others into contending social groups, and even those who had the more prosaic task of recording and reporting strikes themselves.

Data and method

The data base for this project consists of material on some 1,019 strikes that took place betwen March 3, when the Grand Duke Mikhail Aleksandrovich refused the throne and the Provisional Government came to power, and October 25, when the Second Congress of Soviets endorsed the Bolshevik takeover. Some 60% involved individual enterprises of all sorts; the remainder were multienterprise strikes.

For our purposes, the most appropriate unit of measurement for strikes in 1917, and one the data itself compels us to use in drawing aggregate pictures, is not the individual enterprise but the unit commonly used in revolutionary Russia: a work stoppage with common goals. On March 12, for example, a one-day strike-demonstration celebrating the new government took place in Vladimir, involving workers from some twenty-one different enterprises. The

Factory Inspectorate, which continued to function in these weeks, recorded twenty-one separate strikes but we regard this incident as a single strike. Of the 458 strikes recorded by the Factory Inspectorate between March 3 and October 25 included in our data, we thus count only 188 separate incidents. If we were able systematically to use the Factory Inspectorate's single enterprise measure, we estimate that the 1,019 strikes in our data set might balloon more than ten-fold, since so many nonindustrial enterprises were small stores or shops. For industrial strikes, we estimate that a minimum of 2,900 strikes took place between March 3 and October 25 using the Factory Inspectorate's method of counting, approximately 2,400 nonpolitical ("economic") strikes, and some 500 political strikes with demands employers themselves had no ability to grant. This figure seems roughly comparable to the large but unspecified number that the leading Soviet historian of strikes, A. M. Lisetskii, indicates took place in the same period.[1] Soviet labor historians generally rely on the Factory Inspector reports, although recognizing their inadequacies. There has yet to be any definite count of the number of strikes in Russia during 1917, and in all likelihood, there never will be.[2]

Our information is voluminous but of uneven quality. We have recorded separately information we consider "objective" or incontrovertible, and subjective data that might be biased by the perspective of the reporter. Objective information includes factory location, industry and branch, type of ownership and management, the date the strike began, its length in days, and whether the strike was confined to a single factory or extended to more than one production unit. Subjective data include the size of the enterprise and the number of strikers, whether employees or other groups struck along with

1. A. M. Lisetskii, *Bol'sheviki vo glave massovvkh stachek*, (Kishinev, 1974). See also by the same author, "K voprosu o statistike zabastovok v Rossii v period podogotovki velikoi oktiabr'skoi sotsialisticheskoi revoliutsii (mart-oktiabr' 1917 g)," *Trudy Kafedry Istorii KPSS Khar'kovskogo Ordena Trudovogo Kransnogo Znameni Gosudarstvennogo Universiteta imeni A. M. Gor'kogo*, vol. 7 (Kharkov, 1959), pp. 271–83; "O kharaktere stachechnoi bor'by proletariata Rossii v period podgotovki Oktiabr'skoi revoliutsii (mart-oktiabr' 1917 g.)," *Tezisy dokladov ob'edinennoi nauchnoi sessii instituta istorii AN MSSR i nauchnogo soveta ordelenii istoricheskikh nauk AN SSSR po probleme Velikogo Oktiabr'skoi Revoliutsii, posviashchennoi istorii sots. rev. v Moldavii* (Kishenev, 1961), pp. 7–12; "O nekotorykh voprosakh kolichestvennoi kharakteristiki zabastovochnogo dvizheniia v Rossii v period podgotovki Oktiabra," *Kishinevskii Gosuniversitet. Uchenve Zapiski*, 65 (1963), pp. 3–15; "K voprosu o mezhdunarodnom znachenii opyta stachechnoi bor'by proletariata Rossii v period podgotovki velikoi oktiabr'skoi sotsialisticheskoi revoliutsii," *Kishinevskii Gosuniversitet. Uchenve Zapiski* 104, (1968), pp. 299–309; "Predvaritel'nye itogi geografi cheskogo i otraslevogo raspredeleniia stachek v Rossii, ikh deliatel'nosti i resul'tatichnosti (mart-oktiabr' 1917 g.)," *Kishinevskii Gosuniversitet. Uchenye Zapiski* 112 (1969), pp. 365–85.

2. Our data have been collected from available Soviet archives (Ts GIA; SSSR, fond 23), and from all available published sources, including more than two dozen major newspapers, and all major documents, collections and chronicles. Included are the scores of "anniversary" volumes published by various Soviet regional party committees in 1957 and 1967, as well as the important collections issued in the 1920s. A complete bibliography can be found in our *Strikes and Revolution in Russia, 1917* (Princeton, forthcoming).

workers, or against them, information on the participation of trade unions, factory committees, and strike committees. We also include here reports of the "mood" of strikers, whether violence occurred, mediation efforts, and outcome. Most important is a listing of strikers' demands. We have been able to record up to eight demands reported by any source about a particular strike, and have listed them both in fifty-two major categories and in a drastically collapsed set of five categories: wages, hours and conditions, issues of control, issues of dignity, and politics.[3]

In addition to this basic strike data set we have also constructed a file of data organized by province. Here we have aggregated basic strike material for each of Russia's eighty-eight provinces, calculating strike propensities (described below), the distribution of strikes over time and according to demands, length of strikes, outcome, and degree of organization. We have combined this with aggregate socioeconomic data for each province, extracted from tsarist statistical reports and Soviet-period censuses. Included here is information on wages (nominal and real), productivity, age level, gender ratios, literacy rates, and whether or not workers had ties to the land. We include as well information about provincial level votes for the Constituent Assembly elections as a way of presenting general information about the relative mix of political affiliations in different regions. This aggregated data file is the source for our bivariate and multivariate regression analyses, some of which are discussed below.

There seem to be, on the whole, three major problems with our strike material. First, it is incomplete, although sufficient quantitatively to indicate major trends and relationships, which is our primary objective.[4] Second, we have relatively low frequencies for some rather interesting variables.[5] Third,

3. We have arranged our subjective data so that there is one strike record for each strike report: Some strikes were reported in as many as forty different sources – in all, our strikes are recorded in almost 3,000 separate entries. The analysis of reporting bias that this method allows will be discussed in our larger work; the strike analysis reported here is based on a file consisting of a single record for each strike, combining objective and subjective data (including our best guess of the data that varies from source to source, such as the number of workers on strike).

4. This problem simply cannot be remedied, however, on the basis of available resources, and its implications are unclear. While we clearly cannot present a definitive history of Russian strikes in 1917, our data for each strike provide much more detail than that provided by the Factory Inspectorate and generally used by historians up until now. All of our quantitative arguments and interpretations, however, are subject to considerable margins of error.

5. We have information on the participation of women in strikes, for example, in only 41 cases. Of the 1,019 strikes that we know took place between March 3 and October 25, we can estimate the number of strikers with some confidence in only 626 cases. We know relatively little about the existence of strike funds, the role such resources might have played, or the participation of outsiders in support of picketing and other strike activity. Our material on the mood of strikers is similarly incomplete. We found descriptions of workers' attitudes for less than 10% of our strikes, and even here, the diversity of reports makes the data quite inadequate as a description of reality. Again, the problem seems hard to remedy. We are able to use some of our more limited data to interpret biases in reporting, or by isolating all strikes, for example, that report women's participa-

and closely related, our data tend in some important areas to be imprecise, partly because the turmoil of 1917 prevented accurate record-keeping, and because much of value was also lost in the civil war. Factory employment statistics fall into this area, as do figures about wage levels, change in wages over time, productivity, and the like. The fact that 1917 itself was a period of constant change raises further problems about using constant figures across even a six or seven-month span. Many provincial employment statistics, for example, are given as of January 1917, the base month for most Central Statistical Administration data. Obviously, changes had occurred in many places by the following August or September.[6]

These problems have largely dictated the nature of our statistical methodology. For the most part, we use simple descriptive statistical tools: Frequency distributions, rates, and measures of central tendencies (means and medians) furnish much of our quantitative insight. With certain types of data, we can be more statistically rigorous, and we shall present below some of the results of our bivariate and multivariate least-squares regression analysis.

In both kinds of analysis, one of the most useful measures of strike activity has been the notion of strike propensity, a measure that takes into account differences in the numbers of workers employed in the various striking units, whether industry or province. A common measurement of strike activity is the ratio of strikers to workers in a given unit, which we would label, along with Haimson and Petrusha, "strike intensity." As a measure of strike activism we prefer an index that more easily allows us to show comparisons between different major industrial sectors or provinces. This index, commonly called "strike propensity," is the more complex ratio that compares any given industry or province's percentage share of the total number of strikers to its percentage share of the labor force. This method gives a reasonably accurate measure of the relative inclination of different industrial groups in provinces to strike. One can also make industry-by-industry comparisons on this basis between 1917 and previous years.[7]

tion and looking at them independently. In general, however, we simply have had to set aside material that is of marginal statistical significance.

6. Once again, we are limited by the data at hand. In making some calculations, such as those for strike propensities, we have estimated the variations in employment month by month, by distributing equally the annual decrease. This clearly leads to some distortion, but we think this and similar problems are surmountable if we present our findings judiciously, and with ample allowance for error.

7. Using this measure, a strike propensity of 1 equals the propensity of all workers together to strike; it means also that a group's share of strikers is no greater or smaller than one might expect given that group's share of the labor force. Propensities less than 1 signal workers less prone to strike than average (regardless of actual number); propensities several time greater than 1 indicate a strike propensity several times that of all workers taken together. On strike propensity, see K. G. J. C. Knowles, *Strikes – A Study in Industrial Conflict* (Oxford, 1948).

Some general findings

The nature and scope of strikes

The extraordinary changes occurring in Russia's political, economic, and social circumstances in the seven short months between March and October might be distinguished analytically into three general sorts. First and most obvious was the familiar breakdown of political order at the center. From conditions of relative stability at the time the Provisional Government and Petrograd Soviet assumed their respective shares of state power in February, the country found itself by September in utter political disarray. Political structures began to disintegrate rapidly during the first coalition cabinet between May and early July, as the military offensive collapsed, and could not be stabilized when Kerensky and his colleagues assumed power in midsummer on the basis, essentially, of the soviet's program. Even before General Kornilov's mutiny in August, Russia's highly centralized traditional political institutions, concentrated in Moscow, Petrograd, and provincial capitals, no longer exercised effective power on a local level. Simultaneously, the roughly parallel concentration of power in the Petrograd Soviet leadership, functioning through the All-Russian Central Executive Committee, rapidly gave way to the potentially anarchic pattern of local soviet control, exercised by myriad of different groups still generally concentrated, however, in offices or factories located around traditional administrative and commercial centers.

Second, and equally familiar, there was the emergence in the countryside of a spontaneous, irreversible, agrarian revolution, a process of land seizure, gentry expropriation, and deep social polarization occurring so rapidly that Lenin's famous Decree on Land in November was essentially ex post facto. Peasant revolt was fundamentally local in origin (although obviously tied to the failures of tsarist agrarian and social policies), and almost entirely local in execution. But it erupted "upward" in a devastating assault on superordinate principles of law and traditional social relations, crippling the ability of government and soviet leaders alike to create new, more equitable, and more democratic legal and social structures. Revolution in the countryside also acted as a powerful magnet on many workers, particularly in textiles, who kept ties to their villages. Most important, it greatly reinforced, and certainly did much to precipitate, the broader processes of social polarization, both urban and rural, by which Russians everywhere were rapidly defining themselves into competing social camps.

Third, and perhaps less obvious, there were critical changes in Russia's economy and economic relations. Private and foreign capital, hopeful in the spring about investment opportunities in a liberal capitalist system, had by the fall virtually ceased to finance production. Much of Russian industry worked on the basis of goods and orders in "pipelines" being shut off at their source. A growing scarcity of goods, concentrated along with the breakdown of state power in major cities and administrative centers, led quickly to the emergence of black and grey markets, and by the fall to a chaotic system of commodity exchange in which there was for a time virtually no effective legal tender. And obviously, as ordinary and traditional measurements of real value became increasingly unstable, salaries and wages became increasingly problematic, along with the costs of production, a process that, among other things, soon wreaked havoc on efforts to establish orderly and meaningful labor – management relations.

Against this sketchiest of backgrounds, the first important point to be made about the strike movement as a whole in 1917 is that it was at once heavily concentrated in centers of administrative power and in vital industrial sectors in 1917, which gave the very act of striking considerable political significance, but simultaneously well diffused throughout the country, both geographically and in terms of industrial production. The great preponderance of strikes occurred in the cities of Moscow (24%) and Petrograd (12%), as well as in the central and northern industrial regions around them (17% and 7%, respectively). Yet strikes also extended into every province of the Empire in 1917, and virtually every city and town. Our data cover strikes in more than 170 different administrative localities. Fewest strikes are recorded for Western and Eastern Siberia, and for Turkestan, where most of Russia's domestic cotton was produced, but even these areas witnessed a number of work stoppages, and certainly enough so that the strike movement itself became general experience in 1917, just as it had in 1905.

The import of this is several-fold. For one thing, the common experience of strikes for workers throughout the country undoubtedly provided a basis *in action* on which otherwise distant arguments over the nature of Russia's general struggles could easily find specific, local reference. Strike actions everywhere meant participation in the process of confrontation and the development of class consciousness. They engendered as well some ability to perceive through the social realities of local struggles what political activists often discussed at congresses and in the press in essentially theoretical and abstract terms, and hence were an important "primer" of sorts in the nature of revolutionary activism. National leaders of all persuasions could not avoid recognizing the power of labor mobilized from below; others, more locally, could hardly fail to see the complementarity of peasant – worker activism, as well as the absence of effective mechanisms anywhere to negotiate grievances.

Thus, the geographical concentration of strikes around Moscow and Petrograd was undoubtedly a most important reflection of workers' power in 1917, a power that, partly because of this concentration, soon became disproportionate to the size of the Russian labor force relative to the population as a whole. For

173

many in Petrograd and Moscow it *seemed* as if the country as a whole was awash in strikes, even though, as we will show, the reality was not much different than before the February Revolution. Here, moreover, the distinction between strikes and demonstrations was of some considerable importance. The latter may well have been a source of constant concern to government officials, particularly at times of high political crisis during the last week of April – when protestors excoriated the liberal foreign minister Miliukov over Russia's war aims – during the July days, or in Moscow in August, when more than 400,000 demonstrated against Kerensky's Moscow Conference. But the concentration of strikes in the major centers of Russia's war industry production reflected a potential power far greater than the demonstrators', and brought to the fore issues concerning who would exercise this power both within and outside the workplace.

These concerns were all the greater because of the numerical intensity of strikes in 1917, and because of their industrial concentration. Approximately one-fifth of all strikes (and almost 30% of all industrial strikes) continued to be in the metalworking industry, just as they were before the change of regimes in February, despite new wage concessions and the continued relative well-being of workers in this sector. Strikes were spread rather uniformly here between workers in foundries and smelting mills, and those in machine and machine tool construction, but the highest concentrations were in plants with their own blast furnaces (which included both skilled and unskilled workers) and in iron and steel machine manufacturing plants (where skilled workers predominated). Metalworkers were also major participants in some forty-five industrial strikes we record for 1917 involving more than one industrial branch.

What seems at first somewhat surprising is that a very large concentration of strikes, more than 17% of the total, took place in the highly diversified service sector, which included waiters and cooks, maids, chauffeurs, barbers, "handlers," and doormen. We have recorded more strikes by waiters and cooks that by coal miners or oil workers; and strikes by doormen, coachmen, and chauffeurs were publicized as part and parcel of the general labor movement despite the obvious social and occupational differences separating this group of workers from what one generally considers proletarian rank and file.

There are several possible explanations for this, and interesting implications as well. Strikes by service sector employees may well reflect the intense concern of labor as a whole in 1917 for issues involving personal dignity, although statistical evidence here is not conclusive. Service sector workers may also have been more inclined to adopt strikes as a means of protest, rather than less contentious forms, partly as a means of disassociating themselves from the privileged elements they largely served. The broader processes of social polarization, in effect, may well have pressed them in this direction, above and beyond the pressures of their own economic needs, perhaps also making them more receptive to radical than liberal politics.

Other major strike concentrations in 1917 included the fiber-processing industry (textiles, and so on), which accounted for some 13.4% of all strikes; the paper and printing industry, 9.6%; the wood and wood products sector, 6.5%, and the food processing industries, 6.1%. Among paper workers and printers, of whom there were some 80,000 workers in January 1917 employed in 90 paper plants and 211 print shops, typographers accounted for by far the largest number. There were also considerable numbers of strikes among workers in shoe manufacturing plants, tailors, and sawmill workers. These took place largely against private owners (only some 11% of all strikes we have recorded for 1917 were directed at public organizations, municipalities, or the state), but this obviously did not mean that strikes in state-owned factories were any less problematic politically, or that their possible size and duration did not fully compensate for their relative infrequency. It suggests simply that the strike movement in aggregate strike numbers in 1917 was very much an aspect of class conflict, and undoubtedly perceived as such by participants on both sides.

Strikes and strikers

This suggestion becomes far stronger when we look at the number of *strikers* in 1917 in contrast to the number of strikes. It is here, in fact, despite far greater problems of statistical reliability, that we can sense one of the most important political aspects of the strike movement as a whole during the revolution: its enormous number of participants, a large number of whom clearly struck more than once. According to figures gathered by the State Economic Council in early 1917, and refined both by the able statistician S. G. Strumilin and more recent investigators, the total number of all Russian industrial workers in early 1917, including mines and railroad shops, was slightly more than 3,300,000.[8] This is a figure some one million larger than the number used by the Factory Inspectorate for workers under its jurisdiction, but in all likelihood is a reasonable and appropriate figure. Our minimum estimate, in comparison, is that more than 2.4 million workers participated in strikes during the period between March 3 and October 25, a figure equivalent to almost two-thirds of the work force; and as many as 4.5 million participated if one includes January and February 1917, and the last week of October. In other words, there were substantially greater numbers of strikers for 1917 as a whole than there were members

8. See, for example, Tsen. Stat. Upravlenie, *Trudy*, vol. 7, vyp. 1, "Statisticheskii sbornik za 1913–1917," p. 39, and L. S. Gaponenko, *Rabochii klass Rossii v 1917 godu* (Moscow, 1970), pp. 50–2.

Table 1. *Wartime economic strikes and strikers with minimum estimates for 1917 based on the Factory Inspectorate's method of counting (enterprises subject to Factory Inspection only)*

Year	Strikes	Percentage of total	Strikers	Percentage of total	Strikers per strike
1914 (Aug–Dec)	34	83	6,716	70	197
1915	713	77	383,358	71	538
1916	1,046	81	646,785	68	618
1917 (Jan–Feb)	190	14	101,481	15	534
1917 (Mar–Oct)	2,470	83	953,930[a]	62	(508)[b]

[a] Minimum estimates based on 76% of strikes.
[b] For strikes where number of strikers could be estimated only.
Sources: 1914–16: Tsentral'noe statisticheskoe upravlenie, *Trudy*, vol. 7, vyp. 1, "Statisticheskii sbornik za 1913–17," pp. 37, 142–5, 152–5, 162–3. For 1916, "Svedeniia o zabastovochnom dvizhenie," TsGIA, f. 23, op. 16, gives 908 economic strikes with 572,278 strikers. 1917 (Jan–Feb): Iakovleva, "Zabastovochnoe dvizhenie," p. 61. These and other discrepancies are discussed by L. Haimson and E. Brian in "The Wartime Strike Wave in Imperial Russia (1915–16)," Appendix IV, in L. Haimson and G. Sapelli, eds., *Strikes, Wars and Revolutions: The Impact of the War Experience* (to be published in the *Annali* of the Feltrinelli Foundation).

of the work force, a level of strike activity matched only by the "dress rehearsal" of 1905.

Our figures, moreover, are undoubtedly underestimates, based only on counts we regard as reasonable, and leaving aside altogether those instances where we think none of the strike accounts allow acceptable judgments to be made. Just how impressive these figures are can be seen from Table 1, which compares them with wartime statistics. Here, clearly, one can discern an enormous change in the intensity of strike activity after February, even if the number of strikes remained consistent with previous months.

Here too, the significance of industrial and geographical concentration is again quite apparent. More than 58% of the strikers worked in Russia's Central Industrial region; eleven provinces alone accounted for more than 95%. These concentrations continued throughout the year. Of the strikers we can identify clearly by industrial branch between March and October, some 47% were metalworkers and 33% were from the various branches of textile production.

What are we to make of these figures (which again, undoubtedly underestimate the actual numbers)? Two conclusions seem obvious. The strike movement in 1917 reflected a far greater break from the recent past *as a phenomenon of mass participation* than it did as a pattern of work stoppages. This seems true even if we exclude the massive strikes in January and February 1917, as well as political strikes thereafter. And strikes as a form of labor protest

176

seemed to have gained at least as much power from the numbers of workers they could encompass as from the number of enterprises they could force to halt production. This also seems to have been true whether we consider only the March–October period, or examine aggregate figures for the year as a whole. The *political* implications of Russian strikes in 1917, therefore, may well have obtained more from the processes of mass involvement than from the assault of strikes on particular industries or industrial sectors, an aspect of the movement as a whole that, if true, renders its qualitative (and subjective) components at least as relevant (and significant) to the course of revolutionary change as its quantitative ones.

Strike propensities

Aggregate data are, of course, a relatively poor way to measure the tendency of workers to strike, and even more inadequate as a measure of relative activity in different industrial sectors. For this we turn to our measure of strike propensity, calculated in Table 2 and Table 3 for the period 1913–17.

Briefly, what can be said about these figures? First, it is extremely interesting that while the number of strikers in 1917 increased dramatically over previous years, the *relative* position (or rank order) or major industrial branches to each other changed rather little between 1913 and 1917, and was not what either external appearances in this period or the historical literature might lead one to expect. Table 2 shows that, with some exceptions, those industries that were strike-prone in 1917 had been active in strikes before that year. Metalworkers ranked first in strike propensity throughout the period 1913–16, and textile workers were also consistently active, especially if one looks at their economic strike propensities apart from political strikes. Those industries with the lowest strike propensities were equally consistent: The food and mineral industries were consistently at the bottom of the rankings. The most remarkable shift occurred among animal product workers, largely leather workers, who emerged as the most strike-prone industry in 1917. Even though metalworkers in 1917 accounted for the largest number of strikers, approximately 530,000, this represented 97% of the entire labor force in that industry. The animal product workers, on the other hand, provided only 135,000 strikers, but in an industry with 70,000 workers, this meant almost 200% of the labor force went on strike.

It is interesting, also, that a large number of animal products workers were employed in small factories, averaging under one hundred workers each, making mobilization more difficult here than for workers like the metalworkers in large industrial plants, but also suggesting indirectly the pervasiveness of labor discontent. Their quiescence during the war years may thus have reflected the ease with which police could monitor protest in such small plants as much as a real absence of discontent.

Table 2. *Strike propensities, 1913–17, measured as a ratio of an industry's share of strikers and workers*[a]

Industry	Type	1913 SP (rank)	1914 SP (rank)	1915 SP (rank)	1916 SP (rank)	1917[b] SP (rank)
Animal products (leather)						
	Economic	1.12	.66	.45	.27	
	Political	.38	.82	.13	.13	
	All	.07 (8)	.78 (4)	.36 (4)	.23 (4)	3.38 (1)
Metals						
	Economic	1.99	2.12	.99	1.43	
	Political	4.09	3.54	3.22	3.78	
	All	3.16 (1)	3.16 (1)	1.61 (1)	2.19 (1)	1.68 (2)
Textiles						
	Economic	1.10	.90	1.88	1.56	
	Political	.40	.42	.56	.19	
	All	.71 (4)	.55 (6)	1.48 (2)	1.12 (2)	.98 (3)
Wood & wood products						
	Economic	.42	.40	.34	.23	
	Political	.41	.63	.07	.03	
	All	.42 (5)	.57 (5)	.37 (5)	.17 (5)	.91 (4)
Paper & printing						
	Economic	.40	.49	.14	.16	
	Political	1.04	1.50	1.01	.10	
	All	.76 (3)	1.23 (2)	.38 (3)	.14 (6–7)	.46 (5)
Chemicals						
	Economic	1.16	1.89	.01	.40	
	Political	1.41	.93	.00	.01	
	All	1.30 (2)	1.18 (3)	.01 (8)	.27 (3)	.36 (6)
Food & food processing						
	Economic	.31	.20	.18	.16	
	Political	.11	.24	.18	.08	
	All	.20 (6)	.23 (7)	.18 (7)	.14 (6–7)	.07 (7)
Minerals						
	Economic	.19	.26	.27	.19	
	Political	.08	.10	.38	.02	
	All	.13 (7)	.15 (8)	.30 (6)	.13 (8)	.04 (8)

[a] Calculations show relative propensities among these industrial branches only. Mining, mixed products, and other industrial sectors are excluded.
[b] Single industry strikes only. The exclusion of strikes involving more than one industry reduces in particular the strike propensity for metalists, who were especially active in multi-industry strikes.
Sources: 1913–16: TsU, *Trudy*, vol. 7, vyp. 1, Tables II, VI, IX, XII, XV, pp. 36–7, 132–5, 142–5, 152–5, 162–3. 1917: Ibid., Table IV, p. 39.

Table 3. *Strike intensities, 1913–17, measured as a percentge of industry's work force on strike*

Industry	Type	1913	1914	1915	1916	1917
Animal byproducts						
	Economic	18.8	11.8	9.2	8.8	
	Political	8.2	41.5	1.0	2.0	
	All	27.0	53.3	10.2	10.8	193.2
Metals						
	Economic	33.3	38.1	20.0	46.0	
	Political	87.4	177.9	25.3	58.4	
	All	120.8	215.9	45.3	104.3	97.4
Textiles						
	Economic	18.5	16.1	37.1	50.3	
	Political	8.6	21.2	4.6	3.0	
	All	27.0	37.3	41.6	53.3	57.0
Wood & wood products						
	Economic	7.1	7.2	6.9	7.5	
	Political	8.8	31.7	0.6	0.5	
	All	15.9	38.9	7.4	8.0	52.2
Chemical						
	Economic	19.6	33.9	0.3	12.8	
	Political	30.1	46.5	0	0.2	
	All	49.7	80.4	0.3	13.0	20.7
Paper & printing						
	Economic	6.8	8.8	2.8	5.2	
	Political	22.2	74.9	7.9	1.5	
	All	29.0	83.7	10.7	6.7	26.6
Food						
	Economic	5.2	3.5	3.6	5.2	
	Political	2.4	11.9	1.4	1.3	
	All	7.7	15.4	5.0	6.5	4.0
Mineral processing						
	Economic	3.3	4.7	5.4	6.0	
	Political	1.7	5.3	3.0	0.3	
	All	4.9	10.0	8.4	6.3	2.9

Source: See Table 2.

From all this we can draw at least two important general conclusions: (1) The aggregate number of strikers, clearly very high in 1917 in comparison with preceding years and obviously with important political implications, was not always the index of activism it may have appeared, but the consequence of other factors one must examine in detail, such as plant size or geographical concentration; (2) conversely, while the sheer number of strikes undoubtedly conveyed

179

the impression of intense labor activism, the level of discontent among less "visible" workers in smaller industries like leatherworking or woodworking may have been just as intense or nearly so as among groups like the metalworkers, generally associated with the vanguard of labor politics of 1917.

Explaining the tendency to strike

One of the principal tasks of our project is, of course, to sort out the *relative* importance of various factors in affecting the Russian strike movement in 1917, and in this way, try to ascertain those elements common to labor movements everywhere that were of special influence and importance to this particular conjuncture.[9] Obviously a most important general question in this regard is simply why Russian workers went out on strike between February and October 1917. We can approach the question most easily by rephrasing it somewhat, and by inquiring again into elements influencing strike propensities. For each province, we have calculated strike intensities for strikes that involved industrial workers only and that occurred between March and October. We can then use multivariate regression analysis to examine the variation in different provinces in terms of their relationship to other variables for which information is available on characteristics of industrial workers in each province. This regression analysis allows us to ascertain in broadest terms those few elements that were uniformly important in explaining strike behavior.

Our calculations suggest, perhaps not surprisingly, that wage levels, both absolute and in terms of change over time, were one of the most significant factors in explaining strikes in 1917, as they are in nonrevolutionary contexts as well. The higher the average nominal wage in a given province (as of 1916), the greater the tendency of workers in that area to strike. But more importantly, despite the importance of high nominal wages, the more real wages *had fallen* between 1913 and 1916, the more likely it was workers would strike. This holds true regardless of other factors, including the presence or absence of the normally activist metalworkers and the distance from politically volatile Petrograd.

We should point out here that these regressions are ecological: We do not have data on wage levels, literacy rates, or age structures for striking and non-

9. The problems of our data, of course make this a tricky task. Not only are there broad variations in the frequency with which various strike elements appear in our material, there are also the conceptual difficulties of selecting the most appropriate elements for comparison – of deciding, in other words, which of any number of possible variables might actually have had the greatest influence in affecting, say, the propensity of workers in a given region to strike. One great advantage to the techniques of bivariate and multivariate regression analyses, however, is that they provide a reasonable measure of statistical significance. We can thus focus on relationships in which we have some confidence, even if we cannot be as comprehensive as we might like. The conceptual problems can also be bridged somewhat by phrasing questions broadly. Our data can then contribute toward developing answers even if additional work remains to be done.

striking plants, but only aggregate data at provincial and industrial levels. So we cannot say for sure it is workers with high wages who strike most, although we believe this is likely. It could be that low-paid workers in provinces with high wages strike most out of emulation. The industrial data on this point, indeed, is ambiguous. The wage characteristics of workers in the printing and paper industry most closely resemble those of our "ideal type" of striker: The industry enjoyed the highest average nominal wages in 1916, but in real terms, according to government statistics, that wage was only 75% of its prewar 1913 level. Workers in this industry had fared among the worst during the war, and yet their industrial strike propensity is very low. On the other hand, animal products workers enjoyed the fourth highest nominal wage in 1916, a figure that in real terms actually exceeded the 1913 wage; only chemical workers and metalworkers had done better. Yet animal products workers struck at a far greater rate than other workers in 1917. It is therefore evident that even through a high average nominal wage and a negative change in real wages were significant determinants of strike intensities in any given locality in 1917, other factors must have played an important part in the strike process.

On the basis of our multivariate regression analysis, we are quite confident that four factors in all best explain the variation in strike intensities across provinces. Using a regression equation that explains 50% of the variation in strike intensity by provinces, our analysis suggests that strike intensities are highest in those provinces with high nominal wages and the greatest decline in real wages since 1913. Controlling for these wage factors, strike intensities were also greatest in provinces with large concentrations of industrial workers in the population, and more surprisingly, in provinces with low overall urban concentrations. In other words, once one controls for wage levels and industrial concentration, strike rates were higher *away* from urban areas. The mining region of the Donbas and the rural industrial hinterland of the central provinces come immediately to mind here. Factory size also appears to be important (larger factories are associated with higher strike intensities), but this variable and the one for industrial concentration are closely related. Between two provinces with equal concentrations of factory workers, factory size in and of itself makes no additional difference in predicting strike intensities.

Timing and duration

One of the most interesting findings of our study has to do with strike timing, a question we will take up more directly in Part IV of this volume. For Russia as a whole, strikes in 1917 seem to have come in three clusters: between the April crisis and the early weeks of the first coalition government through the first week in July; from the end of July to mid-August; and in late summer and fall, particularly mid-September to mid-October.

Between the second week in March and the third week in April, just before workers and soldiers took to the streets to protest Foreign Minister Miliukov's note on Russia's war aims, we record only one or two strikes a day, on the average. Beginning on April 19, however, and continuing through May, we record strikes at the rate of between twenty and thirty a week; and we record alone fifty-five alone between April 19 and May 1, twelve of which involved workers in more than one enterprise. Then, with the start of the so-called Kerensky Offensive on June 18, strikes fell off again briefly. But from the very end of July until mid-August, strike frequencies again approximated what they were in late April and early May. Finally, after another period of quiescence at the end of August, related in all likelihood to the new German military offensive and fresh signs of Russia's potentially catastrophic economic decline, a third sustained cluster of strikes began, running through the third week of October, and tapering off just before the Bolsheviks came to power.

Although the relationship between these clusters and Russia's revolutionary development is of primary importance to us and is treated extensively in our book (as well as discussed briefly, as noted, in Part IV of this volume), we will restrict ourselves here to one or two observations of possible value in comparative analysis, both for reasons of space, and because of the complexity of the indigenous Russian relationships.

First, we want to note that efforts to conceptualize strikes in Russia during 1917 as one great "wave" unfolding as part of a "developing and deepening" political and social revolution, is at best a great oversimplification. Even the notion of a strike wave seems an inappropriate characterization of Russian strike activity in 1917, if we define a wave as a period in which the frequency of strikes is a least 50% higher than the average for five preceding periods, as Shorter and Tilly have done in *Strikes in France* (1973). Using this definition, the February Revolution clearly did not usher in a wave of strikes, particularly if one adds the January and February 1917 strike to the total for 1916, where they more properly belong in terms of historical rather than chronological, divisions.

Second, one sees relatively little progression in the intensity of strikes from spring to fall measured by the number of strikes themselves. The number of strikes was essentially the same, on the average, in the May–June cluster as in September and October, despite notions current at the time and afterward about strikes running out of control on the eve of the Bolshevik takeover. There were, to be sure, some shifts in frequencies of industrial participation. A somewhat larger number of strikes proportionally took place in May in the textile industry and the service sector; and although essentially the same proportion of metallists' strikes occurred in the spring and fall, strikes in the food products and mining sector (including oil) increased rather markedly in

182

late September and October particularly, in contrast to March and April. Insofar as strikes themselves had particular relevance to the course of events, therefore, the connections must rest on the individual characterisitcs of different kinds of strikes rather than on factors that can be readily perceived statistically.

The same is true with the question of strike duration. Most strikes we have recorded were relatively short, usually lasting less than four days. The mean length of all strikes, moreover, tended to decrease as the weeks went by, despite the concurrent attenuation of social and political conflict; and longer strikes tended to be substantially less successful than shorter ones. Again, this seems contrary to what one might expect, given what we know about the course of events generally in 1917, and reinforces the importance of analysis that differentiates individual or groups of strikes from each other.

Finally, and most important, while strike intensity measured by the number of strikes themselves did not increase from spring to fall, there was, simult- aneously, a very dramatic increase if one measures intensity by the number of strike participants. This is a most interesting and significant discrepancy. We record only 17,600 probable strikers for all of April, the first month this figure had fallen below 10,000, even for economic strikes, since December 1914. For the spring cluster as a whole we record approximately 573,000 strikers, in- cluding some 275,000 participants in the July Day strike, or an average of 7,100 per day. In the September–October period, with strike frequencies again roughly the same as in the spring, the number of strike participants increases to more than 1,229,000, or some 30,000 a day based on conservative estimates, a stun- ning phenomenon, and one that our statistics undoubtedly underrepresent.

This dramatic increase in the number of strikers suggests again that the nature of strikes underwent a change in 1917, and by implication emphasizes the importance of that unquantifiable but vital element, conjuncture, in affecting the nature of labor protest. As we will take up elsewhere, this makes comparisons between "revolutionary" strikes and strikes in stable periods or contexts extremely tricky; and for Russia itself, it also suggests that the Bolsheviks came to power in October facing a very different phenomenon in terms of strike activism than did their predecessors in the Provisional Government, and con- sequently, a very different sort of political and social change.

Goals

Russian workers struck in 1917 for a great variety of goals, overwhelmingly economic, rather than political, in orientation and objective. Our data show such wide-ranging demands as the removal of Cossacks from factory grounds, the introduction of a voluntary piece work system, and the demand that factory owners stop using workers to clean their offices and living quarters. Consistent with our findings on strike propensities, the largest category of workers' demands involved wages, which were an issue in almost half of our recorded strikes. Closely related were specific demands for a change in pay rates, bonuses, and what was reported in approximately 16% of our cases as simply "economic" goals.

Workers also struck with great frequency for reductions in hours, vacation time, the right to organize trade unions, and for management recognition of factory committee powers. Some 55% of all strikers protested work conditions; and in at least twenty-six cases there were demands for changes in managerial personnel, most of which were quite specific. There were also substantial numbers of strikes to secure the rehiring of dismissed comrades and even for arbitration to settle labor – management differences. These demands, of course, were most frequently made along with others; very few strikes in 1917 had only one objective.

What seems particularly interesting about wage demands is their concentration in Moscow, and somewhat less so in Petrograd, and their timing. As Table 4 indicates, March and April were months of relatively few strikes and hence relatively few wage demands, despite our general sense that workers rushed after February to improve material conditions. The formation of the first coalition in early May seems clearly to have encouraged workers to strike for higher wages, just as it seems to have encouraged strikes in general, but July and August saw weeks of relative quiescence in this regard, despite deteriorating economic conditions. Organizational demands, however, were also particularly frequent during the first coalition government in May and June, and then again, perhaps symptomatically, in October, although this might also be simply a function of strike frequency rates in general. The same can be said for correlations between demands and industrial branches. The most demands in all major categories emanated from metalworkers (who also struck more frequently), although there are interesting variations in other sectors. Food, wood, and building workers, for example, seem to have struck at a proportionally higher rate over issues of dignity; wood and construction workers were especially concerned with workers' control, perhaps because gains in this area were won earlier by metallists and others; textile workers seem to have been particularly concerned about working conditions as well as wages, despite especially low pay scales in this sector.

Through regression analysis we can begin to sort out the influences affecting these strike demands, although again, because of statistical limitations, not as comprehensively as we would like. When we examine demands as opposed to strike intensities, one factor stands out in explaining the frequency of strikes that included wage demands. Even though high wages tended to be related to strike intensities as a whole, it was those provinces with the *lowest* nominal wages

Table 4. *Strikes and strikers by cause, 1917*

	Totals		Wages		Hours & factory conditions		Dignity		Workers' control		Political	
	Strikes	Strikers	Strikes	Strikers	Strikes	Strikers	Strikes	Strikers	Strikes	Strikers	Strikes	Strikers
Plants nominally under Factory Inspection	707	1,501,100[a]	71%	58%	23%	37%	7%	32%	19%	42%	4%	38%
All enterprises	1,019	2,406,400[a]	88%	73%	28%	55%	10%	24%	24%	61%	5%	24%

[a] Includes only strikes for which demands are recorded. Figures are overlapped to include strikes with principal demands in more than one demand category.

in 1916 whose strikes most frequently demanded wage improvements. This relationship is independent of any effect of the change in wages – it would seem that it was not deprivation as perceived over time, but rather present material need that encouraged workers to strike for wage gains.

On the other hand, as with strike intensities, this relationship is not obvious if we look at industrial variation. All of the strikes of mineral workers included wage demands, and their nominal wage was the lowest of all nine industries for which we have comparable information in both 1916 and 1917. But miners made the fewest economic demands, and they also ranked low (sixth out of nine) in terms of nominal wages. Clearly variations within industries, especially with respect to timing, tend to obscure relationships such as these, as do the particularities of management–labor relations.

None of the other sets of demands can be as satisfactorily explained by the factors for which we have data at the provincial level. We might expect that the prevalence of demands for job control and for dignity issues might be correlated to areas with veteran, experienced, probably male workers. In fact, multivariate regression suggests that control strikes were indeed most frequent in provinces whose workers had few ties to the countryside, that is, with a proletarianized labor force. But they were at the same time frequent in provinces whose labor force had expanded most rapidly during the war. (These results hold, controlling for overall industrial concentration and urban concentration, which themselves have no significant effect.) This suggests that workers with factory backgrounds but short job tenure were more anxious than others to define the limits of managerial authority. It is diffiult to know whether such strikes were defensive in nature, as management in expanding industrial sites felt they could reduce previous levels of worker autonomy, or whether they were offensive, because workers saw that management in new sites were not secure enough themselves to resist workers' demands for more independence. Firm answers to these speculations suggested by the regression analysis can only come from more intense examination in our longer study.

Even more difficult to evaluate are the results of regressions to explain the frequency of strikes over dignity. Controlling for age levels, industrial concentration, and landholding, it emerges that provinces with the most female workers struck more frequently over dignity issues. But adding literacy to the equation, gender becomes insignificant, and only literacy alone has any effect on dignity demands. But contrary to our hypothesis that dignity issues were raised by veteran and skilled self-confident workers, workers with *low* levels of literacy were more likely to strike over dignity issues. We may take this as a sign that a working-class culture predicated on equality and human dignity was more widespread than is often assumed, but only further examination of the particular strikes involving such demands can satisfactorily explain the phenomenon suggested by this statistical overview.

186

Outcome

Analysing strike outcomes in 1917 is extremely difficult. The definition of "success" and "failure" very much depended on the observer. "Compromise" did not necessarily mean a mutual acceptance of limited gains. Many factories also responded to strikes and strike threats by shutting their gates, sometimes temporarily locking workers out, as occurred at Putilov and elsewhere in Petrograd during the fateful days of late February, sometimes for good. Information on factory closings also is almost impossible to correlate with strikes in a general way, both because we lack specific details and because the data are too sparse. Also, the actual reports of strike outcomes vary enormously.

Still, what is interesting about outcomes in the most general terms in 1917 is that so few strikes end in outright failure. Approximately 54% of all strikes we have been able to analyze can be considered successful in 1917, while less than 10% were not. The rest ended in some form of compromise.

These general patterns seem to be roughly the same throughout the country. There is evidence that the rate of failure was lowest in the city of Petrograd, as we note below, but not as low in the rest of the Northern Industrial Region. Moscow may have had a slightly higher rate of unsuccessful strikes than the country at large, and somewhat higher as well than the Central Industrial Region, which included Moscow province, Tver, Kostroma, Vladimir, Kaluga, Riazan, Tula, and Iaroslavl provinces. Everywhere throughout Russia, however, the compromise rate seems to have been relatively constant.

Although we have only limited data on outcome by industrial branch, it seems clear that the rate of success was relatively low for workers in the metal industry, and much higher for workers in the wood products and paper and printing industries. Strikes seem to have been least successful in the food sector, the metal sector, and also in the animal products industries, especially leather. Again, a very substantial proportion of strikes in all sectors resulted in compromises of one sort or another, especially in the textile industry.

The forms of factory ownership seem to have made some difference here, as did whether a strike was conducted by a single production unit or group of plants. Workers seem to have won the largest number of strikes in state and municipally owned plants. No strikes that we know about here were lost outright. Workers won the least number of strikes against privately held or joint stock firms; and somewhat fewer strikes were won by those in individual plants than by strikers in more than one plant within the same industry. The rate of outright failure also seems to have been much lower in strikes of more than one plant, while the success rate of strikes among workers of different industries seems the same as in individual plants. This may have more to do with specific strike issues than the extent of the strike, and one must again be cautious about drawing the obvious conclusion, which is that solidarity within crafts led to

187

greater success than solidarity across craft lines. Still, there is at least some evidence here that despite the vague nature of most compromise solutions and the increasing hopelessness of Russia's economic circumstances, the strike movement itself may have very much encouraged tendencies in favor of worker solidarity and class consciousness.

It is interesting that strike outcomes seem to have varied rather little on the basis of demands. Approximately 53% of all wage strikes turned out more or less in favor of workers, as did approximately 54% of all strikes over organizational issues, like workers' control. Strikes for improved working conditions and over questions of workers' dignity were also in the 55–60% success range, a bit higher than the rate for all strikes, but not significantly so. Relatively few dignity strikes were apparently lost, but this may have had much to do with strike tactics. Where we have evidence that some degree of violence occurred during a strike, either success rates or compromise rates seem to increase, although our data here are not sufficient to allow confident generalizations.

We should note also that there seem to be some significant variations in success or failure rates month by month, although the outright success-plus-compromise rate is somewhat more steady. Failure rates seem to have been lowest in March and April, and greatest in July; strikes in the second half of the year, from July to October, tended to be less successful. Fewer than half of these strikes were won outright, compared to a 60% success rate in the first half of the revolutionary year. Further, 12% of the later strikes ended in failure. It also appears that the success rate of strikes declined, perhaps noticeable even to contemporaries, on the eve of the Bolshevik coup in October, but since we are only able to examine approximately one-fifth of our strikes in terms of outcome or timing, we must again be careful about drawing conclusions too firmly.

Petrograd and Moscow

The two largest centers of strike activity in 1917 were the cities of Moscow, with 247 strikes (of which at least 57 involved more than one enterprise), and Petrograd, with 126 (including 55 multienterprise strikes). One of us has already examined the strike process in Moscow in some detail,[10] and because strike activity in Petrograd before the war and revolution had been so militant and widespread, our understanding of strikes in the revolutionary milieu of 1917 can be broadened by a comparison of experiences in the two capitals.

Petrograd in 1917 was a larger city than Moscow, and the center of revolutionary politics, yet when we compare both the number of strikes and strikers with the industrial population of the two cities, Moscow appears to be

---

10. Diane Koenker, *Moscow Workers and the 1917 Revolution* (Princeton, 1981), pp. 293–328.

the more strike-prone. According to our data, over 400,000 workers parti-cipated in the seventy-three Petrograd stikes for which we have this informa-tion, while for Moscow we count over 450,000 strikers for 198 strikes. In the aggregate, Moscow registered a total "strike force" of at least 219% of its labor force; Petrograd reported strikers representing 105% of its industrial labor force at a minimum. In other words, Moscow appears to have produced more strikes than Petrograd both numerically and proportionally, although the average size of a strike in Petrograd was clearly much bigger than in Moscow, and it would be a mistake to infer from these figures that Petrograd strikes were less important to the course of events than those in Moscow. Reality, we think, was quite the opposite.

This was partly due to timing. One of the significant features of Moscow's strike movement in 1917 was that the number of strikes and strikers peaked relatively early in the year, even though later Moscow strikes, concentrated in the textile industry, tended to be much larger. Petrograd was different. More than half of that city's strikes began in the second half of the year, from July to October. In contrast, only one-third of Moscow strikes began after June. To be sure, there is evidence that Petrograd also experienced a peak of sorts in May, but its early strikes (those beginning after March 3) were few, and the number of strikes in October was small relative both to Moscow and Russia at large.

The implications of these two different patterns are significant. Along with an increase in political tensions, Petrograd residents could also perceive an exacerbation of labor – management relations, exemplified in the strike process. While the smaller number of late strikes in Moscow does not necessarily imply labor peace, confrontations in that city between labor and management may have been less noticeable and less threatening the late summer and fall, parti-cularly when one considers the relatively liberal outlooks of a substantial portion of Moscow's manufacturing and commercial leadership, some of whose members joined Kerensky after the Kornilov mutiny in attempting to reconstruct the pro-visional regime.[11] The relative absence of late-year strikes in Moscow may thus help to explain the less polarized atmosphere of Moscow's October Days.

Of course, many more features of strikes than sheer numbers and size con-tributed to the overall political climate. We must also compare the composition of the two strike forces, the goals of strikers, and features of the strikes them-selves in order to assess the differences in the strike experiences of the two cities.

To examine the composition of strikes, we again use strike propensities – the share of an industrial group's strikers compared to its share of the work force. We must, however, limit this comparison to industrial workers for whom we

11. On the historical differences between the Moscow and Petrograd bourgeoisie, see in particular Alfred J. Rieber, *Merchants and Entrepreneurs in Imperial Russia* (Chapel Hill, 1982), pt 3.

189

Table 5. *Strike propensities of industrial workers, measured as a ratio of an industry's share of strikers and workers*[a]

Industry	Petrograd	Moscow
Wood	4.29	1.68
Metals	1.43	1.27
Paper and printing	.34	.19
Minerals	.30	.33
Animal products	.27	3.57
Textiles	.09	.22
Chemicals	.02	1.13
Food	.01	.19

[a] Calculations show relative propensities among these industrial branches in branch strikes only.

have the most complete data on size of work force, excluding the active service sector, whose strike frequencies in Petrograd were second only to metalworkers. As Table 5 shows, woodworkers, although numerically few in both cities, were among the most strike-prone of all industries, far more than they had been before or during 1917 in the rest of Russia. Metalworkers in both cities also showed higher than average propensities to strike; textile workers and food workers, many of whom were women, were less prone to strike, although there is no statistical indication that gender was a factor in determining their activism. Food workers may have been particularly concerned with creating hardship for others; and textile workers outside the capitals struck in October in huge numbers.

The similarities in rank order of industrial strike propensities are significant, but even more interesting is how these propensities differ from the all-Russian industrial propensities to strike (Table 2). We are particularly impressed by the relative inactivity of textile workers, with propensities of .09 and .22 in Petrograd and Moscow, but with a greater than average propensity of strike overall (.98 for all Russia). Why did urban textile workers, largely women here as well as in the provinces, strike so little? One possibility has to do with food procurement. We would need to find out more about the process of food distribution in rural factory settlements, but it would not be surprising if urban women were less inclined to strike because more of their time and energies were devoted to burdens of obtaining food for their families.

A second industry whose urban strike propensity also differs from the national average is woodworking. Urban woodworkers tended to have different qualities from workers in the industry outside the cities. Urban woodworkers were mostly skilled craftsmen – carpenters, joiners, cabinetmakers – whereas non-urban woodworkers were primarily lumberjacks and sawmill workers. Indeed, skilled woodworkers struck in only two parts of the country in 1917: in Moscow city, and in the Petrograd region (including the city). But here they struck in great numbers. Elsewhere, semiskilled and unskilled workers dominated strikes in the woodworking industry, and in relative terms, their total was small compared to other industries. We think that the high strike propensity of skilled urban workers suggests the importance of skill (and all the qualities associated with that term in facilitating strikes) in facilitating the mobilizing workers for strike activity. Moreover, skilled urban workers tended to be males, and unlike their female family members, probably did not have to stand in urban bread lines for hours each day.

With respect to goals, our evidence suggests that Moscow workers on the whole were slightly less concerned than Petrograd's about purely wage issues throughout 1917. Further, Moscow workers struck more for better conditions and greater job control than Petrograd's. Moscow's edge in strikes about conditions can be explained in part by the issue of the eight-hour work day, which we have included as a "conditions" demand. In Petrograd, manfacturers agreed collectively to institute the shorter day in their plants; Moscow workers had to strike individually to win this concession. The result: Petrograd experienced very few strikes in March and April that demanded improved working conditions, whereas Moscow reported five or six times as many in this period, although once again we must be very cautious about inferring from this that Petrograders were less concerned about work conditions than their comrades in Moscow.

Moscow and Petrograd also differed in terms of what Shorter and Tilly have conceived of as the shape of strikes. As we have seen, Petrograd experienced fewer strikes per 10,000 workers than Moscow, but at the same time, the average size strike, in strikers per strike, was greater in the capital, particularly considering that the percentage of strikes of unknown size is quite a bit higher in Petrograd than in Moscow. Thus, strikes in Petrograd were less frequent, but much larger when they occurred. Considering the average duration of strikes gives us the third dimension of the "shape" of strikes in the two capitals, although our frequencies on this question are rather small.[12] Here too there is considerable difference: the median strike in Petrograd was short, lasting only three days; 53% of the strikes last one-half week or less. In Moscow, the median length of strike was seven days; only 27% of this city's strikes lasted less than half a week, and 36% of its strikes lasted longer than two weeks. The three factors of frequency, size, and duration give the pictures in Figure 1. Compared with France, Petrograd strikes look like those of the 1940s and 1950s, when

---

12. We know the length for only 30% of Petrograd strikes, and for only 15% of Moscow strikes.

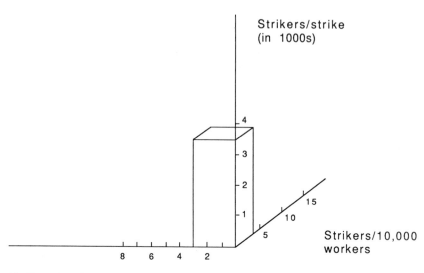

Petrograd

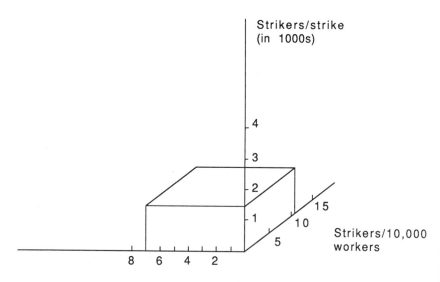

Moscow

Figure 1. The shape of strikes in Petrograd and Moscow

French trade unions were strong and politicized, while Moscow's strikes resemble more the French strikes of a preindustrial era, the 1830s.[13] The different shapes of strikes can partly be explained by the two cities' industrial physiognomy: Petrograd plants were larger on average, so its strikes tended to be larger. Whether organization also affected frequencies and duration is unclear. On one hand, short strikes tend to be more successful than longer ones, and successful strikes tend to be more organized. Petrograd and Moscow each show about the same rate of outright success for their strikes, but our evidence also suggests that Moscow's failure rate was considerably higher than Petrograd's (although we are very wary here of reporting biases). Thus Petrograd's (short) successful strikes might represent the influence of effective organization, just as Moscow's longer strikes.

The direct evidence we have on this question demonstrates roughly equivalent levels of organization. Half of Moscow's strikes reported some sort of organization, and slightly less than half in Petrograd were organized in some way. In some 40% of our cases, organization meant trade unions. Other strike organizers included factory committees and strike committees, formed either as part of a plant's permanent apparatus, or on an ad hoc basis for the purpose of specific strike actions. Somewhat surprisingly, considering the well-known activism of Petrograd factory committees, our evidence suggests that the percentage of Moscow strikes with factory committee involvement may have been double that of Petrograd. On the other hand, Petrograd's share of strikes led by strike committees was double that of Moscow.

A final characteristic of the organization of strikes is the change over time. We would expect the level of organization to increase as workers gained organizational experience over the course of 1917, and Figure 2 demonstrates that this appears to be true. Further, Moscow seems to have improved its organizability earlier than Petrograd. This suggests that Moscow's larger number of early strikes may have been due to earlier organization.

Why, however, should Moscow's workers have organized earlier than

---

13. Edward Shorter and Charles Tilly, *Strikes in France, 1830–1968* (Cambridge, 1974), pp. 52–4.

Worker literacy

	Literate	Illiterate
Moscow (city)	77,980	34,723
Moscow	94,506	69,769
Petersburg (city)	70,746	20,217
Petersburg	6,914	1,615

Source: USSR Tsentral'noe Statisticheskoe Upravelenie. *Trudy*, vol. 26, pt 2 (M., 1926).

% of strikes
with organized
leadership

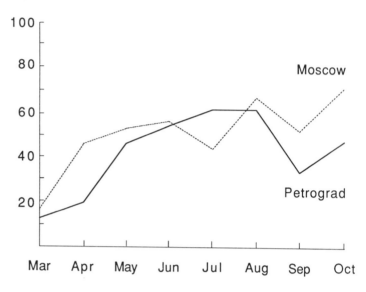

Figure 2. Organization of strikes over time in Moscow and Petrograd

Petrograd's with all the latter's experience in the revolutionary movement? For one thing, Petrograd's labor force had grown more dramatically during the war, bringing new and inexperienced workers into the labor force. And for another, Moscow's special physiognomy, with smaller factories and large numbers of artisans, may also have facilitated quicker organization. Also, one must take into account the ratio of strikes in single factories to those in more than one plant. Multifactory strikes, both within an industry and even more so across industries, clearly require a greater degree of organization and solidarity. In Russia as a whole, we noted that about one-half of all strikes were single-factory strikes. This ratio holds true for Petrograd, but not Moscow, where three-quarters of all strikes were limited to one factory. Petrograd moreover, had proportionally twice as many strikes in more than one plant of the same industry and in plants across industries than Moscow. This evidence suggests that on the whole, Petrograd strikers were better able to forge ties with workers beyond their particular plant, an important component of the strike movement that, again, requires closer investigation of nonstatistical material.

The unevenness of strike organization in both cities during the latter half of

194

1917 suggested by Figure 2 represents, we think, a different picture. We suspect that the "unorganized" strikes here tended more to be wildcat strikes, carried out counter to existing organizations' wishes. There is much evidence to show that by September, workers were often impatient with what they saw as the overly conciliatory tactics of their unions and the indifference of the socialist coalition to labor demands. It is probably significant, therefore, that this decline in strike organization shows up in both capital cities, and that the trend was reversed in both cities in October, as the mobilization of workers for a change in the political system gathered force.

Conclusion

The strike has often served as the dominant image of the labor movement in Russian history. Landmark strikes, such as the general strike that led to the October Manifesto in 1905 or the stoppage in the Lena goldfields that provoked government troops to shoot striking workers in 1912 are an integral part of the Russian revolutionary tradition. The cinema images of Sergei Eisenstein's 1925 film, "Strike" – of misery, blind rebellion, government brutality – have, just as the images of his "October," become part of the folk legacy of the Russian revolutionary movement. The very pattern of the rise and abatement of strikes over time is also often equated with the fortunes of the revolutionary movement itself. Strikes, for contemporaries and historians alike, thus represent a key indicator as well as a major symbol of the Russian revolutionary labor movement.

The symbolic nature of the strike is no less important for 1917. A general strike in Petrograd in February, after all, revealed the powerlessness of the old regime. Equally significant, the movement of strikes throughout 1917, in Petrograd and across the old empire, created a picture of the labor movement that rightly or wrongly shaped the responses of revolutionary leaders on all points of the political spectrum, both in Russia and elsewhere.

Because of the extraordinary power of these symbolic aspects of strikes in revolutionary history, perhaps the most important, if obvious, conclusion to be drawn from the array of material presented here is that the social and political realities of strikes in 1917 do not readily conform to pictures commonly drawn in the literature. It should be clear, for instance, that the familiar division of strikes into political and economic categories makes little sense for 1917, and obscures far more than it clarifies. Our data show that the economic nature of strikes in 1917 had little to do with conceptions of labor activism as a reflexive reaction to hunger and immiseration, or workers' protests as essentially unorganized, irrational, and prone to blind violence, as some historians suggest. It is equally apparent that *all* strikes in 1917, as elsewhere, were fundamentally political regardless of overt goals, an aspect of the sharp contention for social

195

hegemony and power that characterized the very essence of the revolutionary process.

Further, it should also be apparent that despite the vital relationships between these broader processes of revolution and strike activism as a whole, relationships that, as we have noted, are the central concern of our larger study (and about which we have something briefly to say in Part IV of this volume), strikes in Russia during 1917 are also amenable to systematic objective analysis, serious problems with sources and statistical reliability notwithstanding. Yet it is also essential to recognize in making comparisons with strikes elsewhere that the abstraction of 1917 strikes in objective terms may seriously impede an understanding of their nature. Although an index of workers' demands, strikes also reflected a process of changing expectation, social principles, and legal norms; although an aspect of labor protest, strikes also involved the redefinition in a rapidly changing social context of the very terms of struggle; and although a central element, surely, of the traditional processes of labor – management relations, Russian strikes in 1917 also involved the reformulation of social consciousness, and the very sense of what it meant to be a "worker" or member of the "bourgeoisie."

Finally, therefore, a word of caution. Comparative analyses may well be made, but it seems to us that we lack an adequate methodology through which such work might preserve the significance of these indigenous and more subjective factors. In important ways, we would argue, the nature of revolutionary strikes is fundamentally different from the nature of strikes in more stable times. And insofar as Russian strikes in 1917 had influence on workers elsewhere, it may well have been more in prompting a redefinition of social and political contexts than in presenting a comprehensive model of protest.

These and other matters await further study.

8

Strikes in Imperial Russia, 1895–1913: a quantitative analysis

V. I. BOVYKIN, L. I. BORODKIN, Y. I. KIRYANOV

Born at the dawn of the labor movement, the strike remains to this day one of the main forms of proletarian class struggle in capitalist society. At different stages of the labor movement it performed different functions, being remarkably adapted to the solution of the tasks posed by this movement. As a form of worker collective action to counter the intensification of their exploitation by capitalists, strikes connected closely with fluctuations in economic conditions. With the growth of class consciousness of the proletariat, its organization, and the utilization of the strike as a means of political struggle, this connection began to weaken.

The strike cannot resolve the contradiction between labor and capital that engendered it. In the middle of the 1840s, Marx and Engels pointed out that "real strikes in civilized countries are always a subordinate part of the labor movement, because more general combinatioins of workers lead to other forms of actions."[1]

At the same time, the proletariat's constant employment of the strike in its struggle, the different functions performed by it depending on the aims pursued by this struggle, the ability of the strike movement to reflect the level of workers' class consciousness, the proletariat's role in the solution of pressing social contradictions – all this lends special importance to studying the dynamics of the strike movement in the historical analysis of social relations in the capitalist epoch. Lenin said in 1913 that "the Russian workers' strike movement is the best barometer of the entire nation-wide emancipation struggle in Russia."[2]

In Russia, strikes were subject to organized governmental registration from

1. K. Marx and F. Engels, *The German Ideology* (Moscow: Progress Publishers, 1964), p. 425.

2. V. I. Lenin, *Collected Works*, vol. 18, p. 250.

the middle of the 1890s. The government strike statistics that arose on this basis, despite their substantial shortcomings (especially the limitation of registration to manufacturing), represent the most valuable source on the history of the labor movement. Characterizing statistical publications on strikes in 1895–1904, 1905, and 1906–8 undertaken by the Ministry of Trade and Industry, Lenin wrote: "There is such a wealth of valuable material collected in these publications that a complete study and thorough analysis of it will require a great deal of time."[3] Lenin repeatedly turned to these publications and also to the annual "Abstracts of Factory Inspectors' Reports," which contained data of the subsequent period, analyzing on the basis of strike statistics major tendencies and main stages of the liberation movement in Russia at the close of the nineteenth and the beginning of the twentieth century. Of particular interest is Lenin's article "Strike Statistics in Russia," in which he set out "preliminary results" of his elaboration of the published statistical data. Analyzing the dynamics of the strike struggle in Russia in 1905–7, the relationship between its different forms, the degree and character of participation of separate branch and regional contingents of the proletariat, Lenin showed a close connection between political and economic strikes in the course of the first Russian revolution, demonstrated the advanced role of metalworkers, and established the dependence of the effect of economic strikes on their duration and on the general scale of the labor movement.

The task of this paper is to pursue the analysis of the structure of the strike movement in Russia in 1895–1913, (1) to examine interrelationships among its basic aspects and (2) to search for causes of fluctuation in strike activity.

Regrettably, we do not have quantitative indices of political and ideological influences on the strike movement. This compelled us at the given stage of our study to confine ourselves to the examination of the links of the strike movement with economic factors characterizing the industrial situation and the position of the workers.

The main source for the study were the data of the factory inspection of the Ministry of Trade and Industry, published in the annual "Abstracts of Factory Inspectors' Reports" for 1900–13 and also in some special publications.[4] As we have already noted, these cover only factory manufacturing industry (groups I–XII).[5] So, missing from our field of vision were workers of *metallurgical and*

---

3. *Ibid.*, vol. 16, p. 395.

4. *Statistics on Workers' Strikes at Factories and Plants for the Decade 1895–1904* (St. Petersburg, 1905); *Statistics of Strikes at Factories and Plants for 1905* (St. Petersburg, 1908); *Statistics of Workers' Strikes at Factories and Plants for the Three-Year Period of 1906–1908* (St. Petersburg, 1910).

5. Let us recall the names of branches of production and their numerical designation: I. Cotton processing; II. Wool processing; III. Silk processing; IV. Flax processing; V. Mixed production; VI. Papermaking and book printing; VII. Woodworking; VIII. Metalworking; IX. Processing of minerals; X. Processing of animal products; XI. Processing of food products; XII. Chemical production.

mining production, as well as transport, building and agricultural workers, and workers of small-scale, nonfactory industry.

Using annual aggregates for all of Russia, we have calculated correlation coefficients for time series running from 1895 to 1913, a total of nineteen years. The coefficients come in three sets: (1) zero-order, (2) detrended, and (3) first differences, that is, change from one year to the next. Coefficients were calculated on the BESM-6 computer at Moscow State University.

For each year, the variables over which we have computed correlations include:

1. number of strikes in the year;
2. number of strikers;
3. number of working days lost;
4. number of political strikes;
5. number of participants in political strikes;
6. number of economic strikes;
7. number of participants in economic strikes;
8. number of strikes over wages;
9. number of participants in strikes over wages;
10. number of strikes over work hours;
11. number of participants in strikes over work hours;
12. number of strikes over other working and living conditions;
13. number of participants in strikes over other working and living conditions;
14. number of offensive strikes;
15. number of participants in offensive strikes;
16. number of defensive strikes;
17. number of participants in defensive strikes;
18. number of economic strikes ending in workers' victory;
19. number of participants in economic strikes that ended in workers' victory;
20. number of strikes ending in a compromise, partial granting of workers' demands;
21. number of participants in economic strikes that ended in a compromise;
22. number of economic strikes that ended in workers' defeat;
23. number of participants in economic strikes that ended in workers' defeat;
24. nominal wages;
25. real wages;
26. value of gross output (in twelve branches of industry) per worker;
27. value of gross output (in twelve branches of industry) per enterprise;
28. total value of gross output (in twelve branches of industry);
29. number of workers per enterprise.

The zero-order matrix shows a close relationship of numbers of strikes and strikers to other indicators of industrial conflict (Table 1). Correlations range from 0.72 to 0.99, with most over 0.92. The scope of the movement and the increase in the number of striking workers were characterized by the growth of

Table 1. *Zero-order correlations of strike characteristics and economic conditions in Russian manufacturing over years 1895–1913*

												Variables (for identification, see text)																	
1	2	3	4	5	6	7	8	9	10	11	12	13	14	15	16	17	18	19	20	21	22	23	24	25	26	27	28	29	No.
0	98	97	99	98	98	98	97	97	96	97	67	78	98	98	13	23	98	98	98	96	97	91	−31	−14	−30	23	−39	36	1
	0	97	98	99	97	98	95	95	95	98	70	83	97	98	7	20	94	95	98	96	98	94	−35	−16	−33	19	−28	32	2
		0	97	96	93	97	99	99	90	96	56	71	95	98	−1	19	96	97	99	99	94	92	−48	−12	−33	17	−34	32	3
			0	98	96	97	97	97	94	96	63	75	97	97	13	25	97	97	98	96	96	90	−32	−16	−27	24	−40	36	4
				0	98	97	94	94	93	96	68	82	95	96	9	22	93	94	97	95	97	92	−34	−18	−29	21	−27	32	5
					0	98	94	94	99	98	75	84	99	97	12	19	97	97	97	93	97	90	−28	−10	−35	20	−36	35	6
						0	97	98	94	98	73	66	98	99	5	17	96	97	99	96	98	94	−37	−12	−39	15	−28	31	7
							0	95	94	94	52	67	95	97	4	24	97	98	98	98	93	90	−43	−11	−32	18	−43	35	8
								0	99	95	53	83	96	95	3	22	97	98	98	98	93	90	−45	−12	−31	16	−40	32	9
									0	90	79	79	98	95	15	17	96	96	95	89	96	88	−23	−9	−33	20	−35	34	10
										0	76	85	98	99	5	17	96	96	98	95	96	94	−37	−12	−39	14	−28	31	11
											0	94	71	68	19	3	62	62	65	55	76	70	5	−8	−42	6	0	20	12
												0	79	80	8	3	70	72	77	70	87	83	−11	−9	−46	9	3	24	13
													0	98	6	16	98	99	98	95	97	90	−34	−7	−34	21	−37	36	14
														0	0	14	96	98	98	95	97	93	−43	−8	−38	17	−29	33	15
															0	72	7	5	1	−4	12	18	67	−54	−1	−16	−42	−8	16
																0	19	18	17	19	22	27	17	−74	−8	−31	−46	−20	17
																	0	99	97	95	93	86	−36	−6	−30	23	−43	37	18
																		0	98	95	94	88	−38	−7	−32	21	−42	36	19
																			0	98	96	93	−42	−10	−35	18	−33	34	20
																				0	93	91	−50	−11	−33	16	−33	31	21
																					0	95	−30	−16	−40	12	−28	30	22
																						0	−30	−22	−49	0	−23	23	23
																							0	5	3	20	−18	18	24
																								0	−17	57	24	62	25
																									0	14	−25	−43	26
																										0	0	80	27
																											0	−49	28
																												0	29

The whole numbers of the correlation coefficient are omitted, two figures being left after the dot. Thus, −23 means that the coefficient is −0.23.

the number of strikes, the upsurge of the economic struggle was accompanied by the growth of political and offensive strikes, the development of the political struggle brought an increase in the number of economic strikes, and so on. Exceptions to the rule were, however, defensive strikes (variables 16 and 17). The indicators of their number and the number of participants were weakly but directly correlated to all other indicators of the strike struggle (from 0.03 to 0.37). In our view, this is explained by the fact that the development of the movement was conditioned mostly by offensive actions of workers.

Now let us turn to the matrix of correlations of the detrended series (Table 2). Table 2 reproduces the data of the previous table with almost photographic precision: As a rule, the difference between the respective indicators does not exceed hundredth fractions. It follows that the close connection between the indicators existed not only at the level of general tendencies of their dynamics but also of annual deviations of these indicators from their trends.

Table 3 (reflecting year-to-year fluctuations) gives an idea of the degree of conjunction of major share indicators of the strike movement of workers in factory industry of the country in 1895–1913. As before, a close direct connection is observed between the percentage of strikes, percentage of strikers, and the number of lost working days (from 0.97 to 0.99). However, in all other cases connections have a totally different expression than in Tables 1 and 2.

The striker rate was directly and significantly dependent on the proportion of participants in political strikes (0.67). The same is observed in the conjunction of the share of strikers and the share of participants in offensive and defensive strikes (0.57 and −0.34 respectively) as well as the share of participants in strikes that ended, on the one hand, in victory or compromise and, on the other, in defeat (0.43; 0.62, and −0.24 respectively). Thus, political, offensive, and successful strikes tended to occur in the upward phase of strike activity, while economic, defensive and failing strikes occurred in the counterphase. In the course of development of the movement the share of participants in political and offensive strikes rose, and that of participants in economic and defensive strikes declined. The broader the scope of the struggle, the smaller was the share of defeated participants.

It is possible to analyze the connection between the main indicators of the strike movement (the number of strikes and their participants) in different branches of factory production. Correlations of numbers of strikers and strikes in all twelve groups of factory industry are rather significant; only in rare cases does their level drop below 0.90, and then by a small margin.

Now let us examine correlations between indicators of the strike movement, industrial growth, and the economic position of workers. We have only a few indicators for defining industrial development and the economic position of workers throughout the period in question (1895–1913). Among indicators of the first type are the data on the value of gross product in all twelve groups of

201

Table 2. *Detrended correlations of strike characteristics and economic conditions in Russian manufacturing over years 1895–1913*

1	2	3	4	5	6	7	8	9	10	11	12	13	14	15	16	17	18	19	20	21	22	23	24	25	26	27	28	29	No.
0	98	97	99	97	98	98	96	95	96	97	66	76	98	98	20	26	97	97	98	96	95	90	−16	−1	13	26	11	35	1
	0	96	97	99	97	98	93	92	95	98	72	83	97	98	18	23	93	94	98	95	97	94	23	0	19	33	21	40	2
		0	96	95	93	96	98	98	91	95	55	68	95	98	5	21	96	97	99	99	91	89	7	−2	7	19	7	29	3
			0	97	96	97	98	98	94	95	62	72	97	97	19	27	97	97	98	96	94	89	13	−4	10	23	7	33	4
				0	95	97	91	91	99	98	70	82	95	96	20	24	91	92	96	94	96	93	23	0	21	34	22	40	5
					0	95	96	93	99	98	76	82	95	97	22	21	96	96	97	92	97	91	23	5	18	31	18	40	6
						0	98	97	97	99	74	83	98	99	16	20	95	95	98	92	98	94	23	3	16	30	19	39	7
							0	98	88	91	47	60	94	96	7	24	97	98	97	98	88	85	0	−5	−1	12	−3	23	8
								0	87	91	46	59	94	95	5	23	97	97	97	98	87	84	−3	−8	−4	8	−6	19	9
									0	97	80	83	98	95	25	20	94	94	94	89	96	89	27	7	21	35	21	43	10
										0	77	85	98	98	17	20	94	94	98	54	98	94	24	4	19	33	23	41	11
											0	96	70	67	37	10	58	57	64	67	80	76	55	21	43	55	53	57	12
												0	77	78	28	18	65	66	75	95	88	86	51	19	41	54	52	57	13
													0	98	15	17	98	98	98	98	95	89	16	4	12	26	12	36	14
														0	8	17	98	98	99	98	96	92	14	3	11	25	13	35	15
															0	70	96	66	19	20	27	32	51	−23	38	36	29	32	16
																0	21	20	97	96	25	30	16	−57	10	6	0	2	17
																	0	99	98	98	90	83	6	0	3	17	−1	28	18
																		0	99	97	90	84	3	−1	0	14	11	25	19
																			0	98	95	91	13	13	10	24	31	34	20
																				0	91	88	7	−2	6	19	33	28	21
																					0	96	34	6	28	41	94	48	22
																						0	35	1	27	39	47	46	23
																							0	48	94	96	92	88	24
																								0	42	58	0	68	25
																									0	94	0	79	26
																										0	94	94	27
																											0	79	28
																												0	29

Variables (for identification, see text)

The whole numbers of the correlation coefficient are omitted, two figures being left after the dot. Thus, −23 means that the coefficient is −0.23.

Table 3. Correlations of year-to-year changes in strike characteristics and economic conditions in Russian manufacturing over years 1895–1913

Variables (for identification, see text)

1	2	3	4	5	6	7	8	9	10	11	12	13	14	15	16	17	18	19	20	21	22	23	24	25	26	27	28	29	No.
0	99	97	72	65	-72	-64	30	11	-14	6	-41	-25	54	55	-35	-34	50	46	60	62	-41	-23	-31	-14	-29	24	-42	37	1
	0	97	74	67	-74	-67	29	10	-15	5	-39	-24	54	57	-36	-34	46	43	62	62	-39	-24	-35	-16	-30	21	-34	33	2
		0	61	54	-61	-54	32	13	-18	4	-39	-26	51	53	-34	-31	48	41	60	65	-35	-20	-48	-12	-33	17	-34	32	3
			0	98	-99	-98	23	6	-9	7	-35	-19	37	46	-13	-21	12	29	46	30	-26	1	17	-35	-21	14	-28	23	4
				0	-98	-99	21	3	-10	8	-27	-16	34	43	-13	-19	3	25	48	29	-25	0	19	-33	-21	16	-18	22	5
					0	-98	-23	-6	9	-7	35	19	-37	-46	13	21	-12	-29	-46	-30	26	-1	-17	35	21	-14	29	-23	6
						0	-21	-3	10	-8	27	16	-34	-43	13	19	-2	-25	-48	-29	25	0	-19	33	21	-16	17	-22	7
							0	64	-89	-26	-66	-55	17	20	-3	5	-2	31	1	9	24	20	-9	-7	-36	-2	-16	22	8
								0	-61	-76	-36	-35	9	-1	-27	-28	-24	10	8	-33	26	24	-7	4	-5	-12	9	-2	9
									0	39	25	31	9	30	-6	-11	9	21	8	60	-8	-22	-10	-29	42	3	1	-7	10
										0	-9	-33	1	-14	18	47	7	-9	7	-29	-5	-22	18	16	2	-4	-18	-10	11
											0	67	-53	-42	17	7	-8	-31	-8	-38	-25	-5	35	35	6	0	32	14	12
												0	-37	-22	13	-27	24	-1	22	28	-7	-3	26	14	-10	24	11	22	13
													0	84	-88	-65	6	17	26	8	1	-50	-39	-37	-11	20	5	23	14
														0	-75	-78	0	14	43	-10	3	-24	-23	-36	5	22	11	-24	15
															0	74	-6	-14	-33	24	8	63	39	5	-36	-28	-26	-19	16
																0	0	-10	-25	41	-60	23	15	-32	-15	-23	-24	45	17
																	0	-6	0	17	-68	-31	8	-7	-26	41	-58	27	18
																		0	69	0	-71	-34	-6	-20	-20	18	-26	20	19
																			0	43	-49	-35	-18	-5	-5	17	3	19	20
																				0	35	-31	8	32	-14	-25	-23	-19	21
																					0	43	-15	-5	3	-27	15	23	22
																						0	27	-19	-14	-38	-20	24	23
																							0	5	3	20	-18	18	24
																								0	-17	57	0	62	25
																									0	14	24	43	26
																										0	-25	80	27
																											0	-49	28
																												0	29

The whole numbers of the correlation coefficient are omitted, two figures being left after the dot. Thus, -23 means that the coefficient is -0.23.

Russian factory industry as a whole and in each group separately,[6] as well as data on the number of enterprises and the number of workers. Among the indicators of the second type are data on nominal and real wages.[7] Yearly information about nominal wages is given in the "Abstracts of Factory Inspectors' Reports" and about real wages (in the form of indices) in S. G. Strumilin's work.[8]

The indicator of the value of output to a certain extent reflects the economic situation, as do data on the number of workers: The reduction of their number is usually indirect evidence of the growth of unemployment and a crisis of industrial production. Wages are among the most important and most sensitive indicators of the economic position of the proletariat.

Let us begin with describing "internal" connections of the above indicators of industrial development and the economic position of workers.

Table 1 (zero-order correlations) shows that the value of output was closely dependent on the number of workers (0.95), nominal wages (0.94), less significantly on real wages (0.47), and noticeably but inversely dependent on the number of enterprises (−0.34). Nominal wages were closely and directly dependent on the number of workers (0.88) and substantially dependent on real wages (0.48).

Table 2 (detrended correlations), compared with the previous table, introduces substantial adjustments into the picture of internal connections: Only the connection of the value of output with the number of workers was found similar on the whole. A weak negative conjunction (−0.18) is observed between the value of output and nominal wages and between nominal wages and the number of workers; no connection was found between the value of output and real wages or between nominal wages and real wages (0.05). Having common trends in 1895–1913, these indicators were not, however, characterized by synchronous annual fluctuations.

The value of output per enterprise had a substantial connection with real wages (0.57) and a less noticeable connection with nominal wages (0.20). Its close connection with the average size of enterprise appears quite evident.

Let us now examine the connections between the strike movement and indicators of industrial development and the economic position of workers.

---

6. These data are borrowed from the book *Dynamics of Russian and Soviet Industry in Connection with the Development of the National Economy in Forty Years (1887–1926)*, prepared under the guidance of V. E. Varzar and L. B. Afengauz. For more information, see V. I. Bovykin, "Dynamics of Industrial Production in Russia (1896–1910)," *Istoriia SSSR*, no. 3 (1983): 22–3; V. I. Bovykin, *Formation of Finance Capital in Russia: Late 19th C.–1908*, (Moscow, 1984), pp. 22–5.

7. In preliminary calculations we also used the indicator of crop yield, with a lag. However, coefficients of correlation with this indicator were inconsequential. Besides, in the strict sense, the index of real wages "absorbs" it. For this reason we dropped it.

8. See S. G. Strumilin, *Sketches of Russia's Economic History* (Moscow, 1960), pp. 108, 118, 121.

Table 4. *Coefficients of correlation of the number of strikers and the value of output in each of the twelve branches of factory industry in Russia in 1895–1913 (natural series)*

					Branches						
1	2	3	4	5	6	7	8	9	10	11	12
09	00	00	12	09	21	10	56	03	10	08	27

The whole numbers of the correlation coefficient are omitted, two figures being left after the dot. Thus, -23 means that the coefficient is -0.23.

Designation of indicators: 1. number of strikers in cotton processing; 2. number of strikers in wool processing; 3. number of strikers in silk processing; 4. number of strikers in flax processing; 5. number of strikers in mixed production; 6. number of strikers in papermaking and book printing; 7. number of strikers in woodworking; 8. number of strikers in metalworking; 9. number of strikers in the processing of minerals; 10. number of strikers in the processing of livestock products; 11. number of strikers in food processing; 12. number of strikers in chemical production.

Table 1 (zero-order) suggests that there were no substantial connections of this kind.

The connections in Table 2 (detrended) look different. In contrast to the previous table (with the trend), the number of strikers has negative correlations with nearly all indicators used by us – the number of workers, the number of enterprises, gross value of output, and also nominal and real wages – though with a small margin (-0.07, -0.21, -0.28, -0.35, -0.16). Coefficients characterizing the connections of annual fluctuations testify that in a slump of production (reduction of the gross values of output) or decline of the rates of its growth, the strike struggle intensified, and that the growth of industrial production was usually accompanied by a decline of strikes.

Considering that the development of different branches of factory industry (groups I–XII) was uneven in the period under review (1895–1913), it would be interesting to look at the data on the connection of the number of strikers and the value of gross output branchwise. Table 4 shows that such connections existed but had comparatively small magnitudes (usually not more than 0.12; and 0.21 and 0.27 for two of the twelve branches of industry). An exception was metalworking (0.56).

The matrix of detrended correlations (Table 5) points to the presence of negative connections between the value of gross output and the number of strikes in all branches of factory industry, with the exception of metal processing. Indicators were usually within the limits of -0.20 to -0.50 and in chemical production they were practically nil. In metal processing the coefficient had an opposite sign ($+0.43$). This means that with the contraction of production, an

Table 5. *Coefficients of correlation of the number of strikers and the value of output in each of the twelve branches of factory industry in Russia in 1895–1913 (first differences)*

					Branches						
1	2	3	4	5	6	7	8	9	10	11	12
−45	−33	−31	−21	−44	−25	−35	+43	−29	−29	−49	−03

The whole numbers of the correlation coefficient are omitted, two figures being left after the dot. Thus, −23 means that the coefficient is −0.23.

Designation of indicators: 1. number of strikers in cotton processing; 2. number of strikers in wool processing; 3. number of strikers in silk processing; 4. number of strikers in flax processing; 5. number of strikers in mixed production; 6. number of strikers in papermaking and book printing; 7. number of strikers in woodworking; 8. number of strikers in metalworking; 9. number of strikers in the processing of minerals; 10. number of strikers in the processing of livestock products; 11. number of strikers in food processing; 12. number of strikers in chemical production.

increase in the number of strikers was the rule. Metalworkers, on the other hand, waged an especially active struggle at the time of upturns in production. In other words, for the period of 1895–1913 we can state as a general rule an inverse connection between the development of industrial production (value of gross output) and the scope of the strike movement. Only in metal processing, in contrast to other branches, were there positive connections between the respective indicators. But these connections were weak, testifying to the fact that in Russia of the late nineteenth and early twentieth century, there was no strict dependence between changes in economic conditions and the growth of workers' strike activity.

The period under examination includes the years of the first Russian revolution, which were sharply salient for the scope of the strike struggle. This was bound to leave an imprint on the correlations. In order to check the observations made earlier on their basis, we found it necessary to choose a more homogeneous period for our analysis. To this end we decided to confine ourselves to the ten years from 1895 to 1904. Looking at the matrix of differences between the main indicators of the strike movement in Russia in 1895–1913 (Table 6) we can see the extent to which coefficients of this decade differ from the coefficients of most other years (excepting 1909–11). At the same time, the similarity of coefficients in the period under review is noteworthy. Most of the 100 indicators do not exceed the figure 10; only a few rise slightly higher. In his article "Strikes in Russia" (1913) Lenin singled out this period calling it "prerevolutionary."[9]

9. V. I. Lenin, *Collected Works*, vol. 19, p. 535.

Table 6. *Matrix of zero-order coefficients of difference (distance) between 23-dimensional vectors characterizing strikes of factory workers in Russia for each pair of years in the period 1895–1913*

Years	1895	1896	1897	1898	1899	1900	1901	1902	1903	1904	1905	1906	1907	1908	1909	1910	1911	1912	1913
1895	0																		
1896	8	0																	
1897	5	11	0																
1898	6	3	9	0															
1899	6	2	10	2	0														
1900	2	5	6	4	4	0													
1901	9	1	12	3	3	6	0												
1902	5	3	9	2	2	2	4	0											
1903	8	5	11	4	3	6	5	5	0										
1904	9	3	14	4	4	7	2	5	7	0									
1905	99	99	97	97	97	99	98	98	94	99	0								
1906	45	46	44	44	44	45	45	45	41	46	61	0							
1907	26	29	24	26	27	26	29	27	25	30	82	27	0						
1908	21	26	19	24	25	23	27	24	24	27	95	42	16	0					
1909	7	14	4	12	12	9	15	11	13	16	97	43	21	16	0				
1910	6	4	9	1	2	4	4	2	4	5	97	43	26	23	11	0			
1911	9	7	11	5	6	8	7	6	4	8	94	39	23	23	12	4	0		
1912	18	18	18	16	16	18	18	17	14	18	85	30	15	23	17	15	12	0	
1913	35	34	35	33	33	35	34	33	30	34	78	24	24	36	34	32	28	19	0

The whole numbers of the correlation coefficient are omitted, two figures being left after the dot. Thus, −23 means that the coefficient is −0.23.

The value of each coefficient is given as percentage of the maximum distance between 23-dimensional vectors.

What, then, is conveyed by the analysis of connections between major indicators of the strike movement in Russia in 1895–1904? First of all, the main correlations were found to be rather similar to those that were observed over a longer period–from 1895 to 1913. Here too (Table 7, zero-order correlations) the most important indicator (the number of strikes) has a direct and rather substantial connection with the number of strikes, the number of lost working days, the number of political, economic, and offensive strikes (and the number of their participants)–from 0.77 to 0.97. As before, there is a weak connection of the number of strikers with the number of defensive strikes and the number of their participants (0.25 and 0.20).

At the same time, there are some differences. Thus, while the correlation of the number of strikes over work hours with the number of their participants was high as before (0.84 and 0.87), the correlation with the number of participants in strikes over other working and living conditions, and the number of participants in strikes over wages was lower (0.15 and 0.45). Noteworthy is this correlation: even though in 1895–1913 the correlation of the total number of strikers with the number of participants in strikes over other working and living conditions was high (0.83), in 1895–1904 it was insignificant (0.15). From this it can be concluded that the Revolution of 1905–7 substantially broadened the gamut of workers' demands. To the usual demands concerning wages and work hours are added from 1905 on, on an equal footing as it were, demands concerning the improvement of other working and living conditions, demands for decent treatment, social demands related to insurance, medical services, and so on. The Revolution of 1905–7 played an important role not only in the growth of social requirements, but also in the expansion of the respective demands of workers. This found expression in the increase of such demands in the course of the revolution and after it.

The date of the detrended matrix (Table 8) are rather similar to those just quote above.

The matrix of year-to-year changes during 1895–1904 (Table 9), as observed already in the chronologically longer period, produces a different picture. The number of strikers was closely connected with number of lost working days (0.92) and number of political strikes (0.73) and substantially connected with the number of participants in political strikes (0.54), the number of participants in strikes over hours (0.44), and the number of offensive strikes and the number of their participants (0.61 and 0.37). There was a substantial but inverse connection between the number of economic strikes and the number of participants in them (−0.73 and −0.54) as well as between the number of strikes over other working and living conditions and the number of participants (−0.64 and −0.46). Correlation with other indicators was weak, usually not going beyond ±0.24.

Comparison of these data with the respective share data of the matrix for

Table 7. *Zero-order correlations of strike characteristics and economic conditions in Russian manufacturing over years 1895–1904*

Variables (for identification, see text)

1	2	3	4	5	6	7	8	9	10	11	12	13	14	15	16	17	18	19	20	21	22	23	24	25	26	27	28	29	No.
0	87	77	95	91	99	75	82	33	98	64	50	29	99	81	0	-13	94	62	77	46	90	74	32	34	27	22	37	21	1
	0	92	79	77	87	97	82	45	84	87	26	15	86	84	25	20	77	67	57	67	89	80	8	8	4	-1	21	-2	2
		0	76	69	75	89	71	43	74	80	7	13	76	82	15	18	69	63	38	57	88	76	4	0	13	-3	20	-9	3
			0	97	91	64	73	15	91	61	45	34	92	75	-7	-13	93	58	63	43	87	67	42	48	39	34	41	32	4
				0	87	60	69	7	87	61	51	31	88	69	-5	-10	87	50	61	45	86	67	48	52	42	42	45	41	5
					0	77	84	38	98	64	50	26	99	81	3	-13	92	62	80	80	90	75	28	28	22	17	35	17	6
						0	78	54	74	86	14	7	76	73	34	29	64	66	49	46	81	76	17	-19	-9	-18	9	-19	7
							0	68	75	54	14	-5	81	35	23	16	80	75	55	45	81	63	17	15	4	7	28	7	8
								0	27	11	-6	-32	33	81	34	26	26	56	24	8	36	40	-29	-35	-28	-40	-3	-41	9
									0	65	54	32	98	11	-2	-20	90	55	36	82	88	74	28	29	25	18	34	17	10
										0	5	5	66	5	21	31	51	90	36	82	74	63	-6	-15	-8	-9	0	-8	11
											0	58	46	0	-3	-39	44	40	67	-6	30	42	40	37	35	30	41	28	12
												0	25	86	-6	-40	43	13	32	-9	9	19	61	52	56	50	53	44	13
													0	0	-24	-19	69	91	76	44	92	76	29	30	25	20	36	19	14
														0	0	-17	-11	35	39	39	94	85	13	11	17	7	26	5	15
															0	0	83	5	23	60	-14	-19	-32	-45	-48	-37	-29	-48	16
																0	0	46	-13	66	-11	-25	-54	-58	-65	-53	-56	28	17
																	0	74	70	39	78	57	41	44	28	28	38	9	18
																		0	49	53	45	25	-2	-3	-16	-16	0	20	19
																			0	41	50	40	18	16	-36	8	21	-21	20
																				0	42	18	-26	-30	27	-25	-29	18	21
																					0	89	26	26	36	19	38	95	22
																						0	28	17	91	18	50	83	23
																							0	94	87	97	93	98	24
																								0	0	94	92	83	25
																									0	90	88	0	26
																										0	0		27
																											0		28
																												0	29

The whole numbers of the correlation coefficient are omitted, two figures being left after the dot. Thus, -23 means that the coefficient is -0.23.

Table 8. Detrended correlations of strike characteristics and economic conditions in Russian manufacturing over years 1895–1904

Variables (for identification, see text)

1	2	3	4	5	6	7	8	9	10	11	12	13	14	15	16	17	18	19	20	21	22	23	24	25	26	27	28	29	No.
0	88	78	94	91	99	80	82	45	98	69	41	10	99	80	13	7	93	68	77	60	89	70	-14	4	-18	-42	15	-31	1
	0	91	81	81	88	98	82	51	85	88	22	7	87	84	33	35	78	68	56	74	91	82	-44	-33	-29	-59	24	-46	2
		0	79	73	75	90	71	48	74	80	2	6	77	62	21	31	69	64	37	63	85	77	-52	-28	3	-58	29	-58	3
			0	97	90	70	73	28	91	67	33	10	92	74	7	13	92	67	63	61	86	60	-5	22	-5	-28	-4	-23	4
				0	87	68	70	22	87	71	38	1	88	69	12	23	84	60	62	68	85	59	-6	20	-15	-21	-12	-12	5
					0	81	84	50	98	67	43	9	99	80	15	5	91	67	80	59	88	72	-17	-1	-23	-47	22	-33	6
						0	81	56	77	86	14	8	81	82	37	36	70	66	49	70	85	82	-53	-48	-32	-67	34	-53	7
							0	76	74	55	7	-22	80	71	31	32	80	77	53	53	80	61	-15	-7	-43	-42	36	-23	8
								0	38	12	3	-28	44	42	28	16	40	56	30	3	48	56	-42	-35	-20	-66	82	-54	9
									0	69	48	17	98	80	8	-3	89	59	82	58	86	71	-16	0	-14	-44	15	-34	10
										0	6	6	70	78	23	37	56	40	36	85	79	68	-42	-36	-26	-33	-4	-23	11
											0	45	6	3	11	-22	26	16	28	4	19	30	-4	-2	-12	-39	-2	-29	12
												0	37	7	21	-11	27	27	75	7	-15	-6	16	-7	-2	-33	-26	-38	13
													0	85	4	-1	90	61	37	57	91	73	-17	2	-15	-42	18	-31	14
														0	-19	-7	68	37	31	46	94	85	-42	-16	-6	-45	26	-37	15
															0	82	20	62	-4	56	8	-7	-2	-40	-55	-25	6	-12	16
																0	13	52	69	55	75	49	-5	-26	-48	-35	-14	7	17
																	0	82	51	54	49	29	12	21	-27	-45	0	-24	18
																		0		47	48	37	6	0	-38	-31	12	-35	19
																			0		55	32	4	0	-21	-7	17	-19	20
																				0		87	-9	-19	-40	-46	-22	20	21
																					0		-41	-10	-13	-74	4	57	22
																						0	-74	-46	-3	69	23	93	23
																							0	79	-20	66	51	-65	24
																								0	20	8	-65	57	25
																									0	0	-56	71	26
																										0	16	-25	27
																											0	-66	28
																												0	29

The whole numbers of the correlation coefficient are omitted, two figures being left after the dot. Thus, −23 means that the coefficient is −0.23.

Table 9. *Correlations of year-to-year changes in strike characteristics and economic conditions in Russian manufacturing over years 1895–1904*

No.	1	2	3	4	5	6	7	8	9	10	11	12	13	14	15	16	17	18	19	20	21	22	23	24	25	26	27	28	29
1	0	83	73	90	70	70	−90	−70	14	2	16	30	−64	−52	72	47	−49	−10	−13	38	28	20	0	−26	−2	18	−19	−28	−17
2		0	92	73	54	39	−73	−54	20	−13	8	44	−64	−46	61	37	−33	−9	−20	22	5	17	21	−42	−31	−27	−56	16	−44
3			0	66	39	0	−66	−39	18	−4	9	31	−60	−41	53	44	−29	−18	−17	16	−16	1	31	−10	−52	−28	3	−58	29
4				0	88	88	−100	−88	14	1	7	38	−48	−63	60	42	−46	7	−24	18	11	25	−6	−8	3	26	−8	−9	−7
5					0	0	−88	−100	20	−8	−8	51	−32	−65	35	7	44	−27	15	26	53	13	−19	3	−26	−26	9	−15	22
6						0	−88	88	−14	−1	−7	32	−65	−32	36	16	37	−33	11	29	−25	−13	−19	6	−27	8	15	−9	7
7							0	0	−20	8	8	−38	66	37	−61	−24	−33	49	11	37	−4	−6	16	19	−9	8	8	25	−22
8								0	−20	−14	−8	48	−37	−70	−35	−7	−38	58	27	29	−2	55	38	6	−3	27	15	42	−19
9									0	63	−91	−25	−66	−60	26	16	19	−32	−15	14	23	−13	−9	19	−9	−50	8	−19	−13
10										0	−60	−82	−37	−35	9	37	−38	−46	−24	−2	−61	−37	−48	6	−14	4	−50	−12	30
11											0	−36	−43	32	11	−61	−33	6	−11	30	76	−3	−1	−9	−11	3	−26	4	5
12												0	30	−37	36	2	20	−24	−32	27	−19	33	−48	−48	3	47	−50	−32	−13
13													0	−70	−66	9	−33	19	27	−4	57	16	−1	−11	12	4	3	4	−13
14														0	−15	11	−61	−38	−46	6	76	0	−33	−4	−5	−5	−26	−32	−21
15															0	2	28	49	8	−24	−6	−27	0	16	11	−18	27	−59	30
16																0	57	−10	57	15	14	−11	−57	25	1	32	−34	21	5
17																	0	−80	61	37	4	11	−6	−6	23	−8	41	−31	−13
18																		0	67	11	−54	−57	−58	−30	−34	19	−22	31	−21
19																			0	−13	−19	−37	−25	−26	−2	−2	37	31	25
20																				0	30	47	−37	−26	34	22	−5	57	61
21																					0	47	23	−2	39	44	30	−6	20
22																						0	45	23	67	56	−5	10	2
23																							0	65	44	32	30	20	61
24																								0	−71	36	9	−31	−25
25																									0	79	−33	56	−42
26																										0	15	−27	71
27																											0	−20	57
28																												0	−65
29																													0

The whole numbers of the correlation coefficient are omitted, two figures being left after the dot. Thus, −23 means that the coefficient is −0.23.

1895–1913 shows their great similarity. In both cases the correlation of the number of strikers with the number of political strikes and the number of their participants is direct and rather substantial (1895–1913: 0.74 and 0.67; 1985–1904: 0.73 and 0.54). The same can be said about connections with the number of offensive strikes and the number of their participants (respectively: 0.54 and 0.57, 0.61 and 0.37). This shows that the general course of the strike movement was closely "harmonized" with the dynamics of political and offensive strikes.

At the same time, in both cases there was a substantial inverse correlation with the number of economic strikes and the number of their participants (−0.74 and −0.67; −0.73 and −0.54) as well as a marked inverse correlation with the number of strikes over other working and living conditions and the number of participants (−0.39 and −0.24; −0.64 and −0.46), with the number of defensive strikes and the number of participants in them (−0.36 and −0.34; −0.33 and −0.09). Definite differences are observed in correlations with the number of participants in strikes over working time (1895–1913: 0.05; 1895–1904: 0.44), and also with the number of participants in successful strikes (0.44 and 0.22) and in strikes ending in compromise (0.62 and 0.17). We have already discussed the causes of these divergences.

If we compare the correlations of the number of strikers with "economic" indicators, we can note the following. The zero-order matrix for 1895–1913 yields coefficients of correlation with nominal and real wages, and with the aggregate value of gross output, which are low (0.23; 0.00; 0.21). The respective matrix for 1895–1904 only accentuates this observation (0.08; 0.00; 0.21). The matrices of detrended data show a clear inverse connection with both nominal and real wages, coefficients for 1895–1904 being more substantial (−0.35 and −0.16; −0.42 and −0.32). The latter is indirect evidence that in the period preceding the first revolution, questions of material conditions of workers were more prominent in the strike movement than during the period of 1895–1913 as a whole. We have a definite confirmation of this in the increase in the share of strikes over other working and living conditions in the longer period by comparison with the shorter period.

We have additional branch data on the number of strikes and the number of strikers, the number of strikes of different duration (up to 0.5 day, from 0.5 to 2 days, and from 10 to 30 days), and the number of group (collective) strikes. Along with yearly data on the number of enterprises and the number of workers, the value of output of all factory industry and its separate branches, and that of nominal and real wages, we also have for this period yearly indicators of the number of cases when reprisals were inflicted on striking factory workers, such as partial and general layoffs, arrests, and the call-up of soldiers to suppress the strike.[10]

10. See *Statistics on Workers' Strikes at Factories and Plants for the Decade 1895–1904*, p. 38, Table 15.

212

Table 10. *Matrix of correlation of year-to-year changes in branches (twelve groups) of factory industry in Russia, indicators of economic growth and reprisals in 1895–1904*

No.	1	2	3	4	5	6	7	8	9	10	11	12	13	14	15	16	17	18
1	X																	
2	−52	X																
3	48	−11	X															
4	8	21	22	X														
5	50	−39	52	62	X													
6	43	−3	26	64	52	X												
7	−6	28	62	76	60	45	X											
8	4	28	43	91	57	71	87	X										
9	14	11	74	7	10	19	63	38	X									
10	22	0	31	80	59	92	62	88	22	X								
11	65	−3	29	48	35	89	33	53	24	73	X							
12	7	27	58	85	64	63	93	97	47	81	45	X						
13	−55	24	−52	−18	71	−9	−46	−16	−25	−4	−14	−30	X					
14	−58	2	−50	−4	−34	13	−29	−1	−25	19	−13	−12	79	X				
15	34	−63	28	19	58	57	27	31	31	55	38	30	−29	18	X			
16	45	−4	31	72	56	98	53	77	22	94	90	59	−12	6	55	X		
17	−25	23	34	48	44	−21	57	47	21	7	−33	56	−46	−40	−12	−11	X	
18	33	−1	34	74	56	96	56	83	22	98	81	76	−6	15	55	98	−4	X

The whole numbers of the correlation coefficient are omitted, two figures being left after the dot. Thus, −23 means that the coefficient is −0.23.

Designation of indicators: 1. number of strikers in cotton processing; 2. number of strikers in wool processing; 3. number of strikers in silk processing; 4. number of strikers in flax processing; 5. number of strikers in mixed production; 6. number of strikers in papermaking and book printing; 7. number of strikers in woodworking; 8. number of strikers in metalworking; 9. number of strikers in the processing of minerals; 10. number of strikers in the processing of livestock products; 11. number of strikers in food processing; 12. number of strikers in chemical production; 13. nominal wages; 14. real wages; 15. number of partial layoffs; 16. number of general layoffs; 17. number of cases of arrests and exiles to places of domicile registration; 18. number of call-ups of troops.

The conjunction of the number of strikers in different sectors of production is positive and rather substantial in most cases (Table 10). Close connection between the total number of strikers (indicator 0.71 and higher) was characteristic of nontextile production. Thus, in metal processing such connections are traceable with five of the eleven branches of production (with groups of factory industry IV, VI, VII, X, and XII), in processing of livestock products likewise with five branches (IV, VI, VIII, XI, XII), in chemical production and processing of flax and hemp with four branches. At the same time, in the processing of cotton and wool, mixed production, and the processing of mineral substances, these connections did not rise to such a significant level, though "inside" textile production they were rather close. This speaks of a certain "isolation" of the development of the strike movement in the majority of textile groups in the ten-year period under examination (note was made earlier of the reduction of the share of striking textile workers in the total mass of strikers at the close of the nineteenth and the beginning of the twentieth century).

Group (collective) strikes that embraced several related enterprises at a time were evidence of proletarian solidarity. These data show a close direct connection between the number of group strikes and the number of all strikes in general in a particular branch of industry (and, accordingly, the number of participants in them). Thus, the correlations of the number of strikers run from 0.67 (mixed production) to 0.93–0.99 (wool processing, papermaking and book printing, woodworking, processing of metals, livestock products, chemical production).

The connections of the strike movement in different branches of factory industry, on the one hand, and the indicators of economic, social, and political development, on the other hand, are as follows:

The comparison of the number of strikers in different branches of factory industry with countrywide indicators of nominal and real wages (variables 13 and 14 in Table 10) in most cases shows a weak connection, inverse as a rule (from −0.1 to −0.3).[11] Only in three branches – cotton processing, silk processing, and mixed textile products – were the respective indicators substantial: from −0.5 to −0.7. Workers of these branches (all of them textile workers), getting lower wages compared with workers in other lines of production, reacted most "sensitively" to their change.

If we turn to connections of the number of strikes in different branches of factory industry with the number of reprisals against strikers (such as partial or general layoffs, arrest or exile to places of registration, and call-up of soliders) in most cases these connections should be qualified as direct and substantial (0.3–0.7). There were no significant correlations (0.71 and higher) with partial layoffs, arrests, and exiles. Such correlations were found only with general layoffs (in five out of twelve types of production: IV, VI, VIII, X, XI) and call-up of soldiers (in six out of twelve types of proudction: IV, VI, VIII, X, XI, XII). Textiles are noticeably absent (I, II, III, and V). This situation can serve as an indirect indication that the sharpness of the strike struggle during the period in question was accounted for by workers outside the textile industry.

Table 10 points with sufficient clarity to the following regularity: higher con-

---

11. Indicators of this connection in all twelve groups of factory production are as follows: I. −0.55 and −0.58; II. 0.24 and 0.02; III. −0.52 and −0.50; IV. −0.18 and −0.04; V. −0.71 and −0.34; VI. −0.09 and 0.13; VII. −0.46 and −0.29; VIII. −0.16 and −0.01; IX. −0.25 and −0.25; X. −0.04 and 0.19; XI. −0.14 and −0.13; XII. −0.30 and −0.12.

nection of the extent of the movement and the number of strikers in almost all branches of factory industry with general and "harsh" reprisals than with partial reprisals. Thus, in cotton processing the connections with the number of partial and complete layoffs are 0.34 and 0.45, respectively, with the number of arrests (and exiles) and the number of call-ups of soldiers (in connection with the strike), −0.25 and 0.33. In metalworking the corresponding correlations are 0.31 and 0.77; 0.47 and 0.83.

This regularity is confirmed by the coefficients of annual changes in the number of reprisals in the ten-year period (1895–1904). While annual average changes in the number of cases of partial layoffs and arrests were defined respectively as −5.7% and −1.7% (i.e., relatively small figures), the average annual increases in the number of cases of general layoffs of strikers and call-up of soldiers, on the other hand, were 18.9% and 27.5%. These data are eloquent. "Partial" measures give way to more general and "harsher" measures, measures of individual action to means of mass action. Also in evidence is the intensification of repressive policy in relation to strikers and the labor movement as a whole, reflecting the sharpening of social conflicts in 1895–1904.

Let us summarize the results of these correlation analyses:

The data point to the close connection of the main indicators of strike activity in the longer (1895–1913) and shorter (1895–1904) periods, correlation coefficients being higher over the longer period. Throughout the stage under consideration, close connection was observed between the development of economic and political strikes. As is known, Lenin drew attention to this dependence and, at times, the interlocking of economic and political strikes in Russia. An exception were defensive strikes: Connections with them were weak. This is an indirect indication that offensive actions of workers were at the base of the strike movement in Russia during the period under review.

The analysis of relative data showed that the percentage of strikers (in the total workforce) was directly and significantly related to the proportion of participants in political and offensive strikes. Waves of overall strike activity were similar to waves of development of political strikes, even during the shorter period when political strikes themselves accounted for but a very modest share (just a few percent).

One divergence of indicators in the longer and shorter periods is noteworthy. We mean the coefficients of correlation between the total number of strikers and the number of participants in strikes over other working and living conditions. In 1895–1904 this coefficient is a small magnitude (0.15). In 1895–1913 its magnitude rises to the level of coefficients characterizing correlations with the number of participants in strikes over such demands as wages and work hours. This temporary change in correlation reflected the expansion of the range of workers' demands, the rise of their requirements, not only material but also spiritual, that were linked with the period of the revolution of 1905–7 and the following stage.

Correlation analysis makes it possible to see the "conjunction" of the strike movement of workers belonging to different professional contingents, to note the heightened activity or lagging of workers in particular fields of production. Co-efficients of correlation between the number of strikers in the majority of groups of factory industry in 1895–1913 are rather high and similar (not lower than 0.9). An exception are correlations with the indicators for metal processing. These "specific" coefficients of the matrix of correlations characterizing the conduct of metalworkers in the strike struggle are the result of their more active leading role in the labor movement throughout the period under review (beginning with the turn of the century).

The number of strikers, the value of production, and nominal and real wages all rose throughout the period in question. The scope of the movement rested on certain growth of industrial production and certain increase of wages (this is confirmed by the respective data for the shorter period of 1895–1904). The analysis of detrended residuals and year-to-year changes for 1895–1913 shows, however, that the correlation of the number of strikers, this main indicator, with all the three "economic" indicators, though nonsubstantial, was inverse (from −0.15 to −0.35). In practice the aggravation of the economic situation and deterioration of workers' conditions (or lowering of growth rates) frequently led to the development of the strike movement. The data for 1895–1904 confirm this conclusion concerning connections with nominal and real wages, and co-efficients in this case are higher than in the entire period 1895–1913. This points to the gradual weakening of the impact of this factor on the development of the strike struggle. It is significant that the matrix of yearly fluctuations showing negative correlations between the number of strikers and the value of output in eleven branches of factory industry yielded a substantial and direct correlation (0.43) in metal processing: For metalworkers, in contrast to other contingents of the factory proletariat, active strike struggle during upsurges of production was the rule.

Finally, studies of year-to-year variation for the shorter period of 1895–1904 testify to a shift of employers and authorities from partial reprisals against strikers to more general and harsher measures, which reflected the sharpening of social conflicts.

216

9

Labor conflicts in Italy before the rise of fascism, 1881–1923: a quantitative analysis

LORENZO BORDOGNA, GIAN PRIMO CELLA,
GIANCARLO PROVASI

Introduction

The aim of this paper is to provide a synthetic, quantitative analysis of labor conflicts in Italy as they are recorded in official strike statistics from the last decades of the nineteenth century to the ascent of fascism. The qualification, "as they are recorded by the official statistics on strikes," imposes two limits. First, forms of industrial unrest other than strikes, such as boycotts, restriction of output, and absenteeism and sabotage, will not be considered here. If it is true that these various types of conflict are to some extent interchangeable (Knowles 1952, 285), and that restricting one specific manifestation might "merely divert the conflict to other forms" (Hyman 1972, 55), this limitation will be particularly significant in the Italian context, where especially during the first decades analyzed here, the legal and political environment was rather hostile both to unionization and to industrial strikes.

Second, the official statistics provided by the government record only "economic" strikes, that is, "those which aim to obtain better working conditions directly from the employer." Excluded are "political" strikes and those aiming to obtain the passage of some specific legislation or to achieve economic improvements through government measures. It could be, as one Italian scholar put it (Foa, 1975, 1799), that in Italy even more than in other countries the strike movement captured only a portion of labor activity, and that the social strains of the period are better expressed by indices such as migration, crime, and massacres. Nonetheless, this restriction of industrial conflict to economic

This paper is drawn from a longer study by Bordogna and Provasi, "Il movimento degli scioperi in Italia, 1881–1973," in G. P. Cella, ed., *Il movimento degli scioperi nel XX secolo* (Bologna: Il Mulino, 1979). The other countries analyzed in the volume were Britain, France, West Germany, and the United States, and the other authors are G. Baglioni, P. Kemeny, G. Romagnoli, and G. E. Rusconi.

strikes is rather common among writers on the subject, and there is no obvious way to overcome it in this study.

Our analysis will be based on the three basic measures supplied by official sources: the number of strikes, the number of strikers (participation), and the number of workdays lost due to strike activity (volume). The importance of taking into account these three dimensions of strike activity is now generally recognized in the literature as the best approach for developing a comprehensive view and for avoiding the risk of misleading conclusion, such as the well-known Ross and Hartman thesis that postulated the "withering away of the strike."[1]

This paper is divided in five sections. The first one will consider the trends in aggregate strike activity over the entire period as well as some subperiods, paying attention also to the evolution of the unionization process. The second section will be devoted to a brief examination of the "industrial geography" of conflict, and the following one will deal with the problem of the "shape" of strikes. Section four will analyze the determinants of strike activity, comparing and evaluating two contrasting approaches to the Italian experience: one that sees strikes as mainly dependent on, and determined by, the economic conjuncture; the other, which attributes a higher degree of autonomy to workers' industrial action, assigning greater significance to organizational and political factors. Brief conclusions summarizing the general characteristics of strike activity in Italy before the rise of fascism, and its connections with the evolution of the labor movement, will close the paper.

Trends in aggregate strike activity

Over the entire period under consideration aggregate strike activity in Italy at its most intense moments showed a clear and sharp tendency (see Figure 1). From the sporadic episodes of the 1880s involving a few thousands of workers and a few hundred thousands of days lost a year, strike activity increased rapidly and steadily, settling at remarkable levels during the first decade of the new century, and reaching peaks in the post–World War I years, which remain among the highest in Italian history up to the present day (see Table 1). The trend coefficients are in fact all positive and rather strong, showing an average percentage change per year in the number of strikes,

---

1. In fact, Ross and Hartman's thesis about the secular decline of the strike derives not only from the coincidence that their study was carried out during the 1950s (1948–56 is the last period considered), when industrial conflict was actually declining in most of the countries analyzed. It also arises from their failure to take into account all the dimensions of the phenomenon (strike frequency, for instance, was defined as "meaningless", and thus ignored) and to distinguish between the *levels* and *shapes* of strike activity. They were thus induced to confuse a transformation of the shape with a decline of levels of strike activity.

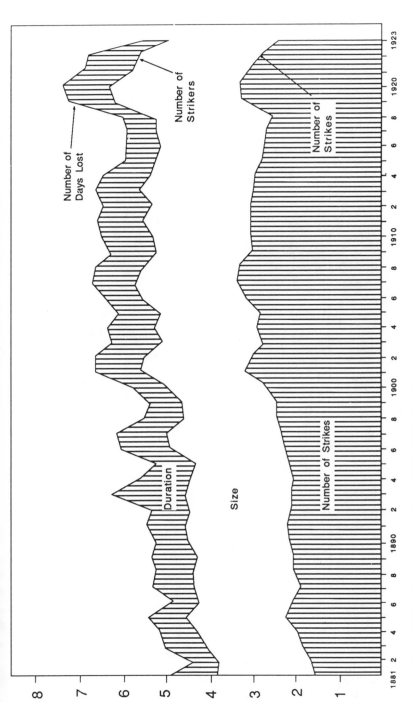

Figure 1. *The strike movement in Italy, 1881–1923 (logarithmic values)*

Table 1. *Numbers of strikes, strikers, and workdays lost due to strikes in Italy, 1881–1923*

Year	Strikes	Strikers (thousands)	Days lost (thousands)
1881	45	8	96
1882	49	8	26
1883	76	13	114
1884	91	24	149
1885	151	43	298
1886	113	21	66
1887	78	27	222
1888	106	30	193
1889	130	24	219
1890	147	40	176
1891	156	43	292
1892	129	34	224
1893	149	44	1,953
1894	117	32	366
1895	133	21	147
1896	211	96	1,153
1897	229	101	1,436
1898	292	44	322
1899	268	45	239
1900	410	93	565
1901	1,671	419	5,078
1902	1,032	344	4,564
1903	596	132	1,881
1904[a]	839	220	2,340
1905[a]	715	155	1,277
1906	1,641	381	2,922
1907	2,258	576	5,541
1908	1,745	371	4,864
1909	1,062	187	1,847
1910	1,118	199	3,300
1911	1,255	386	4,341
1912	1,090	240	2,889
1913	907	465	4,543
1914	864	222	2,568
1915	607	180	872
1916	577	139	838
1917	470	175	849
1918	313	159	1,000
1919	1,871	1,555	22,325
1920[b]	2,070	2,314	30,569
1921	1,134	724	8,180
1922	575	448	6,917
1923	201	66	296

[a] The data for the man-days lost in 1904 and 1905 have been estimated, because they are lacking for the agricultural sector.
[b] The data concerning the occupation of the factories in September 1920 are not included. About 450,000 strikers were involved, and about 6 million labor days lost.

strikers, and days lost of 8.57, 9.45, and 10.30, respectively (see Table 2, last row).

It is not easy to single out the precise determinants that underlay this growth. The explanation does not lie simply in changes in the size of the total active population, which did not increase substantially from 1881 to 1921, so the trend coefficients of strike activity adjusted for the size of the labor force remain virtually stable (see Table 3). Probably more important are other phenomena connected with processes of economic development and social mobilization, such as urbanization, the increase in the proportion of wage and salaried earners, and the displacement of workers from the agricultural to the industrial sector.[2] All of these phenomena were reflected in changes in the internal composition rather than the size of the labor force.

A second feature of industrial conflicts during this period was their irregularity: sudden and dramatic peaks lasting no more than one or two years, followed by equally deep and sudden downturns, in the course of which conflicts almost disappeared.[3] These year-to-year variations, especially marked for the number of participants and the days lost in strikes, distinguished a situation still characterized by the weakness of trade unions with little capacity of planning and coordination by the center. This weakness continued even after the birth, in 1906, of the Confederazione Generale del Lavoro (CGdL), which "never achieved the main characteristic of a centralized organization, that is a direct power over the affiliated unions" (Horowitz 1966, 128). These overall tendencies can be differentiated for several subperiods, during which strike movements assumed changing features. Two such subperiods can be distinguished (1881–1899 and 1900–1923), the second of which can in turn be subdivided (for the years 1900–1914, 1915–1918, and 1919–1923).

1881–1899

The central characteristic of this first subperiod was the generally low levels of conflict, with a very clear increase over the two decades. The yearly values of the number of strikes, strikers, and days lost are in fact consistently

2. For the processes of industrial concentration and their effects on the work force, see Merli (1972, chap. 1), Caracciolo (1975a), and Romagnoli and Manoukian (1972). As for the urbanization process, between 1882 and 1901 the population of industrial towns in northern Italy increased much faster than the Italian population as a whole (Procacci 1972, 13, and Merli, 1972, 127ff.).

3. This situation clearly differed from that of the post–World War II period, when stronger labor organizations and more institutionalized industrial relations, although not producing the "withering away of the strike" predicted by Ross and Hartman (1960), nonetheless helped to regularize and to some extent "discipline" industrial conflicts, in accordance with the recurrent and predictable rhythm of collective bargaining (the variation coefficients are in fact 1.195 and 1.402, respectively, for numbers of strikers and days lost during the 1900–23 period, as against 0.508 and 0.702 for the 1949–73).

Table 2. *Mean number of strikes and trend coefficients by period and subperiod, using raw strike measures*

Period/ subperiod	Strikes	Trend (%)	Strikers (thousands)	Trend (%)	Days lost (thousands)	Trend (%)
1881–99	140	8.24	37	9.60	405	12.83
1900–23	1,042	—	423	—	5,015	—
1900–14	1,147	—	293	—	3,235	—
1915–18	492	—	163	—	890	—
1919–23	1,170	—	1,021	—	13,657	—
1881–1923	644	8.57	252	9.45	2,987	10.30

The trend coefficients have been computed with the formula $Y_t = Y_o (1 = g)t$, which becomes $\log Y_t = \log Y_o + t \log (1 + g)$, where Y is one of the three strike measures and g the average annual percentage rate of change. The trend coefficients have not been reported for the periods in which they are not statistically significant.

Table 3. *Mean number of strikes and trend coefficients per 100,000 workers by period and subperiod (total active population, including agricultural workers)*

Period/ subperiod	Strikes	Trend (%)	Strikers (thousands)	Trend (%)	Days lost (thousands)	Trend (%)
1881–99	0.83	7.91	218.4	9.27	2,401.1	12.94
1900–23	5.77	—	2,301.2	—	27,221.9	—
1900–14	6.47	—	1,649.5	—	18,230.9	—
1915–18	2.65	—	879.5	—	4,791.0	—
1919–23	6.18	—	5,402.8	—	72,139.6	—
1881–1923	3.59	6.88	1,380.9	9.02	16,254.6	9.87

and markedly lower than the average for the entire period (1881–1923), while the trend coefficients are all positive and notably high (8.24%, 9.60%, and 12.83%, respectively), for the three indices. The low levels of aggregate strike activity are probably accounted for not only by the still early stage of industrial development, but also by the severe institutional and legal restrictions to which industrial strikes were subjected. Even when the rights to unionize and to strike were partially liberalized by the Zanardelli legislation (1889), the government continued to view labor action as entirely an issue of public order until the end of the century (Neppi Modona 1969). However, despite recurrent cases of repression following intense outbreaks of industrial conflicts (1884–5, 1893–4, 1896–8), strike activity rose rapidly both in the agricultural and nonagricultural sectors, along with the process of unionization. Although it is not possible to

222

measure the precise degree of connection between the degrees of union organization and the intensity of strikes for lack of a data series on workers' organizations, these decades were marked by significant organizational growth, from the old *societa di mutuo soccorso* to the *leghe di resistenza*, and finally to the first forms of industrial unions and *camere del lavoro* (the first of which was founded in Milan in 1891). By the end of the century more than fifty Chambers of Labor (Camera di Lavoro) were operating and, according to Horowitz (1966, 99), about 150,000 workers had been organized. In 1893 a national Federation of the Chambers of Labor was formed and held several conventions before the birth of the CGdL in 1906, though with little authority over its affiliates. During this period as well, links were forged in the factories and in the country as a whole between the Italian trade union and socialist movements (the Italian Socialist party was founded in 1892; on the process of its organization see Procacci 1972, Barbadoro 1973, Merli 1972).

Three strike waves broke out during this subperiod, in 1885, 1893, and 1896–7.[4] During each of them agricultural struggles played a significant if not central or exclusive role (as in 1893, the year of the Fasci Siciliani and of major conflicts in the Po Valley). In the nonagricultural sector, the main contribution to strike activity came from textile workers (the great majority of them were women, most severely affected by technological changes), the miners (especially concentrated in Sicily), and construction workers. Their struggles frequently followed the classical pattern of labor unrest in periods of depression (Hobsbawn 1974, 153), sometimes assuming the form of broad social and political movements (e.g., Sicily in 1893 and Milan in 1898). The objectives were often defensive in kind: resistance to wage cuts, to the worsening of work conditions, to dismissals and redundancy plans, and restrictions on the right to unionize (Merli 1972, 459ff.).

1900–1914

From a quantitative standpoint, this second subperiod (and actually the entire 1900–23 period) displayed opposite tendencies to the previous one: on the average, there were much higher levels of strike activity, but little or no rising tendency (see Table 1). Levels of conflict were of a different order than those of the late nineteenth century: strikes, strikers, and workdays lost were about eight times higher, and even more than eleven times higher for the last

---

4. Shorter and Tilly (1974, 106–7) define a "strike wave" year as one during which the level of labor conflict is at least 50% higher than the average for the previous five years. In this paper, however, we consider the number of workdays lost, while Shorter and Tilly consider the number of strikes and number of strikers. It seems to us that the number of days lost captures better the total volume of conflicts in a given year. In fact, if we take Shorter and Tilly's criterion literally, the Italian "Hot Autumn" would not be considered as a strike wave.

two of these indices if the whole period up to 1923 is considered. Labor conflict increased dramatically from the very beginning of the period, and remained at higher levels, though with some variations, up to the outbreak of the war.

Leaving aside cyclical factors, such an impressive increase cannot be accounted for solely by the growing economy of the period. Political and organizational factors played an equal, if not more important role. The period began with a general strike in Genoa against the shutdown of the Chamber of Labor by the prefect, which led to the resignation of the national government. During this decade (the period of Gioletti's governments), there was a relative liberalization of the state's handling of industrial conflict, and the extension of full civic rights to the industrial working class and its organizations. Among the signs of the new political climate were the participation of the social groups represented by the reformist Left in the ruling political majority, as exemplified by the support the Socialists gave to the Zanardelli–Giolitti government in 1901–2, the offer of a cabinet position to the Socialist Filippo Turati in October 1903, and the less frequent intervention by police in labor conflicts (see Carocci 1961, Candeloro 1974).

The great strike wave of 1901–2 constituted a real break with previous experience (Procacci 1972). Although the levels of conflict had been rising rapidly during the years of the industrial expansion beginning in the mid-1890s, the 1901–2 wave brought a dramatic upsurge in labor unrest by comparison with the mean for the preceding five years (379%, 403%, and 548%, in the indices for strikes, strikers, and days lost). Again, a major role was played by agricultural workers, who accounted for more than 50% of the total number of strikers and days lost, and who struck at a mean rate twenty times higher than during previous periods.[5] Whereas the main quantitative contribution in the nonagricultural sector still came from traditional industries (textiles and construction), the greatest impact on public opinion was made by the struggles of the railway and public services workers. The first nationwide general strike occurred in September 1904, and despite its partial failure, it demonstrated the capacity of the workers' movement to overcome local limits (Procacci 1972; this strike is not recorded by the official statistics because of its political character).

The second strike wave of the period unfolded in 1906–8. In 1907 the frequency of labor disputes reached its peak for the entire forty years covered by this study, and participation and volume were the highest for the prewar

---

5. In another study it was suggested that only in agriculture did the new century bring out a real cleavage with the former period, while in the industrial sector there had been regular and steady growth in strike activity since the last two decades of the nineteenth century. This is only partially true. In fact, even leaving aside the struggles of the farm workers – although there is no reason to neglect them, given their prominence in the Italian strike movement during the entire period under scrutiny – the growth in labor conflict was quite remarkable (+122% for strikers), though it began after the 1896–7 wave (see Lay, Marucco, and Pesante 1973).

Table 4. *Union membership and union density*

Year	CGdL (thousands)	Total (thousands)	Ratio of total membership and total labor forces
1907	190	684	3.86
1908	262	934	5.25
1909	308	844	4.73
1910	350	817	4.56
1911	386	848	4.71
1912	310	861	4.76
1913	327	972	5.34
1914	321	962	5.26
1915	234	806	4.38
1916	201	717	3.87
1917	238	740	3.97
1918	249		
1919	1159		
1920	2220		
1921	1129		
1922	401		
1923	212		

Sources: See the appendix to this chapter.

period. Along with the prominent role of the agricultural sector, the struggles of the metalworkers and autoworkers, based mainly in Turin, are worth noting not so much for their quantitative contribution as for their results. Typical of the attempts to create a more structured system of industrial relations was the agreement concluded in October 1906 between the Metal Workers Federation (FIOM) and the Italia auto company of Turin. This accord recognized FIOM as the workers' representative and established a closed-shop, conciliation and arbitration procedures, minimum wages for each category of workers, and the workers' right to form a factory committee (Spriano 1972; Castronovo 1971, chap. 1). The social and economic importance of this new industry, still minor in terms of the numbers employed, continued to grow in subsequent years, accounting by 1913 for more than 20% of the total number of days lost. From that moment on, the automobile industry became the key sector of the strike movement in Italy, both in quantitative and qualitative terms.

Strike activity and unionization during the first half of the 1900–14 period displayed similar trends. Following the successful strike in Genoa, and throughout the 1901–2 wave, workers organizations, many of them industrial unions (e.g., FIOM), sprouted and flourished (see Table 4). Their memberships remained unstable, however, as a bitter struggle took place among various factions for control of the movement. The general strike of 1904 and many labor struggles of 1906–7, especially in the Po Valley, were marked by such disputes. In the end, the reformist wing of the Socialist movement prevailed, giving rise in 1906 to the Confederazione Generale del Lavoro (CGdL; see Barbadoro 1973, II, 87 ff.; Procacci 1972, 27 ff.). The decline in competition among the factions,[6] along with the CGdL's collaboration with the reformist designs of the government – union recognition in exchange for industrial peace (Romagnoli 1974, chap. 2; Cartiglia 1976) – contributed to a relative divergence between the growth of union membership (at least in the CGdL) and strike activity: while the first rose, the second remained stable or slowly declined. (The correlation coefficients over 1907–14 are in fact 0.802, −0.538, and −0.450 between CGdL membership and the numbers of strikes, strikers, and days lost, respectively.)

Aside from wage claims,[7] the chief demands pressed during these years included union security (as in the Italia agreement) and reduction in the length of the workday. A ten-hour day was won by the automobile workers in 1906–7.

1915–1918

Aggregate strike activity during the war declined to its lowest levels since the beginning of the century, two to three times lower than the average of the entire 1900–23 period with respect to strike frequency and participation, and almost six times lower with respect to volume. Labor conflict virtually disappeared in the agricultural sector. In the nonagricultural one, the chief contributions came from textile workers and metalworkers. Union membership also declined during the first two years (1915–16), but slowly recovered thereafter. Despite these negative tendencies, the war years were a very innovative period of institution-building in industrial relations, the changes being achieved within the legal framework created by the "Mobilitazione Industriale," established in 1915 as a section of the Ministry of Armaments and Munitions. By the end of the war, the bulk of the textile, chemical, steel, and metal industries – mainly based in nortern Italy and in Naples, and covering almost half of the industrial labor forces recorded by the 1911 census (Caracciolo 1975b) – were under the jurisdiction of this agency. The latter was run jointly by civil servants and employers' and workers' representatives, and its tasks included the regulation of working conditions in industrial enterprises. Strike activity was severely restricted, and workers striking in factories under

---

6. The revolutionary-anarchist USI played a significant role for several years afterward, especially in the struggles of Turin automobile workers in 1913.
7. The 1901–2 wave was no ordinary wage explosion; it ranks with those of 1919–20 and 1969 (Spesso 1966).

Table 5. *Money wages and real wages, 1901–23*
(1913 = 100)

Year	Money wages	Real wages
1901	70.1	79.4
1902	72.0	82.1
1903	72.9	80.7
1904	72.6	79.4
1905	71.8	78.5
1906	74.6	80.0
1907	83.6	85.6
1908	83.1	86.0
1909	94.1	100.2
1910	92.1	95.4
1911	93.2	94.2
1912	96.0	96.2
1913	100.0	100.0
1914	99.7	99.7
1915	100.0	93.5
1916	113.8	85.0
1917	138.4	73.1
1918	170.6	64.6
1919	249.7	93.1
1920	403.1	114.4
1921	529.4	127.0
1922	512.1	123.6
1923	478.0	116.0

Source: Vannutelli, 1961, p. 70.

the Mobilitazione Industriale could be prosecuted under military law. In substance, this was a period of the centralization of labor relations and of unions' involvement in the war production effort, in exchange for their institutional recognition, and of regulation "from above" of labor contracts and factory discipline. Prior to the ascendency of fascism, it provided the most elaborate example of state regulation of industrial conflict. Many elements of this experience were incorporated into the 1926 labor relations legislation (Neppi Modona 1969, chap. 4; Spriano 1972, 337 ff.; Caracciolo 1975b; Arbrate 1977, 53 ff.).

During the war years, working conditions worsened substantially, the hours of labor were extended, and real wages markedly decreased, from an index of 100 in 1913, to 85 in 1916, to 64.6 in 1918 (see Table 5). Nevertheless, the standard of living of working-class families may have actually improved in some branches of industries and industrial centers, such as Turin, because of

227

overtime and the employment of several members of working-class households (Spriano 1972, chap. 8).

1919–23

The immediate postwar period marks one of the most dramatic cycles of labor and political struggles in Italian history, both in its quantitative and qualitative features, as well as in its eventual political outcome: An impressive strike wave during the so-called biennio rosso (1919–20), was followed in 1921, 1922, and 1923 by an equally sudden and deep (though even) decline in the level of labor conflict. The number of strikers and of days lost increased particularly sharply in 1919–20, to levels three to five times higher than the 1900–14 average. In 1902 the numbers of strikers and labor days lost reached their peak for the entire period under our scrutiny, with more than two million workers involved in labor disputes and more than thirty million workdays lost. And these figures do not include the famous factory occupations of September 1920, because this movement's character was officially recorded as political, even though it originated with typical wage demands (Spriano 1964, chap. 2; Maione 1975, chap. 3).[8]

Aside from this exceptional episode, the labor struggles of this period were distinguished by a substantially enlarged base of social support, as well as an increase in militancy. In several cases, labor actions spilled over the traditional boundaries of industrial conflict and assumed the character of social movements. As Gramsci noted at the time, it is impossible to understand the dynamics of this upsurge without taking into consideration the processes of concentration and homogenization of the labor force, as well as the development among the lower classes of a higher capacity of organization and mobilization (Gramsci 1970, 22 ff.; see also Pizzorno 1970). Two points need to be highlighted in this connection: (1) the massive involvement of peasants in the war effort forged bonds of solidarity that facilitated the process of their mobilization in the social struggles of subsequent years; and (2) mass production industries grew enormously during the war, bringing changes in the composition of the industrial labor. There is no question that the key contributors to the post-World War I labor struggles were the steel- and metalworkers (who accounted for 50% of the total days lost in 1919 and 56% in 1922) and the farm laborers (including sharecroppers and tenant farmers).[9] Textile workers became involved

---

8. According to official sources, about 450,000 workers were involved, mainly metalworkers in Turin, with more than six million days lost, making 1920 the second highest year in Italian strike history after 1969, and the first if adjusted for the number of workers employed.
9. There are no precise figures showing the distribution of semiskilled and unskilled jobs in Italian industry during the war years, but the rapid development of mass production and quasi-Tayloristic methods employed in many companies is well known (Caracciolo 1975b, 218ff.;

only in 1921 and 1923, years during which the strike wave among other workers was actually declining.

Trends in strike activity paralleled almost perfectly changes in union membership. From an average of 300,000 members in the last years before the war, and after the lower levels of the war years, the CGdL expanded to more than 1 million members in 1919 and then to a peak of 2.2 million in 1920. Other organizations followed a similar pattern, such as the newborn CIL (the Catholic Trade Union Confederation), which reached a membership in 1920 of more than 1 million in 1920. Here again it is possible to observe the effects of the massive mobilization processes induced by the war, which were reflected in the successes of the Socialist and Catholic parties in the administrative and political elections of 1910, 1920, and 1921. (In the 1919 elections the Socialists received 32.3% of the votes and the Catholics 20.5%.)

Among the central demands of strikers during this period were wage increases and cost-of-living adjustments (causing real wages to rise from an index of 64.6 in 1918 to 127 in 1921), the eight-hour working day, and factory councils.

Given the major changes in the patterns of labor conflicts and labor relations, one cannot discern substantial continuities between strike activity during these years and the prewar experience.[10] Only with the economic crisis of 1921 and the Fascist repression were these changes arrested and reversed.

The industrial composition of the strike movement

Some notable changes took place in the industrial "geography" of labor during the decades under our scrutiny, that is, in the contribution of various branches of industry to strike activity (see Table 6). It is worth re-emphasizing, first of all, the importance of the role played by agricultural workers during the four decades before fascism, and especially in the 1900–23 period.[11] They often contributed one-fourth to one-third of the total number of strikers and days lost per year, and their contribution was especially crucial in almost every strike wave, (when they accounted for up to 50% of the aggregate strike activity).

Castronovo, 1971, chaps. 2 and 3; La Valle 1976, chap. 4). Among the farm laborers there was a decrease of wage workers between 1911 and 1921, and an increase in the number of those (small farmers) self-employed from 52.8% to 45.4% and 18.1% to 32.1% respectively (all figures for male workers only). See Vitali (1968, 30).

10. This thesis is advanced by Lay and Pesante (1974, 404, 408) and Lay and Pesante (1981), though here in a slightly weaker way. Aside from any consideration of a qualitative character, such a thesis can hardly be maintained even on purely quantitative grounds, whether we consider the figures for the entire movement or for the industrial sector only.

11. The importance of this sector in Italian history is underscored by the fact that labor conflict exhibited similar levels after World War II, at least during the 1950s. It would be a mistake to neglect it.

Table 6. *Industrial composition percentage on total strike activity*

Year	Strikes (%)						Strikers (%)						Days lost (%)					
	Agri.	Mining	Const.	Metal.	Text.	Trans.	Agri.	Mining	Const.	Metal.	Text.	Trans.	Agri.	Mining	Const.	Metal.	Text.	Trans.
1901	37.64	6.40	10.17	4.61	14.18	3.51	53.22	5.01	9.31	1.91	10.74	4.77	57.74					
1902	21.51	7.17	16.47	8.04	16.18	1.84	42.73	5.52	10.17	4.65	12.21	1.45	44.37					
1903	7.89	10.57	15.94	8.22	21.31	3.52	17.42	13.64	18.94	9.85	11.36	4.55	18.18					
1904	24.79	7.51	11.92	8.11	15.50	2.74	43.18	10.00	14.09	2.27	10.91	3.64	41.50					
1905	12.17	8.81	16.92	10.63	14.83	3.64	28.39	8.39	14.19	3.87	10.32	18.71	35.20					
1906	20.84	6.40	12.92	8.29	12.98	4.69	30.71	6.56	13.39	5.51	16.01	4.72	22.31					
1907	16.70	4.92	14.45	9.61	15.19	5.18	44.10	3.99	8.68	8.85	12.50	3.30	43.53					
1908	16.39	4.47	14.90	8.83	11.92	4.07	46.63	2.70	14.02	7.28	8.90	2.97	55.61					
1909	12.43	5.27	15.73	10.92	12.71	5.93	25.13	7.49	20.32	7.49	12.30	7.49	17.92					
1910	8.68	6.44	18.52	14.40	11.63	6.08	13.07	7.04	34.17	9.55	10.05	6.53	10.36					
1911	11.79	7.89	14.50	10.84	12.99	7.81	34.46	8.03	7.77	6.22	6.48	5.96	42.94					
1912	16.15	6.88	13.21	10.73	11.74	9.36	40.00	5.00	10.42	7.92	7.08	11.67	31.88	10.90	7.82	20.84	4.71	5.82
1913	10.70	7.94	14.11	11.58	13.45	9.70	17.20	3.01	3.87	6.88	4.09	4.09	15.47	4.53	7.13	18.01	4.60	2.29
1914	9.49	9.49	17.71	13.43	13.54	12.27	22.07	5.86	14.41	8.56	10.81	16.22	18.77	7.28	10.36	7.67	10.13	8.22
1915	11.20	7.25	12.19	16.64	18.95	11.70	26.67	3.86	4.44	12.22	31.67	12.22	22.82	4.24	4.01	8.95	38.19	8.26
1916	10.57	9.53	3.64	16.29	28.25	7.63	10.79	10.79	1.44	23.74	35.97	5.67	12.05	24.82	0.60	10.50	38.31	2.75
1917	5.75	10.42	3.19	11.28	35.96	4.26	3.43	5.71	5.14	13.71	56.00	1.14	2.12	8.01	8.13	13.07	49.59	1.18
1918	3.20	7.67	0.64	20.45	30.67	4.47	0.63	5.03	0.63	43.40	32.70	3.15	0.30	2.60	0.10	28.20	45.40	1.20
1919	11.12	8.23	7.96	11.44	15.34	6.52	32.48	3.47	2.89	25.53	12.54	5.34	15.40	6.02	1.41	49.93	12.95	2.29
1920	9.13	10.87	10.24	11.21	10.24	6.62	45.20	3.84	3.07	8.25	4.97	10.42	46.36	5.95	2.12	7.19	5.09	8.25
1921	7.85	14.29	11.02	12.70	15.43	6.35	10.91	7.46	7.46	13.81	33.15	3.73	4.98	15.60	8.01	19.34	35.48	1.75
1922	4.00	15.63	15.83	15.13	12.70	6.78	5.58	4.24	8.93	57.37	6.25	4.91	4.79	11.64	9.60	55.86	5.61	7.17
1923	0.50	19.90	9.45	18.41	29.35	2.49	1.52	16.67	18.18	13.64	43.94	1.52	0.34	22.97	22.64	8.11	38.51	0.68

In the nonagricultural sector we observe a shift from traditional industries (textiles, construction, and mining and quarry – especially the workers of the Sicilian sulphur mines) to the more modern ones. In particular, the role of the metalworkers, mainly concentrated in Turin, Milan, and Genoa, assuming steadily greater significance from the 1906–7 strike wave onward. In 1913 metalworkers accounted for 20% of the total number of workdays lost, and with the massive concentration and rationalization of industry induced by the war, metalworkers assumed the leadership of the entire strike movement. Thereafter their role remained central in every strike wave.

Workers in agriculture and in the metal industry also provided the core of the Italian union movement during these years. According to the "Statistic Cabrini" of 1902, Federterra (the agriculture workers' union) then had 240,000 members, while the total union membership of all other sectors was 239,000. In 1920 the agriculture workers made up 46% of the CGdL and 80% of the CIL. The membership of the FIOM was much lower before the war (usually no more than twenty thousands), but it reached 160,000 in 1919. To be sure, the prominence of its political role cannot be measured by these membership figures alone.

Participation in every strike wave, except for that of 1919–20, was always limited to two or three sectors. Even in the 1919–20 wave, when there was a wider industrial base, rates of participation and volume of days lost remained at the same levels. The absence of structured and centralized organizations cost heavily. Given the lack of a capacity for nationwide strike planning and coordination, the magnitude of strike mobilizations in most sectors was effectively undermined.

The shape of strikes

The distinction between *levels* and *shapes* of strike activity, a familiar one in the literature since the writings by Forchheimer (1948) and Knowles (1952), although overlooked by Ross and Hartman's study, brings out the fact that not all strikes can be considered as equivalent. There is a clear difference, for example, between a work stoppage involving a few hundred or a few thousand workers for several days or weeks and a general strike involving some hundreds of thousands lasting no more than a few hours. Quite different are their impacts on the economic and political systems, their social meanings, and, probably, the subjective perceptions of those involved. These qualitative aspects of strike movements can be considered through quantitative analysis. Three measures are usually utilized for this purpose: the strike frequency (the number of strikers adjusted to the number of employees, or of total labor force); the average *size* of strikes (the ratio of the number of strikers to the number of

231

Table 7. *The shape of strikes (entire economy)*

	Frequency[a]	Size	Duration
1881–99	0.83	253.4	9.66[b]
1900–14	6.47	257.5	11.07
1915–18	2.66	354.5	5.50
1919–23	6.12	738.8	11.76
1919–20	10.43	925.0	13.78
1900–23	5.77	374.0	10.30

[a] Number of strikes per 100,000 workers.
[b] In 1893 more than 44 workdays were lost per striker (Fasci Siciliani struggles). If this year is excluded, the average duration for the 1881–99 period is 7.73.

strikes), and the average *duration* of strikes (the ratio of the days lost to the number strikers).[12]

In their research, Shorter and Tilly (1971; 1974, chaps. 4 and 12) emphasized the existence of a long-term trend in the shape of strikes in most industrial countries – from "savage" to "modern," or "civilized," types of strikes – that took place either between the two world wars, or following the Second World War, depending on the country concerned. The first pattern resembles a real trial of strength, with rare episodes of long and hard-fought struggles involving small groups of workers, however, the modern one has assumed the domesticated features of the mass demonstration strike (frequent, very large, and very brief), and addresses itself more to the political authorities or public opinion than directly to employers.

On the whole the Italian experience has followed this pattern. The 1880–1923 period fits well the "savage" pattern of strikes, a radical transformation occurring only after World War II. But shorter-term changes in the Italian case show that this is not a linear process of transformation from one polar type to the other. There can be sudden turning points and even, under certain circumstances, a reappearance of a shape typical of previous stages. It is apparent that this dimension of strike activity is more sensitive to economic fluctuations than to the changing characteristics of the political and industrial relations system.

12. These measures are linked by a relationship such as: Strike volume = frequency × size × duration, or:

$$\text{Man-days lost per total labor forces} = \frac{\text{strikes}}{\text{total labor forces}} \times \frac{\text{strikers}}{\text{strikes}} \times \frac{\text{man-days lost}}{\text{strikers}}$$

That is, with the same amount of workdays lost during a certain year, the result can derive from a few strikes, involving small groups of workers in long-lasting and tough struggles, or from many strikes involving large groups of workers in episodes that last just a few hours.

Table 8. *The shape of strikes*

	Agriculture		Remaining sectors	
	Size	Duration	Size	Duration
1881–99	392.9	8.76	249.7	7.83
1900–14	541.4	10.77	208.6	10.99
1915–18	310.7	4.67	346.5	5.57
1919–23	2011.0	8.71	603.6	12.60
1900–23	809.1	9.33	313.9	10.42

For the period under study, several primary features need to be emphasized (see Tables 7 and 8).

1881–1899

The last two decades of the nineteenth century, characterized by a political and institutional environment rather hostile to organized labor generally and to industrial conflict in particular, present the lowest values of the entire period, with the exception of the war years. Strikes were very rare, with less than one work stoppage a year per 100,000 workers, and usually had a narrow base and modest duration, except for the years of strike waves when larger groups of workers were involved in hard-fought conflicts (especially in 1896–97).

1900–1914

The dimension of labor unrest that increases most sharply during the "Giolittian" decade is strike frequency, against which the political institutional environment had played an inhibiting role in the previous period. This is not paralleled, however, by a similar increase in the average size of strikes, although strike duration rose markedly. This is not a pattern conforming to a linear "from savage to civilized strikes" schema, but one explainable by the fact that the liberalization of industrial conflict fostered by Giolitti at a political level was in sharp contrast to the policies followed by employers. The first employers' associations were formed precisely during these years, and they often polemicized against the government's policy of neutrality in labor conflicts (Abrate 1967; Baglioni 1974). The high strike frequency was also connected with the tough interunion competition that characterized the first decade of the century. The same features appear when one considers solely the nonagricultural sector,

233

in which the mean size of strikes decreased and their mean duration increased by 16% and 40%, respectively, over the previous period. In short, the new reformist orientation of the government and the first attempts at the institution-alization of industrial conflict seem to have brought effects opposite to those usually emphasized by writers on this topic: Strikes were more frequent, but also narrower and notably more persistently waged.

1915–1918

A remarkable transformation occured during the war years, marked by a sharp decline in the frequency and duration of strikes, along with an enlargement of their size, especially in the nonagricultural sector (from 208 to 346 workers per strike).[13] The centralization of labor relations and their subjection to strict political controls found its institutional expression in the Mobilitazione Industriale and its national and regional committees. Wages and work conditions for the companies and industries governed by this tripartite body (under ministerial control) were often dealt with at the regional level, without involving the local plant, where military discipline was in effect. This change in labor relations accounted for the decline in the frequency and duration of strikes, while the enlargement of their average size appears con-nected with the introduction of mass production techniques in many industries, especially auto and metal factories. Fiat, for example, which entered the war with a work force of 4,000, had more than 40,000 in 1918, many of them women and unskilled workers on the assembly lines (Castronovo 1971, 152).

1919–1923

Strikes assumed a more modern shape – higher frequency and larger average size – and their duration returned to a more savage stage, so to speak – more than doubling by comparison with the war period. The tone of the "two Red years" is suggested by size and duration of strike activity. On one hand, one observes the mass character of the labor struggles along with the mobiliza-tion capacities achieved by the unions; on the other, the extreme bitterness of the confrontations. These were not mass demonstration strikes aimed at exercising "civilized" pressure on the political system and public opinion generally, but wholesale confrontations in which both sides – workers and employers – were harshly engaged. After having reached its peak in 1919 and 1920, the average size of strikes gradually decreased, yet strikes maintained a

13. The shape of this period is probably the closest to the contemporary one with regard to those countries, such as the Scandinavian ones, where some sort of political regulation of industrial conflict is practiced.

very harsh character until 1922, when the movement collapsed in the face of the repressions conducted by the new Fascist regime.

The determinants of strike activity

Two models explaining the determinants of strike activity will be considered in this section. The first, which can be defined as the economic model, aims at testing the well-known hypothesis that year-to-year variations of the strike movement are dependent on the business cycle. The standard economic model for such an analysis usually includes the following variables: nominal wages, consumer prices (cost of living), unemployment, and a trend factor. The first two predictors are specified as an annual rate of change, and the third is expressed as an absolute percentage. For the first and third predictors, the expected signs are negative. For the second predictor, the expected relationship is positive: With business up, prices are up, bringing more strikes. Nominal wages and cost of living can be replaced by a real wages indicator (for a discussion of the rationale underlying the economic model, see Ashenfelter and Johnson 1969).

The second model, which could be called the political–organizational model, aims at testing the explanatory power of factors that are not economic, but political and organizational. The predictors considered here are union growth and political participation (specified as the annual rate of change of the Italian Socialist party's – PSI – membership). The expected relationships with strike intensity are heavily debated in the literature. On one hand, the unionization variable could in fact be assumed to be an indicator of collective mobilization, positively correlated with strike activity (and specified in terms of the annual rate of change in union membership); on the other hand, it may be seen as a proxy for organizational strength of the trade unions, whose expected sign in a well-institutionalized industrial relations system would be negative (the variable would be better specified here as "union density"). Likewise, the expected relationship for the political participation variable is usually positive, on the grounds that leftist political parties' memberships somehow capture and channelize extrainstitutional discontent. But when these parties are represented in the government, a negative relationship with strike activity would be expected (as is shown by Social-Democratic experience; see Hibbs 1978). In the Italian case, considering the characteristics of the political and industrial relations system, the relationship of strike activity with both the political–organizational variables should be positive.

The unavailability of several historical data series has unfortunately created very serious constraints for our analysis. The data series on wages and prices are unavailable for the last two decades of the nineteenth century; that on union (CGdL) membership begins only in 1907; and the only series on unemploy-

Models and realities

Table 9. *Simple correlation coefficients between strike activity and some economic and political variables*

Dependent variable[a]	Independent variable	1881–99	1901–14	1907–23
Number of strikes	GNP	0.85*	0.06	−0.56*
	Industrial prod.	0.64*	0.16	−0.67*
	Cost of living index	—	0.16	−0.41
	Money wages	—	−0.01	−0.43
	Real wages	—	−0.07	−0.52
	Union membership	—	−0.03[b]	−0.40
	PSI membership	—	0.10	0.14
Number of strikers	GNP	0.70*	0.16	0.07
	Industrial prod.	0.51*	0.16	−0.19
	Cost of living index	—	0.23	0.22
	Money wages	—	0.08	0.18
	Real wages	—	0.01	0.05
	Union membership	—	0.06[b]	0.79*
	PSI membership	—	0.13	0.64*
Number of days lost	GNP	0.49*	0.14	−0.04
	Industrial prod.	0.30	0.16	−0.27
	Cost of living index	—	0.21	0.13
	Money wages	—	0.13	0.10
	Real wages	—	0.08	−0.01
	Union membership	—	0.13[b]	0.72*
	PSI membership	—	0.02	0.57*

* Starred coefficients are significant at a level of <0.05.
[a] The dependent variables are in logarithmic form.
[b] For 1901–14, Chambers of Labor membership; for 1907–23, CGdL membership.

ment we have been able to find covers just the years 1919–23. Thus, although Tables 9 and 10 also give the simple and partialized (for trend) correlation coefficients between the three strike indices and a set of economic, political, and organizational variables for 1881–99 and 1900–14, the regression analysis comparing the two above-mentioned models is limited to the 1907–23 period. Admittedly, this procedure, excluding the first years of the century and including some years of the postwar period, is in some sense anomalous. What is more, it has not been possible to utilize any unemployment predictor. Despite all these limitations, however, several tests on the 1902–14 years, as well as the isolation of the 1919–23 subperiod from the preceding ones by means of analysis of covariance techniques, have permitted us to draw a rather precise idea of the different patterns of relationships prevailing in the pre- and postwar periods. Table 11 presents the findings of these analyses.

236

Table 10. *Partial correlation coefficients between strike activity and some economic and political variables, partialized for time*

Dependent variables[a]	Independent variables	1881–99	1901–14	1907–23
Number of strikes	GNP	0.28	0.36	−0.29
	Industrial prod.	0.18	0.60*	−0.52*
	Cost of living index	—	0.59*	0.19
	Money wages	—	0.07	0.08
	Real wages	—	−0.11	−0.21
	Union membership	—	0.00b	0.86*
	PSI membership	—	0.01	0.76
	Year (simple *r*)	0.88*	−0.02	−0.50
Number of strikers	GNP	0.06	0.42	−0.20
	Industrial prod.	0.05	0.32	−0.45
	Cost of living index	—	0.55*	0.13
	Money wages	—	0.08	0.04
	Real wages	—	0.11	−0.21
	Union membership	—	0.01[b]	0.82*
	PSI membership	—	0.19	0.72*
	Year (simple *r*)	0.76*	0.06	0.18
Number of days lost	GNP	−0.29	0.38	−0.26
	Industrial prod.	−0.22	0.34	−0.48
	Cost of living index	—	0.51*	0.10
	Money wages	—	0.29	0.02
	Real wages	—	0.08	−0.16
	Union membership	—	0.22[b]	0.78*
	PSI membership	—	0.06	0.69*
	Year (simple *r*)	−0.66*	0.05	0.10

* Starred coefficients are significant at a level of <0.05.
[a] The dependent variables are in logarithmic form.
[b] For 1901–14, Chambers of Labor membership; for 1907–23, CGdL membership.

The economic model (1907–23, 1915–18 excluded)

The first conclusion suggested by the findings presented in Table 11 is the relative homogeneity of the relationships between the economic variables and all three strike indices, the main difference lying in the explanatory capacity of the trend factor, which is decidedly higher for frequency of strikes than for the other two indices.[14] This said, the economic model does seem to offer on the whole satisfactory estimates of the strike movement, even if the inclusion

14. The significant and negative value of the frequency is probably due to the processes of industrial concentration and centralization of labor relations that distinguished this period.

Table 11. *Determinants of strike activity (standardized regression coefficient) for pre-Fascist period: 1907–23 (1915–18 excluded)*

	Log FR		Log PR		Log VL	
	1	2	3	4	5	6
R^2	.716	.934	.543	.805	.557	.793
$\bar{R}^2$	.622	.900	.391	.705	.409	.690
SEE	.170	.086	.315	.219	.381	.276
F	7.573[a]	28.128[a]	3.571	8.173[a]	3.772	7.682[a]
df	3,9	4,8	3,9	4,8	3,9	4,8
VN	1.807	2.186	2.234	2.587	2.159	2.692
Wt-1	.571	5.11	.588	.494	.771	.709
	(1.843)	(3.208[a])	(1.421)	(1.7992)	(1.992)	(2.522[b])
Pt	.289	.293	.334	.399	.151	.156
	(1.050)	(2.081)	(.958)	(1.399)	(.440)	(.628)
UMt		.470		.513		.489
		(5.118[a])		(3.255[a])		(3.026[b])
T	−.930	−.919	−.261	−.249	−.402	−.390
	(4.279[a])	(−8.236[a])	(−.947)	(−1.296)	(−1.482)	(−1.982)

Von Neumann statistics excludes positive autocorrelation of residuals.
Wt-1 = annual rate of change of money wages (one year lag).
Pt = annual rate of change of the cost of living (retail prices).
UMt = annual rate of change of union (CGdL) membership.
T = year (trend factor).
[a] Test F for t significant at 0.01 level.
[b] Test F for t significant at 0.05 level; t test within the graphs.

among the independent variables of an indicator of the market position of the labor force might have improved the model. The equations for the number of participants and the volume of strikes, while presenting fairly high coefficients of determination, are statistically unreliable (the F test value is too low). For the frequency of strikes the remarkable explanatory power of the model (more than 70% of the variance is explained) is not attributable in any real sense to the business cycle variables (wages and prices) as much as to the trend factor. When the latter component is excluded, in fact, the R^2 drops to minimal levels. More significant is that the relationship with the wage variable turns out to be the opposite of that predicted by the theoretical model (positive instead of negative), while for the 1902–14 period it shows the expected sign (according to equations not presented here).

In order to examine this relationship in greater detail, we have isolated the effects of wage levels on strike activity for the years 1919–23 from that of the prewar period through an analysis of covariance. The analysis confirms that the wage predictor, negative though insignificant for the 1907–14 years, assumes a positive sign and a higher value only after World War I. This signifies to us that two different patterns of relations are observable: on one hand, the economic model holds for the "Giolittian Era,"[15] even if with modest explanatory power; on the other hand, the logic underlying the postwar period holds for a broader social movement, in which wage demands no longer reflected economically rational evaluations, but themselves became a device for workers' mobilization. It should be noted that these results support the considerations developed previously about the deep cleavage between the strike movement during the Giolittian Era and the postwar social insurgency.

The political–organizational variant

The organizational and political variables, especially the former, seem to play a remarkable role in the determination of strike activity during the entire period. Some technical and substantive qualifications, however, are in order.

To begin with, the effects of the unionization process (UMt) on strikes turns out to be quite strong and statistically reliable. The F test shows that the inclusion of this variable affects the whole pattern of relationships at a statistically significant level for all three of the strike indices. The signs of the relationships are the expected ones; that is, the more rapid the union growth, the higher the strike activity. It is possible, however, that a reciprocal causation process is at work between the two phenomena. In order to test this possibility, an equation with the lagged unionization regressor ($UMt - 1$) was used. The coefficients (not reported here) turned out to be unsatisfactory and statistically unreliable, and thus reinforce the doubt about the existence of a simultaneous causation process. These results do not appear to us without meaning, even if a solid test would demand more sophisticated techniques of analysis (e.g., the 2SLS technique). The fact that strike activity is highly sensitive to union growth during the same years, while insensitive to the lagged unionization regressor, suggests that the organizational factor in this period was not so much a necessary prerequisite for workers' collective action as an essential component of that action itself. More than actions as the flywheel of labor struggles, union growth – like strike activity – was a reflection of workers' mobilization – a mobilization that, as we have seen, is not satisfactorily accounted for by the business cycle.

The same kind of relationships are observable between our strike indices and the political participation variable. The correlation coefficients all have the

---

15. The simple correlation coefficients with nominal and real wages in the 1907–14 period are −0.95, −0.41, −0.53 and −0.96, −0.59, −0.72, respectively, for number of strikes, strikers, and workdays lost.

_xpected (positive) sign, at rather strong and statistically significant levels, even when the trend factor is controlled (see Tables 9 and 10). That is, variations in Socialist party membership also may have had strong effects on labor militancy or, more likely, were themselves – along with union growth and strike activity – part of the same nexus of labor mobilization.[16]

Conclusion

Table 12 summarizes the different characteristics of the strike movement as they have emerged in our analysis. It provides a synthetic overview of the Italian pre-Fascist experience across the series of variables considered in the preceding sections. With the support of this table, we will draw some broad conclusions.

The Italian experience provides a case study of industrial conflict that in its basic characteristics – trends, shape, turning points, objectives, determinants – was marked by strong political influences. In Italy, strike actions could hardly have been the result of the process of economically rational evaluation suggested by bargaining theory. Our findings, especially those of the previous section, are consistent with Snyder's (1975) arguments and results supporting the thesis that the validity of the economic model of strike activity depends on some specific institutional conditions that are not always met in the real world. On the whole, they are not met in the Italian case, and several lines of our analysis converge toward this judgment: a traditionally loose market; a highly complex social stratification in both the society as a whole and within the laboring class itself, connected with the dualism of the Italian economic structure; the permanence of the position of agriculture as the chief employment sector; and the presence of a political and institutional system that remained hostile to organized labor until early in the twentieth century. Together, all of these factors contributed to labor actions in which weak and unstable workers' organizations were obliged to struggle for political as well as economic objectives. In these struggles, the general interests of the entire laboring class usually prevailed over narrower occupational and craft interests, where the horizontal (territorial) organizational principle was more important than industrial unionism, and where trade unions tried to compensate for their weakness on the labor market and within the factories by establishing links with a like-minded political party. In sum, given a context in which workers still had to struggle for collective bargaining and political rights, if not for basic recognition as citizens, it is hardly surprising that strike activity was more responsive to political and organizational variables than to economic ones.

16. The equation including both the organizational (union growth) and political participation variables is not reported because the strong statistical relationship between them raises serious problems of multicollinearity.

Table 12. *Characteristics of the Italian strike movement, 1881–1923 (synthetic table)*

Year	Levels and trend of strike activity	Shape of strikes	Industrial composition	Cycles of struggles	Relations with economic variable	Relations with political and organizational variable	Industrial relations system
1881–99	Low levels but rapidly rising strike activity	Rare, narrow, and relatively long strikes	Traditional sectors (textile, mining, constor and agri.)	Mono-sector waves: 1834–5 and 1893 (agriculture); 1896–7 (traditional industries)	Pattern of strikes during the depression		Collective bargaining not yet established; repressive State interventions
1900–14	High levels of strike activity (cleavage with the previous period) but no trend to rise	Increasing frequency and duration of strikes, but small size. After 1907, the frequency tends to decline	The role of traditional industrial sectors is declining. Rising importance of metal-industries. Great importance of farm workers strikes	1901–2 wave (agriculture); 1907–8 wave (agriculture and metal-industries)	Relationship with the economic variable with expected signs (although weak coeff.)	1901–6: uncertain relation with union membership; 1907–14: positive relationship with union membership; positive but weak relation with PSI membership	Gradual diffusion of collective bargaining; rising strength of trades unions and birth in 1906 of CGdL (national trades union confederation); attempts of centralization after 1906 under the reformist leadership of CGdL; moderate support from the government; aversion from some employers' circles
1919–23	Impressive strike cycle with simultansous variations of all the strike measures and union membership	Strikes are frequent, very touch, and involve very large groups of workers	Strikes concentrated in agriculture and above all in metal industries	1919–20 wave: farm and metal workers struggles	Weak relation with economic variables; positive relation with wages (utilized as mobilizing device)	Strong positive relation with union and PSI membership	Stalemate and breakdown of the industrial relations system; failure of the reformist intermediation design

If the economic model does not apply to a poorly institutionalized industrial relations system, the experience here analyzed, however limited, sheds light on another implicit aspect of Snyder's argument – that of the high sensitivity of strike activity – to changes in the political and institutional framework in which it unfolds. A brief comparison between the Giolittian Era and the post–World War I cycle of labor conflict will help clarify this final point. The Giolittian decade encompassed reformist attempts at involving the working class and its organizations in the operation and administration of the Italian economy. This meant that a process of (partial) institutionalization of labor relations was paralleled by industrial conflicts that, after the big strike wave of 1901–2, came close to the patterns of labor–management relations suggested by the economic model – even if with weak regression coefficients. The economic model, nonetheless, fails to fit the Italian experience. The Giolittian system of institutionalized conflict mediation, which had already been undermined in the immediate prewar years by the combined opposition of farmers, some employers' circles (especially in steel and heavy industry), and the revolutionary wing of the labor movement, definitely collapsed in the postwar period under the pressure of the massive processes of social mobilization induced by the war. To the failure of this reformist strategy was linked the impressive postwar cycle of strikes, in which both wage claims and union growth provided effective vehicles for labor mobilization.[17]

Appendix: Sources and characteristics of the data

Strike measures

For the period under consideration, four successive series of official data are available:

1878–91: in this period the data are based on a reconstruction of the reports submitted by the Prefects (Prefetti) to the Minister of the Interior;

1892–1903: in 1892 an annual systematic survey by the Prefetture was introduced, based on appropriate questionnaires. The responsible agency was the Direzione Generale della Statistica of the Ministry of Agriculture, Industry, and Commerce (MAIC);

---

17. A similar sequence also occured in the Italian post-World War II period. The failure of the reformist experience of Center-Left governments, during which strike activity corresponded to the economic model, was followed by a huge wage and strike explosion (the Hot Autumn and the entire 1968–73 period), reflecting the effects of political and organizational, rather than economic factors (Bordogna and Provasi 1979, 282ff). On the historical analogies between the Giolittian Era and the Center-Left government years, see Carocci (1975, 351ff.).

On the basis of these and other findings in Cella (1979, 296ff., and 593ff.), we suggested that

1904–13: the data are based on questionnaires sent to various local organizations. The Prefetture still provided synthetic reports. The responsible organism was the Ufficio del Lavoro, of the MAIC;

1914–23: the responsible agency was the Direzione Generale del Lavoro e della Previdenza Sociale, Ministry of National Economy.

The aggregate data we have utilized are drawn from the volume *I conflitti di lavoro in Italia nel decennio 1914–1923*, "Supplemento" no. 38 of the *Bollettino del lavoro e della previdenza sociale*, published by Ministero dell'Economia Nazionale, Roma, 1924, pp. 315–16. For the agricultural sector, the data on the workdays lost in 1904 and 1905 are missing, and estimated here. The data on industrial composition are drawn from the several volumes *Statistica degli Scioperi*, published since 1892 by the MAIC (and successive denominations).

The series records only the "economic strikes," that is, "those whose purpose is an improvement of the working conditions directed to the employers and to the owners of the factories where the strikers work." Solidarity strikes are included only when assimilable to the previous ones. There is no such restriction with respect to numbers of strikers and the duration of strikes. Several accurate pieces of information are provided by the statistics, though not all of them cover the entire period: the number of strikes, strikers and workdays lost, causes and outcomes of strikes, duration (by categories), industrial and regional composition, and the role played by the workers' organizations.

On the characteristics of the strike statistics before fascism, a rich source of information is Lay, Marucco, and Pesante, 1973.

Employment

For the period before the ascendance of fascism, the only data available with some continuity and consistency are those on the active population provided by the census surveys (1881, 1901, 1911, 1921). We have drawn them from the reconstruction elaborated by O. Vitali (1970) and have estimated the data relative to the years between the censuses, assuming a year-to-year uniform variation. With this method, the periods of rapid transformation of the labor force cannot be taken into account.

The *Statistica Industriale* of 1903 and the *Censimento degli Opifici e delle Imprese Industriali* of 1911 provide data on industrial employees, but are hardly comparable.

Snyder's argument should be qualified by contrasting the economic model, and the institutional conditions underlying it, with two different political–organizational models: the first one (closer to that depicted by Shorter and Tilly and by Snyder himself) characteristic of institutional settings in which workers and their organizations are excluded from the national polity and consequently have to struggle for recognition and for the establishment of collective bargaining; the other (closer to the situation outlined by Pizzorno, 1978) typical of so-called neocorporatist settings, in which unions not only enjoy full recognition, but are also deeply involved within a thick network of exchange relations with employers and public authorities, resulting in depressing effects on strike activity. In other words, while Snyder maintains that the economic model of strike activity fits only a "well institutionalized" labor relations system, we put forward the idea that it more likely corresponds to a context that is intermediate in institutional (not chronological) terms between a situation of labor exclusion and one of neocorporatist involvement.

Unemployment

As far as we know there is no data series for unemployed workers before fascism. For the years 1918–23, a series of uncertain reliability is presented in Ministero dell'Economia Nazionale, *Bolletino del Lavoro e della Previdenza Sociale* 40 (July–December 1923).

Unionization

The series of the CGdL (1907–23) can be found in L. Marchetti (ed.), 1962. (It is the series utilized by Ross and Hartman.) The Statistica delle organizzazioni dei lavoratori, "Supplemento" to MAIC, *Bolletino dell'Ufficio del Lavoro*, nos. 8, 9, 12, 13, 15, 20, 31, provide figures on the total membership of workers' organizations. Data also exist relative to other organizations, like the Camere del Lavoro. Important are the so-called Statistica Cabrini, in MAIC, *Bolletino dell'Ufficio del Lavoro* (January 1905), pp. 84–5, and the data provided by *Bollettino del Lavoro e della Previdenza Sociale* (1921–II), pp. 220–1. As far as we know, a complete and homogenous series of union membership from 1900 to 1923 does not exist.

Prices and wages

C. Vannutelli (1961, 559–96) provides a series starting in 1901 of consumer price, nominal wage, and real wage indices. We have utilized these series. Other, more recently elaborated wage series, starting in 1911, are provided by V. Zamagni, in Ciocca and Toniolo (1976, 329–78).

Gross domestic product

See Ercolani (1975, tables XII.1.1.A and XII.1.3.A).

Industrial production index

R. Romeo (1972, Table 6).

Political participation

W. Kendall (1975) provides a record of PSI members, which we have integrated for the years 1917 and 1920–3 with G. Galli (1974, 209ff.).

References

Abrate, M. 1967. *La lotta sindacale nella industrializzazione in Italia, 1906–1926*. Milan: F. Angeli. 1977. *Lavoro e lavoratori nell'Italia contemporanea*. Milan: F. Angeli.
Ashenfelter, D., and G. E. Johnson. 1969. "Bargaining Theory, Trade Unions, and Industrial Strike Activity." *American Economic Review* 59: 35–48.

Baglioni, G. 1974. *L'ideologia della borghesia industriale*. Turin: Einaudi.

Barbadoro, I. 1973. *Storia del sindicalismo italiano. Dalla nascita al fascismo*. Firenze: La Nuova Italia.

Bordogna, L., and G. Provasi, 1979. "Il movimento degli scioperi in Italia (1881– 1973)." In G. P. Cella, ed., *Il movimento degli scioperi nel XX secolo*. Bologna: Il Mulino.

Candeloro, G. 1974. *Storia dell'Italia moderna*. Milan: Feltrinelli.

Caracciolo, A. 1975a. "Il processo d'industrializzazione." In G. Fua', ed., *Lo sviluppo economico in Italia*. Vol. 3. Milan: F. Angeli. 1975b. "La crescita e la trasformazione della grande idustria durante la prima guerra mondiale." In G. Fua', ed., *Lo sviluppo economico in Italia*. Vol. 3. Milan: F. Angeli.

Carocci, G. 1961. *Giolitti e l'eta' giolittiana*. Turin: Einaudi. 1975. *Storia d'Italia dall'Unita ad oggi*. Milan: Feltrinelli.

Cartiglia, C. 1976. *Rinaldo Rigola e il sindacalismo riformista in Italia*. Milan: Feltrinelli.

Castronovo, V. 1971. *Agnelli*. Turin: UTET.

Cella, G. P. 1979. (a cura di), *Il movimento degli scioperi nel XX secolo*. Bologna: Il Mulino.

Ercolani, P. 1975. "Documentazione statistica di base." In G. Fua' ed., *Lo sviluppo economico in Italia*. Vol. 3. Milan: F. Angeli.

Foa, V. 1975. "Sindacati e lotte sociali." In *Storia d'Italia*. Vol. 5. Turin: Einaudi.

Forchheimer, K. 1948. "Some International Aspects of the Strike Movement. *"The Bulletin of the Strike Movement of the Oxford Institute of Statistics* 10: 9–24.

Galli, G. 1974. *I partiti politici*. Turin: UTET.

Gramsci, A. 1970. *L'ordine Nuovo, 1919–1920*. Turin: Einaudi.

Hibbs, D. A. 1978. "On the Political Economy of Long-run Trends in Strike Activity." *British Journal of Political Science* 8: 153–177.

Hobsbawm, E. 1974. "Tendenze del movimento operaio britannico." In *Studi di storia del movimento operaio*. Turin: Einaudi.

Horowitz, D. L. 1966. *Storia del movimento sindacale in Italia*. Bologna: Il Mulino.

Hyman, R. 1972. *Strikes*. London: Fontana.

Kendall, W. 1975. *The Labour Movement in Europe*. London: Cox & Wyman.

Knowles, K. G. 1952. *Strikes. A Study in Industrial Conflict*. London: Basil Blackwell.

La Valle, D. 1976. *Le origini della classe operaia alla Fiat*. Rome: Coines.

Lay, A., D. Marucco, and M. L. Pesante. 1973. "Classe operaia e scioperi ipotesi per il periodo 1880–1923." *Ouaderni storici*, no. 22: 87–144.

Lay, A., and M. L. Pesante. 1974. "Ciclo economico e lotte operaie in Europa, 1880–1920. *"Rivista di storia contemporanea*, no. 3: 38, 9–421.

Maione, G. 1975. *Il biennio rosso. Autonamia e spontaneita' operaia nel 1919–1920*. Bologna: Il Mulino.

Marchetti, L., ed. 1962. *La Confederazione Generale del Lavoro negli atti, nei documenti, nei congressi*. Milan: Edizioni Avanti.

Merli, S. 1972. *Proletariato di fabbrica e capitalismo industriale*. Firenze: La Nuova Italia.

Neppi Modona, G. 1969. *Sciopero, potere politico e magistratura*. Bari: Laterza.

Pizzorno, A. 1970. "Sul metodo di Gramsci: dalla storiografia all scienza i politica." In AA. VV. *Gramsci e la cultura contemporanea*. Rome: Riuniti. 1978. "Political Exchange and Collective Indentity in Industrial Conflict." In C. Crouch and A. Pizzorno, eds.,

The Resurgence of Class Conflict in Western Europe since 1968. London: Macmillan.

Procacci, G. 1972. *La lotta di classe in Italia agli inizi del secolo XX.* Rome: Riuniti.

Romagnoli, G., and A. Manoukian. 1972. "Il sistema di fabbrica nella fase inizia le dello sviluppo capitalistico in Italia." *Studie di Sociologia* 10 (April–September): 275–390.

Romagnoli, U. 1974. *Lavoratori e sindacati tra vecchio e nuovo diritto.* Bologna: Il Mulino.

Romeo, R. 1972. *Breve storia della grande industria in Italia.* Bologna: Capelli.

Ross, A. M., and P. T. Hartmann. 1960. *Changing patterns of Industrial Conflict.* New York: Wiley.

Shorter, E., and C. Tilly. 1971. "The Shape of Strike in France, 1830–1960." *Comparative Studies in Society and History,* no. 13: 60–86.

Snyder, D. 1975. "Institutional Setting and Industrial Conflict: Comparative Analysis of France, Italy, and the United States." *American Sociological Review* 40: 259–78.

Spesso, R. 1966. "Dinamica delle conquiste salariali prima dopo la repubblica." *Critica marxista* 4 (September): 138–54.

Spriano, P. 1964: *L'occupazione delle fabbrice.* Turin: Einaudi. 1972. *Storia di Torino operaia e socialista.* Turin: Einaudi.

Vitali, O. 1968. *La popolazione attiva in agricoltura attraverso i censimenti italiani.* Istituto di Demografia dell'Universita di Roma. 1970. *Aspetti dello sviluppo economico italian o alla luce della ricostruzione della populazione attiva.* Istituto di Demografia dell'Universita di Roma.

Zamagni, V. 1976. "La dinamica dei salari nel seltore industriale." In P. Ciocca and G. Toniolo, eds., *L'economie italiana nel periods fascista.* Bologna: Il Mulino.

Vannutelli, C. 1961. "Occupazione e salari dal 1861 al 1961." In AA. VV., *L'economia italiene dal 1861 al 1961. Studi nel primo centenazio dell'Unitè al Italia.* Milan: Ginffré.

10

Strikes and politics in the United States, 1900–1919

P. K. EDWARDS

The traditional view of the relationship between American trade unions and politics was that special factors in the American environment and in the attitude of American workers militated against the involvement of unions in politics and justified the pure-and-simple unionism of the American Federation of Labor. The view, associated with the historiography of John R. Commons and the "Wisconsin School," has been subjected to considerable criticism in recent years. It has been pointed out that socialist influences within the unions were sometimes considerable (Laslett 1970), that at the level of the individual states labor political activity was significant (Fink 1973), and, more generally, that the teleological mode of presentation, whereby unions fulfilled their natural destinies and errors such as political involvement were rejected, was not the best way of understanding historical processes.

The outcome of these and other criticisms has been the emergence of a new approach in which political matters are given much more serious attention. Perhaps the largest claim for the importance of politics is that of Shorter and Tilly (1974, 329): until the 1930s "collective action was as much political as economic, intended equally to build political organization and press political demands and to elevate the standard of living by pressuring individual employers." It will be convenient to use this statement as a starting point for the present discussion. The period 1900–19 is not chosen as a detailed case study; reasons of space preclude that. It is used simply as an illustration of some more general points about the relationship between strikes and politics.

Dimensions of political action

As it stands, the hypothesis that strikes and politics were connected is too vague to be analyzed. Several distinctions must be drawn. They are illustrated schematically in Figure 1.

Figure 1. Typology of relations between strikes and politics

	National politics	State/local politics	Distribution of power in general
Strikes intended to influence			
Other labor movement activity intended to influence			
Strikes influenced by			
General development of labor movement influenced by			

The first distinction concerns the meaning of politics. It has been easy for writers who are skeptical about arguments based on collective bargaining to suggest that bargaining institutions have to be seen in the context of a broader distribution of power in society (e.g., Korpi and Shalev 1979). They thus have the benefit of appearing to take a wider view than the institutionalists without having to define very closely what is meant by politics or the political economy. For example, when Shorter and Tilly (1974, 326) defend their political interpretation of strikes in Britain, they describe them as being "fundamentally localized protests over the local distribution of power." The politics here are plainly very different from the politics of putting pressure on the national government. In the American context it seems useful to make a threefold distinction between types of politics: national politics, politics at the level of the individual states or cities within the states, and politics in the generic sense of having to do with the distribution of power between social groups. The second distinction concerns the activities of workers and unions. Hence it can be argued that strikes were directly aimed at a political target or, more cautiously, that labor movement behavior other than strikes contained political elements such as lobbying of legislatures. Alternatively, it can be suggested that strikes or the more general development of the labor movement were products of various political climates.

Further distinctions can readily be introduced into each of the dimensions in Figure 1. On the political dimension it would be necessary, if a proper categorization were to be achieved, to take account of the different forms of political action: building a distinct labor party, lobbying legislatures, recording legislators' voting patterns and asking labor supporters to vote accordingly, and so on. On the labor movement dimension it would be necessary to take account of, for example, the proportion of strikes aimed at the polity or affected by it: It might be argued that all strikes had political intent, that only a particular

248

sort of strike activity such as that in the public services was affected by the polity, and so on.

It is for those who espouse a political interpretation of strikes to specify which of these many possible meanings they propose. In some cases this is clear. Fink (1973), for example, argues that in Missouri there was a considerable amount of general labor movement activity concerned with lobbying state legislators and that there was also sympathy for third-party movements. In other cases it is less clear. The statement by Shorter and Tilly that has been taken as a starting point is plainly about intentions. And, although it refers to collective action in general, it is made in the context of strike figures and can reasonably be taken to mean that strikes, like other forms of collective action, had a political intent. As might be expected from a programmatic statement, the nature of political action, and the level at which it was directed, are indicated in only general terms, but Shorter and Tilly are plainly not restricting their hypothesis to the level of national politics, and any form of pressing political demands would count in its favor.

As the foregoing explication has shown, their statement is not open to testing as it stands, and instead various of its elements need to be considered. First, no detailed documentation is required to dispose of any implication that a significant proportion of strikes had immediate political intents in the sense, for example, of being deliberately used to secure passage of a particular piece of legislation. No doubt some militants in some strikes saw their activity as having the broad political purpose of putting pressure on the capitalist class in general or of raising the political awareness of the workers. But it is surely questionable whether such a view was predominant among the rank and file and whether it affected the express demands of particular strikes. "Intention" is a strong word, carrying implications of an express link between political aims and the use of the strike weapon. It may be that the historian with the benefit of hindsight can discern a link between the growth of strikes and broad developments within the political economy, but this does not warrant the inference that strikes had a conscious political motivation. Similarly, any direct link between strikes and the building of political organization is surely questionable. Is there any evidence that strikes were used to further the creation of political parties, for example? In short, if we wish to explain a particular phenomenon, namely the movement of strike activity, reference to the supposed political aspiration of the strikers will not advance the explanation very much.

Shorter and Tilly are on much stronger ground concerning the political animus of collective action in a generic sense, which they define as "the application of some population's pooled resources on behalf of that population's collective objectives" (1974, 6). There is evidence that American workers have taken an interest in political matters. In addition to the works mentioned earlier numerous detailed studies demonstrate the importance of political action

249

in a range of localities. To cite but three: Cross (1935, 97–127) discusses the emergence of the Californian labor movement and, among other things, its involvement in political activity to control Chinese immigration; Yellowitz (1965) analyzes the role of labor in the politics of New York State; and Dawley (1976, 199–219) indicates the range of political interests among workers in Lynn, Massachusetts. Yet two points must be made concerning the significance of such studies for Shorter and Tilly's overall argument. First, the studies do not deal directly with national politics. Many writers have commented on the difficulties of creating a national focus in labor politics given the existing two-party system and the problems of generalizing from the successful prosecution of purely local demands to a program and organization capable of achieving widespread support. A national focus obviously attained significance at times, as in the presidential campaign of 1912 when the Socialist party candiate Eugene Debs attained 6% of the popular vote. Yet the overall drift of the labor movement's use of collective action can hardly be said to have had a powerful national focus when set alongside efforts to build unions, to obtain recognition from employers, and to conduct strike action in the face of considerable opposition from employers.

This leads to the second point. Shorter and Tilly say that political action and pressurizing individual employers were "equally" important. Assessing the relative importance of two such complex factors is obviously a matter of judgment. But it should be noted that the aim of many of the studies that criticize the traditional stress on collective bargaining was to correct what they saw as a complete imbalance. By "bringing politics back in" they did not assert or imply that politics were thus of equal significance to collective bargaining. It is difficult to know what criteria to use to judge relative importance, and again the conclusion must be that Shorter and Tilly's statement is not so much not proven as not capable of being proven as it stands.

There are, moreover, some further distinctions to be introduced when "importance" is considered. First, there is a difference between the argument that collective bargaining and political action are, in principal, both likely to attract the attention of a labor movement, and the claim that in a particular country they were pursued with equal vigor. Second, there is a difference between the general importance of politics and the success with which political demands were made. Writers in the Commons school are rightly criticized for inferring from the nonpartisan approach of the AFL that politics were necessarily of secondary importance in America; that is they are criticized for conflating the two elements of the first distinction. But the reverse error must also be avoided: Allowing that politics can be important does not imply that American workers in fact gave them equal importance to their industrial struggles. Similarly, it can readily be accepted that politics were important to the American worker in a general sense without accepting that political demands were as likely to be successful as industrial ones. That is, it was perfectly possible for workers to believe that a political program was in itself desirable, but that the problems of carrying it out were so great that it was preferable to concentrate on economic struggles.

The present importance of these two distinctions is that they add a further set of considerations when the questions of economic and political action are considered. To say that both were important is to say everything and nothing, and what is required instead is detailed analysis taking account of the sort of considerations indicated above. Plainly, this task cannot be carried out here. The main aim has simply been to sustain a "political" interpretation of collective action in America. One or two summary points may, however, be made. First, socialism was plainly not incompatible with the American environment. It declined bacause of internal difficulties (Weinstein 1967, viii), direct repression (Preston 1966; Goldstein 1978), or economic and political developments outside its control (Laslett 1970, 5), or all three. Second, it remains true that the American labor movement did not found an independent political party and that its political activities were generally localized and directed at specific issues. However much it is stressed that business unionism was not the necessary fate of the American labor movement, it remains true that voluntarism and a nonpartisan politics dominated it. My own view on this is that, in addition to factors concerned with the American polity and the alleged individualism of the American workers, an important element in the explanation is the way in which American unions were constrained to concentrate on the workplace because of the intensity of employers' hostility to them (Edwards 1981; 1983a). That is, collective bargaining was not the necessary course of American unions, but a focus on the workplace was forced on them by the behavior of other powerful actors. It remained possible, in principle, to follow the Webbs's method of legal enactment, but given also the hostility of the courts to union interests and the fearsome problems of organizing at the national level, it would have been a brave union leader who was willing to divert a substantial proportion of his resources away from collective bargaining and into the uncertain world of politics.

What, then, of the reverse connection, namely the influence of politics on strike patterns? Snyder (1975; 1977) has taken up Shorter and Tilly's arguments by suggesting that during the "early" period of American strikes, which he defines as 1900–48, political influences on the movement of strike indices would be important, whereas in the subsequent period of institutionalized bargaining, economic factors would be more significant. He produces a series of regression equations in which the dependent variables are the number of strikes and the number of workers involved in strikes, and the independent variables are two economic indices (the unemployment percentage and the rate of change of wages), one measure of union organization (the percentage of

251

workers organized), and two political indices (the proportion of Congress filled by Democrats, and a dummy variable for the party of the president). He suggests that a favorable political climate, as measured by a high proportion of Democrats or a Democratic president, will be conducive to a high level of strike activity.

As shown in detail elsewhere (Edwards 1978; 1981, 67–83), these results are not as decisive as Snyder suggests. There is no dramatic shift in the signs of the coefficients of the economic and political variables between the two periods identified. Neither is it clear why Snyder relies on just two periods with the expectation that there will be a rapid shift in the character of the link between the polity and strike activity. An alternative formulation in terms of three periods, including the earlier period 1881–99 as well as Snyder's two periods, for example, shows that the party of the president variable was, as predicted, significant for the first two periods but not the third, but also that the percentage Democrat variable fails to be signficant in the first two and attains significance only in the third (Edwards 1978, 330). Moreover, it is hardly surprising that the party of the president dummy is significant for the period 1900–48 in view of the Republican incumbency of the White House between 1921 and 1933, when strike activity was very low, and the Democrat incumbency from 1933 to 1948, when the strike rate returned to more normal levels. More generally, the measures of the political climate are very rough, and perhaps not too much should be expected of them. The link between who occupies the White House and the decision of workers in Wisconsin as to whether or not to go on strike is tenuous. Indeed a clearer test of Snyder's model would, particularly in view of the apparent concentration of labor's political activity at the state level, examine the connections between strikes and politics within particular states. As they stand, Snyder's results are insufficiently robust to bear the weight of interpretation required of them.

In short, the burden of proof still rests on those who propose the strong thesis that strikes in America before the First World War had a direct political intent or that they were the reflection of political forces defined in terms of the composition of the legislature and executive branch of the government. This is particularly so since it has been admitted that Shorter and Tilly produced "no evidence" to support their argument about the political interpretation in a strong sense, although it is certainly true that political questions cannot be totally ignored. A rather broader view of the links between strikes and the polity than that implied in the literature discussed is required.

Strikes and the political economy

During the last quarter of the nineteenth century the "labor problem" forced its attention on governments, the judiciary, and middle-class reformers, as well as on employers, in novel and disturbing ways. From the great railway strikes of 1877, through the strikes for the eight-hour day and the Haymarket incident of 1886, to the Homestead and Pullman strikes of the 1890s, and on into a whole series of highly publicized battles during the early twentieth century, workers' struggles took a conflict-laden and often violent course. Yet they did so not simply because workers had become suddenly more militant. Changes in the economic and political landscape were altering the nature of the environment in which workers lived. The emergence of giant corporations (Nelson 1959; Kirkland, 1961) occurred alongside the building of a new administrative state with new regulatory powers (Skowronek, 1982). Labor's struggles were not political in the simple sense of using strikes to attain express political aims. But their development reflected broader changes in the American political economy.

It is not surprising that many of the most significant disputes of the late nineteenth century occurred on the railways. The railways were the nation's first modern business enterprises (Chandler 1977), with enormous concentrations of power. Neither is it surprising that railway disputes attracted the attention of the state, in the shape of the executive and the judiciary. The strikes of 1877 were the first in which federal troops were called out to repress industrial disorder (Yellen 1936, 3). And there was a series of court judgments that curtailed the use of the strike weapon. In 1886, for example, came the first federal injunction preventing interference with the operation of a railway, and in 1894 the courts interpreted their powers extremely widely to ban strikes, an activity supported by the open assistance that the federal government gave to the railway companies in crushing the strikes (Eggert 1967, 125, 182–9). Eggert (1967, 21) argues that the courts were the only parts of the state to adopt a consistent and decisive policy toward strikes. The executive branch tended to respond in an ad hoc manner to the demands of the immediate situation. But although there was no planned or coherent policy on labor relations, a means of dealing with the "labor problem" slowly emerged. The battles of the late nineteenth century on the railways were not repeated. A significant illustration of the changed nature of industrial relations came in 1916 with the demand by the unions organizing workers who actually moved the trains (known as the operating Brotherhoods) for an eight-hour day. The threat of a strike was sufficient to persuade the government to go over the heads of the companies by passing the Adamson Act, which granted most of the unions' demands (see Kaufman 1954, 60–5).

Two general points, which ought to be familiar from the debate about corporate liberalism, emerge from this example. First, the state was not simply the creature of the employers, for it acted at times against their express wishes. And, second, there was no carefully formulated strategy of incorporating the unions. More interesting are the reasons for the state's intervention. Two features of the railways made them different from other industries: the unambiguous nature of their business as involving interstate commerce, and hence the unquestioned right of the federal legislature to pass laws covering it; and their enormous importance to the economy as a whole, for in 1916 they carried 98% of intercity passenger traffic and 77% of the freight traffic (Stover 1961, 238). These features permitted and encouraged the state to intervene, even against the wishes of the companies, to protect some loosely defined public interest. Intervention certainly occurred in other industries when there appeared to be a threat to public health or safety, as in the 1902 anthracite strike when fears of a fuel shortage became acute (Wiebe 1961). But this tended to be a response to an immediate situation, and there was no lasting governmental intervention in the conduct of labor relations in the great majority of industries. The particular position of the railways led to intervention that moved labor relations away from "free" collective bargaining and into a set of conciliation and arbitration arrangements in which the state was always a silent, and sometimes active, participant.

To the extent that a general public policy emerged out of experience with the railways and out of observation of the many labor conflicts elsewhere, it was that collective bargaining was the way forward. But this was more a pious statement that bargaining was in some sense a good thing than a policy that was likely to produce action. The investigation into the railway strike of 1894 had certainly said that employers should be encouraged to recognize trade unions and that the growth of large corporations was a "perversion" of the laws of supply and demand (U.S. Strike Commission 1895, LIV, XLVII). But it had also grappled with a problem with the state's intervening in labor relations: As the commission saw it, employers could be forced to comply with the state's rulings but employees could not, since they always had the right to quit. The solution was that railways were a special case because they were "creatures of the state, whose rights are conferred upon them for public purposes" (p. LI). Other inquires, notably the mammoth report of the U.S. Commission on Industrial Relations (1916; see also Adams 1966), similarly criticized the excessive power of large corporations and revealed sympathy for the workers laboring long hours in poor conditions. One solution that attracted considerable interest was the arbitration of differences, with interested eyes being turned on experiments with compulsory arbitration in countries such as Australia and New Zealand (Coleman 1982). Despite its appeal among reform groups, the craft unions were firmly opposed to it, and collective bargaining emerged as the solution generally preferred among reformers (Ramirez 1978, 4, 160–71; Yellowitz 1965, 142). Yet there were few opportunities for making collective bargaining into an effective public policy.

The main opportunity came during the First World War. The war emergency, with the need to maintain production and the tightening of labor markets, led to unprecedented government intervention through agencies such as the National War Labor Board. Their policy was to reduce the arbitrary power of employers by encouraging collective bargaining, an approach that has led some observers to find in the wartime experience the model for the subsequent reforms of industrial relations carried out during the New Deal (e.g., Nash 1960). Yet, as is well known, unions attained few lasting gains from their cooperation with the war effort, and the 1920s were a period of the reassertion of managerial control and a rapid decline in union membership. Government intervention was based on the established principle of responding to a particular problem using the tools at hand: There was a problem of industrial unrest that required action because of the national needs of the war effort, and collective bargaining was a useful model for dealing with the problem. Even then, however, the government's commitment to bargaining should not be exaggerated. The war emergency was very short-lived, and the NWLB for example was not established until April 1918. This hardly gave time for collective relations to develop. Moreover, what emerges from detailed descriptions of the wartime policy, notably that of Bing (1921), who was a participant in it, is not that free collective bargaining developed under the benign eye of the state but that crises emerged in particular areas and that the military were often directly involved in solving them. Finally, the other side of the coin of the recognition of responsible AFL unions was the suppression of radical union activity in the shape of the IWW, which continued after the war with the Red Scare of 1919–20 (Preston 1966).

The war marked an important stage in the increasing implication of the government in the conduct of the economy. This process reflected far more than the party–political complexion of the legislature or even the political climate of the Progressive Era, with its stress on the evils of the unregulated development of capitalism. Indeed, the importance of reform movements is easily exaggerated. As Yellowitz (1965, 127) concludes, in New York State the reforms that were achieved reflected not the inherent power of labor or the Progressives but the acceptance of their programs as a statement of public attitudes. Now, public acceptance of labor's demands may be seen as success. Yet, as Yellowitz implies, it is not a matter of labor pressing demands on an essentially neutral state, but of the state's having a set of problems of its own and a degree of autonomy in solving them. Acceptance of some elements of labor's program depended on the nature of these problems, in particular the degree to which the state was seen as responsible for controlling the economy. The emergence of a "political economy" meant that economic matters such as the commercial activities of corporations or their ways of dealing with their employees could no longer be seen as a private concern. The state became implicated as a result of its tasks of overseeing the development of the economy. The precise definition of these tasks was a lengthy and continuous process, complicated in America by the division between federal and state responsibilities. It is only by locating labor's political concerns within this process that the relationship between labor and the polity can be understood. Workers may not always have had express political demands. Indeed, it is ironic that it was the most conservative and craft-conscious of unions, the railway Brotherhoods, that were the first to become closely enmeshed with the political apparatus. It was not just the degree of workers' political awareness that was important, but their position within an emerging economic and political system that defined their relationship to the polity.

The state's policies toward labor were not, moreover, all of a piece. As would be expected from the jerky ad hoc development of policy there were different, and sometimes conflicting, elements. As argued at more length elsewhere in relation to the New Deal period (Edwards 1983b), this is to be expected given that the state has two fundamental tasks, which are generally in a state of creative tension, of providing the conditions for further accumulation and legitimizing the existing economic and political order. Thus at one point the use of federal power to suppress strikes may seem to be called for. The growing ability of the state to provide resources may be illustrated by developments in the army: In 1877 the army was small, most of its troops were located well away from urban centers, and since an appropriations bill had not been passed, the enlisted men were not being paid (Eggert 1967, 29); by 1920 there were sophisticated contingency plans to deal with domestic unrest (Preston 1966, 245). At other points, however, suppression may be replaced by a more conciliatory approach if, for example, the public interest seems to be endangered by labor disputes. Differing priorities require different policies, and it is through the working out of the various pressures upon it that the state fashions something that may be called a strategy toward labor relations.

The foregoing discussion has covered many issues in a very short space. Its aim has been to do no more than indicate some of the factors that have to be taken into account when the complex word "politics" is used to describe workers' behavior. The word is a useful slogan for the criticism of an allegedly narrow concentration on collective bargaining. But it has several meanings that, when untangled, suggest that some of the larger claims implicit in the slogan have to be rejected. The literature on labor in politics has undermined some of the simpler assumptions about the voluntarism of American unions. It has not supported the conclusion that political aims were on a par with economic ones. Certainly, if the concern is with quantifiable patterns of strikes, and with the proximate causes thereof, a general appeal to politics does not get the analysis very far. A broader interest in the activities of the state is also important for political interpretations. Yet, ironically, such interpretations have deployed a narrow view of politics as the pursuit of identifiable demands within the arena of national or state legislatures. This needs to be set in the context of a consideration of the role of the state in the management of the political economy. Hence when Montgomery (1979, 83) concludes his essay on "machinists, the Civil Federation and the Socialist Party" by remarking that "in the twentieth century the questions of workers' control and the role of the state had become inseparably intertwined," he does not mean that the pursuit of workplace matters had the immediate aim of affecting the national polity, but that the problem of shopfloor control and the activities of the state in managing the economy were necessarily becoming intimately related. It is within the changing relationships of workers, unions, employers, and the state that the question of politics should be pursued.

References

Adams, Graham. 1966. *Age of Industrial Violence, 1910–15: The Activities and Findings of the United States Commission on Industrial Relations.* New York: Columbia University Press.

Bing, Alexander M. 1921. *Wartime Strikes and Their Adjustment.* New York: E. P. Dutton & Co.

Chandler, Alfred D. 1977. *The Visible Hand: The Managerial Revolution in American Business.* Cambridge, Mass.: Harvard University Press.

Coleman, Peter J. 1982. "New Zealand Liberalism and the Origins of the American Welfare State." *Journal of American History* 69: 372–91.

Cross, Ira B. 1935. *A History of the Labor Movement in California.* Berkeley: University of California Press.

Dawley, Alan. 1976. *Class and Community: The Industrial Revolution in Lynn.* Cambridge, Mass.: Harvard University Press.

Edwards, P. K. 1978. "Time Series Regression Models of Strike Activity: A Reconsideration with American Data." *British Journal of Industrial Relations* 16: 320–34.

1981. *Strikes in the United States, 1881–1974.* Oxford: Blackwell.

1983a. "The Exceptionalism of the American Labour Movement: the Neglected Role of Workplace Struggle." Paper presented to annual conference of the British Association for American Studies.

1983b. "The Political Economy of Industrial Conflict: Britain and America." *Economic and Industrial Democracy* 4: 461–500.

Eggert, Gerald G. 1967. *Railroad Labor Disputes: The Beginnings of Federal Strike Policy.* Ann Arbor: Michigan University Press.

Fink, Gary N. 1973. *Labor's Search for Political Order: The Political Behavior of the Missouri Labor Movement, 1890–1940.* Columbia: University of Missouri Press.

Goldstein, Robert Justin. 1978. *Political Repression in Modern America: From 1870 to the Present.* Cambridge, Mass.: Schenkman.

Kaufman, Jacob J. 1954. *Collective Bargaining in the Railroad Industry.* New York: King's Crown Press.

Kirkland, Edward C. 1961. *Industry Comes of Age: Business, Labor and Public Policy,*

1860–1897. New York: Holt, Rinehart & Winston.

Korpi, Walter, and Michael Shalev. 1979. "Strikes, Industrial Relations and Class Conflict in Capitalist Societies." *British Journal of Sociology* 30: 164–87.

Laslett, John H. M. 1970. *Labor and the Left: A Study of Socialist and Radical Influences in the American Labor Movement, 1881–1924.* New York: Basic Books.

Montgomery, David. 1979. *Workers' Control in America.* Cambridge: Cambridge University Press.

Nash, G. D. 1960. "Franklin D. Roosevelt and Labor: the World War I Origins of Early New Deal Policy." *Labor History* 1: 39–52.

Nelson, Ralph L. 1959. *Merger Movements in American Industry, 1895–1956.* Princeton: Princeton University Press.

Preston, William. 1966. *Aliens and Dissenters: Federal Suppression of Radicals, 1903–1933.* New York: Harper Torchbooks.

Ramirez, Bruno. 1978. *When Workers Fight: The Politics of Industrial Relations in the Progressive Era, 1898–1916.* Westport: Greenwood.

Shorter, Edward, and Charles Tilly. 1974. *Strikes in France, 1830–1968.* Cambridge: Cambridge University Press.

Skowronek, Stephen. 1982. *Building a New American State: the Expansion of National Administrative Capacities, 1877–1920.* Cambridge: Cambridge University Press.

Snyder, David. 1975. "Institutional Setting and Industrial Conflict: Comparative Analyses of France, Italy, and the United States." *American Sociological Review* 40: 259–78.

1977. "Early North American Strikes: A Reinterpretation." *Industrial and Labor Relations Review* 30: 325–41.

Stover, John F. 1961. *American Railroads.* Chicago: University of Chicago Press.

Tilly, Charles, and Roberto Franzosi. 1983. "Review of Edwards, 1981." *Industrial Relations Law Journal* 5: 426–39.

United States Commission on Industrial Relations. 1916. *Final Report and Testimony.* Washington, D.C.: Government Printing Office.

United States Strike Commission. 1895. *Report on the Chicago Strikes of June–July 1894.* Washington, D.C.: Government Printing Office.

Weinstein, James. 1967. *The Decline of Socialism in America, 1912–1925.* New York: Monthly Review Press.

Wiebe, Robert H. 1961. "The Anthracite Strike of 1902: A Record of Confusion." *Mississippi Valley Historical Review* 48: 229–51.

Yellen, Samuel. 1936. 1936. *American Labor Struggles.* New York: Harcourt, Brace & Co.

Yellowitz, Irwin. 1965. *Labor and the Progressive Movement in New York State, 1897–1916.* Ithaca: Cornell University Press.

III

Workers in metal-processing enterprises
in comparative perspective

11

Introduction: from the mechanic to the metallo

MICHELLE PERROT

If the workers of the metal-processing industry, who are largely absent from the strike scene as late as the 1880s, became by the turn of the century major actors in labor unrest, it is first and foremost because of the structural transformations of production that turn metal processing into a key sector of industry. The introduction in means of transportation of mechanical equipment involving the use of coal, and eventually oil, gives a major impulse to the development of mechanical enterprises and shipyards. From the Urals to the Appalachians, the numbers of workers employed in metal-processing and mechanical enterprises swell during these two decades: in St. Petersburg, from 21,000 in 1884 to 60,000 by 1900; in the United States, from 55,000 workers employed in mechanical enterprises in 1870 to 840,000 by 1920. These comparative indices illustrate the transformation of the industrial landscape that provides the common background for the case studies presented here.

Besides these patterns of rapid growth, these case studies of the metal industry bring out another common feature: the changes in organization that, with different degrees of rapidity and scope, metal-processing enterprises undergo everywhere: from Detroit to St. Petersburg, from Milan to Sheffield and Essen. At the beginning of the 1880s, at least in Western Europe, the metal-processing industry largely consists of a myriad of small enterprises, employing workers with a wide range of skills and enjoying a considerable degree of autonomy, which they manage to safeguard by maintaining a certain degree of control of the labor market, control over the dissemination of their skills as well as of the levels of remuneration paid for them. Their monopoly of skill is safeguarded not so much by the intrinsic difficulties of attaining them, as through the imposition of a period of apprenticeship, the very length of which provides a guarantee of status. Levels of remuneration, in turn, are safeguarded through practices of subcontracting, which as late as the twentieth century maintain, even in large plants, a semiartisanal character.

261

The piece rates that have become predominant by this time are not really calculated on the basis of productivity since they do not take account of the time actually spent in production. A shared consensus among the work force restrains excesses of zeal on the part of immigrant workers from the country-side striving for higher earnings, imposing on one and all a more acceptable rhythm of work; Taylor will call it "loafing." (The practice is the object of a celebrated study by Max Weber in 1909.)

The very disorder reigning in the shops – the very sight of which in old photographs appears so unseemly to our eyes, accustomed to a Taylor-made order – actually provides a way of preserving "trade secrets," which constitute for those who hold them a source of power and autonomy. For this is what is really involved at this, as at any, stage of the organization of production processes.

In these industrial establishments that rapidly multiplied from the 1860s to the 1880s, in the climate of easy profits created by the upswing of the Kondratieff cycle in which iron and steel were kings, the mechanic is his own "little master," almost obscuring the presence of the other "real master." Indeed, the mechanic is not the servant but the master of the machine – a molder, adjuster, turner – whose hand and eye, trained by experience and daily contact with his seniors, are worth more than years of schooling. Masters of technique, these mechanics are also men of progress. Avid readers of technical journals and enthusiastic visitors of technical exhibits, they are lovers of modernity, combining individual initiative and enterprise with a sense of group, and even class, identity. The portrait that David Montgomery draws of American machinists probably applied very widely, at least in the West.

As in the 1880s, these mechanics by and large are still only feebly organized, except in Britain, where the Amalgamated Society of Engineers has already managed to establish a "craft administration" and to have it recognized even by the government (Keith Burgess). In St. Petersburg, according to Ratnik's report, 80% of the work forces of metal-processing enterprises consist of immigrants from the countryside, who have come to the city for additional earnings to send home to their families in their native villages. But these work forces also include a minority of workers of urban origin and artisanal back-ground eager for promotion and imbued with a sense of dignity, even if they are impelled to drown their frequent setbacks and grievances in alcohol. Certain perspicacious state officials warn of the danger inherent in this explosive mixture, and suggest potential remedies: a reorganization of work processes that would lead to greater labor productivity, and thereby make possible higher rates of remuneration and better living conditions.

Everywhere the period of the Great Depression, from the 1880s through the turn of the century – compounded in Russia by the effects of the Russo–Japanese war – upsets this fragile economic equilibrium and the climate of prosperity that it has engendered. As so many economists have argued, all crises are conducive to rationalization. The scope and intensity of this one induces systematic reflection about the "space–time" universe of the enterprise. The terms "scientific organization of labor" and "scientific management" are generally applied to the body of theory that it contributes.

Various descriptions of this process generally bring out the prominent roles played in it by engineers, particularly those employed in state enterprises. The crisis provides for them a dreamed of opportunity to apply capacities to innovate hitherto underexploited by conservative employers. Indeed, the crisis sounds the death knell of the era of "bosses' sons" (*fils a papa*). In the course of the second wave of industrialization, employers will have to enroll their heirs in management and engineering schools, and call trained technicians to their aid.

The case of Imperial Russia is especially striking. Managers of large public enterprises (Ratnik), and of private ones (Semenov), make up for the tours of the United States conducted by their Western confreres by reading American (as well as German and British) publications. They translate them in their technical journals and discuss them at the meetings of their technical associations, worshipping Taylor as the potential savior of Russian industry, if not of Russian society. In this connection, Heather Hogan's study shows persuasively how much St. Petersburg, after the turn of the century, looks to the West. Even the Marxists greet the doctrine of scientific management with utmost seriousness, and in later years Lenin and the Agarkov movement will put them to use.

One must recognize that the ideology of the engineering mentality inherent in the Taylorist approach encompasses certain positive, if not necessarily humanist, features: the standardization of machinery and tools, a fuller exploitation of aptitudes and skills, the introduction of wage incentives hitherto unused. In practice, to be sure, rationalization is exploited by private employers to increase productivity and maximize profits at the workers' expense. Work forces are subjected to controls and checks by time setters; piece rates are modified or eliminated; and hourly rates, adjusted to the time spent in the completion of work tasks, are introduced in their place.

To be sure, Russia, where workers' associations are not legally entitled to defend the interests and rights of labor, and strikes necessarily assume more violent forms and almost invariably are eventually repressed, constitutes an extreme case in point. In Western countries, it is by this time somewhat easier to wage strikes, even if workers still die occasionally in labor conflicts (in France, for example, during a strike by construction workers in Draveil, near Paris, in 1908).

But even in those countries (such as Germany) where rationalization does not assume explicitly Taylorist forms, it increases tensions and undermines

263

the power and autonomy of the mechanic. For the earlier practice of subcontracting and the use of piece rates, it substitutes base pay and bonuses that are systematically reduced with the achievement of higher average levels of productivity. It eliminates freedom of movement within, let alone outside, the shop, imposing checks on even the most momentary absences from the bench. No individual initiative is left to the workers in the performance of their tasks. Work cards and work sheets, drawn up in "production bureaus" by white collar workers who direct the work but never perform it, set precisely the nature of tasks and the ways in which they are to be performed. Even the foreman has now been dispossessed in his traditional prerogatives and authority. Dismissals are now justified on the ground of "unadaptability." In the effort to divide work tasks into their component parts, the labor force is reorganized. Jobs defined as "simple" are assigned to immigrants from the countryside, to the young, and even to women hitherto excluded from the performance of preeminently "male" tasks. This implied at all levels of the enterprise an elaborate process of selection and testing of the work force. The profile of the "métallo" – the *ouvrier spécialisé* (O.S.) in France, the unskilled laborer in Britain – is already on the horizon, although it will take Ford's assembly line (which is introduced in Europe only in the 1920s) to put him in his place. It is already evident that he will have nothing in common with the mechanic of old.

To be sure, the process unfolds at varying rates of speed, especially rapidly in the United States, where it has originated, and in Russia, or at least in St. Petersburg, a city of mammoth plants and anxious managers. German industry also undergoes a considerable degree of rationalization, if, as we have noted, in highly indigenous forms. Everywhere else, its introduction is slowed down by workers' resistance (especially so in England), as well as by the inadequate degree of concentration of enterprises. In France, where Taylorism is introduced on an experimental basis in state enterprises (at the St. Etienne arms works, for example) and in a few large automobile plants (Berillet, Renault), hardly more than 1% of the labor force is actually affected. Just as in Italy and Britain, it will take the advent of the war to open the door wide to the systematic introduction of Taylorism. But even in medium-sized enterprises, where resort to the whole arsenal of "scientific management" is hardly justified, one observes by the eve of the war a hardening of discipline and a tightening of control over the performance of work tasks, which set off numerous strikes.

The strike waves that break out in the various countries under scrutiny between 1905 and 1910 indeed share certain common features. Often defensive in character, for the most part confined to one or a few very large enterprises, they tend to be drawn out. For they run into a hardening of resistance on the part of the employers, who exploit what for them is the favorable economic conjuncture to impose their will. This hardening of resistance takes the form

264

of the organization of employers' associations (in Great Britain, the EEF, established in 1896), and especially of a wide resort to lock-outs (especially in Germany, where in 1910 the number of workers locked out actually exceeds the number of strikers!). The percentage of labor defeats in these strikes increases so sharply in most of the countries concerned that workers in fact turn away from the strike weapon, which loses much of its effectiveness now that employers have united to resist it.

Under these conditions, new forms of organization of labor militance emerge at the shop level of the enterprise, where skilled workers – especially sensitive to the issues at stake in the rationalization of work processes – take the lead in resorting to them. "Shop stewards" recruited from their ranks stress the importance of defending "workers' power" in the shop and the threat of overwork implicit in the higher levels of pay ostensibly extended, initially at least, to unskilled workers. David Montgomery and Keith Burgess describe this movement for "job control," which assumes particular importance in British engineering works. Bruno Bezza brings out the appearance of similar motifs in the strike waves in Lombardy in 1905–7, where trade unions seek to gain control of the labor market through the imposition of the "closed shop." Is the same order of phenomena surfacing during these years in large Russian metal plants, especially with the emergence of the first workers' soviets? At least, one encounters a similar stress on *qualitative* demands in the prewar strike wave in St. Petersburg: an insistence on the dignity of labor, workers' complaints of "rudeness," and demands for "polite treatment and address" (including the demand that workers be addressed as "you," rather than "thou").

This workers' resistance mobilized not solely in defense of particular interests. On the contrary, the unions of metalworkers organized in most of the countries concerned emphasize the need to bring together different categories of workers, including the unskilled, on an industrywide scale rather than on the basis of individual trades. The gravity of the threat induces, at least among the most prescient, a process of reflection about the future of unionism. In France, for example, metallists like Menheim advocate an economic analysis of the new strategies of capitalism to target union objectives more effectively. Jack Murphy in England, John Hall in the United States, and Colombino in Italy incarnate these union leaders of a new type who discern the threat that "deskilling" raises for all workers.

There surfaces at the same time a new political consciousness, as metalworkers are drawn to socialism – a new mode of representation of the state's relationship to the economy. The DMW, the powerful Union of German Metal Workers, established in 1891 (discussed in this volume by Elisabeth Domansky), assumes in this regard an especially prominent role. Distinguished in its orientation by the somewhat mechanistic brand of Marxism characteristic

265

of prewar Social Democracy, the DMW – persuaded of the inevitable triumph of socialism inherent in capitalist development – stresses the value of organization at the expense of action. Fundamentally hostile to the idea of a general strike, so fancied by Latins attracted to anarchism, it really considers any strike an ultimately wasteful expenditure of energy. Unions should resort to strikes only on the basis of coldly calculated decisions, carefully timed to favorable economic conjunctures. Strikes should be conducted by the same token with cold rationality – to the exclusion of all uncontrolled demonstrations – and involve only the issuance of "well-grounded demands." Under these circumstances, the union should be able to provide the strikers, whom it views as "technically unemployed," with appropriate financial assistance.

The DMW thus entertains an instrumentalist and functional conception of the strike weapon diametrically opposed to the conception of strikes as a mode of communal expression of the rank-and-file characteristic of "direct action" syndicalism, as well as to the British shop steward movement's view of strikes as a test of "workers' power." One million strong by 1911, the DMW exercises a decisive influence on the behavior of the German labor movement, which now proves far less responsive to the impact of economic and political conjunctures than working-class movements in other countries. As a mass union, the DMW is concerned first and foremost with the "rational management" – through negotiations – of the interests of its members.

According to Elisabeth Domansky's critical view of its policies, the over-optimistic economic orientation of the DMW blinded it to the scope of the ongoing structural transformation of industry, as well as to the political implications of the new tactics of employers – rationalization, lockouts, and the like – which were so clearly designed to sap the very basis of union power. In fact, the DMW now proved unable to bargain effectively. Only a few wage settlements were negotiated during this period, largely in small enterprises (affecting in fact only 13% of German metalworkers in 1914), and most of these agreements were concluded by employers – bypassing the union – directly with their work forces.

Thus, the moderate course of the DMW, which had been designed to anticipate and minimize risks, actually culminated in an internal crisis. After 1909, a grass-roots democratic movement built up within the union to press for greater participation by the rank and file in strike decisions. These internal divisions, cleverly exploited by employers, were partially responsible for the growing number of strike defeats as well as of wildcat strikes during this period.

While the economic crisis contributed to the consolidation of the power of managers and the influence of doctrines of scientific management, the outbreak of the war in turn reinforced the hitherto relatively marginal role played by the state in the running of the industrial economy. Indeed, the aggravation of living conditions induced by the shortages of consumer products and

266

increases in the cost of the living during the war years, was another common feature of the evolution of the various countries under our scrutiny. Given the strategic significance of the metal-processing industry for the war effort, the war and armaments ministries of the various belligerent countries assumed the leadership of the rationalization of production processes, in which the military had traditionally played a pioneering role. The restructuring of the work force connected with the massive hiring of women, of the young, and other new and unexperienced workers, marked these processes with a stamp of legitimacy. In Great Britain and Italy, the war provided a decisive impulse for the massive introduction of previously languishing rationalization processes.

The case of Great Britain, where the most classic forms of economic liberalism now gave way to the energetic interventionism of Lloyd George, is especially striking. In addition to the imposition of restrictions on the right to strike as well as on lockouts, and a wage freeze, hardly compensated by the taxation of rents on housing (a crucial issue at the time), there took place a wholesale reorganization of production processes, most notably in defense plants that were placed under the direct control of the state. This process of restructuring was conducted by "management boards," which introduced Taylorist methods on a wide scale.

A quite comparable situation developed in the regions of northern Italy, studied by Bruno Bezza, where the FIUM (Italian Metal Workers Federation) was completely disoriented by the attitudes displayed by the new work forces that were now recruited into industry. Although the union had emphasized "workers' power" and control of the labor market, these new workers – seeking first and foremost to earn higher wages – displayed little concern with modes of remuneration and their potential perverse effects.

Hence the heterogenous character of the demands advanced during the strike waves that broke out in the various belligerent countries in 1916–17, concerning which the contributions to this volume bring out numerous comparative dimensions. Most of these contributions emphasize the various discontinuities induced by the war. Economic discontinuities stem from the radical changes in the organization of production processes as well as from technological advances. Political discontinuities are caused by the affirmation of the dual role of the state as employer and provider. Social discontinuities result from the disappearance of the mechanic and the emergence of the "mass" worker, along with the creation of new systems of classification of the work force – which in fact bore little relationship to actual skills, laying instead considerable emphasis on seniority in an effort to stabilize the work force and reduce the labor turnovers that would eventually become a major problem in Taylorized plants.

The "metallo," who emerges as a central figures during the war years, and especially in the immediate postwar period, bears little resemblance

267

to the mechanics of old, most of whom will eventually find employment as skilled workers in large plants, while the most enterprising seek refuge in automobile repair shops. This is what will happen in France, for example, where women and foreigners will fill the ranks of the unskilled (*ouvriers spécialisés*, O.S.).

These mutations will exercise considerable effects on unionism. To represent the new "mass" workers, "mass" unions will emerge, less concerned with issues of workers' power and job control than with wage levels and systems of job classification, the arbitrary character of which will be a permanent source of conflict. So will the issue of free time, the only compensation that will not be available for the fragmentation of work tasks and the crisis of identity induced by the dissolution of traditional trades. These new mass unions will now be assigned a more recognized status, and assume the roles of acceptable interlocutors at the national level. From this point of view, the war provides a testing ground for the emergence of new forms of industrial relations. While in Germany, the DWM becomes fully absorbed into the institutional system; in Britain, Lloyd George brings official representatives of labor into his cabinet (even while ruthlessly repressing rank-and-file movements) and practices skillful policies of social reforms, to which those pursued in France by Albert Thomas deserve to be compared.

But here the comparisons end. In one way or another, all of these evolutionary processes will come up against the experience of 1917 and the enigma of the revolution. Possible, desirable, necessary, redoubtable? Provisionally at least, a new historical process is launched.

12

Strikes of machinists in the United States, 1870–1922

DAVID MONTGOMERY

The most impressive fact about machinists' strikes in the late nineteenth century is that there were not many of them. Strike statistics published by the U.S. Commissioner of Labor in 1887 and in 1896 classified strikers by occupation (in contrast to the famous report of 1906 that arranged all strikes since 1881 according to the industries involved). Strikes by coal miners, building workers, clothing workers, iron-and-steelworkers, and printers appeared frequently in the early figures, but not those of machinists. Work stoppages that did close metal fabricating establishments were regularly attributed to molders, and less often to boilermakers and to blacksmiths. Of fifty strikes in Pittsburgh's metal industry (excluding iron and steel smelting and rolling) during 1886, for example, not one was credited to machinists. Moreover, the machinists' strikes that did stand out were largely conducted by members of the craft who worked in railroad repair shops. Large manufacturers of railway cars in Detroit, Pullman, Paterson, and elsewhere were often struck in the 1880s, but most of their employees were woodworkers of some sort. In them – as in the San Francisco shipyards, Connecticut hardware factories, and midwestern agricultural implement works, where important strikes took place before 1894 – machinists left their posts along with others, but there is no hint of any special or leading role they might have played. If any single craft acted constantly and aggressively *as a craft* in nineteenth-century metalworks, it was the iron molders.[1]

In 1922 the Department of Labor again released data that attributed strikes to particular crafts or occupations , and the figures covered the years 1916–21.[2]

1. U.S. Department of the Interior, *Report of the Secretary of the Interior*, 50th Cong., 1st sess., H. Doc. 1, pt 5 (Washington, 1887); U.S. Commissioner of Labor, *Tenth Annual Report...1894. Strikes and Lockouts*, 2 vols., 54th Cong., 1st sess., H. Doc. 339 (Washington, 1896). Throughout this essay I shall follow the American usage, which distinguishes the metalworking industry from the iron-and-steel industry (smelting and rolling).
2. *Monthly Labor Review* 14 (May, 1922): 181–9 (hereinafter cites as *MLR*).

269

This epoch, as P. K. Edwards has shown, exhibited a higher general level of strike activity than any other period in the country's history. In each of the five years between 1916 and 1922 machinists were found among the three occupational groups initiating the largest number of strikes, and during 1918 and 1919 they actually led the list (even ahead of coal miners). Edwards has warned historians, quite properly, that the "number of strikes" is the most arbitrary category in all the aggregate figures provided by the government. Whether a cessation of work against several employers is one strike or many depends on ad hoc clerical judgments. Moreover, the 1922 data does not indicate the number of strikers, and later publications that do after statistics on the size of this period's strikes rank them by industry, not by trade.[3] Nevertheless, it is safe to conclude that between the end of the nineteenth century and the postwar years, American machinists had exchanged a negligible role in the country's strikes for one of great prominence. How is one to explain and evaluate this change?

Paradoxically, machinists waxed increasingly craft-conscious as their craft became more difficult to define. Although by 1900 the name of the trade designated people who cut and shaped metal parts on machine tools, less than half a century earlier it had referred to builders of machinery. Thus an early (1877) attempt at a national union had called itself the Mechanical Engineers of North America, and Machine Builders was the name adopted in 1888 by a national trades' district of machinists' assemblies in the Knights of Labor. One can even encounter suggestive, if not numerous, references from that epoch to "machinists" who worked in small shops with no power-driven machinery. Customarily, machinists from the fifties through the eighties had functioned from a bench, where they had laid out tasks with bluing and scribes and where they also finished work with files, scrapers, or lapping stones. They moved parts to an available lathe, milling machine, drill press, planer, shaper, or grinder as the sequence of operations they had determined required, until they could deliver finished parts (e.g., drive shafts) or assembled units (e.g., wheel carriages) to the foreman. The latter, invariably a machinist himself, served as the estimator of job costs, distributor of assignments, fixer of piece rates (where they were used), troubleshooter, inspector, and disciplinarian for the shop. His instructions to the individual craftsman were little more than descriptions of the mechanical problem to be solved, or perhaps desired dimensions chalked on the surface of shafts or diagrams sketched on the floor. The actual work of the journeymen. therefore, was well summed up by the British title, "fitter and turner."[4]

3. P. K. Edwards, *Strikes in the United States, 1881–1974* (Oxford, 1981), pp. 2–22, 295.

4. Circular no. 1, Central Council, Mechanical Engineers of North America (Terence V. Powderly Papers, hereinafter cited as TVP, microfilm reel 1), *Journal of United Labors*, 10 Aug.

Between 1870 and 1920 the number of men classified as machinists by the federal census grew from 55,000 to 841,000. Net growth of the trade averaged 8% per year as the building of machinery became factory-organized work, and again at the same pace during the decade of World War I. As their numbers increased, machinists in both railroad shops and larger factories increasingly found their days confined to the use of a single lathe, milling machine, boring mill, or other machine tool, on which they performed operations specified by blueprints and written as well as oral instructions. Others remained at the bench as fitters (and in the fabrication of such mechanisms as electrical turbines, final assembly was the most highly skilled work). Paradoxically, the specialization and educational requirements increased simultaneously.[5]

Although employers and trade unionists alike publicly lamented the disappearance of genuine apprenticeship to the machinist's craft, such large enterprises as Hoe Printing Press in New England, Baldwin Locomotive in Philadelphia, and Brown and Sharpe in Providence had many apprentice boys, whom they required in 1890 to study mathematics, mechanical drawing, reading, and spelling in night school, while they mastered all-important machine tools during four-year indentures. A poll of 116 machinery manufacturers conducted by the employers' journal *American Machinist* six years later found, to the editor's surprise, that 85 of them (73%) trained apprentices. Nevertheless, contemporary accounts of apprentices being employed in numbers far too great for proper training or kept incessantly at the same elementary tasks are too numerous to be ignored. The Rhode Island Bureau of Industrial Statistics found that only 14% of the boys hired in machine shops in that state ever became "first-class workmen." Charles Stelzle, who had completed an apprenticeship at Hoe Printing Press in 1890, commented that only a few of the American-educated workers he met in the trade "knew how to read a drawing or to work to scale."[6] Although American-born workers were very numerous in the trade, especially in the East, figures provided by the U.S. Immigration Commission suggest that by the turn of the century, at least, most midwestern journeymen had been trained in Germany or Britain.

1886; W. S. Rogers, "Sketches of an Apprenticeship," *American Machinist* 13 and 14 (10 Aug. 1890 – 28 May 1891); International Association of Machinists, *Proceedings of the Fourteenth Biennial Convention* (Davenport, Iowa, 1911), p. 160; Fred J. Miller, "The Machinist," *Scibner's Magazine* 14 (Oct. – Dec. 1893): 314–34.
  5. U.S. Bureau of the Census, *Sixteenth Census of the United States: 1940. Population. Comparative Occupational Statistics for the United States, 1870–1940* (Washington, 1943), p. 105 (hereinafter cited as *Occ. Stat.*).
  6. Rogers, "Sketches"; U.S. Commissioner of Labor, *Seventeenth Annual Report... 1902. Trade and Technical Education*, 57th Cong., 2d sess., H. Doc. 18 (Washington, 1902); Daniel Nelson, *Managers and Workers: Origins of the New Factory System in the United States 1880–1920* (Madison, Wis., 1975), p. 201, n. 82; Rhode Island, Commissioner of Industrial Statistics, *Second Annual Report* (Providence, 1889), p. 163; P. J. Conlon to *Machinist Monthly Journal* 21 (Feb. 1909): 164–5 (hereinafter cited as *MMJ*); Charles Stelzle, *A Son of the Bowery: The Life Story of an East Side American* (New York, 1926), pp. 40–1.

There was great variety in the earnings of machinists, even within the same firm, and at least some of the differences in pay were related to differences in technical competence. The very nature of the occupation, however, placed a premium on abstract reasoning, as well as practical experience. For its practitioners, the nineteenth-century gospel of self-improvement was linked to simply keeping up with the times. "We recognize," said a Chicago union leader, "that in the machinists' trade, especially, what may to-day seem impossible is a matter of practice to-morrow."[7] Labor spokesmen who emerged from the craft union's official organ, *The Machinists' Monthly Journal*, published a steady flow of technical instruction in its pages, along with news of strikes, union debates, and socialism.

Specialization of work assignments proceeded so rapidly during the late nineteenth century that the organizers of the International Association of Machinists (IAM) devoted much of the time of every convention to debating who was and who was not a member of the craft. In addition to the specialization of journeymen, increasing numbers of operatives, or "handymen," appeared in the shops, performing repetitive work on a machine set up by someone else. The 1897 convention proposed to admit to the union "any competent, sober and industrious machinist" with four years in the trade or a completed four-year apprenticeship, who was of the white race and who was paid at least the minimum wage fixed by the union for his locality. So many specialities had already appeared in the trade, however, that the convention accepted President James O'Connell's recommendation to designate on each member's card which of nine competencies applied to him: general floor hand, lathe hand, vise hand, planer hand, milling-machine hand, slotting-machine hand, diesinker, toolmaker, or boring-mill hand. Six years later O'Connell explained that operators on purely "automatic machinery where no skill is required of the operator, nut-tapping machines, bolt cutters, small simple drill presses used to drill rough holes upon common rough work, power saws, and a simple class of machinery" were definitely "not admitted."[8]

The growing size of metalworking enterprises and the specialization of machine tools and their operators did more than blur the boundaries of the craft: They also stimulated the development of inside contracting. Between 1860 and 1890 this practice spread until it became, in the words of a government study, "practically universal in New England," and commonplace elsewhere in the land as well.[9] In one form, a foreman assigned a large batch of parts to be fabricated, or even a single element like a locomotive wheel carriage,

7. U.S. Commissioner of Labor, *Eleventh Special Report. Regulation and Restriction of Output* (Washington, 1904), p. 145 (hereinafter cited as *Restriction*).

8. *MMJ* 9 (June 1897): 258–9; *Restriction*, pp. 104–5; Mark Perlman, *The Machinists: A New Study in American Trade Unionism* (Cambridge, Mass., 1961), pp. 22–3.

9. *Restriction*, p. 135; John Butterick, "The Inside Contract System," *Journal of Economic History* 12 (Summer 1952): 205–21.

to the worker who offered the lowest bid per unit to do the job. The worker then used the company's machinery and employed one or more workmates from within the plant (usually at a fixed day rate) to assist him. The margin between the helpers' wages and the price paid by the company was the contractor's income. An individual machinst might be a contractor some weeks and a helper for someone else who had a contract at other times.

But inside contracting also functioned on a grander scale. Individuals might contract to turn out one entire product line, sometimes for years on end, using the company's fixed capital, but hiring their own help. Such contractors subdivided the tasks among journeymen, relatives, operatives, and even children, and often waxed prosperous as petty exploiters of their fellow workers. In the Winchester Repeating Arms factory of New Haven, for example, five departments (e.g., small parts and drilling barrels) were in the eighties under the control of contractors who employed an average of forty-three people apiece and earned an average of $4,800 yearly, in contrast to their employees' average of $700. Another five contractors could be found at the same time averaging two employees each and earnings of $1,430 to their helpers' $570.[10]

Many wage struggles of the 1880s, and especially of the 1890s, were shaped by the inside contracting system. Employers seeking lower production costs reduced the price they paid the contractor, often by as much as 5% each year, and increasingly often dismissed contractors for unacceptable work, padding the payroll with relatives, disguising production costs and methods, and other offenses. When contractors responded by cutting the wages of their employees, the latter struck. To avoid such conflicts, and to improve their knowledge of contractors' actual costs, large companies began to pay the contractors' employees directly, sometimes at wages fixed by plantwide standards, and to keep more systematic records, which might reveal the contractors' secrets. In short, although the system of inside contracting had induced many machinists of the 1870s and 1880s to envisage themselves as men on the make, the system also became the focal point of bitter conflicts by the end of the century. Both the employers and the employees of the contractors charged that they were being swindled. Craft unions set out to exterminate the practice altogether, at the same time that employers were seeking to replace it with more direct and systematic controls over their workers.[11]

These two sets of contradictions, those inherent in inside contracting and those that linked growing specialization to rising educational requirements, may help us understand the mentality and behavior of late nineteenth-century machinists. Struggles to preserve handcraft tradition, such as those waged by

10. *Restriction*, p. 216.
11. Ibid.; Dan Clawson, *Bureaucracy and the Labor Process: The Transformation of U.S. Industry, 1860–1920* (New York and London, 1980) is very informative on inside contracting, but interprets its significance in a very different way from that suggested here.

printers when confronted with the linotype machine or by stonecutters faced with planing machines, were quite alien to machinists' experience. Modern technology was their natural habitat; improvements were often their own inventions. Moreover, the large enterprise appeared to them less a menace than a desirable place of employment. Although the earnings of individual machinists varied greatly within almost any firm, highly capitalized factories usually paid better overall than small shops and definitely offered more secure employment. And among the machinists were many ambitious men who hungered to be inside contractors. "Self-made men" were, in fact, numerous among the proprietors of engineering firms. It was not at all preposterous for W. S. Rogers, editor of the *American Machinist* (an employers' journal), to recall of his own apprenticeship in the 1870s: "The height of every cub's ambition is to some day be the Old Man [boss] of some plant."[12]

In 1885, when sixteen-year-old Charles Stelzle started an apprenticeship in New York's great Hoe Printing Press Company, he "determined that some day [he] would be boss of that shop," studied arduously, and sought to finish tasks in record time. Told to cut keyways on a new shaft for a rotary press cylinder in for repair, he worked so furiously and took so many short cuts (including standing on the moving table of the machine) that he completed in five hours a job that the foreman had previously estimated at twelve. Stelzle not only earned the full six dollars piece price for only five hours work, but was also promised that someday the foremanship would be his. His fellow machinists, however, cursed him angrily and warned the naive "cub" that the rate for the job would surely be cut when news of his accomplishment reached the office. Indeed it was: When the next such shaft appeared in the shop, the wage for cutting its keyways had been slashed from six dollars to four.[13]

An older journeyman in Stelzle's department at the time was universally despised by the other workers. This "big Yankee" consistently took the boss's side in disputes, turned off gas jets carelessly left burning by others, ground his tools before starting time, and once even threw on the belt of his lathe the instant the main engine put the drive shafts in motion, "amid howls of derision from all over the shop." In May 1886, when all 900 of Hoe's workers joined the citywide strike movement for shorter hours, the Yankee reported to work. When he sauntered out at noontime for his can of beer, he was viciously beaten by his mates.[14]

---

12. Rogers, "Sketches," *American Machinist* 25 Sept. 1890): 11; Bruce Laurie, Theodore Herschberg, and George Alter, "Immigrants and Social History: The Philadelphia Experience, 1850–1880," *Journal of Social History* 9 (Winter 1976): 227; Herbert G. Gutman, *Work Culture and Society in Industrializing America: Essays in Working-Class and Social History* (New York, 1976), pp. 211–33.
13. Stelzle, *Son*, pp. 43–3.
14. Ibid., pp. 44–5. The Hoe strike is listed in *Report of the Secretary of the Interior* (1887).

In short, though individualists like Rogers, Stelzle, and the Yankee did exist, they found themselves in a minority at Hoe's works, severely chastised for violating their workmates' code of ethics. According to that code, "hogs" and "swifts" who raced or fawned to please the boss were held in contempt, no man ever operated more than one machine at a time, speeds and feeds were not to be set so high as to strain the machines, and those who were paid by the piece regulated their output so that their earnings would not significantly exceed the standard day rate for the trade. Any performance better than that, machinists knew from experience, simply invited a reduction in the price per piece. They also knew that a pace set by a youth might destroy an older man, and that virtually all employers considered a machinist old at forty. Like many other machinists, in fact, those at Hoe ultimately resolved to wipe out piecework altogether, and in 1898–9 under the IAM's banner, they waged a successful strike for that objective.[15]

Just as machinists' conduct revealed a tension through contracting and piece-work, and a mutualistic code of ethics cultivated by workers and enforced primarily through social pressures, so, too, on the level of organized behavior there was a chronic tension between craft exclusiveness and universality. Exclusiveness was rooted in the machinists' sense of social superiority to the workers; universality, or identification with other workers, was stimulated by a keen awareness that metal-fabricating plants employed innumerable molders, boilermakers, pattern makers, polishers, blacksmiths, operatives, and laborers, in addition to themselves. Machinists could not afford to ignore their neighbors on the job. Furthermore, a walk through the streets where they lived was enough to remind them how many other working people shared at least important parts of their fate. Consequently, both the craft union ideal and that of banding together with other workers always found advocates within the trade. For example, in 1874, when the president of the Machinists and Blacksmiths International Union proposed to strengthen the organization by admitting boilermakers, he provoked a controversy that disrupted the whole organization. A broadside from a Buffalo lodge charged that "the admission of Boiler makers would not be advancing in that social and intellectual # scale that is desirable." Terence Powderly, then a young officer of the union who favored the proposal, replied in verse:

> Aristocrats of labor, we
> Are up on airs and graces.
> We wear clean collars, cuffs, and shirts,
> Likewise we wash our faces.
> There's no one quite so good as we

15. *Restriction*, pp. 100–22, 145–8, 205–8. On the Hoe strike see *MMJ* 10 (1898): 577 and 11 (June 1899): 366.

In all the ranks of labor.
The boilermaker we despise,
Although he is our neighbor.[16]

Thousands of machinists turned along with Powderly to the Knights of Labor in quest of "the universal brotherhood of labor." Among the 800 or so delegates to the famous 1886 Richmond General Assembly of the Knights, 86 had come from railroad or factory machine shops, among them James O'Connell, future president of the IAM. Nevertheless, by the turn of the century it was the IAM that had become the dominant organization in the trade. It barred blacks from membership until 1948; innumerable schemes of various members to amalgamate it with related craft organizations never got off the drawing boards; women workers were welcomed into some lodges but routed physically from the shops by members of others; and even a proposal by the union's leaders to admit semiskilled operatives (to subordinate membership) was only narrowly adopted by the 1903 convention. As one Kansas delegate opposed to that motion put it: "The experienced man's whole being cries out against the imposition placed upon him by classing him with inferior workmen."[17]

Even the most exclusive craft unions of machinists, however, affiliated with whatever national congress of labor organizations existed, from the National Labor Union through the American Federation of Labor (AFL), and articulate machinists were always prominent in the labor reform crusade from the 1850s onward. Isaac Cassin, president of the Machinists and Blacksmiths International Union, had appealed in 1860 for the "complete affiliation of every interest, and every class of labor into one common cause," so as to "supersede all strikes, and install an 'Age of Reason' among operators and operatives."[18]

Cassin's faith in the power of organization, his wariness of strikes, his dream of ultimate harmony between intelligent, assertive mechanics and their employers, and his commitment to active citizenship were reechoed by prominent machinists for the next thirty years. His successor, John Fehrenbatch, boasted in 1875 that he and other officers of the M&BIU were "active politicians," aware that "nine-tenths of all the evils that afflict workingmen are brought

16. Machinists and Blacksmiths International Union No. 5, printed brochure dated 28 Nov. 1874 (TVP, reel 1); Terence V. Powderly, *The Path I Trod*, edited by Harry J. Carman, Henry David, and Paul N. Guthrie (New York, 1940), pp. 41–2.

17. *MMJ* 16 (April 1904): 343–44 and 15 (July 1903): 590–1. For O'Connell's recollections of the Richmond General Assembly, see IAM *Fourteenth Convention*, 159. Many British machinists in the U.S. belonged to the Amalgamated Society of Engineers in the early 1900s, and other machinists, especially Germans in brass-working firms, belonged to the United Metal Workers Industrial Union. A good account of the latter can be found in Bruno Ramirez, *When Workers Fight: The Politics of Industrial Relations in the Progressive Era* (Westport, Conn., 1978), pp. 108–22.

18. *Proceedings of the National Union of Machinists and Blacksmiths of the United States of America. Held in Baltimore, Md., Nov., 1860* (Philadelphia, 1861), p. 11.

about through bad legislation."[19] During the 1886 campaign for the eight-hour day machinists in many cities formed Eight-Hour Leagues to press for legislation and to persuade employers and the public that the shorter workday would (in the language of the Cincinnati League), "improve [the worker's] mental and moral condition," allow him to be a good citizen, and make him "more intelligent, and, consequently, more valuable to the employer."[20] Although this rhetoric reminds us that strikes of the craft were still rare, machinists did join into the general working-class enthusiasm for the eight-hour day and in the mass processions that swept through factory districts, shutting down all production in Chicago, Milwaukee, Cincinnati, Boston, New York, and elsewhere. Even in May 1886, however, machinists often refused to march behind red flags or armed contingents of workers, and most of their local assemblies in the Knights seem to have supported General Master Workman Powderly in his denunciations of the Haymarket anarchists.[21]

The next thirty years witnessed important modifications in the attitudes of organized machinists. Although the rhetorical themes of mutuality, exclusiveness, and citizenship remained prominent, a new sense of craft aggressiveness appeared, together with a growing appeal of socialism, and even of revolutionary syndicalism. The driving force behind these changes was a struggle over the reorganization of the relations of production, which converted the machinists' union into the "war dog of the A. F. of L." The protracted deflationary crisis of 1873–97 drove metal trades employers to consolidate enterprises for better control of markets and patents, to standardize and systematize work processes as well as products, and to search relentlessly for lower production costs. Although large enterprises like General Electric or Singer Sewing Machine had powerful resources with which to combat organized labor, they could not eliminate the dozen or more skilled trades needed to fabricate their metal wares, nor did they enjoy economies of scale in production. If anything, firms of 200–300 workers turned out to be the most efficient in this realm.[22] Consequently, owners of machine shops (often inspired by incessant discussions of productivity and methods of payment in meetings of the American Society of Mechanical Engineers) expanded their use of piecework and refined the

19. Circular no. 38, Machinists and Blacksmiths International Union of North America, 6 Nov. 1875 (TVP, reel 1).
20. Steven J. Ross, "Workers on the Edge: Work, Leisure, and Politics in Industrializing Cincinnati, 1830–1890" (Ph.D. diss., Princeton University, 1980), p. 426.
21. Ibid., pp. 482–517; George Schilling, "History of the Labor Movement in Chicago," in Lucy E. Parsons, *Life of Albert B. Parsons, with a Brief History of the Labor Movement in America* (Chicago, 1889), xiv–xxviii; Wisconsin Bureau of Labor Statistics, *Second Biennial Report, 1885–1886* (Madison, 1886), pp. 314–50. Joseph Buchanan, a railroad machinist, led the supporters of the Haymarket anarchists. See Joseph R. Buchanan, *Story of a Labor Agitator* (New York, 1903).
22. For good discussions of this crisis, see David M. Gordon, Richard Edwards, and Michael Reich, *Segmented Work, Divided Workers: The Historical Transformation of Labor in the United*

277

specialization of tasks during the eighties and nineties, routinely cut piece prices on which journeymen earned more than the locally prevailing wage, and squeezed inside contractors for cheaper and better output. To break the resilience of the machinists' ethical code, employers imposed rules of silence, fired troublemakers, rewarded "swifts," and, especially after 1893, locked out obstreperous machinists.

Scientific management and Fordism did not originate this campaign, but grew out of it. The doctrines of Frederick Winslow Taylor had special appeal to metal trades employers at the turn of the century. Through planning the flow of work, the use of time and motion study to analyze and standardize "the one best way" to perform each task, and the payment of premiums, bonuses, differentials, or some other incentives to reward fast producers and weed out the slow, managers hoped to expropriate the knowledge and initiative of craftsmen. The conflicts generated by piece work and contracting, declared Taylor, could all be eliminated if management assumed its proper task of systematically directing the energies of everyone in the firm toward the common goal of greater productivity. Henry Ford's Highland Park plant (opened in 1914) suggested an alternative model of systematic direction, in which all mental or directive elements of production were engineered into the machinery itself (through interconnected specialized machine tools and assembly lines), rather than into standardized work instructions. Both schemes profoundly influenced managerial practice in metal fabricating by 1915, even though many small firms (and especially those manufacturing machine tools, where quality mattered more than price) clung to older production methods. Taylor's teachings proved more generally useful than Ford's approach, which had been designed for a factory of 14,000 workers producing but a single commodity – the model T. Whatever particular techniques were used or teachings applied, the basic thrust of reform throughout the industry was the same: The actual fabrication of parts and their assembly was put into the hands of systematically directed unskilled workers, while skilled tasks were not eliminated, but were concentrated in ancillary roles, like toolmaking, inspection, and setup.[23]

Between 1900 and 1914, workers' resistance to stopwatches, incentive pay, and efficiency engineers flared up in metalworking plants throughout the country. The publication and popularity of Taylor's *Shop Management* (1903) inspired a veritable *Grand Peur* in machinists' ranks, so that opposition to

States (Cambridge and New York, 1982); Alfred D. Chandler, Jr., *The Visible Hand: The Managerial Revolution in American Business* (Cambridge, Mass., 1977); Bruce Laurie and Mark Schmitz, "Manufacture and Productivity: The Making of an Industrial Base, Philadelphia, 1850–1880," in Theodore Herschberg, ed., *Philadelphia: Work, Space, Family and Group Experience in the Nineteenth Century* (New York, 1981), pp. 43–92.
23. For a fuller discussion of scientific management and the workers at this time see David Montgomery, *Workers' Control in America: Studies in the History of Work, Technology, and Labor Struggles* (Cambridge and New York, 1979).

Taylorism spread even more rapidly than its practice. Simultaneously, the National Metal Trades Association (NMTA) and citizens' alliances in many cities proclaimed that harmony and efficiency could never prevail in American industry until the power of the IAM was broken and management won "full discretion to designate the men [it considers] competent to perform the work and to determine the conditions under which that work is to be prosecuted." The NMTA declared that it would "not permit employees to place any restriction on the management, methods, or production" of its members' works and would discuss nothing with any workers who were on strike.[24]

Even in the teeth of this open shop campaign, however, the role of the machinists' union was *not* a purely defensive one. Much of the appeal of Taylorism to employers stemmed from their observation that machinists were becoming more craft-conscious, more assertive, and more determined to translate their mutualistic ethical code into specific rules that every union member was obliged to obey. The IAM grew very rapidly between 1898 and 1901, winning by strike action in March 1900, a nationwide trade agreement with the NMTA itself, which committed employers to recognize the union and institute by stages a nine-hour day. Although the national agreement broke down after only one year, it marked the ascendancy of a craft union of some 56,000 members, ready and able to use the strike effectively and often on behalf of the wages and work rules it prescribed.

Quite abruptly machinists had become leading actors on the country's strike scene. There were three important aspects of their behavior in the stormy prewar years, however, that are not revealed by strike statistics. First, one important legacy of the 1900 victory was the consolidation of a salaried union leadership committed to establishing and preserving contractual relations with employers. Union representatives dealt directly with employers, often relegating shop committees to a minor role or simply overriding their judgment for the sake of the union's institutional needs. Officers sought to compromise with employers on questions of incentive pay, work rules, output restrictions, and other explosive issues of workplace control, on which the rank and file was often adamant. They tried to solidify the unions' power in machine shops that had fewer and fewer journeymen machinists by bringing handymen, women, and other operatives into the ranks, and to persuade employers that union labels on their wares would improve sales – an argument that was persuasive to companies like Starrett Tool that sold directly to machinists.

Above all, James O'Connell and his fellow officers hoped to persuade members and employers alike that a trade agreement with the IAM would not be broken by sympathetic strikes. This undertaking was as important as it was difficult, because all metal trades unions had routinely supported each other in

24. *Restriction*, pp. 197–8.

local strikes of the 1890s. The Iron Molders Unions, then more powerful than the IAM, led the way toward the policy of resisting sympathetic strikes. During the 1900 machinists' strike President Martin Fox of the molders received 150 telegrams from his locals asking permission to walk out in support of the machinists; each request he rejected. The next year, when fifteen unions struck the major agricultural implement firms of the Middle West, the union molders stayed on the job in obedience to their contracts, often making casting for scabs to machine and assemble. From that point until the wave of rebel strikes by molders in 1920, machinists took it for granted that unless their union had an explicit joint bargaining agreement with the local molders' union (and that was rare outside of Chicago), they could expect the foundries to continue in operation during any strike by the IAM. The leaders of the IAM tried to follow the molders' example in respecting "sacred contracts," but they also found their members difficult to control on this score and their conventions regularly deluged with resolutions calling for treaties of alliance or mergers with other metal trades unions. In fact, on some western railroads a movement for "system federations," or grass-roots alliances of repair shop workers of all trades, posed a forceful challenge to the authority of all the international unions of the metal trades, and members of the IAM were especially prominent in that movement.[25]

The second noteworthy development of the prewar years was the rising popularity of socialism among IAM members. Machinists' long-evident sense of themselves as producers at the very cutting edge of industrial progress, their familiarity with political struggles and parliamentary arenas, and their concern for civil society (education, women's suffrage, civic improvement, etc.) as well as the workplace, had all paved the way for socialist ideas. The role of the courts and the police in attacks on their union and the open assault of scientific management on all their notions of ethical work relations attracted more and more machinists to the Socialist party. In 1911 a slate of candidates organized by the party won all the union's international offices. Neighborhoods heavily populated by machinists in Schenectady and Dayton, which had long been Socialist strongholds, were joined by many others in Debs's famous campaign of 1912. The emphasis of Socialists was on political action and mass education in quest of a collectivist future, which they envisaged as the only truly "scientific" organization of society. The party had no distinctive program for union action: some machinists in its ranks championing craft organization, others

25. Montgomery, *Workers' Control.* On sympathetic action of molders and machinists, see *MMJ* 9 (June 1897): 214–6. On molders' unionism, see James E. Cebula, *The Glory and Despair of Challenge and Change: A History of the Molders Union* (Cincinnati, 1976), pp. 28–48; Jacob H. Hollander and George E. Barnett, *Studies in American Trade Unionism* (New York, 1912), pp. 257–8; *Restriction*, pp. 202–8. More than a dozen unions, including the IAM and the molders, did bargain jointly with International Harvester in Chicago. *MMJ* 15 (Sept. 1903): 831–3.

petitioning for amalgamation with related craft organizations, and still others joining the Industrial Workers of the World (IWW). As Max Hayes, the party's most prominent spokesman in the AFL said in 1907 to emphasize the primacy of politics: "It is absurd for Socialists to waste a lot of valuable time in splitting hairs, over the question of industrial organization."[26]

The rising influence of the Socialists provoked their foes within the IAM to mobilize a conservative bloc around President O'Connell, which became as prominent and highly disciplined as the Socialists themselves. The conservatives enjoyed the support of Samuel Gompers and the AFL Executive Council, of Protestant clergy like Charles Stelzle (the former machinist turned leading Presbyterian), and of the Militia of Christ, to which Rev. Peter E. Dietz and other Catholic clergy rallied the "class-conscious children of our Holy Mother Church." Together they fought to ally the union with the Democratic party and warned that socialism meant the obliteration of family ties and individuality by an omnipotent state. As alternatives they proposed "American unionism" and "the living wage," through which fathers might support their own families in "reasonable and frugal comfort." Nevertheless, the conservatives were as hostile to Taylorism as the Socialists, if not more so. American sentiments were not very different from those that Henri De Man observed in Germany in the early 1920s: "As workers, the Christians felt exactly like the infidel socialists whose material conditions of life they shared."[27]

The third development was more evident outside IAM ranks than within them: the movement for industrial unionism. Its social basis in metal-fabricating works was the reorganization of production symbolized by Ford and Taylor. For machine tenders who repeated routine tasks and for assemblers who worked on the line, rather than as precision fitters, the traditions, rules, and standard wage rates of craft unions meant little. The fact that most of them were immigrants, women, or at least transients who were not eligible to vote limited the appeal of Socialist politics. On the other hand, from 1909 onward such workers increasingly often engaged in large strikes. An early and well-publicized instance was the strike at the Pressed Steel Car Company in McKees Rocks, in which the strikers turned to the IWW for leadership. And the company had crushed its skilled workers, when they had struck under the IAM's banner in 1907. Two years later some 3,000 workers of all grades

26. Montgomery, *Workers' Control*, pp. 74–83; John H. M. Lasleto, *Labor and the Left: A Study of Socialist and Radical Influences in the American Labor Movement, 1881–1924* (New York and London, 1970), pp. 144–91. The Hayes quotation is from Ira Kipnis, *The American Socialist Movement, 1897–1912* (New York and London, 1952), p. 237.

27. Montgomery, *Workers' Control*, pp. 74–83; Stelzle; Elizabeth and Kenneth Fones-Wolf, "Trade-Union Evangelism: Religion and the AFL in the Labor Forward Movement, 1912–1916," in Michael H. Frisch and Daniel J. Walkowitz, eds., *Working-Class America: Essays on Labor, Community, and American Society* (Urbana, Ill., 1983), pp. 153–84; Henri De Man, *Joy in Work*, trans. by Eden and Cedar Paul (London, 1929), p. 64.

walked out in protest against a complex group premium system of payment. Although the strike was settled on terms that gave the workers little, it loudly announced the appearance of a new style of unionism in metal fabricating.[28]

The industrial union impulse extended far beyond the domain of IWW influence, was distinctively shaped by the new production methods, and involved both skilled craftsmen and unskilled production workers in a complex interaction. Because one such effort, the Allegheny Congenial Industrial Union, functioned effectively and continuously from 1914 through 1917 at a company that was a model of up-to-date management (the main Westinghouse Electric Company plant in the Turtle Creek valley east of Pittsburgh), that organization provides a revealing case study of the dynamics of industrial unionism in this epoch.

The Socialist party was so strong in the Turtle Creek valley that it had outpolled both of the major parties during the 1912 elections in most of its communities. The local Socialist newspaper, *Justice*, was edited by Fred Merrick, who ardently supported the IWW and direct action generally. In fact, the party had supplemented its 1912 electoral activity with a sustained "free speech" campaign at plant gates and street corners, during which many members were jailed for agitating about grievances and conditions inside the Westinghouse plants. The union these Socialists developed defied the AFL's operating principles, sought to enlist workers of all grades, elect and support shop stewards, and mobilize struggles around demands, rather than negotiate contracts. It called its first major strike in June 1914 – a time when heavy unemployment had put a damper on most strike activity. In fact, the strike was inspired by the company's reduction of hours from fifty-four to forty-five a week, together with extensive layoffs (including some 2,000 salaried employees) and continuous slashing of incentive rates in response to the hard times. After some five months of enduring these practices, union members struck. The 3,000 or so who initiated the walkout were soon joined by all but about 1,500 of the 8,200 then employed, as well as by many people from smaller firms of the valley, which were linked to Westinghouse economically. The strikers demanded a rotation system for handling layoffs and the abolition of all piecework and incentive pay plans. In short, they aimed straight at scientific management's jugular vein. They held out for five weeks, toward the end of which the clerical workers voted to join the strike. Despite the fact that the company agreed publicly to none of the strikers' demands, they ultimately voted to return to work, proclaimed that they had forced Westinghouse to recognize their union, and marched in formation into the plant to resume their jobs.[29]

---

28. Melvyn Dubofsky, *We Shall Be All: A History of the Industrial Workers of the World* (Chicago, 1969), pp. 200–8; John N. Ingham, "A Strike in the Progressive Era: McKees Rocks, 1909," *Pennsylvania Magazine of History and Biography* 90 (July 1966): 353–77.

29. Jacob Margolis, "The Streets of Pittsburgh," *International Socialist Review* 13 (Oct.

For the next three years Westinghouse did deal with the union, which soon changed its name to the American Industrial Union (AIU). It also dealt with others: a company union, which it had created on the eve of the 1914 strike, the IAM, the International Brotherhood of Electrical Workers, and others from time to time. Its official policy was that an employee could belong to any organization and anyone could bring a grievance to a supervisor. Meanwhile war orders not only restored the fifty-four-hour week but led to a doubling of the firm's work force. In the wake of a largely spontaneous wave of strikes in eastern munitions plants in the summer of 1915, both the AIU and the AFL stepped up their activity at Westinghouse (among the organizers sent in by the federation was the young John L. Lewis). In negotiations with a committee of workers' representatives the company offered a fifty-two-hour week and a bonus of 6 % on all wages. At a September mass meeting the workers voted to accept the proposal and remain at work.[30]

A special role was played during these years by one group of machinists: the tool-and-diemakers. This group, whose very name had first entered everyday speech only in the 1890s, had grown in numbers as a consequence of the spread of scientific management (from 9,263 according to the census of 1910 to 55,092 in 1920). Carefully instructed unskilled workers could replace journeymen as operators of machine tools only if their movements were guided by a variety of jigs, fixtures, prototypes or patterns, and form tools. Such aids were made in the tool room by expert machinists, about 2,000 of them at Westinghouse. They clearly envisaged themselves as the elite of the work force: They exercised great judgment in their tasks, virtually never encountered piecework, and worked in a setting where, as two engineers wrote of Ford's Highland Park tool room, "nothing [was] scamped or hurried."[31] Nevertheless, union sentiment was strong among them. They had no standard wage, but rather observed extreme and inexplicable variety in their earnings. They hungered for such traditional union goals as an eight-hour day and protection against arbitrary treatment. Moreover, as war production increased, they often learned of unskilled pieceworkers mastering their repetitious operations so well that they earned as much pay as toolmakers – or even more![32] It is not surprising, therefore, that by April 1916, some 500 of them had enrolled in the IAM,

1912): 313–20; Department of Labor, Federal Mediation and Conciliation Service file 33–37, R. G. 280, National Archives; *The Iron Age* 93 (22 Jan. 1914): 285, 93 (11 June 1914): 1496, 94 (2 July 1914): 56, 94 (16 July 1914): 180 (hereinafter cited as *IA*).

    30. *IA* 96 (7 Oct. 1915): 853; Melvyn Dubofsky and Warren Van Tine, *John L. Lewis: A Biography* (New York, 1977), pp. 28–9.

    31. *Occ. Stat.*, 106; Horace L. Arnold and Fay L. Faurote, *Ford Methods and Ford Shops* (New York, 1915), p. 41.

    32. Cf., Cecelia F. Bucki, "Dilution and Craft Traditions: Bridgeport, Connecticut, Munitions Workers, 1915–1919," *Social Science History* 4 (Winter 1980): 105–24; James Hinton, *The First Shop Stewards' Movement* (London, 1973).

successfully negotiated a 10% raise for themselves, and eagerly awaited 1 May, the date set by the IAM for a nationwide strike of machinists for the eight-hour day.

There was also among the toolmakers a revolutionary minority, epitomized by John Hall (who actually worked in the huge shell-turning building). These men favored the AIU, circulated Merrick's paper *Justice*, and held the IAM in contempt. They believed that only a union of all its employees could deal effectively with a concern like Westinghouse. It was, they noted, the production workers who actually turned out the motors and the artillery shells sold by the company; the toolmakers' role was only ancillary. They also believed that workers needed and would use the power of the strike, as well as the ballot, in order to overthrow capitalism. Although they generally supported the special demands of their fellow toolmakers (including exemptions from the draft in 1918), Hall and his comrades tried to persuade their colleagues that their interests were one with those of the production workers. Their slogan was borrowed from the "Detroit IWW" (i.e., the Socialist Labor party): "Organization, Education, Solidarity." Within toolmakers' ranks, therefore, a tension persisted between these broad aspirations and the parochial struggle to protect the privileges and differentials of the machinists' elite. Both the company and government mediators were aware of this tension and played upon it. On 22 April, the same day that Westinghouse raised the wages of its toolmakers, it fired Hall.[33]

The protest strike that began that day was supported by far more production workers than toolmakers at first. The former had a very different conception of unionism from that offered by the IAM in 1916. Most of them were immigrants or Pennsylvania farm youth with no craft heritage. Experience at Westinghouse taught them that they needed an in-plant organization made up of their own elected delegates, who could not only formulate general demands but could also deal with the reality of scientific management, as it affected their working lives.

The essence of that reality is that scientific management did not reorganize production methods and work relations once and for all; rather, it reorganized them incessantly. Time-study men were always snooping around somewhere. When one department had been rearranged to their (momentary) satisfaction, they turned to the next. Workers were paid by the hour at some times and with incentives at others. New product lines might be begun by journeymen machinists, then put into the hands of the unskilled with some of those journeymen as troubleshooters, once production was deemed ready to roll. Unlike the Highland Park plant with its single product and its engineering cast

33. This account of the 1916 strike is based on: Department of Labor, Federal Mediation and Conciliation Service, File 33–202, Record Group 280, National Archives; *I. A.*, 97 (27 April 1916): 1036, 97 (4 May 1916): 1090, 97 (18 May 1916): 1218, 98 (13 July 1916): 112.

in steel, the Westinghouse works turned out generators, flatirons, streetcars, and shells for the voracious appetites of the czar's cannons. Different standard times, base, and incentive rates existed for each component of each of those products. (An agricultural implement plant of only 300 workers had 22,000 different piece rates in 1903). New designs, changes in work instructions, or a supervisor's belief that a standard was wrong led to retiming. Constant changes of product lines and departmental organization meant constant hiring, layoff, and transfer within the plant, and all that meant a broad scope for favoritism or reprisals by foremen. And everywhere, always, there was pressure to produce faster!

A setting like that made a mockery of craft union practice. What meaning was there to a standard machinists' wage? What worker could pledge to abide honorably by union work rules? What use was the traditional IAM shop steward, whose tasks had been to see that members kept their dues paid up and to report infractions of union rules to headquarters? Mass production workers needed the permanent presence of an active group representative right there on the production floor, all day, every day, and they had to be prepared to defend those representatives against management's reprisals. Moreover, craft union stewards had customarily fought overspeeding of pieceworkers by setting a ceiling on their earnings. If, for example, the local standard wage for machinists was $2.80 per day, any earnings of an individual above, say, $3.00 subjected that individual to a union fine.[34] Such a practice could not be effective in Westinghouse's production departments. Better to have a shop steward who could challenge new times and negotiate better rates for jobs as they appeared on the floor. And for the workers as a whole, the remedy for intensive toil was the eight-hour day.

When *Justice* summoned the Westinghouse workers to a meeting in the Wilmerding baseball park to protest the firings of 22 April, those who came voted a general strike to demand reinstatement of Hall and other activists, company guarantees of nondiscrimination against union members, and the eight-hour day with no reduction in pay. That action set in motion a style of strike behavior that had been commonplace between the 1860s and the 1880s in America, but rarely seen since that time: a militant procession to shut down all local industry. Most of Westinghouse's own workers were already out when the IAM sent a circular to all employers of machinists in the Pittsburgh area to "respectfully request that you establish not later than May 1, 1916, an 8-hour work day with no reduction in pay per day." While machinists all over the county struck in response to their employers' rejection of that appeal, Merrick and the AIU organized a grand May Day parade, which moved through the Turtle Creek valley, shutting down every establishment and bringing altogether some 36,000

34. *Restriction*, pp. 113–4, 145–6, 208–25.

men and women out on strike. When marchers returned the next day to close the Edgar Thompson Works of U.S. Steel (located at the junction of the Turtle Creek and the Monongahela River in Braddock), they engaged in a bloody gun battle with company police. An important indication of the character this strike had assumed lies in the fact that this battle was not at Westinghouse, but at a nearby steel mill, to which marchers had carried the strike.

Troops were rushed to the scene; Hall, Merrick, Anna Bell, and twenty-seven other leaders were arrested on sedition charges (for which most were later imprisoned for long terms); federal mediators tried to find a formula for settlement; and IAM organizers staged rival rallies to those of the AIU in an effort to bring workers back into Westinghouse under their leadership. In a word, to the existing interplay of craft and industrial unions had been added the overt and powerful intervention of the state, which sought to decapitate the industrial union movement, wring some concessions out of the company, and cultivate the IAM as a counterweight to the AIU. Stunned and bloodied by the street fighting and arrests of 2 May, the strikers desperately petitioned the Secretary of Labor to aid "those, on whom this country must depend for its National Defense." "Injustice has dulled our patriotism," their appeal concluded. "Man's equality before the law will make us patriots instead of paupers."[35] Westinghouse refused to budge, cavalry galloped daily through the streets of valley towns, and strikers drifted back to work. On 17 May the IAM declared the strike over.

Only in some twenty-five small shops around the county had some 322 machinists won the eight-hour day.[36] Most Westinghouse workers, who were not in jail, do seem to have been reinstated; labor was in short supply. Less than a year later a new wave of strike agitation swept the area. Federal mediators who rushed to the scene this time were armed with new war powers. They brought business and AFL leaders together in a local Council of National Defense, encouraged the adoption of union standards of pay and hours, and promoted government-sponsored shop committees to handle grievances.[37]

The strike wave of 1916, of which the Westinghouse struggle formed a part, set off the final stage in the evolution of machinists' strikes. As was noted earlier, during the seven years of continuous strike activity at historic record levels (1916–22), metalworkers played an especially conspicuous role (as did textile, railroad, and coal mine employees), and in the crude measure of "number of strikes" recorded, machinists were found consistently among the three leading occupations. The basic contours of the epoch's strikes had

35. "To the Honorable William B. Wilson," Dept. of Labor, Federal Mediation and Conciliation Service, File 33–202, RG 280, typescript.
36. IAM, *Proceedings, 1916,* p. 14.
37. Department of Labor, Federal Mediation and Conciliation Service, File 33/374, RG 280, National Archives.

already been revealed at Westinghouse: the interaction of craft and mass unionism; the ambivalent role of toolmakers; the new style and importance of workplace delegates or stewards; the mass mobilization of working-class communities through marches that closed many factories; the use made of these mobilizations and of workplace organization by revolutionaries to project an image of workers' control of modern industry and a path toward that goal; the emergence of "progressive unionism" as an alternative path to social reform; and the powerful presence of the state – as a customer for industry's wares, as arbiter of standards, and as an instrument of coercion. The profound transformation in the working lives of machinists since the 1860s and 1870s was evident not only in their new importance in the ranks of strikers, but even more in the way they mobilized and the objectives they sought.

Three special features of postwar strikes (1919–22) may be viewed essentially as variations on these long-term themes, variations produced by the imposing, if inconsistent, role of the state in trade union activity and the soaring hopes that stirred not just revolutionaries but millions of workers in various ways in these years, that some new and better form of industrial life was being born.[38] One was the decisive turn of the IAM to progressive unionism. Having ardently supported the war effort and enjoyed significant assistance from governmental war agencies, not to mention the audacity with which workers joined unions when unemployment virtually disappeared, the IAM emerged from the war with more that 350,000 members, funds enough to create its own banks and international trading companies, a firm alliance to farmers' cooperatives, total commitment to nationalization of the railroads through the Plumb Plan, and an effective alliance with unions of coal miners, garment workers, and railway workers to commit the AFL to a program of political action and social reconstruction along the lines then proposed by the British Labour party.[39] These developments encouraged the nineteenth-century dream of organized harmony in economic life to reappear in a guise that borrowed from the vocabulary, and even from the methods, of Taylorism itself. The IAM, said General Secretary E. C. Davidson in 1921, "is working to eliminate economic waste to the public through strikes and lockouts."[40] The next year the union announced jointly with Otto Beyer of the Taylor Society

38. For a more thorough discussion of wartime and postwar strikes, see David Montgomery, "New Tendencies in Union Struggles and Strategies in Europe and the United States, 1916–1922," in James E. Cronin and Carmen Sirianni, eds., *Work, Community, and Power: The Experience of Labor in Europe and America, 1900–1925* (Philadelphia, 1983), pp. 88–116; Montgomery, "Immigrants, Industrial Unions, and Social Reconstruction in the United States, 1916–1923," *Labour/Le Travailleur* 13 (Spring 1984): 101–14; Montgomery, "Nationalism, American Patriotism, and Class Consciousness among Immigrant Workers in the United States in the Epoch of World War I," in Dirk Hoerder, ed., *"Struggle a Hard Battle": Essays on Working-Class Immigrants* (DeKalb, Ill., 1986), pp. 327–51.
39. Montgomery, "New Tendencies," pp. 97–100.
40. *Seattle Union Record*, 19 Jan. 1921.

the Baltimore and Ohio Plan, for systematic union collaboration in the modernization and management of the railroad.[41]

Second, the unprecedented number of strikes in which the union did engage included many that involved tens of thousands of workers for months on end, like the nationwide American Can strike and that in the Philadelphia shipyards in 1921, and especially the 1922 railroad shopmen's strike. Most of these stoppages were joint struggles of several metal trades unions. They were coordinated by local metal trades' councils or (as in the Seattle general strike of 1919) by a city central labor federation. Even though craft union leaders did resist successfully all efforts to amalgamate related crafts into larger quasiindustrial unions, they did frequently cooperate in economic actions, which compelled them to sustain their members in very protracted battles. If strikes of all types are considered together for 1921, the average length was no less than 51 days, and 237 strikes lasted longer than 91 days.[42]

Finally, strikes of machinists that were not authorized by the IAM occurred with great frequency during the postwar years, especially during the last months of 1919 and the first half of 1920 (a year in which more than one-half of all the country's strikers were out without union sanction). Metal trades councils and shop stewards' organizations often led such strikes in defiance of craft union jurisdictions, membership, or rules. In those heady months strikers' rhetoric often linked workplace grievances to political demands, especially freedom for Tom Mooney and other political prisoners. For the moment, the gospel of the One Big Union informed strikers' aspirations like a Sorelian myth.[43] The popularity of such aspirations, however, was not enough to overcome either the established leaders of the IAM or the craft parochialism of much of its membership. The historic tension of craft and class remained ineradicable right through the strikes of the postwar era. The social dynamics that gave that tension its new form were those that had been displayed at Westinghouse.

By the end of the depression of 1920–2, progressive unionism, joint strike action, and the One Big Union myth had all met with defeat.

41. Hyacinthe Dubreuil, *Robots or Men? A French Workman's Experience in American Industry* (New York, 1930), pp. 350–88; Thomas R. Brooks, *Clint: A Biography of a Labor Intellectual, Clinton S. Golden* (New York, 1978), pp. 100–6.

42. *Monthly Labor Review* 16 (June 1923): 238–9.

43. Sylvia Kopald, *Rebellion in Labor Unions* (New York, 1924); Montgomery, "Immigrants, Industrial Unions, and Social Reconstruction."

13

The political economy of British engineering workers during the First World War

KEITH BURGESS

I

It is now generally accepted by historians that the First World War demanded the mobilization of people and resources that was not only unprecedented but largely incomprehensible in terms of prewar assumptions.[1] It was generally expediency that dictated government policy, and the ad hoc way in which the state was forced inexorably to extend its scope of activity meant that major changes were set in motion, and in a context where there was little understanding of the principles of wartime mobilization, and even less of an appreciation of the social consequences that could have scarcely been anticipated. This was especially true of the engineering industry and its labor force, which has been so crucial to the demands of twentieth-century warfare. The engineering industry is defined to include all manner of metal fabrication, and thus would appear to encompass more than might be inferred from the term "munitions work," which was a subsequent government-styled designation that has continued to confuse an understanding of the industry's development during the First World War.[2] Despite difficulties of definition, one estimate shows that in munitions, as a whole, the male labor force rose from 1,869,000 in July 1914 to 2,309,000 by November 1918, while the female labor forces rose from 212,000 to 945,000 during the same period, which marks a total net increase of 1,200,000 workers.[3] The growth in the number of women workers highlights the acute labor shortage during the war, as men were lost

---

1. For a recent survey of the British experience see, for example, Kathleen Burk, ed., *War and the State. The Transformation of British Government, 1914–1919* (London: Allen & Unwin, 1982).
2. Humbert Wolfe, *Labour Supply and Regulation* (Oxford: Clarendon Press, 1923), pp. 100–14, discusses in detail the provisions of the Munitions of War Act.
3. Ibid.

to the armed forces at the same time that existing productive capacity had to be increased and new lines established. This triggered a parallel expansion of trade union membership and a rise in the number of firms affiliated to employers' associations. Thus the membership of a self-consciously craft union like the Amalgamated Society of Engineers (ASE) rose from 174,253 in 1914 to 298,782 by 1918, while the increase in unionization among workers not traditionally defined as "skilled" was proportionally often greater.[4] At the same time, the number of firms affiliated to the Engineering Employers' Federation (EEF), for example, rose from 714 in 1914 to 1,469 by 1918.[5]

This increase in the scale of organization of both capital and labor was itself of considerable significance in widening the scope for industrial conflict. Yet questions remain concerning the more general causes of labor unrest in Britain during the First World War, arising from disagreements over the respective importance of economic, political, and ideological developments, and these apply particularly to the engineering industry. Thus it has been argued, for example, that changing patterns of work and productive relations generally played the *determining* role in shaping the political economy of British engineering workers during the period.[6] In contrast, more recent studies have sought to situate the workplace more widely in terms of its relationship with the changing contours of social structure and politics.[7] On reflection, it would appear that an explanation for industrial conflict during the war must admit a determining role for politics and ideology. In this respect, it has been noted that an *exclusive* focus upon the workplace or labor process takes the organization of work as the touchstone for passing judgment on the forms of economy and society as a whole, thereby elevating *alienation* in work to a higher analytical plane than the relations of *exploitation*,[8] which are more appropriate to a materialist approach to industrial conflict. Relations of exploitation are defined as the the appropriation of the labor of one class by another class, realized because of the latter's differential ownership of, or access to control of, the nonhuman means of production. And because the latter is, in turn, sanctioned ultimately by the state, together with its juridical forms and ideological imperatives, politics and ideology *do* have a determining effect on the workplace or labor process compatible with a materialist analysis. The experience of the First World War

4. J. B. Jefferys, *The Story of the Engineers* (London: Lawrence & Wishart, 1946), p. 292.

5. Jonathan Zeitlin, "The Labour Strategies of British Engineering Employers, 1890–1922," in Howard F. Gospel & Craig R. Littler, eds., *Managerial Strategies and Industrial Relations* (London: Hainemann, 1983), p. 47.

6. This view is argued most rigorously in James Hinton, *The First Shop Stewards' Movement* (London: Allen & Unwin, 1973).

7. See, for example, Alastair Reid, "Dilution, Trade Unionism and the State in Britain during the First World War," in Steven Tolliday and Jonathan Zeitlin, ed., *Shop Floor Bargaining and the State* (Cambridge: Cambridge University Press, 1985).

8. John Roemer, "New Directions in the Marxian Theory of Exploitation and Class," in John Roemer, ed., *Analytical Marxism* (Cambridge: Cambridge University Press, 1985).

emphasizes the advantages of this approach, as the state extended inexorably the scope of its activities in the economic sphere. In consequence, industrial conflict became intertwined with a wider struggle for control of the agencies of the state itself, and capital–labor. conflict became more overtly politicized.

II

An understanding of the wartime period, however, must be prefaced by some appraisal of the prewar background. Thus the terms of settlement of the great engineering lockout of 1897–8 had failed to resolve what was essentially a struggle over the control of production, or more precisely, the division of labor. Since the second quarter of the nineteenth century, the overall trajectory of British capitalist development had rested on the steady diffusion of a particular mode of fixed capital reproduction – machine-made steam power. This had, in fact, created the engineering industry in the first place. As a specific mode of production, its development was determined primarily by a particular set of product and labor market conditions, but this was also influenced by the role of the state. In particular, government legislation during the 1840's, especially the Bank Charter Act and the dismantling of the protectionist system, had helped to secure Britain's position as the "first industrial nation," at the center of world trade in goods, services, and, above all, capital itself. It was this that had made possible Britain's domination of world trade during the third quarter of the nineteenth century by large numbers of relatively small-scale merchants and manufacturers.[9] The result was that Britain's industrial structure before the First World War remained extremely competitive horizontally, and vertically very specialized, in contrast to the marked trend toward amalgamation and vertical integration in Germany and the United States.[10] This was particularly the case in the British engineering industry, which had become oriented to specialization on small-batch production where the diversity of markets abroad created a multiplicity of different customer needs.[11] It was fragmented, heterogeneous, and had a highly differentiated product, where small-scale enterprise remained ubiquitous.[12] It is also important

9. For a persuasively argued study of the importance of relations between government and the City of London in shaping Britain's nineteenth-century economic development, see Geoffrey Ingham, *Capitalism Divided? The City and Industry in British Social Development* (London: Macmillan, 1984), especially chap. 5.

10. See, for example, Alfred A. Chandler, "The Growth of the Transnational Firm in the United States and the United Kingdom: A Comparative Analysis," *Economic History Review*, 2d ser. 32, no. 3 (1980).

11. S. B. Saul, "The Market and the Development of the Mechanical Engineering Industries in Britain, 1860–1914," *Economic History Review*, 2d ser. 20 (1967).

12. Roderick Floud, *The British Machine Tool Industry, 1850–1914* (Cambridge: Cambridge University Press, 1976), e.g., Table 7.3, p. 200; AUEW Offices, London, 1876 Information Schedule, Amalgamated Society of Engineers.

to appreciate that although machine-made steam power remained the dominant technology, this was based upon the adaptation of key artisanal skills to the requirements of mechanized industry.[13]

In the first instance, this was a consequence of the capital development of the industry itself. Structural fragmentation and specialization associated with small-batch production continued to demand increasing inputs of relatively scarce engineering skills. In addition, the growth of strong craft unions like the ASE enabled skilled workers to establish a position of autonomous workplace control, in the context of fragmented and highly competitive production that made it difficult for firms to implement more "systematic" management strategies, even after the formation of the EEF in 1896.[14] This system of "craft administration" thus provided skilled engineering workers with a large measure of autonomous authority in relation to employers and supervisors, in an overall context of relations of exploitation.[15] This autonomy rested not only on their "genuine" skill, in the sense that they possessed manual facility or dexterity combined with practical knowledge acquired by experience, but also upon "constructed" skill as enshrined in the five-year apprenticeship that craft unions like the ASE normally demanded as the precondition for membership.[16] It was generally the skilled journeymen who were also responsible for the training of apprentices, specifying the tasks they had to master as a means of restricting entry into the trade, which was reflected in the ASE's insistence on a 4:1 ratio of journeymen relative to apprentices employed.[17] Finally, the legitimacy of this craft administered system of production had been in some sense recognized in government legislation during the 1870s, when trade unionism was granted a legal identity and the crucial weapon in its armory – "peaceful" picketing – was given juridical protection. It is significant that the latter was only an effective tactic for craft unionism, where "mass" picketing and illegal "intimidation" were largely unnecessary, and the evidence of government inquires and reports indicates that legislators consciously framed the law in the light of this, despite opposition from some employers.[18]

Toward the end of the Great Depression period of 1873–96, amidst increasing complaints about "an excess of production," there was a growing feeling among engineering employers that despite frequently high levels

---

13. Keith Burgess, *The Origins of British Industrial Relations: the Nineteenth Century Experience* (London: Croom Helm, 1975), chap. 1.
14. Zeitlin, "Labour Strategies."
15. B. C. M. Weekes, "The Amalgamated Society of Engineers, 1880–1914. A Study of Trade Union Government, Politics and Industrial Policy" (Ph.D. diss., University of Warwick, 1970), chap. 1.
16. 1876 Information Schedule, ASE. For a discussion of the distinction between "genuine" and "constructed" skill, see Charles More, *Skill and the English Working Class, 1870–1914* (London: Croom Helm, 1980), chap. 1.
17. 1876 Information Schedule, ASE.
18. Burgess, *Origins*, for example, pp. 38, 112–27.

of unemployment, the most dire effects of 'overproduction' threatened the capitalist more than they did the worker.[19] In consequence, firms tried to restrict the work of the relatively expensive fitters and turners to the more technically difficult parts of jobs like lathe work, while upgrading cheaper, unskilled labor to the simpler machine tools like the drilling, planing, and slotting machines.[20] This tactic of increasing the division of labor, in order to lower labor costs *absolutely*, was complemented by attempts to reduce labor costs *relatively* as well by increasing work loads and generally speeding up the pace of work.[21] The greater division of labor also made possible the growth of piecework in place of timework wages, which promised to assist firms in their efforts to speed up the pace of work and reduce costs by progressively cutting piecework rates. The outcome was increasingly to differentiate the function of "fitting," where the highly variable character of the work made payment by results less appropriate, from the related one of "turning" – lathe work – where piecework could be introduced even in small-batch production.[22] These developments led to mounting conflict between employers and workers during the 1880s and 1890s. The ASE responded to the spread of what it called task work, for example, by opposing the employers' drive to extend piecework, in combination with more semiskilled and nonunion labor, to what the society designated as "skilled" work, and this triggered bitter disputes like the prolonged strike during 1880–90 at the armaments firm of Maxim-Nordenfelt.[23] As a result of the ASE's 1892 Delegate Meeting, the society's decision to "follow" the machines, rather than leave them to nonunion labor, led to an escalation of disputes and was the background to the formation of the EEF in 1896, whose determination to reassert "the power to manage" precipitated the great lockout of 1897–8.[24]

Throughout the 1890s and early 1900s, the growing labor unrest in the engineering industry was perceived by government as part of a more general sharpening of capital–labor conflict in Britain during this period. The appointment of a Royal Commission on Labor taking evidence during 1892–3, and the establishment in January 1893 of the Labor Department of the Board

19. For the views of Chambers of Commerce, see the *Royal Commission on the Depression of Trade and Industry*, First Report, Cd. 4621 (1886), Appendix A.
20. Ibid., Third Report, Minutes of Evidence, Cd. 4794 (1886), pp. 144–5.
21. *Royal Commission on Labour*, Cd. 6894–VII (1893), p. 166, for the evidence of ASE district officials.
22. M. L. Yates, *Wages and Labour Conditions in British Engineering* (London: Macdonald & Evans, 1937), p. 97.
23. AUEW Offices, London, *ASE Abstract Report of the Council's Proceedings*, 1 July 1888–31 December 1890, pp. 18–25, for reports of this dispute; also discussed in Burgess, *Origins*, p. 50.
24. British Library of Political and Economic Science, Webb Collection E (Trade Union), *The Employers' Federation of Engineering Associations*, Engineering Conference, 1897; see also Burgess, *Origins* pp. 62–4.

of Trade, testify to the importance that government now attached to the problem.[25] Conflict in the engineering industry was regarded as part of the upsurge in labor unrest associated with the "new unionism," which its employers claimed was "infecting" workers with "pernicious" doctrines.[26] The ASE's demand for a reduction in working hours from fifty-four to forty-eight per week, to be secured by government legislation if necessary, was just one example of how conflict in the economic sphere began to be politicized.[27] In addition, there was the steady erosion of trade unionism's legal immunities in the courts during the 1890s, and the combined effect of defeat in the 1897–8 lockout and the definitive Taff Vale judgment of 1901 persuaded the ASE to throw its support behind the Labour Representation Committee, following the lead of its new General Secretary, George Barnes.[28] By the early 1900s, it appeared to the ASE that the legitimacy of the engineering industry's "craft administered" system of production had come to be threatened not only by the employers but by the state itself. The terms for the appropriation of labor power were clearly seen to be shifting in favor of employers. In terms of workers' attitudes, politics and ideology were coming to play an increasingly important role.

The terms of settlement of the 1897–8 lockout had marked the advent of nationwide collective bargaining between capital and labor in the engineering industry. Yet the expectations of some employers' leaders that this would create the condition favorable to more systematic management proved oversanguine. It is true that by the early 1900s British engineering employers did have at their disposal the technical means for restructuring the division of labor on terms more favorable to themselves. Cheaper and more efficient electric power, the development of high-speed steel, and the development of new, more specialized and multifunctional machine tools like the milling machine, the turret lathe, and precision grinding machine, did make possible a shift to a higher form of fixed capital reproduction where there would be less of a demand for all-round skill.[29] Yet with the possible exception of some large armaments firms, there is little evidence to suggest that the majority of enterprises introduced these innovations as part of a concerted management strategy.[30] An awareness of their potential did lead some of the more progressive firms to implement more "scientific" methods for measuring labor time, hence the

---

25. See, for example, Roger Davidson, *Whitehall and the Labour Problem in Late-Victorian and Edwardian Britain* (London: Croom Helm, 1985).

26. *Engineering*, 5 November 1897.

27. Webb Collection E (Trade Unions), *Abstract Report of General and Local Council's Proceedings* (ASE), 1 January–30 June 1891, pp. 95–103.

28. H. A. Clegg, Alan Fox and A. F. Thompson, *A History of British Trade Unions since 1889*, vol. 1 (Oxford: Oxford University Press, 1964), p. 375.

29. Weekes, "Amalgamated Society of Engineers," chap. 2.

30. Zeitlin, "Labour Strategies," pp. 36–8.

spread of new methods of wage determination like the premium bonus system.[31] Following the Carlisle Agreement in 1902, the ASE Executive did agree to terms for the implementation of the premium bonus system, but this met with widespread resistance from the shopfloor.[32] To the extent that this system was introduced, it hastened the shift in the focus of collective bargaining to plant bargaining by shop stewards, outside the formal remit of the 1898 terms of settlement, which led to a mounting number of disputes just before the war and threatened the very existence of the settlement itself.[33]

The fact remains, however, that the engineering employers were unable to undermine once and for all the industry's craft administrated division of labor because they were unable to *supersede* the product and labor market conditions that had given rise to it in the first place. With the possible exception of some armaments firms, which possessed some degree of market control via "cost-plus" government contracts, most of the engineering industry was unable to supplant intense market competition by *corporate control* of markets, on the U.S. or German model.[34] This discouraged any fundamental shift by British firms to a more sophisticated technology. Thus in 1914, fully 60% of workers employed by the EEF were designated as "skilled," compared with 20% who were "semi-skilled," and 20% who were "unskilled".[35] This highlights the continuing section fragmentation of British engineering employers, despite the formation of the EEF in 1896. This was most profoundly the case at the political level where it was the financial institutions of the City of London who had the ear of successive British governments, which resisted pressure from some industrialists, including engineering employers, for intervention in the guise of "fair trade" or tariff reform.[36] In contrast, the legal immunities of the ASE and other trade unions had been restored by the Trade Disputes Act of 1906 following the "aberrations" of the Taff Vale judgment, and trade unionism was granted further recognition when it became involved in the implementation of liberal welfare legislation like the 1911 National Insurance Act. When the whole of the ASE Executive had to be reelected in 1913,

31. Weekes, "Amalgamated Society of Engineers," Appendix V.
32. Zeitlin, "Labour Strategies," pp. 40–2.
33. J. R. Richmond, "Some Aspects of Labour and its Claims in the Engineering Industry" (Presidential address to the Glasgow University Engineering Society, Session 1916–17).
34. Chandler, "Growth of the Transnational Firm." Unfortunately, much of the recent research on German economic development still awaits translation into English, but for a wide-ranging survey see David Blackbourn and Geoff Eley, *The Peculiarities of German History. Bourgeois Society and Politics in Nineteenth-Century Germany* (Oxford: Oxford University Press, 1984), especially pp. 176–90, 206–21.
35. Yates, *Wages and Labour Conditions*, p. 31.
36. British Library of Political and Economic Science, evidence of employers presented to the 1904 Tariff Reform Commission, for example, the evidence of Bergtheil & Young Ltd., London Engineers and Electric Power Specialists (ref. TC3 1/315). See also Ingham, *Capitalism Divided?*, chap. 7, for the dominance at the political level of the financial institutions of the City of London.

following the society's constitutional crisis of the previous year, a study of the political character of its members indicates that few of them had any reservations about what they perceived as the continuing drift of *political* power toward organized labor,[37] which had come to be recognized as essential for a successful campaign against employer's "encroachments" at the workplace.

The incidence of strike activity in the British engineering industry emphasizes the continuing resilience in the bargaining position of skilled workers during the years between the 1898 terms of settlement and the outbreak of the First World War. In particular, the spread of plant bargaining led to many local disputes, despite the existence of industrywide collective bargaining. The following is a list of such yearly disputes referred to Central Conference representing the trade unions and the Engineering Employers' Federation:[38]

1898–8	1904–22	1910–19
1899–7	1905–12	1911–37
1900–19	1906–29	1912–37
1901–15	1907–56	1913–35
1902–26	1908–21	1914–38
1903–16	1909–21	

Thus it would appear that the benefit to employers of the 1898 terms of settlement proved relatively short-lived. In the context of a period of comparatively low unemployment, at least for skilled workers, the failure of wages to keep abreast of prices after 1905 and especially after 1910 seems to have been combined with the rising expectations associated with the Liberal government in accounting for the persistence of local disputes, especially since the EEF sought to contain wage increases by entering into long-term agreements with the trade unions.[39]

In the case of disputes leading directly to stoppages of work, the issue of wages was by far the single most important cause (see Table 1).[40] What is noteworthy, nevertheless, is that during an inflationary period, when prices tended to move ahead of wages, there should have been so many stoppages arising from conflict over the *control* of work, rather than the terms of its remuneration. Work stoppages fitted the former in all but the first, third,

---

37. Weekes, "Amalgamated Society of Engineers," pp. 343–7; see also Keith Burgess, "New Unionism for Old? The Amalgamated Society of Engineers in Britain," in Wolfgang J. Mommsen and Hans-Gerhard Husung, eds., *The Development of Trade Unionism in Great Britain and Germany 1880–1914* (London: Allen & Unwin, 1985), pp. 181–2.

38. *Committee on Industry and Trade* (Balfour Committee), vol. 1, evidence of Sir John Dewrance, President of the EEF, 1925, Appendix L, p. 546.

39. Engineering seems to have followed the general pattern of strike activity in Britain during these years – see James E. Cronin, *Industrial Conflict in Modern Britain* (London: Croom Helm, 1979), pp. 96–109.

40. *Committee on Industry and Trade* (Balfour Committee), vol. 1, Appendix E, Table 1, p. 542.

Table 1. *Engineering stoppages of work, 1910–14*

Cause of stoppage	Number of stoppages
Wages application	33
Nonunion question	7
Piece prices	6
Manning of machines	4
Reinstatement of men after discharge	5
Demarcation	4
Employment of unskilled labor on skilled work	4
Objection to foreman	4
Working conditions	1
Victimization	3
Objection to payment by results	1
Outworking allowances	1
Payment for overtime	1
Miscellaneous	18
Total	92

thirteenth, and fourteenth of the above categories, notwithstanding the large number of miscellaneous cases. How the experience of "total war" was to transform this conflict into a struggle for control of the state, as well as the workplace, remains to be examined.

III

It is not entirely true that the British government entered into the First World War in a total state of upreparedness, although the plans it had made proved entirely inadequate as the hopes for a quick victory faded during the first year of hostilities. It had been assumed that Britain's military presence on the continent would be limited, and that the burden of her involvement in the conflict would be carried by the Royal Navy. Whether or not the British government's initial adoption of a business-as-usual approach reflected its profound adherence to laissez-faire principles, which has recently been discounted,[41] it is arguable that a naval policy promised a minimum of dislocation to the domestic economy and reduced the political liability that would arise from any decision to deploy a large standing army on the continent. In any case, the effect of this kind of policy assumption was to make the British government slow to come to terms with the demands of the war. With the benefit of hindsight, it can be seen that the demands of war confronted the British state with

41. David French, "The Rise and Fall of 'Business as Usual,'" in Burk, *War and the State*, p. 11.

three major problems that were interrelated. The first of these was how to finance the mobilization of men and materials on the scale required. Secondly, this led to the problem of organizing production in a way that promised to optimize the economy's capacity to sustain a huge increase in the output of munitions, while at the same time ensuring the necessary inputs of raw materials, food, and other civilian production outside the armaments sector but essential to it. And, thirdly, government had to devise means of maintaining the flow of men to the armed forces, as determined by the increasing needs of the military, without reducing the economy's ability to produce or otherwise obtain the arms, raw materials, food, and a whole range of other commodities and services deemed necessary for the prosecution of the war.

As the conflict dragged on, the focus of government policy began to concentrate on the state's need for manpower. It was in this sphere that efforts to reconcile rising losses at the front with the necessity of meeting wartime demands for increased production led the state to become more and more involved in the direction, control, and disciplining of the labor force. In fact, it was the imposition of these external forms of authority upon what had traditionally been a 'free' labor market that was the underlying cause of much of the unrest in the engineering industry during the war years. State intervention and control required a reconstruction of the conventional terms for the appropriation of labor power, which had to supersede, in some degree, relations of exploitation based upon the differential ownership of means of production. In consequence, the role of the state was perceived as much more integral to productive relations generally than had been the case in Britain before 1914. And it was to be expected that state control would impinge most directly on workers in trades engaged in the manufacture of war materials, particularly in the engineering industry. Yet it was in this very sector of the economy where relations between capital and labor had been especially strained during the prewar years.

It soon became clear as the hopes for a quick military victory receded that the output of the engineering trades could not be increased on the scale required, without changes in work practices. Thus the effect of voluntary recruitment to the armed forces had meant that 19.5% of male workers in the engineering industry had enlisted by June 1915, creating severe shortages of skilled labor as munitions production was increased.[42] Voluntary schemes for directing skilled labor to where it was most needed had palpably failed.[43] In the meantime, the Defence of the Realm Act of August 1914 had constituted the legal basis for state control of the labor market. As subsequently amended during the early months of 1915, it not only made illegal strikes on government

42. Wolfe, *Labour Supply and Regulation*, p. 14.
43. Samuel J. Hurwitz, *State Intervention in Great Britain. A Study of Economic Control and Social Response, 1914–1919* (New York: Columbia University Press, 1949), pp. 98–101.

298

work, but also proscribed all "restrictive practices or customs calculated to affect the production of munitions of war." This was subsequently incorporated in the famous Treasury Agreement signed in March 1915 by the government and the officials of the leading unions involved.[44] For many skilled engineering workers, it appeared that the power of the state would now be deployed to supplant the craft administered system of production in the interests of the employers, who were now freed of market constraints by the accident of war, and this threatened to reverse the prewar drift of political power toward organized labor.

The Treasury Agreement was to have been administered by local munitions committees composed of an equal number of representatives of employers and workers, together with an additional number of "impartial persons" appointed by the state. Their brief was not only to settle wage questions but also included "the management and control of industry" itself.[45] The problem with such an ambitious and far-reaching strategy was that a coherent labor policy could hardly be expected to emerge from a series of uncoordinated and localized agreements, while the government had neither the staff nor the experience to implement it.[46] It was the result of the notorious "Shells Scandal" that centered the govenment's attention on the need to improve the administration for mobilizing wartime production, which led eventually to the setting up of the Ministry of Munitions in June 1915 under the direction of Lloyd George.[47]

Faced with a lack of civil servants having the appropriate industrial experience, Lloyd George drew on the "fund of goodwill" he had accumulated with the business community before 1914 in persuading men of business to accept prominent positions in the new ministry. It is estimated that more than ninety directors and managers were "loaned" to the Ministry of Munitions for the duration of the war. Many were to remain on the payrolls of their respective firms, however, and the instances where leading engineering employers like Alfred Herbert administered sectors of production that also happened to coincide with their own business interests made it difficult to distinguish where business control ended and state control began.[48] Given the prominence of many of the more progressive engineering employers on the staff of the

44. Wolfe, *Labour Supply and Regulation*, Appendix 9, pp. 361–4, for the text of the agreement.
45. M. B. Hammond, *British Labour Conditions and Legislation during the War* (New York: Oxford University Press, 1919), p. 79.
46. Joseph Melling, "The Servile State Revisited: Employers, Workplace Conflict and State Intervention in Britain, 1914–16" (unpublished paper, King's College Research Centre, Cambridge, 1983), p.42.
47. Chris Wrigley, "The Ministry of Munitions: an Innovatory Department," in Burk, *War and the State.*
48. Hinton, *First Shop Stewards' Movement*, pp. 29–30.

ministry, the trade unions like the ASE suspected that the need to increase armaments production would serve as the pretext for eliminating the measure of control that skilled workers had exercised over the division of labor, especially since the fifty or so local Boards of Management set up under the ministry's auspices excluded labor representation.[49] The latter was confined to area Labor Advisory Boards that were subsequently established. The extent to which this separation institutionalized capital–labor conflict within the agencies of the state itself is crucial to an understanding of the character of the labor unrest in the engineering industry for the duration of the war.

Under the terms of the Munitions of War Act, strikes and lockouts were declared illegal, heavy penalties were imposed for any breach of the law, and the settlement of differences was left to state-managed compulsory arbitration. In the context of wartime labor scarcity, the prohibition of lockouts and strikes was not regarded by the trade unions as a genuine quid pro quo. The act's principal innovation was the creation of a new industrial category – the so-called controlled establishment – defined as any plant considered essential for the manufacture of munitions. In controlled establishments, all restrictive practices or customs affecting the employment of skilled and unskilled labor were suspended, and not only wages but all aspects of workplace organization, including manning levels, the selection of operatives to be employed, and the more general "ordering of work," were now subject to state control.[50] In order to prevent the "poaching" of scarce labor by firms other than those designated as controlled establishments, workers could be assigned to their place of employment according to the wishes of the ministry, and they were not allowed to seek work elsewhere unless in possession of a leaving certificate issued by their previous employer. Finally, Section 10 of the Munitions of War Act gave the state very wide and undefined powers of control in case any of the more specific provisions proved inadequate. The government's imposition of a Munitions Levy on the profits of controlled establishments, to be merged later with the more widely applied Excess Profits Duty, did not allay trade union suspicions of state-funded "profiteering" because the levy could be written off against capital expenditure and depreciation. In any event, there is considerable evidence to show that the Ministry of Munitions did more to modernize the British engineering industry than the prewar dominance of "free" product and labor markets.[51]

It was generally assumed that the Munitions of War Act represented the maximum degree of control the state could exercise over the labor market, short of outright 'industrial conscription'. Moreover, the terms of the act extended

49. Melling, "Servile State Revisited," p. 82.
50. Wolfe, *Labour Supply and Regulation*, pp. 104–6.
51. Wrigley, "Ministry of Munitions," pp. 48–9.

beyond those firms having plants engaged in munitions woi
the latter meant was never clearly defined, although the act as ⌄
in 1916 specified, in addition to armaments, "any other article⌄
articles intended or adapted for use in war."[52] Thus the repair of railⱽ
belonging to a colliery was classified as munitions work since the wag⌄
being used for war purposes.[53] In this respect, the degree of flexibility p⌄
in the administration of the act implied that the terms "munitions work⌄ and
"controlled establishment" were *political* designations rather than strict
technical categories. This made the potential authority of the local Boards of
Management very great indeed, and explains why the latter were regarded as
such a serious threat not only by munitions workers in the strictly technical
sense but also by other groups as well. In short, government now possessed
almost unlimited power to determine in detail the working conditions and practices to be adopted throughout the engineering industry. It was this politicization of productive relations rather than any inherent technological dynamism
that accounts both for the extent and the changing character of labor unrest in
the industry for the duration of the War.[54]

IV

Once the Munitions of War Act had become law, government was
slow to grasp the scope of the potential conflict that would arise. This tardiness
reflected, in the first instance, differences in the relative power of the distinct
classes or fractions of classes in British society. The government's wartime
financial policy, for example, was in accordance with the dominant orthodoxy
of the Treasury, the Bank of England, and the City of London institutions.
This meant that even during the early phase of hostilities, government expenditure rose considerably above peacetime levels, and by 1916 this represented
an increase of 562% on the first war budget.[55] Government income covered
substantially less than one-third of total expenditure until the very last year
of the war, and the size of the deficit steadily grew, financed by a succession
of war loans. The cost of this strategy was high, however, and the social
consequences immeasurable. Since a large proportion of the massive increase
in state indebtedness was earmarked for nonproductive use, the fires of
inflation were allowed to rage almost out of control. It has been estimated that
government expenditure during the war would have been no more than 50%

52. Wolfe, *Labour Supply and Regulation*, Appendix 13, p. 378.
53. Hammond, *British Labour Conditons*, p. 89.
54. Zeithlin, "Labour Strategies," p. 46; and this view is argued more generally
in Keith Burgess, *The Challenge of Labour, Shaping British Society 1850–1930* (London: Croom
Helm, 1980), pp. 159–64.
55. Gerd Hardach, *The First World War* (London: Allen Lane, 1977), p. 151.

of its actual amount if the "ransom" to financial institutions had not in fact been paid.[56] As it was, the amount of interest required to service the national debt at the end of hostilities exceeded an entire prewar budget.

Until the spring of 1916, the levels of wage increases guaranteed to adult male engineering workers were in the order of an additional four shillings weekly on time rates, or 10% on piece rates.[57] It was only as a result of long hours of work, sometimes in excess of seventy hours per week, that enabled earnings to keep abreast of the rising cost of living.[58] Moreover, the wages of the many women workers who began to enter the industry often became the major source of family income as military recruitment gathered pace. As late as October 1915, the Circular L2 issued by the Central Munitions Labour Supply Committee laid down a minimum of only one pound a week for women employed in "controlled establishments." The fact that this circular had to be reissued during the course of 1916 suggests that it was not always adhered to by individual firms.[59] The minimum wage was below the level required to maintain a family's subsistence, even in terms of prewar prices, yet the government's own figures indicate that retail food prices alone had risen by 32% during the first twelve months of the war in the large cities where controlled establishments were mostly located.[60] Relatively cheap food had been central to the family life-style of the skilled engineering worker before the war. The inflationary consequences of the conflict were now perceived to threaten this standard, evidence of wartime profiteering was widely cited, and persistently long working hours increased the strain on family life.[61]

The first months of the war had not, in fact, witnessed any marked increase in the number of disputes in the engineering industry, reflecting a display of genuinely popular patriotism and the widespread expectation that the conflict would be short-lived. But the number began to mount during the early months of 1915, and eighty-six were so referred to the Central Conference representing the trade unions and the Engineering Employers' Federation during the year as a whole.[62] This was more than twice the prewar average despite the threat of legal penalties. Clydeside was the focus of much of this labor unrest since it was at this time the single largest and probably most rapidly expanding center in Britain for munitions production. In the shipbuilding

56. A. H. Gibson, "A Criticism of the Economic and Financial Policy Pursued by the Government During the War," in A. W. Kirkaldy, ed., *British Finance During and After the War 1914–21* (London: Pitman, 1921), p. 396.

57. Wolfe, *Labour Supply and Regulation*, p. 244.

58. Ibid.

59. Hurwitz, *State Intervention*, pp. 141–2.

60. Simon Litman, *Prices and Price Control in Great Britain and the United States during the World War* (New York: Oxford University Press, 1920), p. 32.

61. Gail Braybon, *Women Workers in the First World War* (London: Croom Helm, 1981), pp. 113–17.

62. *Committee on Industry and Trade* (Balfour Committee), vol. 1, Appendix L, p. 546.

302

trades, for example, the especially heavy demands of naval construction created an acute shortage of skilled labor, at the same time that tradesmen were lost to the armed forces, with the result that a serious crisis developed during August 1915 at the Fairfield shipyard in Govan.[63] The latter was designated as a controlled establishment within the terms of reference of the Munitions of War Act, and the firm's particularly aggressive management sought to use the threat of legal prosecution against strikers in disputes over leaving certificates and war bonuses. When two men were dismissed for "slacking," 430 shipwrights struck in sympathy, with the result that 17 of their shop stewards were consequently convicted and threatened with prison sentences of thirty days unless each paid a ten-pound fine. Although the threat of the latter was sufficient to force the strikers back to work, on the day after the strike had begun, the convicted men sought assistance from the Govan Trades Council to get their sentences remitted and the Munitions of War Act abolished. This marked the beginning of an increasing struggle between skilled workers and both employers and the state over the maintenance of wartime living standards.

Early in October 1915, a delegate meeting representing the skilled trades in the Clydeside engineering and shipbuilding industries decided to form an organization called the Clyde Trades Vigilance Committee. This fused the shipyard workers with the more narrowly defined munitions trades directly making armaments that had established a now defunct Central Labour Withholding Committee early in 1915. It is significant that the former body, which was to be the direct precursor of the better-known Clyde Workers' Committee, was the creation of skilled workers in the shipbuilding trades rather than those directly engaged in the manufacture of guns and shells.[64] Thus it was the more general impact of state control, and not the specific changes in workplace relations associated subsequently with "dilution," that was to prove the underlying cause of labor unrest. In this respect, it is noteworthy that of all workers compulsorily transferred to other employment under government direction, the proportion of shipbuilding trades affected was almost as great as the number of fitters and turners employed exclusively in armaments production.[65] What united the skilled trades was their common hostility to what they regarded as the coercive provisions of the Munitions of War Act. To many workers, for example, the restriction on labor mobility arising from the system of leaving certificates bore a sinister resemblance to the practice of 'character notes' used traditionally by shipbuilding and engineering firms to discipline their labor force, and it is significant that this had been a major issue underlying the Fairfield strike of August 1915.[66] And this lack of mobility applied equally

---

63. Wolfe, *Labour Supply and Regulation*, pp. 127–30.
64. Hinton, *First Shop Stewards' Movement*, pp. 118–19.
65. Wolfe, *Labour Supply and Regulation*, p. 198.
66. Hinton, *First Shop Steward's Movement*, p. 114.

to *all* workers employed in controlled establishments. As the *Women Workers* was to observe in June 1916:[67]

> The foreman's reply to the complaining one is no longer: "If you don't like it you can leave it." If she tries, she will find that no other employer will be allowed to engage her, and unless she can persuade a Munitions Court to grant a leaving certificate, six weeks' idleness must be her portion. And we know what that means to many a woman worker....One great danger of the new conditions is that sweating and bad conditions may be stereotyped.

In the meantime, labor unrest had turned to one sphere of the social relations of production where government had not anticipated the inflationary consequences of its wartime financial policies. In particular, rising house rents during the course of 1915 began to bear especially hard on working people employed in the rapidly expanding munitions centers like Clydeside. Housing provision in Glasgow, for example, was the most obvious manifestation of the spatial segregation of its population on the basis of social class before the First World War, with skilled workers, clerks, and other "respectable" groups aspiring to rented housing that was markedly better than the property occupied by the poorer classes. Even prior to 1914, however, a combination of rising interest rates, the movement of capital into overseas issues, and a lack of effective demand, had led to a worsening housing shortage. This was aggravated further, of course, by the growth of the munitions industries during the war, with the population of Glasgow increasing by almost 24,000 during 1914 alone, although only 373 of the estimated 5,000 additional dwellings required were actually built.[68] Finally, the government's wartime financial policies had the effect of bringing to a virtual halt what little construction had been undertaken specifically for the working class in the period 1900–14.

The result was to intensify the pressure on Glasgow's existing stock of housing, more than two-thirds of which consisted of accommodation with two or fewer rooms per unit. The competition for the remaining housing comprising the city's stock of "superior" accommodation was especially intense, as the war led to an increase in the proportion of the population earning regular and rising money earnings. In this respect, it is significant that the highest increases in rents, varying from almost 12% to more than 23%, affected housing in Partick and Govan and Fairfield, where a large concentration of skilled tradesmen lived adjacent to the expanding munitions firms.[69] This

---

67. Irene Osgood Andrews, *Economic Effects of the War Upon Women and Children in Great Britain* (New York: Oxford University Press, 1918), cited pp. 84–5.

68. Joseph Melling, "Clydeside Housing and the Evolution of State Rent Control, 1900–1939," in Joseph Melling, ed., *Housing Social Policy and the State* (London: Croom Helm, 1980), p. 147.

69. Ibid., p. 148.

group was clearly reluctant to accept living in one or two rooms, which did not meet its expectations and aspirations, particularly "the growth and expansion of those domestic and social virtues upon which the welfare of the community depends."[70] Glasgow's housing crisis was thus perceived to have a *moral* dimension that reflected a specific form of social-class reproduction – skilled workers and their families. Moreover, as a specific form of relations of exploitation, the effect of this housing crisis threatened to disrupt the productive relations of the war economy.

With attempts at eviction of tenants in October 1915 for the nonpayment of their increased rents, there was the possibility of a conjuncture of rent "strikes" and resistance to the government's manpower policies, which might culminate in a major social crisis.[71] Organizations like the local wards of the Independent Labour party and the Glasgow Women's Housing Association were especially active in leading the rent strikes, which also obtained a wide circle of support from among munitions workers like William Reid who was a leading shop steward at Parkhead Forge.[72] In fact, the government faced mounting pressure to resolve the rents question *before* it combined with industrial unrest, thus precipitating a major crisis that might threaten the prosecution of the war itself. Thus there was support from some prominent industrialists for housing "reform." The government itself was alarmed at the inflationary effect of rising rents, and it regarded the prospect of sacrificing the interests of petite bourgeoisie investing in house mortages and in receipt of house rents, by imposing some form of state rent control, as the lesser evil when compared to the threat of widespread disruption.[73]

It was in this context that the government acted quickly and passed into law the Rent and Mortage Interest (War Restriction) Act in December 1915, which froze all rents at their prewar levels. The agitation of engineering workers and their families had thus forced the state to take the unprecedented step of superseding the market prerogatives of property owners in the interests of the working class. The government had been undoubtedly impressed by the moral tone of the rhetoric deployed in this agitation, which centered on "unpatriotic" landlords who were exploiting the wartime sacrifices of the working class. And with the rents issue resolved, the government was subsequently free to concentrate its attentions on the management of its manpower policies, without the attendant danger of triggering a wider social crisis. In fact, the state's speedy handling of the rents issue also served to legitimize

70. Joseph Melling, "Scottish Industrialists and the Changing Character of Class Relations in the Clyde Region, c. 1880–1918," in Tony Dickson, ed., *Capital and Class in Scotland* (Edinburgh: John Donald, 1982), p. 126.
71. John McHugh, "The Clyde Rent Strikes, 1915," *Journal of Scottish Labour History Society* 12 (1978): p. 58.
72. Melling, "Clydeside Housing," p. 149.
73. Ibid., p. 148.

the "patriotism" of the rent strikers, which effectively identified working-class interests with the state's prosecution of the war and its promise of a victorious outcome. This was to prove decisive as unrest in the engineering trades persisted during the winter of 1915–16, and as government made final preparations for a conclusive battle with skilled workers over the terms for the control of the division of labor.

By the end of 1915, it had become clear that the War Munitions Volunteer Scheme had failed to attract the required numbers of skilled tradesmen to munitions work, and that as an alternative to the introduction of industrial conscription, the government decided on the systematic pursuit of dilution as the means for releasing men for the armed forces, while avoiding a head-on collision with an organized labor movement united in opposition ·to the government's manpower policies. In this task, Lloyd George used his personal influence with the trade union leaders who had already signed away any official right to oppose dilution after they had agreed to the provisions of the Munitions of War Act. Thus the position of the ASE Executive was that it did not oppose dilution as such, but it was opposed to any attempt by the employers to use dilution as a means of undermining the skilled workers' control of the division of labor. The ASE Executive insisted that all work performed customarily by skilled workers should continue to be paid according to the normally recognized wage rate when it was transferred to dilutee labor.[74] This position had also been the policy initially of the Ministry of Munitions itself during October–November 1915, but it aroused widespread opposition from engineering employers who were concerned that such a fundamental concession to craft administration should be recognized in legislative form.[75] It was this deadlock that led the ministry to dispatch Dilution Commissioners to Clydeside, authorized to investigate local conditions and implement dilution on a plant-by-plant basis. In order to reduce the expected resistance, the commissioners were to promote the establishment of joint committees of management and unions at each workplace.[76]

In the meantime, the Clyde Workers' Committee (CWC) had been formed during the last week of October 1915, representing a fusion of shipyard and armaments factories. On paper, skilled engineering workers now possessed an organization capable of doing battle with employers and government over the terms for the control of the division of labor in the controlled establishments designated by the Ministry of Munitions. But the CWC was unable to develop an immediate *tactical* response to the government's dilution plans quickly enough, spending much of its time during the last crucial weeks of 1915 in argument over the long-term *strategy* for the nationalization of industry with

74. Hinton, *First Shop Stewards' Movement*, p. 68.
75. Melling, "Servile State Revisted," p. 102.
76. Ibid., p. 108.

306

workers' participation.[77] This reflected the highly politicized character of the CWC's leadership, composed of shop stewards who were activists in either the Independent Labour party, the British Socialist party or the Socialist Labour party.[78] Outright opposition to dilution remained the single policy that the CWC could rely upon for support amongst the skilled rank and file. This was to prove the root cause of its defeat early in 1916.

Whether, in fact, the civil servants at the Ministry of Munitions were intent on using dilution as a pretext for 'smashing' the labor movement is unlikely given the prewar background of their leading lights like William Beveridge and Llewellyn Smith.[79] They had strenuously sought before 1914 to obtain the cooperation of trade union leaders as part of the New Liberalism's grand strategy of social cohesion and social reform. Their first priority was to administer to the needs of the war economy as efficiently as possible, but it would be misleading nonetheless to underestimate the importance they attached to defeating the CWC. As an unofficial and highly politicized body, the latter did not come within the compass of "responsible" trade unionism, hence the government's insistent refusal to negotiate with it, and preference for dealing with the ASE Executive in the discussions preceding the implementation of dilution. The problem for the ministry was that the remit of the Dilution Commissioners to establish joint committees at each workplace, in order to reduce localized resistance, had to come to terms with the positions of authority that the CWC shop stewards had already established for themselves. What the ministry's civil servants failed to do was to allay the suspicion widespread among skilled engineering workers that the *effect* of government-sponsored dilution would yield important advantages to the employers, but at the expense of workers who were expected to surrender what they regarded as the only means available to them for protecting their interest – their control of the division of labor.

Thus the government's handling of the CWC has to be seen in terms of practical expedience. From its very inception, the CWC had been as much opposed to the Munitions of War Act as to dilution as such, which is not surprising given the prominent role played by shipyard workers in the establishment of the committee.[80] It was the latter group who had suffered most

77. Hinton, *First Shop Stewards' Movement*, p. 130.
78. For surveys of these political movements, together with an understanding of their influence on Clydeside, see: Walter Kendall, *The Revolutionary Movement in Britain 1900–21* (London: Weidenfeld & Nicolson, 1969), pp. 105–8; Raymond Challinor, *The Origins of British Bolshevism* (London: Croom Helm, 1978), pp. 127, 130–3; Stuart Macintyre, *A Proletarian Science. Marxism in Britain 1917–1933* (Cambridge: Cambridge University Press, 1980). chap. 1; Iain McLean, *The Legend of Red Clydeside* (Edinburgh: John Donald, 1983).
79. Roger Davidson, "War-time Labour Policy 1914–1916: A Reappraisal," *Journal of Scottish Labour History Society* 8 (1974).
80. Hinton, *First Shop Stewards' Movement*, pp. 118–19.

during the initial phase of the Munitions of War Act's implementation, but who were less directly affected by the threat of dilution. Their support for the rent strikes on Clydeside during 1915 had clearly alarmed the government, yet the resolution of this question in 1915 allowed the government to concentrate specifically on the resistance of skilled *armaments* workers to dilution, and this increasingly came to preoccupy the CWC. The result was to weaken fatally the CWC's effort to generalize its policies of nationalization and workers' participation as working *class* demands, since it had been effectively captured by *one* group within its constituency and thus could be more readily isolated.[81] The government was not disposed, therefore, to hurry and bring about a "premature" confrontation during the turbulent days of November–December 1915, but it moved cautiously in the knowledge that the ground was being prepared for a signal victory.

The government was inclined initially to persuasion rather than coercion. Lloyd George intervened personally and toured the munitions districts, trying to persuade the local union officials to accept dilution. In line with previous government policy, he refused to deal with the shop stewards, with the important exception of Clydeside where the strength of local feeling was such as to leave him with no other alternative. His talk with a deputation of the CWC on 24 December 1915, however, and his speech at a tumultuous public meeting the next day at St. Andrews Hall in Glasgow proved abortive. Even then, the government remained reluctant to discard its policy of conciliation, although the possibility of resorting to legal coercion had been mooted earlier.[82] In January 1916, an amendment act laid down more precisely the conditions under which leaving certificates had to be granted to employees, which included failure to pay the standard rate of wages; any behavior of the employer or his agent toward a worker that justified him leaving; or the existence of another vacancy where the worker could be used "with greater advantage to the national interest."[83] This amendment could be expected to appeal especially to the shipyard and other trades represented by the CWC, with the exception of its leaders and their supporters in armaments works like Parkhead Forge, and it may have been instrumental in isolating the latter and preparing the way for the committee's defeat at the hands of the government.[84]

At the same time, during January 1916, three government-appointed Dilution Commissioners were dispatched to the Clyde and the Tyne. On Clydeside, they worked closely with Willliam Weir, part-owner of a well-known

81. Iain McLean, "The Ministry of Munitions, the Clyde Workers' Committee, and the suppression of the "Forward": an alternative view," *Journal of Scottish Labour History Society* 6 (1972), p. 4; and see Hinton, *First Shop Stewards' Movement*, p. 340, for a map locating the CWC's support in workplaces on the Clyde.

82. Hinton, *First Shop Stewards' Movement*, pp. 140–3.

83. Wolfe, *Labour Supply and Regulation*, pp. 223ff.

84. Melling, "Servile State Revisited," p. 114.

engineering firm, who was not only a keen advocate of progressive managerialism but had been Director of Munitions for Scotland since August 1915. The government was prepared to take legal action against strikes or any incitement to strike under regulations of the Defence of the Realm Act. By February 1916, it considered the CWC sufficiently isolated, and during February and March, dilution was enforced on a plant-by-plant basis in major firms like Parkhead Forge, Weir's, and the Albion. At Parkhead Forge, for example, the skilled workers struck when management revoked the authority of shop stewards to 'ascertain' the pay and conditions of women workers who were being introduced as dilutees. This posed a fundamental challenge to the craft administered division of labor since it implied that it was the prerogative of management and not labor to regulate the terms for the employment of dilutee labor. Yet the employers were unable to carry on production without the presence of skilled workers to train, set up, and superintend the new recruits, which explains the government's rapid deployment of state coercion when it decided to arrest and deport the CWC leaders, and at the same time, suppress the left-wing journal *Forward*. With their leaders gone, and amidst the importation of "soldiers" and "Englishmen" as strikebreakers, the opposition to dilution on the Clyde collapsed.[85]

Yet the bargaining position of the skilled workers on the shopfloor had been far from broken. The employers discovered that shop stewards remained essential to the smooth functioning of dilution, especially since the fixing of wages and regulation of working conditions were in constant flux.[86] Moreover, the dilutees continued to rely on the new *responsibilities* of a smaller proportion of highly skilled workers who had to set up, superintend, and maintain the new division of labor. Thus the shop stewards were able to prevent the employers from using dilution as a means of reducing *overall* labor costs, and thus maximizing their share of the industry's increased output at the workers' expense. The agreements negotiated subsequently in the major Clydeside armaments factories specified that dilutees once fully trained should receive rates of pay that "with the wages paid to the necessary supervisor and the increased wages paid to the men who now solely perform the difficult portion of the operation, will make the cost of doing work not less than it was before."[87] It was this approach that was subsequently to form the kernel of the demand for workers' *control* of industry as a *class* demand. This was to be taken up later in the war in the form of more overtly "revolutionary" shop stewards' activity. By then, the issue of dilution that had so preoccupied the leaders of the

85. Highton Collection, Department of Economic History, University of Glasgow, *Manifesto from Parkhead Forge Engineers to their Fellow Workers* (printed leaflet, n.d., probably March 1916).
86. Richmond, "Some Aspects of Labour," pp. 26–7.
87. Hinton, *First Shop Stewards' Movement*, pp. 140–3.

CWC during the winter of 1915–16 had become an accomplished fact, and productive relations had become politicized to such an extent that industrial conflict shifted more directly to a struggle for control of the institutions of the state itself.

V

It was during the course of 1916 that the full magnitude of the sacrifices demanded by the war became apparent. Not only did dilution proceed under the direct supervision of the Ministry of Munitions, but the responsibility for deciding whether a worker was judged to be indispensable to the war effort was transferred from the individual employer to the state after April 1916, with the introduction of military conscription.[88] Yet this new phase of the government's manpower policy, known as "debadging," had withdrawn a mere 40,000 exemptions from conscription by August 1916, out of some 850,000 issued at the outset, which proved totally inadequate given the heavy losses incurred in the first battle of the Somme. Meanwhile, the skilled munitions workers, having swallowed dilution, insisted via the ASE Executive that as a quid pro quo they should be exempted from military service, and this was agreed to by the Cabinet on condition that they agreed to undertake all necessary work as designated by the Ministry of Munitions.[89] By November 1916, however, there was growing unrest over indiscriminate recruiting in Glasgow and Sheffield, and an important strike took place in Sheffield when a skilled tradesman was conscripted.

Sheffield like Glasgow had witnessed a rapid expansion of munitions production since 1914, and many of the city's heavy engineering firms had shifted directly into arms and other related work. Unlike the situation on Clydeside, however, where the shipyards remained generally separate from the armaments firms, the relatively greater integration of Sheffield's engineering industry made for greater cohesiveness in its labor force. Much of the work carried on was regarded, moreover, as unsuited to female dilutee labor and this made family incomes particularly dependent on men's wages, which magnified the threat posed by compulsory military service to living standards.[90] Yet differences in productive relations should not be overemphasized in explaining the timing and the distinctive character of labor unrest in Sheffield. By November 1916, in contrast to the troubles on Clydeside during the winter of the previous year, dilution had become an accomplished fact in most of the munitions districts, including Sheffield where physically strong male

88. Wolfe, *Labour Supply and Regulation*, p. 39.
89. C. J. Wrigley, *David Lloyd George and the British Labour Movement* (Brighton: Harvester Press, 1976), pp. 169–70.
90. Hinton, *First Shop Stewards' Movement*, p. 165.

laborers were increasingly employed in place of skilled tradesmen. All workers now faced the ultimate threat of compulsory military service, although the more highly organized skilled trades were in a stronger bargaining position to offer resistance. Thus it was a decisive difference in political context that led to the emergence in Sheffield of the leading theorist of "workers' control" in the person of Jack Murphy, secretary to its Engineering Shop Stewards' Committee, who developed the idea of the workplace committee as the basis for an industrywide organization of production, involving the participation of *all* grades of labor.[91] Whereas the terms for the implementation of dilution on Clydeside had been perceived to undermine the skilled workers' control of the division of labor, to the advantage of the employers, the issue at stake late in 1916 had become a question of the *political* terms for allocating the burden of wartime sacrifice amongst munitions workers as a whole.

The danger of widespread disruption affecting the munitions industries was an alarming prospect for the government given the state of the war at the end of 1916. This explains its decision to release the Sheffield tradesman who had been conscripted, and this brought the strike to an end. The government then sought to isolate the skilled tradesmen from dilutee labor by negotiating the so-called Trade Card scheme with craft unions like the ASE late in November.[92] This allowed them to exempt their members from military service, on condition that they did "their utmost" to supply the Ministry of Munitions with skilled workers to serve either in the Artificers' Corps in the army or as War Munitions Volunteers in controlled establishments. The government was thus given a free hand to recruit from among the unskilled and semiskilled in the munitions industries, who were less well organized and still dependent on the craft unions for leadership. This practice was intended to prevent the mobilization of a mass movement directed against conscription and the prosecution of the war, although there was a proviso in the Trade Card agreement that the government could resort again to statutory compulsion if sufficient skilled workers were not provided by the unions for war work.

The advent of the Trade Card scheme marked a remarkable transformation in state manpower policy during the course of 1916 as escalating carnage on the battlefields had intensified labor shortages in the munitions industries. Thus within less than a year, the craft unions had wrenched control, first from the employers and then the state, of the authority to determine whether a worker was to be judged indispensable to the war effort. This outcome reflected, in turn, the intensity of shopfloor conflict as the craft unions fought for control of dilution in the localities. Thus the Engineering Employers' Federation reported no fewer than 186 disputes referred to Central Conference

91. Highton Collection, Department of Economic History, University of Glasgow, J. T. Murphy, *Compromise or Independence?* (Sheffield Workers' Committee, 1917), pp. 10–14.
92. Wolfe, *Labour Supply and Regulation*, chap. 4.

311

in 1916, more than twice the number so referred during 1915, and the highest figure recorded for any year of the war.[93] Contrary to the expectation of some Clydeside employers during the winter of 1915–16, the exemption of skilled workers from military service while dilutees could be freely conscripted had the effect of strengthening the established system of craft administered production. At the same time, however, the government took steps to depoliticize shopfloor power by initiating a concerted attack on "agitators" who tried to exploit grievances as a means of generating popular opposition to the war and preparing the ground for the destruction of the existing social order. Thus by the end of 1916, most of the CWC leadership was either in prison or had been deported to other districts, pacifist agitators like John MacLean had been imprisoned, and the Ministry of Munitions had spent 620,000 pounds in organizing a system of industrial espionage, including the widespread use of agents provocateurs and spies.[94]

It was the combination of military disasters and continuing unrest at home that finally brought about the fall of Asquith and the accession of Lloyd George as Prime Minister in December 1916. Lloyd George's administration was bound to be more systematically interventionist than its predecessor, having none of the inhibitions of Asquith's visibly Whiggish regime. It marked a turning point in the war in the sense that the balance of class interests articulating the institutions of the state shifted more directly in favor of industrial capital, in the first instance, and then subsequently in favor of the industrial working class, as labor unrest continued unabated. This change had been anticipated earlier by measures like the Rent Restriction Act, but it was formally confirmed with the advent of the Lloyd George administration. Its most striking manifestation was the recruitment of his so-called new men, mostly industrialists, to lead the powerful new ministries that were subsequently to increase considerably the effectiveness of the state in its handling of the war.[95] Their recruitment to government marked the culmination of wartime developments leading to a new form of interlocking relationship between capital, labor, and the state; yet, the roots of these new men in the established institutions and practices of British politics were very tenuous indeed. This opened a dangerous lacuna in the implementation *in practice* of the government's wartime policies, which caused a shift of the locus of capital–labor conflict to the arena of competing *ideological* discourses. These centered, above all, on the efforts of Lloyd George's administration to represent its labor policies in the guise of "war socialism," yet the responsibility for implementing this lay with the

---

93. *Committee on Industry and Trade* (Balfour Committee), vol. 1, Appendix L, p. 546.
94. Challinor, *British Bolshevism*, especially pp. 138–41, 147.
95. Peter K. Cline, "Eric Geddes and the 'Experiment' with Businessmen in Government, 1915–22," in Kenneth D. Brown, ed., *Essays in Anti-Labour History* (London: Macmillan, 1974); see also Burk, *War and the State*.

government's new ministries, whose leaders organized labor found difficult to reconcile with Lloyd George's rhetoric. This explains the government's creation of the new Ministry of Labour to complement the work performed hitherto by the more overtly 'coercive' Ministry of Munitions.

The Ministry of Labour appeared to provide organized labor with direct access to political power at cabinet level. But it was both administratively weak and lacked a coherent policy, reflecting the government's intention of limiting its authority by hiving off many of its potential responsibilities to rival organizations.[96] The outcome of war socialism, therefore, more closely approximated a form of *corporatism*, which has been defined as "the unification of self-governing industries by a national committee representing them and other interests, including the state."[97] Yet this was a form of state control that reckoned without competing ideological discourses. In fact, to the extent that corporatism subsumes economics *within* politics, the intensity of this ideological conflict was consequently increased. Thus pledged to the more efficient prosecution of the war, Lloyd George had necessarily to be more thorough in his handling of issues like conscription, but at the same time he had to respond to labor demands like the "conscription of riches" put forward by the War Emergency Workers' National Committee, which indicated the strength of feeling that wartime sacrifices were not being equally shared.[98] The conscription issue, in particular, generated more widespread opposition as the war's demands for manpower continued to rise, with the Trades Councils, for example, becoming a focus for agitation against the class bias of the recruiting drive, which it was feared would lead to industrial conscription in the interests of employers.[99] By the early months of 1917, the situation had become critical because of the success of Germany's unrestricted submarine campaign. It became imperative to restrict the production of nonessentials, especially if they had a high import content, while economizing on the use of manpower in ways that would contribute first to maximum production for military purposes, and second to maintain the export trade.[100]

This gave rise to government measures leading directly to the most *politically* serious labor unrest of the war, particularly in the engineering trades. The first was a bill extending dilution to "private" nonmunitions work, and this was

96. Rodney Lowe, "The Ministry of Labour, 1916–19," in Burk, *War and the State*, p. 112.

97. L. P. Carpenter, "Corporatism in Britain, 1930–45," *Journal of Contemporary History* 11, no. 1 (1976): p. 3.

98. Royden Harrison, "The War Emergency Workers' National Committee, 1914–1920," in Asa Briggs and John Saville, eds., *Essays in Labour History 1886–1923* (London: Macmillan, 1971), pp. 236–8, 247.

99. Alan Clinton, "Trades Councils during the First World War," *International Review of Social History* 15, pt. 2 (1970): especially p. 215.

100. E. M. H. Lloyd, *Experiments in State Control* (Oxford: Clarendon Press, 1924), chap. 22.

followed by the government's announcement of its decision to end the Trade Card agreement with the craft unions, substituting in its place a more rigorous Schedule of Protected Occupations administered directly by the state. What strengthened the government's case against the Trade Card scheme was the increasing efficiency of dilutee labor, once it was trained and acquired work experience, which undermined the craft unions' claim of the right to supply skilled labor for war work.[101] In fact, what constituted acceptable levels of skill became increasingly difficult to define. The situation by 1917, therefore, had become less of a problem of dilution threatening the craft autonomy of skilled workers, but had shifted instead to the threat of war socialism to both the livelihoods and lives of munitions workers as a whole. The continuing upward trend of prices, moreover, had taken their toll of morale, and this was aggravated further by shortages of basic foodstuffs brough about by the unresticted sinking of merchant shipping, while the increasing pace and intensity of work led to general war-weariness.[102] During the first six months of 1917, retail prices exceeded by a ratio of more than 2:1 the levels prevailing in 1914, while wage rates for most workers were rarely more than 50% above their prewar levels.[103]

This was the background to the almost spontaneous wave of strikes that, starting in the Lancashire textile machine–making districts, spread subsequently to engineering workers in Sheffield, the West Midlands, and London.[104] Although the EEF reported only 66 disputes referred to Central Council during 1917, compared with 186 in the previous year, more than 200,000 engineering workers had been involved in strikes by the end of May, equivalent to the loss of 1,500,000 working days. There was especially strong opposition to the government's plan to extend dilution to private work, which was seen as commercially inspired to make firms a quick profit, and which directly threatened a previously unaffected area of craft administration.[105] For the first time, a Joint Engineering Shop Stewards' Committee was formed to coordinate the strikes, and it sought to negotiate directly with the government and repudiated any "interference by the union executives." Arthur Henderson, the Minister of Labour, warned the government that the unrest had been "deepened by the Russian Revolution," and Lloyd George acknowledged that the War Cabinet was aware of the existence of "a very considerable and highly

101. B. A. Waites, "The Effect of the First World War on Class and Status in England," *Journal of Contemporary History* 11, no. 1 (1976): p. 36.

102. Parliamentary Papers, *Commission of Enquiry into Industrial Unrest, North-Western Area*, Cd. 8663, 1917, pp. 19–20; *Yorkshire and East Midlands Area*, Cd. 8664, 1917, p. 5.

103. Arthur L. Bowley, *Prices and Wages in the United Kingdom, 1914–1920* (Oxford: Clarendon Press, 1921), pp. 7–9, 105ff.

104. Hinton, *First Shop Stewards' Movement*, chap. 7, contains a full discussion.

105. Edmund and Ruth Frow, *Engineering Struggles. Episodes in the Story of the Shop Stewards' Movement* (Manchester: Working Class Movement Library, 1982), p. 50.

314

organized labour movement with seditious tendencies."[106] In the workshops, disaffection had spread even to the supervisory grades of labor, with employers alarmed at the prospect of trade unionism establishing autonomous organizations specifically for their non-comissioned officers."[107]

Yet the bases for the strength of the shop stewards' movement in the localities created almost insuperable obstacles in coordinating the strikes and preventing divisions within its own ranks. In fact, it could be argued that its rank-and-file rhetoric prevented its capture of official union structures or the building of alternatives to them, which, in contrast to the situation prior to 1914, had acquired increasing authority as a result of government recognition. Thus when the Joint Engineering Shop Stewards' Committee finally succeeded in calling a conference representative of all the movement in August 1917, the majority of delegates refused to recognize the need for an Executive Committee to provide effective leadership. They agreed only to the creation of an "Administrative Committee" with no independent powers of decision, which led to the localized fragmentation of the movement.[108] This situation played into the hands of the government that was able to negotiate a "pre-emptive" settlement with the ASE Executive. There was to be some modification of the proposed Schedule of Protected Occupations, which included a pledge to call up all dilutees for military service before recruiting skilled tradesmen or apprentices, and the government promised to consult with the unions in implementing the schedule.

The government's tactic of recognizing the preferred position of skilled tradesmen, by giving them preferential treatment in military recruitment, was in line with the earlier Trade Card scheme. But Lloyd George now applied his immense personal presence to this practice of divide-and-rule. He was not only prepared to meet with trade union leaders and negotiate compromises with them, he also worked energetically to formalize arrangements that would give "to labour a definite and enlarged share in the discussion and settlement of industrial matters." What he termed "constructive cooperation" had led, for example, to the appointment of the Whitley Committee in November 1916, and its interim report published in March 1917 had recommended the establishment of local, district, and national joint committees to determine working conditions.[109] Thus the state was seeking to co-opt in *form* the organ-

106. Wrigley, *David Lloyd George*, cited p. 189.

107. For a background discussion, see Joseph Melling, "'Non-Commissioned Officers:' British Employers and their Supervisory Workers, 1880–1920," *Social History* 5, no. 2 (1980); see also Keith Burgess, "Authority Relations and the Division of Labour in British Industry, with Special Reference to Clydeside, c. 1860–1930," *Social History* 11, no. 2 (1986): pp. 228–30.

108. Frow, *Engineering Struggles*, p. 56.

109. For a succinct discussion of "Whitleyism," see Hugh Armstrong Clegg, *A History of British Trade Unions since 1889*, vol. 2, *1911–1933* (Oxford: Clarendon Press, 1985), pp. 204–7.

ization of the shop stewards' movement itself. Responsibility for these joint committees became part of the remit for the much more ambitious plans of the Ministry of Reconstruction, created by statute in August 1917 following the findings of the government's Commission of Enquiry into Industrial Unrest, which revealed the deep-seated causes of labor disaffection in the munitions districts. These pointed to the danger of a resurgence of unrest over the shortage of housing threatening to spill over into disruption at the workplace, and there was specific mention of a "revolutionary minority" who were described as a "serious menace" to the government and the established order of society.[110] During the latter half of 1917, the government did, in fact, act quickly to slow down the wartime rise in the cost of living, via intervention by the Ministry of Food. Substantial increases in wage rates were also granted after the summer of 1917 in the engineering and shipbuilding trades, with the result that during the last year of the war money wages rose rapidly and began to keep pace with the cost of living for the first time since hostilities had begun.[111] In thus presenting itself as the ultimate arbiter of the terms for the appropriation of labor power, Lloyd George's administration sought to make war socialism the means for labor's emancipation from exploitation based upon relations of property, wealth, and power.

The government required time, however, for these concessions and promises to make an impact on the lives and minds of working people. What clearly worried the authorities, especially after October 1917, was the way support for the Russian Revolution was being mobilized to justify demands for labor's emancipation in Britain. Thus despite war socialism, there was no cessation of unrest among engineering workers during the final year of the war.[112] Again, it was the critical manpower losses sustained during the winter of 1917–18, after the huge casualties suffered in the Passchendaele campaign, that precipitated another crisis of civilian morale. The government's award of a $12\frac{1}{2}\%$ bonus to hourly paid workers in the munitions trades, made in October 1917 to rectify anomalies of skilled tradesmen earning less than the semiskilled operatives whom they supervised, led to a series of strikes aimed at extending this award to groups in allied trades. In January 1918, the army's demand for a further 250,000 men led to a new Military Service Act, which authorized government to cancel exemptions on the basis of occupation, and a revised Schedule of Protected Occupations introduced the so-called clean cut for men under twenty-three years of age who no longer had any protection against

---

110. Parliamentary Papers, *Commission of Enquiry into Industrial Unrest, London and South-Eastern Area*, Cd. 8666, 1917, pp. 5–6; *Yorkshire and East Midlands Area*, Cd. 8664, 1917, p. 3; *Scotland*, Cd. 8669, 1917, p. 3.
111. Bowley, *Prices and Wages*, pp. 105ff.
112. Hinton, *First Shop Stewards' Movement*, e.g., pp. 246–7ff.

recruitment. The situation worsened during March 1918 with the beginning of the last German offensive on the western front, and proposals that the War Munitions Volunteer scheme should be offered as the *only* alternative to fighting in the trenches appeared to signal the coming of outright industrial conscription. The Administrative Committee of the shop stewards' movement tried to mobilize opposition not just to the government's "combing out" of this or that trade, but to the continued prosecution of the war itself. Lloyd George's much-used tactic of divide-and-rule seemed to be on the point of collapse as a result of the developing crisis of the war.

During the course of 1918 as a whole, the EEF reported 127 cases of dispute referred to the industry's Central Council, compared with 66 in the previous year, despite the magnitude of the government's concessions to organized labor since the summer of 1917.[113] Yet it can be argued that this continuing unrest at such a critical time had outrun the political development of the shop stewards' movement. In contrast, the government had established a strong position to "manage" the unrest. In objective terms, the shop stewards' movement was by 1917–18 in direct confrontation with the state and the class interests perceived to be supported by it, and its everyday praxis was no longer confined to opposing or even managing dilution in the interests of craft administration. Yet its subsequent debacles emphasize that there had taken place no corresponding shift in political consciousness, and the equivocation of the movement's national leadership demonstrates that it was unsure of its ground. Thus although a revived Clyde Workers' Committee obtained unanimous support "to enforce the declaration of an immediate armistice on all fronts" at a mass meeting in January 1918, a more representative conference of shop stewards held in the following April was opposed to political action to end the war, confining itself to administrative matters.[114] This was also the consensus of workshop meetings.[115] This feeling grew after the Germans launched their last great offensive in the West, which was presented by the government as a battle of national survival, with the result that industrial unrest subsided for a time and the employers succeeded in victimizing many of the leading shop stewards.[116]

It is clear that an explanation for this failure of the shop stewards' movement to realize its "revolutionary" potential must take into account the wider political climate, and not just the internal divisions in the movement that can be reduced simply to variations in productive relations. To argue that it was "locked in the syndicalist categories of workers' control," and ignored the role of state

---

113. *Committee on Industry and Trade* (Balfour Committee), vol. 1, Appendix L, p. 546.
114. Frow, *Engineering Struggles*, p. 65.
115. Hinton, *First Shop Stewards' Movement*, pp. 262–3.
116. Ibid., p. 266.

power, is to beg the question as to why workers' consciousness was so "imperfectly" articulated.[117] Clearly, the efforts made by government after the summer of 1917 to develop new institutional forms for the containment of industrial conflict, for example, through the agency of the Ministry of Reconstruction, created a new ideological discourse that offered hope for the future; and, this promise was seemingly confirmed by the state's *action* in improving the material welfare of the great mass of working people during the last year of war. Government initiatives were thus crucial in preventing the shop stewards' movement from widening its support to the degree required for a fundamental political challenge to the power of the state. Moreover, the reconstruction of the Labour party during 1917–18, with clause four of its new constitution widely interpreted as an indication of its commitment to socialism, appeared to offer working people hope in the constitutional road to an improved tomorrow, and would make unnecessary a Bolshevik-style seizure of power. After all, there was neither a starving peasantry nor a starving proletariat in Britain during 1917–18.

VI

Although the shop stewards' movement may not have realized the revolutionary potential expected of it by some theoreticians of the movement, it had been the most original and significant expression of working-class struggle in the British engineering industry. The shop steward had been a key figure in renegotiating the terms for the division of labor, protecting the interests of skilled workers in the craft administration of production, and preventing employers from using dilution as a means of undermining trade unionism in the industry during the wartime period. At the same time, the shop steward's authority also allowed for some technical modernization of the industry, but not at workers' expense. In the postwar period, the shop stewards' movement fought an often bitter and prolonged struggle to preserve the gains won during the war. This is reflected in the persistently high number of cases in dispute referred to the industry's Central Conference after 1918, especially during the years 1919–21: 1919, 168; 1920, 186; 1921, 193; 1922, 144; 1923, 178; 1924, 167.[118] The effectiveness of the shop stewards' movement had also been significant in convincing trade unionists in the industry that it was now essential to extend union organization and reshape it on an industrial rather than a craft basis, which led to the merger of craft societies in the Amalgamated Engineering Union in 1920. Together with the parallel expansion in the employers' organizations, this widened considerably the scope for collective bargaining in the industry after the war.

117. Ibid., p. 366.
118. *Committee on Industry and Trade* (Balfour Committee), vol. 1, Appendix L, p. 546.

318

Table 2. *Engineering Stoppages of Work, 1919–24*

Cause of Stoppage	Number of Stoppages
Hours	28
Wages-applications for advance	73
Objections to payment by results	18
Victimization	19
To resist wage reductions	26
Nonunion labor	13
Piecework prices	21
Demarcation	10
Three-shift system	2
Employment of semi- and unskilled labor	9
Objection to foreman	2
Objection to employment of trainees	5
Objection to female labor	6
Overtime	2
Objection to withdrawal of bonus systems	3
Outworking allowances	2
Limitation of apprentices	2
Nightshift – limitation of hours	4
Holidays	1
Miscellaneous	41
Total	287

Thus even though wage questions remained the single most important cause of stoppages after 1918, as they also had been in the prewar period, the incidence of stoppages caused by wage *reductions* highlights the change in economic climate (see Table 2).[119]

Stoppages caused by victimization and opposition to payment by results were relatively more numerous than before 1914, reflecting the employers' determination to rid themselves of militants and increase productivity as rising unemployment weakened the workers' bargaining position. At the same time, stoppages caused by the introduction of shift working, the employment of female labor, and the withdrawal of war bonuses, are indicative of the continuing impact of war-induced innovation. During the early 1920s, it is also noteworthy that there were three national engineering stoppages: the 1922 lockout over "managerial functions," a national wages strike by molders, and one by electrical workers caused by the employment of nonunion foremen.[120] The last-mentioned dispute is illustrative of the conflict between the employers

119. Ibid., Appendix E, Table 2, p. 542.
120. Ibid.

and the predominantly manual unions for control of the supervisory grades during the 1920s, and was again a direct outcome of the deteriorating position of supervisory workers during the war.[121] In the context of the difficulties of the interwar period, therefore, perhaps the most lasting legacy of these years of unprecedented labor unrest in the engineering industry was in its effect on the policy-making of successive British governments and, in particular, the priority that was assigned subsequently to the preservation of stable industrial relations.[122] This was a direct consequence of the intertwining of industrial conflict with a wider struggle for control of the state, which had begun at the turn of the century, but which only reached its climax during the First World War itself. The case of the political economy of British engineering workers during the war emphasizes that politics and ideology do have a determining effect on productive relations compatible with a materialist analysis.

121. During the 1920s, for example, there are instances where foremen who refused to surrender their trade union membership and join the employers' client Foreman's Mutual Benefit Society were threatened that their wages would be reduced to the rates of hourly paid tradesmen. See the AEU Central and Special Conferences, Shorthand Notes, vol. 2, 9 September 1921, pp. 398–404, in the AUEW Offices, London, See also Burgess, "Authority Relations and Division of Labour," pp. 230–1.

122. For differing interpretations of the subsequent emergence of "corporatist-style" solutions to Britain's problems of economic and social instability, see, for example: Carpenter, "Corporatism in Britain"; Keith Middlemas, *Politics in Industrial Society. The Experience of the British System since 1911* (London: Andre Deutsch, 1979), chaps. 5–8; Burgess, *Challenge of Labour*, chap. 6–7; Charles Feinstein, ed., *The Managed Economy. Essays in British Economic Policy and Performance since 1929* (Oxford: Oxford University Press, 1983).

14

The rationalization of class struggle: strikes and strike strategy of the German Metalworkers' Union, 1891–1922

ELISABETH DOMANSKY

This study of the strikes led by the German Metalworkers' Union (Deutscher Metallarbeiter-Verband, DMV) and of this union's strategy pursues the dual goal of understanding union action on the one hand and of union interpretation of its strategies of class struggle on the other. Union action must be at the center of research about labor unions because associations of workers were perfectly able and willing to generate their own strategies and to pursue them in practice.[1] They actively intervened in the historical process of labor conflicts rather than being driven by external forces. I start with the conviction that to deny workers and their unions the role as independent actors in a tense and contradictory environment is historically incorrect. It also withdraws dignity and responsibility from workers and their associations.

The DMV was the first German union that organized itself along the lines of an industrial union. The model of industrial unions is commonly considered to be progressive, as opposed to traditional trade unions organized along craft lines.[2] The "modern" principle of the industrial union is stated to be the appropriate organizational form for the phase of "organized capitalism." It is

My special thanks are due to Michael Geyer and Bernd Weisbrod for their extensive help in preparing the English version of this article. The manuscript was completed and submitted to the editors in 1984. It does not reflect the most recent literature nor my own further elaborations on the subject.

1. The following is essentially based on the results of my thesis. Elisabeth Domansky, "Arbeitskämpfe und Arbeitskampfstrategien des Deutschen Metallarbeiter-Verbandes 1891–1924," (Ph.D. diss., Bochum, 1981, microfiche). The thesis will be published as a book in 1989.
2. See, e.g., W. Albrecht, *Fachverein-Berufsgewerkschaft-Zentralverband. Organisationsprobleme der deutschen Gewerkschaften 1870–1890* (Bonn, 1982); Klaus Schönhoven, *Expansion und Konzentration. Studien zur Entwicklung der Freien Gewerkschaften im Wilhelminischen Deutschland 1890–1914* (Stuttgart, 1980). Cf. also Rudolf Boch "Solinger Lokalgewerkschaften und Deutscher Metallarbeiter-Verband. Eine Fallstudie zur krisenhaften Ablösung alter durch neue Arbeiterschichten 1871–1914," (Ph.D. diss., Bielefeld, 1983), pp. 6ff. This thesis has been published in the meantime. Rudolf Boch, *Handwerker-Sozialisten gegen Fabrikgesellschaft* (Göttingen, 1985).

credited with having played a decisive role in the changes in the form and function experienced by the labor struggles around the turn of the century.[3] This view is reflected in various approaches, most of which, however, are reductionist.

Existing studies of strike developments in Germany are characterized by their obvious avoidance of workers' organizations.[4] Along with case studies of spectacular labor struggles, the major emphasis has been on quantitative analyses. The latter have been especially concerned with the relationships between economic cycles and strikes as well as with the effects of long-term structural changes of German capitalism on labor unrest. This approach has brought out secular trends in the development of strikes and formed the basis for comparative studies in an international context. It presents, however, the danger of degrading strikes and strike behavior to a dependent variable of the economic process. Generally, questions concerning perceptions of workers and employers are disregarded. By the same token, political and ideological configurations that determined the decisions and actions of the strikers are neglected.

It is the merit of numerous case studies, on the other hand, to emphasize these aspects. They thus provide a necessary corrective to the prevalent macro-economic perspective. Only recently, however, has an attempt been made to extend this approach to the study of long-term changes in "forms of perception and protest" as well as to develop criteria for a comparative study of European strike movements.[5] Because these studies are largely committed to the approach of "history from below," they seek to explain the workers' actions through the analysis of their working and living conditions, their roots in old traditions, and the like. As a result, they usually remain aloof of union history as well.[6]

Even the latest studies of the history of German unions, however, almost entirely neglect the influence that unions exerted on the living and working conditions of workers, although this was precisely the function that unions

3. Hartmut Kaelble, and Heinrich Volkmann, "Konjunktur und Streik wahrend des Uebergangs zum Organisierten Kapitalismus in Deutschland," *Zeitschrift für Geschichtswissenschaft* 92, 2 (1972): 513–44.

4. For general outline of the present standard of strike research in Germany see Klaus Tenfelde, and Heinrich Volkmann, eds., *Streik. Zur Geschichte des Arbeitskampfes in Deutschland während der Industrialisierung* (Munich, 1981).

5. See, e.g., Michael Grüttner, "Basisbewegungen und Gewerkschaften im Hamburger Hafen seit 1896/97," in Wolfgang J. Mommsen, and Hans Gerhard Husung, eds., *Auf dem Weg zur Massengewerkschaft. Die Entwicklung der Gewerkschaften in Deutschland und Grossbritannien 1880–1914*, vol. 15 of *veröffentlichungen des Deutschen Historischen Instituts in London* (Stuttgart, 1984).

6. See, e.g. Detlev Puls, "Ein im ganzen gutartiger streik." Bemerkungen zu Alltagserfahrungen und Protestverhalten der oberschlesischen Bergarbeiter am Ende des 19. Jahrunderts," in *Wahrnehmungsformen und Protestverhalten. Studien zur Lage der Unterschichten im 18. und 19. Jahrhundert* (Frankfurt a.M., 1979), pp. 175–225.

considered to be the justification of their existence.[7] The same applies to labor struggles led by the unions, their role in the reaching of collective agreements, and the development of union relief funds. This neglect of the central aspect of union actions picks up and reinforces a perception that prevailed in Germany by 1914, that the construction of strong organizations was the unions' main task. Studies of union history, therefore, concentrate on the construction and expansion of organizations, the development of the membership, and the sociopolitical decisions of the unions.

The compartmentalization of research on strikes and unions has led to the widespread assumption that there was an increase in the rationality of struggles for the distribution of material goods after the turn of the century, due to the dominant influence of industrial unions. It is further argued that this increase reflected a higher degree of rationality in capitalist production. This presumed rationality of capitalist production in turn becomes the yardstick for measuring the rationality of labor protest; that is, the more organized forms of labor protest were, the better and the more adjusted they were to the demands of modern society.[8]

Studies that criticized this model point to the loss of influence of unions after the turn of the century. This diminution of influence is seen as a reflection of significant changes in shop organization and of the expansion of employers' associations. Even though these observations are undoubtedly correct, these studies treat workers and their organizations primarily as victims of capitalist rationalization strategies rather than as active participants and antagonists.[9]

Progress can be made in research on unions and strikes in Germany only if the history of the labor movement is no longer seen as mechanically dependent on a presumed logic of economic development. There has to be more research on the activities and politics of unions. But even such research will not provide satisfactory results as long as union politics are studied only in terms of formal political articulations of union politics, for example, official platforms. We also need to examine union activities and union reflections on their activities.

The latter approach enables us to see the specific strike strategy of the DMV as a consequence of its adoption of the principle of an industrial union. The

---

7. See, e.g., Schönhoven *Expansion*; see also Michael Schneider, *Die christlichen Gewerkschaften 1894–1933* (Bonn, 1982). Exceptions are Lothar Wentzel, *Inflation und Arbeitslosigkeit. Gewerkschaftliche Kämpfe und ihre Grenzen am Beispiel des Deutschen Metallarbeiter-Verbandes 1920–1924* (Hannover, 1981), and Rudolf Steinke, "Die Politik des Deutschen Metallarbeiter-Verbandes 1920–1924" (Staatsexamen thesis, Berlin, 1981).

8. See, e.g. Kaelble and Volkmann, "Konjunktur," and Tenfelde and Volkmann, *Streik*, pp. 9–30.

9. Dieter Groh, "Intensification of work and Industrial Conflict in Germany, 1896–1914," *Politics and Society* 8 (1978): 349–97; Ilse Costas, "Arbeitskämpfe in der Berliner Elektroindustrie 1905 und 1906," in Tenfelde and Volkmann, *Streik*, pp. 91–107; Ilse Costas, *Auswirkungen der Konzentration des Kapitals auf die Arbeiterklasse in Deutschland (1880–1914)* (Frankfurt a.M. and New York, 1981).

choice of this organizational model was, in turn, the result of a conscious decision in a particular historical situation rather than a necessary consequence of supposed structural changes in the capitalist system. This study analyzes what has usually been considered to be an inevitable development of union history as the product of the actions and decisions of unionists. This approach may help to demythologize the history of the German labor movement by giving back the workers their politics and, with them, their history.

Industrial union and strike strategy: the scientific approach to the conflict between capital and labor

The industrial union as a cartel for selling labor

In the period of the legal reorganization of the German unions after the Anti-Socialist Law (1878–90), the founding of the DMV (1891) and of the Woodworkers' Union (1893) represented a novelty in the history of the German labor movement.[10] Both groups chose a new kind of organization, that of the industrial union. In contrast to the traditional associations that were organized along vocational lines, they wanted to mobilize the workers of an entire industrial sector rather than only workers of a particular trade. They intended to overcome the separation between workers of different trades as well as that between skilled and unskilled.

The DMV justified this decision by referring to the structural changes in the capitalist system. "In view of the fact that the concentration as well as the cartelization of capital make the class struggle bitterer and more intensive,"[11] only an industrial union was the appropriate organization to represent the workers' interests effectively. This perception was influenced by the founding of the General Association of German Metal Industrialists (Gesamtverband Deutscher Metallindustrieller, GDM) in early 1890. This event, however, only strengthened the conviction that, in the process of capitalist development, the internal differences of the working class would be reduced in favor of increasing homogeneity.

The founding of the union was oriented more toward expected future developments than toward the existing possibilities of union activities. The workers reacted correspondingly. They viewed the new models of organizing an interest group sceptically. During their Halberstadt Congress in 1892 the majority of the German unions voted for the organizational model of craft unions. Coppersmiths, blacksmiths, shipwrights, gold- and silversmiths, and the majority of the molders adhered to the principle of craft organization. They

10. Cf. Schönhoven, *Expansion*, esp. pp. 306ff., and Domansky, "Arbeitskämpfe," pp. 24ff.

11. *Deutsche Metallarbeiter-Zeitung* 11, no. 3 (17 Jan. 1891).

324

joined the DMV only reluctantly in the following years, partly under massive pressure of the industrial union. The highly organized metalworkers in Berlin preferred to retain their localist organization as well. They did not join the DMV until 1897 and only after assurance of complete independence in their strikes by the leadership of the DMV, although this was contrary to the principles of the union. Other local affiliations of the DMV, too, acted with a localist outlook rather than as subordinate institutions of a central union. The unauthorized use of union funds – forbidden by union statutes – demonstrates the case most clearly.

Even the organizations that had joined the DMV did not completely detach themselves from conventional organizational ideas. The founding articles of the DMV expressly called for sections of different vocational groups within the union. Many of them developed lively activities, which were thorns in the side of the DMV, because they constantly tested the unions' integrational ability. Consequently the DMV leadership attempted to restrict supraregional conferences of the union's vocational groups, especially when the leadership suspected such conferences as being held in order to prepare wage negotiations without consulting the union's authorities at the beginning.

The growth and structure of the rank and file also demonstrates that the concept of the industrial union "remained a promise rather than a fulfillment."[12] The DMV only slowly grew in membership during the nineties. At the beginning of the decade, this was partly due to the economic recession. It is true that in 1896, with its 50,000 members, the DMV was the largest German union. But it had only doubled its original size. Like the other unions the DMV succeeded in its "breakthrough to a mass union," beginning in the second half of the 1890s. In 1901 it counted more than 100,000, and by 1911 more than half a million members. This enormous growth, however, cannot disguise the fact that the association's expansion remained both quantitatively and qualitatively behind the expectations linked with the model of an industrial union.

The proportion of all the German metalworkers organized in the DMV reached 8% in 1894 and rose to approximately 17% in 1907. This increase, however, came largely as a result of a higher degree of organization among the workers in small- and medium-sized firms in the finished goods industry. Statistical information gathered by the DMV shows, for example, that before 1905, 70% of the gold-and silversmiths worked in firms of up to 50 employees. In 1907, 98% of the file-cutters, and about 61% of the turners in 1910 worked in firms of this size. On the other hand, the share of molders in firms of up to fifty employees amounted only to 25%. According to a regional breakdown the

12. Fritz Opel, *Der Deutsche Metallarbeiter-Verband während des Ersten Weltkrieges und der Revolution* (Hannover and Frankfurt a.M., 1958), p. 30.

degree of organization of molders was below average precisely in those German states where large-scale enterprises were predominant.[13] The DMV had a difficult time organizing workers of large-scale enterprises. The union completely failed to gain access to the sector of heavy industry before the First World War. Steelworks and rolling mills were first organized in 1907, yet they only constituted 0.5% of the union's membership. Locksmiths, turners, plumbers, and molders represented about two-thirds of the membership. They remained dominant even after 1905, when the membership's structure gradually began to shift in favor of semiskilled and unskilled workers. In 1913, 5% of the members were women, 20% were semiskilled and unskilled, and 75% still remained to be skilled workers.[14]

The workers of the shipbuilding industry – who as industrial workers of a new type ideally corresponded to the principle of an industrial union – constituted only 1% of the DMV's membership. They had decided very early in favor of centralization reaching beyond vocational lines, but they preferred for a long time the Central Association of Shipyard Workers, (Zentralverband der Werftarbeiter), founded in 1897, to the DMV. Obviously the interests of these workers were addressed better by a shop-oriented organization than by an industrial union. The affiliation of the Central Organization of Workers of the Shipbuilding Industry with the DMV was practically forced through by the rest of the unions represented at the shipyards. They refused to support the union, which was in serious financial difficulties due to a strike that the DMV had initiated. They demanded instead that the workers of the shipbuilding industry should join the industrial union.[15] But this affiliation turned out to be a Pyrrhic victory for the DMV. Although the new members made up only an infinitely small portion of the DMV's membership, the shipyard industry was to become the main stage of the DMV's labor conflicts in the years between 1907 and 1913. As these strikes ended unsuccessfully, conflicts between the workers of the shipyards and the DMV leadership were rampant. Thus, the DMV slid into a profound crisis at the very moment when it had managed to organize a portion of those workers for whom its organizational model had been developed.

The main reasons for this crisis were obvious. Contemporary studies criticized the absence of a subdivision focusing on the shop in addition to the local administration, the latter organizing workers according to their residence instead of their workplace. They considered the lack of such subdivisions an inherent impediment against the organization of workers in large-scale

13. Elisabeth Domansky-Davidsohn, "Der Grossbetrieb als Organisations-problem des Deutschen Metallarbeiter-Verbandes vor dem Ersten Weltkrieg," in Hans Mommsen, ed., *Arbeiterbewegung und industrieller Wandel. Studien zu gewerkschaftlichen Organisationsproblemen im Reich und an der Ruhr* (Wuppertal, 1980), pp. 95–116.

14. Ibid., pp. 98ff.

15. Domansky, "Arbeitskämpfe," p. 29.

enterprises.[16] The local union's office was extremely well suited for promoting the amalgamation of all those workers who were employed in the smallest enterprises in a single city, as was the case, for example, for plumbers and the like. It could, however, hinder the growth of solidarity among workers of large-scale enterprises due to the dispersion of their homes. Otto Hommer, who wrote the first history of the DMV in 1912, reported about a large-scale enterprise in Kassel, for example, that employed 9,000 metalworkers of which "2,000 lived in the country in about 100 different localities."[17]

The lack of a shop-oriented organizational unit reflected the absence of a union strategy geared to action at that level. There were two reasons for the lack of such strategies. Action on the local or regional level promised success for workers of small shops organized in craft unions. These workers were most of all interested in improving their working and living conditions through controlling the job market, and they were amazingly successful. Some associations like the coppersmiths', who organized two-thirds of the German coppersmiths, actually controlled the job market of their vocational group.[18]

The DMV carried this idea of job market control from a vocational group over to the entire industrial sector. For workers in large enterprises or heavy industry, however, this goal remained of secondary importance. The majority of workers in heavy industry, whose numbers greatly expanded before the First World War, received by and large high wages, and did not feel threatened either by reductions of jobs or by abuses in apprenticeship. However, these were two of the main problems of the skilled workers employed in nonindustrial production. As a result, the DMV's initiative in 1904 to come to a binding agreement with employers of the metal industry covering working hours, minimum wages, piecework, and measures to prevent layoffs during recessions for the metal industry, bypassed the needs of many industrial workers. The latter were more interested in codetermining the conditions at their workplaces rather than in industrywide job market problems.[19]

The DMV was of very little help in this respect. It paid homage to the optimism of technological progress, which led it to reject all forms of influence on changes in production methods. The union leadership was deeply convinced that the transition from a capitalist to a socialist society would emerge on its own in the wake of the further development of the capitalist system and its productive forces. In this respect the DMV stood on the same ground as the Erfurt program of the Social-Democratic party (SPD) of 1891. The progress of

16. Otto Hommer, *Die Entwicklung und Tätigkeit des Deutschen Metallarbeiter-Verbandes* (Berlin, 1912), p. 68.
17. Ibid., p. 36.
18. H. Gentzke, *Gewerkschaftsbewegung und Arbeitsverhältnisse im deutschen Kupferschmiedegewerb* (Halle, 1914). See also Boch, "Solinger Lokalgewerkschaften," p. 10.
19. Domansky-Davidsohn, "Grossbetrieb."

this development was to be taken into consideration and, when possible, to be pushed forward; by no means was progress to be impeded. The equation of technological and social progress reflected in this economic determinism was the main reason why the DMV rejected any interference with production methods calculated to achieve this supposed progress. "The faster technology develops," the DMV was convinced, "the faster the capitalist modes of production will reach the point where it will have made itself superfluous and will have to be replaced by a higher form of production."[20]

Given this position, the DMV failed to respond to the concerns of two major strata of workers. On the one hand, it offered no perspectives to workers in large enterprises and heavy industry whose concerns increasingly arose from their confrontation with new calculation methods or the introduction of scientific management after the turn of the century. The great labor conflicts of that period not only occurred in the shipyards, but also in the metal industry of southern Germany: in 1908 at Brown, Boveri and Company (BBC) and in the Strebelwerk in Mannheim, and in 1913 at Bosch in Stuttgart. In all these conflicts new methods of calculation used in the piece-rate system were of central importance. Workers who were affected by changes in the work processes had to force the union's leadership to address this issue. At the union's convention in 1909, where the first major disputes over the union's strike strategy took place, some of the delegates pointed out that "recently...this calculation system has been introduced in all the larger firms" and that the union would have "to deal with this issue time and again in the future." They complained that "our officials are no longer familiar with the new working conditions."[21]

In addition, there were groups of traditional workers who had been affected by the transition from artisanal to industrial forms of production. This matter has recently been studied by Rudolf Boch for the first time, using the polishers in Solingen as an example.[22] These were skilled workers who, as Boch points out, while employed as free wage workers, were still integrated in an artisanal work process. They criticized the DMV because it was not prepared to resist the changes in their artisanal production system, but rather offered its support to those workers who were produced by these changes. Seen from the perspective of the Solingen workers, as Boch convincingly shows, the DMV was a union that oriented its action less on the concrete interest of workers than on theoretical assumptions about the development of the forces of production. They even accused the DMV of attempting to compel the workers, when they

20. *Die siebente ordentliche Generalversammlung des Deutschen Metallarbeiter-Verbandes.* Abgehalten vom 12.–17. Juni 1905 in Leipzig (Stuttgart, n.d.), p. 138.
21. *Die neunte ordentliche Generalversammlung des Deutschen Metallarbeiter-Verbandes in Hamburg.* Abgehalten vom 31. Mai bis 5. Juni 1909 (Stuttgart, n.d.), pp. 82, 113.
22. Boch, "Solinger Lokalgewerkschaften."

did not correspond to its idea of an industrial proletariat, to adjust to its concept, if necessary by force.[23]

It becomes evident how problematic the model of an industrial union was. It did not ideally meet the changed needs of a "modern" work force. On the contrary, a paradoxical situation emerged in which the industrial union, as conceived by the DMV, did not address the needs of the modern industrial workers. Rather it corresponded to the perspectives and interests of skilled workers. Consequently the argument that the principle of the industrial union was the most timely and natural organizational form in the phase of high industrialization becomes very tenuous. The characteristic "modernism" of this organizational form was primarily a political and ideological construct that was designed for and accepted by certain strata of workers, who were not in fact industrial workers.

So far it has not been possible to analyze precisely the main groups of supporters of the DMV, simply because detailed statistics about working conditions of the vocational groups in the DMV do not exist. In lieu of such studies a look at the union leadership will have to suffice in order to find out more about what type of worker was actually interested in an industrial union.[24]

After 1890, the generational shift in the German trade unions brought different kinds of workers to the top of the newly founded organizations. The DMV leadership, being between 30 and 40 years old, were distinctly younger than the SPD leadership. Though this also applied to the chairmen of the various craft unions, it appears that the DMV leadership differed from them in that they were confronted earlier with the shift away from artisanal work processes.

Martin Segitz, who at the time of the union's founding was a metalworkers' shop steward belonged to the independent masters of the batter craft, who were organized by the DMV. He consciously experienced the end of an artisanal craft, that of the sheet metal trade. Carl Severing, who in 1901 became a salaried director of the administrative office of the DMV in Bielefeld, completed an apprenticeship as a locksmith in an artisanal shop. Nonetheless, he had already become familiar with the advanced segmentation of the locksmith's work process. The shop where he worked procured semifinished products from wholesale dealers that were further processed according to set patterns. The working conditions of most locksmiths, who represented the largest group in the DMV before World War I, may well have been comparable. Alexander

---

23. Ibid., pp. 3ff., 225ff.
24. See Schönhoven, *Expansion*, pp. 233ff.; Ulrich Borsdorf, "Hans Böckler. Arbeit und Leben eines Gewerkschafters von 1875–1945," in *Schriftenreihe der Hans-Böckler-Stiftung 10*, (Cologne, 1982), pp. 24ff. Uta Stolle, *Arbeiterpolitik im Betrieb* (Frankfurt a.M. and New York, 1980), esp. pp. 233ff., 239ff. See esp. the recent study of Boch, "Solinger Lokalgewerkschaften," pp. 277ff.

Schlicke, who was union chairman from 1895 to 1919, had similar experiences as a precision mechanic. His school education – he attended a Gymnasium up to the Untersekunda – certainly contributed in no small way to rouse the interest and create the ability to view his own living and working conditions in their overall social context.

The impact of structural changes in some parts of the German metal industry on jobs and the job market of particular vocational groups led politically conscious workers of this economic sector to search for answers to the changes in their work situation as well as their market position. The idea of an organizational form that went beyond vocational boundaries received decisive impulses through the SPD's reception of Marxism during the period of the Anti-Socialist Law. Since leading representatives of the DMV experienced their political socialization at this time, it is not surprising that elements of Marxist social theory were essential in helping to create a new organizational and ideological reality, even if they were partially modified and possibly influenced by cooperation with the bourgeois social reformers.[25] In order to avoid the same economistic determinism it is necessary to find out what desires and strategies for solving problems existed and also what the limits of the solutions found were.

A mechanistic interpretation of Marxist theory formed the groundwork for the decision not to fight against the changes observed in the metal industry's job and job market situation. It was, after all, exactly in the course of this development that the transition from capitalism to socialism was supposed to occur. Hence, one of the DMV's self-appointed tasks was to safeguard the "overall interest" of the proletariat against the "special interests" of individual vocational groups.[26] These groups were perceived as unfit to understand the underlying meaning of the historical processes at work in the changes in the modes of production. As long as a capitalist society existed, conformance to the laws of capitalist production rather than a struggle against them provided the security of pushing forward the development of the whole society, while improving the workers' working and living conditions. Efficiency and cost-benefit calculations were, therefore, the new principles that the DMV tried to introduce into the organization of labor conflicts.[27]

The perception of labor as a product like all others led to the decision to organize not as a strike fund but as a cartel for selling labor. That the most promising strategy for representing interests was by securing a monopoly was something the DMV learned not only from Marxist theory but also from the cartelization effects in German industry.

According to this view, an industrial union was the necessary prerequisite

---

25. On the self-perception of the DMV see Domansky, "Arbeitskämpfe," pp. 52ff.
26. See also Boch, "Solinger Lokalgewerschaften," pp. 225ff.
27. See Domansky, "Arbeitskämpfe," pp. 167ff., 172ff., 208ff.

for insuring the organization of all workers. This, in turn, was made possible by the trends in capitalist development. The comprehensive organization of all workers likewise was the prerequisite for the effective functioning of the industrial union as a cartel. The calls for an extension of the organization, for limiting the fluctuation in membership, and for the elimination of the fragmentation of the trade union movement emerged as necessary consequences of this designation of tasks and functions.

The concept of industrial union and strike strategy

The DMV's self-perception as a cartel for selling labor and its efforts at efficiency in this respect made it imperative that the DMV find means for making the value of its product more independent of recurring crises rather than having it defined through temporary scarcity at times of strikes.[28] Just as was the case for employers, the control of demand and price agreements provided the appropriate cartel policy. The attempts of the DMV to influence the job market by introducing union unemployment payments and employment agencies with, at least, proportional representation, have to be viewed from this perspective. They can be understood as part of a union strategy for labor conflicts. The same was true for collective bargaining contracts that the union did not support in the 1890s, only because it considered success on this issue highly unlikely.

Because of their presumed futility, the DMV rejected any form of political general strikes, although general strikes in some European countries demonstrated around the turn of the century that such strikes were not necessarily doomed to failure.[29] The leading representatives of the DMV believed that a general strike could only be successful if very large numbers of workers, and ideally all workers of a country, participated. At the moment when such a mobilization of workers became possible, they argued, a general strike would be superfluous, because the workers would have already taken over political power. Changing social conditions with the help of strikes was unimaginable for a union that expected the restructuring of society to result from the further development of the capitalist system.

Even the rejection of all strikes that displayed the character of mere demonstrations rather than of revolt was mostly based on utilitarian grounds and on efficiency. Thus, the union board led a fierce fight against initially massive resistance on the part of a majority of union members for the abolition of 1 May as a day of rest. The DMV refused to pay support to members who struck for this demand or who were locked out because of May Day celebrations. The

---

28. For a more detailed account see ibid., pp. 151ff., 172ff., 208ff.

29. On politically motivated general strikes, see *Jahrbuch Arbeiterbewegung 1981. Politischer Streik* (Frankfurt a.M., 1981). Ibid also references to older publications on the subject.

DMV leadership maintained that the costs this incurred were at the expense of economic conflicts. It argued that the latter constituted the union's real task.

For similar reasons the union rejected so-called struggles for principles, such as strikes to insure workers' freedom of association as well as strikes over disciplinary punishments of workers. More decisive than the issue of their chances for success was the consideration whether the rehiring of one or more dismissed workers really justified the costs of a strike. The promise of material success was a minimum requirement for the launching of a strike.

The DMV would rather have avoided strikes for the attainment of economic demands altogether. From the beginning they were viewed as only the "ultima ratio" in conflicts between capital and labor. Underlying this position, especially in the early 1890s, was the belief that in a capitalist society workers could never achieve any lasting success. Hence, it was ultimately futile to fight for economic demands through strikes. The ever-recurring crises would periodically wipe out the workers' economic gains. This attitude yielded to a more positive assessment of the chances of success for strikes during the period of the economic boom in the second half of the 1890s. Nonetheless, the union preferred to employ this tool as seldom as possible because this form of conflict was considered to be basically inferior to others. The costs involved were too high. Added to that was the fear of the unforeseen consequences of strikes. The "strike fever" of 1896, especially the dockworkers' strike of 1896–7 in Hamburg, made clear to the DMV how little its conception of calculated settlements of labor conflicts was rooted among the workers and how easily strikes could turn into actions that threatened the very survival of the organization.

Furthermore, as Frank Trommler has shown, the DMV's relation to work was as unclear as that of the SPD.[30] On the one hand, the DMV believed in the "alienation" of workers under capitalism. On the other hand, their view of "work as a source of all culture" led to the equating of absenteeism with "laziness." It was irreconcilable with this view to conceive of the decision not to work as another form of human self-realization. Joint excursions of strikers, steamboat trips, and theatre programs were to be found in Germany only in the early phase of unionized organizations and later outside the union framework. The DMV leadership was completely unsympathetic to the wildcat strikes of the shipwrights, which were often celebrated with bibulous harmonica parties. For the DMV leadership, strikes were an issue of the temporary withdrawl of labor from the job market. As such, they were simply another form of enhancing the value of labor on the market. Strikes were seen as part of the process of selling labor, but not as a temporary suspension of this process.

---

30. Frank Trommler, "Die Nationalisierung der Arbeit," in Reinhold Grimm and Jost Hermand, eds., *Arbeit als Thema in der deutschen Literatur vom Mittelalter bis zur Gegenwart* (Königstein/Ts., 1979), pp. 102–25.

Strikes, therefore, required the same behavior as all other components of cartel strategy: planning, order, discipline.

In the 1890s the development and the implementation of such a strike strategy was one of the major goals of the DMV. It had to be pushed through among the membership to end the "anarchy which predominated in strike matters."[31] Inseparably connected with this strategy was the enforcement of the concept of an industrial union, which was neither that of a strike fund nor an automatic money dispenser as numerous members believed. Their strike behavior in the 1890s clearly showed that many members were not aware of the implications of the union's strike strategy. Up to the turn of the century the union leadership did not cease to complain that most union members staged strikes without taking into consideration the economic situation, the chance of obtaining their demands, the problems of financing the strikes, the strength of the employers, and, last but not least, the interests of other groups organized in the union. The rules governing strikes were worked out only after fierce debates between the union leadership and union members over the integration that the leadership sought to achieve, as well as its endeavor to make cost-benefit calculations the basis of strike behavior.

The precondition for this was for the union leadership to gain control over strikes by its members. The union board gradually succeeded in achieving these objectives at the union conventions between 1893 and 1897.[32] After 1897, strikes could only be initiated with the board's approval: offensive strikes were to be registered three months before being launched, and defensive strikes and lockouts had to be reported twenty-four hours in advance. Strikers were obligated to give weekly reports about the progress of their strike actions. When such a report was not filed, the union board could discontinue support. The right to draw strike support was made dependent upon the length of union membership (at least twenty-six weeks) in order to reduce the possibility of workers joining the union only for the duration of a strike. Neither the membership nor the local union officials could carry out even approved strikes independently. The union bylaws directed them to act according to the instructions simultaneously sent to them with the approval of the union board. The board secured itself the right to send an authorized representative to the strike area, whose task it was above all to check if the labor conflict was carried out along the guidelines set by the bylaws.

More decisive than these rules concerning strike procedure was the provision for criteria according to which the union board determined whether a strike should be approved or not. The leadership had to consider the overall economic situation as well as the special situation of the affected vocational groups.

---

31. *Deutsche Metallarbeiter-Zeitung* 11, no. 20 (20 May 1893): 3.
32. Domansky, "Arbeitskämpfe," pp. 179ff.

Moreover, they had to assess the union's financial situation to determine if it could withstand another strike. Beginning in 1903, the strength of employers' organizations became a crucial criterion, and the limitation of strikes to bread-and-butter issues was prescribed. At least on paper the underlying assumption for this strategy became a generally recognized guideline. Strikes were not to deal with moral questions, with enforcing demands that were "just," but rather with power and interests.

According to the bylaws of 1897, an offensive strike had the best chances of being approved if the overall economic situation was good and unemployment was low. This criterion had to apply to the particular situation of the branch affected by the strike, too. In addition, strikes in response to disciplinary actions were not allowed. The reduction of working hours had to be a primary goal of strikes. The chances for initiating a strike increased if the overwhelming majority of DMV members agreed to it in a secret vote. To start a strike while larger actions were taking place elsewhere was considered hopeless. In all cases it was necessary to prove that attempts had been made before the strike to negotiate with the employers. The responsible locals had to present convincing reports about the situation favoring the strike. Last but not least, approval was always contingent on the financial capacity of the DMV to cover the costs of the strike.

These essential points of the DMV strike strategy remained substantially unchanged until World War I. Just how much the leadership was able to assert its concept of an industrial union and its strike strategy is evident from the decreasing numbers of complaints by the board about violations of strike regulations. Another proof of the successful enforcement of union regulations is the fact that in 1907 the vast majority of union members supported curtailing the Berlin local administration's privilege of being the only local organization entitled to start wage movements independently. Opposition had grown mainly because of the Berliners' practice of using the largest portion of their revenues for their own purposes. Many union delegates hoped to enhance the chances to improve the conditions of provincial workers by containing the wage movement in Berlin. While the General Convention did not take the risk of officially repealing the autonomy of the Berlin organization, it was nonetheless termed a "danger for the general welfare," and the union board was entrusted with the task of negotiating an end to Berlin's exceptional position. With this, the industrial union's principle of putting the general welfare ahead of the interests of particular groups of workers was generally accepted.[33]

Other measures were adopted to support the statutory regulations, aimed at taking the heat out of labor conflicts and making them a scientifically planned exercise. One of them was the decision to participate in state unemployment reports. With better information about the work force, union officials hoped to

33. Ibid., pp. 201ff., 235ff.

334

improve their ability to judge the chances of the success of strikes. Moreover, the DMV tried to revive the system of shop stewards, and in some places to improve it, in order to gain more exact information about conditions inside factories. For the same reason the union leadership encouraged the local administrations regularly to conduct surveys about the working conditions in individual factories. It was argued that this was the only way to formulate "well-founded" demands – that is, demands that were attainable and in the interest of the union.[34]

When preparing strike demands, the union leadership was guided by the principle that maximalist demands ought to be avoided along with the raising of too many issues.[35] The former could arouse unwarranted hopes among the workers, while the latter made employers intractable to negotiations. Since only well-founded demands were supposed to be introduced, it was strictly forbidden to have striking workers put forward their own demands. Demands were only to be prepared by the local union office with the agreement of the district administration. They subsequently were to be submitted to a meeting of strike-ready workers.

The objective of a strike, which was to be as free as possible of emotion, was supposed to be achieved through increasing bureaucratization in the preparation and conduct of strikes. Thus, the correspondence in wage disputes was strictly regulated to the point of specifying what type of seal should be used on certain letters. Modeled after the procedures of the Prussian provincial administration, the correspondence followed strictly prescribed channels that ran from the members of the DMV through the local union office and the district administration up to the union board, and vice versa. The progress of a given wage conflict had to be reported regularly in detailed statements. Local union officials were sworn to treat matters in question "objectively". In order to achieve this goal, it was ruled that only those workers who participated directly in the strike were allowed to attend meetings where strike demands were to be voted on. In those cases when the workers at such as meeting showed signs of becoming strongly emotional, the local union administration had to postpone the vote. Union functionaries were also supposed to make sure that voters were not able to see each other's ballots. The election rules corresponded to those of the state and national elections. There were election committees, voting lists, ballot boxes, and special ballots. Members who were eligible to vote had to identify themselves. Propaganda for or against a strike was forbidden at the polling station.

Once a strike was approved, each striking worker had to report twice a day to a place determined by the strike committee. Only "experienced and calm" individuals were supposed to be picketers and, if possible, they were to exercise

34. Ibid., p. 226.
35. Ibid., pp. 253ff.

this function no longer than two hours in a row. Picketers were instructed not to tolerate any "gathering of curious colleagues" around the picket line. Advice to union members to avoid pubs during strikes and to stay clear of picket lines and of the enterprises struck was aimed at preventing the emotionalization of the strikes, which in the union officials' view might lead to confrontation with the authorities and to more obdurate resistance of the employers.

The image of the employers propagated by the union was also intended to contribute to the deemotionalization of strikes.[36] The employer was perceived as an "official," simply playing his allotted role of developing capitalism to its exhaustion. Thus, the request that union members should refrain from attacking their employers personally was not surprising.

An identification of the interests of workers and employers was implicit in the DMV's social theory. It remained a basis for union actions even when it became evident after the turn of the century that employers increasingly resorted to lockouts as a means in their power struggle against the working class, rather than as interest-oriented economic instruments. Since the union leadership was convinced that the unions were an indispensable part of capitalist society, the DMV leadership could not conceive that the elimination of unions could be a rational goal of the employers' policy.

The DMV felt that the "lockout epidemic" in the decade preceding the First World War was due to a lack of understanding of the progressive laws of social development by narrow-minded employers. The DMV expected that the new generation of employers who were speeding up the rationalization of their factories could not but recognize the importance of union organizations to assure the uninterrupted flow of production. This notion was quickly dispensed in practice. The labor conflict at Bosch in Stuttgart in 1913 was not the first to demonstrate that the development in plant organization was leading to increasing separation of administrative and blue-collar work, which could make interest-oriented unions superfluous because work was now defined objectively. The new managers and employers conceived of working hours and wages as categories that one could objectivize. To determine hours and wages one simply had to develop appropriate methods for measuring these factors, which made all disputes unnecessary.[37]

The rejection of the bonus pay at the 1905 union convention is the sole indication that the DMV sensed this possibility as well. The Incentive Pay System was not rejected because of a worsening of the metalworkers' working conditions, although this was discussed at great length, but rather because of its possible negative consequences for the willingness of the workers to organize

---

36. Ibid., pp. 339ff.
37. Heidrun Homburg, "Anfänge des Taylorsystems in Deutschland vor dem Ersten Weltkrieg. Eine Problemskizze unter besonderer Berücksichtigung der Arbeitskämpfe bei Bosch 1913," *Geschichte und Gesellschaft* 4 (1978): 170–94. See also Stolle, *Arbeiterpolitik*, pp. 146ff.

themselves. Union officials feared that individual competition among the workers would result from that system, similar to what happened under the piece-rate system.[38] Aside from this exception, the DMV attempted to adapt the goals of its strikes to the technological development. It modernized its catalogue of demands. Demands for the abolition of the piece-rate system were replaced in time by requests for its regulation. Likewise the DMV abandoned its demands for the prohibition of work on Sundays and of overtime, because it did not want to hinder work procedures that reflected the "current state of technology."

The DMV strike strategy was, without a doubt, a successful contribution to the establishment of the concept of the industrial union among the workers in the metal industry. Social protest had largely been eliminated as an element of the actions of organized metalworkers by the beginning of the twentieth century. Utilitarianism and cost-benefit assumptions as well as the idea of suprapersonal collective interests of the working class had asserted themselves. With this, the DMV made a decisive contribution to the homogenization of the working class. The costs of this development were very similar to those in the productive sphere. The relations among workers and employers were formalized and depersonalized in the transition from artisanal to factory production. The relation between workers and their representatives underwent the same change during the transition from branch to industrial organization. The relation between the rank and file and the union leadership was shaped by growing anonymity and by hierarchy. There was hardly any direct contact between both sides after the turn of the century. The reasons for the conflicts that arose between the masses of workers and the leadership of German unions shortly before World War I should be understood as symptoms of this alienation process that was accompanied by signs of crises that were analogous to those which resulted from the alienation process in the production sphere.

Therefore we need to ask whether the DMV's rationalization strategy was as successful in achieving material gains for its members as the capitalist strategy was for the profit of the employers.

Scientific management and labor conflict strategy: the repoliticization of the struggle between capital and labor

The changes in labor conflict in the metal industry after 1903

The quantitative analysis of the labor conflicts led by the DMV demonstrates that its range of actions did not increase in accordance with

---

38. Domansky, "Arbeitskämpfe," pp. 245ff. See also Gunnar Stollberg, *Die Rationa-lisierungsdebatte 1908–1933. Freie Gewerschaften zwischen Mitbestimmung und Gegenwehr* (Frankfurt a.M. and New York, 1981).

the consolidation of the union, but actually declined. The number of work stoppages approved by the DMV shows a clear slowdown in growth.[39] While the number of strikes and strikers grew in absolute terms, their number only doubled from 1901 to 1905, and from 1906 to 1910, when compared to the preceding five years. In the years from 1895 to 1899, however, there had been five times as many strikes compared to the period of 1890 to 1894. The same is true of the share of union members who participated in strikes. Until 1903 participants grew steadily. In that year the proportion of striking union members reached 6.4%. This was only slightly exceeded in 1906, 1910, and 1911. In all other years a smaller proportion of union members struck than in 1903; that is, as the union grew, its members became less involved in strike activities.

Single strikes occurring in one locality and in one shop still predominated in work stoppages.[40] Ninety percent of workers involved in defensive strikes participated in strikes affecting one shop only. In the 1890s the same was true of approximately half of the workers participating in offensive strikes. After the turn of the century the share of single-shop strikes dropped by about 13%, but the difference was minimal. Now the majority of strikes affected between two and nineteen shops. So-called general strikes that encompassed all firms of a specific vocational group in one town involved one-fifth of the strikers before and after 1900. They were initiated mainly by plumbers, pipe fitters, batters, file cutters, heating assemblers, molders, and electrical fitters. The plumbers alone staged almost half of the general strikes after 1900. Their activities were due to the small shop size in this trade. In any case, the expansion of the DMV did not make the occurrence of more general strikes more frequent than before the turn of the century. Nor did it improve chances for general strikes in other than the traditional vocational groups.

The number of strikes in large firms increased after 1900, yet the change by comparison with the 1890s does not appear to be so significant as one might assume at first. Between 1901 and 1913 close to 30% of the strikers worked in firms with 100 to 1,000 employees and 27% in firms with more than 1,000 employees.

After 1900 the number of strikers increased especially in enterprises of more than 1,000 but less than 10,000 workers. Strike costs also increased, by 80% in offensive strikes and 50% in defensive strikes. The increase in costs incurred in offensive strikes was due to the fact that after the turn of the century they lasted longer than defensive strikes. Between 1907 and 1913 only 30% of the workers participating in offensive strikes and 54% participating in defensive strikes were able to end their strike within one or two weeks.[41] It is highly questionable

---

39. Cf. Domansky, "Arbeitskämpfe," pp. 79ff.
40. Ibid., pp. 102ff.
41. Ibid., pp. 120ff.

338

that conflict behavior grew more rational if we consider that after 1900, the average length of strikes decreased, but that the shorter strikes had fewer participants.

An analysis of strike results gives rise to similar doubts. The percentage of completely unsuccessful strikes decreased after 1900. This, however, resulted primarily from the centralization of labor conflicts that was enforced by the union, rather than from an increase of union power. As previously stated, the strike strategy was oriented on the achievable and on entrepreneurial strength and, therefore, observed very carefully the limits that were set by its class enemy.

The success of union strategy becomes entirely questionable, if one keeps in mind that after 1903 numerous strikes had to be discontinued because the DMV feared the precipitation of a lockout – a very realistic fear because almost all large lockouts before the First World War were in retaliation to strikes.[42] This was true of the lockouts in the Bavarian metal industry and the Berlin electronic industry in 1905; the lockout of molders and unskilled foundry workers during the wage dispute of 1906; the lockouts in the shipbuilding industry in 1907, 1908, and 1910; the lockouts resulting from strikes at BBC and in the Strebelwerk in Mannheim in 1908; the lockout in connection with the chain makers' labor conflict in Pforzheim in 1910; the wage conflict of casting and unskilled foundry workers in Chemnitz, the metal casters in Leipzig, and in the metal industry of Thuringia in 1911; the lockouts in the province of Saxony and in Thuringia and in connection with the labor conflict at four firms in Frankfurt in 1912, and of the strike at Bosch in Stuttgart in 1913. It is impossible to determine how many strike actions were rejected because of the fear of lockouts. In any case, after 1905 the union leadership warned increasingly against "ill-considered" strikes. The labor conflicts in the Berlin electronic industry in 1905, and at the Strebelwerk in Mannheim and the Howaldt shipyard in Kiel in 1908 were examples of the DMV making conciliatory moves due to the threat of lockouts.

Indeed, lockouts became the dominant form of labor conflict after the turn of the century.[43] The number of workers affected by lockouts increased substantially faster than the number of strikers. From 1903 on, at least one-third of workers involved in labor conflicts were locked out each year. In 1905 more than three-fourths of the participants in labor conflicts were locked out. In 1908, 1910, and 1911, the number of locked-out workers likewise exceeded the number of strikers, though not to such a degree as in 1905.

Strikes stood in the shadow of lockouts also with respect to their scope. Lockouts continuously involved more and larger firms as well as a larger

42. Ibid., p. 144.
43. Ibid., pp. 79ff. See also Michael Schneider, *Aussperrung. Ihre Geschichte und Funktion vom Kaiserreich bis heute* (Frankfurt a.M., 1980), esp. pp. 21ff., 61ff.

number of participants than did strikes. From 1901 to 1913, almost 60% of all locked-out workers were involved in lockouts affecting more than one, and usually all firms of a single town, region, or branch. Two-thirds of the workers locked out were employed in firms with more than 1,000 employees, and nearly half were caught up in lockouts that kept more than 20,000 workers idle. One-third of the workers concerned was involved in labor conflicts that lasted one to two weeks; another third, however, in conflicts that lasted seven to thirteen weeks. Because of their larger scope and length, lockouts devoured substantially more union funds than strikes. They were fourteen times more expensive than defensive strikes, and five times more expensive than offensive ones.

The DMV had to face two specific handicaps in regard to lockouts. It could not influence the decision for or against lockouts; yet, lockouts decidedly restricted its financial resources, and therefore its margin of action. This situation applied to the defensive strikes as well. Indeed, defensive strikes and lockouts jointly accounted for half of all the DMV expenditures on work stoppages during the two decades preceding the First World War, with the exception of six years, four of which were before 1900. More important than the restriction of the union margin of action through lockouts, and even more through the lockouts and defensive strikes combined, is the change in the causes of labor conflicts after the turn of the century.[44] In both decades before the First World War disputes over wages and hours surfaced as the primary causes of offensive and defensive strikes. But after 1900 demands for wage increases clearly prevailed in offensive strikes. This is surprising in view of the union's objective of achieving reductions in hours and its distinct preference for those strikes that sought to achieve this goal. The trend in favor of demanding wage increases was due in part to the strong conviction of workers that the cost of living was rising steadily. They were continuously and primarily concerned with securing their standard of living instead of concentrating on the interests of the union, namely demands for job security, minimum wages, additional pay for night shifts and for works on Sundays, and so on. While in this respect the union tactic was countered by the economic development, the decline in the demands for shorter working hours after 1905 can be traced back to the massive pressure exerted by the employers. In 1905 and 1906, the DMV achieved the highest average reductions in working hours in its strike history: 3.2 and 3.6 hours per worker per week, respectively. With this, however, a limit was reached that the employers stubbornly defended.

A further qualitative change in labor conflicts concerned collective wage agreements. Such agreements were demanded by at least one-fifth of all strikers after the turn of the century. This documents the assertion of the

44. Domansky, "Arbeitskämpfe," pp. 129ff., 240.

concept of collective agreements within the DMV that was pushed through during the general convention of 1903.

The increasing importance of demands in the second half of the decade preceding the First World War to regulate rather than to abolish piece-rate work and to improve pay scales for night shift and Sunday work clearly reflects the technical and organizational conditions of plants in which newly organized workers were employed, as opposed to the traditional union membership. "Classical" demands for wage increases and shorter working hours played only an insignificant role among the causes of the most spectacular labor disputes, the extensive lockouts in the decade before World War I.[45] Resistance to lower piece-rate wages and arbitrarily determined piece rates were more predominant. This was the case in the labor conflicts at BBC, in the Strebelwerk in Mannheim and in the shipbuilding industry in the years from 1907 to 1913. These trends in the patterns of labor conflicts were thus the results of the organizational changes in firms that took place in Germany in those years. The further development of capitalist modes of production threatened the DMV in two ways. First, it was the cause of numerous labor disputes. Second, the employers saw scientific management as their chance to effectively weaken the unions. By introducing scientific management, they could take advantage of the DMV's modernism and of its industrial union model.

The modernism of the DMV brought it into conflict with those of its members who were especially affected by rationalization and intensification of work processes. The industrial union model allowed the employers to exercise maximum pressure, since each strike of a craft group could be escalated to lockouts encompassing all metalworkers. It was possible, therefore, for crises arising in connection with the rationalization of production to turn into major crises within the DMV.

This dismal picture was not brightened by the increase in the number of peaceful wage negotiations after 1904, and in collective wage agreements after 1903.[46] Collective agreements were generally reached only in the small- and medium-sized firms of the construction trades (plumbers, mechanics, heating assemblers) as opposed to larger firms. There were also hardly any supra-regional collective agreements. Most collective agreements were signed in the major cities in southern Germany.

Besides, numerous wage agreements could only be reached with the help of

---

45. Ibid., pp. 349ff.

46. Ibid., pp. 278ff. See also Peter Ullmann, *Tarifverträge und Tarifpolitik in Deutschland bis 1914. Entstehung und Entwicklung, interessenpolitische Bedingungen und Bedeutung des Tarifvertragswesens für die sozialistischen Gewerschaften* (Frankfurt a.M., Las Vegas, and Bern, 1977). Jutta Rabenschlag-Kräusslich, *Parität statt Klassenkampf? Zur Organisation des Arbeitsmarktes und Domestizierung des Arbeitskampfes in Deutschland und England 1900–1918* (Frankfurt a.M. and Bern, 1981).

strikes. Some of the large lockouts before the First World War, like the one in the Bavarian metal industry in 1905, resulted from wage disputes, the goal of which was wage agreements. Even more serious than the fact that collective agreements did not replace wage disputes, and in many cases actually incited them, was that the DMV's scope of action could be restricted by collective agreements. Union members sometimes tended to accept unfavorable conditions in order to conclude a wage agreement. Altogether it can be ascertained that many collective agreements were concluded at the urging of the rank-and-file members, notwithstanding the reluctance of the union leadership.

There were several reasons for this reluctance. In the first place, collective wage agreements exposed the basic weakness of the DMV. The success of workers in small- and medium-sized firms (above all the construction trades) in attaining collective wage agreements made the failure to achieve this concept in big industry – the industrial sector that the DMV wanted foremost to organize – stand out. The GDM and the Central Association of German Industrialists (Centralverband Deutscher Industrieller, CDI) before the First World War flatly rejected all the DMV initiatives to discuss the possible terms of such an agreement. As a result, 87% of all employees in the metal industry were still without signed collective agreements in 1914. In fact, the percentage of metalworkers working with such agreements declined after 1907. Besides, the number of agreements with single firms, which the DMV viewed as "makeshift," far outweighed the local, branch- and districtwide collective agreements for which they strove during the entire period.

Even more important, many of the collective agreements initiated through union pressure were not formally concluded between union and employer organizations. At the very most, in only one-fourth of the settlements the DMV was entrusted with monitoring the compliance with the agreement. In more than half of the cases, supervisory wage commissions composed of workers and representatives of the firm management were appointed for this purpose. The DMV board correctly recognized the danger inherent in such agreements, which helped foster the view that the regulation of working conditions and the shaping of cooperative relationships between employees and employers could be reached without the intervention of the unions.

The restriction of collective wage agreements to artisanal vocations and the exclusion of the unions from being contract partners clearly qualify the conclusion drawn by researchers who cite the collective agreements reached during these years as evidence of union strength. The same obviously applies to the so-called peaceful wage disputes – settlements of differences through negotiations without strikes – that took place on a large scale after 1904.[47] In assessing the importance of these "peaceful" disputes, one must consider that very often they

---

47. Domansky, "Arbeitskämpfe," pp. 323ff.

342

involved petty demands that could hardly create grounds for a strike. On the other hand, certain types of demands were never included in such negotiations. This was especially the case for all issues related to piece-rate work. In fact, the increase in the number of peaceful wage disputes reduced neither the growth nor the severity of labor conflicts after 1904. Half of these disputes were negotiated directly between workers and employers, and in those instances where unions participated, locals rather than the central organizations were involved. Available information also suggests that one-third of the participating employers did not belong to any employers' association and, contrary to the suggestions of the DMV, the participation even of organized employers could not be equated with the actual involvement of employers' organizations.

Although this way of settling wage disputes was not new, the DMV only began to compile statistics about peaceful wage disputes in 1904. More DMV members were implicated in such negotiations than in open conflicts. Partly the union was impelled to present its members an image of greater success than that which it had achieved in open labor conflicts. Even the board's own report at the general convention of 1899 stated: "Our struggle with the industrialists has hitherto resembled guerilla war."[48] Massive criticism of the board's strike strategy – first articulated at a general convention in 1901 – accused it of "killing strikes."[49] The board reacted to this criticism by making collective agreements an official goal of union strategy, thereby meeting the wish of a part of its members. This happened at the 1903 union convention. The documentation provided of the peaceful regulation of wage disputes should be seen in this context.

In addition, the union board continued to pursue its goal of extending the organization's internal system of support. This was especially true of unemployment support, which appeared to the board to be the central means for controlling the job market after its attempts to establish union employment agencies had proven unsuccessful.[50] Union unemployment payments were introduced in the DMV in 1899, after having been regularly rejected at the preceding union conventions. The DMV apparatus for unemployment support and its expansion in 1905 document the general acceptance of a strategy of long-term job market control over the short-term exploitation of opportunities created by economic developments. Through the expansion of the union unemployment support program, its board hoped to attract new members and to strengthen their ties to the organization. That the DMV expected to buttress

48. Deutscher Metallarbeiter-Verband. *Protokoll der IV. ordentlichen Generalversammlung zu Halle a. S. Abgehalten vom 4. bis 8. April 1899* (Stuttgart, n.d.), p. 21.

49. Domansky, "Arbeitskämpfe," pp. 208ff.

50. Ibid., pp. 261ff. But cf. Klaus Schönhoven, "Selbsthilfe als Form von Solidarität. Das gewerkschaftliche Unterstützungswesen im Deutschen Kaiserreich bis 1914," *Archiv für Sozialgeschichte* 20 (1980): 147–93.

its market position as a cartel for the sale of labor has already been demonstrated above. This policy, however, remained quite as unsuccessful as the strike strategy of the union. The introduction of unemployment payments did not significantly improve the ability of the DMV to increase its rosters. Neither could the fluctuation of the DMV membership be stemmed. The latter was ultimately dependent on economic developments. As long as their collective action did not acquire a monopolistic character due to insufficient organization, metalworkers still had to take advantage of market opportunities as individuals. Since only those workers organized in the free unions enjoyed the right of receiving unemployment support, the original hope of reducing the use of scabs was not achieved either.

Unemployment support did, however, help in decreasing the number of labor conflicts. By extending support to members who lost their jobs through disciplinary measures or lockouts, a number of strikes were avoided. Furthermore, the union saved money thereby, as the cost of unemployment support amounted to less than that for strike support. It cannot be overlooked, however, that unemployment benefits also contributed to the reduction of labor conflicts, because in periods of crisis the union was so burdened with payments that it was forced to refrain from labor conflicts. The extraordinarily steep decline in the number of strikes, especially offensive strikes, in 1908–9, as compared to the crisis-ridden years of 1901–2, was mainly due to the strain on union funds, which were badly depleted by benefit payments. For unemployed members alone the union had to provide three million marks. Compensation for strikes – in fact strikes and lockouts together – did not even make up 10% of the total union expenditure for support in both these years. Offensive strikes accounted in fact for only 1% of total expenditure. In 1908 this precarious situation – the union was close to financial ruin – caused the union leadership to clamp down on labor conflicts. By failing to inform the members about the union's financial situation, the DMV helped to fuel the debates at the 1909 general convention over the union strike strategy that arose from this abrupt change of policy.[51]

These debates lasted until the beginning of the First World War. They are hardly to be explained in terms of the tactical mistakes made by the union leadership on individual occasions, but rather in terms of its inability to see labor conflicts as anything but purely economic conflicts. The union leadership clung to this fiction even though the lockouts of 1905–6 and 1910 made it abundantly clear that employers were primarily interested in using labor conflicts as instruments of power politics. Even when in 1906 the GDM responded for the first time to a molders' wage movement initiated by the DMV with threats of a "total lockout," not only of all metal casters but of all metalworkers in the German Empire, the DMV wrote in its yearbook: "We are thoroughly

---

51. Domansky, "Arbeitskämpfe," pp. 349ff.

convinced that the lock-out epidemic which is presently rampant in Germany is a completely temporary occurrence in the economic dispute between capital and labor over wages and hours and that this lock-out epidemic will destroy itself."[52]

The following years would prove the inaccuracy of this appraisal. The implementation of lockouts as an instrument of power politics would eventually lead to a politicization of union members and union leadership alike, although in different ways.

The model of the industrial union in crisis

At the DMV's 1909 union convention in Hamburg, it became evident for the first time that the DMV was divided into two political wings.[53] One faction supported the course followed by the union board; the other carried the banner of union democracy. The latter demanded that the rank and file should take a greater part in the board's decision making, either through strike ballots or other procedures. Despite some serious controversy about certain issues, both factions were united in their dissatisfaction "with the entire development, with the tactics, in short with the entire system dominating the situation in the union lately."[54]

This dissatisfaction resulted on the one hand from the response of the DMV to the organizational restructuring of firms in German heavy industry, a response that was bound to disappoint many of the rank and file. On the other hand, it was due to the fact that in the great labor conflicts of the prewar decade the DMV had failed to prevail over employers. Most union members ascribed this failure not so much to the powerful position of the employers as to a basic flaw in the DMV strike tactics. The rank-and-file critique was directed less at its class enemy than it was at its own organization. How could this happen?

The great labor conflicts in the metal industry between 1907 and 1913 had made it clear that the DMV strike strategy had proven unsuccessful in heavy industry. The union's insistence on negotiating on the level of central organizations only and its claim to run labor conflicts centrally had been exploited by employers for their own ends. They accepted negotiations in order to gain time and to worsen the position of the workers and, furthermore, rarely felt bound by the settlements agreed upon.

The strike at BBC in Mannheim in 1908 was settled by negotiations between the DMV and the "Employers' Association in the Metal Industry in Würtemberg, Baden, and the Bordering Districts." The association refused, how-

---

52. *Der Deutsche Metallarbeiter-Verband im Jahre 1906. Jahrund Handbuch für Verbandsmitglieder*, ed. by Vorstand des Deutschen Metallarbeiter-Verbandes (Stuttgart, 1907), p. 42.
53. Domansky, "Arbeitskämpfe," pp. 349ff.
54. *Die neunte ordentliche Generalversammlung des DMV*, p. 86.

ever, any responsibility for its member firms' readiness to abide by the terms of the settlement. Complaints of the DMV were left unanswered. The settlement existed merely on paper.

In the foundry workers' dispute in Chemnitz in 1911, the employers were playing for time. In deciding who was to be in charge of the negotiations, the buck was passed repeatedly between individual firms and the Employers' Association. In this case, too, the employers did not consider themselves bound by the agreement that was arrived at only after weeks of negotiations. In the molders' dispute in Leipzig, the DMV suffered defeat mainly because the employers attempted to forestall any settlement until the workers were forced to accept minimal offers in the last minute negotiations that took place under the pressure of a lockout threat.

The DMV's strategy ran into difficulties especially in the shipyards.[55] The agreements reached with the German Seashipyards Caucus of the GDM in 1907 were not honored by the individual shipyards. In 1910 negotiations between the DMV and the GDM lasted for four weeks and ended without any material success for the workers. Disputed points were explicitly left to local negotiations. Particularly in the shipyards of Hamburg, the owners argued that further negotiations were superfluous, because everything had been settled at the central level. It was all too obvious that the central negotiations had only aimed at forestalling the conflict and weakening the position of the DMV.

The dispute of 1910, which ended in complete failure, induced the DMV to call for local negotiations from the start and to rely on workers' representatives from individual shipyards in 1913. In contrast to previous practice, a catalogue of demands was drawn up in 1913, which did not deal with all the demands in detail but allowed the workers of individual shipyards to negotiate on wage differentials. This was the first time that the DMV deviated from its concept of central negotiations. The shipyards, however, did not comply. They insisted on central negotiations, although permitting the participation of local representatives of the shipyards and workers. These negotiations did not lead to any satisfactory results, particularly because after two weeks, the employers categorically rejected further negotiations at a local level. The attempt of the union board to initiate central negotiations between the two organizations finally failed because the shipwrights, convinced of the futility of such negotiations, went on strike without the consent of the DMV.

This behavior resulted from the shipwrights' experience with unofficial strikes that had become nearly everyday occurrences in the shipyards. Through

---

55. See the recent study of Marina Cattaruzza, "Das Hamburgische Modell der Beziehung zwischen Arbeit und Kapital. Organisationsprobleme und Konfliktverhalten auf den Werften 1890–1914," in Arno Herzig, Dieter Langewiesche, and Arnold Sywottek, eds., *Arbeiter in Hamburg, Unterschichten, Arbeiter und Arbeiterbewegung seit dem ausgehended 18. Jahrhundert* (Hamburg, 1983), pp. 347ff.

346

wildcat strikes the workers were often able to take advantage of profitable orders for their shipyards. Not only were they often able to secure spectacular wage increases, which were out of reach in disputes conducted along official guidelines, but occasionally they were even able to establish demands that the union board would have rejected as futile, like the rehiring of dismissed workers. The explosive force of these forms of actions increased, because the source of their success was partially based on their violation of DMV statutes. If the statutory registration period for strikes had been observed, strikes in the wake of short-term lucrative orders would have been ruled out altogether.

Other vocational groups came to the same conclusion as the shipwrights; the strike tactics of the DMV might well be in the union's interest, but not necessarily in the interest of its rank and file. This experience induced heating assemblers, engravers, chasers, gold- and silversmiths, as well as shipwrights to consider consolidating their vocational groups within the DMV, or even establishing their own trade organizations again. Given the existence of the DMV, however, the latter course proved impossible. An internal opposition was formed instead. Delegates at the 1909 and 1913 union conventions considered this development to be related to the "increasing hostility in the antagonism between workers and employers in the metal industry." But members of the internal opposition also criticized the union's "wavering policy" and, at the same time, its "dictatorship," its "absolutism." Paul Dittmann, a delegate from Hamburg, called the union leadership a "praetorian guard," and compared it to the janissaries in the Middle Ages.[56]

The opposition failed, however, to offer a clear tactical alternative.[57] Their demand not to be deterred by every threat of a lockout, and instead to take recourse more often to special levies in order to sack up their funds during lockouts, did not present a real solution for existing problems. Neither in 1909 nor in 1913 did a discussion about the aims and contents of union policies take place that would have shown the connection between the immobility and inflexibility of the DMV in class and labor conflicts and the organizational form of industrial union. A large part of the opposition hoped to reach a solution for these problems by democratizing the decision-making process, especially in the organization of labor conflicts. There was disunity over the question whether to attach the demand for "more democracy" in every case to strike ballots, or whether it sufficed to retain the mode of voting used in the past and to bind the board to resolutions of the membership. This was a far cry indeed from the board's notion of democracy. Still, to expect a solution of these problems solely through changes in the decision-making process was somewhat naive, since the problems were in fact deeply rooted in the ideological concept and organ-

---

56. Die neunte ordentliche Generalversammlung des DMV, pp. 86ff., 113.
57. Domansky, "Arbeitskämpfe," pp. 347ff.

izational makeup of the DMV as a labor cartel. The internal union opposition was less concerned with a general revision of union actual policy than with a general "politicization" of the union by giving the rank and file a greater say.

The union leadership, however, failed to respond to the intensification of class conflict. They did not recognize that the latter was the source for the criticism of the rank and file. The leadership did not change tactics but tried to save its organizational priorities, and, implicitly, its own concept for organizing class struggle. It did however, attempt to win a majority over to its policies. A special convention was called in 1913 to confirm the decision of the board to block local funds and withhold support in a dispute arising from a wildcat strike in the shipyards. The board won the day only by a slight margin. In 1909 and 1913 the board tried to discredit the internal opposition by suggesting that it was infected by the ideas of the anarchist-syndicalist movement, but this effort was to no avail.

These attempts aimed at protecting the organization against the danger within. In order to protect itself against the external threat posed by the employers' strengthened position, the union resorted to new policies that were to be increasingly employed during the First World War and under the Weimar Republic: the substitution of industrial disputes by improvements in working and living conditions achieved through welfare policies.[58] In 1907 the DMV compiled statistical evidence on wages and working conditions of workers in steel mills that was submitted to the Reichstag in the form of a memorandum.[59] The DMV chose this course because it believed that steelworkers shunned the unions due to allegedly oppressive working conditions, as well as to the power of employers. By improving the social conditions of the steelworkers, the DMV hoped to increase their readiness to join the union. It was generally believed that better-off workers would be more willing to do so. The fact that already at that point the union board sought for a "political" solution instead of industrial disputes is to be seen as a consequence of its perception of the failure of its original organizational model and objective: to achieve a national labor-force monopoly over an entire industry.

Labor conflicts in war and revolution: the industrial workers' confrontation with the industrial union

The DMV finally achieved in war and revolution what it had failed to achieve in peace. Through the official recognition by government and employers,

---

58. Hans Mommsen, Historische Optionen der deutschen Gewerkschaftsbewegung, in Willy Brandt and Eugen Woodcock, eds., *FS für Eugen Loderer zum 60. Geburstag*, (Cologne, 1980).
59. Domansky, "Arbeitskämpfe," pp. 347ff.

it attained a national monopoly for representing labor in the metal industry. At the same time, the process of restriction of the union's maneuverability, already apparent before the First World War, was accentuated. Furthermore, the DMV union model and strategy seemed hardly appropriate to permanently tie its newly won members to the organization.

With the outbreak of war the DMV board concluded an unconditional truce with the government in the "Burgfrieden."[60] Berlin decided to recognize the unions as representatives of labor in order to enlist the support of the workers for the war effort. The wartime importance of the metal industry helped the DMV to achieve a strong position. The union's chairman, Alexander Schlicke, was appointed to the newly created War Bureau in the War Department as a labor representative, and the "Vaterländisches Hilfsdienstgesetz" (National Auxiliary Service Law) of December 1916 set up arbitration committees for settling disputes over working conditions and wages on a parity basis.

This recognition of the unions had to be paid for in various ways by union members and workers. The unions, and above all the DMV, were confronted with a high incidence of unemployment at the beginning of the war, and forced to alleviate the distress of many families out of their own funds. Organized and unorganized workers alike were affected negatively when the DMV consented in 1915 to restrict greatly the freedom of contract that was all but abolished in the Auxiliary Service Law in 1916. Furthermore, with the "Burgfrieden" the unions had to renounce all strikes in order not to jeopardize armament production. Hence, the metalworkers were deprived of the chance to assert their interests either individually by freely changing their jobs or collectively by strikes.

These restrictions, along with the extremely nationalist stance assumed by the union leadership, caused the prewar rift in the organization to deepen. At both union conventions that the DMV had to hold during the war due to the unrest among its members, it was apparent that a growing proportion of the membership would not recognize the board's sworn policy of "war socialism." On the contrary, they believed the "Burgfrieden" to be more of a "mouse trap" in which the union members "floundered defenselessly."[61] On the one hand, the opposition against the union leadership led to a political division, with the opposition taking sides with the Independent Social-Democratic party (USPD) after the split in the SPD. On the other hand, it led to the alienation of the mass

---

60. Cf. esp. Opel, *DMV*; Wentzel, *Inflation*; Steinke, "Politik." See also Friendhelm Boll, *Massenbewegungen in Niedersachsen 1906–1920* (Bonn, 1981), esp. pp. 145ff.; Dick Geary, "The German Labor Movement 1848–1919," *European Studies Review* 6 (1976): 297–330; Geralnd D. Feldman, Eberhard Kolb, and Reinhard Rürup, "Die Massenbewegungen der Arbeitschaft am Ende des Ersten Weltkrieges (1917–1920)," *Politische Vierteljahresschrift* 13, no. 1 (1972): 84–105; H.-J. Bieber, *Industrie, Staat und Militär in Deutschland 1914–1920* (Hamburg, 1981). See also Steinisch's contribution to this volume.
61. Cited from Opel, *DMV*, p. 49.

349

movements generated during the war and revolution from the DMV and its traditional organized channels.[62]

As early as 1915 the workers, suffering from the deprivations induced by the war, perceived that the "Volksgemeinschaft" proclaimed even by the unions was no more than a product of fantasy. It was evident in various respects, but especially with regard to nutrition, that the class struggle intensified rather than diminished during the war.[63] Beginning in 1915, disputes over working and living conditions increasingly embraced political demands for peace and the parliamentarization of the Reich. These conflicts were supported by both the skilled and traditionally highly organized parts of the metalworkers – particularly the turners of Berlin – and the unskilled and semiskilled workers employed for the first time in the metal industry.

The dilution of the work force in the metal industry was reflected in the restructuring of the DMV membership during the war, but especially in the period following the November Revolution. From the beginning of 1917, following the recognition of the unions in the National Auxiliary Service Law, the membership of the DMV, which had declined at the beginning of the war, began to increase again.[64] At the end of 1918 it amounted to 786,000 and literally soared ahead to approximately 1.6 million members by the end of 1919. Until 1923 DMV membership remained at that level. In 1924, in connection with the effects and aftereffects of inflation, the conflicts arising from the occupation of the Ruhr area in 1923, and also the suppression of the communist uprising in Thuringia and Saxony, union membership fell back to below the 1918 level. Unionization shows a similar picture: While the union had been able to organize two-thirds of all metalworkers in 1919 – nearly 90% were organized when independent and confessional unions are taken into account – in 1924 the degree of organization in the metal industry slumped to about one-third and, thus, was only insignificantly higher than before the war. This reduction in membership and in the degree of organization was rooted primarily in the fact that the DMV failed permanently to retain the new groups of workers who had joined the union during the war and revolution.[65] This was the case for women, youths, unskilled, and semiskilled workers as well as for iron- and steelworkers who, in 1919, had provided the highest growth rates of all groups represented in the unions. By 1924, the traditional vocational groups, especially the locksmiths, dominated the union again. Although it cannot be

---

62. Ibid., pp. 48ff., 65ff.

63. Ibid., pp. 50ff. See also Jürgen Kocka, *Klassengesellschaft im Krieg 1914–1918*, (Göttingen, 1973), esp. pp. 33ff.

64. On the development of the DMV membership during WWI and revolution see Wentzel, *Inflation*, pp. 16ff., 176ff.; Steinke, "Politik," pp. 45ff., 195ff.; Irmgard Steinisch, "Die gewerschaftliche Organisation der rheinisch-westfälischen Arbeiterschaft in der eisen und stahlerzeugenden Industrie 1918–1924," in Mommsen, *Arbeiterbewegung*, pp. 117–139.

65. Steinke, "Politik," pp. 204ff. Wentzel, *Inflation*, pp. 176ff.

ignored that the working conditions of those workers were largely altered by the rationalization caused by the war, in 1924 the union's membership, quantitatively and qualitatively, resembled much more its prewar structure than the one of the interim period between the war and the revolution.

The general decrease in membership certainly has to be attributed to the postwar economic crises, the aftermath of the inflation, the occupation of the Ruhr, and the massive attack led by the employers against the sociopolitical achievements of the revolution. Those factors alone, however, cannot explain the disproportionate decrease in new membership that can be observed, for example, among the Berlin metalworkers who had been particularly active during the war and the revolution. On the contrary, the forms of conflict developed by those workers and their objectives demonstrate that their abandonment of the union was to be attributed to the fact that the USPD leadership in the DMV, which in 1919 had replaced the former union leadership, also failed to include and develop further the new organizational approach pioneered by those workers during the war and the revolution. At the same time it became apparent that the situation of these workers could in no way be improved by conventional means, especially under the conditions of inflation. This interpretation is borne out, on the one hand, by the fact that already at the end of 1922 the core of the new membership in the centers of the iron-and-steel industry started to crumble and, on the other hand, by the increase in anarcho-syndicalist activities in the Ruhr area and in Berlin.[66]

Economic and political strikes of metalworkers during the war closely resembled the prewar strikes waged by other groups of workers as well as by some of the trades organized in the DMV, in particular, the shipwrights. For example, the strikes against forced savings in 1916 ("Sparzwangstreik"); the mass strike against the sentencing of Karl Liebknecht in the summer of the same year; the strikes in the armament factories in Berlin, Halle, Leipzig, Braunschweig, Cologne, Munich, Mannheim, Magdeburg, Halle, Bochum, Dortmund, and other cities all broke out without the instigation of the DMV.[67] In those cases where the union's officials were able to intervene, they tried to limit the strikes to purely economic demands. It would be wrong to characterize the exclusion of the unions, often upon the request of the workers, who preferred to negotiate with the authorities directly, as antiunion. In most of the strike actions during the war, shop stewards played an important role. This was especially true in Berlin, where the idea of a workers' council emerged from the organization of strikes at the factory level. The factory was to be the focus and the basis of union policy.[68] Elements of grass roots democracy generally played an outstanding role in wartime strikes. Decisions were taken by meetings of

66. Geary, "German Labor Movement," pp. 317ff.
67. Boll, *Massenbewegungen*, pp. 145ff.; Opel, *DMV*, pp. 57ff.
68. Opel, *DMV*, pp. 71ff.; Geary, "German Labor Movement," pp. 317ff.

351

striking workers, where demands were discussed and committees elected from the strikers' own ranks.

Not only the forms, but also the objectives of these movements show signs of a reorientation in the way in which labor disputes were conducted. Demands that resulted directly from wartime deprivations were to be found along with traditional demands of the working class. Demands for the protection of workers' autonomy and freedom of association emerged once again. In addition, there were demands with respect to management prerogatives. Demands also included those for the discontinuation of disciplinary measures and the withdrawal of the planned forced savings program for young people. The resistance of adults, especially women, to the measures for disciplining young workers – a portion of their wage was to be retained and deposited in a savings account – demonstrates that their concept of appropriate living and working conditions could well go beyond a restricted understanding of these objectives. These motifs recall the prewar strikes directed against the "bad treatment" of workers that the unions had tried to repress before the World War.

The abolition of the piece-rate system and demands for wage increases to squeeze the wage differentials constituted a second category of strike objectives. Wage demands leveled out the differences between skilled and unskilled workers and those between similarly qualified workers exercising different functions. In the course of the revolution it was even possible to reach comprehensive wage settlements for individual branches of the Berlin metal industry.[69]

Common to all wartime strikes was the tendency to abolish the distinction normally made between economic and political strikes. This tendency continued well into the immediate postwar years. The DMV leadership, however, realized that this tendency endangered its own position and, therefore, felt compelled to campaign just as before the war, for the enforcement of its strike statutes that had hardly been altered, and generally to press home the demand for discipline among its members.[70] The oppositional forces, unable to assert themselves, failed to achieve their goal of restructuring the union along the lines of the workers' councils, a program hardly convincing for the more traditional groups in the DMV. Disappointment over the return to conventional forms of union politics may well have been as decisive for the exodus of large numbers of the new union membership as the frustration of socialist expectations.

Those labor conflicts that were in line with the statutes showed a drastic change after 1920, due to the increase in the cost of living during the inflation. From 1919 to 1922, the traditional demands with respect to wage increases, extra wages, and hours prevailed. Already in 1919 it became evident that the

69. Wentzel, *Inflation*, p. 58.
70. Ibid., pp. 55ff.

successes achieved in squeezing wage differentials could not be maintained. In the labor conflict in Berlin in the summer and autumn of 1919, employers succeeded in introducing wage differentials again. In the great dispute in the metal industry of southern Germany in 1922, employers gained their first success in their attack against the eight-hour day.[71]

The most drastic change in labor conflicts, however, was that from 1920 onward, strikes conducted by the DMV, especially offensive strikes, dwindled into insignificance compared to wage settlements without work stoppages. In 1919, 7.5% of all workers involved in disputes participated in offensive strikes; in 1920, only 1.5%; in 1921, 3.6%; and in 1922, 0.7%.[72] Due to the spiraling inflation in these years, wage disputes likewise developed a "self-propelling force."[73] The need to adjust wages to the increasing cost of living could not be disputed. Conflicts shifted to issues of wage differentials and of working hours. In both areas the employers were able to assert their interests. In this respect, two labor conflicts were of special importance during this period.

In 1919 state arbitration in a conflict in the Berlin metal industry provided for five wage groups, instead of six as demanded by the Metal Industrialists of Berlin, or three as demanded by the Berlin DMV. Although both parties accepted this proposal, the conflict expanded because a compromise could not be reached about the classification of workers into the separate wage groups. Another arbitration committee based its classification of workers into five groups on formal qualifications rather than on job description. Furthermore, the committee did not work on the basis of existing pay scales, and in the end imposed wage reductions on numerous workers. This was in line with the employers' strategy of no "minimum wages." The DMV was completely unprepared for this method of reducing the cost of labor by the differentiation of wage groups, which threatened to replace the traditional methods of cutting wages.[74] The metalworkers were also unsuccessful in their struggle to retain the eight-hour day. The first battle was fought in early 1922 in the southern German metal industry. In this dispute workers did not succeed in maintaining the forty-six-hour week.[75]

The DMV did not only fail in these open conflicts with the employers, who had regained their economic and political strength. As the traditional conflicts over wage increases declined, new criteria had to be developed for the adjustment of wages to the cost of living. Although this problem only surfaced in

71. Ibid., pp. 129ff.
72. Steinke, "Politik," p. 115.
73. Ibid., p. 116.
74. See esp. Wentzel, *Inflation*, pp. 55ff.
75. Wentzel, *Inflation*, pp. 129ff. See also Gerald D. Feldman, and Irmgard Steinisch, "Die Weimarer Republik zwischen Sozial – und Wirtschaftsstaat. Die Entscheidung gegen den Achtstundentag," *Archiv für Sozialgeschichte* 18 (1978): 353–439.

the period of inflation, it essentially evolved out of the concept of collective bargaining. If long contracts were not to be detrimental to the workers, the problem of wage fixing had to be reconsidered. Some of the prewar collective agreements of the DMV already provided clauses for updating wage increases. The DMV did not, however, develop any new perspectives for union action in this area. It rejected the introduction of a "social wage" or "family wage," according to social criteria that General German Federation of Trade Unions (ADGB) recommended, as well as the introduction of a "flexible wage scale" designed to automatically adjust wages to price changes. Critics of both concepts feared that such procedures would undercut union prerogatives.[76] They asserted their position in the DMV even though the "flexible wage scale" was already being tested in the metal industry in Dresden, for example.[77] By doing so, the union deviated in a decisive area from its principle not to obstruct the general trend of economic developments without arriving for a fundamental reorientation in its strategy.

Hence, the DMV found itself in a frozen position even before the period of hyperinflation and the Ruhr Conflict. It had failed to rebuild its organization on the council model. The attempt of the left wing of the DMV to employ union labor disputes, not only for economic demands but also for the democratization of the economic process itself, had foundered. On the other hand, the DMV deviated at least partially from its traditional line of adapting to innovations in the production process. In addition, the wage-price development in the inflation period deprived the unions of their traditional goals and methods in labor conflicts.

The early uncompromising reliance on state support, however, paid off for the DMV. The legal recognition of collective bargaining, the workers' councils, and the arbitration committees secured a monopoly for the DMV and other unions as representatives of workers at a time when the employers once again tried to change course, after their temporary alliance with the unions in the "Zentralarbeitsgemeinschaft" (Stinnes-Legien Agreement) had helped to defuse radical tendencies among the workers.[78] The DMV acquired its monopoly as the metalworkers' representative without a thorough organizational penetration of its constituency. The political recognition of the union can only be seen as a "victory," if we disregard the fact that the degree of union organization was not substantially higher than before the war despite this legal recognition, and that unionization no longer provided substantial benefits for the workers. In

---

76. Steinke, "Politik," esp. pp. 119ff.
77. Ibid., p. 116.
78. Gerald D. Feldman, "German Business between War and Revolution. The Origins of the Stinnes-Legien-Agreement," in G. A. Ritter, ed., *Entstehung und Wandel der modernen Gesellschaft. Festschrift für Hans Rosenberg zum 65. Geburtstag* (Berlin, 1970), pp. 312–41.

disputes between capital and labor, as the DMV had always stressed in the prewar period, "questions of power" were at issue. To attempt a solution to these questions without a fundamental restructuring of Weimar society according to the workers' ideals proved to be an illusion.

15

Scientific management and the changing nature of work in the St. Petersburg metalworking industry, 1900–1914

HEATHER HOGAN

On the eve of World War I, strike protest in the St. Petersburg metalworking industry was distinguished by a frequency and intensity that was rarely displayed by other workers in the capital or by workers elsewhere in the empire.[1] To a significant degree, it will be argued, this extraordinary level of labor–management conflict was linked to a process of structural change that had been unfolding in the financial, commercial, technological, and managerial organization of the industry, as well as important alterations in the process of production. Reforms had been implemented in response to the sharp economic downturn of the 1900–10 period and to the outbreak of serious labor unrest in 1901 and again in 1905.

The new strategies adopted by Petersburg employers to meet these various challenges were broadly similar to those associated with the managerial reform movement, then enjoying great popularity in the West. Interestingly, however, the ideas of "scientific management" were first explored and partially implemented in Russia by managers and engineers in the state-owned factories. These men were scarcely the representatives of progressive capitalism searching for ways to maximize profits, but instead officials of the state's bureaucracy charged with the production of military goods and the maintenance of orderly and harmonious labor–management relations within the state's factories. Only in the wake of the first revolution would private entrepreneurs embrace the new methodologies, but at a time when state managers had begun to retreat from a consistent implementation of such practices. This paper explores several

I wish to thank the editors of *Russian Review* for allowing me to republish parts of an essay that first appeared as "Industrial Rationalization and the Roots of Labor Militance in the St. Petersburg Metalworking Industry, 1901–1914," *Russian Review* 42 (1983): 163–90.
    1. See the contribution to this volume by Leopold Haimson, "Structural Processes of Change and Changing Patterns of Labor Unrest: The Case of the Metal-Processing Industry in Imperial Russia (1890–1914)," especially pp. 394–400.

356

problems related to the changing nature of work in St. Petersburg: the reasons why a shift occurred from the state to the private sector as the focal point of the managerial reform movement in Russia; the extent to which rationalizing methodologies were actually introduced into Petersburg's metalworking factories; and the ways in which worker protest in the prewar period may be understood as a response to a change in relative power between labor and capital brought about by the deskilling of the labor force, the intensification of the work process, and the consolidation of the financial, commercial, and managerial structures of the heavy industry of the capital.

Until the turn of the century, Petersburg's metalworkers did not play a conspicuous role in the strike protest that marked the last decades of the nineteenth century, nor did they participate in the great strike wave that enveloped the textile factories of the capital in 1896–7. Enjoying substantially higher wages and shorter hours than their unskilled and often illiterate comrades in the textile mills, and benefiting from the favorable labor market conditions that attended the tumultuous expansion of heavy industry between 1893–9, Petersburg metalworkers rarely challenged in overt and collective ways the prerogatives of management or the established patterns of work and industrial relations.

This apparent quiescence was broken dramatically by the "Obukhov defense" of May 1901. Protesting the dismissal of several workers because of their absence on May Day, Obukhov workers demonstratively downed tools and left the factory, to be met by armed police units. A bloody clash ensued, leaving seven dead, scores wounded, and the remains of Russia's first barricades on the streets of the capital. Within days, unrest spread to several other large metalworking factories. At the Baltic Ship Construction Factory, the Aleksandrovskii Engineering Works, the Nevskii Ship Construction and Engineering Plant, and elsewhere, workers struck, demanding not only the recognition of May Day as a legal holiday, but insisting on wage increases and the introduction of the eight-hour day. Strikes and unrest continued through May and into June, while stunned state officials and private employers struggled to suppress labor protest by means of arrests, dismissals, and partial concessions.[2]

Detailed investigations of the incident were undertaken at the behest of the Naval Ministry. A. N. Chikolev, an assistant to the managing board of the Baltic Works and a recognized expert on the "worker question," was selected to carry out a study of eleven major metalworking plants of the capital. A per-

2. L. M. Ivanov, ed., *Rabochee dvizhenie v Rossii v 1901–1904 gg: Sbornik dokumentov* (Leningrad, 1975), pp. 387–94. For a brief overview of the 1901 strikes see N. V. Iukhneva, "Iz istorii stachechnogo dvizheniia peterburgskikh rabochikh posle Obukhovskoi oborony," *Uchenye zapiski LGU*, no. 270 (1959): pp. 201–16.

ceptive critique of Chikolev's findings was contributed by Major-General K. K. Ratnik, the director of the Baltic Works since 1893.[3]

Chikolev argued that socialist agitation lay behind the recent disorders. Radicals had gained a sympathetic response to demands for an eight-hour day, a general increase in pay with the establishment of a minimum wage, and the abolition of overtime, only by appealing to the "inert mass" of workers on the basis of their purely "local" concerns and by reference to a few particularly vexing aspects of their employment at a given plant. Asserting that the eight-hour day was inappropriate to Russian conditions, rejecting demands for wage increases as making "no sense," and finding appeals for a one ruble a day minimum wage "arbitrary," Chikolev's approach to labor's grievances must be recognized as fundamentally dismissive. Yet in examining those conditions that provided fertile soil for socialist agitation, he accurately identified a principal cause of the unrest: an industrial crisis at the turn of the century led to the curtailment of production and the abolition of overtime, and hence to the deprivation of those supplemental wages metalworkers had typically earned. Accustomed to this higher level of earnings, workers suddenly found themselves in difficult financial straits. Labor protest, therefore, had been rooted in the particular economic conjuncture of the times.[4]

With the exception of several minor recommendations for change (e.g., a reduction in the workday by one-half hour, a modest upward revision of piece rates, the abolition of the search), as well as a general admonition to directors of state and private factories of similar type that they work together to standardize conditions of employment and institute uniform rules, little in Chikolev's report indicated that the demands voiced by workers should be viewed as legitimate.[5] Still less in his study suggested that Baltic's workers were capable of independent, purposive action or that managerial assumptions about labor unrest required serious reexamination. Ratnik's conclusions were strikingly dissimilar. Eschewing reference to "outside" socialist agitation and rejecting Chikolev's depiction of workers as an "inert mass," Ratnik discovered the deeper sources of worker radicalism in the increasing complexity of Baltic's work force.

Focusing on the social origins and dominant characteristics of his work force, Ratnik found that the largest group consisted of workers from the peasant *soslovie* (estate), some 80% of the total. Of these, slightly more than half retained an allotment of land in the countryside. While scarcely living in luxury, these peasant-workers were relatively better off than others at the factory, for they often derived a supplemental income from their land. Despite the fact that landed workers might spend their adult lives in an urban-industrial

3. A. L. Blek, comp., "Usloviia truda rabochikh na peterburgskikh zaodakh po dannym 1901 g.," *Arkhiv istorii truda v Rossii*, 1921, no. 2, pt. 1: 65–85.

4. Ibid., pp. 70–1.

5. Ibid., p. 73.

environment, they typically married in the village or sought a "country-girl" in the city, and endeavored to establish a household that would nurture children in the values of rural Russia. If raised in the city, their children were trained under the watchful eye of a parent or fellow countryman (*zemliak*), usually in one of the trades of the "hot shops" – that is, those metallurgical departments that relied on the physical strength of the worker, did not require a long apprenticeship that would attenuate ties to the land, but paid relatively good wages (e.g., blacksmithing). Ratnik concluded that landed workers and their children were the most stable, materially secure, and conservative element at the factory; their bonds to the village had not been broken and for this reason, he seemed to argue, they were not among the ranks of the worker militants.[6]

Of those peasant-workers without an allotment, Ratnik found that a significant number lacked even a family farmstead – these were poor, landless peasants whose ties to the countryside were purely formal and who were well on their way to becoming permanent urban dwellers. Particularly difficult was the plight of the young people in this group who had been forced to leave the land because their families could no longer feed them, but who were nonetheless obligated to send back part of their earnings to the village. Because these youths had not been raised in the ways of the factory, they were unable to compete with their urban counterparts for the best-paying jobs or to select the most advantageous trades to enter. Thus they typically served as assistants to the skilled cadres, but their wages advanced at a slower pace. Ratnik argued that the income of these workers demanded the most serious reexamination; he implied that by improving their economic well-being and by strengthening their bonds to the land, the stability of this group within the factory could be fostered.[7]

Almost 17% of the work force belonged to the petty townsmen and artisanal estates, and these workers, as well as the children of the landless peasantry who had grown up in the city, constituted the most unstable and undisciplined element in the factory, according to Ratnik. "In large part literate and in their own way well-read," these workers were the "most developed," even "gifted" segments of the labor force and typically occupied those positions that were the best paid and least demanding of physical labor. As pattern-makers and joiners, draftsmen and machinists, as *masterovie* (trained workers), but never *rabochie* (common laborers), they received "good wages" that were, however, inadequate to their "broadly-developed urban needs." It was this skilled, urbanized youth, argued Ratnik, yet to suffer material hardship or assume responsibility for a family, who insistently rejected the authority of the "less developed" older generation and who provided the workers' movement with its most militant

6. Ibid., pp. 80–2.
7. Ibid.

elements.[8] Ratnik stressed, moreover, that the material situation of workers from the lower urban estates was extremely unstable, in large part because they would sooner accept poverty if they lost their regular job than take up the position of common laborer that they so disdained. For this reason, alcoholism flourished among them. Nonetheless, the Major-General concluded:

> If restless and in many respects even dissolute, this group of workers from the petty urban bourgeoisie and artisans is the most able, providing from its ranks a large part of the intelligent crew leaders (*ukazatelei*), assistant foremen and even foremen, and therefore, the improvement of their daily lives, not only materially, but also morally, deserves special attention as the best technical support of production.[9]

Ratnik's analysis was compelling: He had described the emergence of a significant category of workers who retained no meaningful ties to the country-side, but formed instead the nucleus of an urban proletariat. Literate, tech-nically proficient, with broadly developed urban tastes, at times fulfilling lower level supervisory positions, and displaying a keen sense of professional pride, these workers, and most particularly their children, provided the activist core of the labor movement. Moreover, Ratnik emphasized, the productive viability of Baltic Factory rested squarely on their shoulders. It was a stunning recog-nition, one that necessarily undermined complacent notions of Petersburg's metalworkers as an inert and undifferentiated mass and dispelled confidence in the view that a temporary, if severe, industrial crisis was the root cause of the recent disorder. Ratnik's concern with the "material and moral" needs of the urbanized segments of his work force – and hence the fundamental legitimacy he accorded worker demands for improved wages and hours – thus reflected the perception that state managers had to adjust to changing realities.

The Major-General's insights led him to explore ways to respond to labor's grievances. Striking in Ratnik's approach was his focus on issues of mechan-ization and labor productivity and his apparent realization that more advanced technologies and higher rates of productivity would permit the substantive gains for workers that he deemed urgent and desirable. Thus, for example, Ratnik examined the possibility of reducing the workday without reducing wages by studying the level of mechanization at the factory, and the earnings and comparative hourly productivity of piece-rate workers on regular days (10 hours) and Saturdays ($7\frac{1}{2}$ hours); he concluded that acceptable levels of output could be maintained on an $8\frac{1}{2}$-hour shift.[10] Yet equally striking was the meshing of these "rational" and "quantitative" methods of analysis with

8. Ibid., pp. 81–2.
9. Ibid., p. 81.
10. Ibid., pp. 74–7.

the more familiar assumptions of tsarist bureaucrats. When Ratnik sought the "proper" beginning for the $8\frac{1}{2}$-hour day, he considered the marital and housing situation of his workers and determined a start-up time that would be most supportive of a stable family life. Similarly, Ratnik linked the "worker question" with the state of the peasantry and argued that the well-being of urban workers ultimately depended on the health and viability of the rural sector and that wage levels would only rise when an impoverished peasantry ceased to flood the urban market.[11]

To the extent that Ratnik coupled the satisfaction of demands for better wages and shorter hours with an improvement in the productivity of his factory, he provided a congenial environment for those concerned with issues of industrial rationalization, and as we shall see, the engineers at Baltic Factory would be among the advocates of Taylorist methods in the 1905–7 period. But Ratnik's approach differed markedly from these later technocratic reformers. Indeed, the Major-General's memorandum illustrates the worldview of those state bureaucrats who did not reject the further industrial development of Russia, but who were clearly troubled by the ways in which industrialization and urbanization threatened social stability and who therefore struggled to articulate a strategy that might insure labor peace and public order, as well as preserve the absolute authority of officials managing the state factories. Ratnik explored, on the one hand, new methods that would enhance the factory's productivity and thereby make possible those material gains that he perceived as crucial to the resolution of labor–management conflict, and on the other, searched for ways to buttress those aspects of working-class existence – decent and affordable housing, a secure and orderly family life – that would contribute to the stability and "morality" of his work force in the unsettling, even corrupting conditions of an urban-industrial environment. Such a strategy, he hoped, would cultivate the discipline and loyalty of those skilled workers on whom the process of production depended. And yet despite the acuity of his perceptions and the urgency of his concerns, Ratnik's views were not embraced by the Naval Ministry, nor did they have much impact on working conditions at the Baltic Factory until some years later.

Acute capital scarcity and sharp declines in the domestic demand for heavy industrial goods defined the economic crisis experienced by the metalworking industry in the first years of the twentieth century. Although the distress was partially alleviated by defense contracts let in conjunction with the Russo–Japanese War of 1904–5, heavy industry continued to stagnate through the rest of the decade. The troubled condition of the economy led to important changes in the structure of the industry. The development of syndicates and later

11. Ibid., pp. 77–8, 83.

monopolistic agreements permitted most of the "giants" to survive the tight market, but forced smaller enterprises into bankruptcy. Capital scarcity impelled numerous other firms to close, while it encouraged still others to seek reorganization as joint-stock corporations or refinancing under the direction of major banking consortiums.[12] Taken together, the problems of the early twentieth century led to the pronounced concentration of the Petersburg metalworking industry, as well as to its dependence on financial institutions heavily backed by foreign investors. It also introduced industrialists to the unfamiliar challenge of competition on a limited private market, since the government, too, had been forced to curtail its investment in the industrialization of the country.[13]

Metalworkers experienced the crisis as falling wages, mounting unemployment, and the loss of occupational mobility, both laterally into other metalworking factories and vertically into more skilled or even supervisory positions. The once relatively privileged world of the metalworkers was threatened: Losing not only their comparatively high wages, metalworkers sustained a sharp blow to occupational pride and social status within the working-class community. The literate, technically proficient, yet highly volatile stratum of urbanized workers identified by Ratnik now confronted unemployment or the common labor it found so degrading.

These as yet inchoate feelings of loss and deprivation were further shaped by the temporary recovery of industry in 1904 and by the outbreak of revolution in early 1905. With industry flooded by urgent defense contracts, metalworkers could once again earn overtime wages, but faced stiff pressure from unrelenting foremen trying to get the work out at rates acceptable to their bosses.[14] By January 1905, shopfloor tension had mounted and flowed easily into the massive strikes enveloping the captial. Metalworkers now freely complained about exhaustion and fatigue, but coupled their grievances with accusations that foremen "belittled the human dignity of the workers."[15] They insisted, moreover, that workers be treated respectfully and addressed politely, with

12. Between 1901 and 1904, sixteen machine-construction factories were liquidated, and another ten collapsed between 1905 and 1909. N. Vanag and S. Tomsinskii, comp., *Ekonomicheskoe razvitie Rossii* (Moscow and Leningrad, 1930), pp. 25–6. Reflecting the trend toward consolidation, the number of joint-stock corporations in the Petersburg metalworking industry grew from nineteen to forty-two between 1900 and 1913. E. E. Kruze, "Promyshlennoe razvitie Peterburga v 1890-kh–1914 gg.," in B. M. Kochakov et al., eds., *Ocherki istorii Leningrada*, vol. 3 (Moscow and Leningrad, 1956), p. 17.

13. The economic crisis and its impact are discussed in greater detail in Heather Hogan, "Labor and Management in Conflict: The St. Petersburg Metalworking Industry, 1900–1914" (Ph.D. diss., University of Michigan, 1981), pp. 54–63.

14. See, for example, Leningradskii gosudarstvennyi istoricheskii arkhiv (henceforth LGIA), f. 1267, op. 1, d. 992, 11. 6–8, for the problems building at the Obukhov Factory.

15. A. L'vovich, "Trebovaniia rabochikh Baltiiskogo i drugikh morskikh zavodov v ianvarskie dni 1905 godu," *Arkhiv istorii truda v Rossii*, 1922, no. 4, pt.1: 86–7.

the formal *vy* (you), not the condescending *ty* (thou). And in the days immediately following Bloody Sunday, they presented long lists of demands insisting on a reduction in hours, the establishment of grievance committees, and changes in the wage structure.[16] Fueling unrest in the capital's heavy industry, then, was a pace and intensity of work that was largely the product of long hours and the high-pressure tactics of foremen, but was also a consequence of the loss of occupational status experienced by skilled metalworkers as a result of the economic downturn at the turn of the century. Also at issue was the gap perceived by metalworkers between the respect legitimately due them by virtue of their technical proficiency and urbanized ways and the contemptuous attitudes regularly displayed toward them by supervisory personnel. In short, the skilled, urbanized strata observed by Ratnik had begun to assert self-consciously its own dignity and self-worth and had begun to struggle against the historic rightlessness of Russian labor in polity and society.

As the state's managers confronted what surely must have appeared an all-enveloping chaos in their factories in 1905, many displayed the same essential sympathy toward worker demands demonstrated by Ratnik in 1901. Thus the Major-General was joined by F. Kh. Gross, the director of the Izhorskii Works, in the belief that a reduction in hours was both desirable and possible. Gross was also willing to reconsider established wage policy by eliminating the ceiling on piece-rate earnings, while Ratnik moved quickly to remove several particularly offensive foremen and lower level supervisors.[17]

Yet as Gross responded to one set of grievances, it became clear that he failed to find ways to satisfy others. Due to increased pay for overtime and the higher earnings workers now received on piecework, but also because of the curtailment of orders that attended the end of the Far Eastern war, the factory had been unable to control costs and therefore faced a shortfall of hundreds of thousands of rubles by the end of the year. By September, these intense economic pressures forced Gross to cut back on the workweek to avoid general layoffs.[18]

Nor had the concerns of supervisory personnel been addressed. In March a group of Izhorskii engineers submitted a detailed critique of worker demands, along with pointed criticism of upper management's attitudes toward the technical staff. Two essential themes emerged from this report. First was the strong

16. Ibid., pp. 86–8; see also A. M. Pankratova et al., eds., *Revoliutsiia 1905–1907 gg. v Rossii: Dokumenty i materialy. Nachalo Pervoi Russkoi revoliutsii, ianvar'-mart, 1905 g.* (Moscow, 1955), pp. 135–6, 190–1. At the same time, metalworkers presented a range of political demands. For a more comprehensive examination of the evolving attitudes of metalworkers toward the autocracy and the issue of substantive political change, see my forthcoming study *The Metalworkers of St. Petersburg, 1890–1914.*

17. M. M. Mikhailov, "1905 god na Izhorskom zavode," *Krasnaia letopis'* 1931, nos. 5–6 (44–5): 244; L'vovich, "Trebovaniia rabochikh," p. 88.

18. Mikhailov, "1905 god," *Krasnaia letopis'*, 1931, nos. 1–2 (46–7): 239–40.

sense of wounded professional pride and a conviction that management failed to appreciate and rely on the expertise of its technical personnel.

> Up to now, we either remain passive spectators to the unrest in our shops, or we are called to meetings in the capacity of so-called informed persons, [as] the executors of the administration's plans, but not as technologists, consciously working in some branch of factory operations with the right of a decisive voice.[19]

Moreover, engineers stressed that in their capacity as foremen and departmental managers they were the first to receive worker demands – and one might add, the first to bear the brunt of worker hostility. Yet despite this pivotal position in labor–management relations, engineers complained that their opinions were rarely solicited or typically ignored by their superiors.[20]

These concerns were coupled with an assertion that worker demands for shorter hours and higher wages had to be satisfied at least in part. This would be possible, however, only if labor productivity was substantially increased – a change that would require, in the opinion of the engineers, a much greater technical independence for foremen and managers and a genuine improvement in the organization of work and the technology of production at the factory. To this end, they suggested that two commissions be established, each composed of foremen and technical personnel and under the chairmanship of the director or his appointed deputy. One would discuss matters pertaining to labor–management relations; the other would examine technical problems. All decisions would be made by majority vote.[21]

Gross and his immediate superior in the Naval Ministry were not sympathetic to these suggestions; indeed, the proposals were viewed as an "impermissible" encroachment on the authority of the director and were dismissed summarily.[22] At the heart of the conflict, however, was more than a challenge to Gross's authority or criticism of his technical competence. The issue hinged on two differing conceptions of labor–management relations, and more generally on two clashing views of the future structure of Russia's economy and society. Gross, like Ratnik, was uncomfortable with the ways in which the industrial transformation of Russian society was undermining constituted authority; and as if to confirm his larger fears, some dozen members of his engineering staff joined the general strike of October in support of the liberationist movement.[23] Throughout the crisis of 1905, Gross had endeavored to maintain a personalized, if unilateral, control over his factory, responding

19. Mikhailov, "1905 god," *Krasnai letopis'*, 1932, no. 3 (48): 190.
20. Ibid.
21. Ibid., pp. 191–2.
22. Ibid., p. 192.
23. Ibid., p. 194. Mikhailov described the conflict between Gross and his engineers

to labor protest by advocating a gradual amelioration of working conditions, and reacting to the political and professional pretensions of his engineers by forcing their dismissal. In fundamental contrast, the engineers embraced wholeheartedly the further capitalist transformation of state and society, and their position suggested – if only tentatively – the emergence of an entirely new vision of labor–management relations, one that placed supreme value on the development of labor processes and labor relations fully subordinated to the impersonal imperatives of technical rationality. In their essentially technocratic and productivist worldview, social conflict would be transcended, and the industrial primitiveness of Russia overcome, when *both* labor and management accepted the discipline of impartial, "scientifically-determined" patterns of industrial organization and authority.

While the evidence is scattered, one can document the emergence of such a vision from a variety of sources. The self-conscious assertion of the especially important role of the engineering professional can be seen, for example, in an editorial that appeared in *Vestnik Obshchestva Tekhnologov* in the spring of 1905. Here the themes of intense international competition and the importance of science-based technology to industry were woven together to stress the need of "backward" Russia for the trained engineer. Only those nations that adapted to the most modern technological advances would survive the ruthless economic struggle, and crucial to survival were the services of the technologist. This central figure in the life of the nation was not only an economic actor, however, but bore an important social responsibility as well. He had to concern himself with overall developments and with a broad range of national problems, among the most vexing of which was the "worker question" and the difficult position of the engineer between the "hammer and anvil" of labor–management conflict. The engineer had to extricate himself from these conflicting pulls. He had to define an independent course, sound "his own" voice, and let go of the "coattails of private entrepreneurial interests."[24]

More concretely, one sees this new worldview through the arguments presented by the state's engineers in support of a range of rationalizing methodologies in the winter of 1905–6. At the Baltic Factory, for example, engineers debated intently the merits of various "progressive" wage incentive plans, the virtues of the "Taylor system," ways to reorganize the work process to improve efficiency, and methods to overcome labor conflict. Important here was the perception that a "proper," objectively defined wage policy would resolve the conflict that was embedded in long-established patterns of work practiced by both labor and management. Thus in the past, argued one

as reflective of the struggle between "American" and "Prussian," "progressive" and "conservative" forms of capitalism. See especially, pp. 192–4.

24. *Vestnik Obshchestva tekhnologov*, 1905, no. 3: 115–16.

engineer, any increase in labor productivity usually led to rate cutting by the administration, and, in turn, to worker efforts to control carefully the pace of their work. A "progressive" system schooled workers in another way. By increasing the intensity of labor, they would be assured of a premium. Management would be disciplined as well. A higher wage bill encouraged technical rationalization, while an "objectively" defined wage policy eliminated those arbitrary cuts in piece rates that generated tension. Yet equally important in the discussion at Baltic was the dissatisfaction displayed by engineers with current managerial routines: some bemoaned the absence of "system" and "order," while others complained that the "regime [at the Baltic Factory] was developed by bureaucrats (*chinovniki*) and not by technical personnel (*rabotniki*)."[25]

Similar concerns shaped the thinking of engineers at the state's Obukhov plant.[26] Locating conflict at the point of production, Obukhov's reformers argued that the "improper" wage policy that had heretofore been utilized at the factory encouraged workers to control productivity. A confused policy of rate setting lay at the heart of the problem, as did the discretionary actions of foremen. Shop personnel had been given too much responsibility and too little guidance, which not only permitted workers to control the pace of the labor process, but led to a personalization of conflict on the shopfloor, since workers focused their anger on those who set their rates. But a comprehensive wage reform, the introduction of a rates bureau, and a complete uniformity in administrative measures for the entire factory promised to "remove personal responsibility from each. This must bring about a significant improvement in personal relations with workers."[27] Moreover, concern with speeding the work process was seen as an important ongoing stimulus "to a whole series of reorganizations in the methods of work and in the technology of the factory." In sum, the Obukhov reformers set the goal of completely rooting out old patterns and habits of work. Said one, "The old had to be forgotten, [so that] the new order could not even give occasion to allude to the old."[28]

Yet there was resistance to the new vision as well. Some departmental managers at Baltic found the so-called American methods offensive and threatening, one describing them as "exploitative" and hence inappropriate for a state factory, another dubbing them "keen-witted" and "sly," but unjust

25. LGIA, f. 1304, op. 1, d. 2691, 11. 76–100; quote on 1. 154.
26. This discussion draws on two reports, one written in April 1906 and entitled "A Memorandum on the Work of the Commission on Questions Regarding the Regulation of Labor–Management Relations at the Obukhov Steel Factory," and the second written in April 1908, which reviewed the 1906 reforms as well as several changes made in 1907, entitled "The System of Paying Workers Employed at Obukhov Steel Factory." The first report (LGIA, f. 1267, op. 1, d. 1701, 11. 92–103ob) was appended to the second (11. 76–90).
27. Ibid., 1. 103.
28. Ibid., 1. 78.

to the worker.[29] One can also detect a certain tension in the foremen's response to the projected creation of a rates bureau or the establishment of "progressive" wages. Such innovations would deprive them of a key aspect of their power over workers, namely the setting of piece rates, and thereby diminish their authority on the shopfloor and their importance in the managerial structure.[30] Perhaps more to the point, however, the reforms were resented because they implicitly condemned the staff as backward and arbitrary , and explicity sought to depersonalize labor–management relations. As such the ideas of the reformers could only clash with the views and interests of those state officials who were concerned with the "morality" and "stability" of their work force and the "loyalty" of their personnel in a period of rapid socioeconomic and political change. Thus despite the intense discussions and activity in the winter of 1905–6 at the state's plants, a policy review conducted in 1908 at Obukhov revealed that many of the proposals had not been fully implemented, and the development of plans for a rates bureau at Baltic only in 1911 reflected the slowing pace of innovation at this factory.[31]

In the years following the 1905 Revolution, growing numbers of private employers looked closely and carefully at the experiments begun at the state's factories and ultimately adopted rationalizing strategies more consistently and extensively. Substantive change in the organization of work unfolded in four major areas: first, a new wage policy; second, changes in time management; third, a reorganization of various commercial, bookkeeping, and accounting procedures; fourth, the introduction of labor-saving technology, which simultaneously increased productivity and altered the composition of the work force. Private employers were demonstratively less concerned with the "exploitative" nature of wage incentive schemes and less nostalgic about the depersonalization of labor relations than their counterparts in the state plants. Moreover, they accepted the technocratic and productivist vision of their engineers not because it promised to "harmonize" the interests of labor and management, but because it provided a methodology to intensify the labor process and hence increase the profitability of their operations.

In most Petersburg metalworking factories, a new wage policy was introduced in the 1906–14 period. Important to the spread of new approaches was not only the example of the state plants, but the actions of the Petersburg Society of Mill and Factory Owners, the principle employer association in the capital.

---

29. LGIA, f. 1304, op. 1, d. 2691, 11. 113–14, 149. Any incentive piece-rate system was called American.

30. See, for example, ibid., 11. 108, 118–19, 131, 134, 136, 137, 140, 149.

31. On Obukhov, see LGIA, f. 1267, op. 1, d. 1701, 11. 79, 88–90; on Baltic see LGIA, f. 1304, op. 1, d. 57, 11. 34–38.

In March 1908, a circular distributed by the society to its member firms discussed the wisdom of an industrywide change in wage policy, from the commonly practiced computation of wages by the day to the introduction of wages by the hour. The directive advised employers that such a policy offered a convenient method for the establishment of a "correct system of shop-hourly pay" and, along with it, rates on piecework. It might also facilitate the establishment of uniform rates in plants of similar type in the future, while simultaneously discouraging workers from lateness, absenteeism, and demands for a shorter workday on Saturdays or the numerous pre-holidays. Moreover, private employers were encouraged to use a half-kopeck, not a full kopeck, as the accounting unit, in order to guarantee sufficient "elasticity."[32] The new, "rational" methods soon elicited a response. By June, reports from the factories began to appear in the metalworkers' press noting the introduction of the hourly wage, and a 31 May session of the union's governing board confirmed that the majority of plants had made the shift.[33]

The Society's directive encouraged employers to reexamine their wage policies and paved the way for experiments with "progressive" wage incentive schemes. The available sources do not permit a detailed discussion of the types of wage systems introduced at private metalworking plants; in virtually all cases, reports are limited to simple, unqualified statements that "American wages" or the "American system" was introduced. Only in two cases were specific schemes identified. The Nevskii factory used the Halsey system, while the Kreiton factory implemented the Rowan plan.[34] In the labor press the *amerikanka* connoted any premium system built on economies of time and sometimes referred to the use of work cards, order sheets, "blanks," or the like, which specified the time in which a task was to be performed. Using this broad definition, at least ten plants may be identified as employing wage incentive schemes in the 1906–14 period: Feniks, Kreiton, San-Galli, Vulkan, Struck, Siemens-Halske, Obukhov, Baltic, Nevskii, the Pneumatic Machine Plant, and the Sestroretskii Arms Factory.[35] More generally, a survey conducted

32. LGIA, f. 1440, op. 8, d. 183, 11. 40–41.

33. *Vestnik rabochikh po obrabotke metalla*, 5 June 1908, pp. 6, 11; no. 3 (n.d.), p. 10. Not all plants made the changeover to hourly pay immediately, however.

34. N. P. Paialin, *Zavod imeni Lenina, 1857–1918* (Moscow and Leningrad, 1933), p. 258; *Vestnik rabochikh po obrabotke metalla*, 5 June 1908, p. 2.

35. *Rabochii po metallu*, 13 June 1907, p. 14; 26 July 1907, p. 8; 25 October 1907, p. 13; *Edinstvo*, 5 March 1909, p. 15; 19 March 1909, p. 14; 15 June 1909, p. 16; 10 August 1909, p. 2; LGIA, f. 1267, op. 1, d. 1701, 11. 76–90, 92–103ob; Paialin, *Zavod imenin Lenina*, p. 158; *Nash put'*, 4 March 1911, p. 13; *Metalist*, 5 December 1913; p. 14. Although not specifically identified as such, the evidence suggests that some form of incentive wage was utilized at the A. I. Semenov and Atlas factories (see the special supplement to *Vestnik Obshchestva tekhnologov*, 1912, no. 11: 1–18, 30–49) and probably at the New Aivaz plant as well (see *Novaia rabochaia gazeta*, 18 September 1913, p. 13).

by the Metalworkers' Union in 1909 noted that "a whole series of attempts were made to transfer to the American system in the 1907–8 period."[36] Throughout the 1906–14 period, other factories adopted new procedures for rating, issuing, and recording work. By some accounts, the establishment of rates bureaus became the idée fixe of many industrialists. In the capital, bureaus existed at the Lessner, Nevskii, Nobel', New Admiralty, and Semenov plants, and perhaps at Obukhov and Baltic.[37] Workers were threatened and concerned by such bodies. The pace of work was not only substantially intensified, but the ability of workers to influence rate determination was diminished. The worker could no longer bargain with the foreman directly, but was told to direct his complaints elsewhere or that he had no reason to complain since rates had been set "scientifically." Nevskii workers pointedly expressed their feelings in regard to such bodies by calling them "funeral bureaus."[38]

Further innovation was apparent in a new array of printed forms given to workers when they were issued a task. These were variously called order sheets (*nariadnye listi*), control sheets (*kontrol'nye listi*), or a check or card system. Typically, the workers had to note when they began and ended a task. Some forms specified the time allotted for a task, others defined the procedure and materials the workers were to use.[39] These new requirements also generated anxiety within the workers' ranks. Thus in 1914, workers at the Putilov Wharf downed tools when an order system (*nariadoviia sistema*) and notation of tags (*poiarlykam*) was instituted in place of the old method of calculating piece rates according to receipts.[40]

A diverse body of evidence thus indicates a wide-ranging set of reforms in wage policy. Most Petersburg plants replaced the day wage with an hourly wage following 1905, and many employed wage incentive schemes rather than simple piece rates. Innovative payment plans often entailed the institution of special rates bureaus and the utilization of new printed forms. These reforms were frequently part of a larger process of reorganization, including the expanded employment of technical and office personnel both to record and

---

36. Soiuz rabochikh po metallu, St. Petersburg, *Materialy ob ekonomicheskom polozhenii i professional'noi organizatsii Peterburgskikh rabochikh po metallu* (St. Petersburg, 1909), p. 108; see also *Obshchestvo zavodchikov i fabrikantov Moskovskogo promyshlennogo raiona. Biulleten' rabochego dvizhenia*, 30 May–1 July 1907, p. 4, which noted the broad usage of piece-rate wages by the hour with a premium fixed for rapid work in the St. Petersburg metalworking industry.

37. L. V. Filippov, "Iz poezdki po angliiskim zavodam," *Vestnik Obshchestva takhnologov*, 1910, no. 11: 487; *Edinstvo*, 1 April 1910, p. 22; *Metallist*, 7 April 1912, p. 16; *Nadezhda*, 31 July 1908, p. 13; special supplement to *Vestnik Obshchestva tekhnologov*, 1912, no. 11: 5.

38. *Edinstvo*, 1 April 1910, p. 22.

39. *Vestnik rabochikh po obrabotke metalla*, 5 June 1908, p. 2; *Rabochii po metallu*, 11 July 1907, p. 14; *Pravda*, 10 November 1912, p. 10; *Nadezhda*, 28 September 1908, p. 19; *Nash put'*, 4 March 1911, p. 13.

40. *Trudovaia pravda*, 3 July 1914, p. 3.

document the work process and to increase supervision over the labor force. A "rational" wage policy promised management reduced costs and increased productivity. Workers, though, perceived these changes as falling piece rates, a faster pace of work, and a new and disconcerting discipline effected by an enlarged managerial staff.

As management began to scrutinize more closely the problems of cost and productivity, the question of factory time came into sharper focus. Attention to the systematic "soldiering" of production-line workers led employers to examine the pace and structure of the workday generally. Major reforms in the area of time management included the abolition or restriction of the traditional "free time" – that five to fifteen minutes before the start of work in the morning or after dinner when workers conversed, put their tools in order, or simply relaxed without fear of a fine. Automatic time clocks began to appear in some of the capital's metalworking factories that "red-lined" minutes of lateness and afforded a strange contrast to the old practice of hanging "numbers" – square or oval tags – on hooks on a board.[41] Workers complained bitterly that such methods lengthened the workday: Putilovtsy destroyed a newly installed "fine" bell, while angry Obukhov workers hurled rocks at the turnstiles that led to the new timeclocks.[42]

Equally troubling was the intensified supervision of foremen: "The strengthened staff of foremen vigilantly follow each move of the worker: God save you if you talk with a neighbor, take a smoke, leave the bench, sit in a group, or still worse, glance at a paper. Fine, Fine, Fine!"[43] Some workers grumbled that this supervision even extended into the bathroom, while others felt that the new restrictions on tea and *kipiatok* in the shops was detrimental to the workers' health.[44] And the practice known in early American textile mills as "the stretch-out" – work on more than one machine or operation at the same time – was now employed by some metalworking plants of the capital.[45]

Perhaps most disturbing was the arrival of "time-work" specialists on the shopfloor. While it is difficult to determine the extent to which time study was employed in St. Petersburg metalworking factories, there is no doubt it was the cause of considerable anxiety within labor's ranks and that the per-

41. *Materialy ob ekonomicheskom polozhenii*, pp. 121–22.

42. On the 1912 conflict at the Putilov Works concerning lateness, checking-in procedures, and the new 'fine' bell, see S. B. Okun, comp., *Putilovets v trekh revoliutsiiakh* (Leningrad, 1933), pp. 179–83; and M. Mitel'man, B. Glebov, and A. Ul'ianskii, *Istoriia Putilovskogo zavoda* (Moscow, 1961), p. 365; on the Obukhov disorders, LGIA, f. 1267, op. 15, d. 78, 1. 142.

43. *Materialy ob ekonomicheskom polozhenii*, p. 122.

44. *Pravda*, 13 July 1912, p. 11; *Luch'*, 26 September 1912, p. 4; *Edinstvo*, 5 March 1909, p. 12; 10 August 1909, p. 13.

45. *Vestnik zhizni*, 23 May 1906, p. 52; *Luch'*, 13 December 1912, p. 4. This practice suggests the simplification of work processes and the gradual transformation of the metalworker into a machine tender.

sonnel who practiced it were often met by anger and resentment. At the Glebov Factory, the director had his "foremen go around with watches and check upon the workers," while at the Metal Factory a worker complained that "our fattened foreman comes up to the bench, takes out a watch and says to the workers: set it with more traction, at a faster pace and take it with greater force (*vziat' s truzhku*)."[46]

Young technical students on assignment in the factories were often practitioners of time study; their age and their methods combined to give particular offense to the work force. At the Baltic Factory such students, acting as assistant foremen, administered tests to incoming workers and observed their performance with stopwatches. The Nevskii Factory employed students in its rates bureau, and it was these young technicians who studied the machine tools and the workers, and who then calculated speeds and wage rates. In 1913, a sixty-day strike at the New Aivaz Factory broke out over the issue of time study, a conflict that began when the student Balik was carted out of the shop in a wheelbarrow.[47]

Taken together, management's heightened concern to influence the utilization of factory time deeply affected the patterns that had once defined the workday. The customs that had animated the shops and grew in the moments of a break were gradually circumscribed, to be reshaped by the more exacting requirements of the punch clock and stopwatch. Management sought structures to instill a new discipline, methods to break peasant-workers into the rhythms of industry, and ways to compel skilled workers to stay at their benches. Employers believed they were combatting entrenched attitudes and customs that impeded the development of industrial Russia.[48] But for workers, the intrusion of management ever more deeply into the shop culture was both threatening and demoralizing.

Integral to many reforms in wage policy and time management were the collection and analysis of production-line data. However, the business practices of an earlier era were inadequate to these new tasks. Few managers had records on hand to document expenditures on materials and labor; few knew in any detail the costs of production; few had bothered to monitor workflows carefully; few employed the requisite technical and administrative staff to generate this information. Such is the impression gleaned from the specialized press, which in the post-1905 period began to provide practical guidelines for the implementation of the most basic reforms in business practice and bemoaned the

---

46. *Rabochii po metallu*, 15 March 1907, p. 10; *Kuznets*, 20 December 1907, pp. 14–15.

47. *Edinstvo*, 5 March 1909, p. 13; *Metallist*, 26 January 1912, p. 14; *Severnaia pravda*, 17 August 1913, p. 1.

48. On the benefits to be reaped from the Taylor system by an industry still dependent on peasants steeped in rural ways, see "Znachenie sistemy Teilora," *Fabrichno-zavodskoe delo*, no. 1 (July 1913): pp. 16–17, reprinted from *Utro Rossii*.

primitiveness of many accounting procedures. It also offered a plethora of forms to serve as models for the reorganization of business practices. Often the substitution of written for oral communication stood at the center of such reforms, designed to systematize business operations, provide simple and clear indices of productivity, and develop a greater responsiveness at all levels to managerial directives. Diverse aspects of the commercial and production process could now be more closely scrutinized. Formerly, accurate records on the cost of producing individual articles were rarely maintained, but now management was introduced to cost-benefit analysis and more refined accounting methods. Earlier, pay office clerks labored over torn and dirty workbooks and the barely legible notations of foremen; now worksheets supplemented the workbook. These far more detailed printed forms gradually allowed for the gathering of crucial data on the organization of the production process and permitted it to be passed "upward" to management for analysis and subsequent action. New forms specified the worker's name and number, the rates and time of work, the materials and instruments used, and sometimes the methods by which work was to be performed. Further systematization included the installation of time clocks, with the punch card constituting an additional record of account with the worker. Office procedures became more specialized, and simple mechanical devices were applied to routine operations. Filing systems organized blueprints and drawings for the needs of the planning department; heretofore such documents had remained in the shops, under the physical control of foremen and workers.[49]

The collection and cataloging of such material necessarily entailed the expansion of technical and administrative staff. Although adequate statistical data on the employment of such personnel are generally lacking, there is evidence of their increasing role in Petersburg metalworking factories. Perhaps most telling from the point of view of labor–management conflict were the numerous reports in the labor press that documented the increasing tension that accompanied the expansion of supervisory personnel throughout the 1907–14 period.[50] Such an increase was especially felt between 1907 and 1910, when the work force was cut due to the curtailment of production, while the administrative staff remained the same or was enlarged. This trend was further evidenced by the promotion of workers to the post of foreman. Workers frequently complained that "former comrades," now working for management,

---

49. See, for example, F. Vebner, "Kak uznat' deistvitel'nuiu stoimost' proizvodstva," *Kommercheskii deiatel'*, no. 2/3 (1910): 107; no. 4: 12–21; no. 5/6: 10–14; and no. 7/8: 9–12; "Organizatsiia zavodoupravleniia," special supplement to *Vestnik Obshchestva tekhnologov*, 1912, no. 11: 1–49; S. Sharpant'e, "Vedenie fabrichnoi otchetnosti (po Liliental'iu)," *Zapiski Imperatorskogo russkogo tekhnicheskogo obshchestva*, no. 11 (1911): 377–86 and no. 12: 425–32.

50. *Edinstvo*, 10 August 1909, p. 12; *Metallist*, 26 January 1912, p. 15; *Pravda*, 3 November 1912, p. 12.

had betrayed them; their hostility found pointed expression in a 1910 decision to exclude such workers from the Metalworkers' Union.[51] Finally, the expansion of technical education made an increasing number of trained professionals available to industry; between 1896 and 1902 the number of higher technical schools doubled, as did enrollment at existing institutes, in all producing a fourfold increase in the number of engineering students.[52]

The Semenov Factory – widely considered a model machine-construction plant – provides one of the best illustrations of the integration of diverse aspects of the rationalization process described above: the utilization of advanced technologies, the subdivision and functional specialization of work and staff, the increase in written documentation to structure factory operations, the expansion of administrative staff with an attendant increase in overhead expenses, and the application of elements of Taylorism (e.g., time study, progressive wage systems, even Barth's slide rules for machining problems). The goal of these reforms was the elimination of a factory's "accidental dependence" on the human personality and the substitution of a "system" for the discretion of individuals.[53] And so as managerial control began to replace the diffuse control exercised by the various participants in the work process, the "art" of skilled foremen and workers and the value of long years of training and experience were degraded.

The application of advanced technologies to the work process was a constituent element in the rationalization of the metalworking industry.[54] As production processes were mechanized and standardized, a more refined division of labor became possible. The subdivision of work led to the simplification of individual operations, which in turn permitted employers to hire less skilled labor. The role of the skilled worker in the factory was narrowed. Caught between an expanded cadre of semi- and unskilled labor "below" him and an enlarged contingent of technical personnel "above" him, the skilled metalworker confronted a permanent loss of status and sharply reduced possibilities for advancement.[55] For management, such a developmental strategy promised to relieve the industry of its dependence on the skilled, highly paid, and often militant metalworker. In his place, factory owners could tap Russia's

---

51. *Nash put'*, 9 June 1910, p. 12; 7 November 1910, p. 14; and 4 March 1911, p. 14; *Proletarskaia pravda.* 14 December 1913, p. 3. On the decision of the Metalworkers' Union see, *Nash put'*, 7 November 1910, p. 11.

52. Harley Balzer, "Educating Engineers: Economic Politics and Technical Training in Tsarist Russia" (Ph.D. diss., University of Pennsylvania, 1980), p. 369.

53. Special supplement to *Vestnik Obshchestva tekhnologov*, 1912, no. 11: 1–18.

54. On capital investment in the physical plant of the metalworking industry, see Hogan, "Labor and Management in Conflict," pp. 110–17.

55. I am indebted to Leopold Haimson for focusing my attention on this sense of "compression" experienced by the skilled metalworker as the composition of the work force began to change.

abundant reserves of unskilled, female, and adolescent labor – labor that was cheaper and presumably more docile.

To be sure, innovation in these areas was gradual, indeed only just beginning, and the impact on work force composition was still relatively modest; nonetheless, reports from the factories in the immediate post-1905 period began to register workers' alarm, as management turned to unskilled cadres. Women replaced men at the Cable Factory, and adolescents took over adults' jobs at the Cartridge-Case Plant.[56] In some places common laborers were put on machine tools, not to train them to become metalworkers (*slesari*), but "with a view to economy."[57] Other plants expanded the use of adolescents, and when adult workers left or were fired, they were replaced by assistants (*podruchnye*) "who, after a year and a half of work, were already considered genuine lathe-operators."[58] At the Pipe Factory automatic machine tools were installed, which not only lowered rates but, workers assumed, would soon displace the skilled.[59] The use of common labor in place of skilled was noted as well in the tram repair parks and at the Vulkan Factory.[60] In yet another case, workers at Siemens-Halske complained that the administration, trying to reduce costs as much as possible, had placed inexperienced workers "who perhaps have never seen a machine-tool before" on the benches, and this had "naturally" led to the increase in accidents at the factory.[61]

Throughout the interrevolutionary period, the labor press voiced concern about these emerging trends. A July 1907 article spoke of "major technological changes which are displacing workers,"[62] and an informal survey of thirty-eight plants conducted by Malinovskii in the late summer of 1909 sketched the following picture. These plants had reduced their work force by 7% in the past year and a half. Virtually all dismissals had been accompanied by a decrease in rates, and at the same time adult workers were replaced by adolescents, men by women, trained workers by common laborers. Although technical modernization was sporadic, various improvements were noted in the forge shop at Putilov (new riveting presses had dramatically increased the speed of this operation), new machine tools and cranes were introduced at the Cable Factory and at Langenzippen, and a range of improvements had occurred at the Aleksandrovskii Plant.[63]

56. *Materialy ob ekonomicheskom polozhenii*, p. 108.
57. *Edinstvo*, 1 December 1909, p. 14.
58. *Edinstvo*, 12 March 1910, p. 13.
59. *Nash put'*, 25 June 1910, p. 12.
60. *Nash put'*, 11 August 1911, p. 13; *Metallist*, no. 4, 10 November 1911, p. 11.
61. *Luch'*, 7 December 1912, p. 4.
62. *Rabochii po metallu*, 26 July 1907, p. 9.
63. *Edinstvo*, 18 September 1909, pp. 7–8. One must also note that metalworkers did not suffer unemployment due to deskilling in the prewar period. The industry still required skilled cadres, both to set up and maintain the new technologies and to work in the many "unreformed" factories of the capital.

Unfortunately, available statistical data on female employment are not particularly illuminating. But two sets of figures offer a crude index. *Metallist*, citing factory inspectorate material, reported that the number of women in metalworking had increased by 33% between 1901 and 1910, while the male component grew by only 8%.[64] Similar data for 1913, exclusive of the state plants, indicated a 3.3% rate of female employment, up from 1.3% reported in the more comprehensive city census of 1900.[65] Articles in *Pravda* from late 1913 and early 1914 suggest that 10,000–15,000 women were employed in metalworking, thereby constituting 8–12% of the work force.[66]

Although female employment remained modest until the war, many metalworkers were more troubled than the actual number of female workers might warrant. This anxiety rested, in part, on the "intrusion" of women into a once exclusively male world; also at issue was the perceived threat of displacement and dilution. Thus for some the factory began to seem like an "odious women's city," and many "grey" workers were quick to curse the "old women" who "get in" everywhere.[67] Others evinced a greater sensitivity to the plight of women in the shops. Commented one metalworker: "To our shame, the relations of the rank-and-file worker to women are frequently shockingly crude."[68] These concerns were manifested in other ways as well. In the prewar period, the labor press carried an increasing number of articles on female labor, while the Metalworkers' Union made an effort to recruit members among women by lowering dues. Another striking indicator of shifting attitudes was the election of two women to the governing board of the union in 1913.[69] And probably as much a reflection of the interests of skilled workers undergoing a process of displacement as a sensitivity to the needs of women, strike demands began to insist on minimum wage rates for female metalworkers.[70]

Similar concerns came to light in regard to apprenticeship programs. This training had never been subject to control by labor organizations, but had rested on the practices of individual factories or on the state's vocational education system. Worker efforts to structure the training received by apprentices were therefore severely constrained. But in the prewar period, strike demands reflected an attempt to regularize apprenticeships by specifying the time a young worker spent at each stage of the training and the wages that were

64. *Metallist*, 22 May 1913, p. 4.

65. E. E. Kruze, *Peterburgskie rabochie v 1912–1914 godakh* (Moscow and Leningrad, 1961), p. 78; N. Semanov, *Peterburgskie rabochie nakanune pervoi russkoi revoliutsii* (Moscow and Leningrad, 1966), p. 44.

66. *Proletarskaia pravda*, 13 December 1913, p. 1; *Put' pravdy*, 23 January 1914, p. 4.

67. *Metallist*, 14 December 1913, p. 2.

68. *Metallist*, 10 August 1913, pp. 5–6.

69. See, for example, *Metallist*, 14 December 1913, pp. 2–4; 15 March 1914, pp. 3–4; 12 April 1914, pp. 9–11; *Severnaia pravda*, 23 August 1913, p. 1.

70. This demand was put forth by workers at the New Aivaz Factory. See *Severnaia pravda*, 10 August 1913, p. 3.

to be earned.[71] As work processes were simplified, however, training could be accomplished in a much shorter period of time; and rather than serving to teach a worker the skills vital to the trade, management held workers in the apprenticeship category longer than necessary in the new conditions to secure cheap labor. And as young workers entered the shops in increasing numbers, tensions sometimes flared; not a few apprentices suffered beatings at the hands of adult workers.[72]

Also indicative of the simplification of work processes and the expanded utilization of unskilled cadres was the lowering of piece rates. During the years of reaction, rate cutting was already apparent, although this could be explained in part by the downward pressure exerted on wage levels by continuing economic stagnation and high unemployment. More indicative of the changes underway was the pattern of rate cutting in the 1912–14 period, a time of industrial expansion and inflation. Thus in the most technically advanced metalworking factories – leading machine-construction plants like Nobel', Erikson, New Aivaz, and Vulkan – protests against rate cuts of as much as 30–50% occurred in the prewar years.[73] At a meeting of the board of the Metalworkers' Union on 1 November 1913, moreover, workers reported that the majority of recent strikes had been caused by decreases in rates.[74]

Diverse processes thus combined to alter the work force and to erode the male camaraderie and pride in skill that had heretofore defined the shop culture of Petersburg's metalworking factories. The long-established customs and rhythms of the workday seemed now to be changing quickly, as the plants of the capital traversed the distance between the old factory regime and the "modern" industrial enterprise. These processes were scarcely complete by 1914. They were still unfolding and still apparent in only the most advanced of the capital's industry. Nonetheless, resistance to these trends was beginning to assume a central place in the strike movement of the Petersburg metalworkers.

Many factors contributed to the prewar militancy of the *metallisty*, not least of which was an erosion of the established patterns of deference to constituted authority reflected so well in workers' demands for polite address. Also important were the duma forum, the labor press, and various labor organizations, all of which expanded the avenues open to workers for the articulation of

---

71. See, for example, Iu. I. Korablev, ed., *Rabochee dvizhenie v Petrograde v 1912–1917 gg., Dokumenty i materialy* (Leningrad, 1958), pp. 114–15, 119, 120; *Pravda*, 23 May 1912, pp. 10–11; Tsentral'nyi gosudarstvennyi istoricheskii arkhiv (henceforth TsGIA), f. 150, op. 1, d. 667, ll. 271.

72. *Edinstvo*, 19 April 1910, p. 4.

73. Tsentral'nyi gosudarstvennyi arkhiv Oktiabr'skoi revoliutsii (henceforth TsGAOR), f. 111, op. 5, d. 454, 1913, ll. 5, 57–58; *Metallist*, 1 September 1912, p. 13; *Za pravdu*, 30 November 1913, p. 3.

74. *Za pravdu*, 26 November 1913, p. 3.

their common grievances. Significant too, was the frustration experienced by many workers when their deputies were silenced, their leaders harassed by arrest, exile, or imprisonment, and their organizations closed by an all-too-watchful autocracy. In these years, moreover, the economically and politically motivated strikes of metalworkers became closely intertwined, and it seemed that the workers' search for economic and social rights was leading to a confrontation with an archaic political regime. But in important respects, this assault on the established premises of state and society tended to obscure the conflict surrounding the emergence of a substantially new socioeconomic order. The rationalization of work processes; the consolidation of the financial, commercial, and industrial structure of the Petersburg metalworking industry; and the emergence of a self-conscious stratum of professional engineers were symptomatic of the larger capitalist transformation of Russian society. The fierce, and by 1914 increasingly political, protest of the *metallisty* was motivated in large measure by efforts to intervene in this transformation. Thus to the volatile mix of those factors that agitated metalworkers on the eve of war and revolution, an intense conflict over the shifting relations of labor and capital must be added.

Direct evidence of labor's struggle against rationalization and its larger socioeconomic and political implications is thin. The archives of private metalworking plants are incomplete and do not contain records comparable to those available for the state-owned factories. Worker resistance to rationalizing trends was typically indirect and rarely expressly articulated, although protest against the lowering of piece rates, various demands in regard to women, apprentices, and the unskilled, as well as worker insistence on paid leaves and a reduction in work hours was suggestive of the contours of the conflict underway.[75]

Also contributing to the difficulty of assessing these newly emergent phenomena is the fact that Taylorist methods were seldom adopted in toto in the United States, Russia, or elsewhere. Taylor's excessively detailed procedures and his costly staffing requirements were scarcely practicable for most manufacturers. Far more applicable were the general principles of the scientific management movement as a whole: the stress on rational workflows, strategies to permit the full utilization of increasingly capital-intensive plants, and methods to facilitate the standardization and simplification of work processes. As we have seen, these principles were broadly, if singly, discernible in the heavy industry of the capital.

Yet what was central to the evolving relationship between labor and capital in the metalworking industry was not that the majority of plants had adopted

---

75. Worker demands that sought paid vacations or an eight- or nine-hour day suggested resistance to the increasing intensity of labor. See, for example, *Pravda*, 22 May 1912, p. 12; 11 May 1913, p. 3; TsGAOR, f. 111, op. 5, d. 455, 1913, 1. 300; LGIA, f. 1440, op. 8, d. 341, 1. 7; *Metallist*, 26 October 1912, p. 11.

Taylorlike methodologies by the eve of the war or that the typical metalworker had directly experienced displacement or time study or progressive wage schemes; rather, it was the perception on the part of metalworkers that such changes would soon transcend the confines of individual factories and transform work relations in the industry as a whole. This increasingly shared perception was based on worker correspondence in the labor press, conversations with comrades at other plants, and regular interactions with workers in various labor organizations; and it was reflected in the unusually high levels of financial contributions and collective support given by metalworkers to individual strikes fought over issues of worker dignity, factory order, and the human rights of labor.[76] Through such a daily imbibing of and participation in the collective experience of metalworkers, the nature of the challenge that confronted them all was grasped. Thus, what might have appeared as a disparate series of reforms carried out piecemeal fashion in individual factories, came together in a frightening totality of changes unfolding throughout the industry generally.[77]

Indicative of the sense of unease and imminent danger that gripped some workers was the comment of a Semenov worker in early 1912: "While almost none of us have come to an understanding of this system [a variety of Taylorlike reforms], nonetheless we feel that something advances upon us (*nadvigaetsia*), and that it will be necessary to respond."[78] By the summer of 1913 such fears doubtless seized other Petersburg workers as they read the appeals of their comrades at New Aivaz, who had struck to protest management's program of technical rationalization, time study, rate cuts, the expanded employment of female and unskilled labor, and the displacement of skilled metal workers.

> New Aivaz is the first major factory where the American system of Taylor has been introduced, with its division of labor, machine-ism (*mashinizm*), and time study. Our conflict is a struggle against this oppression. To win our strike is to secure all Petersburg from the savage extremes of the American system, to take the first step in the subsequent difficult and crucial struggle. What will become of "New Aivaz" if the workers of Petersburg leave it without their help? It will not be a factory, but a "workhouse" with its horrible bondage; it will be a brutal laboratory of human exploitation, where the latest work

76. On strikes of solidarity, see, for example, *Metallist*, 1 September 1912, p. 5; 15 June 1913, p. 5.
77. David Montgomery writes of the comparable phenomena in the United States following the economic crisis of 1907: "During the next two years the metal trades experienced what might be called the 'Great Fear' of Taylorism, somewhat like the mass anxiety that gripped the French peasantry in 1789. Opposition to scientific management spread much faster than did its practice." David Montgomery, *The Fall of the House of Labor* (Cambridge, 1987), p. 247.
78. *Metallist*, 23 February 1912, pp. 8–9.

in technical science will be bought at the price of hunger, humiliation, sweating, illness, and premature death.[79]

Metalworkers were not only alarmed by the accumulation of reforms at the point of production, however, for they had come to see that these reforms were linked to a far larger process of change that was altering the relations of power between labor and management. The increasing size and scope of the corporations employing metalworkers, the monopolization and financial restructuring of the industry, and the formation of influential employer associations combined to empower industrialists to resist the demands of labor more successfully than in the past. Strengthened economically by the strategies they had adopted, employers were able to defeat a remarkable number of strikes and to carry out a growing number of debilitating lockouts by 1914.[80] Directly from their own strike experience, therefore metalworkers began to perceive the greater power of employers; sustaining defeat after defeat on the enterprise level, metalworkers began to shift their protest to the larger political arena.[81]

Fueling conflict in the metalworking industry, then, were the specific changes unfolding on the shopfloor and the repressions of the decaying autocracy, but also and equally a struggle surrounding the emergent power of an important segment of the industrial bourgeoisie. And giving this conflict its violent intensity was the frustration experienced by workers as strike defeats demonstrated to them their declining ability to shape the work environment that had, after all, contributed so profoundly to the conscious assertion of their human dignity. A mastery of skill, an adaptation to the city, and a keen sense of difference from the "grey" and transient mass of peasants was the collective heritage of Petersburg metalworkers since the turn of the century, and it was now threatened by the increasing power of employers to restructure working-class life in the capital.

79. *Severnaia pravda*, 1 September 1913, p. 3. For a detailed discussion of this strike, see Hogan, "Labor and Management in Conflict," pp. 484–509.
80. Data compiled by Balabanov on the basis of factory inspectorate reports for all Russia indicate that metalworkers lost 56.7% of their economic strikes in 1912, 63.1% in 1913, and 75.4% in 1914; moreover, those economic strikes ending in compromise settlements fell from 38.5% in 1912 to 29.1% in 1913, and to 20.1% in 1914. In other words, metalworkers won a mere 4.5% of their economic strikes in 1914. M. S. Balabanov, *Ot 1905 k 1917. Massovoe rabochee dvizhenie* (Moscow and Leningrad, 1927), p. 238.
81. On the increasing number of political strikes by metal workers, see ibid., p. 235.

16

Structural processes of change and changing patterns of labor unrest: the case of the metal-processing industry in Imperial Russia (1890–1914)

LEOPOLD H. HAIMSON

If we turn back the clock to the early 1890s, or more precisely to the sketches drawn for us (largely by radical members of the intelligentsia) of the *masterovye*, the skilled workers employed in St. Petersburg's mechanical and metal-processing plants, we can draw a number of concurring generalizations about the characteristics that then distinguished these workers – and more generally the world of the *zavodskiye* (the workers, skilled and unskilled, employed in various plants of the capital's heavy industries) – from the largely unskilled and lower paid workers employed in the city's light industries, (most of them in textile and food-processing enterprises):

1. One of these concurring generalizations centers on the learning process involved in skilled metalworkers' *mastering* of their trade and the key role that this process of mastering ultimately played in these workers' gains of greater autonomy in the production process, as well as in their economic, social, and cultural advancement. Greater autonomy because, in the semiartisanal conditions that still distinguished the operations of St. Petersburg's mechanical and other metal-processing plants (including even the larger ones), the acquisition of the various skills attendant on the mastery of the trade implied for a machinist and other skilled workers employed in mechanical and other metal-processing plants the assumption of *greater control over their own work*: greater independence in the exercise of the various decisions involved in the work process, in the tempo at which this work was performed, and more generally in the degree of freedom attained in this work performance from interference by supervisory personnel. This degree of autonomy was maximized during this period of rapid industrial expansion and of consequent shortages of skilled labor by the greater bargaining power that a skilled worker could almost automatically assert, given the demand for his services, in his relations with supervisors. By the same token, mastering one's trade afforded during these years significant possibilities for social as well

380

as economic advancement. This mastery opened the way not only to higher levels of pay, but also, in many cases, to supervisory positions in the production process: to those of *starshyi* (senior worker) and *master* (foreman), if not of "engineer." Indeed, as of the beginning of the 1890s, many of the "engineers" in St. Petersburg's metal plants, especially among those of foreign origin, were in fact merely workers who had attained especially high levels of skill.[1]

If, for one reason or another, a metalworker who had successfully mastered his trade could not achieve a degree of economic-cum-professional advancement or a degree of autonomy in the performance of his work commensurate to his levels of skill in the plant in which he was employed, he had during these years the genuine choice of moving on to a better and often more highly paid job in another plant of St. Petersburg's rapidly expanding metal industry. Indeed, as the memoirs of many worker revolutionaries of this period confirm, this was a period of extraordinary labor mobility, as more highly skilled, and/or independent-minded and rebellious, metalworkers moved quite swiftly and easily from job to job, in their search for a more congenial work environment as well as for higher pay.[2]

2. A crucial dimension to worker mastery of the trade was the attainment of at least a minimal level of literacy, but also in many cases knowledge of arithmetic, if not geometry: to read and adapt the mechanical drawings and designs that these workers had to apply in making their products; to measure the cuts to be used in the metals utilized in making them; and so on. And all contemporary descriptions concur about the respect if not yearning for knowledge, indeed the intellectual curiosity, that the very nature of their jobs induced in this stratum of St. Petersburg's workers – particularly among members of the younger genera-

1. The specific character of the labor environment in which a skilled worker of the metal industry moved during these years, especially in St. Petersburg – the expectations that it awakened, but also to a considerable degree fulfilled – was reflected in the language itself. The word *masterovye* generally applied to the skilled workers of the metal industry (and distinguishing them from the *rabochie* employed in factories, but also from the *chernye rabochie*, the unskilled laborers, working in their *own* plants) and is close in its etymology to *master*, a term equally applicable to a foreman and to the "master" of any particular skill.

2. These generalizations are most sharply drawn in Plekhanov's classical, if somewhat stylized, discussion of the differences in mentalities, attitudes, and mores between St. Petersburg's skilled and unskilled workers, and of the sources of the attraction of skilled workers to the revolutionary movement. See G. V. Plekhanov, *Russkii rabochii v revolutsionnom dvizhenii (po lichnym vospominaniam)*, originally published in a series of two articles in *Sotsial-Demokrat* (Geneva) in 1890–2. See inter alia the memoirs of I. V. Babushkin (*Vospominaniia Ivana Vasil'evicha Babushkina (1893–1900)*, Leningrad, 1925); G. M. Fisher (*V Rossii i v Anglii, nablindeniia i vospominaniia peterburgskoga rabochego, 1890–1921 gg.*, Moscow, 1922); A. S. Shapovalov (*V bor'be za sotsializm; vospominaniia starogo bolshevika – podposhchika*, Moscow, 1934); and S. I. Kanatchikov (*Iz istorii moego bytiia*, vol. 1, 2, Moscow, 1929–34). The reader may also wish to consult Reginald E. Zelnick, "Russian Rebels. An Introduction to the Memoirs of the Russian Workers Senan Kanatchikov and Matvei Fisher," *Russian Review* 35, nos. 3, 4 (July, October, 1976); and Allan Wildman, *The Making of a Workers' Revolution: Russian Social Democracy, 1891–1903* (University of Chicago Press, 1967).

tion who by the 1890s were already attending Sunday and evening schools in significant numbers to perfect their levels of knowledge and skill, but even among the older ones who did not.[3]

3. These minimal levels of knowledge required for skilled metalworkers' proper performance of their tasks made for a process of natural selection in the original sources of their recruitment: a disproportionate number, even among those (the vast majority) who had immigrated from other parts of the country, had been drawn not from the countryside, let alone from agriculture, but from other urban and/or industrial environments. (Many of these workers were in fact distinguished from a legal standpoint by their appurtenance to the *meshchanstvo*, the hereditary petty bourgeois and artisanal class of Russia's society of *sosloviia*, rather than to the *krestianstvo*, the peasant hereditary estate.)

By the same token, contemporary accounts, especially those of intellectuals, emphasize the rapidity of these workers' process of urbanization, and the *indivisibility* in this process of their rising levels of cultural, social, and economic aspirations and achievements. Indeed, some of these accounts emphasize the indivisibility of the political motivations that animated those workers who were drawn into revolutionary circles from their desires to emulate the material attainments, but also the mores (the "way of life," including the modes of dress) of the members of privileged "census" society with whom these workers were congregated in such close proximity in the urban environment of the capital.[4]

4. Just as economic and social aspirations and attainments were ultimately inseparable from the expansion of cultural and eventually political horizons, so, some of these contemporary descriptions emphasize, the *knowledge* to which these workers aspired was ultimately indivisible. This was particularly the case for the young workers attending Sunday and evening schools, who in the course of this learning process were almost irresistibly impelled to question the traditional cosmogony and the whole structure of superordinate authority that it supported – from the existence of God to the equally unchallengeable rule of the tsar, His ostensible representative on earth. But to a less dramatic degree, this erosion of traditional beliefs (and mores) was also seen to affect older skilled workers who were less formally exposed to the invasion of modern secular knowledge and its contradiction of traditional assumptions.

In some of the workers' memoirs of this period, one is confronted with a far less idealized (and I believe, far more realistic) image of the world of the *zavodskie* of this period, even in the capital. These memoirs lay considerably greater stress on the persistent hold, especially among the older generation of

---

3. On this point, see especially the memoirs of I. V. Babushkin, M. Fisher, and S. Kanatchikov.
4. Plekhanov strongly argues this proposition in his essay, sharply criticizing those intelligentsia agitators on the St. Petersburg scene who deprecated skilled workers' aspirations for material and social attainments.

skilled workers, of traditional values and "superstitions," including traditional religious dogmas and belief in the superordinate authority of the tsar. But these accounts also lay much greater stress on the various manifestations of anomie to which the erosion of traditional beliefs and mores gave rise: drunkenness, theft, violence, and more generally the psychological disorientation, if not the sense of despair, that the new ways of the city and industrial experience frequently induced.

But even more important, some of these reminiscences (especially those recorded by workers who did not so easily gain a sense of mastery of their work and the self-confidence that could be drawn from it) differ from the accounts of intellectuals in painting the world of the plant as one in which bonds of solidarity were at best rare, if not entirely absent. Indeed, as some memoirists describe it, foreign foremen and skilled workers (Balts, Finns, Poles, but especially Germans) displayed open contempt for the ignorant and "uncultured" Russian workers under their charge, and induced in them, in return, a complex mixture of hatred and envy. Russian skilled workers displayed equal contempt for the barbarousness of the *derevenshchiki*, the ignorant "peasant" types often hired directly from the countryside to perform the more menial and/or more demanding physical tasks in their plants (not to mention the *rabochie* working in the nearby factories of other branches of industry). Even Russian skilled workers spent much of their time drinking, brawling, stealing each other's tools, ridiculing and tormenting each other, in the pecking order of superordinate relations so sharply drawn by their respective levels of knowledge and skills and their degrees of assimilation of urban culture and its values.[5]

These features of social and psychological fragmentation, if not total chaos, of the world of the *zavodskie* were greatly accentuated throughout the 1890s by the enormously rapid rate of its expansion: St. Petersburg's metal industry grew from some 21,000 workers in 1884 to over 60,000 by the turn of the century (and that of the Empire as a whole from 103,000 in 1887 to over 250,000 by 1900). Obviously, this tremendous rate of expansion (far exceeding that of other branches of industry, expecially in the capital) made for tremendous vertical as well as horizontal mobility within the plant and from plant to plant – a mobility that helped satisfy skilled workers' rising levels of aspirations – but it also made for a tremendous wave of immigration into the world of the *zavodskie* of workers, skilled but especially unskilled, recruited from outside the capital.

Neither of these conditions, of course, was conducive to the forging of bonds of solidarity among the workers employed in St. Petersburg's metal plants. In fact, in combination with the characteristics of the metal trades that we have

5. The most striking pictures are drawn for us by Shapovalov, whose memoirs are especially valuable because he was one of the rare metalworkers recruited into the social democratic study circles of the period who found it difficult to master the skills, the knowledge – and the self-confidence – required to become a successful *masterovyi*.

already discussed, these patterns and tempos of industrial expansion were reflected throughout the 1890s in two, only seemingly contradictory, features of St. Petersburg's labor movement.

On the one hand, the city's skilled and semiskilled metalworkers, especially the younger ones who attended Sunday and evening schools, provided one of the chief sources of recruitment into the circles of enlightenment and propaganda organized by the Populist, and eventually the Marxist, groups of the revolutionary intelligentsia, and indeed themselves sought to keep such circles in operation even in the absence of intelligentsia leadership.

On the other hand, the metalworkers of the capital hardly engaged throughout this period in *any* industrial strikes. They failed to do so (notwithstanding the appeals of the intelligentsia leadership of the St. Petersburg Union of Liberation of Labor) even when, in 1896–7, vast numbers of the *rabochie* – the largely unskilled workers employed in the city's textile and tobacco factories – were spontaneously drawn into a wave of labor unrest that eventually impelled the government to legislate the eleven-and-a-half-hour labor day.[6] The contradiction, I repeat, was only a superficial one, because those metalworkers who had been drawn into the circles of enlightenment and propaganda – along with a sprinkling of other semiartisanal and artisanal workers (printers, tailors, etc.) – were probably even more culturally estranged thereby from the vast mass of St. Petersburg's working class. It is indeed notable that the ideal image of self to which most of these workers were attracted through their contacts with members of the intelligentsia, even in the Marxist circles of the period, was – beneath the veneer of the phraseology of proletarian class consciousness – that of themselves becoming a workers' *intelligentsia* (rather than identifying in any genuine sense with the benighted *chernorabochie*, the unskilled laborers in their own plants, let alone those of nearby factories).[7]

It was only at the turn of the century that this situation began to change, and that the first real manifestations of labor unrest surfaced in the world of the St. Petersburg *zavodskie* – not, at least as yet, due to any significant changes in the character and organization of their work tasks, but rather because of the sudden contraction of their visions of economic opportunity resulting from the sudden deep recession that the metal industry experienced at the time. It was, in large measure, this economic recession at the turn of the century (and the cuts in base pay, but especially in piece rates and opportunities for piece and overtime work, and for job *advancement*, which this recession induced) that, along with the first manifestations of an opposition movement in "census" society (most notably among the university students of the capital), provided the major catalyst

6. This point is recognized even in the memoirs of I. V. Babushkin, one of the activists of the Union of Struggle for the Emancipation of Labor during this period.
7. For fuller discussions of the psychological dynamics of this interaction, see Allan Wildman, *Making of a Workers' Revolution*, and Reginald Zelnick, "Russian Rebels."

384

for the outbreak of strikes among the city's metalworkers, first and foremost among those employed in state rather than private plants.

More generally, from 1900 to 1904, in sharp contrast to the previous five years, the metal industry in the Empire as a whole displayed the highest indices of strike intensity recorded by the Factory Inspectorate among the various industrial groups under its jurisdiction: its workers, who in 1900 accounted for less than 15% of the labor force under Factory Inspection, were responsible for almost 40% of the rather modest total of 210,000–odd strikers recorded by the Inspectorate during this half decade. (The metalworkers of *St. Petersburg* contributed significantly to this number, however, only in 1901 and 1903.)

The Factory Inspectors' statistics of this period also afford us a few tell-tale signs of the nature of the conflicts to which the economic restrictions suffered by workers of the metal industry gave rise on the factory floor, as well as of the growing bonds of solidarity that metalworkers now displayed in the face of these economic constrictions, and as a result of the relative stabilization that the labor force of the industry underwent during these years. (Even after the economic recovery that the metal industry experienced in 1903 and especially in 1904 following the outbreak of the war with Japan, its labor force increased only modestly, the number of metalworkers under Factory Inspection rising between 1900 and 1905 by only a relatively modest 8%.) The tell-tale signs of changing patterns of labor unrest among metalworkers are to be found in the exceptional proportion of strikes over order in the enterprise (21.7% of the total number of strikers recorded in the metal industry during the years 1900–4, as against 13.5% in Russian industry as a whole). They are also to be found in the proportions of solidarity and political strikes among metalworkers (12% of their strikers as against a national average of 7.9%), and finally in the proportion of defeats that metalworkers experienced in their strike actions (60.3% of the total number of strikers in the industry as against a nationwide average of 51.6%). However, it is equally suggestive that the metal industry did *not* record during this period (not, it appears, at any time up to the post-Lena period) any exceptional indices of strike intensity in *strikes over hours*. (The proportion of the total number of strikers recorded in this category among metalworkers during the years 1900–4, 28.1%, was actually *lower* than the Empirewide average of 30.1%).

St. Petersburg metalworkers undeniably played a catalytic role in the inception of the Revolution of 1905, and the metal industry as a whole contributed a disproportionate number of *political* strikers during Russia's First Revolution (although standing in first place in its indices of strike intensity even for this category of strikes only in 1905). However, metalworkers, especially after 1905, did not record nearly as impressive proportions of the participants in economic strikes recorded by the Factory Inspectorate.

As Table 1 indicates, the percentage of participants in economic strikes that metalworkers contributed to the wave of labor unrest sharply declined in 1906,

Table 1. *Percentage of total number of participants in political and economic strikes in all branches of industry under Factory Inspection contributed by workers of the metal industry, 1905–7*

	Political strikes		Economic strikes	
Year	Strikers contributed by metalworkers (%)	Rank order of strike intensity of metal industry (among 12 industrial groups)	Strikers contributed by metalworkers (%)	Rank order of strike intensity of metal industry (among 12 industrial groups)
1905	21.2	1	22.5	1
1906	25.4	3	10.3	7
1907	31.3	2	16.2	6

Proportion of metalworkers among total number of workers under Factory Inspection in 1905: 16.2%.

and even in 1907 was not disproportionate to their numbers in the total labor force. But what is especially noteworthy is that even in 1907, a year when the workers of *all branches of industry* in St. Petersburg guberniia contributed a proportion of the total number of strikers recorded in the country as a whole most nearly comparable to those observable in the post-Lena period, St. Petersburg's *metalworkers* stood in but *fourth place* among the workers of the capital (behind the workers of the cotton, wool, and flax industries) in their aggregate indices of strike intensity (including both political and economic strikes).

Yet, even if we do not witness at any point during the 1905–7 strike wave the peculiar interplay and mutual reinforcement of political and economic strikes that would become so characteristic of labor unrest among metalworkers by the eve of the war, we do observe the first modest signs of things to come. They surface in the 1906 strike statistics in the indices for the proportion of participants in economic strikes in the metal industry involved in two specific subcategories of strike actions: conflicts with supervisory personnel and strikes over the *system* of allocating pay (rather than over actual levels of pay). In combination, these two subcategories account in 1906 for some 17% of the participants in economic strikes in the metal industry, twice the national average.

Mainly involved in this modest upswell of strikes over *forms* of remuneration in these statistics were the dozen or so defensive strikes that broke out in St. Petersburg in the fall of 1906 in large private mechanical and metal-processing firms (most of them corporately organized) over the substitution for the traditional system of base pay, calculated on a daily basis, of a new system of hourly

386

rates. These were the first manifestations, at least in the form of labor unrest, of the responses among metalworkers to the initial steps in the introduction of a new system, based on new criteria to determine the levels of pay awarded for their labor – a new system of pay that was itself but a component part of a more comprehensive effort to redesign on a systematic basis the character and organization of work processes, largely under the influence of Western conceptions of scientific management.

There is little I need to add here to Heather Hogan's description of this new system of remuneration – including the "American" method of calculating piece rates, with its bonuses for the amount of time taken in the completion of work tasks – except to expand on the impact this new system had on the workers who were subjected to it, and the responses that it eventually evoked in the course of the post-Lena strike wave.

In their letters and reports to the labor press, and eventually in the grievances and demands that surfaced in their strike actions, metalworkers who were subjected to these applications of the doctrines of scientific management, and particularly to the innovations in work processes that they entailed, complained of being nervously and physically exhausted by them, but most of all, of being continuously harassed – indeed treated like "cattle" or "slaves" – by the foremen who sought to administer them. In fact, these innovations eliminated areas of autonomy in the performance of their work that skilled workers had traditionally regarded as their own; or more precisely, as some of the perquisites to be gained through their mastering of the work process. This was particularly the case in those plants of the private sector that went furthest in the process of simplification and standardization of work tasks, and in the specification (on work cards and worksheets) of *how* these tasks were to be performed.

But more generally, in those plants that introduced on a systematic basis the new progressive systems of wage rates and bonuses advocated by the exponents of scientific management, skilled and semiskilled workers were deprived of another equally important dimension of the sense of autonomy that their mastering of the work process had traditionally won for them: that of controlling the time, the rhythm, of their own work. We should clearly emphasize that the central issue in this connection was *not* piece rates per se, to which skilled metalworkers had already become accustomed during the 1890s (and which many of them actually *sought* because of the higher pay that they provided), or even, in a strict sense, the *time* they took to perform their tasks (many of these workers also had become accustomed to, and indeed taken pride in, working faster in order to earn more). At issue, rather, was the sense of loss of control over their own time – their own pace – in the performance of their work. The issue of time was made all the more dramatic because of the variety of efforts on the part of employers to achieve greater labor discipline that were also connected with time:

the time clocks and turnstiles that were now much more generally introduced to discourage lateness in reporting for work; the efforts to control the time consumed by workers in their breaks for tea or to go to the toilet; and the fines for violations of the new rules of internal order that were imposed in this connection, as well as for absenteeism from work. And even more highly symbolic in this regard (and thus even more loudly denounced by the labor press) were the efforts, as yet very modest, to introduce and eventually apply time studies of work performances.

In those mechanical plants in the private sector that went furthest in the efforts to achieve greater productivity and economies of labor and a smoother production flow through the simplification and standardization of work tasks and the attendant greater mechanization of the production process, and especially in those enterprises in which this process involved the introduction of specific mechanisms to specify how tasks were to be performed, skilled and semiskilled workers felt most sharply deprived of their sense of autonomy and control over their own work. But in order to fully understand the impact that these innovations had on these specific strata of workers, we should also bring to mind that attendant to their introduction, there also took place in these plants certain significant changes in the character and composition of both the work force and supervisory personnel. These changes further contributed to the erosion among the skilled, and especially the semiskilled, workers employed in these enterprises of their status or potential status as *masterovye*, masters or potential masters of their own work.

This sense of constriction, if not of invasion, was induced from below as well as from above. From below, because the simplification and standardization of work tasks made possible the employment of various types of unskilled workers for the performance of tasks that had traditionally been reserved for skilled and semiskilled workers: unskilled laborers (*chernorabochiye*), worker assistants (*podruchnye*), "apprentices" (now in name only *ucheniki*), and last but not least, women. We should note that up to the outbreak of the war, the increase in the proportions of such workers, and especially of women, in the mechanical and metal-processing industry remained actually quite modest. (It did increase dramatically, however, during the years of the First World War.) That it aroused such loud protest during the prewar period, was due to the fact that the employment of such workers, and especially of women, to perform more than menial tasks was so unprecedented, and injurious to male workers' sense of self-esteem.

Far more pervasive was the invasion from above induced by the appearance at these plants of the various engineers, cost accountants, and bookkeepers, who were now hired to introduce and supervise the implementation of the various innovations in the character and organization of the work processes. The evidence (some of it quoted by Hogan) suggests that the increase in the numbers of these new types of supervisory personnel was more substantial in

388

mechanical than in other metal-processing enterprises (although even in most mechanical enterprises they did not reach dramatic proportions until *after* the outbreak of the war). To explain the reaction that the phenomenon aroused among machinists and other skilled workers in mechanical plants even before the war, especially in the private sector, we have to take further account of two of its major features.

The first was that, in many cases, the persons hired to perform these various supervisory and control functions assumed their positions of authority over the work force, not on the basis of accumulated experience on the factory floor (i.e., through the traditional life path from apprenticeship to *masterovyi* and eventually to senior worker [*starshina*] and foreman), but through training in engineering and business schools, generally inaccessible even to the children of skilled workers. Not only did the appearance of this new breed of men thus introduce a new dimension of social distinction and friction in the relationship between workers and supervisory personnel, but even more basically it also induced a constriction, new at least in degree, in the sense of possibility that young workers could entertain of themselves advancing in the course of their working lives to supervisory positions in the production process. We should also note that this erosion of the sense of possibility of professional advancement within the enterprise, by moving to another enterprise (greatly accentuated during the years of recession by the contraction of the labor force), also occurred precisely at a time when a new generation of young metalworkers was also appearing on the factory floor. These young workers were literate, better educated, and at least potentially more competent than ever before, partly as a result of the higher levels of education that many of them now also attained, not only in elementary and evening and Sunday schools, but also in some cases in the new secondary technical schools that were opening in growing numbers, especially in the capital.

But there was yet another dimension in the resentments to which these changes in the character and organization of work processes gave rise, and particularly to their eventual translation into labor unrest, especially among young workers. Notwithstanding the appearance of a new breed of men to introduce the various innovations that the reorganization of production processes entailed, actual supervision on the shopfloor from day to day continued to be exercised – in many if not in most plants – by foremen of the old type, who had risen to their positions through the traditional path of accumulated work experience. Yet even when they did not lead to their actual replacement, the new relations of production effectively delegitimized the position of these foremen of the old type, sapping their power and especially their moral authority in the eyes of the workers, especially young workers under their charge. For these new relations and systems of administration of production deprived these foremen as *well* of the power and the autonomy that they had traditionally enjoyed: their

389

traditional prerogatives of assigning work tasks and deciding (in interaction with the workers themselves) how these tasks were to be performed; and determining the wage levels (and in particular, the piece rates) to be awarded for these work performances.

These considerable areas of discretion that foremen had traditionally enjoyed had frequently made for displays of arbitrariness of which the workers victimized by them had sometimes bitterly complained, but by the same token they had greatly reinforced the foreman's *authority* in the eyes of most workers. Even more to the point, the traditional discretionary authority of the foremen had established informal, yet highly flexible, patterns of labor relations that reflected with a considerable degree of accuracy and sensitivity the actual relations of power and authority on the factory floor, and thus provided significant safety valves for the avoidance and/or defusion of labor conflicts. By the same token, the new depersonalized relations of production that had now been introduced (ironically, in part precisely to reduce the element of arbitrariness in labor relations, and thus to reduce labor conflicts) not only had the effect of greatly reducing the power and moral authority of the foremen, but also of removing the safety valves provided hitherto by these more traditional patterns of labor relations, and the informal bargaining process for which they had allowed between foremen of the old type and the workers under their charge.

Under the circumstances, all that was left of the traditional patterns of labor relations was their *negative* features: the brusqueness and the rudeness with which foremen of the old type sought to apply the new depersonalized system of wage rates and the new rules of internal order, almost as unfamiliar to them as to the workers under their charge. These displays of rudeness and arbitrariness were now felt all the more sharply by young workers, not only because so many of them were now more literate, more "cultured" than their foremen, and therefore more demanding of courteous and polite address, but also because the foremen of the old type were now so largely deprived of the aura of personalized authority and of the sense of assurance with which their traditional areas of personal discretion and power had hitherto infused their roles.[8]

It was in the context of these changes in the social compostion of the work force and supervisory personnel and of the new dimensions introduced into labor relations by the changes in the character, organization, and supervision of production processes in the metal industry (greatly reinforced up to 1910 by the effects of the contraction of its labor force), that workers of this industry, and especially young semiskilled workers, developed really for the first time a full sense of being industrial workers (rather than *masterovye*). And it was on the

---

8. These appear to have been the patterns of interaction with supervisors that generally underlay the outbreak of the often very bitter and drawn out strikes over order among St. Petersburg metalworkers in the spring and early summer of 1913. The only notable exception was the strike at Aivaz, which did in fact break out over the conduct of time studies.

basis of this new sense of identity that these workers forged new bonds of solidarity, and articulated and *generalized* the grievances induced by the situation that was now defined for them in the workplace and by the contraction of their sense of economic and social possibilities.

These last observations, and more generally the prominence that the younger generation of metalworkers have assumed in this discussion, impel us to take note of two, at first sight somewhat puzzling, features suggested by the strike statistics at our disposal concerning the character and dynamics of labor unrest in the metal industry during the post-Lena period.

The first is that in St. Petersburg's mechanical industry, the hotbeds of labor unrest during these years tended to be the newer rather than the older plants of the private firms of that industry: new Lessner rather than old Lessner, the new Siemens plant on the St. Petersburg side rather than the old Siemens plant in Vasileostrov. It was in these newer plants of St. Petersburg's mechanical industry – whose work forces were generally distinguished by higher proportions of young, often recently hired semiskilled workers – that labor conflicts by and large originally broke out. The workers in these enterprises drew in their wake the work forces of the older plants of the same firms (which tended to include higher proportions of older, more highly skilled *masterovye*), sometimes only after several weeks or months, marked by an initial reluctance on the part of the workers of these older plants to become involved in the strike actions.[9]

These frequent time lags, especially in the outbreak of nonpolitical strikes, and the differences in their incidence between the newer and older enterprises of St. Petersburg's mechanical industry are explicable, in part at least by the differences of age and status between the skilled and semiskilled workers that they respectively employed, but also by the fact that it was in the more recently established of these enterprises that the novel forms of the organization of work processes and work relations that we are considering were generally most fully imposed, and by the same token evoked the greatest resentments among the workers who were subjected to them.[10] This fact, in turn, helps account for another seemingly puzzling feature that labor unrest among metalworkers assumed during the post-Lena strike wave. It is that so few of their strike actions were explicitly directed at the abolition of the progressive hourly rates per se. In 1906, when hourly rates were originally introduced in certain of the capital's private plants, no less than a dozen strikes led by St. Petersburg's Union of Metallists

9. This is the pattern suggested by the reports on labor unrest published during this period by the labor press, as well as by those recorded by the Department of Police and the St. Petersburg Society of Manufacturers and Mill Owners.

10. These observations surface in several of the histories of St. Petersburg metal plants prepared, on the basis of the reminiscences collected from workers employed in them, in the course of a project directed by Maxim Gorki in the late 1920s and early 30s. (*Istoriia zavodov*). They are most strikingly drawn in the manuscripts on the old and new Lessner plants ("Istoriia zavoda im. Karla Marksa, byvshchyi Lessner") deposited in TSGAOR (Moscow), *f.* 7952, *op.* 4, *d.* 48 and 49.

had broken out over this issue (all of them ending in labor defeats); the introduction of this new system represented at the time to the workers employed in these plants a genuine *break* with earlier work practices. By the eve of the war, however, this was no longer the case. Aside from the very large and steadily rising number of political strikes, the wave of labor unrest that unfolded in mechanical and metal-processing enterprises was distinguished (in St. Petersburg by the spring of 1913, in the rest of the country by the early fall of 1913) by disproportionate numbers of participants in strikes for a shorter labor day, as well as in conflicts with supervisory personnel. It may well be argued that these types of strike actions in fact constituted just as direct challenges of their employers' authority by the workers implicated in them, given the concern for the restoration of labor discipline, and even more precisely the desire to discourage demands for shorter hours, which had been one of the prime motivations of the St. Petersburg Society of Factory and Mill Owners in seeking to promote the new system of pay rates. But another order of explanation is that in their growing challenge of existing authority, the new generation of young metalworkers who constituted the real "inciters" of labor unrest during the prewar period were not principally motivated by a conscious desire to restore the old factory order and its moral economy, and were in fact articulating grievances and claims grounded in their recently discovered, or at least reinforced, sense of working-class identity, rather than in the self-image of would-be *masterovye*, shape by the traditions of a world that most of them in fact had never directly experienced.

Be that as it may, the statistics compiled by the St. Petersburg Society of Manufacturers and Mill Owners enable us to draw a relatively precise and differentiated picture of the character that labor conflicts actually assumed in the metal enterprises of the capital during these years.[11] Specifically, these statistics that, unlike those of the Factory Inspectorate, provided separate breakdowns of the strike actions recorded in St. Petersburg's dozen odd electrotechnical plants and in other mechanical enterprises bring out, for both 1913 and 1914, quite distinctive patterns of labor unrest among the work forces employed in these two subgroups.

Sharply distinguishing the patterns characteristic of St. Peterburg's mechanical enterprises in 1913 from those observable in its electrotechnical subgroup was the large proportion of strike actions (almost $\frac{2}{5}$ of the total) classified in these statistics as neither "political" nor "economic," but as "demonstrative" strikes – the terminology used by the St. Petersburg Society to distinguish strikes over order in the enterprise, including conflict with supervisory personnel. In contrast, almost no strike actions were recorded in this category for St. Petersburg's electrotechnical plants (and only a few for any other of the groups

---

11. These statistics are recorded in the reports for 1913 and 1914 of the St. Petersburg Society deposited in TSGIA (Leningrad), *f.* 150, *op.* 1, *d.* 667 and 669.

of the St. Petersburg Society), almost all of the strikes in electrotechnical enterprises being classified as either "political" or "economic," including a disproportionate number of strikes for shorter hours. By 1914 the number of "economic" strikes reported in the capital's Electrotechnical Group (just as in most other groups of the St. Petersburg Society) declined very sharply, as labor unrest in the capital generally assumed an overwhelmingly political character. But even during the six and a half months preceding the outbreak of the war, the statistics of the St. Petersburg Society continued to record a significant number of "demonstrative" strikes in its Mechanical Group. (The only other industrial enterprises for which such strikes were now listed were a few large textile and chemical factories.)

In seeking to account for these different patterns of labor unrest within St. Petersburg's metal industry, we need to recall that its electrotechnical plants, almost all of them affiliated with foreign firms, were by and large the most advanced and technically proficient enterprises of the capital. They employed the most coherent, highly skilled, and highly paid work forces (including large numbers of young graduates of the city's technical schools), and also disproportionate numbers of technicians and other supervisory personnel, many of them foreigners, administering, at every stage, production processes (inspired in many cases by the new doctrines of scientific management) that had originally been introduced at the home plants of these foreign firms. In contrast, most of the city's other mechanical and metal-processing enterprises were relatively more backward as well as more diversified. Old patterns of production and production relations coexisted in them (in different and sometimes even in the same shops) with new production processes; and the functioning of these production processes was still largely if not entirely supervised on the shopfloor by the now delegitimized foremen of the old type, whose profiles and patterns of interaction with the workers under their charge we have sought earlier to describe.

This brings us to another difference in patterns of labor unrest within the capital's metal industry that these reports of the St. Petersburg Society and those of the Department of Police also suggest. It is that equally distinctive of the character of the strike actions of the work forces of electrotechnical enterprises during this period (as well as of the "filialy" of foreign firms in other branches of the mechanical industry) was the absence, even in nonpolitical strikes, of the phenomenon of *tsekhovshchina* – of the fragmentation of labor unrest among workers in different shops, and indeed different trades. Even in older mechanical and metal-processing plants – typically engaging in more diversified forms of production in which older and more traditional processes and relations of production coexisted and indeed intermingled with the new – the phenomenon of *tsekhovshchina* was by and large no longer apparent by the eve of the war in political strikes, the workers of different shops overwhelmingly

393

joining by this time in this type of strike action. But this phenomenon was still manifest (and indeed continued to surface even during the 1917 Revolution) in *economic* strikes, especially in very large enterprises such as the Putilov works (making for a deceptive swelling of the strike statistics recorded for them). In electrotechnical enterprises, however, as well as in the more modern filialy of foreign firms in other sectors of the mechanical industry, the phenomenon of *tsekhovshchina* was largely transcended by the eve of the war even in strike actions classified as "economic"; especially so in strikes over hours and over order in the enterprise, in which overwhelming proportions if not the entire work forces of these plants were almost consistently involved.[12]

All of this suggests that it was in these newer and more modern plants, and specifically in those in which the various strategies of scientific management were most consistently applied, that the workers who were subjected to them had also developed most fully by this time a sense of *working-class identity and class solidarity*, which they displayed even in the conduct of their economic struggles. It is hardly surprising that this should be so, given the fact that the various dimensions of these strategies of scientific management – including the introduction of more uniform patterns of production and of more uniform forms of control and remuneration of work tasks – had contributed to the emergence of less diversified work forces, as well as to a more unified treatment of them. But the end results is also ironic, given the initial assumption entertained by exponents of doctrines of scientific management that the achievement of these very objective – the creation of more coherent work forces and especially a more consistent and uniform treatment of them – would also lead to the defusion of the sources of labor conflicts, and thus eventually contribute to labor peace.

These subtle differences in patterns of labor unrest are not brought out in the contemporary statistics published by the Factory Inspectorate. They present the data for strikes by causes only in aggregated form for all branches of the metal industry, and indeed distinguish among geographical concentrations of metalworkers only in the data provided for overall strike intensity, without specification of the chief causes attributed for strike actions. But even these geographical breakdowns are worthy of attention, for they suggest that in all areas of the Empire in which metalworkers – and especially those employed in machine construction – were represented in large numbers, they struck throughout the post-Lena strike wave in altogether disproportionate numbers by comparison with workers of other industries. Recorded in Table 2 are the indices we have drawn from these statistics of the proportions of workers striking in 1914 in the metal industry, as against all other industrial groups under Factory

12. These observations are drawn from the contemporary strike statistics of the St. Petersburg Society as well as those of the Department of Police deposited in TSGAOR, *f.* 102 (DP), IV, *d.* 61, and in *f.* 111 (St. Petersburg Okhrannoe Otdelenie).

Table 2. *Percentages of work forces striking in 1914 in metal industry as against workers in all other groups under Factory Inspection*

Location	Indices for workers in metal industry (group 8)	Aggregate indices for workers employed in all other industrial groups
St. Petersburg gub.	542.7	212.6
Lifland	395.3	153.1
Estland	267.1	38.1
Tver	250.2	31.5
Moscow	177.8	16.4
Kherson	66.1	18.1
Nizhegorodskaia	63.3	2.0
Saratov	31.7	3.3
Bakinskaia	131.4	86.2
Donskaia	27.8	10.6
Orlovskaia	96.4	13.9
Kharkov	181.6	6.2
Empire as a whole	215.9	44.1
Empire without St. Petersburg gub.	117.6	29.1

Inspection, in various areas of the country where mechanical enterprises were significantly represented.

These indices suggest that the aggregate data that the Factory Inspectorate provided on the character and intensity of labor unrest in the metal industry as a whole were to a considerable degree representative of patterns of labor unrest not only among metalworkers of St. Petersburg *guberniia*, but also among metalworkers in other parts of the country, especially those employed in machine construction. (Throughout the post-Lena period, workers outside St. Petersburg *guberniia* accounted for over 50% of the total number of strikers recorded by the Factory Inspectorate for the metal industry as a whole; and substantially more so, we would suggest, in nonpolitical than in political strikes, given the disproportionate concentration of political strikes in the capital.)

With this reassurance of their broadly representative character, let us consider what the aggregate data provided by the Factory Inspectorate about the chief causes of strikes suggest about patterns of labor unrest in the metal industry during the post-Lena strike wave, by comparison with all other industries (see tables in Appendix 1).

First and foremost, these figures bring out the extraordinary and disproportionate involvement of metalworkers throughout the prewar period in political strikes, most notably so in the capital, the other data at our disposal suggest, but also to a lesser degree in all other areas of European Russia (with the exception of the Kingdom of Poland) where substantial numbers of workers employed in mechanical plants were represented. In 1912 (when the metal industry was responsible for but 15.7% of the total number of workers under Factory Inspection) metalworkers accounted for 56.5% of the number of strikers and 56.2% of the days lost in political strikes recorded among all workers under the jurisdiction of the Inspectorate. For 1913 these indices rise, respectively, to 67.9% and 69.5%. And even in 1914, when political strikes spread much more widely during the six and a half months preceding the war among workers employed in other industrial groups (especially so in the capital), metalworkers still accounted for 62.6% of the total number of participants and 59.4% of the number of days lost in political strikes.

The indices for the intensity of specific categories of economic strikes in the metal industry during the post-Lena period are equally distinctive – bringing out consistently the disproportionate numbers of metalworkers involved, by comparison with workers of other industries, in strikes over hours and conflicts with supervisory personnel. Our other indices – particularly those for the numbers of days lost per worker, and especially per striker, in different categories of nonpolitical strikes – are even more notable for the changes that they bring out in the character and dynamics that these strikes assumed among metalworkers between Lena and the outbreak of the war.

In 1913, the first year of the post-Lena strike wave in which strikes over hours surfaced as a major phenomenon in the aggregate data of the Factory Inspectorate, metalworkers accounted for 58.3% of the total number of strikes, and 92% of the days lost recorded in this catagory of strikes, and the mean duration of their strikes over hours (almost entirely over the length of the labor day) climbed to a remarkable 26.4 days per striker as against an average of 3.2 for workers in all other industries. A number of extraordinarily persistent strikes for a shorter workday (some of them lasting as much as two or three months) were pressed, largely during the spring and early summer of 1913, by the work forces of a number of St. Petersburg's mechanical and metal-processing plants, the phenomenon spreading by fall among metalworkers employed in other parts of the Empire. Workers of the metal industry also accounted in 1913 for 48.9% of the number of strikers and 62.1% of the days lost in conflicts with supervisory personnel, the mean duration of this category of strikes climbing in the metal industry to 13.5 days per striker (from 6.9 in 1912) as against an average of but 9.0 per striker for workers in all other industries.

In 1914 metalworkers accounted for 53% of the total number of strikers and days lost in conflicts with supervisory personnel. The degree of their involvement in strikes over hours also continued to rise: The metal industry recorded during the six and a half months preceding the outbreak of the war as large a number of strikers in conflicts over the length of the labor day as in all of 1913. Consequently, notwithstanding a notable spread of strikes over hours among workers in other industries, metalworkers still accounted in 1914 for 43.2% of the number of strikers recorded in this category of strikes (as against but 25% of the number of participants in strikes over wages).

However, this element of continuity masks a major change in the patterns of labor unrest that metalworkers displayed during these last prewar months. It was the abrupt decline in the mean duration of their strikes over hours (from an average of 26.4 days per striker in 1913 to but 7.3 per striker in 1914). This phenomenon was in fact observable in all other categories of the ostensibly economic strikes in which metalworkers still engaged during this period, including conflicts with supervisory personnel (in which the mean duration of their strike actions declined from 15.3 days per striker in 1913 to 5.5 in 1914), and strikes over wages (whose mean duration also declined from 9.0 days per striker to 3.5). As a reverse trend was apparent in degree of persistence with which workers in other industries pressed their strikes over hours and over wages during these last prewar months, the proportion of the total number of days lost in these two categories of strikes among workers under Factory Inspection accounted for by metalworkers correspondingly declined: to but 16.1% of the number of days lost in strikes over hours and to a remarkably low 9.6% of the days lost in strikes over wages (far below the 17% accounted for by metalworkers of the total number of workers under Factory Inspection).

Russia's metalworkers afford us a prime example of the extraordinary degree to which labor protest among its politically more militant strata of workers was channelized by the eve of the war into explicitly political-demonstrative strikes (these strikes accounted in 1914 for 82.4% of the number of days lost in all strike actions recorded among metalworkers). But they also provide a dramatic illustration of the extent to which, among such highly politicized workers, *all other forms* of labor conflicts – including strikes over hours – now demonstrated by the feverish staccato pace at which they were conducted, the character of additional manifestations of revolutionary unrest.

The dynamics that labor conflicts assumed even in ostensibly nonpolitical strikes and also the special symbolic significance that strikes over hours came to display, for workers and employers alike, are also glaringly reflected in the statistics on the outcomes of these strike actions. For 1914, the data of the Factory Inspectorate about the results of economic strikes among workers of the metal industry bring out that but 4.3% of their participants were involved in labor victories, 20.2% in compromise settlements between strikers and employers, and a staggering 75.5% in outright labor defeats (involving no concessions whatsoever to the strikers' demands). Our indices for the outcomes of the strikes over hours that metalworkers conducted in 1914 are even more stunning: only 0.7% of their participants were recorded in labor victories, 1.8%

in compromise settlements, and no less than 97.5% in outright labor defeats (!).

This discussion, as well as that contributed earlier by Heather Hogan, may have focused attention on the structural changes in the character of production processes and in their modes of supervision and compensation that Russia's metal industry experienced largely after 1905, and on the effects of these changes on the patterns of labor unrest that metalworkers so strikingly came to display by the eve of the First World War. It remains for us to explore, however, the role that conjunctural factors, political and economic, also played in unleashing this storm of labor protest, and in eventually channelizing it into more explicit and generalized patterns of revolt against all forms of the exercise of superordinate authority.

Appendix 1

Table 1.1. *Indices of strike intensity in different categories of strikes in enterprises of metal industry under Factory Inspection, January–December 1912*

	Number and proportion of strikers			
	% of metalworkers striking	% of strikers	% of economic strikers	% of all strikers in Empire
Political-demonstrative strikes	91.8	83.8	—	56.5
All economic strikes	17.8	16.2	100.0	34.2
Incl. strikes over:				
Wages	10.5	9.4	59.3	30.2
Hours	1.5	1.4	8.6	56.0
Order in Enterprise	5.7	5.2	32.1	39.8
Incl. conflicts with supervisory personnel	2.8	2.5	15.6	0.3
Totals	109.5	100.0	100.0	51.0

	Number and proportion of days lost				
	Days lost per worker	Days lost per striker	% of all days lost	% of economic days lost	% of days lost in Empire
Political-demonstrative strikes	0.8	0.9	26.0	—	56.2
All economic strikes	2.4	13.6	74.0	100.0	43.9
Incl. strikes over:					
Wages	1.8	17.4	56.2	75.9	41.9
Hours	0.2	12.3	5.7	7.7	39.5
Order in Enterprise	0.4	6.9	12.1	16.3	42.9
Incl. conflicts with supervisory personnel	0.2	6.8	5.7	7.7	44.0
Totals	3.3	3.0	100.0	100.0	46.5

Proportion of total number of workers under Factory Inspection accounted for by metal industry: 15.7%.

Table 1.2. *Indices of strike intensity in different categories of strikes in enterprises of the metal industry under Factory Inspection, January–December 1913*

	Number and proportion of strikers			
	% of metalworkers striking	% of strikers	% of economic strikers	% of all strikers in Empire
Political-demonstrative strikes	87.4	72.4	—	67.9
All economic strikes	27.6	22.9	100.0	32.9
Incl. strikes over:				
Wages	19.7	16.3	71.3	28.9
Hours	2.2	1.8	7.8	58.3
Order in Enterprise	5.8	4.8	20.8	47.2
Incl. conflicts with				
supervisory personnel	4.0	3.3	14.5	48.9
Totals	120.8	100.0	100.0	52.5

	Number and proportion of days lost			
	Days lost per worker	Days lost per striker	% of all days lost	% of economic days lost	% of days lost in Empire
Political-demonstrative strikes	0.9	1.1	22.7	—	69.5
All economic strikes	3.1	11.2	74.9	100.0	37.7
Incl. strikes over:					
Wages	1.8	9.0	43.1	57.6	28.2
Hours	0.6	26.4	13.9	18.6	92.0
Order in Enterprise	0.7	12.7	17.8	23.8	58.2
Incl. conflicts with					
supervisory personnel	0.6	15.3	14.9	19.9	62.1
Totals	4.1	3.4	100.0	100.0	41.0

Proportion of number of workers under Factory Inspection accounted for by the metal industry: 16.6%.

Table 1.3 *Indices of strike intensity in different categories of strikes in enterprises of the metal industry under Factory Inspection, January–December 1914*

	Number and proportion of strikers			
	% of metalworkers striking	% of strikers	% of economic strikers	% of all strikers in Empire
Political-demonstrative strikes	177.8	82.4	—.	62.6
All economic strikes	25.3	11.9	100.0	31.5
Incl. strikes over:				
Wages	10.9	5.0	42.9	25.0
Hours	8.9	4.1	35.2	43.2
Order in Enterprise	5.5	2.6	21.9	34.1
Incl. conflicts with				
supervisory personnel	5.3	2.5	20.9	53.0
Totals	215.9	100.0	100.0	56.0

	Number and proportion of days lost				
	Days lost per worker	Days lost per striker	% of all days lost	% of economic days lost	% of days lost in Empire
Political-demonstrative strikes	2.9	1.6	62.9	—	59.4
All economic strikes	1.6	6.1	33.8	100.0	13.5
Incl. strikes over:					
Wages	0.6	5.5	13.1	38.8	9.4
Hours	0.6	7.3	14.1	41.7	16.1
Order in Enterprise	0.3	5.5	6.6	19.5	29.4
Incl. conflicts with					
supervisory personnel	0.3	5.6	6.5	19.1	53.0
Totals	4.6	2.1	100.0	100.0	27.6

Proportion of number of workers recorded accounted for by metal industry: 17.6%.

17

Social characteristics, attitudes, and patterns of strike behavior of the metalworkers in Italy during the First World War

BRUNO BEZZA

The new class of Metalworkers and the First World War

The First World War induced great changes in the character of the working class and in industrial relations. The slow evolution of industrial relations since the turn of the century, and the very foundations of the social structure were abruptly upset – so much so that it was said that "the war was veritably a typhoon that radically changed the structure of Italian society and modified, at the same time, its social texture." A new working class emerged, forged in the miliarized factories, changed in its organic composition, younger and more impatient than the one that had fought the big trade unions battles during the Giolitti period.[1]

The Great War altered the patterns of industrial relations that had slowly become established in the Giolittian era. During the war, hiring contracts and collective wage agreements assumed a political and legal significance unknown in earlier legislation. Trade unions and employers discovered different, often compulsory mechanisms for mediating labor conflicts. The more progressive members of the political and administrative classes, and later employers and trade unions, sought to put some order in the customs and regulations that had built up through the years, and to set up an organic and binding system of industrial relations. The great structural changes that took place in industry thus made possible the emergence of a uniform set of rules governing social relations in industrial firms.[2]

The First World War also generated such a number of social, economic, and structural changes in the working class, as to create a clear divide in the

---

1. G. Procacce, "Intervento," in *Movimento operaio e socialista. Bilancio storiografico e problemi storici. Convegno di Firenze, 18–20 gennaio 1963,* (Ed. del Gallo, 1965), p. 310.
2. See A. Camarda, "Classe operaia e grande guerra. A proposito di alcuni recenti studi," in *Studi Bresciani,* 1981, no. 4: 136–44.

character and conditions of employment. Although, before the war, the characteristics of the work forces in mechanical, engineering, and metallurgical firms had differed greatly from one enterprise to another, skilled craftsmen constituted in most of them a factor of central importance. Only years of apprenticeship could produce a high degree of skill and the worker who actually achieved this status jealously guarded it, since it afforded him a high bargaining power and autonomy in the workplace. Clearly, this highly paid workers' elite presented an objective check to workshop rationalization and to the introduction of technical innovations; hence, the hostility between skilled craftsmen and rank-and-file workers, and the mistrust by males of female workers whom they regarded as competitors. This situation was of serious concern to the Union Secretariat of FIOM (Federazione Italiana Operai Metallugici, Italian Union of Metalworkers), because of the strong centrifugal pressures that it induced among members of the work force. Eventually FIOM was driven to make desperate efforts to achieve control over the labor market.

As the number of industries mobilized for the war effort grew, the number of workers employed in them grew exponentially, even in the short term. The numbers of women and children displayed the largest percentage growth. In industrial centers like Milan, offers of employment far outran demand. This generated an influx into the labor force of unskilled workers, most of rural backgrounds, who were generally assigned extremely repetitive and simple tasks. Thus, skilled craftsmen lost the importance they had once held, as technological innovations and labor market pressure increasingly curtailed their roles.[3]

According to contemporary experts, the operation of the production cycle required a type of worker capable of operating a specific machine throughout the working day. These workers had to be so interchangeable as to make possible the introduction of several production shifts, during which a standardized productivity could consistently be maintained through the elimination of differences in working capacity and the attainment of common standards of tolerances, gauges, and properties in the pieces produced. Paradoxically, one could say that the new type of "skilled" worker (*ouvrier spécialisé*) was to operate only one type of lathe, or even only a specific make of lathe, to produce exclusively a specific piece.

Yet, it is evident that only big enterprises could undertake the task of plant rationalization and retraining on-the-job required for the employment of these new skilled workers. A typical example of this restructuring was the creation of maintenance and tools departments to handle tools sharpening and maintenance work. Hence, the more rationalized the operations of the enterprise, the greater

---

3. See the statistical data in the review "Citta di Milano" for the years 1915–18 and A. Camarda and S. Peli, *L'altro esercito* (Milan: Feltrinelli, 1980), pp. 57–64.

the division of labor that was the essential factor in achieving higher productivity. To quote A. Touraine, "The initiative of the worker who operates the machine is becoming less and less needed, while the machine itself is becoming more and more autonomous."[4]

This new condition did not entail merely technical changes. It also involved a shift from production methods requiring workers to possess specific kinds of skills to ones for which such skills were no longer indispensable. The role of the traditional craft worker was made obsolete by such rationalization. When a machine broke down, an engineer was called in to repair it, and a special department was entrusted with the preparation of tools and the adjustment of machinery. Another department was to determine production times and methods, as was already the case for workshop accounting, previously integrated into piece mastering.

We could describe this transition phase as one in which more time was spent in preparatory work, the economy of time achieved in actual production and the reduced need for higher skills more than making up for it. The new production system no longer allowed for idle time. Whereas previously a skilled craftsman, knowing all the components that made up the final item, could touch up the piece if it was imperfect, now work coordination and new precision lathes provided substitutes for most of his professional skill.

The increase in the number of unskilled workers and female labor was especially impressive in Milan's armaments industry, but it also eventually encompassed the chemical and textile industries. The numbers of skilled workers and semiskilled machine operators suffered the same decline as that of skilled craftsmen. This was due in part to the restructuring processes of the factories that led to a reduction in the transportation work force, once particularly large, and in part to the fact that skilled and semiskilled workers were made redundant by the new technical processes. Semiskilled workers were to make their comeback in the workshop at a later stage, although in roles severely diminished by the new production systems. Thus, they ceased to represent within the factory a step in a career of which mastery of a "trade" once was the final goal.

Before 1914, unionism had involved the organization of workers by trades. Common attitudes toward the union were shared by a high percentage of the members, whose proportion of the work force fluctuated between 2% and 4%. The Great War was a transition phase during which union membership passed the 5% mark until, at the end of the war, trade unions became a mass movement. However, this new phase marked the final decline of skilled craftsmen and of their professional solidarity. It saw the emergence of unskilled workers who had

4. A. Touraine, "L'organizzazione professionale dell'impresa," in G. Friedman, and P. Naville, *Trattato di sociologia del lavoro*, (Milan: Ed. Comunita, 1963); A. Touraine, *L'evoluzione del lavoro operaio alla Renault* (Turin: Rosenberg Y Sellier, 1976).

no professional identity and displayed little solidarity, and who contributed, therefore, to make this a period of contradictions and instability in the development of unions. While union membership sharply increased, the mass of new members used the organization merely as a tool for demanding higher wages, rather than as an instrument for the promotion of social, professional, and moral values. It was no coincidence that the professional dissatisfaction of unskilled workers, semiskilled workers, and semiskilled machine operators always manifested itself in economic demands, thus causing serious conflicts within the FIOM sections between their leaderships and rank and files, making life hard for the regional committees. However, it is also true that FIOM relinquished control over factory discipline in exchange for wage increases and the official sanctioning of its role. In point of fact, FIOM proved powerless when unskilled workers and female labor were fined, or when political and union activists were sent to the front to fight.

An analysis of industrial labor conflicts during the war is very difficult. Unlike those of the prewar period, wartime labor conflicts did not bring to the foreground any basic general tendencies. Rather, there were numerous single-objective struggles over wages, regulations, or normative procedures, often reaching their climax in explosive street demonstrations, such as the one that took place in Turin in August 1917. To identify the main aspects of this fragmentation of labor conflicts, it is necessary to piece together, at least from a quantitative point of view, patterns of strike behavior, as well as the actions taken by unions.

Two patterns of considerable interest emerge from such a quantitative analysis. The first is the intensity of labor unrest in "mechanical construction" enterprises, a sector that had witnessed broad and rapid changes in technology and the composition of its work forces, and in which FIOM had important strongholds (Turin being the main example). The second pattern is that, whereas the number of strikes tended to decrease (due in part to the repressive regulations of the Industrial Mobilization), workers' participation in them increased rapidly. The conditions and objectives of labor conflicts had become more general, and the structures of work forces less polarized than in preceding years.

These considerations help explain the important role played by wartime labor conflicts in laying the ground for the workers' mobilization during the *biennio rosso* (the red biennium). Yet, the percentage of planned strikes, according to the figures supplied by Buozzi at the Seventh Congress of 1918, remained at a very low level: 15.3% in 1915, 4.4% in 1916 (the year of the most massive involvement of metalworkers in strikes over the introduction of female labor and the labor discipline imposed by the Industrial Mobilization), and 10.6% in 1917.

In the four wartime years, FIOM was faced with a rapidly expanding and changing world in which it was difficult to organize and to devise a strategy of

405

labor demands. The General Confederation of Labor (Confederazione Generale del Lavoro) began to address the more general problems of concern to the workers (the rise in the cost of living, excess profits, the war levy). Afraid of being left out, FIOM decided to join, as a third party, the Industrial Mobilization. It declared that "the proletariat would not tolerate an Industrial Mobilization that would be only to its expense," noting however that "while... in drawing up the Industrial Mobilization documents, only the industrialists have been heard, it cannot be said that our opinion has gone unheeded."[5]

The first results of FIOM's involvement were that union disputes that could not be settled within the enterprise were arbitrated by the regional committees of the Industrial Mobilization and by the national committees upon third petition; all contracts of employment were frozen until three months after the end of the war; and resignations, dismissals, and workers' transfers from plant to plant were subject to the rulings of the regional committees of the Industrial Mobilization.[6] Sixteen disputes were settled by the Lombardy regional committee of the Industrial Mobilization in 1916, 171 in 1917, 210 in 1918 (making a total of 417, compared to the 948 disputes settled at the national level). In the metalworking sector of Lombardy the number of disputes from 1915 to 1918 totaled 181, slightly under 50% of all disputes settled. These percentage figures are very interesting: metalworking and mechanical engineering enterprise in Lombardy accounted for less than half of the disputes settled, even though 80–90% of them were mobilized, while the other industrial sectors had much lower mobilization levels. This pattern is even more paradoxical when we consider the number of disputes settled by ordinance. In Lombardy, from 1916 to 1918, there were as many as 178 out of a national total of 458, while disputes settled by the national committee amounted to 67 out of a total of 186. If we add up all disputes settled on second and third petitioning from 1916 to 1918 in Lombardy, we reach a total of 662 out of a national total of 1,592. And of the 662 disputes in all mobilized industrial sectors in Lombardy, only 181 were in the metalworking and mechanical engineering sectors.

In this relatively untroubled labor climate, industrialists chose to keep the basic wage almost unchanged, confining wage increases to gains in productivity. These wage increases were generally associated with the introduction of more advanced machine tools, especially in the case of Fiat and other progressive firms, giving rise to increases in the number of skilled workers of a new type, at the expense of the traditional skilled craftsmen.[7]

This trend was reflected in the agreements signed in Turin at Fiat, Itala,

5. M. Antonioli, and B. Bezza, eds., *La Fiom dalle origini al fascismo* (Bari: De Donato, 1978), p. 447ff.

6. A. De Stefani, *La legislazione economica della guella* (Bari: Laterza, 1926), *as vocem*.

7. For all these themes it is essential to consult the Fiom documents kept in the Archivio Centrale di Stato in Rome (*Mostra della Rivoluzine fascista*, files 13 and 14).

Scat, Frejus, Diatto, Rapid, Lancia, Fiat San Giorgio, Garrone & C., and Fiat Acciaierie in January 1916.[8] For the first time, the various qualifications were grouped into four levels: (1) calibrators, toolmakers, inspectors, model makers; (2) unskilled machine operators; (3) unskilled workers; (4) women and apprentices. In Lombardy, too, although more slowly, a new workers' classification identical to that adopted in Turin was established. Ordinance 429136 of 10 September 1918 of the Lombardy regional committees for Industrial Mobilization specified three basic categories: skilled, semiskilled, and unskilled workers.

Before Italy entered the war, the objectives of FIOM, officially sanctioned at the Florence Congress in 1910, focused on wage increases, fewer working hours, the establishment of a minimum wage in the various industrial areas, and limitations on overtime. When the Industrial Mobilization regime came into force, FIOM endeavored to "make it as painless as possible." "In part, our efforts were rewarded," acknowledged Buozzi, though he went on to say that "Industrial Mobilization turned out to be only a militarization of the workers.... Despite the enormous demand for labor, wartime wages did not even rise enough to keep up with the increase in the cost of living."[9] The contractual objectives that had been given a new emphasis at the Turin National Congress of 26 June 1916, were disregarded. The union was forced to relinquish the objective of an eight-hour day and to accept a ten-hour working day, five and a half days a week, in addition to frequent allowances for night-work and overtime, as well as a freeze on traditional piece rates associated with the introduction of more advanced production processes.[10] Admittedly, there was some positive results, such as the compulsory enrollment of the workers in auxiliary (i.e., mobilized) factories, beginning in the second half of 1917 in the National Health Superannuation Fund. But this was still a long way away from the modern social security system that would have made up for the shortcomings and indecisiveness of the union's contractual policy.[11]

At the FIOM Congress of November 1918, the Colombino report confirmed that the union had proven powerless in its attempt to establish an overall wage policy. In the view of the union leader, the organization had been unable to achieve increases in the basic wage and a periodic review of piece rates in order to modify the minimum threshold of union scale wages. Indeed, the union had ceased making demands for standardized wage parameters, because "the variety... of the processes, rates, piecework systems, measurements of the nominal wage, by individual enterprises, if not individual workshops, was such

8. M. Antonioli and B. Bezza, *La Fiom*, pp. 738–9.
9. Ibido, pp. 447–8.
10. See Comitato Centrale per la Mobilizazione Industriale, *Assetto delle industrie che lavorano durante e dopo la guerra* (Milano, 1917).
11. See Ministero della Guerra, Sottosegretariato armi e munizioni, Comitato Centrale per la Mobilizazione Industriale, *verabali della seduta del 26 novembre 1916* (Rome, 1916).

as to make it all but impossible to set the minimum wage for each category."[12] In point of fact, FIOM's wage policy continued to display a reformist optimism resting on the notion of a "fair price of labor," and an aversion to disputes over work organization, which might stand in the way of "efficiency" and "progress." We should stress the deep concern of FIOM's leaders to link wartime wage variations with postwar problems. Specifically, with an eye to postwar conditions, they sought not to restrict unduly "workers hierarchies" for the benefit of rank-and-file workers, and to preserve the "metal workers' class" through a minimum wage policy, differentiated according to individual processing systems and workshops.[13]

This contractual policy involved calling for increases in basic wages correlated with increases in productivity, so as to erode the significance of piecework percentages.[14] However, neither the entrepreneurs nor the Industrial Mobilization accepted this policy of wage demands. Increases granted in basic pay or partly consolidated into it continued to rest on specific criteria: rises in the cost of living, premium rates, professional-qualification premia, and so on. Even so, the total amount was ludicrously low compared to the high earnings that could be achieved by piecework. In addition, piecework union rates, instead of remaining at the same level, increased with factory rationalization and the consequent review of the piecework calculation system. This made for a steep rise in the portion of salary linked to piece rates, which made rank-and-file workers, given their low minimum "basic" wage, the chief beneficiaries of this complex operation.

We need only consider, in this connection, the evolution of ordinary piecework. At the outbreak of war, Industrial Mobilization extended the terms of factory contracts of employment until three months after the end of the war, and froze the rates for traditional piecework. The latter turned out to represent, in informal factory bargaining, a kind of minimum threshold of piecework earnings. In the big firms and in the more advanced sectors, special premium rates were used to reward the time saved in the completion of work tasks, resting on new systems of wage calculation (Taylor, Gantt, Rowan, etc.).[15] On this portion of the salary, the only one that could be negotiated at factory level, were concentrated the demands of works committees and of independent groups of workers. Under the piecework system (*cottimo a pezzo*), the skilled craftsman had been the centerpiece and the chief beneficiary of the entire work organization. Under the time-rate system (*cottimo a tempo*), on the other hand, the main figure became the semiskilled or unskilled machine-operator.

At the 1918 FIOM Congress, Colombino stated: "The most common piece-

12. M. Antonioli and B. Bezza, *La Fiom*, p. 479.
13. See Archivio Centrale di Stato (Roma), *Mostra della Rivoluzione fascista*, f. 13.
14. M. Antonioli and B. Bezza, *La Fiom*, p. 488.
15. See Archivio Centrale di Stato (Roma), *Mostra della Rivoluzione fascista*, f. 13.

work system adopted in the majority of our factories, assesses the work to be performed on the basis of a specific price; from this figure the worker had to draw his hourly wage. The extra amount produced through higher productivity will represent extra pay for the worker."[16] However, for the new processes, either mass-produced or with a high technological input, Industrial Mobilization gave entrepreneurs ample power to fix standard piece rates as they saw fit. Because of rationalization and the greater size of plants, entrepreneurs were forced to modify the pyramidal structure of the old workshop hierarchical organization by separating from the production process the higher stratum of skilled craftsmen, thus creating a special category: percentage workers.

These workers did not obtain piecework status through production rates or a production time system. Their earnings were based on a percentage of the piece rate paid within the department, the workshop, or the plant. In the car manufacturing industry, calibrators, toolmakers, inspectors, and model-makers made up this new category in which craftsmanship had found its last refuge. In the bargaining between workers and foremen, piecework earnings were high in rationalized factories: "In workshops where mass-production is better organized, it is no longer a matter of discussing a 100–150% piecework bonus; the figures now mentioned are one, one and a half of two lire per hour."[17] In short, the accepted norm was beginning to be a workshop production rate, rather than a piece rate, so that the workers would bargain, in individual disputes, over the production premium rather than the piece rate of the basic wage.

These new wage systems reflected accurately the social stratification that was taking place in the more advanced Turin and Milan metalworking and iron workshops. They redistributed piecework qualifications and rates according to new schemes, and tried out organizational solutions in workshops relations and hierarchies that vastly changed the structural typologies of the firms. In these types of firms, the character and importance of informal bargaining conducted, whether on an individual basis, by groups of workers, or by the works committees, reflected the revolutionary changes that had upset the relation between basic or minimum wage and piecework earnings.

A quantitative analysis of strikes in the iron and metalworking industries

Figure 1 shows the overall pattern of the cycle of labor conflicts from 1901 to 1923. The data are based on a fairly uniform statistical survey. The figure points out regional contributions to the cycle (Lombardy, Piedmont,

16. M. Antonioli and B. Bezza, *La Fiom*, p. 478.
17. Ibid., p. 481.

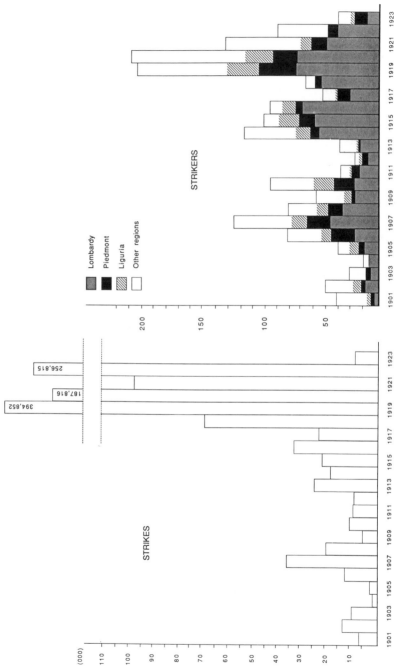

Figure 1. Strikes and strikers in the metalworking industry, 1901–23 (absolute figures)

410

Liguria, and other regions), and brings out three significant cycles of labor conflicts with different characteristics:

1. *1906–10.* The number of strikes exceeds that of the previous period and is comparable to the number recorded in the subsequent period. The average number of strikers exceeds that of the previous period but is lower than in the subsequent period. In the immediate prewar years (1911–13) the number of strikes declines sharply, while the number of strikers decreases only slightly.
2. *1914–18.* The number of strikes is comparable to that of the 1906–10 cycle, but the number of strikers steadily climbs (except for a slight decline in 1917), reaching its peak in 1918.

    Attention should be drawn to the discrepancy between the curves for strikes and strikers: the first declines while the second rises, that is, the coefficient of participation is on the way up.
3. *1919–23.* This cycle is anomalous by comparison with the characteristics of the previous cycles, and is presented here solely for demonstration purposes. It comprises two contradictory phases absent in the previous cycles: an ascending phase (in the number of both strikes and strikers), and a subsequent descending phase (with the exception of the 1922 anomaly).

In Figure 2 we consider the numbers of strikers in the metalworking industry according to subsectors (iron industry and metalworking industry, mechanical engineering, and shipbuilding). In Figure 3 we consider the number of strikes in the same subsectors. The graphs illustrating strikes and strikers are not synchronous. Specifically, in the iron industry in 1918, the graphs tracing the evolution in the numbers of strikes drop to the lowest point for the whole period, whereas those for strikers reach the peaks attained in the first five-year period (1914–18). In 1920 we observe the largest number of strikes, whereas the lower number of strikers already reflects the turnabout trend begun four years earlier. In the metal constructions industry, the graphs of strikes and strikers are never parallel, except in 1918. In mechanical engineering, the most interesting sector (car manufacturing industry, heavy and light mechanical industry), the trend appears quite synchronous, except for some anomalies in 1920 (when the number of strikes decreases slightly, while that of strikers increases sixfold by comparison with the previous year). In shipbuilding, the two graphs are totally divergent, except in 1918, 1921, and 1922, the three years that provide the very key to our interpretation, as we will see further on. Figure 4, which illustrates the trend in the percentages of strikes, strikers, and working days lost in all industries accounted for by the metalworking sector, also shows several anomalies. The figure suggests the limited significance of the metalworking sector in accounting for the general trend of strikes, strikers, and working days lost. Despite the sharp increase in these indices of labor unrest for all industries during the period from 1919 to 1922, the proportion accounted

411

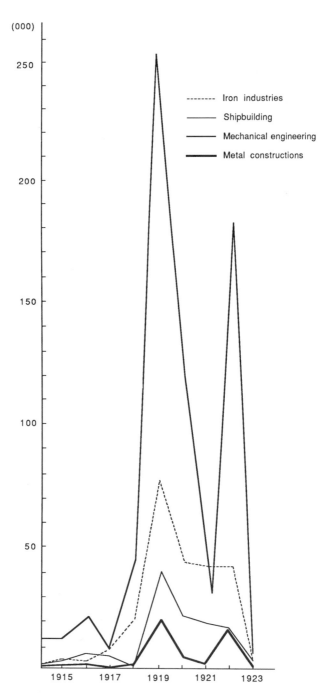

Figure 2. Strikers per subsectors (absolute figures)

412

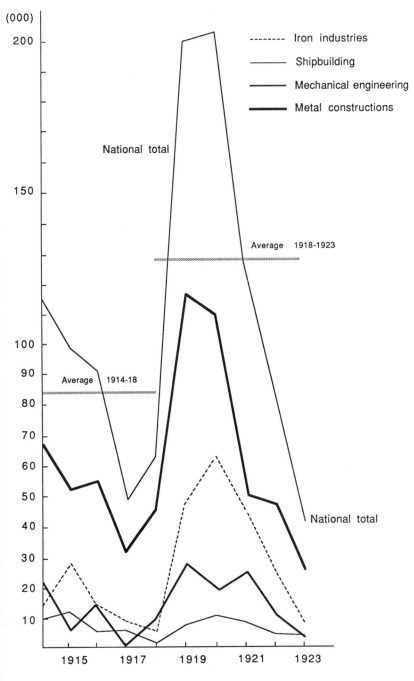

Figure 3. Strikes in the metalworking industry (absolute figures)

413

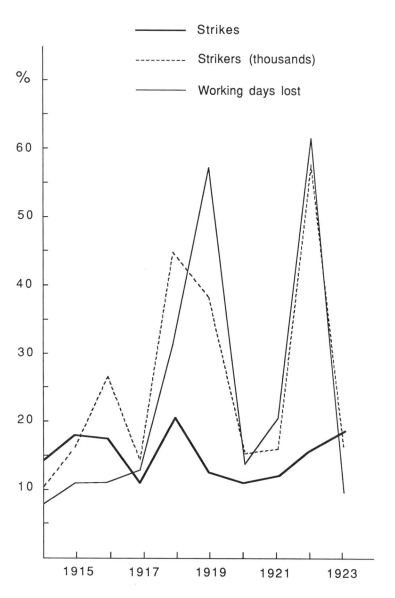

Figure 4. Percentage of strikes, strikers, working days lost in the metalworking sector over total industrial strikes

for by metalworking enterprises remains almost unchanged. It would be interesting to disaggregate and compare the figures for individual sectors: They would probably reflect the steadily increasing importance of the textile sector. However, the sharpest contrasts emerge in the periods 1914–15, 1918–19, and 1921–3. In the first period, a drop in the number of strikes in metalworking (in absolute figures), coincides with an actual increase in their proportion of the total; in the second, a slight rise in the absolute number of strikes among the metalworkers coincides with a sharp percentage fall; in the third period, despite the sharp drop in absolute figures (a two-thirds decrease), the percentage figures increase notably.

In Figure 5, we have taken into consideration the linear correlation between the numbers of FIOM members (data supplied by FIOM Secretary Bruno Buozzi) and the numbers of strikers. The number of members increases sharply in 1914, slowly in 1915, and steeply in 1916 and 1917, reaching approximately 152,000 by the end of 1920. (We have to point out, however, that in August/ September of that year, membership reached the figure of 194,000.) This graph for the numbers of union members is synchronous with that for strikers (although there is an obvious time displacement), until 1920 when it declines more slowly then the other graph. The data for 1922 reflect an atypical regional case that involved mainly the Piedmont mechanical engineering subsector. The fall in membership is largely caused by the drop in 1922 in the number of members in the car manufacturing industry of the Turin area.

Figures 6, 7, 8, 9, and 10 bring out regional and national trends in the numbers of various categories of strikes, strikers, and working days lost. Figures 6, 7, and 8 show the incidence of four significant regions (Lombardy, Piedmont, Liguria, and Campania) in the national totals of strikes, strikers, and working days lost. The figures illustrate the preponderance of Lombardy by comparison with the other three regions.

In Figures 7 and 8, the peaks in the intensity of labor unrest for each region never coincide. The incidence of strikes, strikers, and working days lost in Piedmont is not very significant during the first five-year period. Lombardy records the highest number of strikes from 1914 to 1922; its numbers of strikers are highest for the years 1914, 1915, 1917, 1919, and 1922; Piedmont leads in 1920.

Figures 9 and 10 give a clearer picture of the trends. Their volumetric projections are based on the percentage averages of the two five-year periods 1914–18 and 1919–23. Although the first five-year period (we should really speak of a four-year period, because in the case of Italy, 1914 is to be assigned to the prewar period) shows a very steady trend, the following period can be broken down into three widely different subperiods. The first of these subperiods, 1919–20, while still influenced by the expansion resulting from wartime production and the consequent model of industrial relations, is called, because

415

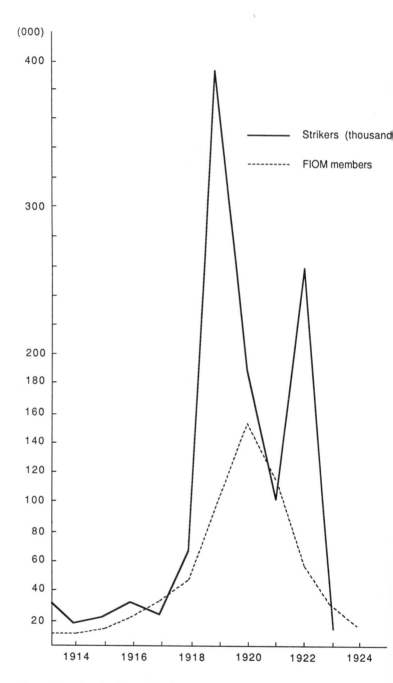

Figure 5. Strikers in the metalworking sector and Fiom members

416

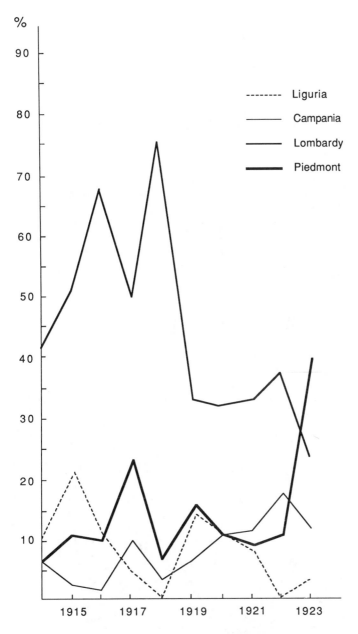

Figure 6. Regional percentage of strikes in the metalworking sector

417

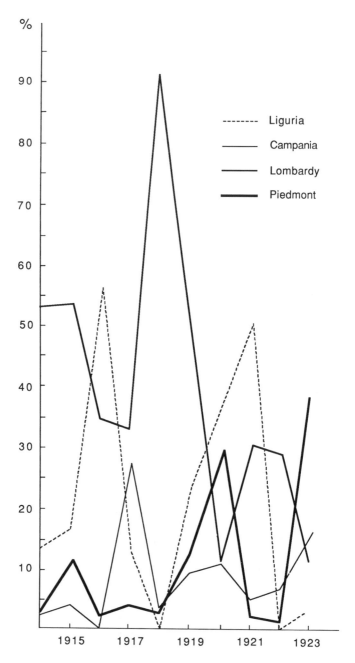

Figure 7. Regional percentages of strikers in the metalworking sector

418

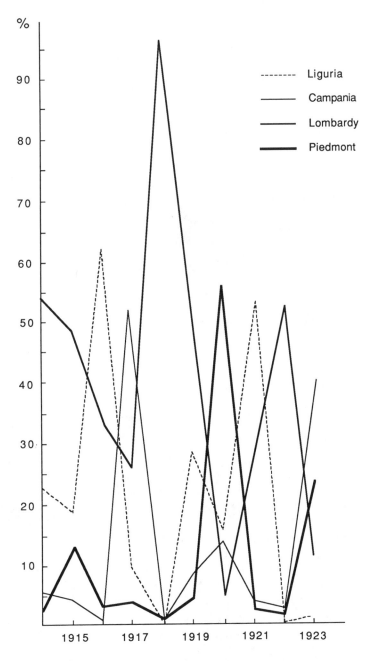

Figure 8. Regional percentages of working days lost in the metalworking sector

419

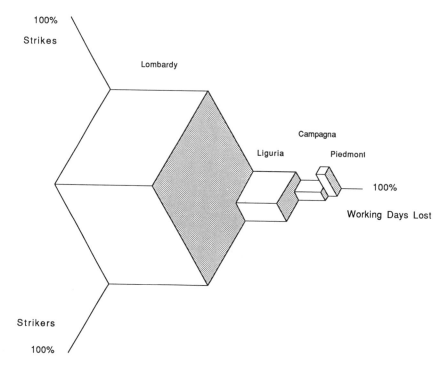

Figure 9. Strikes, strikers, working days lost: percentage average for 1914–18 period

of the sharpness of its labor conflicts, the red biennium; the second, 1921–2, is marked by deflationary economic policies, and by 1922 by wage reductions and widespread dismissals in the mechanical constructions industry of the Turin area (mainly Fiat); the third period, which begins in 1923 and ends in 1925–6, is marked by the consolidation of the Fascist State, deviations from the eight-hour working day, defensive strikes of Lombardy metalworkers in 1924–5, and the resumption of labor conflicts in Piedmont. These events culminate in the dramatic epilogue of 1926, with the agreement of Palazzo Vidoni, followed by the dissolution of the General Confederation of Labor.

However, a comparison between the two five-year periods may be useful, even if percentage averages may be misleading with respect to the overall picture. The relationship among the various regions emerges with great clarity: very high figures of labor unrest for Lombardy in the first five-year period and slightly lower ones in the following period; Piedmont goes from last place in the first period to second place in the second period; Liguria remains at the same level in both periods, whereas the figures for Campania increase.

420

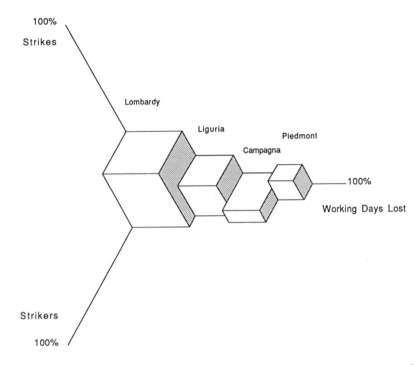

Figure 10. Strikes, strikers, working days lost: percentage average for 1919–23 period

An additional remark about the contribution of the four regions to the national totals is useful. From 1914 to 1918, they contribute 84.26% of the strikes, 90.58% of the strikers, and 91.88% of working days lost. From 1919 to 1923, the figures are 77.15%, 75.04%, and 81.20%, respectively. The latter figures illustrate the spreading of labor conflicts and the greater uniformity in workers' behavior throughout the country.

Figures 11, 12, 13, and 14 show the average length of strikes, their severity, and size. These indices are obtained by dividing the number of strikers by the number of strikes (size), the numbers of working days lost per striker (severity), and the number of working days lost per strike (length). These three indices have been used for the four subsectors for which they are available: iron- and metalworking, metal construction, mechanical engineering, and shipbuilding. Here, as in the previous figures, two peak years stand out: 1919 and 1922. We know that the data for 1919 are mainly attributable to Lombardy, Liguria, and other regions not considered here; those for 1922 are mainly attributable to Lombardy, Campania, and these other regions.

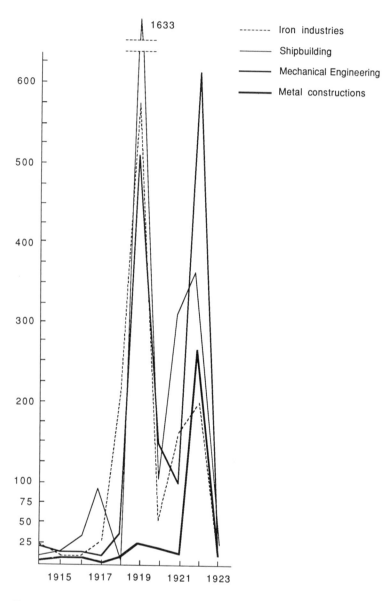

Figure 11. Average length of strikes in the metalworking sector (:100)

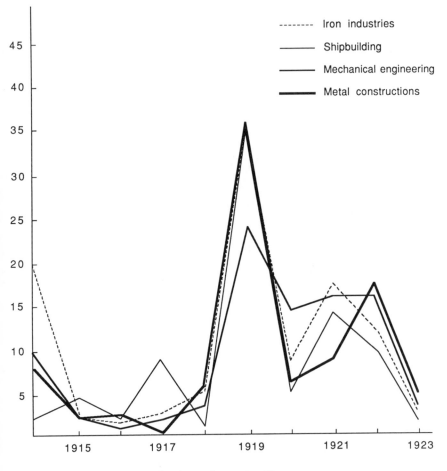

Figure 12. Severity of strikes in the metalworking sector

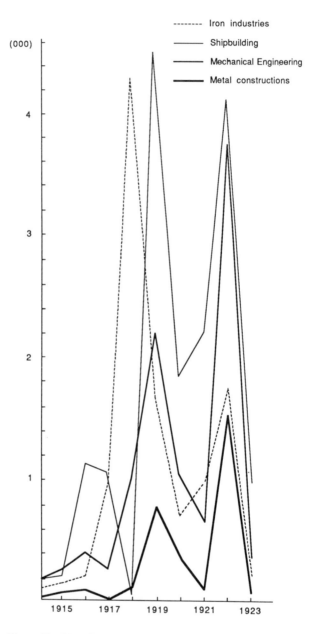

Iron industries
Shipbuilding
Mechanical Engineering
Metal constructions

4

3

2

1

1915   1917   1919   1921   1923

Figure 13. Size of strikes in the metalworking sector

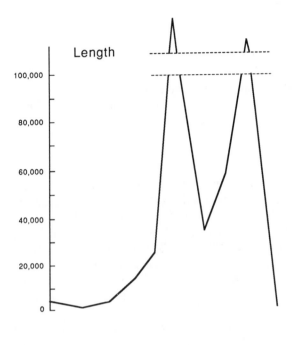

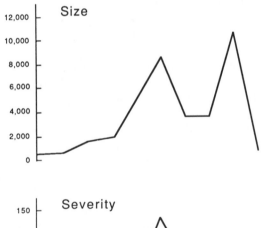

Figure 14. Length, size, severity of strikes in the metalworking sector (absolute figures)

425

All indices of the severity of the strikes rise sharply in 1919 (except for a small peak in shipbuilding in 1917 attributable to the general strike of metalworkers in Naples) and, less consistently, in 1921 and 1922. It should be noted, however, that official statistics do not encompass the occupations of factories in 1920, because they were officially considered as due to political unrest.

Conclusions

If we consider the whole period of activity of FIOM, from 1901 to 1923, the last year for which a statistical survey of strikes were carried out, it is difficult to identify a cycle of labor conflict (see Figure 1).

The years 1906–10 were perhaps the most interesting of the Giolitti era (1901–13): 1905, 1906, and 1907 saw a significant number of labor conflicts whose fundamental objectives were the recognition of the trade union movement through the establishment of the closed shop and union monopoly of the labor market. These objectives were pursued through 1909 and 1910 and largely abandoned in 1911–13. The depression cycle began with the strikes in Piombino and on the island of Elba, with the labor conflicts in the Turin manufacturing sector in 1912, in the Milan railway rolling stock sector in 1913, and again in the Turin car manufacturing sector in 1913. This depression cycle was marked by the shift of the revolutionary union movement from the rural to the urban world, by conflicts between organized and unorganized workers, by the establishment of the big trusts of the iron industry, and the emergence of large employers' organizations.

The First World War witnessed a rapid spread of strikes across the country, with some industrial regions as leaders: Lombardy, (with steadily increasing figures), Liguria, Piedmont, and Campania. However, the figures for the last three regions bring out the explosive aspects of the conflicts, rather than cyclical trends. For the calmer periods of the economic conjuncture, the graphs tend to level out, dropping to the minimum values of other nonsignificant regions.

A comparison between the regional figures of labor conflicts and those of degrees of labor organization, shows that the stronger the organization (Piedmont), the greater the fluctuations observable in the cycle of conflicts. Where the organization is weaker (Lombardy), the cycle is down to median figures. In Liguria, where the level of organization was generally strong, there were two strike waves not comparable to the other regions considered. It should be mentioned that in these three regions different branches of the metalworking world were represented: car manufacturing and mechanical construction in Turin and Piedmont; shipbuilding and iron works in Liguria; metal processing, mechanical construction, and micromechanics in Lombardy. The three regions thus feature different strata of workers and different industrial relations, as well as different political worlds and cultural traditions.

426

Between 1914 and 1918, patterns of labor conflicts were distinguished by the greater intensity and the shorter length of strikes. The settlements of disputes were favorable to the workers. A model of industrial relations that was strictly binding for the parties was established, whose legal – institutional contents were reasonably advantageous for the working class. The new features of industrial labor conflicts included quickly growing participation in, and frequency of, strike actions, which reached their peak in 1919–20; a greater incidence of metal enterprises in the total number of industrial conflicts (after 1918 it exceeded 35%); and an attenuation of the differences in the cycles of regional conflicts, reflecting greater uniformity in the patterns of demands. The proportion of industrial strikes accounted for by the four regions considered declined from 84.26% in the 1914–18 period to 67.15% in 1919–24; that of strikers from 90.58% to 75.04%; and of the number of working days lost from 91.88% to 81.20%.

Reflected in these changes in strike patterns was a revolutionized industrial structure that paved the way for the trade union revolution. The average number of workers per plant increased from two to twenty-five times (in the case of Milan), and more advanced technology was introduced, particularly in the crucial sectors of metalworking and mechanical construction. On the other hand, the trade union movement modified its representation system: in 1917 with the establishment of works committees; in 1919 with that of works councils. It also created a regional organizational structure, enlarged its national secretariat, and collected membership fees through plant management. At the same time, the bargaining power of FIOM was sanctioned by the Industrial Mobilization bodies that granted FIOM a power of intervention that it had not previously enjoyed. Yet, during these years, the social basis of FIOM was continuously in ferment: The new plant organization system and the new techniques of work organization reduced the importance of the skilled craftsman, while the so-called cadres secondaires acquired a role and preponderance that changed the hierarchical picture of the workshops. The inflow of youths and women with low qualifications, low union membership, little recognition within the work organization, and a completely different set of values, exercised centrifugal effects on the union movement.

If we consider the relationship between the numbers of strikers and union members, we observe that until 1918 the strength of the movement tended to be a factor that regulated conflicts, whereas in the following years (except for 1919 and 1920), the unfavorable economic cycle (deflationary measures, deviations from the eight-hour working days, wage reductions) determined the pattern of strike actions (all of a defensive nature), as trade union membership dropped to an all-time low.

The 1919–20 period illustrates the changes in the relationships between employers and workers. The rise in the indices of labor unrest was sharper with respect to numbers of strikers than for the numbers of strikes and working days lost. These differences bring out a change in the forms of strikes. The labor conflicts of the wartime period had been distinguished by their considerable length and limited participation, whereas strikes in the following two-year period (except for the occupation of factories) became shorter in duration, but reflected a higher degree of participation and a broadening of the scope of labor unrest.

References

Sources

Relazione presentata a S. E. il Ministro dell'Interno nel mese di marzo 1879 dalla Commissione d'inchiesta sugli scioperi nominata con R. D. 3 febbraio 1878. Rome, 1885.

Atti Parlamentari. Camera dei Deputati. *Relazione della dommissione. Disposizioni relative agli scioperi.* Seduta 23 aprile 1884, XV Leg., la sessione 1882–83–84, Documenti-disegni di legge e relazioni, n. 114-A.

Ministerio di Agricoltura, Industria e Commercio. (d'ora in poi MAIC). Direzione Generale della Statistica. 1892. *Statistica degli scioperi avvenuti nell'industria e nell'agricultura durante gli anni dal 1884 al 1891.* Rome.

Direzione Generale della Statistica. 1894–8, 1900–4, 1906. *Statistica degli scioperi avvenuti nell'industria e nell'agricultura negli anni 1892 e 1893–1903.* 10 vols. Rome.

Direzione Generale della Statistica e del Lavoro, Ufficio del Lavoro. 1914. *Classificazione decimale delle industrie.* Rome.

Ufficio del Lavoro. 1907–8, 1911–14, 1916. *Statistica degli scioperi avvenuti in Italia nell'anno 1904–7, 1910–13.* 8 vols. Rome.

Ufficio del Lavoro. 1911. *Statistica degli socioperi avvenuti in Italia dal 1901 al 1905 (in apendice gli scioperi dal 1906 al 1908 e dal 1901 al 1909).* Rome.

Ufficio del Lavoro. 1910. *Statistica sommaria degli scioperi avvenuti in Italia nell'anno 1909.* Rome.

Ministero dell'economia nazionale. Direzione Generale del Lavoro e della Previdenza Sociale. 1924. *I conflitti di lavoro in Italia nel decennio 1914–1923 (dati statistici),* suppl. al n. 38 del Bollettino dell'Ufficio del Lavoro e della Previdenza Sociale. Rome.

Periodical publications

MAIC Ufficio del Lavoro 1904–16. *Bollettino dell'Ufficio del Lavoro.* Rome.

Ufficio Centrale di Statistica 1916–19. *Bollettino dell'Ufficio del Lavoro.* Rome.

Direzione Generale del Lavoro e della Previdenza Sociale 1920. *Bollettino del Lavoro e della Previdenza Sociale.* Rome.

Ministero del Lavoro e della Previdenza Sociale Direzione Generale del Lavoro e della Previdenza Sociale 1920–3. *Bollettino del Lavoro e della Previdezna Sociale.* Rome.

Historiography

Antonioli, M., and Bezza, B., eds. 1978. *La FIOM dalle origini al fascismo. 1901–1924* Bari.

Barbadoro, I. 1980. *Il sindicato in Italia. Dalle origini al congresso di Modena dell Confederazione.* Milan.

Berta, G. 1982. "Un caso di industrialismo sindicale: la Fiom del primo novecento" *Societa e Storia*, a. 5, no. 15.

Bezza, B. 1982. "La nouva classe operaia, la nascita della contrattazione collettiva e la FIOM durante la prima guerra mondiale" *Giornale di diritto del lavoro e delle relazioni industriali*, no. 16.

Bigazzi, D. 1980. "Gli operaia della catena di montaggio: la FIAT (1922–1923" *Annali della Fondazione Giangiacomo Feltrinelli, 1979/1980.* Milan.

Bordogna, L., and Provasi, G.C. 1979. "Il movimento degli scioperi in Italia (1881–1973)" In G.P. Cella, ed. *Il movimento degli scioperi nel XX secolo.* Bologna.

Camarda A., and Peli, S. 1980. *L'altro esercito. La classe operaia durante la prima guerra mondiale.* Milan.

Cicerchia, G. 1950. "Andamento in Italia, nel secolo XX, del salario reale dell'operaio rispetto al costo della vita" *Rivista Italiana di Demografia e Statistica* 4, nos. 1–2.

Davite, L. 1982. "I lavoratori meccanici e metallurgici in Lombardia dall'Unita alla prima guerra mondiale." *Classe* 5 (febbraio).

De Benedetti, A. 1974. *La classe operaia a Napoli nel primo dopoguerra.* Naples.

Lay, A., Marucco, D., and Pesante, L. 1973. "Classe operaia e scioperi: ipotesi per il periodo 1880–1923" *Quaderni Storici*, a. 8, no. 22 (gennaio–aprile).

Maione, G. 1975. *Il biennio rosso. Autonomia e spontaneita operaia nel 1919–1920.* Bologna.

Marmo, M. 1978. *Il proletariato industriale a Napoli in eta liberale.* Naples.

Musso, S. 1980. *Gli operaia di Torino, 1900–1920.* Milan.

Neppi Modona, G. 1969. *Sciopero, potere politico e magistratura (1870–1920).* Bari.

IV

The effects of short-term variation

18

Introduction

CHARLES TILLY

Industrial conflict is volatile

The temporal patterns of strikes do not resemble those of births, or school attendance, or traffic accidents. Births, school attendance, traffic accidents, and many other repetitive social phenomena display a kind of quantitative inertia: One year's pattern usually resembles the previous year's quite closely, and large changes only occur gradually.

Strikes differ emphatically from such cumulative social phenomena; they veer rapidly in location and number from one period to the next. To be sure, the frequency of strikes varies with the season in construction, schoolteaching, and a number of other trades that have annual production cycles. The periodicity of labor contracts affects the rhythm of industrial conflict. And to the extent that the business cycle follows a regular pattern – a much-disputed subject – so do the ebb and flow of strikes. Yet a glance at almost any national strike series shows large swings in frequency and amplitude from month to month and year to year. Indeed, strikes often arrive in great waves that wash over an entire region or country.

The volatility of strike activity resembles that of open political struggle. As represented by demonstrations, marches, meetings, petitions, partisan attacks, and related forms of contention, political struggles shift rapidly from pallid to intense, from small to immense. War, revolution, rebellion, and other forms of strategic interaction likewise swing quickly. When multiple parties struggle openly for advantage, volatility becomes the rule.

Why should that be? Three related features of strategic interaction contribute to its rapid variations in intensity. First, the involvement of multiple parties means that the action of one party often accelerates or retards the action of another; repression strikes quickly, A's moment of weakness incites B to act, escalation begins, and so on. Second, timing makes a big difference; antagonists monitor each other's vulnerability and strength from time to time, while watching the changing probabilities that third parties will intervene. Third, the interaction produces clear winners and losers: Only a slight advantage will win large rewards, and only a slight disadvantage will mean substantial losses. Therefore the incentive of the weaker party to attack generally declines with the relative strength of the other party; conversely, the closer two antagonists come to equality, the greater incentives they both have to attack. And relative strength shifts speedily as a function of mobilization, demobilization, and coalition-formation. Multiple parties, timing advantages, and changing relative strength of the parties combine to produce rapid alternations in the levels of strategic interaction.

These features of industrial conflict become obvious to anyone who looks closely at individual strikes. Despite the temptation to treat the frequency of strikes as an expression of the mood or will of workers alone, whether a strike occurs in a given firm depends on the give and take between workers and employers, not to mention third parties such as unions and government officials. Gerald Friedman (1985) has shown that French workers commonly used short large strikes to incite government intervention in labor disputes, and thereby reduce their own chances of failing. American workers, on the other hand, had less to gain from governmental involvement, and more often opted for long, well-financed strikes by small groups of skilled workers. The Knights of Labor failed, in effect, by adopting French tactics on the American scene.

Timing strongly affects the likelihood that a strike will succeed, and therefore the probability that it will happen at all. The threat of a strike in a season of peak production sometimes induces bosses to make concessions, or to call in troops; in those cases, struggle occurs, but no strikes. Workers who are relatively strong often get satisfaction without a strike, while those who are relatively weak risk a great deal if they dare to strike. The correspondence between the individual interests or desires of workers and the frequencies of strikes therefore remains quite imperfect.

Strike activity, furthermore, varies along three different quantitative dimensions: frequency, size, and duration. (Analyses of strike intensity sometimes adopt a fourth sort of measure, total person-days in strikes, but it is simply a multiple of frequency, size, and duration.) How often strikes occur, how many workers take part in the average strike, and how long the average strike lasts are logically independent of each other, and have no strong tendency to vary together. In fact, strikes have often gotten larger as they have grown shorter; the rise of the massive one-day warning strike as an instrument of union action exemplifies exactly that tendency. All parties to strikes have some influence over the combinations of frequency, size, and duration the strikes display: more or less frequent, larger or smaller, longer or shorter. The mixture of the three, in fact, is itself an object of strategic interaction. For example,

434

the duration of strikes results not from the holding power of workers alone, but from the time it takes for both parties to arrive at readiness to strike a bargain; how long a strike will last becomes part of the bargain.

Any student of fluctuations in industrial conflict therefore faces serious substantive and technical problems. Substantively, careless analysts of industrial conflict often interpret the intensity of strike activity as a direct measure of worker militancy, solidarity, or discontent. Yet any sound analysis must avoid imputing the fluctuations to changes in the condition of a single collective actor – workers or others. The analyst must take into account a continuous stream of strategic interaction, much of which takes place outside of strikes. Technically, each treatment of strike data runs the double risk of confounding correlations with causes, on one side, and of losing significant connections in the maze of complexity, on the other. Since many of the putative causes of industrial conflict (such as cycles of demand and threats of unemployment) covary, every analysis requires delicate threading through a web of reciprocal causation.

Six countries' strikes, 1890–1924

These warnings certainly apply to the six-country experience we are analyzing here. Figures 1–6 present the curves of total strikes and total strikers for the six countries in each of the years for which we have statistical evidence. In France (Figure 1) we see an irregular rise in numbers of strikes and strikers from 1892 to 1910, a slowing of strike activity from 1911 to 1914, a decisive drop in 1915, followed by a dramatic rise up to 1919–20; the middle years of World War I mark a sharp break in an otherwise upward movement of industrial conflict. Italy (Figure 2) displays a similar pattern, except that the prewar peak arrives around 1907, the wartime reduction of industrial conflict is less marked, and the decline in strikes and strikers after 1920 is much more precipitous than in France. Germany (Figure 3) has something in common with France and Italy, including a sharp drop in strikes between 1914 and 1916, but the prewar rise is more irregular and less emphatic, and no notable decline appears before 1926.

In Great Britain (Figure 4) we find a rather different pattern. Although Britain resembles other countries in having a significant decline in strike activity from 1913 to 1916, the curves of strikes and strikers from 1890 to 1913 describe a bumpy valley rather than an upward slope. In the postwar period, furthermore, the number of strikers shoots up much faster than the number of strikes.

The United States' (Figure 5) experience with strikes and strikers was much more regular than that of the other countries: gentle decline from 1890 to 1898, rapid rise to a new plateau from 1899 to 1903, fluctuations along that plateau

Figure 1. Strikes and strikers in France, 1890–1924 (Source: Shorter and Tilly)

until 1920 with a minor peak in 1917, rapid falloff thereafter. In the United States, the number of strikers (and therefore the number of strikers per strike) rises irregularly through much of the period, peaking in 1917 and then decreasing rapidly. Unlike any of the other countries, the United States shows no sign of a wartime decline in strike activity.

Russia's (Figure 6) experience – at least so much of it as we have strike statistics for – stands out from all the rest. In Russia from 1895 to 1914

436

Figure 2. Strikes and strikers in Italy, 1890–1923 (Source: Bordogna, Cella, and Provasi)

numbers of strikes and of strikers swing dizzily from year to year, with the most visible troughs in 1904 and 1910, and a decisive increase from 1910 to the beginning of the war. Until research that is now in progress yields results, we can only speculate that Russian strikes declined radically during the early months of 1915, rebounded toward the end of the year, then mounted irre-gularly to peaks around the two revolutions of 1917. The annual totals for 1915 and 1916 – down in 1915, up again in 1916 – are consistent with that speculation. In Russia, as in most of the other countries we are examining, strike waves dominated year-to-year movement in industrial conflict, and

437

Figure 3. Strikes and strikers in Germany, 1899–1924 (Source: Mitchell)

typically brought major confrontations between organized workers and national authorities.

Using a conventional standard – that the numbers of both strikes and strikers exceeded their mean of the previous five years by at least 50% – the following were the years of strike waves in the six countries during those years between 1890 and 1924 for which we have the necessary data:

> *France, 1890–1924:* 1890, 1893, 1899–1900, 1904, 1906, 1919
>
> *Italy, 1890–1923:* 1896–7, 1900–2, 1906–7, 1919–20
>
> *Germany, 1899–1924:* 1890, 1900, 1905–6, 1910, 1919–20
>
> *Great Britain, 1890–1924:* 1890, 1911, 1919

438

Figure 4. Strikes and strikers in Great Britain, 1890–1924 (Source: Cronin)

United States, 1890–1924: 1903
Russia, 1895–1914: 1903, 1905–6, 1912–14

Thus out of the years for which we have statistics, 30% were wave years in Russia, 27% in Italy and Germany, 20% in France, 9% in Great Britain, and only 3% in the United States. By this crude standard, industrial conflict was most volatile in Russia, and least so in the United States. The rank order corresponds roughly to the entrenchment of organized labor in national, politics: least in Russia, most in Britain and the United States.

Revolutions, wars, and strikes

Some of the international differences, however, depend on exposure to the major political events of the period: the Russian revolutions of 1905

439

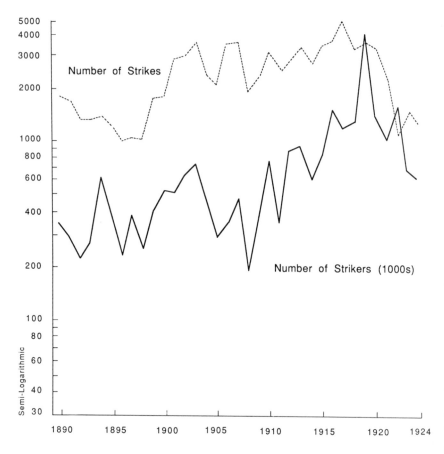

Figure 5. Strikes and strikers in the United States, 1890–1924 (Source: Snyder)

and 1917, the Great War of 1914–18. In the case of Russia, we can hardly speak of the revolutions as "causing" strikes, since widespread strikes constituted part of the revolutionary action. Over the twenty years from 1895 to 1914, 40% of all the strikes and 25% of all the strikers reported by the Factory Inspectors appeared in the revolutionary year of 1905. But in other countries the Russian revolutions, especially the revolution of October 1917, set a model for workers to follow on the path to power. The Social-Democratic congress of Iena, in 1905, cited the Russian example in declaring the general strike a major instrument of working-class struggle. Similarly, Western Europe's widespread, often insurrectionary, strikes of 1919 and 1920 owed plenty to the Russian model.

The links between war and strike activity were more subtle, but no less

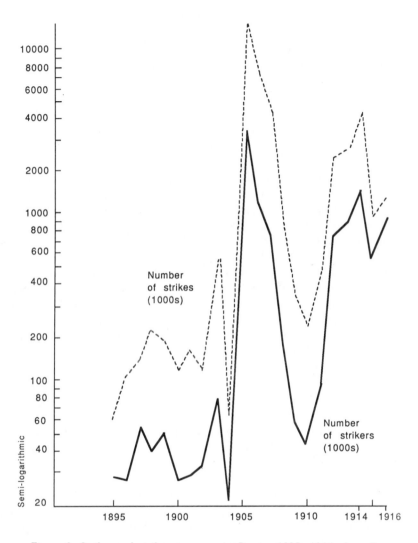

Figure 6. Strikes and strikers per year in Russia, 1895–1914, from Factory Inspectors' reports (Source: Haimson and Petrusha)

important. When industrial countries go to war, on the whole, strike activity declines. At least it typically declines at the start of a war. That happens for a number of reasons: because young workers enter military service and other workers who are less well organized replace them; because labor shifts to government-controlled war industries; because governments work out compacts with management and organized labor in order to pursue the war effort; and because governments' repressive capacities and propensities generally increase in wartime.

World War I provides a case in point. The war itself was a long time in coming. It grew most immediately out of a series of conflicts in the Balkans and the Mediterranean; European expansion into the domains of a weakening Ottoman Empire precipitated much of the action. However, the struggle of Austria-Hungary and Russia for control of Slavic peoples coupled with the industrial and strategic rivalry of Britain with Germany to produce sharp divisions within Europe as well.

Austria's annexation of Bosnia and Herzegovina and its promotion of Bulgaria's independence (October 1908) widened a set of fissures that had already opened, but the subsequent French advances in Morocco filled them with steaming sulphur. Italian conquests in North Africa and the Mediterranean followed. Through a chain of linked events, Bulgaria, Serbia, and Greece were soon at war with Turkey (1912); that conflict, in its turn, soon had Austria defending its interests by means of threats and alliances. The Austrian declaration of war on Serbia (28 July 1914) ushered in the general war. By the end of the year, Germany, Austria, and Turkey were at war with Serbia, Russia, France, Belgium, England, Montenegro, and Japan. Italy, the former ally of Austria and Germany, only entered the war against them in 1915 and 1916, respectively. The United States completed our set by declaring war on Germany in April 1917. By that time, open war had been spreading for five years.

It had less than two years to run. During 1914 and 1915, Turkey, Austria, and (especially) Germany had generally held their own or advanced, while Russian forces retreated well into their own territory. During 1916 and 1917, the war as a whole came closer to stalemate, although the Russians failed in a major offensive and then fell back before major German assaults, while the Allies made inroads in Turkey's Asian territories. During this period, organized workers committed themselves more actively against the war in Russia and Germany. The demand for peace loomed large in Russia's February Revolution. Then German socialists sent delegations to Stockholm for the international's peace-oriented conference of June 1917. From that point on, the socialists pressed increasingly for a negotiated peace.

Following its two revolutions, Russia withdrew from the war through an armistice with Germany on 15 December 1917. Germany and Austria proceeded to invade and occupy Poland, Lithuania, the Ukraine, Baltic Russia, Finland, and Transcaucasia. On the western front, American forces first intervened seriously in June 1918. Toward the same time, the Allies stepped up their air war against Germany, and sent expeditionary forces to Russia. Turkey, Bulgaria, and the Austro-Hungarian Empire began to collapse, as the Allies started advancing against Germany in the West. On 11 November

442

1918, the western war ended, and the wars elsewhere began to wind down. Although battles recurred along the Russian borders until 1920, by the middle of 1919 the general war was over. The chronology of war had a decisive impact on the rhythm of strike activity. Over Europe as a whole, the beginning of a country's war effort muted overt industrial conflict. Our six countries show, however, how variable and incomplete were these effects in 1914–18. When citizens felt direct threats from other countries' troops at the same time as their governments maintained domestic control, strikes dropped to very low levels. In Great Britain, the number of new strikes fell from 140 in May 1914, 118 in June, and 99 in July to a mere 15 in August, the month Britain entered the war. Yet when governments began to lose wars and face sharper internal opposition – as they did dramatically in Germany and Russia during the later years of World War I – industrial conflict revived. Russia went through that cycle twice in rapid succession, first in the face of astonishing losses to Japan in 1905, then in response to the battering it took in the World War. In the revolutions of 1905 and 1917 alike, broad strikes and ineffectual repression prefaced the revolutionary assault on national power. In Germany, after Russia's October Revolution, mutinies and strikes merged in the abortive revolution that drove the Kaiser to abdicate in November 1918.

Even for the eventual winners, as Hugues Lagrange argues in the case of France, changing evidence of the government's wartime competence or incompetence affects the frequency of strike activity. In Great Britain, despite mounting repression and state intervention in labor disputes, industrial conflict intensified from month to month during most of 1917 and 1918 (Lind 1973, 132–52).

Labor historians of the period often adopt a rough distinction between "economic" and "political" strikes. Writers who use these terms ordinarily have a twofold distinction in mind. We might classify the demands that workers make with respect to whether (1) they concern long-term or short-term alterations in the conditions of work and workers; wage levels, for example, are short-term, while the right to organize is long-term; (2) their scope is confined to the local worksite or national in scope:

	Local	*National*
Long-term	local power	national power ("political")
Short term	local working conditions ("economic")	national working conditions

Where exactly we draw the line between economic and political in such a diagram matters little. To the extent that the long-term power position of labor (whether weak or strong) is stable and individual employers are the primary

443

decision-makers with respect to local working conditions, we can expect economic strikes to predominate.

To the extent that the crucial decisions visibly take place at a national scale (through some combination of worker organization, capital structure, and state intervention) and the power position of labor is uncertain, we can expect political strikes to become more prominent. A state's wartime measures, in moving crucial decisions to a national scale and threatening the power position of labor, therefore tend to politicize strike activity. As a war draws to its close, both capitalist and organized workers often begin to press their suspended or repressed claims on the state. If the state has lost power – especially by starting to lose the war – its ability to meet those claims has declined just as it has become more vulnerable to claims; hence a war-shaken state often faces massive, politicized industrial conflict.

We can also expect to see contrasting temporal patterns in industrial conflict at the two extremes. Economic strikes should rise and fall in response to local fluctuations in production, employment, and worker organization, while political strikes should respond more clearly to changes of national power and policy, including changes of regime. Our authors have not formalized this simple model, but all of them keep some version of it in mind. For the most part, the contributors to this section eschew formal modeling of causal relationships in favor of integrating fluctuations of strike activity into a more general narrative of a country's economic and political fortunes.

The contributions

The articles in Part IV of this book deal with short-term variation in strike activity at both scales: local and national. Before sorting out general themes of the papers, let us look at them individually.

Placing German experience in comparative perspective, Friedhelm Boll raises a number of questions about the relationship between business cycles and strike activity. He concedes that a broad relationship exists, but asks which features of the cycles actually promote industrial conflict, and which theories of causation thus make sense. In particular, he challenges the model of evolution from spontaneous to organized, from defensive to offensive, from primitive to modern.

James Cronin concentrates on the end of World War I and its political aftermath. Turning away from its conventional interrogation about the possibility of revolution in postwar Britain, he argues "that the crisis in Britain between 1917 and the early 1920s was in essence a crisis in the system of effective political representation brought on by wartime shifts in the balance of political and industrial power." As elements of the crisis, Cronin sees the accumulation of anger among soldiers and sailors – both discharged and under arms – at

444

war's end, the increasing organization of less skilled workers, the diminution of divisions (including income differentials) within the working class, and accelerating inflation. All of these elements, he argues, cumulated to produce a more unified and powerful working class. That class confronted employers who had recently seen a great increase of state involvement in industry, unions that had faced great resistance among their own members to their wartime bargaining away of shopfloor rights, and a state that was creaking under a rapidly increasing burden of responsibilities and shaking as a consequence of major shifts in the system of political parties. The postwar strike wave, in Cronin's view, resulted from the changing balance of power and possibility in Britain.

Hugues Lagrange asks why strikes became so rare in France at the start of World War I, only to proliferate toward the war's end. He points out that in the surge of strikes during May and June 1917, industries that were ordinarily less militant and organized – textiles, garments, leather, and food – not only led the way but also featured strikes involving many workplaces. He lays out evidence against cost-of-living changes as the sole explanation of wartime fluctuations in strikes. Later, however, he opts for a combination of price rises and losses of governmental legitimacy (largely, but not exclusively, as a result of setbacks at the front) as the explanation.

Leopold Haimson's trio of papers in this volume helps supply the necessary chronology. The third paper deals especially with the differences between the strikes of 1911 and the much more extensive round of strikes in 1912–14. Haimson stresses the great concentration of national political activity and of strikes in Moscow and, especially, St. Petersburg. He sees a crisis of the entire system as emerging from the convergence of distinct crises within the ruling class and within the working class. Inflation and the widespread demand for labor compounded the crises. The massacre in the Lena goldfields of Siberia (where, on 4 April 1912, troops fired on strikers and killed 170 of them) spread moral indignation over a wide range of the Russian population; demonstrations and sympathy strikes occurred almost immediately in St. Petersburg, Moscow, and other cities, and May Day brought massive strike-demonstrations in Russia's major centers. The Social Democratic party, finally, provided a vehicle for the effective communication of workers – especially skilled urban workers' – grievances and aspirations, and used workers' support to position itself for a seizure of power. The convergence of crises, argues Haimson, paralyzed a state that would probably have been able to deal with each problem singly.

Looking closely at the year of revolution, Diane Koenker and William Rosenberg discern three phases of industrial conflict: (1) a prerevolutionary phase in which strikes were illegal and "hence explicitly political," but occurred within a well-defined system of property and production; (2) the spring and summer following the February Revolution, when strikes became part of the exuberant exercise of democratic rights to transform workplaces and material welfare; (3) the fall preceding the November Revolution, during which strikes polarized social classes and undermined democratic order. In support of their analysis, they cite the spread of strikes outside of major urban areas, the correlation of strike activity with declining wages, the great increase in the number of strikers per strike, the rise in strikes against state-owned enterprises and municipal authorities, and the resemblance of 1917's strike patterns to those of the previous revolutionary year, 1905. All in all, according to Koenker and Rosenberg, the changing industrial conflicts of 1917 reflect a radicalization of workers, and a polarization of national politics.

Comments and conclusions

These articles deal with strikes in two rather different ways: as direct objects of study for their own sake and as components of major events such as wars and revolutions. Papers stressing the first theme include Boll on business cycles and strikes, and Lagrange on strikes and war. The remainder emphasize the place of strikes in some larger economic and (especially) political transformation: Cronin on the British crisis of 1917–22; Haimson on Russia from 1911 to 1914; Koenker and Rosenberg on Russia in 1917.

The two approaches, to be sure, complement each other. Yet on balance they lead to different sorts of conclusions. Boll and Lagrange both reject narrowly economistic explanations of industrial conflict, and insist on the deep influence of national struggles for power on the character of strikes. They make little effort to examine general interpretations of German or French history on the basis of their findings. Instead they ask what kinds of *explanations* can reasonably enter general accounts of those histories. Conclusions: mistrust both these explanations that portray current patterns of strike activity as direct expressions of workers' attitudes and interests, and those that depend on a continuous, economically-driven process of "modernization."

Cronin, Haimson, Koenker, and Rosenberg do not deny the impact of national power struggles on industrial conflict – far from it. They attempt, however, to reverse the relationship, seeking greater insight into political transformations by means of evidence about industrial conflict. As Cronin sees wholesale transformations of British politics emerging from the accommodations of World War I, the other authors discern the mounting conflicts and political improvisation that eventuated·in the Bolshevik seizure of power.

In general, our authors work implicitly with a model of national social structure including five actors: capitalists, workers, unions, other citizens, and the state. Considering their salience in other accounts of the same countries, landlords, peasants, farmers, petty bourgeois, and intellectuals figure little

446

in these analyses. Further actors such as political parties enter the analysis insofar as they ally themselves with one or more of the primary actors.

Most of the analyses suggest, furthermore, that very different European states made similar efforts to cope with World War I, seeking early to incorporate capitalists and organized workers into the war effort. But the states differed enormously in their strategies for that incorporation, and in their capacity to accomplish it. To the extent that they succeeded, they deferred industrial conflicts to the war's end, and accumulated commitment – often conflicting commitments – that became the stuff of postwar politics. To the extent that they failed, the war effort itself became an object of struggle. Where the war effort significantly weakened the state, the state became vulnerable to rebellion and revolution. Russia, once again, marks the extreme case, but a case in point nonetheless.

In this sense, our papers argue against treatments of Russian experience as sui generis, as an expression of a mentality and destiny having nothing in common with Russia's nonrevolutionary neighbors. They suggest that the neighbors, too, could have had successful revolutions under some conditions that were, in 1914 or later, not utterly unthinkable. In a modest way, the papers challenge us to rethink our theories of revolution.

References

Bond, Brian. 1983. *War and Society in Europe, 1870–1970*. Leicester: Leicester University Press.

Burawoy, Michael. 1985. *The Politics of Production. Factory Regimes Under Capitalism and Socialism*. London: Verso.

Conell, Carol. 1980. "The Value of Union Sponsorship to Strikers." Ph.D. diss., University of Michigan.

Cronin, James E. 1979. *Industrial Conflict in Modern Britain*. London: Croom Helm.

DeNardo, James. 1985. *Power in Numbers. The Political Strategy of Protest and Rebellion*. Princeton: Princeton University Press.

Friedman, Gerald. 1985. "Politics and Unions. Government, Ideology, and Unionization in the United States and France, 1880–1914." Ph.D. diss., Harvard University.

Geary, Roger. 1985. *Policing Industrial Disputes: 1893 to 1985*. Cambridge: Cambridge University Press.

Korpi, Walter, and Michael Shalev. 1980. "Strikes, Power and Politics in the Western Nations, 1900–1976." In Maurice Zaitlin, ed., *Political Power and Social Theory*. Greenwich, Conn.: JAI Press.

Lind, Joan. 1973. "Foreign and Domestic Conflict: The British and Swedish Labor Movements, 1900–1950." Ph.D. diss., University of Michigan.

Marwick, Arthur. 1974. *War and Social Change in the Twentieth Century. A Comparative Study of Britain, France, Germany, Russia and the United States*. London: Macmillan.

447

William G. Roy, 1984. "Class Conflict and Social Change in Historical Perspective." *Annual Review of Sociology 10:* 483–506.

Snyder, David. 1974. "Determinants of Industrial Conflict: Historical Models of Strikes in France, Italy and the United States." Ph.D. diss., University of Michigan.

Tarrow, Sidney. 1983. *Struggling to Reform: Social Movements and Policy Change During Cycles of Protest.* Center for International Studies, Western Societies Program, Occasional Paper no. 15. Ithaca, N.Y.: Cornell University.

19

Economic cycles and labor conflicts in Germany during the first quarter of the twentieth century

FRIEDHELM BOLL

Germany has never been the classic country for researching labor conflicts and least of all for researching strike action by quantitative methods. Thus, only a few studies on the subject have been published. The time that has been best studied in the context of economic cycles and labor conflicts is the period before 1914.[1] The findings fit well into the international context, for they confirm the impressive dependence of strike frequencies on economic cycles.[2] A closer look, however, shows some problems in interpreting the results. These problems have to do with the choice of comparative indicators.

First of all, with regard to strike indicators, the fact that they oscillate between greater extremes than the series of economic cycle indicators is of importance. Thus, it is not a comparison of absolute figures that is required but one of the relative decline and increase, that is, a study of their relative changes.

Further, it is significant that positive results only arise if the number of strikes (and lockouts) is compared with economic cycle indicators, rather than the number of people involved. Therefore, Perrot's observation on France applies here: The economic cycle is the strongest influence on the *decision* to take strike

---

1. It has to be pointed out that the rather strong tradition of strike research within the circle of the Kathedersozialisten was not continued after 1945. This older type of literature can be found mainly in the *Handwörterbuch für Staatswissenschaften*, vol.1 of *Arbeitseinstellunge* (Jena, 1909). For all recent literature see the bibliography in K. Tenfelde and H . Volkmann, eds., *Streik* (Munich, 1981), pp. 315–29. For the dependence on the economic cycle see particularly H. Kaelble and H. Volkmann, "Konjunktur und Streik während des Übergangs zum organisierten Kapitalismus in Deutschland," in: *Zeitschrift für Wirtschafts – und Sozialwissenschaften* 92 (1972): 513–44; I. Costas, *Auswirkungen der Konzentration des Kapitals auf die Arbeiterklasse in Deutschland (1880–1914)* (Frankfurt and New York, 1981); H. Volkmann, "Modernisierung des Arbeits-kampfes?" in H. Kaelble et al., *Probleme der Modernisierung in Deutschland* (Opladen, 1978), pp. 110–70. esp. pp. 153–62.

2. H. Perrot, *Les ouviers en grève, France 1871–1890* (Paris, 1974); idem., "Grèves, Grévistes et conjonctures: vieux problemes, travaux neufs," *Mouvement social* (avril–juin 1968).

action but all other questions, such as the form of participation, organization, duration, regional and branch involvement, depend on national or other factors. This statement becomes even more important because it is apparently valid regardless of trade union influence on a strike. Also, it applies especially to those times that were still characterized by very weak union movements (France and Germany before 1885).

The abilities of and opportunities for workers to choose the optimal timing of demands for improvements in their working conditions and their wages are apparently not dependent on an especially high degree of unionization, but on the level of education of the workers. Before going into that aspect, the economic cycle indicators will be discussed. The question of which economic cycle indicators predict most precisely the development of strikes has become one of the central questions of quantitative labor conflict research.[3] A number of theories are based on them. A close correlation between strikes and consumer goods prices or the cost of living, respectively, would mean that during periods of price increases the rate of strikes should be highest. Thus a decreasing real wage would be the most important indicator for the workers to put their demands. Only in the United States, however, is this correlation of a significant degree.[4] In Germany and France the correlation between strikes and industrial production is much more convincing.[5] This means that it was not the direct reaction to decreasing real wages that triggered the strike, but more the tactical consideration of what would be, economically speaking, the most favorable timing. For Britain and France this result has been confirmed insofar as the rate of strikes shows a clear dependence on the situation of the labor market. Workers, it seems, notice the upward trend of the economy especially through increased demand for labor, which is seen as the best time for labor conflicts.[6]

The dependence of strikes on certain economic cycle indicators as described can undoubtedly be interpreted in the way Volkmann did: Not the protest reaction to decreasing real wages but the calculated, rational reaction timed to coincide with the most favorable economic development can be seen as the initial strike situation for the majority of labor conflicts, particularly for aggressive strikes.[7] Thus, besides the *protest model* there is the *adjustment model*, which French researchers usually call the *aggressive model*.

3. Kaelble and Volkmann, "Konjunktur," p. 517; Perrot, "Greves," pp. 114ff.; E. Weede, "Der Streik in westlichen Industriegesellschaften. Eine Kritische Übersicht der international vergleichenden und quantitiven Streikforschung," *Zeitschrift für die gesamte Staatswissenschaft* 135, lst Book, pp. 1–16.

4. Kaelble and Volkmann, "Konjunktur," p. 526.

5. Ibid.; E. Andréani, *Grèves et Fluctuations. La France de 1890 à 1914* (Paris (edition Cujas), 1968), p. 127.

6. Kaelble and Volkmann, "Konjunktur," p. 526.

7. Perrot, "Grèves," p. 123.

It is only a short step from making this distinction between protest and adjustment models to relating these models to the respective trade union organization and to developing interpretive models like *Organisierter Kapitalismus*. Kaelble and Volkmann chose to do that. They related the tactical reaction of the workers, which had been adjusted to the economic situation, to the strengthening of the German unions before 1914. And they suggested an adjustment model of strike behavior corresponding to so-called organized capitalism. They assumed that the tactical orientation of striking workers, and their adjustment to the economic cycle reflects a learning process that had not only been furthered by the unions but would hardly have taken place without them. Thus the question that becomes a central focus of discussion is: How conscious were the workers of the economic cycle?

We know from French research that the workers' consciousness of changes in the economic cycle and their best tactical use differed significantly from branch to branch. Workers in the trades with a craft tradition, that is, the construction, wood, and engineering industries, were clearly more advanced than the workers in the textile and earth-moving industries. But this consciousness developed much earlier than and thus independently from the influence of the unions.[8] Between 1870 and 1890, when at the most 10% to 20% of strikes in France were organized by unions, a clear dependence of strikes on industrial development can already be shown (because no other indicators are available, measured in import rates of raw materials). However, even more interesting is a comparison of the years 1896–1914. For this period, Andreani established a correlation coefficient of a simple linear correlation of +0.83 between strikes and industrial production in France, although unions participated in only 72% of these strikes at most. Also comparing the curves of labor conflicts influenced by and not influenced by unions did not show any difference in their dependence on the economic cycle.[9] Seeking the best timing for a strike – which the French unions had made their tactic in the same way as the German or British unions – had thus been successfully pursued even without union influence.

Although these conclusions do not necessarily apply to Germany, they should engender caution regarding a suggested dependence on union influence for deciding the right timing according to the economic cycle. Kaelble and Volkmann's calculations of the dependence of labor conflicts in Germany on economic cycles rendered worse rather than better results than those for France. This occurred despite the fact that in the case of Germany the strikes were all organized by unions. The dependence index here amounts to +0.36 for industrial production and +0.73 for share prices.[10] Thus,

---

8. Perrot, "Grèves," pp. 119ff., which also applies to what follows.
9. Andreani, *Fluctuations*, pp. 118, 244.
10. Kaelble and Volkmann, "Konjunktur," p. 526.

in the case of Germany too, the question regarding the awareness of economic cycles has to be put in a much more differentiated way than hitherto.

In principle, one has to assume that workers offering their labor learned very quickly how to judge the economic situation and the corresponding value of their labor. They did not need any remedial help by the unions for that. During the nineteenth and the early twentieth century, no firmly established organizations were needed for that either. Unskilled, semiskilled, and skilled workers changed their jobs so frequently that a thorough knowledge of the labor market was an automatic by-product. The awareness of one's own market value, the mutual information on towns and regions with high or low wages, and the improvement of one's own situation through changing jobs were part of the basic experience of each worker in these days. Extremely high mobility rates in factories and unions are telling proof of this kind of individual conflict solution. High workplace mobility was thus an important precondition in order to defend oneself. Sickness, age, large numbers of children, or the necessity for wives and children to work, as was the case in the textile industry, meant a serious decrease of this mobility and was bound to reduce the worker's ability to react according to the economic situation. On the basis of these considerations, it does not seem very sensible to take the timing of labor conflicts in accordance with the economic situation as a yardstick for the development of a capitalist society organized in associations.[11]

A further distinction has to be made regarding the dependence of strikes on the economic cycle. All the available studies show that there is a much closer connection between aggressive strikes and economic cycle indicators (raw material imports, share prices) than between the latter and defensive strikes. This also very clearly applies when looked at branch by branch. Thus there is further proof that strikes serve a double function, that is, as aggressive and as defensive weapons.[12] French research into labor conflicts, which is a better developed discipline than the German, has also shown these differences to pertain to individual strike waves. For example, the strike waves in 1919–20 and 1947–8, following the world wars, were more of the aggressive type, but the strikes in 1936 and 1968 match the model of a protest strike.[13] Apparently, there is no development from a protest strike toward an aggressive strike in the French case, especially as after 1945 another change took place when the more dominant aggressive labor conflict (1948–68) reverted toward the protest type of strike (1968–78). Recent studies in particular have empha-

11. As do Kaelble and Volkmann. For labor mobility see: D. Langewiesche, "Wanderungsbewegungen in der Hochindustrialisierungsperiode. Regionale, interstädtische und innerstädtische Mobilität in Deutschland 1880–1914," *Vierteljahrschrift für Sozial- und Wirtschaftsgeschichte*, 1977: 1–40.
12. Andréani, *Fluctuations*, p. 208; Perrot, "Greves," p. 119.
13. H. Lagrange's contribution.

sized that these are not opposing but parallel trends with one type of labor conflict simply being temporarily more dominant than the other. Corresponding studies do not yet exist for Germany. However, first indications from research into strike waves lead us to expect that in the German case, too, the view will have to be abandoned that there was an evolutionary development in the function of labor conflicts. The evidence rather points toward the parallel development of different strike functions.

In discussions about explanatory models going beyond epochal developments, models such as organized capitalism and modernization theory, the influence of centralized organizational leadership on strikes is often too strongly emphasized. As already illustrated with the workers' awareness of economic cycles, the freedom of decision making that local and regional organizations had before 1914 – that is, the workers and labor forces of factories – was much greater than generally assumed. According to the official statistics of the German Reich, 42.9% of all striking workers downed their tools during the strike wave of 1910–13 without giving proper notice. If this high degree of violation of contractual obligations is taken as a yardstick for spontaneous strikes, the history of labor conflicts in the prewar period can by no means be regarded as having been "domesticated" (controlled) by the unions.[14]

The period from 1914 until far into the 1920s was characterized by an increasing gap between central union policy on the one hand and local autonomy of labor forces in factories, union subdivisions, and individual mobility on the other hand. To mention only one example in place of many: Union statistics at the time were apparently entirely insufficient. They show only 67.7% of all strikes in 1919–20 with just 12.8% of the workers indicated as involved in strikes by the statistics of the German Reich.[15] The decrease in union influence that can be seen from this had already started in 1915, when after an official decision by the central executives, local organizations and factory staff began to conduct their strikes under their own direction. This autonomy of rank-and-file labor had, at the beginning, nothing to do with a conflict about

14. H. Volkmann, "Un analisi comparata dei cicli conflittuali 1910–1913 e 1919–1920," *Sindacato e classe operaia nell'eta della Seconda Internazionale* (Florence, 1983), pp. 119–52. Tenfelde emphasized this recently once more with regard to the miners' strikes of the pre- and postwar period; see K. Tenfelde, "Linksradikale Strömungen in der Bergarbeiterschaft 1905 bis 1919," in H. Mommsen and U. Borsdorf, eds., *Die Bergarbeiter und ihre Organisation in Deutschland* (Colonge, 1979), pp. 199–223. It is particularly important to clarify that only a minority of strikes were started by the union organization; the majority, on the other hand, were started by the labor forces' democratic decision – which as the older form of organization had always been an obstacle to the union organization and also became the basis for the left-wing radicalism of the revolutionary period. A study that would deal with the unions' behavior during labor conflicts would presumably show even clearer how widely spread rank-and-file autonomy had been in other industrial branches at the beginning of a strike. See Tenfelde, "Crisi del sindacato? Relazioni industriali in Germania negli anni precedenti lo scoppio della prima guerra mondiale (1914)," in *Sindacata e classe operaia*, pp. 93–118.

15. Volkmann, "Un analisi", p. 133, tab. 6 (political strikes are included).

the political direction of the unions. It is noticeable, however, that the labor force of individual factories or parts thereof often proceeded autonomously in downing their tools spontaneously – either on their own initiative or in support of union-led wage movements.[16]

During the World War, when communication was more difficult and political pressure increased, labor conflicts can be divided into three types. Besides the increase of short-term individual strikes, the deteriorating political situation also came to a head in another dimension of labor conflict – the political mass strikes after 1916. This form of labor conflict had been much discussed in Germany before 1914, but only in wartime conditions was it practiced, showing many of the characteristics of the later strike period: a high degree of participation by striking individuals and by factories, relatively short duration, often good though informal organization by oppositional groups. It is not surprising therefore that this political strike movement always emerged in the strongholds of the internal organizational opposition. Here the preconditions for communication were so clearly developed in the form of an opposition press and system of meetings that the spark of the political antiwar movement could be conveyed to the work force in factories. A precise count of the strikes with an expressly political element shows that these strike movements largely took place where the strongholds of opposition were located (usually with an opposition Social-Democratic party paper). It was only during the strike in January 1918, when in fifty-seven German cities a total of one to two million workers took to the roads, that this political movement took over some of the strongholds of moderate social democracy.[17] If one adds together strikes and other forms of protest such as demonstrations, unrest, and petitions, a concentration of these protests during times of military setbacks is clearly recognizable. Apart from inflationary peaks, war events also had a strong influence on the outbreaks of strikes.

The social situation during the World War became very tense and thus thoroughly changed a third dimension of labor conflict: the readiness of the individual to enter into conflict. Even before the beginning of the war, changing jobs was a highly important form of conflict solution. From the middle of 1915 onward, because of the tight labor market, job mobility gained even more in importance. A mobility rate of more than 300% for the labor force of factories was no longer rare. It was for good reason that these factories were

---

16. The strikes during the First World War in Brunswick and Hanover are such examples of rank-and-file autonomy mentioned by F. Boll, *Massenbewegungen in Niedersachsen 1906–1920* (Bonn, 1981), pp. 207ff.

17. This calculation is based on a count of all primarily politically motivated strikes mentioned in the "Geschichte der deutschen Arbeiterbewegung," in F. Boll, *Frieden ohne Revolution? Friedensstrategien der deutschen Sozialdemokratie vom Erfurter Programm 1891 bis zur Revolution 1918* (Bonn, 1980), p. 207.

compared to a dovecote.[18] New groups of workers, particularly women and young people, were increasingly drawn into the industrial labor market and, of course, into the continuous bargaining over the value of their own labor, especially as they could not be silenced by the threat of being sent to the front.

However, high individual mobility of workers not only weakens the organization of factory production but also the fighting strength of the unions. Even before 1914, but more so during the war, the unions had tried to stem the fluctuation of membership, which was closely connected with labor mobility, by strongly extending the union's insurance system.[19]

The employers' demand to restrict labor mobility for the duration of the war thus met the interests of the union leaderships. The Auxiliary Service Law was passed with the agreement of nearly all German union leaders and contained strict regulations on labor mobility. It sharply reduced the individual's ability to enter into conflicts and thus became the cause of a new conflict at the level of the individual's autonomy at his or her place of work – something the individual is particularly aware of. Arbitration committees were set up in the wake of the Auxiliary Service Law with equal representation of employers and employees. Their files are overflowing with individual complaints against employers who had refused to accept the resignation of an employee.

Labor conflict during the World War was characterized by increasing numbers of individual strikes, strikes becoming more politically oriented (even to the degree of political mass strikes), and increased labor mobility. All these new developments played their part in the increasing alienation between the central leadership and the rank and file of the unions.

The new leaders of the workers who had emerged from these rank-and-file activities were able to create their own new representative bodies during the revolution of 1918–19 in the shape of the workers or factory councils. These were the new instruments of power that carried the strike wave up to the Kapp putsch (1920) and led it against the old centralized union leaderships. When the German government, which was led by the Social-Democrats as the senior coalition partner, put an end to the Workers' Councils, the new leadership elite quickly lost its influence – especially as it had only managed in a few exceptional cases to conquer the power apparatus of the old unions.[20]

The employers in Germany had already recognized earlier that they were vulnerable when the labor market became tight during periods of economic

18. G. D. Feldman, *Army, Industry and Labor in Germany 1914–1918* (Princeton, 1966).
19. K. Schonhoven, *Expansion und Konzentration. Studien zur Entwicklung der Freien Gewerkschaften im Wilhelminischen Deutschland 1890 bis 1914* (Stuttgart, 1980), pp. 150ff.
20. G. Hogl, "Gewekschaften und USPD von 1916–1922. Ein Beitrag zur Geschichte der deutschen Arbeiterbewegung unter besonderer Berücksichtigung des Deutschen Metallarbeiter-, Textilarbeiter- und Schumacherverbandes" (Ph.D. diss., Munich, 1982). H. Potthoff, *Gewerkschaften zwischen Revolution und Inflation* (Dusseldorf, 1978).

upswing. Therefore, there were many attempts after 1890 to regain the ground lost during the economic recovery, and especially to control the labor market itself much more. Employers' organizations thus established their own labor exchanges everywhere, with which they tried in particular to influence the sectors of large industry. They managed quite often by blacklisting to discipline striking workers or exclude them from further employment in their traditional industry.[21] The trade unions' counterstrategy was to foil the employers' objective and establish labor exchanges with equal representation. But they only succeeded in industries with predominantly small- and medium-sized companies.[22] Large companies were clearly underrepresented in labor conflicts in Gemany, which explains the relatively small average number of employees directly involved in a strike – about 109 compared with 215 in France and 291 in Britain – and demonstrates the sharp class divisions of the Kaiserreich. The above average number of lockouts emphasizes this situation even more.

It is therefore not surprising that the strike wave of 1919–20 was regarded not only as an economic struggle, but also as a fight for the control of the power of the state. The power of the state was seen as a means of counterbalancing the structural inferiority of the union organizations.

Let us return to my initial remark: It is not accidental that the reliance on French and British research sheds light on the backwardness of German historiography regarding the relationship between strikes and the economic cycle. There is a particular shortage of studies differentiating regions and industrial branches to throw light on this complex relationship and the workers' awareness of the economic situation. The teleological view has been predominant in German strike research so far. With the existence of such studies this view would presumably wane and the awareness of the multifunctional character of strikes would increase once more. Thus the theoretical study of explanatory models would find a new basis with plenty of material.

21. Costas, *Auswirkungen*; K. Saul, *Staat, Industrie, Arbeiterbewegung im Kaiserreich* (Dusseldorf, 1974), pp. 66ff.
22. F. Boll, "Streikwellen im europaischen Vergleich," in W. J. Mommsen and H. G. Husung, eds., *Auf dem Wege zur Massengewerkschaft. Die Entwicklung der Gewerkschaften in Deutschland und Grossbritannien* (Stuttgart, 1984), pp. 109–34, here p. 123.

456

20

The crisis of state and society in Britain, 1917–1922

JAMES E. CRONIN

When David Lloyd George surveyed the political scene in the famous Fontainebleau memorandum of March 1919, he claimed to discern a "spirit of revolution" in every country in Europe, not excepting Great Britain.

> The whole of Europe is filled with the spirit of revolution. There is a deep sense not only of discontent, but of anger and revolt, amongst the workmen against prewar conditions. The whole existing order in its political, social and economic aspects is questioned by the masses of the population from one end of Europe to the other. In some countries, like Germany and Russia, the unrest takes the form of open rebellion; in others, like France, Great Britain and Italy, it takes the shape of strikes and of a general disinclination to settle down to work – symptoms which are just as much concerned with the desire for political and social change as with age demands.[1]

The forces that were toppling regimes and dynasties in central and eastern Europe were thus seen to be active also in Britain. Of course, they were unlikely to have such dramatic effects on the English side of the Channel. And yet neither Lloyd George nor anyone else could doubt that they would bring about far-reaching changes in the nature of British politics and society. Indeed, the extraordinary trajectory of Lloyd George's own political career from 1916 to 1922 is quite incomprehensible to anyone who fails to recognize the essential fluidity and sense of crisis that characterized British political life in that era and that permeated the consciousness, not simply of Lloyd George, but also of the mass of rather dull and ordinary politicians with whom he dealt.

But what was the precise nature of the crisis affecting Britain after the Great War? It was clearly not a revolutionary or even prerevolutionary situation in any

---

1. "Some Considerations for the Peace Conference before They Finally Draft Their Terms," *Memorandum Circulated by the Prime Minister on March 25, 1919,* Cmd. 1614 (1922), cited in Arno Mayer, *Politics and Diplomacy of Peacemaking* (New York: Vintage, 1967), pp. 581–3.

meaningful sense.[2] Although there was lots of talk of revolution in Britain, and plenty of discontent to fuel such rhetoric, there was never any question of a collapse of state authority. Since such a collapse is normally considered to be the essential ingredient in the making of any revolution, it would seem a mistake to speak of the crisis in such terms. But does that mean there was no crisis to speak of at all? Does it, more precisely, justify the arguments of those historians who seek to minimize the extent of unrest and refuse even to recognize a crisis during these years?[3]

The point of this paper is to suggest that it does not. What the improbability of social revolution in 1917–20 does justify and indeed requires is a reformulation of the argument concerning the crisis of those years in terms that can capture its dimensions but that do not prejudge its outcome. In particular, it is essential to abandon the sort of analysis that implicitly portrays political conflict as a set of binary choices among polar opposites. Revolution and reaction were not the only options confronting ordinary people in Britain after the war. In fact, it could be argued that such options were never put before the working class in Britain. What was before them, however, was a range of political strategies and possible outcomes that, though probably not encompassing such extreme positions, would nevertheless have included a variety of more limited and more realistic choices embodying quite different visions of the postwar social and political order.

Shifting the focus away from the narrow, and by now also quite sterile, question of the possibility of revolution in Britain after World War I to the more open-ended question about the range of actual political possibilities, has a second analytical benefit. It affords a different angle of vision from which to review and evaluate the impact of war upon society. Basic to this perspective is the effort to assess the effect of social, economic, and political changes during 1914–18 upon the power, the collective capacity, of various social and political groups. From this point of view, what is most interesting and significant about the Great War was not so much how it affected the well-being of workers, employers, or others – although this obviously mattered a great deal to them – but rather how it shifted the balance of social power within and between them, and thus altered the possibilities for political action.[4] More specifically, we shall

2. On the genuinely revolutionary situations on the Continent, see Charles Bertrand, ed., *Revolutionary Situation in Europe, 1917–1922* (Montreal, 1977); and J. Cronin, "Labor Insurgency and Class Formation: Comparative Perspectives on the Crisis of 1917–1920 in Europe," in Cronin and C. Sirianni, eds., *Work, Community and Power: The Experience of Labor in Europe and America, 1900–1925* (Philadelphia: Temple University Press, 1982), pp. 20–48. For the problems confronting revolutionaries in Britain, see Walter Kendall, *The Revolutionary Movement in Britain, 1900–1921* (London: Weidenfeld and Nicolson, 1969); and R. Chalinor, *The Origins of British Bolshevism* (London: Croom Helm, 1977).

3. Arthur Marwick, *Britain in Our Century* (London: Thames and Hudson, 1974) is the latest book to argue such a position.

4. This approach could also be defended in more theoretical terms, though such an

use this approach to argue that the crisis in Britain between 1917 and the early 1920s was in essence a crisis in the system of effective political representation brought on by wartime shifts in the balance of political and industrial power.

Consider, for example, the contradictory impact of the war upon workers, employers, and the state considered as very broad categories. In terms of living standards and conditions at work, the war was a very mixed affair for workers; in terms of political and industrial clout, however, it brought about immense gains. For businessmen, on the other hand, the political and economic effects were largely the opposite: profits increased enormously and investment in plant and equipment boomed; but politically businessmen were placed very much on the defensive. The war had an equally ambiguous impact upon the state itself, for while it greatly expanded its social and economic reach – what Michael Mann calls its "infrastructural power" – it also increased the demands and expectations placed upon the state.[5] It thus made its successful functioning more dependent than ever before upon the state's ability to secure the consent of key groups in civil society. Such summary judgments as these, of course, serve as much to mask as to illuminate the considerable variations that were evident in the impact of the war upon British society. To get at these, let us disaggregate a bit more and look in some detail at who won and who lost during the years when Britain first became organized for "total war."

Among the workers, surely the most telling distinction was between those who fought and those who did not. Over the course of the war, approximately eight million men were mobilized, and most of these were inevitably drawn from the working class.[6] In the first six months of the war, nearly two million volunteered. The great bulk of these were taken into the army. Not only were most of them workers, but many came from occupations, industries, and regions noted for their level of organization and industrial militancy. Miners, for example, enlisted in very large numbers.[7] So, too, did metalworkers and engineers, workers in the chemicals industry and, it appears, many dockers.[8] Particularly interesting was the way recruitment and enlistment followed and

exercise would go well beyond the purpose and the confines of this essay. A sense of what it would look like, however, can be glimpsed in two papers with which I am in general agreement: Charles Tilly, "Models and Realities of Popular Collective Action," *Working Paper no. 10*, Center for Studies of Social Change, New School of Social Research (March 1985); and Scott Lash and John Urry, "The New Marxism of Collective Action: A Critical Analysis," *Sociology* 18 (1984): 33–50.

5. Michael Mann, "The Autonomous Power of the State: Its Origins, Mechanisms and Results," *Archives europeennes de sociologie* 25 (1984): 185–213.

6. Marc Ferro, *The Great War, 1914–1918* (London: Routledge and Kegan Paul, 1973), p. 227.

7. John Keegan, *The Face of battle* (New York: Viking, 1976), p. 219.

8. Arthur Marwick, *The Deluge* (London: Bodley Head, 1965), p. 56; Jonathan Schneer, "The War, the State and the Workplace: British Dockers during 1914–1918," in J. Cronin and J. Schneer, eds., *Social Conflict and the Political Order in Modern Britain* (New Brunswick: Rutgers University Press, 1982), pp. 96–112.

reflected the patterns of working-class social life. Workers in one town or workplace, or even one club, would enlist together, becoming popularly known as the "pals" from this, that, or the other locality. Groups of this sort came from numerous working-class areas – from "Llandudno and Blaenaw Festiniog" in Wales, from "Shoreditch, Islington, West Ham and Bermondsey" in London, and from most of the industrial districts of the north and the midlands.[9] Kitchener's army was thus an army of the working class. So, too, was Fisher's Navy. The ranks of the sailors did not expand in anything like the proportions as those of the soldiers, however, so the wartime Navy did not represent such a broad and current sample of the working class. Sailors came instead from the Navy's traditional recruiting grounds and, given the technical demands of work in the Navy, from the more skilled, literate, and "respectable" sections of the working class.

The effect of all this on organization and on political attitudes was inevitably very complex. In the first place, the siphoning off of such large numbers of industrial workers – and the younger and healthier ones at that – no doubt created a gap in the workshops and in the trade unions. Within the army, the mass infusion of workers, coming in as they did not as individuals but in groups, meant an infusion of working-class mores, attitudes, and styles of life. And despite a good deal of rhetoric to the contrary, the confrontation between these new recruits and their upper-class officers seldom led to a new awareness and sympathy on either side. On the other hand, it did not normally result in open resistance either. Thus, for the most part, the ordinary British soldier remained discontented, but generally not disposed to do much about it. There were momentary exceptions, such as occurred at Etaples in the summer of 1917.[10] After the war, moreover, the soldiers would demonstrate frequently and forcefully for demobilization. But during the war itself protest for most soldiers would be limited to a studied effort at "keeping out of harm's way," a sort of "militarized ca'canny," as it has recently been called.[11]

The Navy, though, was a different story. There agitation could build upon the traditions of organization on the "lower deck" and upon the stability and career orientation of many of the sailors.[12] Unrest broke out in July 1917, and was centered primarily at Rosyth, where the "lower deck associations" formed a joint committee to press their grievances and, more importantly, to demand direct negotiations with representatives of the Admiralty. Agitation continued

9. Keegan, *Face of Battle*, pp. 218–19.
10. Gill and G. Dallas, "Mutiny at Etaples Base in 1917," *Past and Present*, no. 69 (Nov. 1975): 88–112; and Dallas and Gill, *The Unknown Army: Mutinies in the British Army in World War I* (London: New Left Books, 1985).
11. David Englander and James Osborne, "Jack, Tommy and Henry Dubb: The Armed Forces of the Working Class," *Historical Journal* 21 (1978): 593–621.
12. See, in general, Peter Kemp. *The British Sailor: A Social History of the Lower Deck* (London, 1970).

through the remainder of the war, and was finally rewarded with the creation by the Navy of what was called the "Welfare Conference System," a sort of Whitley Councils scheme for the forces. For a variety of reasons, the system would be abandoned in the 1920s, but its setting up was a clear recognition of the power within the Navy of the rank and file on the lower decks.

The significance of the unrest in the armed forces is difficult to judge, both on its own and in terms of its effect upon the civilian workforce. Compared to France, where troops mutinied en masse in 1917, or Russia, where the soldiers and sailors became the backbone of the revolution, or Germany, where, on the one hand, it was the sailors who precipitated the revolution of 1918 and, on the other, it was the organizations of ex-soldiers who were instrumental in suppressing the left after the war, what happened in the British army and Navy was pretty tame. But again, it is not clear that the proper standard of comparison is one drawn from the experience of other nations. Judged against previous British experience, the discontent looks far more important. It was a sign, if nothing else, that the class awareness and antipathies that characterized civil society also permeated the army and the Navy and that the experience of wartime would only harden and polarize class relations. It was a sign, more importantly, that those in authority read as very threatening, for if the forces were not a solid bulwark for the social order, how was that order to be protected? Lastly, the alienation of so many soldiers and sailors from their officers and from their political and military leaders that sent them to war would mean that in the long term these ex-servicemen would not form in Britain a loyal phalanx of patriotic veterans, capable of being mobilized politically by the parties of the right. Rather, they would, for the most part, be reintegrated into the occupations and communities from which they had come without great difficulty, and in a fashion that would probably reinforce the solidarities of the workplace and the neighborhood and, still more significantly, the broader class solidarities to which these gave rise. In the short term, and particularly between the ending of hostilities and the reintegration of former servicemen into society, the presence of large numbers of angry soldiers and sailors waiting to be demobilized or, perhaps even worse, of equally large numbers demobilized but unable to find work and demonstrating vociferously about it, would add considerable intensity to the postwar political and social crisis.[13]

The changes experienced by working people who remained at home were no less dramatic. To begin, there were the gaping holes in the labor force left by those who joined up. To fill these required massive occupational shifts within the working population and an increase in the levels of labor force participation

13. Stephen Ward, "Intelligence Surveillance of British Ex-Servicemen, 1918–1920," *Historical Journal* 16 no. 1 (1975); Directorate of Intelligence, "Survey of Revolutionary Feeling during 1919," Public Record Office, *CAB 24/96, C.P., 462*, and "Survey of Revolutionary Movements in Great Britain in the Year 1920," Public Record Office, *CAB 24/118, C.P. 2455.*

461

for older and younger men and for women of almost all ages. The under-
employed got full-time jobs, old men postponed retirement, and young men
left school early to take up work in the factories, in the mines, on the docks,
or wherever they were most needed. But surely the greatest change concerned
women. According to one estimate, the number of women in paid employment
increased from approximately 3.2 million in July 1914 to just about 4.8 million
in April 1918. Since these figures excluded women in small dress shops and in
domestic service – in which 1.7 million were employed before the war – they
probably understate the overall level of female employment and slightly over-
state the shift occasioned by the war. Still, in 1917 the Ministry of Labour
estimated that one in three women workers was filling a job formerly held
by a man. This suggests that close to two million women had moved, either
from the home or from more traditional women's job, like textiles or domestic service, into work that had been the preserve of male workers before
1914.[14]

The shifting demography of the labor force had quite profound consequences and helped in major ways to further the reshaping of the British
working class. That process had been underway well before the war, but the
changes brought on by the war accelerated it a good deal. Since there has been
considerable discussion and debate about this transformation, it would seem
useful to be a bit more precise about its starting and ending points. Whether
one chooses to talk about the existence of a "labour aristocracy" or not, there is
a very broad and general agreement that the mid-Victorian working class was
rent by sharp divisions between the skilled and the less skilled, the organized
and the unorganized, the "rough" and the "respectable." These distinctions
may at times have been crosscutting, and there were clearly many local variations
in how each group was defined, but the picture of extreme fragmentation is
reinforced in almost all accounts.[15] The working class in twentieth century
Britain stands in considerable contrast. While there have been many local
variations and all sorts of minor, but often quite invidious, distinctions made
within the working class both at work and in the community, the overall image
it has presented to the outside world is one of solidity and cohesiveness. One

14. The estimate quoted comes from A. W. Kirkaldy, *Industry and Finance* (London:
Pitman, 1921). The best contemporary account of the overall phenomenon is I. O. Andrews, *The
Economic Effects of the World War upon Women and Children* (Oxford: Oxford University Press, 1921).
The most useful historical discussion of the topic is Gail Braybon's *Women Workers in the First World
War* (London: Croom Helm, 1981), though Marion Kozak's dissertation, "Women Munition
Workers during the First World War" (Ph.D. diss., University of Hull, 1976), also contains a
wealth of interesting material on the political and trade union organization of women.

15. The literature on the "labour aristocracy" is by now quite enormous. Perhaps the
best place to start, however, is with the most recent contributions of Eric Hobsbawm, who largely
initiated the modern debate. See his *Workers: Worlds of Labor* (New York: Pantheon, 1984), esp.
essays 12–14; and idem., "Artisan or Labour Aristocrat?" *Economic History Review* 37 (1984):
355–72.

may debate the particulars, and argue whether this distinctive world of the working class owed its apparent coherence to structures in the workplace or in the urban landscape, and one may certainly argue over the political impact of the values and style of life that have come to be identified with that world. But few would question its existence.[16]

What is clearly debatable is just how and when it came to be and, related to that, the political consequences of the transformation. There are two main positions on these issues. The first sees the transition as more or less forced and violent and, in consequence, as having dramatic political effects; the second views the change as gradual and smooth, with far less serious political ramifications.[17] In both positions, however, the key transforming agent is technological change at the workplace. The difference in interpretation stems from differing assessments of the pace and impact of technical development. The evidence is frankly somewhat contradictory. It is clear that from about 1890 onward, British employers became increasingly concerned with the technical backwardness of industry and with their own lack of control over the details of production. They began to flirt with notions of scientific management and became committed rhetorically to breaking the control of skilled workers in the workplace.[18] This battle for control raged intermittently from the early 1890s through the Great War, but two rather dramatic confrontations punctuated this protracted struggle. The first was the engineering strike of 1897–8, which by any standard was won by the employers. The second was the dispute over "dilution" – the practice of replacing skilled men with unskilled men or women workers – that flared up early in the war within the munitions industry.[19] Taken together with the less visible, but continual, tug of war in the shops, this record can without difficulty be read as suggesting that the transformation of the labor process was indeed wrenching and, for some, politically radicalizing as well. And so it has been intepreted by one group of scholars.

Such an interpretation has been countered by other scholars who stress the lack of technical change within British industry in general and in engineering in

16. The most evocative description of that world remains Richard Hoggart's *The Uses of Literacy* (London: Chatto and Windus, 1957). Hobsbawm has attempted to chart out the transition to this world in "The Making of the Working Class, 1870–1914," in *Workers*, pp. 194–213. The present writer has sought to chart its subsequent transformation in *Labour and Society in Britain, 1918–1979* (New York: Schocken, 1984).

17. See the essays by Richard Hyman and Richard Price for the first position, and those by Alastair Reid and Jonathan Zeitlin for the second, in the collection of essays edited by Wolfgang Mommsen and H.-G. Husung, *The Development of Trade Unionism in Great Britain and Germany, 1880–1914* (London, 1985).

18. E. J. Hobsbawm, "Custom, Wages and Workload," in *Labouring Men* (Garden City: Anchor, 1963).

19. J. Melling, "'Non-Commissioned Officers': British Employers and their Supervisory Workers, 1880–1920," *Social History* 5 (1980): 183–221; J. B. Jefferys, *The Story of the Engineers* (London: Lawrence and Wishart, 1946); and James Hinton, *The First Shop Stewards' Movement* (London: Allen and Unwin, 1973).

particular. Any breaking of the control of the skilled men over production would have had to be accompanied by a wave of investment in new machinery and new methods of production and by a sharp increase in supervisory personnel. Although investment occurred and the number of foremen and supervisors increased, in neither case was the change particularly dramatic. Hence the economic preconditions for a thoroughgoing transformation of the workplace simply were not there. The effect was to allow the skilled men, especially in engineering and shipbuilding, to retain most, if not all of their prerogatives, and thus effectively to keep control of the shopfloor prior to the First World War.[20] More important, the success of this prewar resistance put them in a very strong position from which to resist "dilution" or, in more current terms, "deskilling," during the war.[21] Even though the skilled men and their unions were forced to accept the introduction of women and unskilled men into certain classes of work previously reserved for the skilled, they largely dictated the terms on which this was done and made sure that it would be done only for the duration of the war. In this they were aided by the very same factors as before the war, for the exigencies of war did not allow for the wholesale disruption of workplace routines or for the introduction of any qualitatively new technologies, both of which would have been necessary to dislodge the skilled men in any permanent fashion.

This debate over the fate of the skilled workers has produced some interesting research, and has undoubtedly served to refine the historical understanding of the place of craftsmen within modern industry. As a vehicle for understanding the overall evolution of the structure of the working class, however, it has served far less well, for it unduly narrows the focus of analysis. The skilled were but a part of the working class, and their ability to maintain their status and their role in the organization of production in the face of the employers' challenge does not mean that their relation to other workers remained as it had been. For while the skilled were trying desperately to maintain what they had previously achieved, the less skilled were organizing to gain what had previously been denied them; and in this they were remarkably successful. The key, of course, was union organization. Just as the status of the skilled was largely a matter of organization and bargaining, so the spread of organization to those who had not served apprenticeships or been otherwise certified as skilled increased the status and industrial leverage of those workers

20. On the indifferent success of management initiatives before 1914, see E. Wigham, *The Power to Manage: A History of the Engineering Employers' Federation* (London: Macmillan, 1973); and the essays in H. Gospel and C. Littler, eds., *Managerial Strategies and Industrial Relations* (London: Heineman, 1983).
21. See Keith Burgess, "The Political Economy of British Engineering Workers during the First World War," this volume.

too.[22] So while the skilled typically retained their privileged positions, the less skilled improved theirs; the result was that the gap between the skilled and the unskilled was noticeably lessened.

It would seem that this broader transformation in the relations between skilled and less skilled workers constitutes the proper context in which to place the struggle over "dilution" and the entry of women into industry during the war. And in that context both phenomena were of critical importance. The need to replace skilled men with women or men without recognized skills vastly improved the status of the latter two groups. It was thus accompanied by a great jump in the organization of both groups and considerable advances in their wages and improvements in their conditions of work. Moreover, these improvements occurred not just in jobs closely related to the waging of the war, but throughout the economy. The change can be represented statistically in terms of the relationship between the wages of skilled and unskilled workers in various trades. Before the war, unskilled workers in construction earned 66% of what a skilled worker made. In shipbuilding they made 55% of the skilled rate, in engineering almost 59%, and on the railways just 54%. By 1918, however, the unskilled worker's wages had increased to 80% of the skilled worker's in construction, to nearly 74% in shipbuilding, to 76% in engineering, and 79% on the railways.[23] These figures, of course, apply to men and not to the women who moved into industry. The women continued to receive less, and very few of those replacing men got the male rate. Nor did the wages of those who remained in the traditional centers of women's work – like textiles and clothing – share fully in the wartime increase of wages. Nevertheless, women workers did gain considerably. One writer estimated that women replacing men had experienced a "real advance of 50%" even after inflation, while those in other sorts of employment more or less kept pace with the increasing cost of living.[24]

Within the working class, therefore, one effect of the war would seem to have been to level upward, and hence to reduce the enormous disparities that had existed between the skilled and the organized on the one hand, and all the rest on the other. The war thus made the working class a somewhat more solid and, at least economically, relatively more compact social formation. It was by no means a "homogenous" class by the end of the war, but it was a far less segmented and socially fractured class than it had been prior to the lengthy

22. On the social construction of the concept and reality of "skill," see Charles More, *Skill and the English Working Class* (London: Croom Helm, 1980); and on the spread of organization to the less skilled, see my earlier essay in this volume.

23. Calculations based on the data in K. G. Knowles and D. J. Robertson, "Differences between the Wages of Skilled and Unskilled Workers, 1880–1950," *Bulletin of the Oxford University Institute of Statistics* 13 (1951): 109–127.

24. M. A. Hamilton, cited in Braybon, *Women Workers*, p. 77.

process of transformation that began in the 1890s and culminated in the Great War.

This lessening of the divisions within the working class was reinforced by the fact that almost all workers shared a common set of economic problems during the war. Of these the most serious was inflation. The cost of living rose by about 10% from July 1914 through the end of the year. It increased still faster in 1915 and 1916, and by July 1917 had risen by a full 80%. Prices jumped even more the next year, so that when war ended in November 1918 the cost of living stood at almost 125% of its prewar level. It was very hard for workers to keep up. Indeed, they did not. By the end of 1916 most workers had lost about a quarter of their real wages. Steady work and lots of overtime earnings softened the impact on individual workers, and particularly on families in which more people were working, but the loss was nonetheless real and it stimulated demands for increases and, in some cases, strikes designed to extract them from employers or from the state. The effect was that workers began to recoup what had been lost in the first two-and-a-half years of the war. Wages rose about as fast as prices during 1917 and 1918 and actually surged briefly ahead in 1919–20. They would subsequently fall back a bit before stabilizing at a level slightly above that of 1914 during the early 1920s.[25]

The success of most workers in resisting the ravages of inflation was significant for at least two reasons. It was a sign, in the first instance, of the augmented power of workers as a whole. Underpinning that power, of course, were the tight labor market created by war and war mobilization, and the spread of organization to hitherto unrepresented groups of workers. After the temporary dislocations of late 1914, unemployment fell for the duration of the war to around 1%, which meant that viturally everyone could find a job. This by itself began to increase union membership, but even more significant were the efforts of unionists to use the conditions of war to bring within their orbit previously unorganized sections of the work force. The result was a jump in unionization from 4.1 million in 1914 to 8.3 million in 1920, which represented an increase in union density of from 25% to 45% of the labor force.[26]

The second, crucially important fact about the popular battle against inflation was its impact on relations within the working class. Inflation transcended boundaries based upon skill, occupation, age, and even sex; it thus confronted all workers with a common problem, an enemy against whom to rally. And because it was in the course of that struggle that the narrowing of wage differentials within the class occurred, the resentment of the skilled and better-

25. Calculations based upon data published by the Department of Employment and Productivity in *British Labour Statistics. Historical Abstract* (London: HMSO, 1971), Tables 12 and 89.

26. G. Bain and R. Price, *Profiles of Union Growth* (Oxford: Basil Blackwell, 1980), p. 37.

paid at the disproportionate gains of the less skilled and worse-paid was more muted than it might otherwise have been. It is indeed difficult to imagine any other context in which wage differentials could have been diminished so greatly with so little reaction from those whose privileges were being eroded. To be sure, there were many skilled workers who voiced their objections to unskilled workers making more on piecework than skilled workers on time rates and who complained bitterly at the improved status of women workers; and the sustained union campaign after the war to drive women back into the home or into their previous employment ghettos was distasteful and divisive.[27] Still, the net effect of wartime changes in intraclass relations would seem to have been in the direction of greater solidarity, both sociologically and politically.[28]

Class sentiments and allegiances were also reinforced by the war's impact upon working-class communities. The locally rooted character of working-class culture in Britain has often been noted, but seldom have those roots been more in evidence or more important than in 1914–18. Not only did men join the forces with their workmates and neighbors, and fight and die as such, but those left behind were also forced to rely upon each other to an unusual degree. The absence of adequate public provision for social services meant that the expanded social needs of wartime – for the care of children and the sick, for example – would have to be met largely from the resources of the community and the various self-help organizations that had flourished within it. But this was not all, for during the war communities were also faced with particularly pressing problems regarding food and housing. For the first three years of the war, food prices ran ahead of the prices of all other commodities. Rents also increased dramatically, at least in those areas, like Glasgow and other engineering and shipbuilding centers, where the needs of war production caused an influx of new workers. In response to both problems, working people organized and protested in and through their communities. The most prominent example was the famous rent strike in Glasgow in 1915, but community-based protest was widespread. Its ubiquity and effectiveness were recognized by the government, which was moved to impose controls on both rent and food.[29] These were highly significant victories, and they had a major impact in mitigating, indeed overcoming, the potentially disastrous demo-

27. Braybon, *Women Workers*, pp. 173–215. See also Kozak, "Women Muniton Workers," who shows how the support of the skilled male unionists for equal pay was based largely upon their calculation that the demand for equal pay would have the effect of pricing women out of the labor market.

28. B. Waites, "The Effect of the First World War on Class and Status in England," *Journal of Contemporary History* 11 (1976): 27–48.

29. David Englander, *Landlord and Tenant in Urban Britain* (Oxford: Oxford University Press, 1983), pp. 193–297; J. Melling, *Rent Strikes: People's Struggle for Housing in West Scotland, 1890–1916* (Edinburgh: Polygon, 1983); Cronin, *Labour and Society in Britain*, 31–2; and Julia Bush, *Behind the Lines. East London Labour, 1914–1919* (London: Merlin, 1984).

graphic consequences of the war upon the civilian population.[30] They also had the political effect of pitting workers as whole communities, often with women in the forefront, against the government.

On balance, then, the sum of economic and social changes stimulated by the war would seem to have had the curious effect of increasing the cohesiveness and augmenting the power of working people. That cohesiveness was, of course, threatened by all sorts of latent and historical divisions and antipathies; and that power was fiercely contested by employers and by the state. But they were real nonetheless. And they were made even more real, or more significant, by the changes that occurred in the power and cohesiveness of the employers and the state over the same span of time.

For employers, the war brought good news and bad. The good news was that business was booming and profits were up. The bad news was that the war brought with it a decisive shift in the relationship between business and the state. Before 1914, employers had virtually free rein inside their shops. They may have had difficulty exercising effective control over their skilled workers, but that was due not to interference from outside but to the structural weaknesses of British industry. With the coming of war, employers' freedom and control were sharply curtailed. As the dimensions of the effort needed to win the war gradually became clear to those in authority, they realized the necessity of a sustained and a strenuous effort to direct the nation's material resources toward war production. This implied controls over prices, over the allocation of material and over labor. Making these controls effective, in turn, dictated that politicians exert controls over businessmen's profits and their relations with workers.[31]

The imposition of controls proved difficult and politically explosive. The major difficulty was the absence of any mechanism to undertake the detailed supervision of economic activity. Government made good this lack by cobbling together an apparatus of control made up largely of those with expertise in the industries affected. This meant primarily businessmen, who constituted the primary membership of the District Armaments Committees set up in various regions and largely responsible for the war effort.[32] Trade unionists were also called upon for government service, though more often than not they were involved in such things as the distribution of food and other necessities. However, unionists were also called upon to bargain away, for the duration of the war at least, the shopfloor privileges of their members and also their right to

30. J. M. Winter, "The Impact of the First World War on Civilian Health in Britain," *Economic History Review* 30 (1977): 487–507.
31. Jonathan Boswell and Bruce Johns, "Patriots or Profiteers: British Businessmen and the First World War," *Journal of European Economic History* 11 (1982): 423–45.
32. K. Middlemas, *Politics in Industrial Society* (London: Andre Deutsch, 1979), pp. 113–14.

strike. This they did in the famous Treasury Agreement of 1915, and the leaders of the unions spent much of the rest of the war trying to deliver on the promises made so rashly at that moment. As the spread of the "shop stewards' movement" and the mounting record of strikes suggest, they were largely unable to do so. On the contrary, the apparent co-optation of the union officials, channeled discontent into forms that were, if not quite revolutionary in their impact, at least very hard to control, and it arrayed ordinary workers behind leaders who in normal times might have had rather more difficulty obtaining such a large following.

One key factor undermining the authority and effectiveness of union officials was the widespread belief that businessmen were profiting tremendously during the war and that government intervention consistently favored the interests of employers. This was ironic, for businessmen believed that the major consequence of state intervention was to diminish their control vis-à-vis the workers. Whether or not their perceptions were entirely accurate, they perceived that in the counsels of the state during the war, "The workmen's interests are paramount, and the masters' entirely neglected."[33] As evidence they could point to the ready access of the Trades Union Congress to government ministers; to the state's readiness to give in to demands for wage increases, for rent control, and for restrictions on profits; to the growth of union membership and the waxing power of the shop stewards; and perhaps most galling of all, to the government's insistence that employers recognize and bargain with the unions.

In response, businessmen developed a marked hostility to the state and its interventions and proceeded at the same time to create several political organizations reflecting this stance. Employers had entered the war extremely disorganized, and they had little time to organize themselves in the short period between the onset of war and the beginnings of serious government intervention. When intervention arrived, therefore, they perceived themselves to be at a considerable disadvantage, particularly when they compared their weakness with the outward strength of the unions, who were not only organized by trade but also on a national basis. The situation gave rise to a variety of efforts – often directly encouraged by government – to put together a national organization of businessmen. After a good deal of bickering and jockeying for position, the Federation of British Industries (FBI) emerged in 1916 as the "peak organization" of British business. Even then, numerous employers and employers' associations, particularly the Engineering Employers' Federation, contested the FBI's right to speak on behalf of industry as a whole either on trade matters or, most important, on questions of industrial relations. The

---

33. The complaint comes from businessmen in East Anglia, cited in Middlemas, *Politics*, p. 111.

dispute became sharp enough to force the creation in 1919 of a second group, the National Conference of Employers' Organisations (NCEO), with the sole responsibility for dealing with labor. Together the FBI and the NCEO represented a real augmentation of the potential collective political clout of business. Their founding, however, was a testament to businessmen's lack of organized strength during and just after the war, and there is some doubt as to whether, even between the wars, very much of that potential was realized or effectively utilized.[34] Businessmen did succeed during the early 1920s in rolling back the power of the state and restoring to employers much of the discretion and control lost during the war. But this success probably owed more to the effectiveness of the City of London, and, within the state, of the Treasury, in convincing politicians and the public of the need for "fiscal responsibility" and of the impossibility of paying for social reform, than it did to the organized efforts of businessmen and employers. Worse still, this very achievement served to remove the major stimulus to the political organization of business and so hindered its further consolidation.[35]

What brought about this contradictory outcome for business was the contradictory impact of state intervention. But what about the effect of state intervention on the state itself? Was it equally contradictory, equally troublesome for the leaders and managers of the state apparatus? The answer again depends largely upon one's point of view. To businessmen, the state's authority during wartime seemed unprecedented and highly threatening. To workers, the state's newly acquired ability to dictate the terms under which they would labor seemed not merely unprecedented but often unreasonable as well. But to those inside the state or on top of it, the new powers obtained by the state seemed to carry with them all sorts of new dangers and problems.

Three particular problems loomed very large at the time, and they seem no less important in retrospect. First, because the state had so little experience at controlling economic life, and virtually no administrative structure with which to do it, the practice of state intervention during the war was riddled with inefficiencies and inequities. This gave rise to almost incessant complaints about treatment by the state. Second, by attempting to control so much of the nation's economic activity, the state in effect asserted its responsibility for the deficiencies that resulted. Worse still, as war progressed, people found it hard

34. John Turner, "The Politics of Organised Business' in the First World War," in Turner, ed., *Businessman and Politics. Studies of Business Activity in British Politics, 1900–1945* (London: Heinemann, 1984), pp. 33–49.

35. Kathleen Burk, "The Treasury: From Impotence to Power," in Burk ed., *War and the State. The Transformation of British Government, 1914–1919* (London: Allen and Unwin, 1982), pp. 84–107; J. Cronin, "Coping with Labour, 1918–1926," in Cronin and J. Schneer, *Social Conflict and Political Order*, pp. 113–45; R. H. Tawney, "The Abolition of Economic Controls, 1918–1921," originally published in 1941, reprinted in J. M. Winter, ed., *History and Society: Essays by R. H. Tawney* (London: Routledge, 1978), pp. 129–86.

to distinguish those deficiencies that stemmed from what the state had done during the war from those that flowed from the normal workings of the market economy. Working people thus came to hold the state responsible for social problems and injustices generally, and began increasingly to locate the source of their difficulties in politics and to define their solutions in political terms as well.[36]

What made these issues so difficult to handle, however, was yet another problem whose significance has yet to be fully appreciated: the parallel crisis of the British party system. The relationship between parties had begun to change well before the First World War, but prior to 1914 most voters had retained their historical allegiance to either the Liberals or the Conservatives. Labor had made a few inroads in the more solidly working-class districts, but before the war had served very much as junior partner to the Liberals. The war, however, led to the destruction of the Liberals and produced a rapid decay of organization among Conservatives. By the end of the war the government was led by a coalition headed by Lloyd George that, in effect, submerged both the major parties and threatened the identity of both. Party identities were further confused by the emergence of the Labour party. The threat from the Left inspired numerous schemes for rallying together the forces of order in defense of property. But under whose leadership? Lloyd George clearly wanted it to be his; in the end, it was to be a reshaped Conservative party that would do the job. In the meantime, the absence of a "party of order" with clear links to the electorate left the state exposed and, to many, lacking in legitimacy.[37]

The net effect of these several interrelated problems was to produce a genuine sense of crisis among Britain's political elite. The state's actions during the war had conjured up a level of expectations and a set of forces with which the nation's rulers had not previously had to contend. The very existence of these new demands and mobilized constituencies was a sign that the old balance of social and political power had been drastically altered. It meant, too,

---

36. The process is very well documented in the various reports of the Commission of Enquiry into Industrial Unrest of 1917. See "Summary of the Reports of the Commission," *British Parliamentary Papers*, Vol. 15, (1917–18).

37. On the general transformation of the party system, see Kenneth Wald, *Crosses on the Ballot* (Princeton University Press, 1983); and Martin Pugh, The Making of Modern British Politics, 1867–1939 (Oxford: Basil Blackwell, 1982). On the Liberals, see Roy Douglas, *The History of the Liberal Party, 1900–1984*, 2d ed. (London: Macmillan, 1984); on the Conservatives, see J. A. Ramsden, *The Age of Balfour and Baldwin, 1902–1940* (London: Longman, 1978); on Labour, see Ross McKibbin, *The Evolution of the Labour Party, 1910–1924* (Oxford: Oxford University Press, 1974), and J. M. Winter, *Socialism and the Challenge of War* (London: Routledge and Kegan Paul, 1974). On the continuing efforts to put together an effective anti-Labour coalition, see Robert Scally, *The Origins of the Lloyd George Coalition* (Princeton: Princeton University Press, 1975); Kenneth Morgan, *Consensus and disunity: The Lloyd George Coalition Government, 1918–1922* (Oxford: Oxford University Press, 1979); and Maurice Cowling, *The Impact of Labour* (Cambridge: Cambridge University Press, 1971).

that the system of political representation inherited from before the war simply would not do. What would come to replace it? From 1917 until 1922, nobody really knew; and this uncertainty fanned the worst fears of those in authority. All around them was revolution; at home, it was clear, the old way of doing things would have to change as well. Can anyone blame Britain's leaders for imagining the worst, for worrying that the alternative to the world they knew before 1914 was disorder, chaos, bolshevism? In retrospect, such fears seem out of place, but in 1917 they would not necessarily have appeared so.

Does this mean that there really was a revolutionary situation in Britain at the end of the First World War? Not at all, for as argued earlier, the range of options realistically open in 1917–20, though wide, did not include revolution on the Continental or Russian model. What was at stake, therefore, was not capitalism or the authority of the state, but rather the social and political order that had prevailed before 1914. The essence of that old order was the effective disfranchisement – politicaly and industrially – of the bulk of the British working class. The effect of the Great War was to initiate a lengthy process of augmenting the power and raising the status of working people. That process was not to climax until after the Second World War, when British workers truly and for the first time became full-fledged citizens of the society in which they lived. In getting that process started, however, the First World War disrupted all the old ways of doing things and opened up enormous new possibilities. It was this sense of irreversible change, of the impossibility of returning to the prewar order and the very real possibility of remaking the world, that defined the conjuncture of 1917–20 and that underpinned the amazing political and industrial militancy of those years.

21

Strikes and the war

HUGUES LAGRANGE

"In general, one can say that no revolution is possible where the authority of the political body remains intact; that is, in modern circumstances, when one can have utter confidence that the armed forces will obey civil authority."[1] The First World War brought both coercion, in the form of moral proscription and the threat of sanctions, and the reasons for protest. Exacerbating frustrations even as it reinforced the legitimacy of public authority, the war forged closer and yet more fragile ties between civil and political society. For this reason, the war provides a privileged moment in which to examine the relationship among economic, political, and ideological phenomena. The following pages deal with the study of strike movements not because they played a determinative role in the developments of the war, but because they illustrate the notion that even under extreme conditions, work conflicts are not always purely instrumental actions. What was the meaning of the social consensus of 1914, witnessed by the disappearance of strikes in that year? Why was that consensus no longer so solid in 1917 and 1918 as it had been at the beginning of the war? Did this consensus depend on the absence of political polarization, or did it flow directly from the interplay of moral constraints imposed by the war? At the point when they reappeared, in 1917 and 1918, did the strikes respond to a logic of economic protest, to the appeal of the Russian Revolution, or to marching orders from the defeatists? Did they inscribe themselves within the dominant political configuration? Did they presage the conflicts of 1919–20?

The war bonded French society, papering over political divisions at the outset and engendering the formation of a social consensus. However, these two processes, though inextricably linked at the beginning of the war, have distinct origins; the war pressed on civil and political society with neither the

1. Hannah Arendt, *Essai sur la Revolution*, NRF, (Paris, 1967), p. 167.

473

same weight nor at the same moments. (Political society includes the institutions of the state, political parties, the syndicates, and various permanent movements and associations.)

The outbreak of the First World War bore two essential consequences in the realm of politics. On the one hand, civil authority lost its autonomy via-à-vis military authority.[2] At the same time, the legislative branch lost all capacity to control the executive;[3] the recourse to a "political state of siege" had transferred all authority to the executive.[4] On the other hand, political bodies were forced to bury their differences and unite in order to govern effectively. In the principal belligerent nations, socialists and social democrats had voted for war credits and entered into governments of "sacred union."[5]

The war had a contradictory impact on civil society. On the one hand, the population was asked to rally around the leaders of the moment; to express any reservations about the government's actions in conducting the war seemed almost treasonous. The press was censored, and public demonstrations were forbidden. If a strike broke out in the war factories, mobilized workers could be sent to the front. On the other hand, the war exacerbated economic tensions, bringing inflation to unprecedented levels, displacing populations, drawing women into the factories on a grand scale, militarizing work in the munitions factories, and developing a social inequality in the face of death.

The war left its mark in the frequency of the most fundamental social acts, those that derive the least from political circumstances: The number of marriages and births, but also that of suicides and crimes fell. If the rate of these individual actions fell off so drastically, such a drop was no less apparent in the case of collective action. When war was declared in August 1914, the frequency of strikes fell to under fifty per year, that is, to the level of 1864, when the ban on unions was finally lifted. The strike, without being illegal, seems to have become politically and morally difficult.

2. In Germany, the replacment of Falkenheyn by Ludendorff in 1917 appears itself to have been the prelude to an absorption of civil power by the military command (Hindenbury-Ludendorff).

3. Thus, on 2 August 1914, the president of the French Republic signed a decree that placed all the *départements* under a state of siege.

4. The regime of "political state of siege was organized under the law of August 9, 1849 and completed by the law of April 3, 1878. It could be declared by decree 'in case of an imminent danger'" J. M. Mayeur, *La vie politique sous la Troisième République 1870–1940* (Paris, 1984), p. 236.

5. In France, R. Poincaré gave the official word during his 4 August 1914 message to the chambers. Although it raised some doubt among syndicalists like Merrheim, Monatte, and Bourderon from the end of 1914 on, the participation of Section Française de l'Internationale Ouvrière (SFIO) members – A. Thomas, J. Guesde, and M. Sembat – was for the most part understood and accepted. "'Events have overwhelmed us' acknowledged the CGT's appeal of 1 August 1914. At Jaures's funeral, Jouhaux recovered the revolutionary tones of 'the nation in danger,' and praised the working class 'which has always sustained itself on the revolutionary traditions of the soldiers from the Year II, who went forth to bring liberty to the world.'" (Mayer, 1984, p. 236).

474

The evolution of strikes during the war

It is difficult to follow precisely the development of strikes during the First World War. The war disrupted services at the labor statistics bureau and a certain number of conflicts went unrecorded. This underreporting undoubtedly affects the statistics for 1919 as well, although to a lesser extent. Some historians feel that the underestimation of both the number and magnitude of strikes particularly distorts the figures for 1918.[6] The stakes of this debate are quite high, for the strikes of 1917 and 1918 do not carry the same meaning. Since no one has yet undertaken systematic study of this underestimation, it is impossible to know the extent of underreporting in this period. We do know that it also affects the statistics for 1917; in the dossiers deposited at the Archives Nationales (series F7, files 12970–13023) there are records of conflicts that the *Statistique des Grèves* for 1917 appears to ignore. (Thus, the *Statistique* fails to mention an important conflict at St. Chamond in the Loire on 3–6 December, in which 160,000 strikers were involved.) Even though it is certain that this underestimation is not consistent throughout the war, it probably alters the shape of the strike curve completely.

A simple graph (Figure 1) shows that, in effect, the frequency of strikes rose in a fairly regular manner from August 1914 until September 1918. (This tendency also is evident in Germany and the United Kingdom.) Even if we look at the acceleration in strikes only from the spring of 1918, it is difficult to claim that this acceleration had upset the previous rate of strikes, for the statistics are deceiving at the level of relative amplitude. But the surprising phenomenon, which we will examine here, is the appearance in June 1917 of a strike movement far more important than those of 1916 or 1918. The peak of 1917 is evident both in the number of strikers involved and in the frequency of strikes; the latter figure is, of course, less sensitive to gaps in the statistics, because it does not depend on the size of the firms affected.

The strike curve was abnormally flat until spring 1916, from which point it rose slowly until suddenly, in the spring of 1917, the calm was broken by an outburst of strikes. Two strike movements of apparently less importance unfolded in the spring and fall of 1918.

With respect to the number of strikes and days lost recorded in peacetime, the figures for 1917 are average; with 696 strikes and 1,481,600 strike days, 1917 is comparable to the years 1890–1900, and falls well below the years

6. J. L. Robert (1977, pp. 52–53) supports this view by citing the work of G. Hatry, "Les delegues d'atelier aux usines Renault" in P. Fidenson, ed., *1914–1918: l'autre front* (Paris, 1977), and that of Ch. Morel, "Le mouvement socialist et syndicalist en 1917 dans la region parisienne," diplome de maitrise.
7. The omission of the conflict at St. Chamond removes only one unit from the frequency series even as it cuts out 160,000 units from the strikers' series.

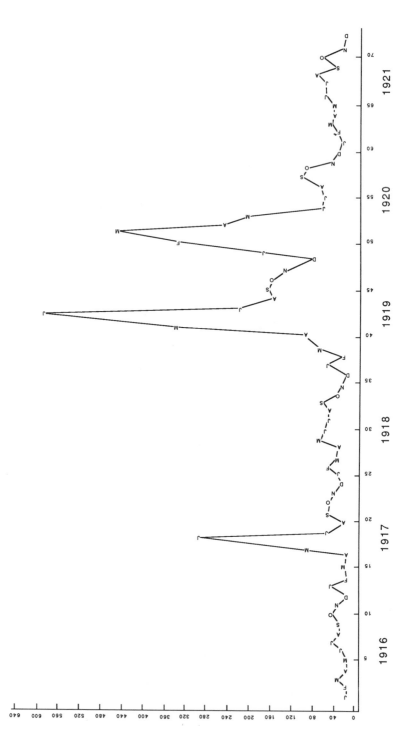

Figure 1. Development by month of the frequency of strikes, 1916–21

immediately preceding the war. Nonetheless, we will insist on two points: (1) the occurrence in 1917 of seven times more strikes and thirty times more days lost than in 1915, and (2) the extraordinarily high rate of conflict in the single month of June, even when compared with the prewar period.

Beyond the quantitative difference that distinguishes 1917 from the rest of the war, 1917 stands out as much in the nature of the industries affected as in the extent of the strikes. During the four years of war, "the highest number of strikes occurred in the textile industry: 360, with 125,272 strikers. Then came the metals industry: 234 strikes and 95,004 strikers; transport: 183 strikes and 31,127 strikers; the garment trade, with 168 strikes and 81,612 strikers."[8] The number of conflicts, and even more, the size of strikes in the war-related metals industries, was slight in relation to the level of strike activity in women's industries, which were traditionally more calm.

"In May and June of 1917, unrest gripped all of France, particularly the most heavily industrialized areas. Collective work stoppages no longer struck only the isolated establishment, but entire industries. The strike did not confine itself to several areas, but. . .all of France, or at the very least; its major cities were affected. The war industries were not the most seriously hit;. . .work conflicts were relatively rare and isolated events in munitions at this time. On the other hand; conflicts were numerous and widespread in the least-organized branches of industry."[9] Table 1, which gives the number of firms in each sector affected by the strikes of May–June 1917, is quite eloquent on this point. Thus, "in metal-working, the conflicts retained their purely individual character, as the 62 strikes recorded involved only 73 firms, that is, barely more than one firm per strike. In the garment trade, 66 strikes touched 1,536 firms, that is, an average of 23 firms per conflict."[10] The number of firms involved in each conflict was also quite high in leather and skins (9.2), and above average in food processing (3.5).

Independent of the absolute level of strike activity, the conflicts of 1918 were clearly far less extensive (measured as the ratio of firm affected/the number of strikes) than those of 1917 (see Table 2). In 1918, the metals industry was for the first time at the forefront in terms of frequency of strikes, and these conflicts

8. According to the *Statistique des Grèves, Ministere du Travail*, vol. 23 (1915–18), p. VI. The factories on war contracts belonged for the most part to the sector "metals industries." I have counted the conflicts and days lost as they affected those metallurgical firms employed on war work, broadly understood (those firms that were the object of any intervention by the Ministry of Munitions or by a military labor inspector) in 1917–18. In 1917, there were 70 conflicts and 146,879 days lost in establishments employed on war work, and 34 conflicts and 40,900 days lost in 1918. For a detailed account of these strikes, see Annex at the end of this chapter.

9. W. Oualid and C. Picquenard, *Salaires, tarifs, couventions collectives et grèves* (Paris, 1927), p. 344.

10. Ibid., p. 345. This exposition is more interesting to us than Oualid and Picquenard's analysis of the causes of labor militancy, which lays the heaviest emphasis on economic causes and differs greatly from our analysis.

Table 1. *Strikes in May–June 1917 in the major professional groups affected*

Branch of industry	Number of strikes	Firms affected	Number of strikers
Garment trade	66	1,536	51,251
Textiles	98	257	31,459
Metallurgy	66	79	35,777
Leather and skins	34	113	19,995
Chemicals	11	50	15,529
Food processing	15	53	10,483

Source: Oualid and Picquenard, *Salaires, tarifs, conventions collectives et grèves* (Paris, 1927), p. 345.

Table 2. *Strikes in May 1918 in the major professional groups affected*

Branch of industry	Number of strikes	Firms affected	Number of strikers
Metallurgy	11	29	24,340
Textiles	7	45	8,357
Leather and skins	9	11	1,534
Garment trade	3	23	788

Source: Oualid and Picquenard, *Salaires, tarifs, conventions collectives et grèves* (Paris, 1927), p. 345.

involved an average of nearly three firms per strike (outside of the struggle in the Loire).

The strikes of 1917 and 1918 differ as much in the composition of the movements as in the modalities of their size. In relation to the distribution of workers in industry prevalent at the time, 1917 was utterly atypical. Why did the strikes assume such importance in sectors outside the industrial core – skilled and male – in industries where, unlike the metals industry, traditions of struggle were not strong, and the ideas of revolutionary syndicalism little known? One might put forth a circumstantial explanation: The contracts with the military formed a context favorable to the development of militancy in the garment and textile industries, for the government concerned itself far less with wages and conditions in these industries than it did with conditions in munitions. But this was in fact not the case. In textiles, as in metallurgy, wages rose swiftly enough during the war. To be precise, the wages of unskilled workers rose more quickly than those of skilled workers, tending to reduce the prewar wage gap (according to surveys conducted by the conseils des prud'hommes in 1911, 1916, and 1921, this reduction only occurred between 1916 and 1921). No divergence in the rate of wage increase distinguishes the several branches of industry, but in all branches such a divergence does distinguish skilled and unskilled workers. From a morphological standpoint the strikes of 1917 appear peripheral, both in the sectors of industry affected and in the structure of the work force mobilized by these strikes.

The impact of the economic context

One of the most widely accepted hypotheses is that the moments and the intensity of collective action during the war were determined by heightened economic tensions. In one oft-read analysis Oualid and Picquenard write, "The disproportion between a cost of living which rose incessantly and the smaller, less regular increases in wages formed the principal source of workers' demands, which discontent was further inflamed by the enormous profits reaped by certain industrialists on war contracts."[11] J. L. Robert expresses a similar conviction, though in a more Machiavellian fashion. "The most extreme rise in prices seems to have come in May–June of 1917. Under these conditions, one can say that despite wage increases won through struggle, workers suffered a severe deterioration in purchasing power during the First World War, to the point where it became doubtful that they could renew their capacity for labor."[12] For reasons having to do with both the quality of the statistics – the record of prices, like that of wages, is not above criticism – and with the rather weak correlation between strikes and the cost of living, a close comparison of the fluctuations in strikes, the cost of living, and wage levels leads one to a more nuanced conclusion.

Aside from the official publications of the *Statistique Generale de la France*, we have L. March's detailed study of the cost of living, written as part of the Carnegie Endowment series on the war.[13] March constructed two separate retail price indices, one each for Paris and the provinces. From 1919 onward, the Parisian index was calculated monthly, whereas the provincial index remained a quarterly one throughout the period 1916–21. Developments in the two indices were somewhat divergent; the provincial index rose more quickly than the Parisian one. However, fluctuations in the Parisian index were especially uneven: Only Parisian prices registered a strong leap forward between April

11. Ibid., p. 358.
12. J. L. Robert, p. 41. According to calculations by J. Singer-Kérel, *Le coût de la vie à Paris, de 1840 à 1954* (Paris, 1961), workers' average buying power hardly would have deteriorated during the first years of the war.
13. L. March, *Mouvement des prix et salaires pendant la guerre* (Paris, 1925).

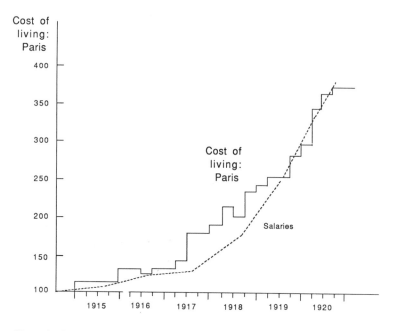

Figure 2. Indices of cost of living and wages

and July 1917, and, in spite of the state's "regulatory" interventions, a further series of sudden price changes from month to month in 1918–19.

If we accept the argument put forward by Oualid and Picquenard, that the strikes responded to the disparity between wages and the cost of living, then at the very least there should have been powerful strike movements in the spring of 1917 and the fall of 1918. By contrast, there should have been few strikes in 1919 and 1920, for the increase in wages at that point tended to surpass rises in the cost of living (see Figure 2). This was not the case, however. This fact does not eliminate the hypothesis that the strike is one means by which wages are indexed to prices – quite the contrary – but one cannot conclude that the failure of wages to keep pace with the cost of living in this period inevitably signalled the launching of a strike.[14]

Did the increase in strike activity coincide with a rise in the cost of living? This appears to have been the case in the second quarter of 1917;

14. It is useful to separate the process of indexation from its effects. From this point of view, one must distinguish two phases over the period 1917–21. From spring to the summer of 1919, the increase in the cost of living was more rapid than the increase in workers' wages; from summer of 1919 up to the end of 1921, their rates of increase remained in step. The gap registered in the first phase fits with the hypothesis that moral inhibitions brought on by the war postponed the indexation, which first came into full operation at the end of the postwar movements.

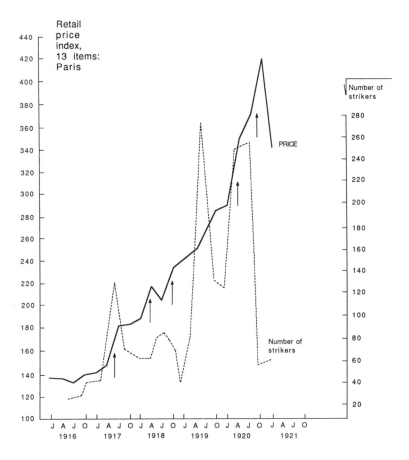

Figure 3. Number of strikers and cost of living in Paris

retail prices rose by 25% during the strongest strike movement of the war. The increase in the cost of living during the first quarter of 1918 also corresponded to a rise in the number of strikes, and this tendency is even more apparent during the first quarter of 1920. On the other hand, the number of strikes rose during the second quarter of 1916, even as the price index fell, and decreased during the third quarter of 1918, when prices were rising rapidly. June 1919, the month with the highest number of strikes in this period (590), was a time when retail prices fell by 8% in Paris and held steady in the provinces. In sum, the relationship between a push toward strikes and the rising cost of living, when examined across the spectrum of monthly flucuations, appears utterly inconclusive (see Figure 3).

481

Despite all of this, can we say that the rising cost of living exerted some influence on the development of strikes, an influence that cannot be reduced to a simple comparison of the most outstanding points on the monthly index? If this is true, can we evaluate what must be the peaks in strike activity, marked by movements in the price of consumer goods, and distinguish that part of the movement which stems from the social context from that which has political origins (by political, I mean variations in the war's death toll, military successes and reverses, changes in morale, the rupture in the *Union sacrée*, and pacifist agitation)?

The simplest model, suggested by an examination of the data, runs as follows:

(1) $G_t = a \cdot \Delta\, px_t/px_t + b$,

where G = increase in the number of strikes in t,

px/px = the increase in retail prices in t.

a, b = coefficients

Strikes would increase in response to the relative increase in retail prices. In order to understand the relative roles of economic, social, and political factors, it might be useful to distinguish the various elements in the strike series, and outline the possible reasons for any delays in responding to the rise in prices. Strikes have a quasiritualistic seasonal component, as is clear from the flurry of activity between March and June and the paucity of conflicts in the winter.[15] This seasonal aspect is neutralized by the differentiation of the series when studied over a twelve-month period.

Keeping these factors in mind, I made two series of calculations using first the monthly statistics, then the quarterly ones, with an eye toward estimating the impact of variations in the cost of living on the development of strikes. What emerged from all this? The results were quite different depending on whether the monthly or the quarterly figures were used: (1) the coefficients for the impact of variations in the cost of living were significant in the quarterly equations but not in the monthly ones (see appendix at the end of this chapter). Integrated over a sufficiently long period of time (three months or a year), strikes appeared to be more frequent during periods of inflation than when retail prices were stable. This relationship disappears when the interval of time under the integral is shortened. (2) Based on the quarterly figures themselves, that part of the fluctuation in strikes that can be attributed to changes in the cost of living, although significant, is quite modest indeed. The fact that this

15. This rhythm seems to be the reflection, in industrial life, of a cosmic influence that should not be expressed by a metaphorical shorthand as simple as a rising of the sap. In a discussion of suicide, Durkheim explains this seasonal rising less by the arrival of summer than by a force that accures through a sense of exclusion from social life that grows more intense in the summer.

482

relationship disappears altogether when the monthly figures are used seems to be a purely statistical phenomenon; the relationship between strikes and the conjuncture is not a simple mechanical one of the sort in which there would be a certain variability in the time lapse separating a price increase from the building of a strike movement. The strike is a likely response to the increasing cost of living, not a temporally fixed reaction to economic stimuli.

But this is not the essential point. Before the First World War, variations in retail prices do not exert an observable influence on the level of strike activity. One possible explanation of the limits of economic determinism, suggested by earlier works, is that the war itself initiated a new system of relations among strikes, prices, and wages. This relationship does not appear new to us because it is by now a common notion that strikes are a form of protest against the high cost of living. But this was not so in 1914, when the strike appears to have comprised two distinct forms of action: on the one hand, the actions of skilled workers, and on the other, the actions of unskilled and less well organized workers. The actions of the formers were characterized by the ability to negotiate in situations where they held some bargaining power. If labor was scarce, or if demand in that sector was strong enough to assure that a strike action would interrupt the flow of profit, then the strike corresponded less to the cost of living than to production and employment levels.[16] The actions of the unskilled, which became important during the First World War and are the only type of action considered in our calculations, are above all a response to the increased cost of living. It was precisely the less-skilled sectors, with no great traditions of syndicalism and in which wages were lowest in 1911, that engaged in the most strikes and experienced the greatest progress in wages during the war. The strike was no longer the weapon of a working-class elite, but had become a more banal mass action, the tempo of which was determined by the cost of living.

Pacifism and the military conjuncture

Whatever form it takes, a purely economic explanation misses an important aspect of the strike phenomenon. On a graph of strikes from which the economic element has been abstracted, several sharp peaks remain that of necessity call for a different explanation (see appendix). The totality of factors mediating between economic frustrations, the formation of a will to strike, and the realization of a collective action distends the bond between the economic context and the strike. Even if the principal source of a working-class action is an economic complaint that expresses directly a real material need, it is vital to see that collective actions have other conditions that can be both positive and

16. Cf. Lagrange, 1982.

Number of military casualties, prisoners,
marriages and strikes: 1914 - 1919

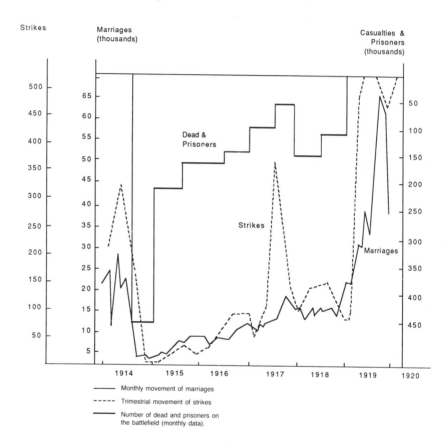

Figure 4. Number of military casualties, prisoners, marriages, and strikes, 1914–19

negative, tending both to incite and inhibit the action. The following pages examine these social and political conditions.

As we have seen, the outbreak of war brutally interrupted social life, which only partially recovered its normal course, and did not regain its peacetime rhythms before 1921. Leaving aside the strike wave of May–June 1917, the pattern of strikes, like that of marriages and divorces, traced a curve that lay in an inverse reflection of the war's death rate (see Figure 4). Any decrease in the number of deaths in the field coincided with a progressive resumption of social life. With the end of the war, these curves rose well above their 1914 level; the

484

war appears to have deferred the aspirations of the population, only to then call forth a postwar movement of compensation.

These curves suggest that the pattern of strikes – taken as an indicator of social consensus – was shaped by the war, but the nature and strength of that relationship remains uncertain. Is there a precise relationship between the intensity of the war and the evolution of strikes, a relationship that may ultimately be discerned through indicators less crude than the number of victims?

Military successes and fluctuations in morale

The first problem in doing a correlative study is to find a sufficiently nuanced scale by which to measure the evolution of the war. To assess the war's impact by a scale that measures the number of victims, for example, poses the classic problem of accounting for various mediating factors. Hypotheses about the effect that the intensity of combat had on conduct at the home front imply that the population perceived the levels of intensity without too many distortions. Recent historical studies, in particular the work of J. J. Becker,[17] indicate that the civilian population was, in fact, aware of fluctuations in the level of combat.

G. Letainurier, prefect for the Yonne, drew a monthly curve representing morale in his *département* from August 1914 until June 1916. When one follows its variations, this curve holds a more general validity. On a small scale, it offers an adequate and probable outline of France's swings through optimism and pessimism in the face of war.[18] The chronological sequence of military events, the advances and retreats of the French army in the field all find expression in the peaks and troughs of this curve.[19] Whether it was from newspapers, however censored and controlled, or from the tales of soldiers on short-leave, public opinion reflected the vicissitudes of the war with remarkable precision. This exact correlation, described by J. J. Becker, allows us to partially extend the prefect's curve for the Yonne, especially when we recall that, as was the case in the beginning of the war, military reverses translated into declines in patriotic fervor and military successes produced a renewed patriotic sentiment. Thus, after the battle of Verdun in 1916, morale remained somewhat low into the

17. J. J. Becker, *Les Français dans la grande guerre* (Paris, 1980), p. 213.
18. The Yonne is one of the rare *départements* where the internationalist tendencies of French socialism were relatively strong from the beginning of the war.
19. Morale dropped to an extremely low level at the beginning of the Battle of the Marne (in the first two weeks of September 1914), rose (enthusiastically) after the French victories, and collapsed again following the short German offensive. Germany's victory over Russia in April 1915 left morale at an extremely low level. It rose temporarily at the time of Joffre's offensives in September 1915, fell during the first months of the German attack on Verdun of February–April 1916, and rose once again in response to French resistance.

early winter. It fell further still, first in May[20] and then in October 1917, and was also quite poor in May 1918, when the German offensive tore through the French line and pushed all the way to Château-Thierry. Morale does not appear to have risen again before the end of the war.

Were the strikes influenced by shifts in morale, that is, indirectly by the outcome of the various battles? The curves reproduced on the graph show that strikes mounted whenever the war was less devastating to France (measured by the number of deaths on the battlefield). In the logic of this relationship, whenever a battle went favorably, and partial victories reinforced the hope that the war might end soon, those social strata that by tradition or political education were least disposed to accept the war had to demonstrate their will, to reaffirm their own identity and grievances through the strike. This affirmation of identity, made possible for the workers at the moments of military success, must have actually included larger social groups, because at those moments of victory, the war was no longer a foreign aggression that claimed unquestioning defense, but an offensive action that no longer enjoyed the support of all, nor held the same legitimacy.

What can we conclude from this? At the beginning of the war, while morale passed through extreme highs and lows, the pattern of strikes held quite steady, with only a handful of conflicts until the end of 1916. In 1917, there is a clear coincidence in the decline in morale following the Nivelle offensive and the development of strikes, but this relationship does not recur in the autumn.[21] The spring of 1918 saw a more limited development in strikes, when morale fell so low after the German offensive at Château-Thierry.

Far from coinciding with military victories, strikes appear to have fed on military setbacks. At least this was clearly the case in May–June 1917 (see Figure 5). As the military reverses correspond to a weakening in patriotic feeling, this conclusion seems to justify the notion, elaborated by some historians, that strikes were also a means of expressing the desire for an immediate peace; that the strikes conveyed a current of revolutionary defeatism that could not have emerged at the beginning of the war.[22]

One explanation for the peaks in strike activity in the spring and fall of 1917,

---

20. In March 1917, the Germans reappeared in the west, following the defensive tactic abandoned by Falkenheyn. They made "a strategic retreat to a powerfully fortified line called the Hindenburg line." (Madaule, 1966, p. 128) On 16 April 1917, General Nivelle finally succeeded in wresting from the French command the decision to launch an offensive that was to founder in a bloody mess at the Chemin des Dames. This failure provoked a grave crisis in morale among the soldiers of the French army and, in the month of May, an impressive series of refusals to "go over the top."

21. The Italian debacle at Caporetto on 24 October appears to have increased French pessimism.

22. J. J. Becker says, more prudently, that opinion shows "signs of uncertainty," but underlines the fact that the National Defense Loan, which was a fairly good indicator of patriotic feeling, had few responses.

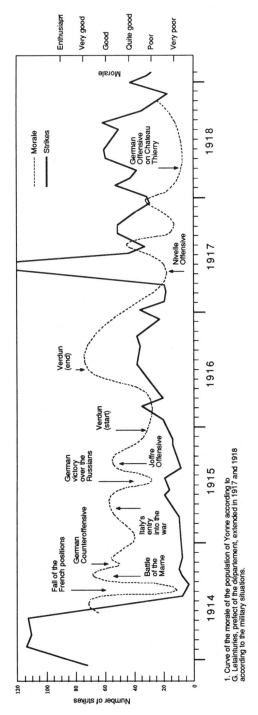

1. Curve of the morale of the population of Yonne according to
G. Letainturies, prefect of the département, extended in 1917 and 1918
according to the military situations.

Figure 5. Evolution of morale and of strikes

often put forth because it unites a substantial psychological probability with an apparent factual compatibility, is that of the impact that events in Russia had on movements in France; the Bolshevik success reawakened antipatriotic sentiment. R. Rémond writes:

> The Russian Revolution "stirred feelings, hitherto contained by the Union sacrée, which cut into the will to fight to the bitter end.... The left wing of the socialist movement regained its vitality, revolutionary defeatism re-awoke and joined with the desire for peace. In France, and especially in Italy, where some segments of opinion had shrunk from entering the war, the tumultuous divisions re-asserted themselves. Centrifugal forces, working in conjunction with physical and nervous exhaustion, explains why 1917 was the difficult year, the year of unrest, of strikes in the French munitions factories, and of mutinies which seized the units at the front.[23]

Rémond's explanation includes many factors, and it is difficult to ascertain the relative weight he assigns to each. Nonetheless, he suggests that the Russian Revolution, in reactivating those revolutionary sentiments buried in the Union sacrée, accounts for the rise of strikes in 1917.

Can we say that the Russian Revolution played a determinative role in the development of the conflicts of spring 1917? If the impact of the February Revolution were important, then how do we account for the fact that the Bolshevik seizure of power produced no comparable resonant movement? Moreover, the strike wave peaked in May–June 1917, which coincides badly with the events of February–March in Russia; the movement of May–June was five times more powerful than that of October, when the Bolsheviks came to power.[24]

Aside from this temporal inadequacy, the argument rests on a fragile set of assumptions. The Russian revolutions are alleged to have awakened pacifism and revolutionary defeatism, and the exacerbation of these feelings is said to have encouraged the strikes. If this were the case, then the areas with strikes in 1917 must also have been those that exhibited a decline in patriotic zeal.

To confirm or disprove this notion of a relationship between labor militancy and the weakening of patriotic sentiment, I juxtaposed maps of the two phenomena. Relying on prefectoral reports, J. J. Becker mapped the morale of the populace in towns and in the countryside at the end of June 1917. His maps

23. R. Rémond, *Le XXe siecle de 1914 a nos jours*, vol. 3 of *Introduction a l'histoire de notre temps* (Paris, 1974), p. 29.
24. Moreover, to explain the weakness of strikes in October, one cannot invoke G. Clémenceau's accession to power, which indisputably affirmed the authority of government, but did not occur until November 1917. By contrast, it is not improbable that the French military intervention in support of the White Army in September 1918 favored the strikes. The intervention in Russia, an act whose legitimacy was not necessarily acknowledged by the workers, summoned to a distant front soldiers exhausted by more than three years of war (which at the very least would appear to have been the occasion for acts of insubordination).

are especially interesting because they describe morale at the home front after the Nivelle offensive, the point at which a wave of mutinies swept the French army and an unusually strong strike movement shook the rest of the nation.

Morale in the cities was worst in a group of *départements* comprising for one part a vast triangle with the Aube, the Isere, and the Allier as its endpoints, and for the other part the Vaucluse, the Herault, the Tarn and Garonne, the Pyrenees Orientales, the Haute-Vienne, the Seine-Maritime, the Seine, and the Meurthe and Moselle. This geography of flagging patriotism correlates very well with the map of cities "contaminated" by pacifist agitation in the spring of 1917 (according to figures from the same author). Regions where the population was struck by a certain discouragement were also those in which pacifist agitation found the liveliest response in working-class milieux.

Without it being possible, or even necessary, to know whether pacifist

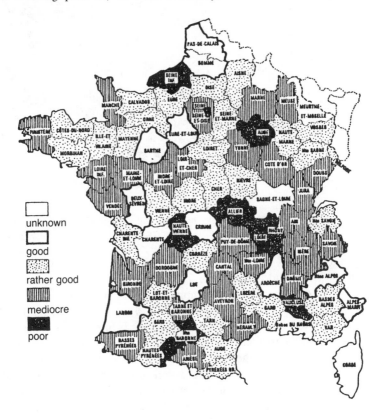

Map 1. Morale of the French population at the end of June, 1917. Annexed or occupied départements apparently not taken into consideration: Bas-Rhin, Haut-Rhin, Moselle, Ardennes et Nord

489

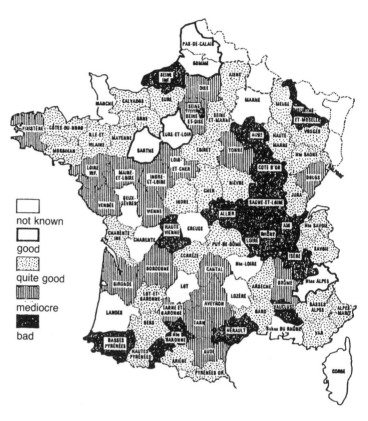

Map 2. Morale of the towns at the end of June 1917. According to J. J. Becker,
Les Français dans la grande guerre *(Paris, R. Laffont, 1980), p. 213.*

agitation caused the drop in morale or vice-versa, it appears that the two
phenomena found favorable terrain in the zones described (see Map 4).

On the other hand, this geography diverges visibly from that of the strikes in
1917. With the exception of three *départements* in the regions of the Rhône-
Alps, the Seine, the Seine-Maritime, and the Haute-Vienne, where the number
of strikes was particularly high, the areas of flagging morale or pacifist agitation
do not coincide with the strike zones in 1917. It therefore seems unlikely that
the strikes were yet another expression of the extreme Left's hostility to the
conduct of the war. If the strikes of 1917 bear witness to a spectacular rupture
in the social consensus of 1914, then this rupture occurred at a deeper level, a
level less marked by expressions of political will (see Maps 1 and 2).

Although ideological determinants were clearly absent in 1917, things went a
bit differently in 1918. We cannot compare strike zones for 1918 with a map of

490

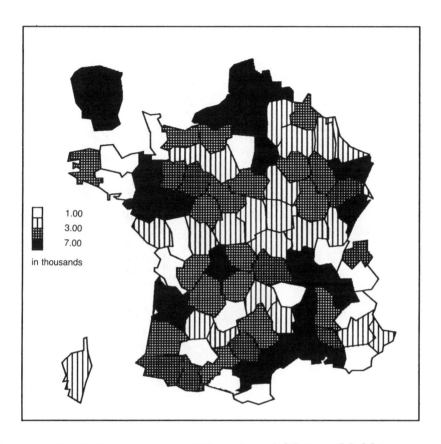

Map 3. Number of strikes in 1917 according to S.G.F. (source B.D.S.P.)

French morale because no such map exists for that year. (And there is no reason to believe that such a map would correspond to that of 1917.) A. Kriegel drew a map describing those areas that tended to favor the Third International. In comparing this map with that of strikes in 1918, we see that the geography of strikes has altered, moving into line with the zones of minority socialist strength. Outside the most heavily working-class areas, those *départements* that supported the Third International (in 1920) also lost the most days to strikes in 1918. (See Maps 5 and 6, on the frequency of strikes in 1918 and political orientaions in 1920.) This cartographical review demonstrates that although ideological determinants emerged perceptibly in the geography of strikes for 1918, they played no role in the strike wave of spring 1917. This corroborates the analysis of differences in morphology and the changing dynamic of strikes between those two years.

491

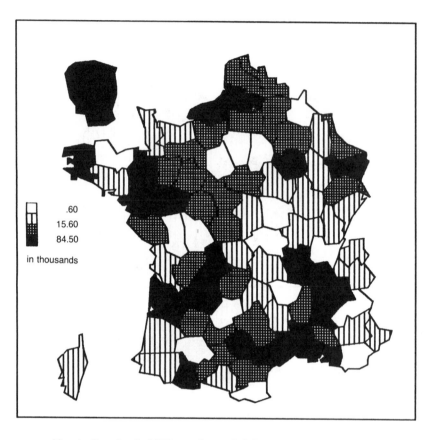

Map 4. Days lost in 1917 according to S.G.F. (source B.D.S.P.)

The recourse to consciousness, to the beliefs of the actors, almost seems to furnish an acceptable explanation because it is immediately comprehensible. Unfortunately, this theory is grounded in the notion that the strike is always a means to an end: here, a means by which a fraction of the working class expressed its hostility toward the government's conduct of the war; elsewhere, and sometimes simultaneously, a means to express dissatisfaction with the deteriorating conditions of life. The strike is sometimes, but not always, an instrument; the most spectacular movements, those of 1917 among them, grew out of another logic.

The development of a strike movement in 1917 calls for another sort of explanation. Why did this strike wave assume such exceptional size, given that the war did not appear to be ending and given that the constraints on strikes quite strong in all the belligerent countries – especially France, an occupied

492

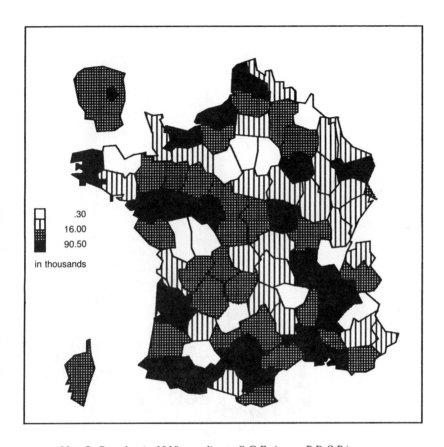

Map 5. Days lost in 1918 according to S.G.F. (source B.D.S.P.)

nation struggling to regain its lost territory? Somehow, the forces of constraint must have been temporarily suspended.

What happened in the spring of 1917? Beginning with 16 April 1917, the date of the Nivelle offensive, there are 161 acts of collective indiscipline on record, acts that in essence consist of refusals to "go over the top." "From a geographical standpoint, the 161 cases on record divide into 125 for the region of the April offensive, and 36 cases in various parts of the *zone des armées*. [Of these] 36 cases, 12 came from units which had recently left the region around the Aisne and the Monts de Champagne after the offensive."[25] Clearly, the mutinies were numerous among those units that had experienced numerous defeats. "Cases of insubordination were most common in the divisions which

25. Pedroncini, p. 71.

493

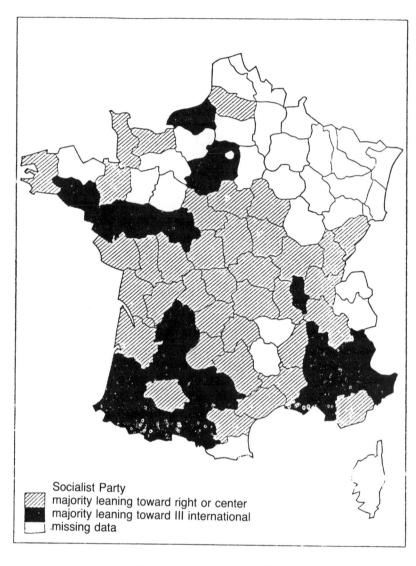

Map 6. Mandates of the federations in February 1920. According to A. Kriegel, Aux origines du communisme Français *(Paris, Mouton, 1964), p. 335.*

took part in the second phase of the battle, fought from the beginning of May on both the Chemin des Dames and the Monts de Champagne," writes Pedroncini.[26] And he adds, "It was the offensive, sometimes because of its failure under conditions where there could be no doubt as to the reasons for that failure, sometimes because of the fear that once again it would be useless, that determined the zone of collective actions and the limits of disobedience."[27] The depths of the military crisis, which lasted a bit beyond Petain's appointment as head of the general staff, threw into question not the goals of the war, but the way in which it was being fought. This crisis in the legitimacy of the military command cannot be compared to a simple military defeat. The acts of insubordination mean that to risk facing a firing squad seemed less dangerous than to obey orders; they indicate that the military and political authorities conducted themselves in such a manner that to desert was no longer an act of treason. The mechanisms by which the war, as a situation of adversity, had excluded any demonstration of autonomy no longer functioned; those on strike could feel neither the threat of sanctions nor moral opprobrium. The strikes, undoubtedly stimulated by the rising cost of living – especially in Paris – witnessed for a brief moment the collapse of the moral interdiction that had previously contained them.

Political polarization and social consensus

It seems that the strike movement of 1917 and the mutinies at the front should not be dismissed as singular events, linked solely by their coincidence in time. Rather, these two events should be seen as indicators within the framework of larger social and political phenomena: the dissolution of social consensus, political polarization, and the loss of legitimacy suffered by military and political authority. In a deliberate fashion, these developments had proceeded without reference to events in political society, as though the development of strikes, or absence of any such development, occurred independently of the political situation. However, one of the war's first effects had been to weld civil and political society. Can we hypothesize that this social consensus had broken down before any return to normal political divisions had come about?

It is useful to distinguish two phenomena in which temporal interference does not supress diversity: (1) the division between Socialists and the Right, and (2) the divisions that cut across the Socialist party and the syndicalist movement on the subject of working-class activism. The breakdown of the Union sacrée began with Malvy's resignation in September 1917, and was sealed in Novem-

26. Ibid., p.73.
27. Ibid.

ber by Clemenceau's accession to power. Political confrontation remained quite marginal until the Union sacrée was fully broken. Before this, only a small minority of the political and syndicalist Left openly adopted a posture favoring an immediate peace without annexations.[28] No constituted power contested the government's political authority, even if there were occasional doubts regarding the government's conduct of the war. Beginning in the winter of 1917–18, however, the situation changed; the prolongation of the war called forth a resurgence of those political divisions that at first it had effaced. The major line of cleavage shifted, cutting through the heart of the Left; the the conflict deepened between revolutionary syndicalists and reformists, between "Zimmerwaldian" or "Kienthalian" Socialist and partisans of the Second International. To be sure, the war powerfully inhibited any expression of political conflict right up until the armistice, and the breakdown of the Union sacrée as primarily an abstention or retreat by the Socialists and not an active, radical opposition. The will to action emerged only on the extreme left of the French socialist movement, which sought to establish the legitimacy of its beliefs through social agitation. The final act in this process of political polarization was the formation of the Bloc National, which, in anticipation of the December 1919 elections, regrouped the Right in coalition with a fraction of the radicals.

The process of polarization unfolded in three stages: (1) The formal rupture of the Union sacrée came in September 1917, as the gap widened between the Left and the extreme Left, inclined toward the Bolsheviks; (2) the armistice of November 1918 freed political life from the constraint of the war, but at the hour of victory, the opposing voices were unable to speak out clearly; (3) the formation of the Bloc National consummated the split between the Socialists and the nationalist Right, whereas the extreme Left gathered strength.

Although closely linked, the process of political polarization and the emergence of a will to action on the socialist Left remain distinct phenomena. The strikes unfolded in the spring of 1917, with the Union sacrée unbroken and no organized political force to encourage them. When, in 1918, the political situation grew strained and a will to action openly emerged on the extreme Left, strikes were less frequent and lacked the contagious dynamic characteristic of the movement in 1917. Even in the Isère, where strikes were more numerous and more massive in 1918 than in 1917, the movement that developed in the defense plants broke off abruptly; not in victory, but under the threat that all mobilized workers would be recalled to the front. J. J. Becker writes that in the Gard, the movement of spring 1918 presented a mixture "of determinations and evasions."[29] In the Paris region, the strike movement, which was extremely

28. G. Herve and the readers of "La Guerre Sociale;" several syndicalists close to P. Monatte.
29. Becker, p. 242.

widespread in the metallurgical industries, came to a sudden halt (after the joint intervention of the majority and minority syndicalists).

Why is it that these strike movements, through which pacifist ideas were widely disseminated, were less powerful than comparable movements in Germany? It is as though the difference had more to do with the asymmetry of the agressed-upon/aggressor relationship, then victor/vanquished relationship than it did with the emergence of an extreme Left seeking to transform the war into revolution. This diachrony in the political maturation of the working classes and their élan offers close analogies with the rhythm of two periods after the war. Syndical and political organizations could provide no goals for the strikes of 1917, and when in 1918 they proposed such goals, the strikes were timid and spread only with difficulty. It seems that it was not so much a lack of political will that prevented the strikes from developing as they did in Germany, but rather a lack of legitimacy. One cannot comprehend the obvious weakness in the process whereby strikes spread in 1918 without returning to the argument that in France at that time the war still possessed a considerable inhibiting power. So long as the struggle continued, neither the collapse of the Union sacrée nor the undeniable determination of the syndicalist and political minority sufficed to produce a broad strike movement, even when the economic context favored such a movement. The "deficit" of strikes in 1918 is a second event no less strange than the "excess" of spring 1917, which suggests that a change in the political legitimacy of authority is an important condition for the success of mass actions, whether or not they possess a revolutionary character.

The war established a marked discontinuity, negatively at the outset, with a deficit of strikes like the deficit in births and marriages noted previously, and this deficit appeared even more pronounced when the enemy was strong and victorious. Although the war strongly influenced the pattern of strikes, these movements did not follow every rise and fall in the curve graphing morale or that for the military situation. The shift in political authority seemed linked to the conduct of the war, but this change did not directly coincide with the success or failure of arms. Changes in political authority became a decisive element in the breakdown of social consensus only in exceptional circumstances, of which the Nivelle offensive is a typical example. In time of war, the threshold above which authority is damaged can be defined with some precision. This change in the legitimacy of political authority explains the strike waves that I have called strike crises.[30] These are movements that, whether encouraged by the economic context or not, are born of a breakdown in the sense of legitimacy that allows a government to coerce the population, and of the absence of any political stakes or will. These movements build in short

30. Cf. Lagrange (1982, b).

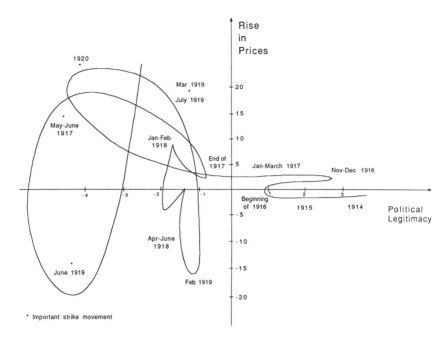

Figure 6. Relationship between political legitimacy, rise in prices, and strikes.

phases from the moment that the dissociation of civil from political society forbids their instrumentalization.

In order to briefly summarize those conditions that stimulate strikes in wartime and those that inhibit them, we can graph the moments of labor militancy in relation to two coordinates, which cannot account for the totality of determinants but only the most fundamental ones (see Figure 6).

Aside from the extraordinary movement in prices in June 1919, the area defined by the conjunction of a rise in prices with a shift in the inhibiting force of authority – due to the conduct of the war in 1917 and to the end of fighting in 1919 – is a propitious one for the development of strike pressure.

Appendix: results from a serial analysis of the strikes

The equations were derived by the Box Jenkins method. The variation in the number of strikes – calculated in the same way for two months or two quarters – that is, over a one year interval – is linked to these same variations, delayed by one quarter or one month (G_t^*), and to changes in prices – relative

($\Delta px_t/px_t$) or absolute (Δpx_t) – over the course of the same year. Those specifications for the quarterly equations that use values delayed by a year for the dependent variable (G^*_{t-4}) are significant. The coefficients of the auto-regression have a mechanical origin: The strikes lasted twenty days longer in this period, and it was therefore necessary to overlap the strikes from one month to the next. This caused a process of auto-regression that seems elsewhere to have disappeared on the quarterly statistics.

In the quarterly equations, the coefficients for the variable increase in retail prices are also substantial. It is on these figures that I base the idea that during the first year of the war, strikes took on the character of a protest against the rising cost of living. The substitution of the especially high number of strikes for June 1919 (594) alters neither the nature nor the relative value of the coefficients in any obvious fashion.

In the equations for the monthly statistics, the coefficients for the auto-regression are highly significant (for the reason indicated above). By contrast, the coefficients for the economic variable are not. Moreover, it should be noted that the sign for this variable remains positive, as one would expect from a protestor's standpoint. An attempt to take into account, in ad hoc fashion, both the movement of June 1917 and those of June 1919 and March 1920, by means of a silent variable, visibly increased the role of variance explicated above.

The analysis of the self-correlation of the remainders showed no strong correlations of the first or second order; the self-correlations of a superior order are on occasion stronger.

22

Labor unrest in Imperial Russia on the eve of the First World War: the roles of conjunctural phenomena, events, and individual and collective actors

LEOPOLD H. HAIMSON

The analyses presented in the second part of this volume have centered attention on the role played by structural processes of change – in the character, organization, and relations of production and the social characteristics of the work forces involved in them – in accounting for changing patterns of labor unrest in Imperial Russia after the turn of the century. In other of my writings to date, I have laid emphasis on the role played by other structural processes: most notably, in the case of the workers of St. Petersburg, on the demographic changes attendant to the emergence after 1905 of more stable, and more coherent working-class communities in certain parts of the capital, and their effects on the patterns of strike actions displayed by the workers concentrated in them.[1]

This is not to suggest, however, that any adequate interpretation of the dynamics of this labor unrest can in fact be drawn by focusing exclusive attention on structural processes of change. Even from a purely statistical standpoint, as we shall see, our analyses have exposed major differences between the 1912–14 strike wave, and the strikes that unfolded in 1911, and indeed during the three months of 1912 immediately preceding the Lena goldfield massacre. And as the contributions of William Rosenberg and Diane Koenker to this volume amply suggest, the dynamics of industrial strikes in the course of the Revolution of 1917 would unveil equally important differences as well as similarities with those that we scrutinized between Lena and the outbreak of the war.

Given these facts, it appears obvious that in seeking to explain not only the specific timing of the post-Lena strike wave, but also the patterns of labor unrest that distinguished it right up to the outbreak of the war, we need to take account not only of more long-term structural processes of change but also

1. See L. Haimson (in collaboration with Eric Brian), "Processus demographiques et greves ouvrieres: Le cas de Saint Petersbourg," in *Annales* (Economics, Societes, Civilisations), no. 4 (Fall 1985).

of shorter-term factors and their differentiated impact on various strata of workers. Let us immediately take note, in this connection, of two major conjuctural features that sharply distinguished the conditions of the immediate prewar period from those of the revolutions of 1905 and 1917.

The first was the degree of concentration, indeed of constriction, of the political and social crisis – and especially of all significant manifestations of public unrest – among the upper as well as the lower strata of society within urban Russia; and within urban Russia, in a few large urban centers, including, first and foremost, the capital of St. Petersburg. To be sure, by the eve of the war, a sense of political and social disaffection had spread very broadly in urban, commercial, industrial (but not rural) Russia. But it was only in large urban centers – partly because of their mixed populations, including the presence in large numbers of members of the intelligentsia, who played an important role in articulating and to a degree melding the dissatisfaction felt by other groups in society – that this dissatisfaction actually poured out into significant displays of public turmoil and protest. Even when they did not provide direct immediate support for the strike movement, these displays of public protest unquestionably encouraged in a growing number of workers a sense of the possibility to act.

In these respects, St. Petersburg stood out as a special case. Its political atmosphere was kept charged by the deliberations of the State Duma, marked as they increasingly were as the war approached by denunciations on the part of representatives of the liberal, as well as radical, opposition of the repressive acts of the tsarist regime, including its repressions of the labor movement. These denunciations were widely reported and amplified not only in the open labor press, but also by the various moderate and liberal newspapers of the capital, whose militance was itself energized by the increasingly vocal opposition sentiments voiced by large segments of "census" society, most notably the large numbers of professional people concentrated in the city. Finally, we should take note of the crucial agitational role played in the mobilization of labor unrest by the activities conducted *outside* of the Taurus Palace (but also covered by parliamentary immunities) by radical Duma deputies, and especially those of the Bolshevik faction. From these various directions, the workers' movement in the capital became the object from the very outset of the post-Lena period of a degree of attention, as well as public sympathy and support, that it did not begin to encounter in any other urban center. And this attention, especially at the outset, played an important part in reinforcing among St. Petersburg workers a sense of the possibility to act, and indeed of the *legitimacy* of their acts (and by the same token, of the *illegitimacy* of the efforts of the organs of authority to suppress them).

But throughout this period, the relationship between the *krizis verkhov* and *krizis nizov* – the political and social crises brewing in the upper and lower reaches of the population – was not a one-way affair. From the very outset,

501

the intensity and especially the highly politicized character that the wave of labor unrest assumed in the capital (partly because of the large number of "advanced," politically militant workers, distinguished by our various objective indices, congregated in it) greatly contributed to the intensity of the opposition movement in census society, largely because it *reinforced its own sense of possibility*. And it was ultimately this dialectic – this process of dynamic interaction between the two crises – that made for the electric quality, the extraordinary feverishness (even by comparison with other urban centers), that the political and social crisis assumed in St. Petersburg by the eve of the First World War.[2]

But perhaps even more important in the further unfolding of this dialectic, it was the feverishness of the opposition movement in census society, and in particular the loudness of the denunciations from the Duma platform and in the liberal and radical press of the arbitrary actions taken to suppress labor unrest and the open labor movement, that – *in combination with the very massiveness and uncontrolled character that the wave of labor unrest increasingly assumed* – crippled the capacity and ultimately the will of officials responsible for the maintenance of order to suppress labor unrest in the capital effectively (and especially to violate systematically the legal norms still protecting the open labor movement, and in particular the open labor press). Indeed, these combined pressures induced the government to recoil, at least up to the July Days of 1914, from summarily lifting these legal protections, and from carrying out the even more drastic and broader coup d'etat advocated by its own Minister of Internal Affairs – for fear that such extreme measures might in fact set off the very revolutionary processes that they were intended to contain.

In these various respects, we repeat, St. Petersburg on the eve of the war stood out as a world apart. In the provinces, by and large, governors and the chiefs of gendarmerie under their supervision did not face problems of such monumental dimensions. Neither did they lack the will to repress, without hesitation, political and even economic strikes (not to mention the organs of open labor movement); nor to menace, and when necessary to suppress, the rare opposition newspapers that dared, in any way to express sympathy for workers' strike actions and the aspirations that animated them.

In contrast to the prewar period, the dynamic interplay between the *krizis verkhov* and the *krizis nizov* during most of the 1905–7 strike wave – and the eroding effects that *in combination*, they could exercise on the capacity and will of organs of authority to repress the strike movement – unfolded over a much broader map, particularly in urban Russia. They would do so again in 1917,

---

2. For a fuller discussion of this interplay between the unfolding of the political and social crises in the upper and lower strata of Russia's urban society, see Leopold Haimson, "The Problem of Social Stability in Urban Russia, 1905–1917," *Slavic Review* 23, no. 4 (December, 1964), and 24, no. 1 (March, 1985).

drawing into the wave of labor unrest strata of industrial workers that, in the immediate prewar period, had not become so intensively involved in it, partly at least because they *did not dare to do so*. (We shall momentarily return to this crucial point.)

The second set of conjunctural features that distinguished the post-Lena period and contributed to the contemporary revival of labor unrest was economic. One of its features was a price inflation, set off, as is so often the case, by the resumption of economic expansion, but accelerated (especially as far as food prices were concerned) by the crop failure in Eastern European Russia and Western Siberia in 1911. In fact, one of the major motifs in those strike actions that Russian workers, especially low-paid workers, launched over wage issues at the end of 1912 and the beginning of 1913, was unquestionably a desire to catch up with the rise in the cost of living, in the now seemingly more favorable setting for the launching of economic strikes created by the new industrial expansion.[3] Indeed, the comments on the labor scene published in the Bulletins of the Moscow Society of Manufacturers and Mill Owners originally advanced the comforting notion that this was the chief factor underlying the new wave of labor unrest, only to withdraw this proposition as the strike wave unfolded, in the face of the extraordinary number of political strikes recorded in their own strike statistics.[4]

But even though price inflation does not really provide an adequate explanation for the character and underlying dynamics of the strike actions of the post-Lena period, and especially of those conducted by the strata of advanced workers among whom labor unrest was so disproportionately concentrated during these years, it seems to me undeniable that the renewed industrial expansion of the prewar period *did*, especially at first, contribute a favorable environment for the revival of various forms of labor unrest, including even political strikes. In this respect as well, the precise effects of the industrial expansion on various strata of industrial workers were almost as variegated as those of the political conjuncture. These differentiated effects stemmed not only from the differences in the regularity and tempo of this expansion in various branches of Russian industry, but also from the relationship obtaining in these various branches of Russian industry (and in the specific occupations represented within them) between the consequent demand for and the actual supply of labor. In this respect, the skilled workers who were in such short numbers and such great demand in rapidly expanding industries were in an

---

3. For the most detailed, and probably the most reliable, recent estimates of this price inflation, and of its effects on the real wages of industrial workers, see the calculations of S. G. Strumilin in *Ocherki ekonomicheskoi ekonomiki istorii Rossii i SSSR* (Nauka, 1966), pp. 90ff., and in Strumilin's *Problemy ekonomiki truda* (Moscow, 1957), p. 463.

4. See *Obshchestvo zavodchikov i fabrikantov Moskovskogo promyshlenogo raiona v 1912 godu* (Moscow, 1913), and *Biulleten, Rabochee dvizhenie*, nos. 16, 17, and 18, issued by the Moscow Society for 1912 and 1913.

especially favorable position in the labor market, and there is little doubt that at the outset of the post-Lena strike wave, the sense that these skilled workers (especially those employed in the exceptionally rapidly expanding metal-processing and mechanical industry) drew from their favorable position greatly encouraged and sustained them in their strike actions.

Indeed, if only because of the acute shortages of skilled labor in their industry, and the orders piled up by the firms in which they were employed (delays in the delivery of orders, particularly from the state, entailed financial penalties, aside from other financial losses), these metalworkers may in fact have expected, at least at first, to win their strike actions in quick order, and at the beginning many of them did so, especially outside the capital. When the character of their strike actions changed, the climate in which they were fought grew on both sides increasingly bitter – private employers as well as state enterprises resorted to increasingly harsh measures against their striking workers and especially those identified as inciters, troublemakers. Even then, however, more militant workers could steel themselves with the reassurance that if they were fired (or indeed arrested, and subjected to administrative exile outside the capital), they could eventually obtain comparable jobs in other cities (and indeed be able to resume their labor agitation in these new settings).

In these respects, as well, the metalworkers of the capital (and those of the metal-processing industry generally) lived a world apart from the unskilled workers employed in the new giant textile *manufaktury* established in the middle of nowhere – at the end of railroad sidings in the countryside of Moscow *guberniia*, for example. And this distinguishing feature, too, helps to account for the enormous differences we have observed between the apathy that such workers generally displayed and the intensity of strike actions among metalworkers during these years.

But not even the effects of the conjunctural features that we now have reviewed (in combination with those of the more long-term processes discussed earlier) can fully account for the timing of the post-Lena wave, or even for the character and the relative intensity of the strike actions that distinguished it. The year 1911 already unfolded in the setting of an economic conjuncture that, at least as far as the metal industry was concerned, did not differ sharply from that of 1912. The year 1911 was also already marked by as yet modest but growing and increasingly vocal displays of political disaffection and opposition on the part of census society, and indeed by demonstrations, especially among students of the higher educational establishments of the capital. Yet, not only did 1911 fail to record outbursts of labor protest comparable in intensity to those that would break out in the spring of the following year, but what is even more important, neither the character nor the dynamics of the strike actions recorded in the course of the year (admittedly a substantially greater number than in 1910) begin to compare, even from a purely statistical standpoint, to those that would unfold from the spring of 1912 onward.

Indeed, underlying our sense of the sharp dividing line separating labor unrest in 1911 from what was to follow is not merely the much lower general level of labor unrest recorded that year, or even the still extremely modest number of political strikes that were involved in it. Even more important in the perspective of our quantitative studies is the fact that neither in isolation, nor in interaction, do the objective indices used with such effectiveness in our analysis of the strikes of the post-Lena period help account to even a comparable degree for the intensity of the strike actions recorded among various strata of workers during this last pre-Lena year. (Our three major indices of wage levels, degrees of concentration in St. Petersburg and in other cities of over 200,000 in population, and in enterprises employing over 500 and over 1,000 workers—which after interaction, account statistically for 64% of the variations in the overall intensity of strike actions recorded in 1912 – account for only 9% of these variations in 1911!)

Obviously, it took not only the longer-term processes or even the more short-term conjunctural features that we have discussed, but the catalytic effect of an *event*, the Lena goldfield massacre – and the indignation that this event and the clumsy handling of it by the government aroused not only among industrial workers but also among liberal and radical circles of census society – to set off the wave of sympathy strikes, and eventually of mutually reinforcing political and "economic" strikes, which our analysis has sought to describe and in some measure to explain.

Is it necessary to add that all we have sought to argue up to this point is that in the dynamics of labor unrest during the post-Lena period we observe the interplay between processes of longer and shorter duration – or more precisely, between structures, conjunctures, and events – that constitutes the very essence, and ultimate mystery, of the unfolding of historical processes?

This comment, however banal, applies with particular force to the study and analysis of strikes; so much so that it induces me to add one last cautionary note. It is that no more than they provide accurate indices of the underlying dynamics of strike actions in *any and all* periods of Russian labor history, do the objective factors that we have found so closely associated statistically with the intensity of strike actions during the immediate prewar period provide, with any reasonable accuracy, indices of the conscious attitudes of individual workers, or even of their stabler and more basic ways of apprehending reality that we associate with the term "mentalite." The caution obtains with respect to any act, but it applies with particular force to strikes, since they involve forms of collective action that require workers (whether in a particular factory, geographical area, or entire branch of industry) *to act in concert* with other workers. For such collective actions to be launched, it is by the same token

505

necessary for a collectivity (and not merely for individuals) not only to share a sense of deprivation, or even to collectively translate this sense of deprivation into specific common grievances, but also to draw the collective conclusion that it is *possible* as well as necessary for them to act; or more precisely, to press their grievances in the specific form of collective action that strikes entail.

Obviously, the unfolding of such a process – and the reaching of such a collective decision – is not merely a function of collective mentality, or even of the sharing of conscious attitudes by a group of workers, but also of the nature of the settings in which these decisions are reached; that is, of the character of these workers' immediate environments. We have already noted the immense differences observable in this regard between the urban and rural settings of prewar Russia, and within urban Russia itself: in the degrees of constraint (as well as of encouragement) that employers, local authorities, and other groups in society could bring to bear on more militant workers, but even more importantly on the behavior of *their fellow workers*, on whose participation the launching, let alone the successful pursuit, of strike actions ultimately hinged.

But even the lines of analysis that we have drawn up to this point in seeking to account for the dynamics of the translation of collective deprivation into a sense of collective grievance, and of collective grievances into the forms of collective action that strike actions entail, have been in the last analysis too simple, too one-sided, too mechanistic. For in the relationships between collective mentality, conscious attitudes, and collective actions we observe just as clearly the interplay – the dialectic – that we noted earlier between structures, conjunctures, and events. Specifically, the statistical results obtained in our analysis confirm the obvious proposition that in this period and setting of labor history, just as in any others, strike actions once set off had their own dynamics, influencing the behavior but also the conscious attitudes, and sometimes ultimately the mentalities, not only of the worker activists initially involved in them, but also of other strata of workers who were drawn into the wave of labor unrest by the force of their example, if not directly by the efforts of these more militant workers to enlist them in their strike actions.

We observed these dynamics of labor action in the evolution of labor unrest among workers in the metal industry during these years, as well as in the "drawing power" that metalworkers were able to exercise on other workers, especially in those large urban centers in which they were congregated in large numbers. But this radiating effect of labor action, and specially of the tangible examples that the strikes in the capital provided of labor militance – of the "proper" behavior for "conscious" workers to adopt, and of the *possibility* and the need to act – was quite tangibly felt by the eve of the war among the more socially and physically isolated cotton workers of the province of Kostroma, whose strike actions launched in May–June 1914 continued to be pressed

506

(unlike those of St. Petersburg workers) into late August 1914, well after the outbreak of the war. This indeed was a harbinger of things to come: of the much broader sociological and geographical map over which labor unrest would unfold by 1917 – providing a major catalyst for the last of the revolutions that Russia experienced in the early twentieth century.

Focused as our attention has been in this volume on the role of objective factors, and particularly on those aspects of the evolution of labor unrest in Imperial Russia that lent themselves to the quantitative analyses that we have sought to summarize, we have made little reference to the role played in labor unrest by the programs, the strategies, the tactics, and the efforts at the political organization of the workers' movement by individual and collective actors. In substance, we have paid little attention to the role played by what was defined in the social democratic language of the times as "conscious" as against "spontaneous" forces (and has now come to be termed by some Soviet historians as "subjective" as against "objective" factors). I have been seeking to describe these more explicitly political dimensions of the labor history of this period in other of my writings. Yet no discussion of the evolution of labor unrest in Imperial Russia during these years, however, can be nearly adequate without recognition of the fact that it was during the post-Lena period, even more than during the years of Russia's First Revolution, that politically "advanced," "conscious" workers – not only among the more militant strata of the working class on which we have focused attention, but also in more inert working-class environments – did so on the basis of a political identification with and commitment to social democracy – indeed with what they conceived to be *their own* "workers" party.

It is also the case that the evolution of the political and social consciousness, and especially of the political and social behavior of many of these workers, particularly among the young, was marked, at least by the end of 1913 and the beginning of 1914, by a growing responsiveness to Bolshevik appeals (if not, in most cases at least by an explicit, let alone unshakable, sense of identification with the Bolshevik faction and its leaders). I have arqued more fully elsewhere that the basic sources of the undeniable successes recorded on the labor scene by the Bolshevik faction, especially by the eve of the war, lay – as is always the case of political successes – in the ultimate correspondence between the vision of contemporary Russian realities advanced by Lenin and his followers (and the political attitudes and patterns of behavior that the Bolsheviks sought to legitimize in response to these realities) and the grievances and aspirations that their own direct and immediate experience of these same realities now fostered among various strata of Russian workers. But this is not for a moment to deny that Bolshevism played during this period – in a variety of ways – a significant role in the articulation and mobilization of these workers'

507

grievances and aspirations, and indeed in their *translation* into the specific and relatively organized forms of collective action involved in the launching and conduct of individual and collective strikes. Within the limits of space dictated by this essay, I can only list the specific roles that Bolshevism played in this connection.

First and foremost, there was the basic vision that Bolshevism drew of a world of workers and peasants arrayed in revolt against a superimposed and oppressive political and social structure of arbitrariness and privilege, and the translation of this vision into the various highly flexible formulations of the Bolshevik program – from the dictatorship of proletariat and peasantry, to the Bolshevik "uncut" slogans of "democratic republic," "eight-hour day," and "confiscation of gentry lands." This vision provided a translation and also a synthesis – in the form of a coherent, explicit, and generalized worldview – of the variety of grievances against the exercise of superordinate authority that now animated the strata of "advanced" workers on whom we have focused attention. Indeed, it provided an image, however vague, of a "bright future" to inspire and steady these workers' revolt.

Perhaps even more important, at least from the standpoint of this analysis, Bolshevism offered Russia's workers during this period a strategy, or more precisely the image of a strategy, to achieve this brighter future, and especially to legitimize and assign wider meaning to the specific forms of labor unrest to which their possibilities for revolt were as yet largely confined. This image of a strategy, formulated by the time of the Poronin conferences of the Bolshevik Central Committee in 1913, was that of a growing and ultimately irresistible strike wave assuming a more and more highly organized and generalized character, which would culminate in a general, nationwide, political strike, leading to an armed uprising, the overthrow of autocracy, and the establishment of a "democratic republic." We should note that in 1905 the model of such a strategy – focusing on the strike weapon as a major, indeed the *primary* vehicle in the unfolding of revolutionary processes – had not been advanced either by the Bolshevik or the Menshevik factions of the RSDRP. Its formulation by Bolshevik leaders on the eve of the war clearly provided a rationale and a long-range objective for the more militant participants in the post-Lena strike wave, and especially for those involved in the launching of political strikes.

Hardly at issue in this connection is the question of how realistic or timely the Bolshevik prewar strategy was, let alone the tactics and forms of organizational activity that were applied to achieve it. Suffice to state that notwithstanding the Mensheviks' contemporary denunciations of Bolshevik tactics, and more generally the sense of growing alarm they expressed about the "statechnyi azart" – the reckless and suicidal course being pursued, in their view, by the strike movement – the image of this strategy increasingly inspired the efforts of militant workers to organize political strikes and demonstrations as the war approached, and indeed provided an ostensible purpose for such massive displays of collective action as the St. Petersburg general strike of July 1914. It gave a broader meaning to the efforts of "inciters" to initiate such collective actions, and to the individual acts of the many thousands who participated in them.

And finally, there was the organizational contribution provided by Bolshevism to the mobilization and sustenance of the leadership of the strike movement. This contribution lay not so much in the Bolsheviks' activities in the underground, let alone in their futile occasional efforts throughout this period to establish regional, and eventually nationwide, underground centers to provide the coordination for their "nationwide political strike leading to an armed uprising." The police were almost invariably informed of these efforts through their myriad of informers and double agents in the underground, and awaited only the most opportune moment to catch in their nets the greatest possible numbers of participants. Rather, the Bolsheviks' positive contribution to the organization of labor unrest lay in part in the participation of Bolshevik militants in the ad hoc, amorphous, cellular "committees" at the factory or shop level that provided whatever elements of leadership the Bolshevik underground actually maintained at the grass roots. Even more important, the Bolsheviks' contribution to the organization of the strike movement lay in their systematic exploitation of what was called at the time "legal possibilities." These were the various forms of activity and organization of the "open" labor movement – protected, however flimsily, by legal immunities – that most Bolshevik stalwarts had despised in earlier years as manifestations of Menshevik "liquidationist" tendencies, but which Lenin and his colleagues now called on them to "use" for revolutionary purposes: the open labor press, in which militant workers heard their grievances and aspirations articulated and legitimized, and more "backward" workers were called upon, indeed "shamed," to emulate them; the trade unions and clubs of enlightenment that provided the legal covers for the gatherings at which Bolshevik worker militants, in St. Petersburg at least, sought to coordinate the efforts to organize political strikes and demonstrations on a citywide basis; and last but not least, the various opportunities for agitational and organizational work, most firmly protected by legal immunities, that were available *outside* as well as inside the State Duma, to the six labor deputies of the Bolshevik faction.

The significance of the roles played throughout the prewar period by these six labor deputies (including Roman Malinovskii, the double agent who acted as their chairman from the fall of 1913 to the spring of 1914) cannot possibly be overestimated. These deputies provided, especially in the more isolated areas of the Central Industrial Region, the chief agitational and organizational conduits for Bolshevik activity, and indeed, in some cases, managed to assume

509

the roles of genuine political leaders of and spokesmen for their constituents. (Such a role was assumed and maintained, to an equal if not superior degree, vis-á-vis their local constituents, by the Georgian deputies of the Menshevik faction in the State Duma.)

It is at this level, far more tangibly and concretely than at the more general level of the political leadership of a figure like Lenin, that historians of the labor movement find themselves confronted, in their search for adequate explanations for the intensity and character of labor unrest among various groups of workers, with the significance of the role played by individual personalities – a significance that is ultimately as irreducible as the role of events. Consider, in this connection, the role of a Shagov, the dynamic and magnetic Bolshevik labor deputy of Kostromskaia *guberniia* (whom even the governor of this province indignantly described in his confidential reports to the Minister of Internal Affairs as the veritable "dictator" of this province), and the weight to be attached to this one person's agitational and organizational activity in accounting for the massiveness of the strike wave that swept through the cotton mills of Kostromskaia *guberniia* in the spring and summer of 1914. Consider the contrast provided in this respect by the almost complete apathy throughout the post-Lena period, including these last prewar months, of the workers employed in the cotton mills of neighboring Vladimirskaia *guberniia* (including those of the industrial center of Ivanovo-Vosnesensk who had displayed such great revolutionary militance in 1905), and the weight to be assigned in accounting for this dramatic contrast to the inactivity of the Boshevik deputy of Vladimirskaia *guberniia*, F. N. Samoilov, who was almost completely immobilized by illness during most of this period.

If we are ultimately induced to attribute so large, if necessarily unmeasurable, a place to the role of individual personalities and events, let alone to that played by historical conjunctures, what precise significance is ultimately to be attached to the broader and more impersonal structural phenomena and long-term processes on which we have laid such considerable attention in our comparative analysis of the 1905–7 and 1912–14 strike waves? Let me try to provide, however tentatively, an answer to this inevitable question. It is that notwithstanding the vastly greater pressures and constraints to which they were subjected in the new political conjuncture created by the outbreak of the war, the strata of militant workers distinguished by our various objective indices would again display during the war years the highly distinctive patterns of labor unrest that surfaced for them in our quantitative analyses of the post-Lena period, and account for an even more disproportionate number of the political strikes recorded up to the outbreak of the February Revolution. Specifically, the groups of workers on which we have focused attention in our studies of structural changes between the turn of the century and 1914 – the workers of the metal industry, and among them those employed in mechanical and machine construction enterprises; the workers of the capital, and in particular those of the Vyborg district; and within the Vyborg district itself, the work forces for the very same mechanical enterprises in the private sector that by the eve of the war had become the hotbeds of St. Petersburg's labor unrest – would reemerge from the fall of 1915 onward as the most explosive and politically most militant elements of the workers' movement, and provide during the February Days the spark that ignited the Revolution of 1917.[5] In the subsequent course of the revolution, as the studies of my colleagues suggest, these same strata of workers would continue to furnish the most militant and radicalized participants in labor unrest, and indeed provide the hard core of the Bolsheviks' working-class support. To be sure, in 1917 no more than in 1914 would these workers – by themselves – prove capable of making a revolution or indeed provide an adequate mass basis for one, but the political and social effects of their patterns of collective action would constitute one of the most important dimensions of the historical scenario that unfolded in the course of the Revolution of 1917, and of the differences that distinguished it from that of the Revolution of 1905.

5. One of the preliminary findings of the analyses we are currently conducting of labor unrest during the First World War is that in 1916 the workers of St. Petersburg's metal industry accounted for over 75% of the total number of participants in political strikes recorded by the Factory Inspectorate in the Empire as a whole.

23

Strikes in Russia, 1917: the impact of revolution

DIANE KOENKER AND WILLIAM G. ROSENBERG

Analyzing the impact of 1917 on strikes in Russia is something like retrieving spilled mercury. Revolutionary change created such fluid circumstances that strikes and protests often changed their nature in the very course of occurring; and just as one is about to get an analytical grasp on events, their form shifts and they skitter from reach, changing size and shape even as they continue to remain the same elemental material.

Changes in Russia's political environment altered the meaning of strikes from the first. Largely illegal and hence explicitly political before the overthrow of the tsar, strikes in 1917 simultaneously became a "routine" element of democratic labor–management conflict and an implicit challenge to the ability of both soviet and government leaders to develop stable social relations and workable democratic institutions. As in other areas of life in 1917, the exercise of democratic rights weakened democratic structures, a paradox of political transformation common to most revolutionary situations. Thus, strikes in the spring, which had as their goal the consolidation of revolutionary gains through improving material welfare and eliminating arbitrary and authoritarian social relations in the workplace, became in the fall a central aspect of social polarization and the breakdown of democratic order, and an important social basis for the Bolsheviks' coming to power.

The same can be said about Russia's economic circumstances and the rapidly changing conditions of work that led in a brief time to fundamental changes in patterns of industrial management and management–worker relations. It is fair to say, we think, that before 1917 strikes in Russia took place within a rather well defined socioeconomic system, in which they were logically and tactically an appropriate weapon of struggle, even if frequently unsuccessful. The response of industrial management might not have been uniform or entirely predictable, but the broader rules governing management–labor conflict were relatively stable. The question of ownership rights, the sanctity of private pro-

512

perty, the prerogatives of management to set the terms of labor discipline, and so forth were not fundamentally in question. Neither for the most part, were the privileged socioeconomic circumstances of Russia's industrial bourgeoisie.

In contrast, 1917 brought fundamental changes in all these areas. The socioeconomic circumstances of Russia's industrial bourgeoisie began themselves to change rapidly, perhaps even more rapidly than those of workers. The sanctity of private property, ownership rights, even formal legal procedures, began to weaken, as of course did the power of local and state authorities to contain the boundaries of conflict and enforce laws or established administrative procedures. This occurred, it must be stressed, not only as a result of new political values, and perhaps not even primarily the result of political change itself, but also because of Russia's rapidly deteriorating economy and because 1917 involved not least of all the failure *before* October of essential elements in Russia's particular form of capitalism: its system of finance, its methods of commodity exchange, its very methods of industrial protection. Although these cannot be detailed here, it is important to emphasize that in these circumstances, the willingness – even eagerness in some cases – of Russia's industrial bourgeoisie to tolerate strikes undoubtedly increased. Strikes could be used by management to legitimize shutdowns that might otherwise have been politically untenable. They were also a reason for factory owners to insist on restructuring their debts, or to seek other more favorable business terms from private or state banks, or even from the succession of increasingly weak government ministers. In essence, the very nature of industrial conflict changes in 1917 along with the socioeconomic circumstances of *both* workers *and* the industrial bourgeoisie, a factor that requires one to examine the strike movement itself with special attention to the possible changes in its very meaning as an aspect of workers protest and worker–management conflict.

Central here, of course, are the crucial historical relationships in revolutionary Russia between the goals and values of workers and strikers themselves, those of moderate socialist parties (and particularly their representatives in the government after the formation of the first coalition in May), and those of the Bolshevik party. It is hardly appropriate to assume, as the Soviet historian A. M. Lisetskii and others are prone to do, that all strikes in 1917 are necessarily a sign of intense class antagonism, or that workers became radicalized primarily as a result of Bolshevik politics. What is more important about an analysis of strikes in a moment of revolutionary conjuncture is precisely to ascertain what the relationships *were* between activist workers and the leading parties, to clarify the importance of these relationships on strike movements themselves, and thus to help clarify as well the social and political character of revolutionary outcomes.

These issues obviously cannot be examined in a few pages. We can call attention here only to certain major aspects of the changing character of strikes

513

in the course of 1917, and indicate only generally their political, social, and economic implications. Most important among these, we think, are the ways in which the character of strike participation changed radically during 1917 in a context of relatively stable strike activity; a significant change in the import of strikes over factory order, hours, and working conditions; and the relationship between the changing clusters of strike activity in 1917 and the development of revolutionary politics. At the risk of oversimplification, we will attempt here a few observations about each.

To assess the changing character of strike participation in 1917, it is important to ascertain whether the revolutionary period brought significant changes in the overall patterns of prewar strike activity. Not only did the outlooks and actions of leading political actors turn on their perceptions of these continuities, the whole question of revolutionary Russia's relationship to its immediate past helped define the political climate in 1917, and hence the expectations and apprehensions of ordinary individuals as well as broader social groups.

At first glance there seems to be little change. The number of strikes over "economic" issues we can date with some accuracy between 3 March and 25 October 1917 (inclusive) fits rather well into the ascending pattern of strike activity in 1915 and 1916, and also that of the first two months of 1917. By economic strikes we mean strikes over issues management itself was able to resolve, although as we show in detail in our book, these strikes often had important political implications. Elsewhere in this volume we have indicated that we use a different measurement of strikes for 1917 than that used by the Factory Inspectorate, but if we project the level of industrial strike activity on an enterprise by enterprise base, the recording system used by the Inspectorate, the resulting figure (2,470) suggests strikes in 1917 were part of an intensifying wave of labor activism that began in 1915 (when the Inspectorate recorded 713 economic strikes) and that built further in 1916, when 1,046 strikes were recorded. Similar conclusions can be drawn from examining the number of strikers, as opposed to the number of strikes. From 383,358 strikers in economic strikes in 1915 and 646,785 in 1916, we estimate the number of strikers in economic strikes between 3 March and 25 October to have been no less than 953,930. We thus see a steady progression in the frequency of economic strikes and the number of workers they involved from roughly the spring of 1915 through the Bolsheviks' coming to power two and one-half years later, broken only by a brief hiatus from mid-March to mid-April 1917 but otherwise unaffected by the collapse of tsarism or the assumption of power of the Provisional regime.

What we have learned about the nature and intensity of strikes and also of their manifest objectives in 1917 supports this hypothesis. More than two-thirds of all strikes directed against employers between 3 March and 25

514

October 1917 had to do in some way with wages. Most strikers simply demanded increased pay, but many demanded a change in pay rates, bonuses, or some combination of similar goals. In the aggregate, wage strikes involved at a minimum some 73% of all estimated strikers.

Yet they were also fundamentally different, and for purposes of understanding Russia's own historical development, as well as for setting comparative analysis in a proper conceptual framework, this is far more important. In their work on strikes in Russia during the 1912–14 period, Haimson and Petrusha have shown the importance in all categories of economic strikes of urban concentration, the size of industrial enterprises, and the average level of pay for all workers. Of the slightly more than 3,000 economic strikes between January 1912 and July 1914 (approximately 38% of the total number of strikes), some 68% were over wages, 14% over hours, and 18% over questions of factory order, including conditions of work. Haimson and Petrusha observe that the only strong correlation helping to explain the intensity of strikes over wages was the concentration of workers in enterprises over 1,000 employees, and that only in 1914. In strikes over hours, analyzed by industrial groups, they observe strong positive bivariate correlations between strike intensity and the proportion of literate workers, workers recently arrived from the countryside, workers employed in St. Petersburg, and the proportion of those in cities from 100,000 to 200,000 in population (1913), and urban areas generally (in 1914). When these factors are subjected to multivariate regressions, size of enterprise and level of pay as well as urban concentration and pay prove most important, while strongly negative correlations emerged between the intensity of strikes over hours and workers' ties to the land. Finally, examining strikes over order, Haimson and Petrusha find strong bivariate correlations between strike intensity and wages, and to a lesser extent, to urban concentration. The most significant interaction emerging from multivariate regressions is, again, factory size and level of pay. Workers in St. Petersburg province accounted for a remarkable 24% of these strikes over factory order and for some 30.4% of their participants, although for economic strikes in general the role of St. Petersburg did not prove to be exceptional.

In contrast, Haimson and Petrusha show that the relative intensity of political strikes in this period, a much larger category, correlates strongly to the level of urban concentration and average wages, and most importantly, the province of St. Petersburg, which accounted for an extraordinary percentage of political strikes (and strikers) in this period, especially in the months just before the outbreak of war. According to Factory Inspectorate statistics, moreover, some 88% of all Petersburg strikes themselves were over political issues between January and July 1914, involving more than 90% of all strikers.

What is important here in addition to the role of the capital, Haimson and Petrusha point out, is the absence of significant bivariate relationships between the intensity of political strikes and the size of industrial enterprises. Positive correlations emerged with literacy, and strong negative correlations with workers' ties to the land. "By and large," they observe, "it was those branches of Russian industry whose work forces were distinguished by their disporportionate degree of concentration in urban areas, and particularly by their higher levels of pay and literacy, and their weaker ties to the land, that, to an increasing degree as the war approached, were more intensely involved in political strikes." When these factors are subjected to multivariate regressions, finally, the most important interactions prove to be between the concentration of workers in large urban centers and average wages.

Although strike intensity is only one component of the strike process and the limitations of space prevent us from examining these issues in detail, it is still possible against this background to begin to discern the impact on *aggregate* strike activity of Russia's revolutionary conjuncture and *changes* in strike activity over time in 1917.

Most striking is the diminished, even negative importance of urban concentration. Also of great interest, although less surprising, are the continued roles of average nominal wages and change in real wages, factors that emerge in our multivariate regressions as perhaps the two most important general determinants of overall strike action in 1917. What we find when we analyze strike intensities for the March–October period, for example, is that the strongest correlations exist between a high average nominal wage in 1916 combined with a decline since 1913 in real wages, on one side, and the level of intensity of strikes for any goal, on the other. Industrial concentration (also expressed by factory size) plays a positive role as well, but urban concentrations had an apparently negative effect on strikes, at least in relative terms. A familiar assumption that strikes in 1917 tended to occur with the greatest intensity in settled urban areas would appear to be unfounded. The 1917 data suggest that the geographic spread of strikes was a profound characteristic of labor activism in that year.

Some additional interesting correlations emerge when we separate wage strikes from strikes over factory conditions (order), control (hours), and dignity, a category of protest that may have been included among strikes over order before 1917, but in any event was now far more extensive, warranting separate consideration and analysis. In strikes over wages, a strong negative correlation emerges between the tendency of a province's workers to strike for wage issues and the average nominal wage in 1916.

In contrast, what matters in strikes over issues of workers' dignity are not wages or relative economic position, but levels of literacy and concentration of women workers. Areas where literacy levels among workers were low (a characteristic of women workers but not exclusively so) demonstrated a greater inclination to strike over matters relating to their personal self-respect and dignity.

516

Concerning strikes over job control and factory organization, issues that seem to be related to dignity demands, we find that landedness, a sign of a peasant rather than a hereditary industrial labor force, has a negative effect on the appearance of such demands, as we might expect. But when we control for industrial and urban concentrations, which do affect overall strike intensities, we find that neither of these factors affects the presence of control demands very much, but that a high rate of labor expansion (measured between 1913 and 1916) is positively correlated with strikes over control issues. The last correlation might well signal the mechanism by which a sense of strikes as weapons to gain power (job control) in the workplace spread throughout Russia during the years of war and revolution, for memoir literature suggests that expanding labor forces were not just fueled by migrant peasants but by geographically mobile urban skilled workers as well.

Even these limited observations, however, allow us to suggest several significant aspects of the *overall* impact of 1917 on strikes in the *aggregate*, emphasizing once again the risks of oversimplification. Most important, it seems evident that while the establishment of civil liberties and democratic forms of political protest in 1917 significantly vitiated strikes as explicit political instruments – and in the process dramatically reduced the leading role St. Petersburg (now Petrograd) had earlier played in strike activity generally – the nature of strikes as efforts to secure economic improvement also changed in ways that relate to the development of revolutionary politics. It hardly needs to be argued, of course, that Petrograd became the center of revolutionary politics in 1917, and the scene of major massive political demonstrations, far larger and far more consequential than any that took place elsewhere in Russia between March and October, with the exception only of the Moscow protests accompanying Kerensky's State Conference in August. But we think it possible that precisely because other forms of politics became more important here, the character of the strike movement in the capital changed after March to reflect more ordinary forms of economic struggle. Strikes became an acceptable (legal) component of workers' efforts to improve their welfare, and used in this way, became an aspect of their commitment to seeking economic gains within the framework of the new democratic order.

We would suggest, however, that this in turn may have been a fact of great consequence for the evolution of revolutionary politics in 1917, and particularly the development of moderate socialism, on one hand, and bolshevism, on the other. The vital role of the Petrograd Soviet in Russian national politics meant that unauthorized political strikes by workers in the capital, particularly the heavy concentration of metallists, would have challenged not so much the authority of the government, but of the soviet itself, which was controlled by socialist moderates until the end of August. This was especially the case after soviet leaders joined the first coalition cabinet in early May, and helps explain why the soviet even attempted to restrain demonstrations in May and June, and moved vigorously to suppress the July Days uprising, led by Bolshevik soldiers. It remains unclear whether strikes elsewhere in Russia were affected by Petrograd politics in precisely the same manner, and it is perhaps significant that the massive Moscow demonstrations protesting Kerensky's State Conference in August were called as a general strike, the largest of the revolutionary period. But in any event, the fact that political issues were largely *removed* from the strike arena, *at least in their explicit form*, transferred indirectly to the moderate socialists the burden of assuring that strikes as legal democratic weapons of economic struggle would become an effective means of securing workers' improvements.

It is not unimportant in this regard that Petrograd Soviet leaders managed from the start to reach an agreement with manufacturers over one of the most contentious issues of the prerevolutionary period, that of workers' hours. As Haimson and Petrusha point out, strikes over hours and factory order before 1917 contested the essential prerogatives of industrialists and entrepreneurs to control their own enterprises, both from interference by the state and from the demands of workers to control essential aspects of production. The agreement establishing an eight-hour day helped direct strikes away from essential political issues, contributing in the process to the creation of a seemingly less contentious strike arena. The government's legalization of factory committees in April, and the efforts of the socialist minister of labor Skobelev and others to establish workable conciliation (or mediation) boards had a similar effect. All of this reduced the apparent value of strikes as instruments to alter Russia's political order.

But precisely because of this, the commitment of workers generally to civil liberties, political democracy, and especially their moderate socialist leadership in revolutionary Russia depended at least to some degree on the strikes becoming *effective* instruments of democratic labor protest in 1917, something economic circumstances themselves would not allow. As Russia's quasi-capitalist order continued to deteriorate in 1917, weakened by war, the collapse of international trade and finance, and the regime's inability to sustain viable markets, even successful wage strikes in 1917 – the great majority – could not bring significant improvements in workers' welfare. In these circumstances, the well-known process whereby Lenin and the Bolsheviks discredited moderate socialism and secured control over soviets in Petrograd, Moscow, and elsewhere in late summer and early fall *had* to impact on strikes, as did the ability of Bolshevik leaders to conceptualize in political terms the broad processes of social polarization. As these efforts helped transform deep social antagonism into a coherent and irrepressible movement for new and more radical revolutionary change, even economic strikes were transformed in the very process of their occurring into a significant component of labor's political radicalization.

Here, finally, we think it possible to appreciate the interactions between factors of economic position and workers' propensity to strike in 1917. If workers in those areas where wages had fallen significantly by the start of 1917 tended to strike most, what impact did the catastrophic fall in real wages *during* 1917 have on the workers' willingness to strike and on their perceptions of what could be gained by doing so? Here a look at what happened to wages becomes important. We have used wages up through 1916 to explain strike intensities because that figure best reflects workers' positions on the eve of revolution; 1917 wage levels can be construed as a result as much as a cause of 1917 strikes. But in fact when we see what happened to workers economically during 1917 itself, the differences among industrial strike propensities becomes clearer. Only chemical workers' real wages were higher in 1917 than they had been in 1913, although even they had fallen since 1916. Metalworkers' nominal wage position dropped to third in 1917; in relative terms, their real wage, which had in 1916 been 7% higher than in 1913, dropped in 1917 to only two-thirds of their prewar level. Animal products workers similarly were slightly ahead of their prewar position in 1916, but by 1917 their real wages were also down to two-thirds of the prewar level.

In terms of nominal success or failure, especially on wage issues, strikes in our 1917 sample tended to be successful. But the figures on declining real wages make strike victories look hollow indeed. Part of the revolutionary process of 1917 surely included a growing realization, between March and October, that strikes were an ineffective means of reallocating society's resources, that more direct political means would have to be sought.

This factor in turn helps us to appreciate all the more the absence of a relationship between urban concentration and strike intensities. It is possible that the negative correlation of strikes with urban concentration represents the *spread* of labor activism as much as anything else, and this can possibly also explain the lack of significant relationships (positive or negative) with factors such as landedness, gender, and age. We can note in passing that with respect to urban concentration, 1917 resembles 1905 much moe than it does 1912–14, as Haimson and Petrusha have shown.

This brings us, finally, to the important issues connected with the impact of Russia's revolutionary circumstances to *changes* in strikes over time in 1917. In Part I of this volume we indicated the essential elements of change as they pertain to the nature of strikes and strike propensities: the grouping of strikes into three rather well-defined clusters, May–June, late July to mid-August, and mid-September through October; relatively little progression in the intensity of strikes from spring to fall if measured by the number of strikes themselves but a dramatic increase over time in the number of strike participants, with the daily average of strikers now at least four times what it was in the spring. These patterns, we believe, reflect not only changes in revolutionary Russia's socioeconomic circumstances over time, but also, and perhaps more consequential, the impact of revolution on the quality and nature of strikes as instruments of labor protest.

Thus, the spring cluster is notable for having a relatively high proportion of strikes in enterprises with less than 100 workers and in industrial sectors that had lagged behind in securing wage and other benefits during 1915 and 1916. Plant owners in large manufacturing and industrial enterprises were essentially conciliatory, undoubtedly raising workers' confidence in the Petrograd Soviet. Strikes in the aggregate most likely proliferated at precisely the moment socialists joined the provisional regime in early May because workers expected that Russia's bourgeois elements everywhere would now be even more responsive to their demands, that earlier promises would now be fulfilled, and that the regime itself, along with its supporters in industrial and commercial circles, would now yield further to new displays of workers' strength. The mean length of strikes tended to be longer in May and early June than at any other time of 1917; a relatively high number occurred in the so-called service sectors, like retail shops and banks; and only a handful took place in state-run enterprises. To some extent, at least, strikes in the spring appeared to reflect an eagerness to participate in, rather than struggle against, the existing sociopolitical order.

Summer was a time of profound transition. Bourgeois Russia began to consolidate itself in opposition to further revolutionary change, a hopeless effort in the countryside, but one that in industrial areas found ready expression in resistance to workers' demands. The soviet leadership found itself forced to ally itself with champions of military discipline and civil order like General Kornilov, the new army commander, and to condemn bolshevism after the July Days as an assault on the integrity of Russian and soviet democracy. This crystallization of what can properly be called a civil war mentality corresponded to the emergence of equally fervent signs of proletarian consciousness among Russia's three million or so industrial and service workers, and the consequent breakdown after General Kornilov's mutiny in late August of virtually any confidence whatsoever in the ability of socialist moderates, in or outside the government, to consolidate or strengthen workers' gains.

Thus, the fall witnessed a threefold increase in strikes in state-owned plants in comparison with the spring, and a doubling of strikes against municipal authorities, while the number of strike protests in the private sector actually seems to have declined, perhaps as much as 15%. Striking workers clearly came to regard state and soviet authorities themselves, as well as industrialists and manufacturers, as the proper adversaries in their struggles.

Strikes also spread geographically; and the number reported as "city wide" in September and October grew from fourteen in the spring to more than forty, resembling much more the massive political strikes of the 1912–14 period than the essentially economic protests of earlier in the year, although many were still not explicitly political in content. Of great interest is the fact that some 27% of all strikes for which we know factory size in October took place in plants or production units with more than 1,000 employees. Thus, strikes were becoming more intense, more concentrated, and more politically and economically debilitating.

This view is confirmed when we submit all of our strike data for the period between 7 July and 25 October to multiple regression analysis, a measure of the dominant forces underlying strikes, and compare it to results obtained for the period 3 March through 6 July 1917. For the first half of the revolutionary year, we find that the highest strike intensities occurred in areas with the highest nominal wages and also a decline in real wages (a characteristic, of course, of Petrograd itself and to a lesser extent of Moscow). These wage effects appear to dominate all other factors, so much so that once they are controlled for, factory size and even the element of urban concentration do not affect strike intensity levels. Past strike experience, however, measured by participation in the strike movement from 1913 to 1916, also turns out to be significantly correlated with strike intensities in this period. We can thus say with a high degree of certainty that the most strike-prone areas of Russia before 7 July were those that had struck most before the February Revolution, had high wages, and a falling real wage. When we subject our data from July to October to multiple regression analysis, however, we find that *none* of the correlations between wage levels and strike activity continue to hold. Nor can the composition of the post-July strike force be explained by any of the conventional factors usually associated with this form of protest: not by wages, past strike experience, urban concentration, skill level, or factory size.

Particularly interesting in this regard is evidence suggesting that strikes grew in intensity *despite* efforts of trade unionists and perhaps even of factory committees, rather than because of them, even though all strikes were more organized in the fall than the spring, and in some cases maintained by strike funds. It is possible our evidence here is distorted, and that our statistics reflect more a bias in reporting than an actual shift in the perspective of trade unionists or factory committee representatives; but it is also possible that although these groups, dominated by skilled and politically conscious workers well aware of the impending dangers of economic collapse, became increasingly more radical in many places and openly identified with the Bolsheviks, a further tendency within many production units may have been for these organizations to attempt to restrain more radical impulses, perhaps becoming themselves in the process targets for attack.

In sum, what we see in the development of strikes over time during 1917 is a clear and statistically supported correlation between strikes and the processes of political radicalization, and the alteration in the meaning of strikes from action reflecting at least some degree of support for Russia's new political order and

521

the workers' own soviet leadership, to actions reflecting deep dissatisfaction, alienation, and the willingness to accept radical alternatives. And in terms of their overall relationship to the political aspects of Russia's revolutionary process in 1917, it might be said that even though strikes were not directly tied to major events or "turning points," as much of the literature suggests, their *power* as weapons of protest on the eve of October lay as much in symbolism as in substance, a sign of decaying faith in Russia's existing political and moral economy, rather than evidence of workers' willingness to use the traditional weapons of a bourgeois democracy to improve their welfare or resolve the nation's fundamental problems.

V

Conclusion

24

Conclusion

LEOPOLD H. HAIMSON

The contributions to this volume have repeatedly brought out, it seems to me, the impressions drawn in its introductory section concerning the similitudes that surfaced in patterns of labor unrest in the course of the major strike waves that unfolded in various countries of Western and Central Europe at the end and in the immediate aftermath of the First World War, and in Imperial Russia already by the eve of the war. Specifically, these contributions appear to confirm the view that what distinguished these strike waves from previous waves of labor unrest was the degree to which, at least among the strata of workers who were most militantly involved in them, all forms of labor unrest – including ostensibly economic strikes – came to focus explicitly over issues of power and authority. Even more notable was the acuteness of the sense that these strata of workers came to display of the inextricable link between their position in the workplace – and particularly the issue of control over the character and pace of their own work – and their position in the polity as a whole. It was the sense of this inextricable connection – so sharply demonstrated by the participants in these labor struggles even when they did not resort to the weapon of political strikes – that induced several of our contributors to assign to these waves of labor unrest a much more highly politicized character, and especially to detect in them more open, direct, if not generalized challenges of existing structures of authority, than had been the case of earlier strike waves in these countries' labor experience.

In the introduction to this volume, we also sought to outline certain common patterns in the evolution of European nation-states and of their industrial economies in the late nineteenth and early twentieth centuries that appeared to have contributed to these new patterns and dynamics of labor unrest, as well as to describe the ways in which the experience of the First World War had accelerated the impact of these longer-term processes. We also noted how these processes – the involvement of the state in the industrial economy,

525

including the regulation of labor relations; of industrial workers in political life as a distinct group in the polity; as well as the impact on labor relations of the efforts of employers, and eventually of the state, to rationalize the industrial economy to achieve greater productivity and economy of costs – had particularly affected the very strata of workers who would eventually emerge as the most militant participants in these strike waves: workers of metal-processing and mechanical enterprises, those employed in large cities, and especially in those capitals where workers of the metal industry were concentrated in large numbers.

But even if the general patterns that we observed in the evolution of labor unrest during these years appear by and large confirmed by the various contributions to this volume, we are left with a number of unanswered questions to which I would now like to return with the aid of the insights that these contributions have afforded us about the timing of these various strike waves, as well as the specific character and dynamics that they assumed in the countries under our scrutiny.

First and foremost, given the broad similarities in the processes of change that European workers experienced in the late nineteenth and early twentieth centuries, what factors contributed to the apparent lag in the translation – at least up to the outbreak of the First World War – of the effects of these processes into patterns of labor unrest among workers of Western and Central Europe, by comparison with those of the Russian Empire? And particularly, given the attention we have assigned to workers of the metal industry, what factors contributed to the lag in the intensity of the response on the part of metalworkers outside of the Russian Empire – whether in the form of strikes over order, or of their transmutation into political strikes – to the changes in the character and organization of work processes to which many of these workers were in fact so much more sharply subjected during the prewar period than those of Russian metal-processing and mechanical enterprises?

In our search for answers to these exceedingly difficult questions, let us first take note of the fact that the various contributions to this volume have sharply qualified the view of the growing "institutionalization" of labor conflicts as a predominant pattern of European experience during the years preceding the outbreak of the First World War. The contributions on workers of the metal-processing industry, in particular, strongly suggest that in all European countries in which efforts to "rationalize" production processes and relations were successfully and systematically pressed, they did arouse a growing sense of grievance not only among the skilled workers who were exposed to them, but also and perhaps even especially among the younger semiskilled – but also often more highly educated – workers who were now recruited in growing numbers by firms engaged in these reorganizations of work tasks. But our contributors have also pointed out that in many of the countries concerned

(Germany being the most notable case in point) the translation of these grievances into labor protest increasingly assumed, especially from 1905 to the
outbreak of the war, a disorganized, inchoate, if not muted character – labor
protests over these issues often taking the form of wildcat strikes, but also
remaining frequently disguised in the more traditional and conventional form of
claims over wage issues.

One order of explanation, advanced especially by our German contributors,
for the character that these labor conflicts assumed, and especially for their
failure to escalate into major strike waves on the eve of the war, is the increasingly ferocious resistance that employers and employers' organizations
displayed during these years against all forms of labor protest, and especially
against strikes over order in their enterprises. The resistance became especially effective, given the greater control over their markets, and hence lesser
vulnerability to strikes, that these firms had achieved as a result of the processes
of consolidation that they had undergone since the turn of the century. Hence
the ability and will that employers, especially those of large metal and mechanical firms, displayed individually and in concert in resorting to the use of
blacklists, lockouts, as well as "yellow" unions, to stifle labor protest and to
destroy the effectiveness of existing trade union organizations.

Friedhelm Boll's observation that the number of industrial workers in Germany affected by lockouts in 1910 exceeded that of the number of participants
in all strike actions clearly suggests the massiveness and effectiveness that these
tactics had assumed among German employers by the eve of the war. By the
same token, James Cronin's observation that the ability of British trade unions
during these years to resist the efforts of engineering firms to introduce major
reorganizations of work processes was due in large measure to the highly
fragmented character of the British engineering industry, confirms the degree
to which the success of these efforts on the part of employers in other European
countries (and their ability to crush and neutralize labor protest) stemmed from
the processes of industrial consolidation – including the emergence of trusts,
cartels, and other forms of syndication – that metal-processing firms had
experienced in certain of the industrial countries of the continent.

Indeed the picture drawn for us by contributors to this volume of the
condition of the organized labor movement in most of the countries under our
scrutiny by the eve of the First World War is one of stagnation, if not of
disarray. Existing trade union organizations proved increasingly ineffective in
countering the militant tactics of employers, and became increasingly reluctant
to engage them in labor conflicts.

The picture is persuasive as far as it goes, but in and of themselves the
militant tactics of employers' organizations and their impact on the ability of
trade unions to organize labor conflicts do not provide an adequate explanation
for the lag in the translation of the grievances generated by the reorganization of

productive processes and relations into labor unrest among metalworkers of Western and Central Europe comparable to the role played by metalworkers in the prewar strike wave in Imperial Russia. After all, it should be recalled that employers of Russia's metal-processing industry and especially the member firms of the Mechanical Council of the St. Petersburg Society of Manufacturers and Mill Owners were increasingly resorting, partly under the inspiration of their German confreres, to equally militant tactics by the eve of the war – including the use of blacklists, collective lockouts, and eventually successful appeals to political authorities to have state enterprises join them in these concerted actions. Yet neither these militant tactics nor the great weakness and vulnerability of trade unions (on the eve of the war there were but 50,000–60,000 trade-union members in Russia, as against over 200,000 in 1906), deterred the build-up of labor unrest, especially among St. Petersburg workers; they merely contributed to its radicalization.

This is why, even if one focuses exclusive attention in this analysis on the mutual confrontations between labor and management – abstracting from the broader political and social environments in which they unfolded – one has to consider the orientations that the leaderships of existing working class organizations, and especially those of trade unions, displayed during these years. Several of the analyses in this volume have suggested, in this connection, that one of the factors that substantially contributed to the dampening of labor unrest in various countries of Western and Central Europe during this period was precisely the orientation to labor conflicts that the existing leaderships of their trade unions – ostensibly so much more powerful, and better financed and organized than those of the Russian Empire – had come to display toward labor conflicts. At issue was not merely the reluctance of traditional craft unions to adapt to the influx of large numbers of semiskilled and unskilled workers into various branches of heavy as well as light industry, but also the strategy and tactics – indeed the basic conception of their roles and of the nature of labor conflicts – displayed by the leadership of existing industrial unions, including those under the influence of Social Democracy. The impassioned critique of the tactics of the German metalworkers' union presented in these pages by Elisabeth Domansky is especially instructive in this regard.

As Domansky describes it, precisely because of the strong Social-Democratic orientation of its leaders, the German Metal Workers Association viewed its role, given the existence of the capitalist order, as that of selling a commodity – the labor of its members – seeking to control its supply on the labor market, but also to act ultimately in conformance with the laws of supply and demand. In and of itself, this orientation made the leadership of this and other Social-Democratic unions more sensitive to issues of wage levels and other "material" benefits than to working conditions, all the more so given the fierceness

528

with which employers of the German metal industry now resisted any claims infringing on their "managerial prerogatives."

But as Domansky suggests, and the experience of Social Democratic unions in other countries confirms, there was another, perhaps even more basic ideological dimension in the reluctance of the leadership of this union to resist the changes in the organization of production processes – including the use of bonus systems for economies of time – that German metal-processing firms were introducing under the influence of doctrines of "scientific management." It was that precisely because of their Marxist orientations, these union leaders felt at most ambivalent about them. Indeed, how could they reject these innovations outright, given the fact that they were calculated to accelerate the very processes of capitalist development that, according to Marxist theory, were laying the grounds for the eventual advent of socialism: the gains in labor productivity and the emergence of more homogeneous work forces, attendant to the "rationalization" and mechanization of work processes, making for the "generalization" of relations of production as well as for the development of productive forces. We should emphasize that the reconciliation with the "realities of capitalist development" that these attitudes reflected was by this time as characteristic of "orthodox" as of "reformist" currents in many European Social-Democratic parties and trade unions, with ultimate implications that would not be unveiled until the advent of the First World War.

This observation also applies by and large to the attitudes that both of these currents of European Social Democracy displayed toward the use of the weapon of political strikes. To be sure, the circles of the Socialist International increasingly entertained during these years the notion of resorting to concerted general strikes to prevent the outbreak of a generalized military conflict on the European continent. But with this exception, orthodox no less than revisionist spokesmen of most European Social-Democratic parties viewed political strikes as an irrational instrument for the attainment of any conceivable political aims. As long as a capitalist order remained firmly in place, those political objectives that could reasonably be attained by Social Democracy could most effectively be pursued through the electoral process and parliamentary struggle. Once conditions became ripe for the advent of socialism, resort to political strikes would merely distract the working class from concentrating its efforts on the seizure of political power and the overthrow of the capitalist state.

Obviously, the attitudes of the leaders of Social-Democratic unions that we have described substantially contributed to the dampening among their rank and files, as well as among unorganized workers, of the grievances induced by the changes in the character and organization of production processes to which they were subjected – given these unions' lack of recognition, if not actual "delegitimization" of these grievances. Indeed, one can hardly escape the impression that the more firmly trade union organizations displaying such orientations were entrenched, the greater was the deterring effect that they came to exercise by the eve of the war on the capacity of organized and unorganized workers to translate their grievances about the changes imposed in their conditions in the workplace into effective forms of collective protest.

The example provided by James Cronin of the on-the-whole successful opposition by British trade union organizations, which did not share this orientation, to the systematic introduction of such changes in British engineering firms, at least up to the outbreak of the war, constitutes in this respect a major exception that partially proves the rule. And so, in a somewhat different perspective, is the exception provided by the prewar experience of the Russian labor movement.

I do not in the least wish to minimize in this connection the essentially spontaneous character of the onset of the wave of labor unrest that broke out in April 1912 in response to the Lena goldfield massacre, nor the degree to which also from the outset the workers who were drawn into this strike wave were reinforced in the sense of possibility and legitimacy of their collective actions by the sympathy with which they were greeted by broader strata of Russia's urban society. Nor is it possible to ignore the degree to which this sense of possibility continued to be nourished right up to the outbreak of the war by the evidence of mounting public disaffection among other social groups with the existing political order, at least in urban Russia. But neither does it seem possible to deny the significance of the role played in the radicalization and politicization of this labor unrest by the availability of a political leadership to assign to it – and specifically to the use of political strikes – an ostensibly wider meaning and purpose.

This, it seems to me, was the essential role played during these years by Lenin and his followers, as well as the basic reason for their success in wresting control of the open organizations of labor from their Menshevik opponents. I have emphasized, in this connection, that through the media of the open labor press, of the trade unions, of the clubs of enlightenment, and the propaganda and agitation conducted under existing legal immunities by their six labor deputies, the Bolsheviks advanced the vision of a steadily mounting strike wave culminating in a general political strike, and eventually an armed uprising leading to the establishment of a "firm" democratic regime. This vision provided for participants in political and in economic strikes, and especially for the militants involved in the launching and organization of these labor actions, a thread linking their acts, wherever they occurred – in however isolated settings and whatever their immediate outcomes – to the *svetloe buduschchee*, the bright golden future, that would open after the overthrow of the existing order.

Under the circumstances, it mattered little in the unfolding of the post-Lena strike wave that throughout this period, Bolshevik underground organizations, almost invariably infiltrated with agents of the secret police, reeled under the impact of periodic arrests – and in fact functioned effectively only as amorphous cellular organizations at the factory level. It mattered little not only due to the ability of the open organizations of labor to furnish whatever minimal degree of coordination the Bolsheviks were in fact able to provide for labor unrest, but chiefly because their essential message, while echoing these workers' own instincts – own grievances and claims – also provided a contextual meaning and a larger purpose for the translation of these grievances and aspirations into increasingly militant patterns of labor unrest.

For Western European workers, this broader contextual meaning and purpose emerged only in the holocaust created by the First World War. We discussed earlier the variety of ways in which the war experience accelerated the longer-term processes that we saw at work in the evolution of the European nation-states since the turn of the century – the involvement of the state in the regulation of the industrial economy, including its mediation or arbitration of labor conflicts, and the absorption of established working-class organizations into the life of the polity, culminating in most belligerent countries in the involvement of the leaderships of their trade union organizations and majority socialist parties in the institutional framework created to mobilize these countries' industrial economies. We also observed how, within this new institutional framework, the pressures to achieve greater productivity in support of the war effort, as well as to draw into defense industries workers of lesser skills, including large numbers of women, greatly accelerated – this time with official sanction, if not official trade union support – the processes of rationalization and mechanization of work tasks in which many industrial firms had been engaged since the turn of the century.

It is not difficult to discern how under the conditions eventually created by the endless and unprecedentedly massive bloodletting at the front, the mounting material deprivations and social strains at the rear, and the eventual erosion of the legitimacy of the existing structure of authority that the war induced, the grievances of industrial workers, especially in defense industries, instinctively turned – in this setting – not only against their employers but also against the state, and indeed also against their own official working-class organizations, which had assumed such unprecedented responsibility for their fate, but also claimed to represent them. All the more so, given the emergence by the end of 1915 and the beginning of 1916 – partly in response to the appeals of the Zimmerwald Center and the Zimmerwald Left – of insurgent leaderships in the socialist parties and trade union organizations of most belligerent countries, which now provided for labor unrest a political rationale and purpose: to bring the war to an end, and almost in the same breath to overturn the existing structure of authority – including the industrial order created by

531

capitalism – that was held accountable for the destruction and suffering that the war had induced.

The general outlines of these processes are relatively well known, but the various contributions to this volume have helped us to flesh them out, and particularly to shed light on the specific character and dynamics that the strike waves in which they culminated assumed in the various countries under scrutiny. They have shown, for example, how even in countries like Britain, in which trade unions had remained relatively successful right up to the outbreak of the war in maintaining a degree of control over the organization of work tasks and their forms of remuneration in engineering firms, the pressures that the war generated finally opened the door for deskilling and more generally for the rationalization of work processes. They have helped account, by the same token, for the inherent logic that emerged within the institutional framework of the war economy for the linking on the part of the insurgent leaderships of labor and socialist parties, but also of workers at the bench, of their struggle for control over conditions in the workplace with control of the industrial economy, and hence of the polity as a whole.

Last but not least, they have helped explain how in the context of this process of generalization and of radicalization of their grievances and aspirations, political strikes emerged in the eyes of many of the workers who participated in these strike waves as a legitimate, but also seemingly effective – indeed logical – weapon. In fact, in the context of the war economy, *all* strikes automatically assumed political, if not a potentially revolutionary character. By the same token, *all* strikes could legitimately, indeed tangibly, be linked to the broader purpose of bringing the war, and the industrial order that had brought it about, to an end.

This logic was most palpable to workers in metal-processing enterprises working for defense, to workers in large cities who were most deeply absorbed in the polity, and especially to workers in those capitals of the belligerent countries – where the seat of political power lay – in which metalworkers were concentrated in large numbers. As we have seen, it was these strata of workers who became most militantly involved in these strike waves. It was also among these workers that we observed most clearly the mutual reinforcement of the various motifs in conflicts with authority that these strikes waves brought out, and eventually, in those countries most severely bled and tried by the war, the fusion of these motifs into generalized revolutionary struggles to overthrow their existing political, social, and economic orders. The culmination of these dynamics in the revolutionary and/or protorevolutionary processes that certain of these European countries experienced at the end of the First World War lie well beyond the problem areas that the contributors to this volume have sought to explore (although we shall seek to address them in a subsequent volume in this series). But let me hazard, even at this point, a few observations concerning

532

the relationships that the strike waves in Imperial Russia, on which we have focused such considerable attention, bore to the revolutionary processes that culminated in the capital city of Petrograd in the February Days of 1917.

Accounts of the February Revolution, and especially those published in the West in recent years, have ranged widely in seeking to identify the actors who triggered this revolution – from the women who rioted in the lines of breadshops in various working-class districts of the capital, to those women textile workers who went on strike on the occasion of the International Women's Day, 23 February, and called on the men employed in nearby metal-processing plants to join them, to the soldiers of the Petrograd garrison who by the evening of the twenty-fourth began to go over to the side of the revolution, to the leaderships of the various opposition and revolutionary parties that by the night of the twenty-sixth took the first hesitant steps toward the organization of the Petrograd Soviet and the Provisional Committee of the State Duma – the original loci of the Dual Power that eventually presided over the opening phase of the revolution.

Yet, when one pieces together the reports of the Petrograd Department of Police, which up to the last sought to keep the existing structure and symbols of existing authority in place even while recording the process of its disintegration, one cannot avoid another, overwhelming impression. It is that the actors who in a narrow sense made the revolution, or more precisely, made others conscious of the fact that it had actually broken out – were the workers of the Vyborg district, and indeed those of the very metal-processing and mechanical enterprises who had been the most militant participants in labor unrest in the capital since the very onset of the post-Lena strike wave, and reemerged by the summer and fall of 1915 as the most militant participants in its political strikes and demonstractions.

These workers – those of Novyi Lessner, Minnyi Zavod, Aivaz, and a few other metal-processing and mechanical plants of the Vyborg district – triggered the revolution when, after going out on strike one more time, on 24 February 1917 – some of them admittedly in response to the appeals of the women employed in nearby textile enterprises – they decided in an irresistible mobilization and unleashing of collective will to cross the Neva, which separated their district from the city's heart and center of authority, and to head for the city's main artery, Nevsky Prospekt – since the late nineteenth century, the magnet for revolutionary demonstrations. To achieve this aim, a few of them infiltrated across the bridges guarded by police and mounted Cossacks and gendarmes, while others crossed on the frozen waters. Joined by the workers of other metal-processing enterprises whom they roused on the other shore of the frozen river, they eventually poured onto Nevsky, and even after they were beaten back from it by the forces of order, persistently regrouped in nearby arteries and made their way back, continuing to do so even after they had begun to suffer casualties – most of them making their way home only late in the night. And they did so again in the morning of the twenty-fifth, this time joined by a larger number of workers from various other districts of the city, as well as by a few male and female students from a number of educational establishments who, wearing Red Cross brassards, sought to assist the casualties. To be sure, many other scenes were played out during these two crucial opening days of the February Revolution, including those, especially on the Vyborg side, that provided the first signs of the defection of the soldiers of the Petrograd garrison to the side of the insurgents. But it was these scenes on Nevsky Prospekt that contributed most sharply to the realization by various political actors, and eventually by wider strata of the city's population, that a revolution was finally in the making and in fact had actually broken out.

Let me elaborate the point with an example – or more precisely, the extension of an example – itself perhaps apocryphal. One of the memoirists of the February Days, Sukhanov as I recall, recounts the incident that allegedly occurred on 25 or 26 February, on one of the bridges separating Vyborg from the center of the capital. A gendarme – after he had aimed his rifle in the direction of one of the striking workers infiltrating across the bridge, and had it summarily pulled out of harm's way by a soldier standing nearby – plaintively exclaimed that no one had told him that the revolution had occurred. In the same vein, I would suggest that the scenes on Nevsky Prospekt that I have described provided for the leading political circles of the capital and other major bystanders, if eventual participants – including many of the soldiers of the Petrograd garrison – the veritable "representation" that the revolution, which many of them had been awaiting for so long, had actually broken out.

We should note that the workers of these metal enterprises on the Vyborg side braced themselves for the collective decision that led to this eventual outcome – that is, mobilized their will to cross the river on 24 February, and to do so again in the morning of 25 February at a time when no major organized political actors, including the Bolsheviks' Petrograd City Committee, had called upon them to do so, and when none of the agencies entrusted with the preservation of order expected any significant outbreak of labor unrest. The Bolsheviks had called on the workers of Petrograd to strike and demonstrate on 9 January, the anniversary of Bloody Sunday. The workers of the metal plants on the Vyborg side had struck on 9 January, and singing revolutionary songs and unfurling a few red banners as they headed out of their factory gates, had gone home. The Labor Groups of the War Industrial Committees and the Menshevik Defensists had called on them to strike on 14 February, the day of the convocation of the State Duma, and to head across the river for the Taurus Palace to demonstrate their support for the duma opposition. The workers of these metal plants had struck on the appointed day, and again went home. Following these fiascoes, even the Bolsheviks had ceased to call for new

534

demonstrations, and decided to postpone the eventual day of reckoning at least until May Day.

What then impelled these workers of the Vyborg district to steel themselves to make their way across the Neva on 24 February, when literally no other major political actors, or organs of authority, expected them to do so? It is with specific reference to the mobilization of collective will that the launching of this action required, as well as its recognition by other actors as the inception of the revolution, that the various other events and actors sometimes identified with its outbreak assume, it seems to me, their full relevance and significance. Their significance is not so much that they contributed to the disaffection or even to the political radicalization of the workers of these metal enterprises of the Vyborg district. For as we already noted, many of these workers had already amply demonstrated their disaffection in the course of the post-Lena strike wave, and had consistently proven thereafter to be among the politically most militant, most radicalized, and most stalwart of the workers of Petrograd. (Indeed, the Vyborg side had remained, even in late 1914 and early 1915, one of the few districts of the capital in which organizations of the revolutionary underground, most notably the Bolsheviks, had continued to function, however feebly, at the grass-roots level.) What the riots in the lines of bread shops, the appeals of the women of nearby textile factories to strike on International Women's Day, and the widely publicized denunciations of the government's handling of the supply crisis by the Food Supply Committee of the State Duma (which undoubtedly contributed to the triggering of these food riots) chiefly added to the revolutionary equation was that they reinforced the sense of possibility, and by the same token of ultimate necessity, involved in the making and acting out of these workers' decision to cross the Neva and head for Nevsky Prospekt. And this decision reflected the crystallization of these workers' own "representation" that the time had come for them to make a revolution.

Other actors and events thus contributed an element of irresistible conviction but also of ultimate legitimation to the reaching, however inarticulate, of this collective decision, which no previous appeals by the revolutionary underground had done. By the same token, the cries of "give us bread" ("daite khleb") that many of these strikers originally issued on this occasion at the forces of order that sought to disperse them clearly appeared to them more irrefutable – and therefore more irresistible – denunciations of the illegitimacy of the existing structure of order and authority than the calls for the overthrow of autocracy, or even for bringing the war to an end, that they had cried out in their earlier political strikes and demonstrations. The decision of hundreds of thousands of other workers to join them on Nevsky on 25 and 26 February, the rapid escalation of their voices to outright insurrectionary appeals, their stubborn confrontations of the forces of order, and the eventual response of the soldiers of the Petrograd garrison, and finally of the broader political circles of the capital to their appeals, also demonstrated – on this occasion – that through their very decision to make a revolution, these workers had in fact made one.

In the light of the scenes that I have sought to describe if not to explain, as well as of the longer-term processes that led up to them, I hope that the aridity of certain of the conceptual categories that have traditionally been applied in historical debates about the origins of the Revolution of 1917 may however become apparent. The February Days of 1917 were par excellence "a spontaneous" phenomenon, at least in the sense that no political parties, indeed no formally organized political actors, dictated them, or in fact foresaw their timing. Yet, the actions of the metalworkers of the Vyborg district on 24 and 25 February appear to me – if any collective actions can be so termed – as preeminently conscious acts, launched on the basis of a conscious decision, by conscious historical actors.

If any collective actions can be described as dictated by objective processes, surely these patterns of collective action – whose origins and dynamics in the behavior of the strata of workers employed in these very plants of the Vyborg district we have traced back to the prewar strike wave, and found consistently associated in our quantitative analyses with various objective indices reflecting the unfolding of these longer-term processes – clearly deserve to be so termed. Yet it took the interplay of structures, conjunctures, and events for these patterns of collective action to culminate in the February Revolution, and thus for the scenario of strikes, war, and revolution – to which this volume has been devoted – to unfold in the Russia of 1917. And by the same token, it took the "subjective" elements and chemistry of human instincts, consciousness, and will for these processes to be ultimately translated into the patterns of collective action, as well as the "representations," which the making of this revolution entailed.

In however different forms, all of these dimensions of human experience, it seems to me, were also involved in the waves of labor unrest in other European countries, at the end and in the immediate aftermath of the First World War, which culminated in the challenge on the part of the workers who participated in them of the entire structures of order and authority that had hitherto shaped and contained their lives.